T0330698

The Routledge Companion to Financial Services Marketing

Interest in financial services marketing has grown hugely over the last few decades, particularly since the financial crisis, which scarred the industry and its relationship with customers. It reflects the importance of the financial services industry to the economies of every nation and the realization that the consumption and marketing of financial services differs from that of tangible goods and indeed many other intangible services.

This book is therefore a timely and much-needed comprehensive compendium that reflects the development and maturation of the research domain, and pulls together, in a single volume, the current state of thinking and debate. The events associated with the financial crisis have highlighted the need for banks and other financial institutions to understand how to rebuild trust and confidence, improve relationships and derive value from the marketing process.

Written by an international team of experts, this book provides the latest thinking on how to manage such challenges and is vital reading for students and researchers in financial services marketing, policy-makers and practitioners.

Tina Harrison is Senior Lecturer at the University of Edinburgh, UK and editor of the *Journal of Financial Services Marketing*.

Hooman Estelami is Professor of Marketing at Fordham University, USA and editor of the *International Journal of Bank Marketing*.

Routledge Companions in Business, Management and Accounting

Routledge Companions in Business, Management and Accounting are prestige reference works providing an overview of a whole subject area or sub-discipline. These books survey the state of the discipline including emerging and cutting edge areas. Providing a comprehensive, up to date, definitive work of reference, Routledge Companions can be cited as an authoritative source on the subject.

A key aspect of these Routledge Companions is their international scope and relevance. Edited by an array of highly regarded scholars, these volumes also benefit from teams of contributors which reflect an international range of perspectives.

Individually, Routledge Companions in Business, Management and Accounting provide an impactful one-stop-shop resource for each theme covered. Collectively, they represent a comprehensive learning and research resource for researchers, postgraduate students and practitioners.

Published titles in this series include:

The Routledge Companion to Fair Value and Financial Reporting
Edited by Peter Walton

The Routledge Companion to Nonprofit Marketing
Edited by Adrian Sargeant and Walter Wymer Jr

The Routledge Companion to Accounting History
Edited by John Richard Edwards and Stephen P. Walker

The Routledge Companion to Creativity
Edited by Tudor Rickards, Mark A. Runco and Susan Moger

The Routledge Companion to Strategic Human Resource Management
Edited by John Storey, Patrick M. Wright and David Ulrich

The Routledge Companion to International Business Coaching
Edited by Michel Moral and Geoffrey Abbott

The Routledge Companion to Organizational Change
Edited by David M. Boje, Bernard Burnes and John Hassard

The Routledge Companion to Cost Management
Edited by Falconer Mitchell, Hanne Nørreklit and Morten Jakobsen

The Routledge Companion to Digital Consumption
Edited by Russell W. Belk and Rosa Llamas

The Routledge Companion to Identity and Consumption
Edited by Ayalla A. Ruvio and Russell W. Belk

Dramatic changes in technology, regulations and consumer behavior are transforming the financial services industry around the world. This book provides an excellent and comprehensive perspective from several experts on how marketing practices need to change in this dynamic industry.

Sunil Gupta, Professor, Harvard University, USA

This book makes a most valuable contribution to research and professionals operating in the financial services industry. In particular, it focuses on the unique nature of the industry, and the diverse range of traditional and emergent issues it is currently facing. In this respect, the book is highly topical and fully reflects the dynamic nature of these issues and the associated challenges.

Barry Howcroft, Professor, Loughborough University, UK

While most financial institutions focus their energy on adhering to the new regulatory environment, this book brings the attention of practitioners and academics back to its origins, namely how to create outstanding customer value in a fast changing environment by providing services for financial security, stability and flexibility. It offers a comprehensive perspective on how to regain trustful relationships with customers and stay competitive against the upcoming new players in the market.

Peter Maas, Professor, University of St. Gallen, Switzerland

This essential guide to financial services marketing provides a comprehensive, expert and critical picture of a vital area of economic life. Researchers and practitioners alike will find it indispensable.

Karen Rowlingson, Professor, University of Birmingham, UK

The Routledge Companion to Financial Services Marketing

Edited by
Tina Harrison and
Hooman Estelami

Routledge
Taylor & Francis Group

LONDON AND NEW YORK

First published 2015 by Routledge

2 Park Square, Milton Park, Abingdon, Oxon OX14 4RN

605 Third Avenue, New York, NY 10017

Routledge is an imprint of the Taylor & Francis Group, an informa business

First issued in paperback 2022

Publisher's Note

The publisher has gone to great lengths to ensure the quality of this reprint but points out that some imperfections in the original copies may be apparent.

British Library Cataloguing in Publication Data
A catalogue record for this book is available from the British Library

Library of Congress Cataloging-in-Publication Data
The Routledge companion to financial services management /
edited by Tina Harrison and Hooman Estelami.
pages cm. – (Routledge companions in business, management and accounting)
Includes bibliographical references and index.
1. Financial services industry–Marketing. 2. Financial institutions–Marketing. 3. Bank marketing. I. Harrison, Tina. II. Estelami, Hooman.
HG173.R68 2014
332.1068'8–dc23
2014019505

ISBN: 978-0-415-82914-4 (hbk)
ISBN: 978-1-03-234021-0 (pbk)
DOI: 10.4324/9780203517390

Typeset in Bembo
by Cenveo Publisher Services

Contents

Contents

Contents

List of figures

List of tables

List of contributors

Dr. Zuriah Abdul Rahman is a Professor in Insurance and Islamic Insurance (Takaful) at Universiti Teknologi MARA, Malaysia. She has served for nearly three decades in various capacities as an academic at Universiti Teknologi MARA; her most previous position is the Director of the Arshad Ayub Graduate Business School. Her contribution to academia and the industry include appointments to various advisory capacities as a subject expert on the Board of the Islamic Banking and Finance Institute of Malaysia, Malaysian Insurance Professional Council and the Finance Accreditation Agency, professional institutions established under the Central Bank of Malaysia to support and accelerate the growth of the industry. Her scholarly activities and services have included cross border assignments particularly, in the United States, as a researcher and an invited speaker under the American Fulbright Scholar program, Durham University Visiting Fellow UK, accreditation assignments for ABEST21, Japan, and in Indonesia as conference speaker sponsored by IRTI, Islamic Development Bank, Saudi Arabia, to name a few. Her works include books and journal articles, on Islamic Finance, Takaful, Risk Management and Wealth Management with national and international publishers.

Roberta Adami is Senior Lecturer in Finance at Westminster Business School and a Visiting Professor at the University of Bologna. Prior to her academic career, she worked as a Financial Analyst at Citibank Global Asset Management and later as a Credit Risk analyst at Tokai Bank Europe, in London. Roberta has spoken at numerous conferences, published articles related to the management of pensions and has a proven research track record with a number of articles published in international journals. Her current research interests are in pensions, income distribution and inequality, pension funds performance and capital markets.

Dr. John K. Ashton is a Reader in Banking at the Bangor Business School at Bangor University. Prior to his current position, John has held positions at the University of Leeds, the University of East Anglia and Bournemouth University. John was a founding member of the ESRC Centre for Competition Policy at the University of East Anglia and has been a member of the International Institute for Banking and Financial Services at the University of Leeds. John's research interests are in the pricing of financial services, financial regulation and competition policy. He has published in the *Journal of Banking and Finance, Regional Studies, Small Business Economics, Corporate Governance: An International Review, Journal of Marketing Management, Industrial Marketing Management* and *The Journal of Public Policy and Marketing*. John also disseminates his research findings as widely as possible and has been interviewed for the financial, scientific and national press as well as national and local radio. His research work has been reported in a diverse assortment of media publications ranging from the *Times Higher Educational Supplement* and *The Daily Mail* to *The Financial Times* and *The Times*.

Dr. George J. Avlonitis is a Professor at the Department of Marketing and Communication at the Athens University of Economics and Business (AUEB). He is also Director of both the Marketing Laboratory (The Athens Laboratory for Research in Marketing) and the Postgraduate Program "Marketing and Communication" of the same Department. He is the Deputy Chairman of the Academic Council of AUEB and served as President of the European Marketing Academy (EMAC) for the biennium 2008–10, as Vice President from 1990 to 1993, and Chairman of the Global Sales Science Institute (GSSI) from 2010 to 2012. He has published more than 180 articles in international conference proceedings and the most prestigious international scientific journals of Marketing including *Journal of Marketing, Journal of the Academy of Marketing Science, International Journal of Research in Marketing, Journal of Product Innovation Management*, etc. He is also on the editorial board of six international journals and has received Best Paper Awards on multiple occasions.

Dr. Hazel Bateman is a Professor of Economics and Head of the School of Risk and Actuarial Studies in the Australian School of Business at the University of New South Wales. She is widely published in the area of the economics and finance of pensions and superannuation. The overall themes of her research are the adequacy and security of retirement saving and benefits, and issues associated with the increasing risk and responsibility faced by retirement savers under the increasingly prevalent defined contributions arrangements. Hazel has been a consultant on retirement incomes to a range of Australian and international organisations including the OECD, the World Bank, the Social Insurance Administration (China) and the Korean Institute of Health and Social Affairs. She has served on the Australian Government's Superannuation Roundtable and is currently a member of the editorial board of the *Journal of Pension Economics and Finance*.

Jens Baumgarten is a Partner in the New York office of Simon-Kucher & Partners and responsible for its financial services clients in North America and UK. His consulting work focuses primarily on value management, strategic pricing and sales optimisation. He has carried out national as well as international projects for clients in the US, Canada, UK, Europe and Asia. Besides financial services, his industry experience covers software, technology, telecommunications, automotive and utilities. Jens has published numerous papers and articles on strategy, marketing, sales and pricing in the financial services sector in the US, Germany and the UK. He is also a frequent speaker at conferences and seminars, where he covers topics in the areas of strategy, marketing, and pricing. Jens holds an MBA degree from the University of Dayton (Ohio, USA) and studied business at the University of Augsburg in Germany, where he majored in Marketing, Management & Organisation and Business Psychology.

Dr. A. Sinan Cebenoyan is Professor of Finance and Director of the Center for International Financial Services and Markets at the Frank G. Zarb School of Business at Hofstra University. He received his M.Phil. and Ph.D. in Finance from New York University and his B.A. and M.A. in Economics from Bogazici University in Istanbul. Before coming (back) to Hofstra, Dr. Cebenoyan taught at the Stern School of Business at New York University, the University of Baltimore, Fordham University, State University of New York at New Paltz, and Hofstra University. He specializes in financial institutions, capital markets and corporate finance. He has been the recipient of the Dean's Research Award at the Frank G. Zarb School of Business, Hofstra University. His publications have appeared in the *Review of Economics and Statistics, Financial Management, Journal of Banking and Finance, Journal of Financial Services Research, Financial Review, Managerial Finance, Research in Banking and Finance, Multinational*

Finance Journal, Global Finance Journal and Real Estate Economics. He has also served as a referee for a number of finance journals.

Dr. James Devlin is Professor of Financial Decision Making in the Department of Marketing at Nottingham University Business School. He is also Associate Dean (International Relations) for the School and Director of the Centre for Risk Banking and Financial Services. James also serves as a Trustee of the Board of Governors of *ifs* University College. He has been involved in research in the areas of consumer decision-making, marketing and policy issues in financial services since joining the University of Nottingham in 1991. Prior to this, James worked in the financial services industry for Lloyds Private Banking. James completed his PhD in 1996 and has subsequently been lead researcher/principle investigator on a number of projects funded by bodies including the Economic and Social Research Council, Financial Services Authority and Financial Services Research Forum and has also been involved as co-researcher in projects funded by the Office of Fair Trading, TSB and others. James has published many research articles covering policy issues in financial services and beyond, as well as marketing financial services and other marketing issues. James has also worked at Cass Business School (1998–2000) and the University of Nottingham Malaysia Campus in Kuala Lumpur (2000–2003).

Dr. Dahlia El-Manstrly, PhD, is a Lecturer in Marketing at the University of Edinburgh Business School. Before joining the University of Edinburgh, she was a doctoral researcher and then associate lecturer at the University of Glasgow, where she obtained an MSc in management research and a PhD in marketing. She taught marketing and other related subjects at the University of Huddersfield, where she obtained her MSc in marketing. She also worked as a research assistant at Leeds Metropolitan University, where she managed large-scale survey projects, and was an assistant lecturer at the University of Suez Canal (Egypt). Her research interests and activities centre on understanding consumer behaviour in cross-cultural and services contexts, including research on service loyalty, service failures and switching costs. She reviews for major marketing journals including *International Marketing Review, Psychology and Marketing,* and *Journal of Marketing Management* and prestigious marketing conferences such as the US-based Academy of Marketing Science (AMS), Academy of Marketing Science World Marketing Congress (AMSWMC), the Australian and New Zealand Marketing Academy (ANZMAC).

Dr. Christine Ennew is Provost and CEO of the University of Nottingham Malaysia Campus and Pro Vice Chancellor at the University of Nottingham. She is also Professor of Marketing in Nottingham University Business School. She has been actively involved in financial services research for most of her academic career. Her research interests lie in the area of services marketing and specifically financial services. She has focused her research on key strategic themes, including service quality and delivery, loyalty and retention, and service failure and recovery, and has completed a range of FSRF funded projects, most notably in relation to the development of the Trust Index. She has also undertaken business oriented research specifically in the areas of customer satisfaction, marketing relationships and trust, including on behalf of a number of major banking organisations. She has published some 100 articles in refereed journals, presented over 60 refereed conference papers and produced four books. She has worked closely with a variety of organisations in the financial services sector during her career including providing marketing training for Bank of Scotland and TSB and consultancy work for Lloyds-TSB, NatWest, AIB Bank, HSBC, Yorkshire Bank, Royal Bank of Scotland, Clydesdale and Co-operative Bank, amongst others.

Dr. Kent Eriksson is a Professor in Applied Business Studies at the Center for Banking and Finance at the Royal Institute of Technology, Sweden. His work involves applied research and development in banking and insurance, and he is also involved in policy and regulation work in the EU and Sweden. He was previously on the board of directors of the Financial Supervisory Authority in Sweden. Dr Eriksson has published in journals, such as the *International Journal of Bank Marketing, Strategic Management Journal* and *Journal of International Business Studies.*

Dr. Hooman Estelami is a Professor of Marketing and Director of the Fordham Pricing Center at the Graduate School of Business, Fordham University in New York. He is the author of three books: *Marketing Financial Services; Marketing Turnarounds;* and *Frontiers of Distance Learning in Business Education.* He is the editor of the *International Journal of Bank Marketing,* and previously served as the associate editor of the *Journal of Product and Brand Management.* His areas of specialisation are financial services marketing, pricing, customer service management and distance education. He has received multiple awards for his teaching and research and has advised a wide range of corporations on target marketing, pricing and service enhancement strategies. He received his Ph.D. in marketing from Columbia University and his MBA from McGill University. His research has appeared in a wide range of journals including: *International Journal of Research in Marketing, Journal of the Academy of Marketing Science, Journal of Financial Services Marketing, Journal of Retailing, Journal of Business Research, Journal of Service Research, Journal of Product and Brand Management, International Journal of Bank Marketing, Journal of Consumer Behaviour, Journal of Promotion Management* and *Marketing Education Review.*

Dr. Jillian Dawes Farquhar is Professor of Management at London Metropolitan University. Her interest in financial services began with providing consultancy services for building societies and moved on to advise the Financial Services Authority on the financial consumer. She edited the *International Journal of Bank Marketing* for seven years strengthening its reputation as a cutting edge interface for practitioner and academic research in financial services marketing. Her book, the *Marketing of Financial Services,* was published in 2010, capturing the aftermath of the financial services crash. She regularly comments in the media on financial services and marketing issues. Her current research includes branding, quality in research methods and selective demarketing.

Dr. Anthony Gandy FCIB is a Reader at *ifs* University College. He holds a Ph.D. from the London School of Economics and has been a Research Fellow at the University of Minnesota. He lectures on Bank Strategy, Banking Regulation and Channel Strategy. He also has a varied professional career working as strategy manager for a Japanese investment bank, as a financial journalist and, for many years, a consultant to a number of blue-chip financial/financial technology companies. He researches and publishes on banking strategy, technology and regulation, in both academic and professional environments and has written a number of books on technology and banking, banking strategy and competition in the early computer industry.

Xue Gong is a Research Fellow at the Consortium for Trustworthy Organizations at Fordham University. She holds an M.Sc. in Media and Communication Management from Fordham Graduate School of Business and a B.A in Journalism from Nanjing University in China. She is also a member of the Honour Society of Phi kappa Phi and the American Marketing Association. During her undergraduate studies, she also studied Media Convergence at the Missouri School of Journalism at the University of Missouri-Columbia as a visiting scholar. Her research interests include organisational trust, leadership and consumer welfare. She has been consulting and writing on organisational trustworthiness during her time working at the Consortium for Trustworthy Organizations. She has also published in the *International Journal of Bank Marketing* and is currently working on a trust measurement validation study which examines the psychometric structure of the organisational trust instrument.

Dr. Orla Gough was Professor of Pensions and Financial Services and Head of the Department of Finance and Business Law at the University of Westminster. Her research publications have been multidisciplinary, spanning the areas of finance, social policy, human resource management and marketing. It focuses on pensions, with specific reference to occupational pension schemes' liabilities and benefit structures, and related issues in the financial services industry. Professor Gough has published a substantial number of research papers in a wide range of journals, including over 20 in peer-reviewed journals and over 75 in non-peer-reviewed publications. She was successful in gaining substantial research grants from the UK's Economic and Social Research Council (ESRC), British Academy and Leverhulme Trust. Professor Gough's knowledge of, and expertise in, financial services enhanced her research-led teaching particularly on specific modules related to courses on Personal Financial Management and International Financial Services. Professor Gough brought over 25 years of experience in public and private equity markets and work with clients such as Standard Life, AXA and the Royal Bank of Scotland to bear on her research. She sadly passed away on 12th July 2014. Through her own research output and her work with the Pensions Research Network she leaves a rich legacy for the future of pensions research and a forum for continued interaction between academic and practitioner communities.

Dr. David R. Harness is a Senior Lecturer in Strategic and International Marketing at Hull University Business School. He holds an undergraduate degree in management from Aston University, an M.Phil. (Birmingham City University) and a Ph.D. (Huddersfield University) which examined end stage product life in the context of services on which he has widely published. Prior to his current position he had worked at Leeds University Business School. His commercial experience was gained in retail banking and he has conducted consultancies in a range of industries in the areas of service product management, value marketing, customer care and relationship marketing in the UK and overseas. His research interests are in service product management; specifically product elimination and service quality. More recently his research has focused on the role of power between SMEs and other trading partners in adopting corporate social responsibility practices. He has been published in a number of journals including: *Journal of Business Ethics, The Service Industries Journal, Journal of Product and Brand Management, Journal of Financial Services Marketing, International Journal of Bank Marketing, Journal of General Management* amongst others. He is co-author of "Marketing Orientation, Transforming Food and Agribusiness Around the Customer" and has written chapters in edited books covering financial services, sports marketing and service product management.

Dr. Tina Harness is a Principal Lecturer in Human Resource Management and Head of Department of Business Management at York St. John University. She previously worked at Leeds Metropolitan University as a Senior Lecturer in Human Resource Management. She holds a Ph.D. in Human Resource Management from Huddersfield University. Her PhD thesis examined the strategic development of the human resource role. Her commercial experience was gained in the nuclear power industry and the NHS. Her specialist teaching areas include Human Resource Management, Organisational Behaviour and Research Methods. She has taught on a range of Masters and professional programmes both at home and internationally. Current research interests comprise Strategic Human Resource Management and Relationship Marketing. Previous publications have appeared in the *Service Industries Journal, Journal of Product and Brand Management, and the Journal of Financial Services Marketing, Journal of General Management* and *Journal of Qualitative Research.*

Dr. Tina Harrison is Senior Lecturer in Marketing at the University of Edinburgh Business School, Scotland, UK. She is author of *Financial Services Marketing* (Prentice-Hall), editor of an online talk series in *Financial Services Marketing* (Henry Stewart) and Editor-in-Chief of the *Journal of Financial Services Marketing*. Her research interests encompass marketing and consumption of financial services, including segmentation, relationships and retention, pensions and the Internet. She has lead several research projects on these topics with funding from financial institutions and research councils, including a major three-year project on pensions and the internet funded by the UK's Economic and Social Research Council (ESRC) and a two-year ESRC-funded seminar series on the topic of *Financial Services and the Consumer: Challenges and Issues in a Context of Change.* She has also conducted a wide range of consultancy projects for financial institutions. Her research has been presented at conferences and published widely in leading international journals including: *European Journal of Marketing, Information and Management, Journal of Marketing Management, Journal of Business and Industrial Marketing, Marketing Intelligence and Planning, Financial Accountability and Management, International Journal of Bank Marketing* and *Journal of Financial Services Marketing.*

Dr. Arvid O. I. Hoffmann is an Assistant Professor of Finance and co-director of the Marketing-Finance Research Lab at Maastricht University as well as research fellow at the Network for Studies on Pensions, Aging and Retirement (Netspar). While working at Maastricht University, he has held visiting positions at the Leavey School of Business (Santa Clara University), the Helsinki School of Economics (Aalto University) and the Foster School of Business (University of Washington). He holds a Ph.D. in Economics and Business (2007) and an M.Sc. in Business Administration (2003) from the University of Groningen. Dr. Hoffmann's research interests are interdisciplinary and bridge the fields of marketing and finance. In particular, he is interested in behavioural economics and finance, consumer financial decision-making, financial services marketing, household finance and individual investor behaviour. He has published his research in such journals as the *Journal of the Academy of Marketing Science*, the *International Journal of Research in Marketing*, the *Journal of Business Research*, the *Journal of Banking and Finance*, the *Journal of Behavioral Finance* and *Theory and Decision.*

Dr. Bruce A. Huhmann is an Associate Professor of Marketing and the Daniels Fund Ethics Initiative Chair at New Mexico State University. After working in banking and marketing research, he earned his Ph.D. in Marketing at the University of Alabama. He teaches undergraduate courses in Internet and social media marketing, consumer behaviour, retail management and organisational ethics as well as doctoral seminars in advertising research. Dr. Huhmann is best known for his work on guilt appeals, which appeared in the *Journal of Advertising*, and his studies on consumer processing of advertising rhetoric, which have appeared in the *Journal of Consumer Research*, the *European Journal of Marketing, IEEE Transactions on Professional Communication* and in the book *Go Figure: New Directions in Advertising Rhetoric.* His investigation into how direct-to-consumer pharmaceutical advertising uses emotion rather than information to persuade consumers appeared in the *International Journal of Advertising.* His research into financial services advertising appeared in the *International Journal of Bank Marketing* and the *Journal of Financial*

Services Marketing. His other research studies have been published in the *Journal of Business Research, Journal of Public Policy and Marketing* and the *Journal of the Academy of Marketing Science* and numerous conference proceedings.

Dr. Robert Hurley (Ph.D. Columbia University) is a Professor at Fordham University and Executive Director of the Consortium for Trustworthy Organizations, a non-profit entity dedicated to providing tools and solutions for leaders to build trustworthy organisations that can sustain excellence across all stakeholder groups. He is also a core faculty member in Columbia Business School's High Impact Leadership Program. His work on trust has appeared in *Harvard Business Review, MIT Sloan Management Review, The Wall Street Journal* and the *Financial Times.* Dr. Hurley's book *The Decision to Trust* was named one of the best leadership books of 2011 by the *Washington Post.* He has also written two book chapters on trust in the financial system (Oxford University Press and Edward Elgar). In total Dr. Hurley has published over 30 articles and book chapters. Dr. Hurley's consulting experience has included work on innovation with NASA and managing change and executive development with Avon Products, First Tennessee Bank, IBM, Merrill Lynch, Citibank, Kraft Foods, Kinkos, Mercedes Benz, Sheetz Convenience Stores and State Farm Insurance. His teaching and consulting has included work in India, United Kingdom, Poland, Portugal, Italy, Japan, China, Switzerland, Hong Kong, Australia, France and the United States.

Dr. Paul A. Igwe teaches Economics at Plymouth University International College. He is an Associate of Plymouth Business School, University of Plymouth, UK. His past roles include: Enterprise Research Fellow with University of Plymouth Enterprise Ltd, Research Fellow at the African Enterprise Development projects, Service and Enterprise Research Centre at Plymouth Business School and part-time Associate Lecturer in International Business, Plymouth Business School.

Dr. Kostis Indounas received his Ph.D. in Marketing from the Athens University of Economics and Business, Greece. He is currently an Assistant Professor of Marketing at the same University. His works have appeared in academic journals such as *Industrial Marketing Management, Journal of Service Management, Journal of Business and Industrial Marketing, Business Horizons, Journal of Retailing and Consumer Services, European Journal of Marketing* and *Journal of Services Marketing* among others. He has presented at international conferences such as *AMA, EMAC and the World Marketing Congress.* His teaching, research and consulting interests are in the areas of pricing, services marketing, marketing for non-profit organisations, business-to-business marketing and new product development.

Dr. Fernando Jaramillo is Associate Professor and Chair of the Marketing Department at the University of Texas at Arlington. He earned his Ph.D. from the University of South Florida. He also teaches graduate level courses at Universidad San Francisco de Quito and Universidad de Chile. Dr. Jaramillo's research interests include marketing strategy, sales force management, leadership, business ethics and financial services. His research has appeared in multiple journals including the *Journal of Personal Selling & Sales Management, International Journal of Research in Marketing, Journal of Business Research* and the *Journal of Marketing Education.* Dr. Jaramillo is also a member of the editorial review board of the *Journal of Personal Selling & Sales Management, Journal of Business Research* and the *Journal of Marketing Theory and Practice.* Dr. Jaramillo has received best paper awards from the *Journal of Marketing Theory and Practice* and the *International Journal of Bank Marketing.*

Dr. Nikos Kalogeras is an Assistant Professor of Marketing-Finance and co-director of the Marketing-Finance Research Lab and M.Sc./IB in Marketing-Finance programme at the Departments of Finance and Marketing and Supply Chain Management, School of Business and Economics, Maastricht University (UM), the Netherlands/EU. He is also an Adjunct Professor of Marketing-Finance and Decision Sciences and he holds the Research Chair in Business Economics in MAICh/CIHEAM. Further, Nikos is a research associate in the European Centre of Corporate Engagement (Dept. of Finance/UM), Financial Engineering Laboratory (Technical University of Crete, Greece) and Services Science Factory (SSF/UM). His research interests mainly deal with individual market participants' (producers, consumers, investors, managers) behaviour regarding strategic marketing and financial decisions. His scientific publications appear in *Journal of Service Management, European Journal of Operational Research, Theory & Decision, Food & Chemical Toxicology, Journal of Food Engineering, Agribusiness: An International Journal, Journal of Food Products Marketing, Journal of International Food & Agribusiness Marketing, Supply Chain & Finance, Journal of Computational Optimization in Economics and Finance*, among others.

Dr. Wei Ke is a Director in the Banking Competence Centre of Simon-Kucher & Partners and based in its New York office. He specialises in strategic issues at the marketing-operations interface. Acting as the Resident Methodology Expert, he advises leading financial services institutions in Europe and North America on pricing optimisation, customer pricing psychology, quantitative marketing models, and risk management for both sides of the balance sheet. Besides advising the financial services industry, he has developed customer-centric pricing and marketing optimisation solutions for a national department store chain and a multi-billion dollar entertainment company in the US. He has also developed optimisation and forecasting solutions for clients in self-storage, healthcare, shipping and solar energy industries. He has frequently been published in leading financial services journals, including *Bank Accounting & Finance, BAI Banking Strategies* and the *American Banker*. He has also co-authored business school teaching cases on retail pricing, and has developed MBA course materials for decision modelling in consumer retail and financial services. He received his Ph.D. in Decision, Risk, and Operations from Columbia Business School and his Bachelor of Science in Electrical Engineering & Applied Mathematics, summa cum laude, from Columbia University.

Dr. Paul Sergius Koku is a tenured Full Professor in the College of Business in Florida Atlantic University. He is involved in several professional associations which include The American Bar Association, The American Finance Association, American Marketing Association, Academy of Marketing Science, The Florida Bar, The Federal Bar-Southern District of Florida and The Institute of Operations Research and Management Sciences. He is an active researcher who engages in interdisciplinary research. He has worked on a wide range of issues including but not limited to issues on poverty eradication, interface between finance and marketing, corporate governance, innovation management in the pharmaceutical industry, market forces and quality control, information asymmetry, ethics, social activism, boycotts and religion and consumption decisions. He has often commented on boycott activities in the national and international media, and his papers have appeared in several peer-reviewed journals and book chapters. Professor Koku holds a B.A (summa cum Laude) with concentration in Finance from University of the Virgin Islands. He also holds MBA (Marketing) from Oregon State University, MBA (Finance), MA (Applied Economics), and a Ph.D. in Finance and Marketing, all from Rutgers University. Professor Koku also holds the *Juris Doctor* degree from the University of Miami School of Law.

Dr. Manoj Kumar is a Professor at Flame School of Business, Pune, India. Earlier, he was a faculty member in the Area of Finance and Accounting at Indian Institute of Management (IIM) Rohtak and IIM Lucknow. He received his doctorate degree from Indian Institute of Technology (IIT) Bombay and has published in the peer reviewed international journals such as *Journal of Intellectual Capital, Journal of Financial Services Marketing, Journal of Modern Accounting and Auditing, Vikalpa, Decision, Management Review, Indian Management* and *The ICFAI Journal of Applied Finance.*

Dr. Jonathan Lean is Associate Professor of Strategic Management at Plymouth University. His research interests include small business and enterprise support policy, enterprise education, entrepreneurial learning and development and simulations for management learning. He has worked on a number of funded research projects for the European Commission and the British Council amongst others.

Dr. Jordan Louviere is a Research Professor in the Institute for Choice in the Business School at the University of South Australia. Jordan is widely published in consumer decision-making and choice behaviour, the design of statistical experiments for studying and modelling discrete choices, choice-based measurement methods such as Best-Worst Scaling and the external validity of stated preference methods. His work has been funded by the Australian Research Council, the National Health and Medical Research Council of Australia, the US National Science Foundation, the Canadian Social Sciences and Humanities Research Council and many other public and private sector funding sources. He has consulted with numerous private and public sector organisations in the US, Canada, Australia and Europe. He won the American Marketing Association's Charles Coolidge Parlin Award for lifetime achievements in marketing research in 2010 and is a Fellow of the Academy of the Social Sciences in Australia and a Fellow of the Australia-New Zealand Marketing Academy.

Dr. Dominik Mahr is an Assistant Professor of Strategic Marketing and Innovation Management. His research interests are in new services adoption, customer co-creation, digital media, knowledge creation, health care, mobile services and strategic marketing. His publications have appeared in journals such as *MIS Quarterly, Journal of Product Innovation Management, Research Policy, Journal of Service Research, BMJ Quality & Safety, Health Policy and Journal of Service Management.* Prior to his academic career, Dominik has worked as a strategy and marketing consultant in the automotive, high-tech, and healthcare industry.

Dr. Lynette McDonald has recently retired from teaching post-graduate and undergraduate public relations courses at the University of Queensland and taken an adjunct position at the University of Southern Queensland in the Australian Centre for Sustainable Business and Development. A former public relations professional working in local government and in PR consultancies, she became interested some years ago in the powerful effects of "companies doing good": corporate social responsibility (CSR). She started researching CSR in 2006 and has a number of academic publications on CSR, including those in the International Journal of Bank Marketing. She has supervised CSR research for both PhD and Masters' program students and has worked with post-graduate students to develop stakeholder-oriented CSR strategies for firms.

Dr. Phil Megicks is Professor of Marketing and Strategy at Plymouth University, UK. Phil has extensive experience of teaching and research in marketing education and has authored a large number of books, refereed articles and conference papers in the field of marketing planning and strategy particularly with regard to the small business and service industries. Notably he has investigated the application of different aspects of strategy in the retail, travel agency, estate agency, accounting and financial services sectors. In the context of services organisations his research also straddles the boundaries of knowledge management supply chain management particularly in terms of improving operational effectiveness.

Dr. Stefan Michel is Professor of Marketing and Service Management and the Executive MBA Program Director at IMD in Switzerland. His major research interests are in marketing strategy, service innovation and pricing. He has written several books, book chapters and numerous newspaper articles on these subjects, as well as many academic articles that have appeared in leading journals such as *Harvard Business Review, Journal of the Academy of Marketing Science* and *Journal of Service Management*, where he won the best paper of the year award twice in a row. Prior to joining IMD, Professor Michel taught at Thunderbird School of Global Management in Arizona (USA) and Business School Lucerne in Switzerland. He is an invited Global Faculty at the Center for Service Leadership, Arizona State University and serves on the non-executive board of Bossard, a publicly traded distribution company in Switzerland. Professor Michel holds an MBA and a DBA from the University of Zurich, both summa cum laude.

Dr. Atul Mishra is a Lecturer in International Business and Strategy in Plymouth University. His research interests include microfinance and microenterprise, in particular, in the context of rural non-farm economies. He has worked on related projects funded by DFID and ILO.

Dr. Sanjay Kumar Mishra is Assistant Professor of Finance in the Faculty of Management, Shri Mata Vaishno Devi University Katra, India. He has over nine years of experience in research, teaching and training. He received his MBA from Kumaun University Nainital, India with distinction and first rank in the University and obtained his Ph.D. in finance from Shri Mata Vaishno Devi University Katra. Much of his research focuses on behavioural biases and how such biases influence financial decisions. His research papers have been published in *Journal of Financial Services Marketing* and *Decision*, among others. He is a member of the editorial board of *Journal of Financial Service Marketing*, and serves as referee for many international peer reviewed journals.

Dr. Peter Moles is Senior Lecturer in Finance at the University of Edinburgh Business School. Prior to this he worked in the City of London as an investment banker where he had a number of different roles in buy and sell side, acting as a relationship manager, consultative marketing executive, transactions manager, researcher and syndicate manager. His research interests are in risk management (principally financial risk management, including foreign exchange management problems) and in how management decisions are made and the difficulties associated with managing complex problems. Recent published research is on derivative usage and short selling, decisions concerning capital structure and issues related to investment management. He has published in the *Journal of Derivatives, Journal of Financial Transformation, Multinational Finance Journal, Annals of Actuarial Science, Journal of Applied Corporate Finance, International Business Review* and *International Transactions in Operational Research*. He is author of the *Handbook of International Financial Market Terms* (Oxford University Press).

Dr. Jay Mulki is an Associate Professor of Marketing at D'Amore-McKim School of Business, Northeastern University, Boston and an Adjunct Senior Research Associate in the University of South Australia, Adelaide. His primary research interests are in the areas of personal selling and sales management. He has published over 40 studies in journals such as *Journal of Business Research, MIT Sloan Management Review, Psychology & Marketing, Journal of Personal Selling & Sales Management, Journal of Marketing Theory & Practice*, and *Journal of Business Ethics*. He is on the editorial board of *Journal of Personal Selling & Sales Management, Journal of Marketing Theory & Practice* and *Journal of Business Research*. He has an undergraduate degree in Chemical Engineering from the Mysore University, India and Ph.D. in Marketing from the University of South Florida.

Dr. Jonas Nilsson is Assistant Professor of Business Administration at the School of Business, Economics and Law at the University of Gothenburg, Sweden. Prior to joining the University of Gothenburg he worked at Umeå University, where he also finished his Ph.D. His research mainly focuses on consumer behaviour within two separate contexts – financial services and pro-social consumer behaviour – with a specific interest in so called Socially Responsible Investment (SRI) initiatives. He has published a number of academic articles and book chapters on how consumers integrate social, ethical and environmental concerns into their investment behaviour. Dr. Nilsson has been funded by the Wallander scholarship, a research grant for outstanding doctoral research. He also serves on the editorial board of *the Journal of Financial Services Marketing*.

Dr. George J. Papaioannou is Vice Dean and C.V. Starr Distinguished Professor of Investment Banking in the Zarb School of Business at Hofstra University. He earned a B.A. in economics with honours from the Athens School of Economics and Business Sciences, an M.B.A. from Duquesne University, and a Ph.D. in Finance from The Pennsylvania State University. His research interests include topics in corporate finance, investment banking and international finance. His teaching concentrates on corporate finance and investment banking. He has conducted research on stock listings, corporate financial policy, mergers and acquisitions, the Greek stock market and security offerings. His papers have appeared in *Financial Management, The Financial Review*, the *Journal of Financial Research*, the *Journal of Financial Education, Managerial and Decision Economics*, and other refereed journals. He was also a contributor to *The New Palgrave Dictionary of Money and Finance*. Dr. Papaioannou has authored the study *Development of Direct Financing in Greece* and edited two volumes of proceedings. Dr. Papaioannou is a Trustee of the Multinational Finance Society and member of the editorial board of the *Journal of Financial Services Marketing*. He was co-founder and director of the Merrill Lynch Center for the Study of International Financial Services and Markets. He has taught Finance at Erasmus University, Rotterdam; the University of Piraeus; and ALBA Graduate Business School, Greece.

Dr. Leyland F. Pitt is the Dennis Culver EMBA Alumni Chair of Business at the Beedie School of Business, Simon Fraser University, and an Affiliate Professor in Industrial Marketing at the Royal Institute of Technology, Sweden. He has also taught in executive and MBA programs at schools such as the Graham School of Continuing Studies (University of Chicago), Columbia University Graduate School of Business, Rotterdam School of Management, and London Business School. His work has been published in such journals as *Information Systems Research, Journal of the Academy of Marketing Science, Sloan Management Review, California Management Review, Communications of the ACM* and *MIS Quarterly* (for which he also served as Associate Editor). In 2000 he was the recipient of the Tamer Cavusgil Award of the American Marketing Association for best article in the *Journal of International Marketing*, and in 2010 he won the Elsevier Award for the best paper in *Business Horizons*.

Dr. Vesa Puttonen is Professor of Finance at Aalto University School of Business in Helsinki where he teaches Marketing Financial Services. He has consulting experience with several financial and non-financial corporations. Puttonen has worked as senior vice president at the Helsinki Stock Exchange and managing director at Conventum Asset Management. He is a faculty member of MBA Programs in Helsinki, Hong Kong, Singapore, Poland, China, Taiwan and South Korea. He was a visiting scholar at New York University's Stern School of Business. Puttonen has published several books and articles on different fields of strategic finance, risk management, behavioural finance and investing. He has published in journals such as *Financial Analysts Journal, Financial Management, Journal of Banking and Finance, Management Science* and *Journal of Financial Services Marketing*. Puttonen is a board member at Oras Invest, Rocla, Suomi Mutual and Taaleritehdas. He is the chairman of the board of the Finnish Ice Hockey League.

Dr. Anoop Rai is Professor of Finance at Hofstra University. He received his B.A. (Honours) and M.A. in Economics from Delhi University, India, and his M.B.A. from the University of Notre Dame. He earned his Ph.D. in International Business with minors in Finance and Economics at Indiana University. Before joining the faculty at Hofstra, Dr. Rai taught as an assistant professor at the University of Vermont and a graduate instructor at Indiana University. Professor Rai's current research interest centres on international banking and financial markets. His articles have been published in the *Journal of Banking and Finance, Journal of International Money and Finance, Journal of Economics and Business, Journal of Futures Markets, Journal of Financial Research Services, Journal of International Financial Markets, Institutions and Money, Financial Management* and *Journal of Risk and Insurance*. He also serves as Associate Editor for the *Journal of Multinational Financial Management*. Professor Rai has taught at several other institutions as a visiting or adjunct professor, including at the Rotterdam School of Management, The Netherlands, the University of Catania in Siciliy, Italy, New York University and Rutgers University, Singapore.

Dr. Hussain G. Rammal is a Senior Lecturer in International Business, and Associate Director of the Australian Centre for Asian Business at the University of South Australia. He obtained his B.Com from the University of Melbourne, MBA from Flinders University and PhD from the University of Adelaide. Dr Hussain's research interests include: internationalisation of service firms, international business negotiations and governance structures in Islamic financial institutions. His research has been published in many international business and accounting and finance journals including *International Business Review, Accounting, Auditing & Accountability Journal, Management Decision, Journal of Financial Services Marketing* and *European Journal of Finance*.

Dr. Julie Robson is Head of Strategy and Marketing Department at the Business School, Bournemouth University, UK. She has over 25 years of experience in financial services marketing both as an academic and a practitioner. Her interest in this sector started with her Ph.D. which examined the image and marketing strategies of building societies. A number of marketing management roles in the insurance sector then followed. During this time she also helped to develop several professional groups including the General Insurance Market Research Association (MRS) and the Financial Services Marketing Group (CIM). More recently her research has been extended to include marketing within the banking, insurance, broker and Islamic finance sectors. Her current research focuses on B2B relationships, strategic groups and the gap between academic and practitioner research.

Karen Robson, MA, MBA is a Ph.D. Student at the Beedie School of Business at Simon Fraser University, Canada. She holds a BSc in Psychology from Queens University, an MA in Psychology and an MBA from Simon Fraser University. A recipient of the Joseph-Armand Bombardier Doctoral Scholarship, her work has appeared in journals such as *MIS Quarterly Executive, Journal of Marketing Education, Journal of Advertising Research* and *Journal of Public Affairs*.

Dr. Jennifer Rowley BA (Hons), MSc, MSc, PhD, is Professor of Information and Communications in the Department of Languages, Information and Communications, and Faculty Head of Postgraduate Studies at Manchester Metropolitan University, UK. Her research interests are diverse and include digital marketing, place branding, digital information behaviour, social media marketing, higher education, and information and knowledge management. Jennifer is editor of *Journal of Further and Higher Education* and Associate Editor, *Journal of Marketing Management*; she also serves on a number of editorial boards and refereeing panels, including those of the *Journal of Information Science, Online information Review, Internet Research*, and *Management Decision*.

Dr. Salvador Ruiz de Maya is full Professor of Marketing at the University of Murcia, Spain. His research and consultancy interests encompass consumer information processing and emotions, family decision-making, food consumption, and social responsibility. He has published more than 50 papers in academic and practitioner journals, including *Journal of Interactive Marketing, Journal of Advertising, Journal of Business Research, Marketing Letters, Ecological Economics, Journal of Business Ethics* and *Journal of Service Research* among other. He also has presented his research in European and American universities where he contributes to Masters and PhD programs. A regular attendant of and reviewer for international marketing and consumer conferences, for some of which he has also served in the organising committees or as track chair, he also is an ad hoc reviewer for journals such as *International Marketing Review, Journal of Advertising* and *Journal of Business Ethics*.

Dr. Harjit Singh Sekhon is Senior Lecturer of Marketing at Coventry Business School. Before entering academia he held a number of marketing and marketing research posts in the UK's financial services sector and continues to have a keen interest in financial services marketing. He holds a doctoral degree from the University of Nottingham and has published many peer-reviewed papers on the topics of trust, trustworthiness and fairness in financial services. His work has appeared in various marketing journals of national and international repute including *European Journal of Marketing, Journal of Marketing Management, Journal of Services Marketing, Journal of Strategic Marketing and Journal of Financial Services Marketing*, as well as leading marketing conferences. As well as publishing work, he was previously the Associate Editor of *International Journal of Bank Marketing*.

Dr. Joon Yong Seo is an Assistant Professor of Marketing at the College at Brockport, State University of New York, where he teaches Marketing Research and Consumer Behaviour. Before he earned his MBA and doctoral degree in marketing, he worked for Prudential Investment & Securities, Seoul, Korea. His research interests include marketing of financial products and, consumer judgment and decision-making.

Dr. Sandeep Singh is Professor of Finance at the College at Brockport, State University of New York, where he teaches courses in Finance and Investments. His research interests include asset allocation, retirement withdrawals and marketing of financial services. His research has appeared in journals such as the *Financial Analysts Journal, International Journal of Bank Marketing* and the *Journal of Financial Planning*. His work has been cited in popular press such as the *New York Times, USA Today* and the *Los Angeles Times* to name a few.

Dr. Susan Thorp is chaired Professor of Finance and Superannuation at the University of Technology, Sydney. Her Chair is funded by the Sydney Financial Forum (through Colonial First State Global Asset Management), the NSW Government, the Association of Superannuation Funds of Australia (ASFA), the Industry Superannuation Network (ISN) and the Paul Woolley Centre for the Study of Capital Market Dysfunctionality. Her research focuses on long-horizon wealth management, especially consumer financial decision-making. Her publications include studies of risk communication, retirement savings portfolio management, annuitiation and retirement income streams. She is a member of the Quantitative Finance Research Centre at UTS, and the National Centre for Econometric Research, QUT. Professor Thorp obtained her BEc (Hons) from the University of Sydney, and her PhD from the University of New South Wales.

Dr. Eva Tomaseti-Solano is Lecturer of Strategic Marketing and Consumer Behaviour at the Polytechnic University of Cartagena, Spain. She completed her Masters degree in Retailing and Marketing and her PhD at the University of Murcia, Spain. She developed part of her research as PhD student at Bradford University, United Kingdom. Her research encompasses consumer behaviour in the area of product innovation evaluation, social networks and family decision-making. She has published in practitioner books in the area of consumer behaviour in Spain and in research outlets such as *Advances in Consumer Research*. A regular attendant of and reviewer for international marketing and consumer conferences, including *ACR North American Conference* and the *European Marketing Academy Conference*, she also has been an ad hoc reviewer for the *Journal of Business Research*.

Dr. Kathryn Waite, is Assistant Professor of Marketing at the School of Management and Languages, Heriot Watt University. Her research interests include understanding consumer use of the Internet for financial services decision-making, purchase and transaction and in particular consumer information search behaviour. Her PhD investigated the evaluative criteria used by bank customers when searching a bank website for information. This was a fresh approach as prior studies had tended to focus on website evaluation for shopping and not information search. She is interested in understanding techniques for marketing complex online services and has conducted research in the pensions sector.

Dr. Alex Wang, is an Associate Professor in the Department of Communication at the University of Connecticut's Stamford campus. His research has focused on issues related to consumer information processing, integrated marketing communications, Internet advertising, and corporate social responsibility (CSR). His research has appeared in journals such as the Journal of Advertising Research, Journal of Public Relations Research, Journal of Financial Services Marketing, and Corporate Communications: An International Journal. He is the author of two books and has won several awards for his research, and has industry experience in advertising, electronic publishing and public relations.

Adeela Waqar is a Research Fellow at the Consortium for Trustworthy Organizations at Fordham University. She holds an MBA majoring in Management and Finance from the Fordham Graduate School of Business Administration and is a member of the Phi Kappa Phi Honour Society. She is a trained accountant by profession having been a member of the Association of Chartered Certified Accountants UK and has worked in PwC, GlaxoSmithKline and Premier Oil London. Her work has appeared in the *International Journal of Bank Marketing*. As part of the Consortium for Trustworthy Organizations she was actively involved in creating an Organizational Trust Measurement survey and publishing the Trust Digest.

Dr. Jonathan A. J. Wilson is an academic at the University of Greenwich Business School London, with 20 years of industry and academic professional experience, which has taken him throughout Europe, the Muslim world and Asia. He is Editor-in-chief for the *Journal of Islamic Marketing*, which is an international academic journal publishing work that examines the new wave of Muslim minority and majority marketing. He is a regular contributor in the *Huffington Post*, the *Marketeers* and *Aquila Style* magazines. His area of expertise spans across: Advertising, Branding, Public Relations, Marketing Communications, Consumer Behaviour, Leadership and Management, Culture, Creativity and Hybridization, Halal, Islamic economies and the Muslim world. He has spoken on over 70 occasions internationally, delivering keynotes, public talks, and research findings. His work has received awards, and international media coverage from the *Times, Guardian, BBC World, Thomson Reuters, Sky News Arabia, Astro Awani* and *Republika* amongst others. He is also an Associate Member of the UK All Party Parliamentary Group (APPG) on Islamic Finance & Diversity in Financial Markets.

Dr. Steve Worthington specialises in the issues surrounding the distribution of financial services particularly by electronic channels and in the organisation and control of the payments systems through which these transactions are carried out. He retired as in 2014 as a Professor of Marketing at Monash University in Melbourne, Australia and has published his research widely, both in academic journals such as the *International Journal of Bank Marketing* and the *Journal of Retailing and Consumer Services*, and in more practitioner focused publications such as *The Financial Times, The Australian Financial Review, Payment Cards* and *Mobile Banking*. He has also written a number of case studies and text book chapters concerning both bank and retailer provision of financial services. A frequent presenter/chairman at industry conferences, he is also consulted by the media as an independent commentator on the delivery of financial services to consumers and has been involved in banking inquiries set up by governments in both Australia and the United Kingdom. He has completed a commissioned paper for the Australian Centre for Financial Studies on regulatory interventions and their consequences in the Australian payment system. He has also researched and published on the payment card markets in China and Japan.

Dr. Georg Wuebker is a Senior Partner with Simon-Kucher & Partners and Global Head of its Banking Competence Centre. His areas of specialisation are corporate strategy, marketing strategy, price optimisation/bundling, value-based product development, loyalty programmes and sales. He has conducted numerous national and international projects for more than 50 financial institutions in the last ten years, and is the co-author of several books, including the following; *Price Management in Financial Services*; *Value Pricing*; *Optimal Bundling*; *Power Pricing for Banking*; and *Preis-und Produktmanagement in Regionalbanken*. He has also published more than 200 articles on pricing and marketing strategy in trade journals and newspapers such as *The Banker, Thexis, NZZ, Financial Times, Die Bank, Bankmagazin, Versicherungswirtschaft, FAZ* and *Handelsblatt*. He has served as a lecturer to several educational programmes at leading universities in Europe, including the Executive MBA workshops at the ETH Zurich, the University of St. Gallen, the WHU – Otto Beisheim School of Management, and EBS. He participates on a regular basis as a keynote speaker in international finance conferences and training seminars. Georg studied Business Administration and Economics in Hull (UK), Osnabrueck (Germany) and Austin (Texas, USA). Dr. Wuebker was awarded his doctorate degree by the University of Mainz and his diploma from the University of Osnabrueck. He has also served as a Visiting Fellow at the University of Texas at Austin.

Dr. Annie Pei-I Yu is Assistant Professor of Marketing in the Department of Business Administration at the National Chung Cheng University, Taiwan. She received her Ph.D. degree in Marketing from the University of Edinburgh and also holds BA and MBA degrees from the National Kaohsiung First University of Science and Technology, Taiwan. She teaches courses in *Brand Management* and *Channel Management* at the MBA level, and Undergraduate courses in *Marketing Management* and *Consumer Behaviour*. She was the winner of the Marketing Research category of the 2009 Emerald/EFMD Outstanding Doctoral Research Awards. She is interested in the nature of consumers' relationship behaviour and motivation for relationship engagement and her research focuses on financial services marketing, consumer-brand relationships, the interaction of brand community members and their influence in branding.

Introduction

Financial services marketing in a post-crisis era

Tina Harrison and Hooman Estelami

Formal academic study of financial services marketing has been an ongoing endeavor for several decades. Countless researchers have examined the wide range of topics related to financial services marketing theory and practice, resulting in thousands of research papers and numerous specialized journals and books. The field of financial services marketing has now reached a new plateau: it has matured to a state where established views on how financial services are to be marketed are being challenged and new horizons have appeared. Drastic changes in the economic climates around the world and the adoption of revolutionizing technologies in financial services are rapidly changing the landscape in which marketers operate.

Because of the drastic changes that have affected financial services markets over the past decade, it has become essential to consolidate expert thinking on critical topics in the field. The need for such coverage has become more apparent since the global financial crisis, which has helped the public, regulators and marketing practitioners better appreciate the critical role that financial services have in facilitating the economic health of nations. With financial services markets being instrumental to a range of economic activities of the population, from transaction processing and lending, to risk management and investing, market failures can quickly translate into catastrophic meltdowns. The economic and political environment that emerged from the financial crisis has increased general awareness on the societal responsibilities that financial services marketers need to accept in their profession. There is now renewed interest to define what constitutes good marketing practice for a financial services organization.

Although several journals and textbooks dedicated to the topic of financial services marketing exist, there is a need to consolidate knowledge in a comprehensive yet concise form. Such a task would be impossible without drawing from the pool of experts who have conducted high-quality research related to their own specialized topics in financial services marketing. Topics related to product development, brand management, communication strategies, pricing, consumer decision-making and industry structure are among the many areas in which research continues to grow. The understanding of each topic area can only be achieved by experts who have dedicated their careers to the issues involved. In designing this book and selecting the chapters it was critical to draw from such expertise and to ensure that the materials are presented in a way that efficiently communicates the state-of-the art knowledge. This book is intended to serve as a "go to" source for the most current knowhow on a range of financial services marketing topics, equally relevant to researchers and practitioners in the field.

What is unique about financial services marketing?

Financial services marketing is distinct in many ways from other branches of marketing. Most of the distinction is driven by the unique characteristics of financial services when compared to other forms of services or manufactured goods. Financial services touch every aspect of our consumption as they facilitate economic activity for households and businesses. Without financial services one would not be able to purchase goods with ease (for example, through the use of credit), manage risk (for example, through the purchase of insurance policies) or plan for the future (for example, through the purchase of investment products).

Furthermore, financial services, by themselves, do not have a physical presence and cannot be visualized, touched, felt or smelled. Assessing the quality of a financial service is challenging if not impossible, requiring consumers to rely on other informational cues such as the brand name and price as indicators of quality. Such reliance can easily lead to miscalculations and error in financial decisions.

To further compound the degree of consumer confusion one needs to also acknowledge the fact that financial services are uninteresting to most consumers and therefore do not arouse much attention and focus in decision-making. This differentiates financial services decisions from consumer decisions in other contexts where products or services that possess a higher level of attractiveness may need to be decided on. For example, for most individuals interest levels in decisions associated with purchasing automobiles, homes, clothing or electronics products are considerably higher than interest levels associated with decisions related to banking, insurance or investments. Moreover, most financial services represent a means to an end, rather than end in themselves; their purchase is often contingent on the purchase of other goods and services (a mortgage) or the result of a legal requirement (automobile insurance).

One of the other unique aspects of financial services is the challenge in establishing value. The value of many financial services may be directly affected by general economic forces. For example, the interest rate associated with a deposit account cannot be evaluated on its own and can only be assessed in light of general economic indicators such as the base (or prime) rate and expected rates of inflation. The issue of value quantification is further complicated by the fact that for many financial services price is a highly complex construct, often consisting of many attributes and dimensions. Even a commoditized financial service such as a mortgage product may have over a dozen attributes, such as the interest rate, prepayment penalties, assessment fees and closing costs. For most individuals, the multidimensionality of price for financial services disables the accurate processing of the communicated information, resulting in suboptimal decisions.

All of the above characteristics make it difficult for consumers to engage in informed rational decisions, placing many consumers in a vulnerable position and making them dependent on the advice of experts. This increases the risk of the transaction, elevates the importance of trust and places greater emphasis on people and relationships in the process of marketing and consumption.

Financial services marketing at a crossroads

Since the 1960s, research has shown that individuals, regardless of their level of training or cognitive skills are bound to make financial decisions that significantly deviate from optimal rational economic thinking. In the early periods of such inquiry, the focus was primarily academic in nature and mostly interested in challenging fundamental assumptions of economic theory (some of which date back nearly two centuries); research eventually evolved in a more action-oriented direction. It became essential to identify how consumers may systematically make suboptimal decisions on financial matters. This line of questioning helped inform new ways of thinking on how financial services organizations can help consumers better understand their financial needs, eventually resulting in improved financial decisions. In addition, it mobilized a large volume of research on financial literacy and consumer education. The resulting research has informed regulatory measures intended to ensure that consumers are provided with the essential information needed to make good financial decisions.

Despite decades of research on tradition in financial services marketing, at no point earlier has the field had such pressing need for a unifying source of information on financial services marketing practices. Following the global financial crisis there has been a growing interest in understanding how financial services marketing practices result in specific outcomes, some of which may provide growth opportunities for financial institutions, others may translate into economic disasters. The financial crisis awakened the public's awareness of the vulnerabilities faced when financial systems fail. Set against this context, it became necessary to gather expert perspectives on marketing practices in financial services. As the pressure for corporate accountability increases it has become apparent to many that financial services providers need to establish – not only for themselves, but also for the mass of customers – how they truly add value in the exchange process.

In the years following the global financial crisis the level of trust that the public places on financial services marketers and the financial system understandably dropped. Survey studies in multiple countries have shown that financial services marketing professionals were not considered to be the most trustworthy and customers' evaluations of the ethical standards of professionals in the financial sector had reached a low point. Recognizing the public distrust of the industry, regulators around the world have become much more hands-on in controlling the activities of financial services marketers.

At the same time, the financial ordeals in which many financial services organizations found themselves have resulted in consolidations, mergers, and in some cases, corporate bankruptcies. The net effect has been increased market concentration for many financial services categories. For example, in the 1990s approximately 15,000 commercial banks operated in the United States but due to mergers, consolidations and bank failures, fewer than 8,000 have survived. Similar patterns of consolidation and market concentration are evident globally in financial categories such as insurance, credit cards and mortgages. Similarly, in many European and Asian countries, competition has become more concentrated for most financial services categories. The net effect has been a reduction in the number of available choices for consumers, an effect that contradicts the initial motivations for deregulatory measures put into motion nearly two decades ago.

The evolutionary changes in the dynamics of financial services markets have resulted in gradual shifts in the focus of academic research conducted. There is growing interest in understanding how financial services marketers can add value to society as a whole and to individual customer experiences. There is also a growing interest in understanding how the delivery of financial services can evolve with the introduction of new technologies. As a result, topics that have emerged in the field, many of which were not as prominent a decade earlier, include issues such as the societal impact of financial services, image building through corporate social responsibility initiatives, mobile banking and financial innovations. It has become more important for the discussions related to the marketing of financial services to cover not only what should be done to optimize profits for the firm, but also what should not be done, in order to avoid customer distrust and public scrutiny. Concerns for social equity and responsibility have become a growing branch of research in the field. In addition, it has become essential to understand the dynamics of how the business-to-business (B2B) financial markets operate. This is especially true considering the fact that while a significant volume of financial transactions occur in the business-to-consumer (B2C) domain, the area of B2B financial services marketing has for a long time been a black box, unexamined due to limited research and data constraints.

It is important that an edited volume such as this has sufficient coverage of the diverse range of topics that are emerging in the field. It is also important that the fundamental areas related to the practice of financial services marketing concerning product development, pricing, advertising and distribution, be thoroughly covered through multiple chapters, reflecting the views of several experts. This allows the reader to gain a richer and deeper understanding of related topics from multiple perspectives in each sub-discipline. Such coverage has enabled a more holistic presentation of the underlying knowledge, far exceeding the depth of discussion provided in any conventional textbook chapter or review article.

Intended readers

This book is intended to serve as a reference for contemporary research on various financial services marketing topics by drawing from the base of knowledge from experts in each sub-discipline of financial services marketing. It provides students, researchers, practitioners and policy-makers with a comprehensive overview of the key practical and theoretical issues impacting the marketing and consumption of financial services. The book has been organized in such a way as to address the needs of readers from a range of perspectives. These include:

Academic researchers: The book is intended to serve as a reference for academics who actively conduct research in financial services marketing. Established researchers and doctoral students looking for a single source covering the emerging research questions will find chapters providing in-depth coverage, the current state of thinking and emerging debates in financial services marketing thinking. The chapters, all written by authoritative experts on each topic, provide a comprehensive resource to identify relevant findings from previous studies and obtain a clear picture of emerging issues, research opportunities and new frontiers.

Marketing practitioners: The book is intended to inform practitioners who are looking for insights into how to manage the challenges of acquiring and retaining customers. Focus is placed on a range of manager-controlled marketing variables. The chapters have been written in a manner intended to enable marketing action and therefore current views on issues relevant to today's financial services marketers are provided. Practical implications are included in the chapters and relate to the various activities that constitute current financial services marketing practice.

Public policy advocates: Given that public policy issues have become a growing focal point in financial services markets around the globe, the coverage provided in this book is also intended to support the needs of public policy advocates and regulators. Several chapters related to regulations, financial decision-making and malpractice address these needs.

The goals of this book

The primary goal of this book is to provide a basis for researchers to understand the state-of-the-art in all relevant topic areas in financial services marketing. At the same time, given the emerging trends and evolving needs in financial services markets, it is recognized that new grounds and emerging topics need to be covered. As a result, the chapters cover the wide range of existing and upcoming issues that have become the focus for researchers in financial services marketing. To practitioners, this would provide a basis to identify ways to add value in the exchange process by improving the services they offer existing and potential customers. This line of thinking would also allow marketing professionals in financial services organizations to re-examine their innovation processes and develop new financial services that would most benefit customers. The discussions facilitated through the words of the authors in this book can inspire further thinking on how a financial services provider can profitably add value to the customer experience. The various sections of the book help structure such conversations and are outlined in eleven parts.

The dynamic financial services marketing environment

This introductory section sets the scene for the book. The first chapter in this section by Rai, Papaioannou and Cebenoyan provides a discussion and analysis of the current financial services marketing environment, its impact on the competitive landscape and implications for marketing and the customer. Updates and critique of regulatory developments and the impact they have had on competition are also provided in this chapter. The second chapter in this section, by Worthington, discusses how new entrants to the competitive arena of retail banking in the UK have prospered. This chapter questions the extent to which banking requirements of today would need to rely on traditional banking models. Both chapters in this section reflect on the financial crisis and provide a critical discussion of the impact on the competitive landscape, implications for regulations and the future challenges for the industry.

The financial services consumer and financial decision-making

The chapters in this section focus on some of the unique aspects that have an impact on consumers' decision-making processes in the context of financial services decisions. Traditional models of consumer behavior assume a rational consumer making informed decisions. Due to a number of factors, financial services consumers do not or cannot make informed rational decisions. Indeed, for some financial services, the decision is limited or the consumer may delegate the decision to an expert, creating a separate set of decisions around the choice and selection of experts. This section of the book addresses these unique sets of issues. It begins with a discussion by Huhmann of the impact of financial literacy on behavior. Then follows an examination of consumer decision-making by Bateman, Louviere and Thorp, drawing on interdisciplinary research from three decision-making contexts. Ruiz de Maya and Tomaseti-Solano explore household financial decision-making and how such decisions are affected by the composition of the household, in particular the role of the wife. The next two chapters explore pension purchasing from different aspects. Gough and Adami address the question of what motivates individuals to invest in a pension, identifying the key triggers for decision-making. Kalogeras, Hoffmann and Mahr focus on the extent to which consumers are guided by financial and non-financial attributes in their decision-making and the implications of such. The final chapter in this section, by Mishra and Kumar, examines the role of financial knowledge in decision-making.

Managing financial services relationships and the customer experience

Building on the previous section, this section explores in more detail the development and ongoing management of the customer–firm relationship and the customer experience. There are a number of unique factors to consider in the context of financial services including the contractual nature of the relationship, the role of trust and the extent to which consumers feel able to terminate a relationship. This set of factors all combine to create unique challenges and implications for the development and management of financial services relationships. The chapters in this section emphasise these issues and in particular provide a critique of the theoretical understanding of relationship marketing, loyalty, trust and service quality. In the first chapter in this section, Yu and Harrison explore what motivates financial providers and consumers to develop a relationship and the many types of relationship that can exist. Ennew and Sekhon examine the dimensions of trust and trustworthiness and report on the results of a longitudinal tracking study of trust in the UK financial services sector. Based on a qualitative study, El-Manstrly explores the antecedents of customer loyalty in the UK banking industry and highlights the positive and the negative reasons for staying. Finally, a key element in the establishment of the customer experience and relationships is service quality and the role of people in the delivery of the service experience. Eriksson presents a framework for delivery of a quality financial services experience.

Developing and managing the financial services offering

Research in the area of financial services product development and management is limited and has tended to apply models of innovation and product development from physical goods to financial services. Recent research has demonstrated that the unique characteristics of financial services call for alternative approaches and fresh insights. The chapters in this section focus on critical areas within the lifecycle of the financial services product. Michel's chapter draws on the latest research and thinking in relation to innovation in the development of new financial services, emphasizing co-creation of value in the service innovation process. In the following chapter, Farquhar and Robson discuss the importance of branding in the ongoing management of the financial product and present a brand-building framework aimed at improving customers' experiences with the brand. In the final chapter in this section, Harness and Harness discuss the end stage of the lifecycle including issues associated with the elimination of financial services and the challenges of management of the ongoing customer relationship.

Financial services pricing strategies

Little has been written about financial services pricing strategies and their impact on financial services consumers. In mainstream marketing, price is an important factor in consumer decisions and is often used by consumers as a signal of the quality of the offering. In the context of financial services, price may manifest itself in a number of ways; it may not always be transparent to the consumer and may not always relate to the direct costs associated with the production and marketing of the offering. Additionally, prices are at times restricted by external factors, outside the control of financial institutions themselves. These conditions create a number of challenges for financial institutions in the use of price as a marketing variable and for consumers as a decision criterion. Drawing on the latest research in this area, the chapters in this section critically discuss consumer interactions with prices and the management of prices by financial institutions. Estelami first discusses how consumers form their perceptions of financial services prices and the factors that influence such perceptions. Avlonitis and Indounas then discuss how financial services organizations arrive at their prices, the pricing methods used and the factors that exert an impact on price management. In the last chapter in this section, Ke, Wuebker and Baumgarten consider how the bundling of financial services prices may make financial offers more attractive and relevant to customers and present strategies for price bundling.

Communicating and promoting financial services

A number of factors pose challenges to financial institutions in the communication and promotion of their offerings, including intangibility, regulation and a disinterested consumer. Early research on this topic tended to focus on the application of traditional methods of promotion to financial services. Recent research recognizes the specific nature of consumer behavior in this context and the implications for communication and advertising. The chapters in this section thus address the theoretical gaps in the literature that suggest practical solutions for institutions in communicating their positioning to the marketplace. The first chapter, by Robson and Pitt, provides an overview of communication and advertising approaches largely from a financial provider perspective, including their uses and effectiveness in relation to financial services. Wang then discusses the impact and effectiveness of communication from a consumer perspective using the AMO (Ability, Motivation, Opportunity) model to explain the degree of consumer information processing of financial services communications and their ultimate effectiveness.

Distribution and delivery of financial services

The distribution and delivery of financial services has received much attention in the literature. Although research has focused on consumer adoption of new technologies such as Internet and mobile banking, the impact of the changing distribution and delivery landscape is not fully explored in past research. New methods for delivery of financial services affect the nature of the customer relationship and the depth of ongoing interactions between financial services providers and customers. The chapters in this section discuss the impact of new distribution and delivery mechanisms on financial institutions and relationship building strategies. In the first chapter, Jaramillo provides a critique of the impact of technology on the financial services distribution and delivery landscape. This is followed by a closer look at mobile technologies by Gandy, in particular the impact of mobile technology on the payments system. Finally, Waite and Rowley present the concept of the e-servicescape, a framework for developing and managing the customer experience in online banking.

Corporate financial services marketing

Although many of the marketing concepts discussed throughout the book are relevant to retail and corporate customers, it is important to recognize that the majority of published research has been conducted in the retail financial services domain. This has left a gap in our understanding of corporate financial services marketing. This section of the book looks at the unique aspects of corporate financial services marketing, including decision-making in an institutional context. Moles first examines the corporate-bank relationship, in particular the factors of communication, commitment and trust. Singh and Seo focus on the unique aspects of cooperation and competition that exist in situations where financial institutions and corporations represent partners and competitors.

Alternative banking models

Several alternative banking and finance models have developed that are beginning to challenge the assumptions of traditional banking and finance methods and offer key lessons for traditional financial institutions. An area of growing academic interest has been that of Islamic banking. The Islamic banking system is different from traditional banking systems in that it is based on Shariah guidelines, which are derived from the teachings of the Qur'an. These guidelines affect how banking and insurance products are presented to customers and they influence matters such as the realization of returns on deposits, lending practices, and the determination of premiums for insurance policies. Considering the global growth of the Islamic banking sector and the expanding markets it serves, two chapters in this section address issues related to banking and insurance marketing in the unique context of Islamic banks. Rammal provides an overview of Islamic banking and the key principles underpinning it, then Wilson and Abdul Rahman discuss risk and insurance in an Islamic context. The final chapter in this section, by Mishra, Igwe, Lean and Megicks, focuses on microfinance, which is also a form of banking distinct from traditional banking models. Microfinance banking models are used in developing countries to empower the poor to become economically active, therefore reflecting the positive societal impact that alternative banking services can have.

Marketing malpractice and financial fiascos

Misselling, marketing malpractice and financial fiascos have all received significant media attention in the last few decades, yet the academic debate on this area remains limited. There is a critical need for the industry to reflect on its past practices, to learn lessons and to identify solutions. In this section of the book, Ashton conducts a critical analysis and assessment of the scale and scope of mis-selling in the UK. Hurley, Gong and Waqar then debate the core issue of trust in banking, the factors contributing to the breakdown of trust and how to restore it. In the final chapter, Puttonen provides an analysis and categorization of the various forms of marketing malpractice witnessed through a series of case examples. The section raises a number of questions about the moral and ethical implications of marketing and the unique role that the financial services industry occupies in terms of its fiduciary responsibility.

Moral and ethical issues in financial services marketing

This final part of the book pulls together a range of topics that are emerging under the umbrella of moral and ethical issues in financial services marketing. Research in this area is a recognition of the specific role of financial services in promoting and protecting the social and economic welfare of society and, the desire for consumers to exercise their own moral and ethical values in the choice of financial services providers, to balance out economic goals and objectives with social and ethical motives. In the first chapter, McDonald provides a critical review of research in the area of CSR (Corporate Social Responsibility) in financial services. Nilsson examines the specific phenomenon of Socially Responsible Investing (SRI), the motives for financial providers and investors and SRI strategies. In recognition of the importance of sales people and advisors in the financial services relationship, Mulki discusses the ethics of the sales process. The last two chapters of the book explore the issue of financial exclusion. Koku examines challenges and issues associated with marketing financial services to the poor. Devlin takes a broader perspective of financial exclusion and examines the many forms that exclusion can take as well as the social and economic consequences. Both chapters provide recommendations on how to reduce exclusion.

Conclusions

While research traditions in financial services marketing have existed for several decades, there is no doubt that new avenues for inquiry have begun. Many researchers, with focus on traditional and emerging topics, have been hard at work for several decades. However, the topics of interest today are distinct from those of a decade earlier. The constant push of technology has created new opportunities for research by changing the way we interact, the growth in demand for unique financial solutions, the economic climates around the globe and the public desire for a higher level of accountability. Understanding the evolving dynamics of financial services markets is essential to keeping pace with inevitable changes in financial services markets. The result is a growing demand on practitioners to innovate financial solutions for customers and a need for academics to explore emerging dynamics that evolve from such innovations.

In order for financial services to have impactful and positive effects on society, one must take into account the benefits that such services provide to every customer. The practice of financial services marketing must maintain focus on adding value to customer experiences while recognizing the long-term impact that financial services can have on the well-being of the public. Ideally, financial services should be reflective of the latent needs of the marketplace while generating sustainable and profitable relationships with individual customers. The desire to maximize profitability needs to be balanced against the costs associated with adding value to the customer experience. It is essential that practitioners and academics identify ways to reach such a delicate balance and it is hoped that this book has provided the resources needed for financial services professionals and researchers to achieve this objective.

Part I

The dynamic financial services marketing environment

1

Impact of regulation on competition in commercial and investment banking

Anoop Rai, George J. Papaioannou and A. Sinan Cebenoyan

Introduction

Financial institutions play a unique role in the saving–investment process of an economy by participating in the creation of credit and mediating the flow of funds between savers and investors. They also assist central banks in their implementation of monetary policy by serving as conduits in achieving money supply and interest rate targets. The failure of a major commercial bank can have a significant negative impact on these functions and disrupt the saving–investment process, hurting the real sector of the economy.

In their intermediation function, commercial banks rely on insured deposits for a large amount of their funding, often enjoying explicit protection from governments that seek to protect small savers in the event of a bank failure. They also enjoy implicit protection in the form of "too big to fail" (TBTF) policies that compel central banks to save large banks to avoid negative externalities on the economy. These protections can lead to moral hazard problems inducing managers to issue riskier loans, knowing that insured depositors have few incentives to monitor loan quality, especially when the presumption of TBTF is present. In addition, the banking sector is characterized by information asymmetry where the opacity of loan portfolios prevents depositors and investors from properly identifying bank quality. To mitigate the problems, most central banks have taken on the responsibility of monitoring banks. As a result, financial institutions tend to be highly regulated entities around the world. Regulation, however, has significant consequences for market competition in financial services and the structure of the financial services industry.

This chapter provides an overview of the major regulatory changes in the commercial and investment banking industry with primary focus on the United States (US) and the European Union (EU). It predominantly covers the period since 1990 when dramatic developments in regulations, policy and practices transformed banking on a global scale. This transformation was two-fold. First, the traditional banking system transitioned to a securitized banking system (Carey et al. 2012). Second, commercial banks aggressively expanded their operations into securities business and investment banking. The first transformation was driven by the development and proliferation of derivative financial products, of which securitized debt is one class. The second transformation was driven by the gradual and total deregulation of the securities business, especially in the US, which allowed banks to expand into the securitized debt markets.

Both activities moved banks away from the spread-based traditional banking to fee-based broker type banking.

The chapter is structured into five sections, the first section gives a brief overview of the theoretical underpinnings of regulation and competition in banking. The second section reports on the main regulatory developments in the EU and presents empirical evidence of their impact on the banking industry and markets. The third section presents the regulatory developments in the US with some pertinent empirical findings on competition. The fourth section discusses the transition of commercial banks into investment banking and its impact on the structure of the investment banking industry and markets. The chapter ends with a summary of the main conclusions and possible implications of recent changes in the regulatory regimes.

Regulation and competition

A lack of enforcement of regulations or regulatory forbearance has been identified as one of the major factors in the market failure of financial institutions in recent years, yet at the same time, regulation is considered to have a dampening effect on free markets. In a competitive market, participants must be allowed to succeed as well as to fail, which may be hindered by regulatory intervention. A number of economic, political and social rationales have been provided as justification for regulating financial institutions: the avoidance of excessive concentration of economic and political power in the hands of a few firms, "too much" competition leading to excessive risk taking and in turn leading to failures and bailouts, expensive monopoly prices, and abuse of uneducated consumers, being the most important. The underlying expectation that post-crisis analysis and regulation should prevent failures under previous regulatory regimes does not seem to be fulfilled.

Most often, the principal loss following financial industry failures is the public's trust in the financial system, which can hurt the saving–investment process and wealth generating capacity of the economy. Although financial contracts can be written to protect the negotiating parties, it is impossible to entirely eliminate the possibility of one-party losses due to information asymmetry or moral hazard. Therefore, regulatory constraints can be thought of as the social price paid to secure a sufficient level of trust (understanding and restoring trust in banks is discussed in detail in Chapter 30).

Central banks are assigned the difficult task of ensuring the safety and soundness of financial institutions while encouraging competition. However, fostering competition to increase efficiency has the potential to stir instability. On the asset side, the presence of deposit insurance can increase risk-taking by bank managers because depositors have fewer incentives to monitor the portfolio of banks, especially in declining markets. On the liability side, excess competition can lead to a higher probability of runs because of the adverse relationship between investors and depositors, increasing the fragility of the banking system (Vives 2011). At the first sign of distress, both depositors and investors, including uninsured depositors, have incentives to be the first to withdraw deposits or curtail funding.

The finance literature has used multiple metrics to measure competition: concentration, barriers to entry, market structure, contestability and within industry competition. However, none of these measures provide an accurate and consistent estimate of competition. For example, the Herfindahl-Hirschman (HH) index is used as a measure of concentration in many economic studies covering industrial and financial sectors. Yet the HH Index can fail to capture the degree of competition, especially in the banking industry.[1] In many European countries the banking industry is dominated by few large banks with branches throughout the region. Nevertheless, there is healthy competition among the banks in many of the countries, partially because of strong regulations and monitoring by central banks.

Market structure is another important factor in the study of competition. Is competition enhanced when there are a large number of small banks or when there are a small number of large banks? The empirical literature has focused on the Structure-Conduct-Performance hypothesis to decide whether a country with few large banks signifies the presence of market power or whether bank efficiency leads to increased market share, which then eventually leads to concentrated markets. Market structure studies also examine whether mergers and acquisitions are the preferred means to increase consolidation and concentration.

Barriers to entry, whether by regulation or cultural factors, can also impact competition. Besanko and Thakor (1992) have shown that the potential for entry alone can make a significant difference to competitive behavior (as demonstrated in Chapter 2 in relation to new entrants). Barriers to entry are also impacted by regulatory forbearance. Kaas's (2004) theoretical model shows that foreign bank entry may be limited when barriers to entry are eliminated if regulatory policy favors social optimality rather than private optimality. In his model, efficient banks that are better at assessing credit quality may not find it profitable to move into countries with less-efficient banks if local governments are unable to close inefficient banks. If less-efficient local banks are allowed to fail, foreign bank entry increases and overall bank lending becomes socially optimal.

It has been argued that insured deposits and costly equity in a competitive market encourage banks to compete for ever-riskier investments leading to increased number of failures and possibly bailouts (see Allen and Gale 2004a, 2004b, among others). Allen and Gale (2004a) show that banking systems dominated by a few large banks are likely to be less fragile than banking systems with many small banks, as they are able to diversify. However, competition has also shown to increase stability, making the competition-stability relationship complex (Anginer et al. 2012). Their analysis finds that greater competition encourages banks to take on more diversified risks, making the banking system less fragile to shocks.

The banking industry in Europe and the US is characterized by healthy competition in the presence of strong oversight by central banks and other regulatory bodies. However, there are sufficient institutional differences and historical precedence that warrant studying the two regions separately to assess the impact of regulations on the competitive behavior of banks. The next section examines changes to European regulations and its impact on competition.

Developments in European banking regulation

The market structure of European banking differs significantly from that of the United States. Nearly all the countries are dominated by a few major banks, some of them government-owned, with branches scattered throughout the region. In larger countries such as Germany, France and Italy, the large banks co-exist with many cooperative and small local banks. The regulatory environment in Europe is also different from the US with most countries having one regulator, usually the central bank, to monitor financial institutions. Each central bank also has its own history with respect to its formation and legacy.

European central banks began their convergence to a single unified banking authority with the Treaty of Rome in 1957, which helped establish a free-trade zone. The process of liberalization continued until the introduction of the Euro, when the European Central Bank (ECB) was established in 1999 as the sole regulatory agency to set monetary policy and ensure the safety and soundness of the banking system throughout the EU. The path to harmonization has been challenging because of the diverse cultures and banking systems.

The initial goals of European banking regulation were to unify the markets and allow establishment of branches across borders, level the playing field on regulation and ensure a competitive environment while protecting consumers. The first major piece of legislation toward conformity was the First Banking Directive instituted in 1977. It was followed by the Second Banking Directive and the Financial Services Action Plan in 1992. Although the directives are not legally binding, it is incumbent among the countries to modify their internal laws to comply with the recommendations.

First Banking Directive of 1977

This major piece of regulation removed the initial barriers between countries by adopting the following changes: banks could provide banking services across borders in countries belonging to the European Economic Community (EEC),[2] rules were harmonized for the establishment of branches, supervisory standards were made uniform, and rules were also harmonized for the treatment of non-EEC banks wishing to offer banking services in EEC countries.

Second Banking Directive of 1992

The first directive still required branches to obtain permission from the host country and fall under host country supervision. The second directive set out to create a single banking license and a real internal banking market based on the principle of home country control.[3] A bank authorized in one state was freely allowed to set up branches in other states, banks were subject to supervision by home country regulators and non-EEC banks could also expand into EEC countries once they were authorized to set up in one state.

The second directive came on the heels of the Maastricht Treaty in 1989, which set the course for the creation of a single currency. The two directives set in motion the dismantling of barriers in the financial services industry in Europe. Over time, other directives were adopted that led to a nearly uniform market across all countries. For example, in 1993 the Investment Services Directive allowed investment firms to offer brokerage and dealer services, individual portfolio management, reception and transmission of investor orders and underwriting activities in other countries. It was replaced in 2007 by the Markets in Financial Instruments Directive (MiFID), which created a single market for investment services and activities and ensured harmonized protection for investors in financial instruments, such as stocks, bonds, derivatives and various structured products. It underwent further refinement in 2011 as a result of the financial crisis. In 1994 there was the establishment of deposit insurance up to €10,000. In 1999 the Financial Services Action Plan (FSAP) was established, aimed at integrating the banking and securities sector by 2005.

The implementation of FSAP encompassed several regulatory reforms between 1999 and 2006. Most of them took place after 2001 following the bankruptcy of Enron, Worldcom and Parmalat, revealing widespread fraud and accounting irregularities. The goal was to liberalize the various financial services sectors while imposing fair and honest standards in financial transactions.

The financial crisis of 2008 added another impetus to the integration and harmonization of banking regulations in Europe. The crisis began with bank failures in Iceland followed by Ireland, Greece and Spain. The cause was heavy bank borrowing in the form of deposits and other liabilities, which were then invested in mortgages and other speculative assets. In Greece, Portugal, Italy and France banks suffered heavy losses on sovereign debt that ultimately lost value as credit premiums rose sharply and debt had to be restructured (as in the case of Greece). As most sovereign debt required zero capital under Basel rules, banks held large portfolios of sovereign debt, never anticipating that sovereign bonds would be downgraded.

The regulatory reforms that followed the 2008 crisis changed focus from the integration of markets to the prevention of crises and protection of consumers. The result was the creation of several supranational agencies with a mandate to consider integration and risk management. A major change was the recognition that supervision of banks by home countries alone was not sufficient. Instead, supervision required management at the European level.

Three new European agencies were created on January 1, 2011, to work with the European Central Bank (ECB). Their mission was to monitor financial institutions throughout the EU and serve as an independent advisory group to the European Parliament and the Council of the European Union. The European Banking Authority (EBA) is focused on the stability of the financial system, transparency of markets and financial products and protection of depositors and investors. The European Securities and Markets Authority (ESMA) is focused on ensuring the integrity, transparency, efficiency and orderly functioning of securities markets, as well as enhancing investor protection by fostering supervisory convergence among securities regulators. The European Insurance and Occupational Pensions Authority (EIOPA) is focused on the protection of insurance policyholders, pension scheme members and beneficiaries.

Similar to the approach taken in the US, European authorities have also acknowledged that the current architecture of national supervisory agencies is insufficient to monitor large banks with substantial cross-border trades. As a result, on September 12, 2013, the European Parliament passed the Single Supervisory Mechanism (SSM) law, which was approved by the Council of the European Union (EU) on October 15, 2013. For the first time, this law will permit the European Central Bank (ECB) to supervise banks that are considered "significant" at a regional level and bypass national regulators. The model is similar to a provision in the Dodd-Frank Bill passed in the US in the aftermath of the financial crisis. This law empowered the Fed and the Federal Stability Oversight Committee (FSOC) to directly monitor financial institutions identified as Significantly Important Financial Institutions (SIFIs). The Fed defines banks with assets greater than $50 billion to be SIFIs.[4]

In Europe, under the new SSM law, the banks will be deemed as "significant" if they have assets greater than €30 billion, they have assets greater than 20 percent of the GDP of the member state with a minimum of €5 billion, they are deemed as one of the three most significant credit institutions within a member state, they have significant cross-border assets and liabilities, and they are currently receiving financial assistance from a national or European agency.

The ECB expects approximately 150 out of the estimated 6,000 banks in Europe to fall under one of the criteria. Although small in number, they represent about 80 percent of the banking sector. The ECB began its supervisory role on November 4, 2014.

Empirical evidence of competition

Studies on bank regulation and competition have found European banks are quite concentrated but at the same time also exhibit competitive behavior. Table 1.1 shows the Herfindahl-Hirschman index and the five-bank concentration rate (CR5) of banks in the EU based on data from 2005 to 2009.[5] The US Department of Justice considers HH scores of lower than 1,000 to indicate negligible concentration, HH scores between 1,000 and 1,800 to indicate moderate concentration and scores above 1,800 to indicate high concentration in the banking industry. Similarly, CR5 values of less than 50 percent are associated with lower concentration.

Germany, Italy, Spain, Austria, Luxembourg and the United Kingdom all have HH scores of lower than 500, indicating very low concentration. Bulgaria, Ireland, France, Hungary, Austria, Poland and Sweden all have HH scores below 1,000. The CR5 ratio provides the same evidence. The rest of the 14 countries have scores greater than 1,000, indicating high concentration. Between 2005 and 2009, there has also been a slight increase in the overall ratios for 16 of the 27 countries. Although policy-makers in the US and Europe are expressly in favor of

Table 1.1 Herfindahl-Hirschman Index for credit institutions and share of total assets of largest five credit institutions. MU16 = countries using Euro as currency. EU27 = EU with 27 countries.

	Herfindahl Index for Credit Institutions					Share of Total Assets of Largest Five Credit Institutions				
	2005	2006	2007	2008	2009	2005	2006	2007	2008	2009
Belgium	2,112	2,041	2,079	1,881	1,622	85.3	84.4	83.4	80.8	77.1
Bulgaria	698	707	833	834	846	50.8	50.3	56.7	57.3	58.3
Czech Republic	1,155	1,104	1,100	1,014	1,032	65.5	64.1	65.7	62.1	62.4
Denmark	1,115	1,071	1,120	1,229	1,042	66.3	64.7	64.2	66	64
Germany	174	178	183	191	206	21.6	22	22	22.7	25
Estonia	4,039	3,593	3,410	3,120	3,090	98.1	97.1	95.7	94.8	93.4
Ireland	644	649	690	794	881	47.8	49	50.4	55.3	58.8
Greece	1,096	1,101	1,096	1,172	1,184	65.6	66.3	67.7	69.5	69.2
Spain	487	442	459	497	507	42	40.4	41	42.4	43.3
France	727	726	679	681	605	51.9	52.3	51.8	51.2	47.2
Italy	230	220	328	344	353	26.8	26.2	33.1	33	34
Cyprus	1,029	1,056	1,089	1,019	1,086	59.8	63.9	64.9	63.8	65
Latvia	1,176	1,271	1,158	1,205	1,181	67.3	69.2	67.2	70.2	69.3
Lithuania	1,838	1,913	1,827	1,714	1,693	80.6	82.5	80.9	81.3	80.5
Luxembourg	312	294	276	278	288	30.7	29.1	27.9	27.3	27.8
Hungary	795	823	840	819	861	53.2	53.5	54.1	54.4	55.2
Malta	1,330	1,171	1,177	1,236	1,246	75.3	70.9	70.2	72.8	72.7
Netherlands	1,796	1,822	1,928	2,168	2,032	84.5	85.1	86.3	86.8	85
Austria	560	534	527	454	414	45	43.8	42.8	39	37.2
Poland	650	599	640	562	574	48.5	46.1	46.6	44.2	43.9
Portugal	1,154	1,134	1,098	1,114	1,150	68.8	67.9	67.8	69.1	70.1
Romania	1,115	1,165	1,041	922	857	59.4	60.1	56.3	54	52.4
Slovenia	1,369	1,300	1,282	1,268	1,256	63	62	59.5	59.1	59.7
Slovakia	1,076	1,131	1,082	1,197	1,273	67.7	66.9	68.2	71.6	72.1
Finland	2,730	2,560	2,540	3,160	3,120	82.9	82.3	81.2	82.8	82.6
Sweden	845	856	934	953	899	57.3	57.8	61	61.9	60.7
United Kingdom	399	394	449	412	467	36.3	35.9	40.7	36.5	40.8
MU16	640	634	659	687	663	42.8	43.1	44.4	44.7	44.6
Unweighted Avg	1,052	1,022	1,032	1,091	1,076	56.7	56.4	56.7	57	57
EU27	614	592	596	665	632	42.6	41.5	41.5	45.2	44.3
Unweighted Avg	1,135	1,106	1,106	1,120	1,102	59.3	59	59.5	59.6	59.5

Source: EU Banking Structures, Table 3, European Central Bank, September 2010. Available at www.ecb.int/pub/pdf/other/eubankingstructures201009en.pdf. Reproduced with permission.

preventing concentration as a means to check TBTF banks, concentration has continued to increase primarily because of the closure of many banks after the crisis.

Empirical studies support the presence of increased concentration in European banking but do not find competition to be stifled. Angelini and Cetrelli (2003) examined 900 banks from 1984 to 1997 covering the first two directives and found that increased concentration had not significantly impacted competition. They attribute the potential threat of the entry of other EU banks allowed by the Second Banking Directive as one explanation. Claessens and Laeven (2004) studied 4,000 banks in 50 countries in the 1994–2001 period and found that concentration was not a significant variable in curtailing competition. They also found that fewer restrictions on entry and access spur competition and contestability was a more influential factor on competition.

Beck et al. (2004) found further nuances in the relationship between concentration and competition. They reported a negative relationship between concentration and access to credit for developing countries but an insignificant relationship for countries with higher GDP per capita, well-developed institutions, efficient credit markets and a high share of foreign banks. Uhde and Heimeshoff (2009) found mixed results. They examined concentration and risk issues using a large sample of EU25 banks between 1997 and 2005 and found that bank profitability and the probability of bank insolvency are positively related to banking sector concentration.

Casu and Girardone (2009) found that the main EU banking markets have become progressively more concentrated and have used their increasing market power to lower their prices at a slower rate than the drop in their marginal cost. They found no evidence that cost efficiency gains preceded the rise of market power.

Finally, the crisis of 2008 highlighted the challenge of policy-makers in coping with the principle of "too big to fail". Gropp et al. (2011) showed that implicit adoption of that principle in OECD countries had the unintended consequence of forcing smaller banks to pursue riskier operations to counter the advantage from the implicit guarantees extended to big banks.

Developments in US banking regulation

This section provides a brief history of US and global regulations and their effects on competition in commercial and investment banking markets.

Regulation of US financial institutions (FIs) is possibly unlike any other country's experience. Until the 1860s, banks were regulated solely by the states in which they were chartered. The National Currency Act (1863) and National Bank Act (1864) established national bank charters for the first time. The Federal Reserve was established in 1913. Table 1.2 provides a summary of major US regulations. It reveals a pattern of recurring cycles of crisis-regulation-deregulation-crisis. Though the history of US banking regulation gives the impression of a patchwork of putting out fires, its evolution seems to follow a storyline.

Three sections of the Dodd-Frank Act, which was enacted in the post-2008 crisis, are of particular importance for the conduct of retail commercial banking and investment banking operations. The first is the creation of the Consumer Financial Protection Bureau established in 2011. Its regulatory powers are poised to have a significant impact in the design of retail banking products and services and restrict practices of poor transparency and dubious value to consumers. The second provision purports to introduce greater transparency in the trading of over-the-counter derivatives. The requirement for central clearing and exchange-based trading of derivatives will affect the ability of investment banks to negotiate bilateral contracts without posting prices. The third far-reaching provision of the Act is the so-called Volcker Rule. The rule, which will become effective in July 2015, is aimed at reducing depositor risks by

Table 1.2 Major banking legislation Acts in the United States.

Year	Legislation	Important regulatory provisions
1927	The McFadden Act	Branching made consistent between nationally and state chartered banks. Liberalized national banks' securities underwriting activities.
1933	Banking Act (Glass-Steagall Act)	FDIC established. Separated Investment and Commercial Banking. Interest rate ceilings for deposits. Allowed state-wide branching.
1935	Banking Act	Restricted entry into banking.
1956	Bank Holding Company (BHC) Act	BHC's restricted to banking activities. Prevented BHC's from owning banks across state lines.
1978	International Banking Act	Brought domestic branches of foreign-owned banks into regulatory conformance with domestic banks.
1980	DIDMCA (Depository Institutions Deregulation and Monetary Control Act)	Interest bearing deposit (NOW) accounts permitted. Allowed Fed to set reserve requirements.
1982	Garn-St. Germain Depository Institutions Act	Introduced money market deposit accounts. Allowed thrifts lending and deposit taking powers. Allowed failed thrifts to be acquired by commercial banks. Reaffirmed limitations on bank powers in insurance and underwriting activities.
1987	CEBA (Competitive Equality in Banking Act)	Redefined the definition of a bank to limit the growth of nonbank banks.
1989	FIRREA (Financial Institutions Reform Recovery and Enforcement Act)	Limited savings banks' nonresidential real estate activities. Introduced QTL. Equalized capital requirements of thrifts and banks. Resolution Trust Corporation created.
1991	FDICIA (Federal Deposit Insurance Corporation Improvement Act)	Introduced Prompt Corrective Actions, requiring mandatory interventions by regulators. Introduced risk-based deposit insurance premiums. Limited too big to fail bailouts.
1994	Riegle-Neal Interstate Banking and Branching Efficiency Act	Permitted BHC's to acquire banks across state lines.
1999	Gramm-Leach-Bliley Act (Financial Services Modernization Act)	Eliminated restrictions on banks, insurance companies and securities firms entering into each other's area. Allowed Financial Services Holding Companies.
2010	Dodd-Frank Act (Wall Street Reform and Consumer Protection Act)	Systemic risk to be controlled by Financial Services oversight council. Power to government to break up systemically risky FIs. Created Consumer Financial Protection Agency. Shareholders given proxy vote on executive pay. OTC derivatives to be traded through clearinghouses. Curtails deposit-insured banks' operations in hedge and private equity funds.

prohibiting banks and affiliated entities from operating as licensed dealers to engage in proprietary short-term trading (except in government bonds) and acquiring or retaining an interest in or sponsoring a private equity or hedge fund. In general, banks may not own more than 3 percent of the ownership interest of the fund and the bank's aggregated ownership interest in such funds may not exceed 3 percent of the bank's Tier 1 capital. Banks are allowed to engage in certain hedging activities as well as in underwriting, market making and riskless trading for customers, though they must provide documentation that trading and hedging activities are in compliance with the law. These restrictions should have the effect of shifting the prohibited activities to non-banking firms and thus affect the structure of the investment banking industry.

Empirical evidence of competition

The empirical literature mirrors the conflicting results of theory. Early evidence of US data tends to favor the "charter value hypothesis" (Marcus 1984, Keeley 1990), whereas later cross-country evidence points in different directions. For instance, De Nicoló et al. (2004) and Boyd and De Nicoló (2005) find a positive association between concentration in the banking sector and banks' overall default risk, thus suggesting that more competition should be associated with more stable banks. Similarly, Beck et al. (2006) find that countries with higher regulatory entry barriers to the banking sector run a higher risk of suffering a systemic financial crisis, but they also find that higher concentration in the banking sector is associated with a lower probability of crisis. Finally, the results of Berger et al. (2009) provide support for the hypothesis of a non-monotonic effect of competition on bank risk, but whether the positive or negative effect dominates depends on the risk measure used. For example, they find a negative effect of competition on banks' asset risk, whereas the effect of increased competition on overall default risk is positive.

DeYoung et al. (2009) report that:

despite general agreement on the broad forces driving consolidation and M&As in the financial sector, there is little consensus regarding this consolidation on industry performance. For example, the extant literature provides inconsistent evidence regarding whether, on average, the participating financial firms benefit from M&As, whether the customers of these firms benefit, or whether societal risks have increased or decreased as a result of this activity.

For the United States, Wheelock (2011) finds little change over time in the average concentration of local banking markets or the average number of dominant local banks, even during the financial crisis when numerous bank failures and several large bank mergers occurred. Concentration did not increase substantially on average. Hakanes and Schnabel (2011), show that stricter bank capital requirements raise firms' risk-taking and increased capital requirements may destabilize the banking sector.

In summary, possibly due to sample, time and modeling differences, neither the theory nor the empirical evidence outlined provide us with a consensus opinion on the effects of market structure in banking and its effects on efficiencies, risks and competition.

The financial crisis of 2008 was an important test for the viability of the securitized banking system and the deregulation of securities business. The crisis reopened the question of whether the repeal of the Glass-Steagall Act in 1999 had contributed to the financial crisis. At the core of the debate lies the role commercial banks played in the securitization of mortgage loans of dubious quality and whether this contributed to the erosion of underwriting standards in issuing home loans. Indeed, there is academic evidence that lenders produced mortgage loans of progressively lower quality during the years leading up to 2007 (Demyanyk and Van Hemert 2011). The reason was the growing appetite of investment banks for securitized paper on which they could earn issuance fees and trading commissions in the secondary market. Screening loans for credit risk as in the traditional bank system became less important as banks could offload the risk to the open market through securitization (Purnanandam 2011).

Notwithstanding this evidence, it must be noted that banks had been granted the power to operate in securitized markets at the start of the deregulation process in the late 1980s. It is debatable, therefore, whether the full repeal of the Glass-Steagall Act in 1999 is solely responsible for the excesses that followed and led to the 2008 crisis.

Commercial banks in the securities business

Deregulation of securities business

No other sector of US financial services has been impacted more by banking deregulation than that of the securities business. As noted in Table 1.2, the Glass-Steagall Act was repealed by the Financial Services Modernization Act (FSMA) and signed by President Clinton on November 14, 1999. The FSMA (also known as the Gramm-Leach-Bliley Act) expanded the Banking Holding Company Act to allow the creation of a new corporate vehicle, the Financial Holding Company (FHC), which could engage in banking, securities and insurance business. National banks and state chartered banks that elected not to obtain the FHC status could engage in securities business through subsidiaries under certain conditions.

The road to full deregulation covered a long period from the early 1980s to the late 1990s. First, bank holding companies were allowed to run brokerage business in 1983, whereas in 1987 Section 20 subsidiaries of banks were permitted to underwrite and trade municipal revenue bonds, mortgage and asset backed debt and commercial paper (Tier I powers).[6] Initially, Section 20 affiliates were allowed to participate in securities business under a cap of 5 percent of total revenue from permissible activities, which favored only the big banks. Indeed, JP Morgan Chase and Bankers Trust were the first to apply and receive Section 20 securities powers. In 1989 and 1990 Section 20 subsidiaries were allowed to underwrite corporate debt and equity (Tier II powers) and the revenue limit was raised to 10 percent. In 1996, the limit was increased to 25 percent and the Federal Reserve removed the strict firewalls between investment and commercial banking departments. The higher revenue limit enabled more banks to enter the field of securities business whereas the removal of the firewalls increased synergies and lowered the information costs incurred by underwriters in setting the offer price of new securities.

Empirical evidence of competition

In the thirty years following the initial steps toward the deregulation of the securities business, commercial banks have come to dominate the securities business and investment banking at the expense of securities firms. A look at how the dominance of the banks was realized leads to an interesting observation. Although banks possessed certain specialized advantages in the conduct of investment banking services, they eventually relied on an acquisitive strategy to position themselves at the top ranks of the investment banking industry.

Commercial banks were expected to benefit from the deregulation of securities business for several reasons. With regard to deal origination, commercial banks were well-placed to exploit their lending relationships with borrowers. Lending relationships and credit analysis of clients also endowed banks with greater inside information about client business. Therefore, banks could have an advantage over their security firm rivals in price discovery and value certification. This advantage can result in lower fees and higher prices for issuers dealing with their relationship bank. The certification advantage is, however, mitigated by the possible conflict of interest. A bank, acting on behalf of a loan client, may withhold negative information in order to facilitate a new issue or an acquisition deal to ensure recovery of doubtful loans. In this case, counterparties to the deal may decline to participate unless they are given a price discount. This can result in new issues or acquisition deals at inferior prices than when the intermediary is an unrelated investment bank.

The expectation that banks would benefit from entry into the investment banking business received early empirical support in studies that showed positive price reaction for bank stocks around the time of various announcements of deregulation-related legislation (Hendershott et al. 2002, Czyrnik and Klein 2004). The positive price reaction was found to be increasing with the bank's size and profitability, a sign that big banks stood to benefit the most. The market's positive assessment of bank deregulation was corroborated by evidence that the price certification advantage of banks was more than enough to offset the negative effect of any perceived conflict of interest. Banks acting as underwriters for loan clients were found to produce higher offer prices in bond offerings, especially when the issuer was a relatively small and risky firm (Gande et al. 1997, Gande et al. 1999, Yasuda 2005), although Rotten and Mullineaux (2002) find no appreciable difference in bonds underwritten by banks or independent securities firms. The evidence in favor of the certification effect is also supported in studies of equity offerings (Hebb 2002, Fields et al. 2003). The benefits of the certification effect are also shown to extend to underwriting fees. Gande et al. (1999) report an overall decline of fees, whereas Rotten and Mullineaux (2002) find relatively lower fees charged by banks to riskier debt issues. Yasuda (2005) reports lower fees to debt issuers with links to the underwriting bank.

Although early evidence did not suggest significant differences in the fees of equity issues (Gande et al. 1999, Fields et al. 2003), a later study by Kim et al. (2008) presented evidence that bank fees have been lower than the fees charged by securities firms in the issuance of debt, seasoned equity offerings (SEOs) and initial public offerings (IPOs). Commercial banks are also found to be favored in underwriting mandates by their capacity to extend credit in tandem with investment banking deals (Drucker and Puri 2005) and their lending relationships (Bharath et al. 2007).

Therefore, commercial banks would be expected to exploit these advantages to gain market share at the expense of securities firms. However, studies show that other factors, besides lending relationships, can affect the issuer's choice for a lead underwriter. For example, underwriter reputation and analyst coverage and quality are influential in winning underwriting clients (Krigman et al. 2001, Brau and Fawcett 2006). To avoid the appearance of a conflict of interest, commercial banks often relinquish the role of lead manager to securities firms when the issuer is the bank's loan client (Song 2004). Prior underwriting relationships also matter for new issue mandates, which would favor the established investment banks (Ljungqvist et al. 2006). Finally, there is evidence that reputable underwriters who provide strong analyst quality and coverage can impose greater underpricing and charge higher fees (Loughran and Ritter 2004 and Fang 2005). Overall, the advantage of commercial banks in producing more cost-efficient underwriting services is mitigated by other competitive factors that favor established securities firms.

Market structure effects

The early evidence of the market structure effects due to the entry of commercial banks was rather mixed. Gande et al. (1999) report that the five-firm concentration ratio and the Herfindahl-Hirschman index for debt issues declined between 1985 and 1996 and the drop in concentration was even more dramatic for debt issues of lower quality. Later evidence shows positive market share gains for banks in the markets for IPO, SEOs and debt (Kim et al. 2008).

Table 1.3 Average four firm concentration index for select underwriting markets.

	1990	1990–2010	1990–1999	2000–2010
Convertibles	0.8409	0.6204	0.6632	0.5893
High Grade Bonds	0.7582	0.5498	0.6029	0.5015
High Yield Bonds	0.9586	0.5465	0.5928	0.5045
Common Stock (SEOs)	0.4820	0.5160	0.4969	0.5333
Initial Public Offerings (IPOs)	0.5610	0.5365	0.5113	0.5594

Source: The table is constructed from raw data reported by the Investment Dealer Digest and Bloomberg.

More comprehensive evidence is presented in Table 1.3. It shows the average four firm concentration index (FFCI) in five underwriting markets in the US over two decades.

It is clear that the concentration in the three debt underwriting markets was very high at the start of the deregulation. The most dramatic decline in market concentration is observed in the debt markets, consistent with the predictions that banks had a strong informational advantage in the underwriting of debt securities due to the lending relationships. On the other hand, SEOs and IPOs exhibit much lower and stable concentration through the twenty-year period compared to debt offerings. Concentration in these markets rises for SEOs and remains about the same on average for IPOs during the decade of 2000–2010. The IPO-related data confirm Corwin and Schultz (2005), who report relatively stable Herfindahl-Hirschman index scores for IPOs in the period 1997–2002.

Changes in ownership and organizational structure

Following deregulation, US and foreign commercial banks eventually dominated the US and global investment banking markets through organic growth and, more often, through acquisitions of established securities firms. Deregulation enabled US banks to compete in the securities business with their foreign universal bank rivals, whereas the latter were set free to expand into the US investment banking markets.

The ranks of the top independent securities firms were depleted by the torrent of acquisitions by commercial banks and their equity capital losses in the financial crisis of 2008. Although the names of the top-ranked investment banks are those of commercial banks, it is the acquired established securities firms of the yesteryear that provided the underlying strengths and the networks of clients and investors. The financial crisis of 2008 that followed the debacle of the housing market had dramatic consequences for commercial and, especially, investment banks. Weakened by losses in the crisis of 2008, the leading securities firms, Bear Stearns and Merrill Lynch were sold to JP Morgan and Bank of America, respectively. A third, Lehman Brothers was forced into bankruptcy. Two more, Goldman Sachs and Morgan Stanley sought refuge under the Federal Reserve System by obtaining bank charters.

The acquisitive strategy of the banks can be explained by the demands of the business model needed for successful investment banking operations. Chief among the requisite ingredients of the model are relationships and reputation (Brau and Fawcett 2006, Fang 2005) as well as the successful integration of multiple services and markets, i.e., underwriting, corporate finance advising, trading, market making and research (Morrison and Wilhelm 2008). These operations require specialized human capital and intangible assets that cannot easily be developed in-house. These resources were recognized long ago as significant barriers to

Table 1.4 Acquisitions by major commercial banks up to 2010.

Acquiring bank	Year of acquisition and acquired bank or securities firm
Citigroup	1998 Travelers [*Smith Barney; Shearson; Salomon Bros.*]
	2000 Schroders (UK)
	2000 Lewco Securities
	2005 Legg Mason Wood Walker
JP Morgan Chase	2000 Chase Bank [Chemical Bank]
	2004 Banc One
	2008 Bear Sterns
Bank of America	2000 Nations Bank [*Montgomery Securities*]
	2004 Fleet Bank [Bank of Boston (*Robertson Stevens*); *Quick & Reilly*
	(*L.F. Rothchild*)]
	2009 Merrill Lynch
CSFB	1989 First Boston
	2000 Donaldson, Lufkin and Jenrette
UBS	1998 SBC [*Warburg (UK); Dillon Reed*]
	2000 Paine Webber
	2006 Piper Jaffray
Deutsche Bank	1989 Morgan Grenfell
	1999 Bankers Trust [*Alex Brown*]
Royal Bank of Scotland	2007 ABN-AMRO [*Baring Bros.* (parts of business)]
Barclays	2008 Lehman Bros. (US operations)
Dresdner	2000 Wasserstein Perella Group
Wells Fargo	2003 Wachovia [*Prudential Securities*]

Firms in brackets are those that were part of the acquired firm; names in italic are those of securities firms.

entry and mobility by Hayes et al. (1983). Therefore, banks used their heavy balance sheets to buy these assets indirectly by acquiring established securities firms. The end result of these developments is the emergence of the commercial bank plus investment bank model (Papaioannou 2010).

Table 1.4 shows the major acquisitions and mergers involving commercial banks and securities firms. The table includes only those transactions where the acquirer and acquired firm are underwriters ranked in the Top 15 positions by market share in equity and debt. It is clear that the major commercial banks expanded and enhanced their capacities in investment banking by directly or indirectly acquiring securities firms with significant presence in the various underwriting markets.

Table 1.5 provides further insights into the transformation of the global investment banking industry following its deregulation in the US. In 1990, only one of the investment banks ranked Top 10 in global bond and equity underwriting and global target advising, that being First Boston operating under Credit Suisse. By 2000 the number of commercial banks ranked in the top ten positions of these markets had increased to six, of which two were US banks. In 2010, the number of Top 10 global investment banks operating under the control of a commercial bank had risen to seven, of which three were US banks. Over the same twenty-year period, the number of top independent (i.e., not controlled by a commercial bank) securities firms had declined from nine to two (Goldman Sachs and Morgan Stanley).

Table 1.5 Top 10 ranked investment banks in 1990, 2000, 2010.

1990		2000		2010	
Global Bonds & Equity	*Global Target Advisors*	*Global Bonds & Equity*	*Global Target Advisors*	*Global Bonds & Equity*	*Global Target Advisors*
Merrill Lynch	**CS First Boston**	Goldman Sachs & Co	Morgan Stanley	**Barclays**	Goldman Sachs & Co
CS First Boston	Goldman Sachs	Morgan Stanley	Goldman Sachs & Co	**JP Morgan**	Morgan Stanley
Goldman, Sachs	Morgan Stanley	Merrill Lynch & Co	**Credit Suisse**	Morgan Stanley	**JP Morgan**
Salomon Brothers	SG Warburg Group PLC	**Citigroup**	**JP Morgan**	Goldman Sachs & Co	**Credit Suisse**
Morgan Stanley	Lazard Houses	**CS First Boston**	Merrill Lynch	**Deutsche Bank AG**	UBS
Kidder, Peabody	Salomon Brothers	**JP Morgan**	UBS	**BOFA Merrill Lynch**	**BOFA Merrill Lynch**
Lehman Brothers	Merrill Lynch	Lehman Brothers	**Citigroup**	UBS	**Deutsche Bank**
Nomura Securities	Wertheim/ Schroder Group	**Deutsche Bank AG**	**Deutsche Bank AG**	Citi	Lazard Ltd
Bear Stearns	Rothschild	**UBS**	Lazard Ltd	**Credit Suisse**	**Barclays**
Prudential-Bache	Lehman Brothers	**ABN AMRO Bank**	Lehman Brothers	**RBS**	**Citi**

Names in bold signify investment banks controlled by a commercial bank.

Conclusions

The banking system in Europe and the US has undergone important transformations by moving into capital market operations and investment banking. The opening up of the securities services to commercial banks in the US had several important consequences. First, it allowed US banks to compete for capital market deals with their foreign universal bank rivals. Second, it allowed foreign banks to enter the US securities business and capture significant market share in various investment banking markets. Third, it allowed banks to use their heavy balance sheets to acquire their smaller independent investment banks, which were also weakened by the financial crisis of 2008. Fourth, the presence of banks in the securitized markets dramatically increased the volume of these markets and gave rise to unregulated shadow banking. This along with the housing market bubble contributed to the financial crisis of 2008.

The new securitized and commercial plus investment banking system presently dominates the global financial landscape. However, it faces considerable challenges. Fully integrated banks are faced with the challenge to manage the multiple conflicts of interest across their various business segments. The 2008 crisis and several subsequent incidents (for example, the London Whale losses in JP Morgan Chase) have weakened the public's trust in the capacity of banks to manage their far-flung operations. The Volcker Rule in the Dodd-Frank Act threatens the trading profits of banks by restricting their proprietary trading and involvement in hedge and private equity funds. That could also deprive banks of the synergies these operations have with underwriting and corporate finance advisory services.

Further restrictions on capital deployment are also expected when the final form of regulations of the Basel III accords takes shape. The new focus will be on the quality of the capital base of banks to withstand credit risk shocks and on strengthening the overall risk protection provided by capital. This involves a greater emphasis on common equity along with new requirements to accommodate conservation and countercyclical capital buffers. Additional capital will have to be set aside for down cycles. Beyond the higher capital requirements, there will also be enhanced stress-testing and disclosure of risk exposures, particularly with regard to off balance sheet vehicles and securitization activities. The new rules will apply to all banks deemed large enough to threaten the world financial system in case of failure. Aside the capital adequacy rules of Basel III, large banks are also likely to face additional capital requirements imposed by national central banks, as is the case with the Federal Reserve in the US. A similar trend is in progress in the EU in relation to the supervision of large and systemically significant banks.

The future viability of the new banking model depends on how strictly the recently legislated regulations will be implemented in practice and how these rules and the inherent conflicts will impact the bank-client relationships and, hence, the banks' profitability and risk.

Notes

1 The HH Index is a measure of industry concentration and is defined as the sum of the squared market shares of all firms in an industry. If one bank dominates an industry, the HH Index = 100^2 = 10,000 to indicate a 100% monopoly. If two firms equally dominate an industry, the HH Index = $50^2 + 50^2$ = 5000. If two firms own 70% and 30% respectively, the HH index = $70^2 + 30^2$ = 5800. The lower the index, the less concentrated the market. See www.justice.gov/atr/public/guidelines/hhi.html

2 In 1977, the EEC consisted of twelve countries: Belgium, France, Federal Republic of Germany, Italy, Luxembourg, the Netherlands, United Kingdom, Ireland, Denmark, Greece, Spain and Portugal.

3 Although home country control was one of the objectives in the First Directive, it was never implemented.

4 As of April 2013, the Fed has identified 37 commercial banks in the US with assets greater than $50 billion and labeled them SIFIs. As of November 2013, the FSOC has identified three insurance firms and eight financial market utility firms in the US as non-bank SIFIs.

5 Concentration rate is another measure of concentration used in economic studies as a proxy for competition. CR3 and CR5 measure the percentage of market share of the top three and top five firms, respectively. In the banking industry, the percentage is computed by taking the total deposits, loans or assets of the largest three or five banks and dividing by the total deposits, loans or assets of all banks in the industry, respectively.

6 Section 20 of the Banking Act of 1933 permitted banks to organize non-permissible activities as long as they were not the principal business of the bank's subsidiary.

References

Allen, F. and D. Gale, 2004a. Competition and financial stability. *Journal of Money, Credit and Banking* 36, 453–80.

——, 2004b. Financial intermediaries and market. *Econometrica* 72, 1023–61.

Angelini, P. and N. Cetrelli, 2003. The effects of regulatory reform on competition in the banking industry. *Journal of Money, Credit and Banking* 35, 663–84.

Anginer, D., A. Demirgüç-Kunt and Min Zhu, 2012. 'How does bank competition affect systemic stability?' World Bank Policy Research Working Paper No. 5981. Available through SSRN: http://ssrn.com/abstract=2013865

Beck, T., A. Demirgüç-Kunt and R. Levine, 2006. Bank concentration, competition, and crises: First results. *Journal of Banking and Finance* 30, 1581–1603.

Beck, T., A. Demirgüç-Kunt and V. Maksimovic, 2004. Bank competition and access to finance: International evidence. *Journal of Money, Credit and Banking* 36, 627–48.

Berger, A.N., L.F. Klapper and R. Turk-Ariss, 2009. Bank competition and financial stability. *Journal of Financial Services Research* 35, 99–118.

Besanko, D. and A. Thakor, 1992. Banking deregulation: Allocational consequences of relaxing entry barriers. *Journal of Banking and Finance* 16, 909–32.

Bharath, S., S. Dahiya, A. Saunders and A. Srinivasan, 2007. So what do I get? The bank's view of lending relationships. *Journal of Financial Economics* 85, 368–419.

Boyd, J.H. and G. De Nicoló, 2005. The theory of bank risk-taking and competition revisited. *Journal of Finance* 60, 1329–43.

Brau, J. and S. Fawcett, 2006. Initial Public Offerings: An analysis of theory and practice. *Journal of Finance* 61, 399–436.

Carey, M., A. Kashyap, R. Rajan and R. Stulz, 2012. Market institutions, financial market risks, and the financial crisis. *Journal of Financial Economics* 104, 421–24.

Casu, B. and C. Girardone, 2009. *Does competition lead to efficiency? The case of EU commercial banks.* Available through SSRN: http://ssrn.com/abstract=1200362 or http://dx.doi.org/10.2139/ssrn.1200362

Claessens, S. and L. Laeven, 2004. What drives bank competition? Some international evidence. *Journal of Money, Credit and Banking* 36, 563–83.

Corwin, S. and P. Schultz, 2005. The role of IPO underwriting syndicates: Pricing, information production, and underwriter competition. *Journal of Finance* 60, 443–86.

Czyrnik, K. and L.S. Klein, 2004. Who benefits from deregulating the separation of banking activities? Differential effects on commercial bank, investment bank and thrift stock returns. *The Financial Review* 39, 317–41.

Demyanyk, Y. and O. Van Hemert, 2011. Understanding the subprime mortgage crisis. *The Review of Financial Studies* 24, 1848–80.

De Nicoló, G., P. Bartholomew, J. Zaman and M. Zephirin, 2004. Bank consolidation, internalization, and conglomeration: Trends and implications for financial risk. *Financial Markets, Institutions and Instruments* 13, 173–217.

DeYoung, R., D. Evanoff and P. Molyneux, 2009. Mergers and acquisitions of financial institutions: A Review of the post-2000 literature. *Journal of Financial Services Research* 36, 87–110.

Drucker, S. and M. Puri, 2005. On the benefits of concurrent lending and underwriting. *Journal of Finance* 60, 2763–99.

Fang, L., 2005. Investment bank reputation and the price and quality of underwriting services. *Journal of Finance* 60, 2729–62.

Fields, P., D. Fraser and R. Bhargava, 2003. A comparison of underwriting costs of initial public offerings by investment and commercial banks. *Journal of Financial Research* 26, 517–34.

Gande, A., M. Puri and A. Saunders, 1999. Bank entry, competition and the market for corporate securities underwriting. *Journal of Financial Economics* 54, 165–95.

Gande, A., M. Puri, A. Saunders and I. Walter, 1997. Bank underwriting of debt securities: modern evidence. *Review of Financial Studies* 10, 1175–1202.

Gropp, R., H. Hakenes and I. Schnabel, 2011. Competition, risk-shifting and public bail-out policies. *The Review of Financial Studies* 24, 2084–2120.

Hakanes, H. and I. Schnabel, 2011. Capital regulation, bank competition, and financial stability, *Economics Letters*, 113, 256–58.

Hayes, S., M. Spence and D. Marks, 1983. *Competition in the Investment Banking Industry.* Cambridge, Mass.: Harvard University Press.

Hebb, G.M., 2002. Conflict of interest in commercial bank equity underwriting. *The Financial Review* 37, 185–206.

Hendershott, R.J., D.E. Lee and J.G. Tompkins, 2002. Winners and losers as financial service providers converge: Evidence from the Financial Services Modernization Act of 1999. *The Financial Review* 37, 53–72.

Kaas, L., 2004. "Financial market integration and loan competition: when is entry deregulation socially beneficial?" Working Paper Series No. 403, European Central Bank.

Keeley, M. 1990. Deposit insurance, risk, and market power in banking. *American Economic Review* 80, 1183–1200.

Kim, D., D. Palia and A. Saunders, 2008. The impact of commercial banks on underwriting spreads: Evidence from three decades. *Journal of Quantitative and Financial Analysis* 43, 975–1000.

Krigman, L., W. Shaw and K. Womack, 2001. Why do firms switch underwriters? *Journal of Financial Economics* 60, 245–84.

Ljungqvist, A., F. Marston and W. Wilhelm, 2006. Competing for securities underwriting mandates: banking relationships and analysts recommendations. *Journal of Finance* 61, 301–40.

Loughran, T. and J. Ritter, 2004. Why has the IPO underpricing changed over time? *Financial Management* 33, 5–37.

Marcus, A.J., 1984. Deregulation and bank financial policy. *Journal of Banking and Finance* 8, 557–65.

Morrison, A. and W. Wilhelm, 2008. The demise of investment banking partnerships: Theory and evidence. *Journal of Finance* 63, 311–50.

Papaioannou, G., 2010. Commercial banks in underwriting and the decline of the independent investment banking model. *Journal of International Business and Law* 9, 79–104.

Purnanandam, A., 2011. Originate-to-Distribute model and the subprime mortgage crisis. *The Review of Financial Studies* 24, 1881–1916.

Rotten, I. and D. Mullineaux, 2002. Debt underwriting by commercial bank-affiliated firms and investment banks: More evidence. *Journal of Banking and Finance* 26, 689–718.

Song, W., 2004. Competition and coalition among underwriters: The decision to join a syndicate. *Journal of Finance* 59, 2421–44.

Uhde, A. and U. Heimeshoff, 2009. Consolidation in banking and financial stability in Europe: empirical evidence. *Journal of Banking and Finance*, 33, 1299–1311.

Vives, X., 2011. Competition policy in banking. *Oxford Review of Economic Policy* 27, 479–97.

Wheelock, D., 2011. Banking industry consolidation and market structure: Impact of the financial crisis and recession. *Review–Federal Reserve Bank of St. Louis* 93, 419–38.

Yasuda, A., 2005. Do bank relationships affect the firm's underwriter choice in the corporate-bond underwriting markets? *Journal of Finance* 60, 1259–92.

2

'Challenger banks': Are they for real?

The impact of new entrants on financial services competition

Steve Worthington

Introduction

This chapter will examine the possibilities for new entrants into retail banking in the United Kingdom, such as those representing 'value brands' (for example, Virgin Money), those whose origins lie in the traditional retail sector (for example, Tesco Bank), and new entrants with entrepreneurial backgrounds (for example, Metro Bank). The chapter will discuss what the possibilities are for these new entrants, from whatever their origins, to both enter and prosper in the financial services market, that is, whether they can offer a 'real' competitive threat to the more 'established' players who have traditionally dominated the market.

Chapter 1 discusses the impact of regulation on competition in commercial and investment banking. Deregulation facilitated the formation of 'conglomerate' financial institutions, where a broad range of services and products were made available to clients, through different arms of the same bank. Following the financial crisis, further legislative changes have been put in place to reverse some of these impacts of deregulation in an attempt to restore confidence in the financial services institutions, in part by changing the structures within those institutions and in part by restricting their marketing practices. Banks, for example, are being encouraged to disaggregate their various activities and construct walls between their various divisions, so that investors' and depositors' funds are not used irresponsibly.

In this context, there has been a growing pressure for retail banking activities to be made separate from investment banking activities by the so-called 'ring fencing' of the two activities from each other. In a speech in February 2013, the Chancellor of the Exchequer in the United Kingdom gave a speech on the future of banking in which he suggested that the proposed 'ring fence' should be 'electrified' with draconian sanctions if retail banking was not protected from riskier investment banking operations. The Chancellor said 'My message to the banks is clear: if a bank flouts the rules, the regulator and the Treasury will have the power to break it up altogether – full separation, not just a ring fence' (Financial Times 2013). He underlined his determination to open up the United Kingdom's retail banking sector beyond its current domination by the large, well established banks by facilitating the entry of 'challenger banks' to create a more competitive retail banking system, that would be more focussed on customers.

This situation where the market for banking services is dominated by a relatively few large 'players' is to be found in a number of countries; despite regulators and consumer groups calling for more competition, the challenges for new entrants are substantial. This chapter discusses those challenges beginning with the challenge of encouraging customers to move one of their key relationships (the personal current/cheque account) from one provider to another; the so-called 'switching' process. It then goes on to consider where new entrants might come from, to detail which 'challenger banks' have emerged so far in the United Kingdom and what their prospects might be.

Background to the situation

In the context of the United Kingdom (UK), the Office of Fair Trading (OFT) released a review of the personal current account (PCA) market in January 2013 (Office of Fair Trading 2013b). The PCA is equivalent to a check or transaction account in many other countries; it is a keystone product in the retail banking sector and often the starting point for the establishment and subsequent development of a relationship between the financial services provider and the customer (see Chapter 9 by Yu and Harrison). In 2013 the UK had 46 million PCA holders. However, according to a study by the Payments Council, the industry body in charge of managing the account switching system, less than three percent of these account holders switched their PCA provider in 2012, thus limiting the competitive impact of new entrants into this market.

The OFT review concluded that in the UK market, further significant changes were still required to tackle longstanding competition concerns and a lack of focus on customers' needs. The OFT found that since it last looked at PCAs in 2008, the major banks had increased their share of the market, that entry by new competitors remained infrequent and that consumers still only rarely switched their PCA to an alternative provider. The conclusion was that overall a combination of a lack of competition, low levels of innovation, ongoing customer apathy/inertia in the face of unclear costs and a lack of diversity in the choices of PCAs available meant that this market was not working well for consumers or indeed the wider economy.

The OFT in January 2013 made new recommendations to make PCA costs more transparent, the switching process more reliable and to improve the way in which managed overdrafts are provided. It called upon all providers to make rapid progress in implementing these recommendations, as well as being more proactive in ensuring that their products and services are better aligned with the needs of their customers. The OFT Chief Executive commented:

> Personal current accounts are critical to the efficient functioning of the UK economy. Despite some improvements, this market is still not serving consumers as well as it should. Customers still find it difficult to assess which account offers the best deal and lack confidence that they can switch accounts easily. This prevents them from driving effective competition between providers. Major changes are taking place in the personal current account market. For these changes to improve the effectiveness of competition in this market, banks and building societies need to act to improve the quality and value for money they provide their customers. The retail banking sector needs to become more competitive and customer-focussed to ensure that further action by the competition authorities is not required.
>
> *Office of Fair Trading 2013a*

Since September 2013 banks in the UK have been required to reduce the amount of time it takes to switch PCAs from one month to just seven days, all at no cost to the customer.

The issue of switching between providers is a vital one for new entrants, as according to the OFT (Office of Fair Trading 2009), the PCA market is the cornerstone of the UK's retail finance system and an essential service for 90 percent of the adult population. Thus, new entrants cannot rely on an 'unbanked' target market from which to gain customers. They must instead hope to win new customers by luring them away from their existing providers; hence customers' perceptions of the difficulty of switching providers will impact strongly on their willingness to switch to a new entrant.

Research conducted by the OFT (Office of Fair Trading 2013b) showed that perceptions of switching among consumers who have never switched PCAs before had not changed significantly since 2008, when only 26 percent had considered switching; by 2012 the percentage who had considered switching had actually reduced to 25 percent. Similarly, for those who have never switched, there has also been no real change in the level of confidence in the switching process running smoothly; in 2008, 52 percent were 'very' or 'fairly confident' about the process, but by 2012 this percentage had also fallen, to 50 percent.

This could be partially explained by changes in perceptions requiring time to occur, particularly if they are not based on the individual's own experience. However, even when individuals have had experience of switching their PCAs between providers, the perceptions of the switching process did not change significantly between 2008 and 2012: in 2008, 75 percent of those who had switched their PCA in the previous 12 months said that it was a relatively 'easy' process, but by 2012 this figure had only grown to 81 percent. Also, in terms of referrals/advocacy, there has been no real change in the likelihood of those who have already switched recommending others who have not switched to change their PCA provider. Thus the overall message arising from the OFT's research, is that switching levels remain low and are either constant or displaying a very gradual increase over time. The findings also suggest that although actual switching of PCAs from one provider to another has gradually increased, it still remains low in terms of the overall proportion of account holders.

The new entrants

How significant are the effects of the global financial crisis on the future structure of the banking sector? Clearly, the ramifications of the financial crisis have led to major changes in the capital, liquidity and accounting regimes for banks. But might the crisis also open up the sector to new competitors on a scale not seen before? Is the distrust of mainstream banks now so deep that ambitious companies in other sectors have an unparalleled opportunity to become major providers of banking services? Chapter 30 discusses the challenges ahead in re-building trust for traditional banks. Many of the potential new entrants to banking are however already well-placed in terms of established consumer trust.

Opportunities for 'non-banks' to enter the market have been discussed many times before. It has been said that 'Banking is essential to a modern economy. Banks are not. If some other entity performs the functions of banking faster, smarter or cheaper, it will replace banks' (Furash 1993: 20). Commentators forecasted that companies from outside banking would use their stronger grasp of information technology and customer service to shake-up financial services, taking lucrative business away from cautious and insular banks (see Worthington and Welch 2011).

In many markets, retailers have been perceived as the biggest threat. Their strong brands, marketing know-how, existing retail networks and store and loyalty cards offered a potential entry platform. In the UK, leading retailers took up the challenge and have been offering financial services for many years. For example, Marks & Spencer (M&S), a leading clothing, food and household goods retailer, entered the market as far back as the late 1980s and Tesco and Sainsbury's, then the two largest UK supermarket chains, launched banking services in the mid-1990s. In the US, Walmart has shown interest in entering the financial services market and made a bid in 2007 to acquire a banking licence; a bid that was subsequently abandoned under fierce opposition from some American lawmakers and community banks that were wary of Walmart's power as a retailer. This has not stopped Walmart from entering the market for financial services and it now has MoneyCenters in-store and offers both credit cards and a checking and debit card service called Bluebird, in partnership with American Express. Bluebird is directly aimed at Walmart customers (140 million visit Walmart every week) who are disillusioned with or excluded from traditional banking services. In China banking regulators are also inviting retailers to apply for banking licenses and their desire to enter this market is understandable as there are large margins to be made in Chinese banking.

Disruptive value brands, such as Virgin, that operate across structurally diverse consumer sectors (air travel, music retailing and mobile telephony) have also identified opportunities in financial services. Virgin Money launched in 1995 with an index tracking unit trust (mutual fund) and has since considerably expanded its range of services. However, prior to the crisis, the 'non-banks' concentrated on a select range of financial services and often operated through partnerships with existing banks. For example, the UK retailers concentrated principally on credit cards and other forms of consumer credit, simple savings accounts and insurance policies that could be sold directly. Tesco and Sainsbury's operated through joint ventures with Royal Bank of Scotland (RBS) and Halifax Bank of Scotland (HBOS) respectively, while M&S, after initially operating on its own, moved into a partnership agreement with the Hong Kong and Shanghai Banking Corporation (HSBC).

The crisis may have extended the opportunities for 'non-banks'. Tesco and Virgin Money in particular aspire to move from being niche players in financial services to full-service providers of retail banking. Both have sought to expand their offerings and the introduction of current accounts (PCAs) and mortgages are planned or in progress. Tesco bought out RBS's stake in its financial services joint venture in 2008 and re-branded Tesco Personal Finance as Tesco Bank. Virgin Money purchased a small regional UK bank (Church House Trust) in 2010 to expedite its acquisition of a banking licence and provide a platform for launching a retail banking business. In early 2012 Virgin bought, from the UK Government, the viable assets of the ailing Northern Rock bank, taking over the healthy loan and depositor base of Northern Rock and converted its existing 75 bank branches into Virgin Money outlets. Since taking over in 2012, Virgin has added 1.7 million new saving and mortgage accounts to its business and it is preparing to enter the PCA market, following Tesco and M&S.

Furthermore, these 'challenger banks' are ambitious in their visions for retail banking. Virgin Money talks of an ambition 'to offer a new kind of bank in the UK – one where everyone benefits'. Tesco says it will focus on 'being simple, straightforward and rewarding loyalty'. Moreover, Tesco and Virgin are not alone. In 2010 it was announced that another new entrant, Metro Bank had received a banking licence from the Financial Services Authority. The activities of each of these three new entrants are now analysed below.

Virgin Money

Virgin moved into financial services in the mid-1990s and originally operated as a niche player in personal financial services, with many of the services actually supplied by third parties but carrying the well-known Virgin brand. Virgin Money was initially founded as Virgin Direct in 1995 as a joint venture between a member of the Virgin group of companies and the insurance group Norwich Union, with the aim of offering equity savings products directly to the UK retail consumer market. It was one of the pioneers of index-tracking funds which carried low fees compared with actively managed funds, and it attracted £42 million invested funds alone in its first month of operation. In 1997, Virgin launched the One Account in a joint venture between

Virgin Direct Personal Financial Services and the Royal Bank of Scotland. The One Account was the UK's first current account mortgage direct to the retail market. However, in 2001, RBS bought out Virgin Direct Personal Financial Service Limited's stake in the joint venture and the management team transferred to RBS.

In 2002, Virgin Direct subsequently re-branded as Virgin Money and increased its product offering, adding a credit card offered in partnership with Bank of America and additional savings, personal loans and insurance products. In 2003, Virgin Money welcomed its millionth customer and launched the Virgin Credit Card in Australia, which was followed in 2006 by the launch of a Virgin Money Credit Card in South Africa. In April 2004, Virgin Group Investments Limited acquired full ownership of Virgin Money with Sir Richard Branson investing £90 million to buy out the existing shareholders. In January 2010, Virgin Money announced a recommended offer for Church House Trust, a small regional bank offering deposits and mortgages. The acquisition of Church House Trust gave Virgin Money a banking licence in the UK, which allowed it to offer its own banking products without the need to partner with established financial institutions.

In January 2012, Virgin Money acquired Northern Rock, the Newcastle-based ex-Building Society which had been nationalised by the British Government following a run on the funds as a consequence of the credit crisis. The earlier purchase of Church House Trust in 2010 had been expected to trigger Virgin's launch into mortgages and current accounts. However, this was repeatedly delayed as Virgin struggled to find a business model that would allow it to compete with the biggest UK banks. Virgin acknowledges that without the purchase of Northern Rock, it would have been difficult for Virgin Money to build a strong foothold in the UK market. Northern Rock had 75 branches and these were rebranded as Virgin Money stores in 2012.

Virgin Money aimed to offer PCAs with 'free banking' (i.e. no monthly or annual fees), however Richard Branson cautioned that free banking should have quotation marks around it, as customers would pay by accepting a small upfront fee, rather than the 'hidden charges' levied by the major banks. Following the acquisition of Northern Rock, Virgin Money had 4 million customers and 2,100 employees and aspirations to grow to 8 million customers and 200 branches. As a step in that direction, the first new Virgin Money Store opened in July 2012, which gave customers their first taste of the Virgin Money branch of the future.

As of 2014 Virgin Money was offering a range of financial services encompassing payment cards (credit, prepaid and travel cards), savings and investment products, general insurance products (motor, home, travel and pets), pensions, financial planning and mortgages. Work was continuing on developing a range of Virgin Money PCAs. In terms of product strategy, Virgin Money claims that it aims to bring simplicity to the UK banking market, which has traditionally been a complex sector, and that Virgin Money's focus will be on a strong retail deposit base with an approach to banking that is founded on developing a sustainable, savings based business.

Tesco Bank

Tesco, like Virgin, has been providing financial services for nearly two decades. The supermarket group began offering financial services in 1996 when it launched the Tesco Clubcard Plus, an in-house debit card, which paid interest on the funds deposited in it and rewarded its users with Clubcard loyalty points. In February 1997, Tesco announced the creation of Tesco Personal Finance (TPF) as a joint venture with the Royal Bank of Scotland (RBS). Tesco PLC and the Royal Bank of Scotland Group PLC held an equal number of shares in the holding company, Tesco Personal Finance Group Ltd. However, one of the shares held by Tesco was a non-voting share and, as a consequence, RBS was the ultimate holding company. In December 2008, Tesco completed its acquisition of RBS's stake in TPF for approximately £950 million, with TPF becoming a wholly-owned subsidiary of Tesco PLC and in October 2009, TPF was re-branded as Tesco Bank.

At the time of the acquisition of the RBS stake in TPF the UK financial services profit pool was estimated to be worth at least £20 billion per annum. The Tesco Personal Finance product offering at that time had material market positions in two of the core categories of financial services products: credit cards (6.9 percent of the market) and car insurance (4.3 percent of the market). Less meaningful market positions were held in home insurance (2.0 percent) and savings (0.8 percent), hence it was claimed that there was considerable opportunity to exploit Tesco's innovative capabilities and customer service skills, to both build share in existing categories and to enter new product segments successfully.

By 2013 Tesco Bank had become the UK's largest supermarket bank with 6.5 million customer accounts across a range of financial products and services. Its principal activities are credit cards, savings, personal loans, mortgages and general insurance, including car, home, pet and travel. Tesco Bank also operates a network of automated teller machines (ATMs) and customers can purchase products in-store, online or by telephone. In mid-2012 Tesco Bank also launched a range of mortgages, both at fixed rates and a base rate tracker. By 2013 it had over 3000 employees and according to the Tesco Annual Report 2012–13, for that financial year Tesco Bank generated £1.02 billion of revenue and a trading profit of £191 million (4 percent of the Tesco Group total), with a trading margin of 18.7 percent.

The 2012–13 Tesco Annual Report also describes Tesco Bank as having been in a period of transition since its creation in 2008. It now has a completely new infrastructure and is poised to move towards offering a full-service retail bank experience to Tesco's customers. As of 2014, Tesco Bank has 7 million customer accounts and is preparing to launch its first current account product (PCA) this year.

Tesco Bank also welcomed the initiatives being taken in the UK to make it easier for customers to switch their PCA between providers. Tesco Bank's ambition is to be Tesco customers' core provider of banking services. With regards to PCAs, Tesco intends to be its customers' main banking relationship and wants its customers to say 'I bank with Tesco'.

Metro Bank

Metro Bank was the UK's first new 'high street' bank in over 100 years when it was launched in July 2010, having been granted a banking licence by the Financial Services Authority (FSA). It promised to revolutionise the retail banking market. By the end of 2013, Metro Bank had opened twenty bank branches and planned to have a total of 200 by 2020. It had also attracted over 140,000 customers and businesses, based primarily on its customer service ethos. The bank operated typical retail store opening hours with extended evening opening. By May 2013, 136,000 customers held a PCA with Metro Bank, which, after only three years in operation, demonstrates just how difficult it is for new entrants to gain new customers in this key PCA market.

Metro offers PCAs, savings products, personal loans, credit cards and mortgages and various extra 'services' such as safe deposit boxes and free coin counting machines. Metro Bank has free online banking, instant in-branch issuance of bank cards and assistance with switching accounts from other providers. Its customer service focus is summed up by its tag line 'No stupid bank rules' and it encourages its customers to 'Love your bank at last'. Metro Bank's key point of differentiation is its focus on its customers, by offering them very high levels of service and convenience.

Metro Bank's business banking offers working capital, commercial mortgages or expansion funding for both start-ups and established businesses, clubs, societies and charities, with a dedicated business banker in each branch. Notwithstanding, Metro Bank has found attracting new customers problematic: in the four months following its initial inception it had only provided about 100 mortgage loans. The bank's lending capacity is limited by its reliance on retail deposits to fund the loans. These retail deposits often follow the opening up of a PCA by a new customer. Metro Bank acknowledges that there is a lack of public confidence in the switching process and that this is preventing customers from changing to the new providers.

Metro Bank views itself as a retailer of financial services and as a retailer it is open 7 days a week. The physical presence is important; Metro Bank claims that 93 percent of all its new accounts are opened in its bank branches. Metro believes that what matters most is the customer experience and hence its goal is to reclaim the banking values of the past by focussing on a more retail-orientated structure, hence the longer branch opening hours.

Analysis of 'challenger bank' competitiveness

An obvious way of structuring the analysis of the 'challenger bank' prospects is through a conventional Strengths, Weaknesses, Opportunities and Threats (SWOT) framework. The analysis looks first at the opportunities and threats facing the challenger banks in the financial services market environment. It then considers the new entrants' own strengths and weaknesses. How well the challenger banks fare will depend on their ability to minimise the effects of any external threats or internal weaknesses and use their strengths to capitalise on opportunities.

Opportunities

Market size

Given their current scale relative to the market, the sheer size of the personal banking market clearly presents a major opportunity. However, none of the new entrants have achieved a significant presence in the mortgage and current account segments. Even in those major segments where the new entrants do have a presence – retail deposits and consumer credit – it remains small relative to the market as a whole.

Table 2.1 Tesco Bank, Virgin Money and Metro Bank: SWOT analysis

Opportunities	Threats
• Overall market size. • Consumer anger at mainstream banks. • Disposals planned by government required under EC State Aid rules.	• Lower growth prospects for key personal banking segments. • Fall in structural profitability of banking (stronger capital and liquidity requirements). • Competitive dynamics/customer behaviour.
Strengths	Weaknesses
• Strength of brands. • Successful diversification records. • Product innovation. • Existing customer relationships/infrastructure.	• Lack of branch networks. • Lack of core skills. • Small size relative to the largest banks.

Source: Author's own analysis.

Impact of the financial crisis

The change that may justify a shift in the ambitions of the new entrants is clearly the fall out from the financial crisis. In the wake of the crisis, it is assumed that the level of consumer anger at and distrust of mainstream banks has significantly increased the opportunities for new entrants, particularly with regards to consumer appetite to consider alternative providers, including those from outside the banking sector. Above and beyond the market size, it is this change that appears to underpin the ambitions of Metro, Tesco and Virgin to move from a selective offering of financial services to full-service retail banking.

Divestments

A further major opportunity presented by the crisis is the possibility of acquiring an existing bank or branch network. Both Lloyds Bank and RBS have been required to make disposals as part of the conditions imposed by the European Commission under EC State Aid rules. As an example, the acquisition of Northern Rock brought substantial retail savings and mortgage portfolios to Virgin Money.

With regards to the required Lloyds and RBS divestments, the former looks potentially more attractive in terms of achieving greater competition in the personal current account segment because it is estimated that whoever wins the Lloyds divestment will have an extra 4.6 percent market share in the PCA market, gained through a network of at least 600 nationwide branches. In the case of RBS, the disposal is more focussed on SME banking and the mid-corporate market.

Threats

If the financial crisis has created new opportunities, it has also introduced new threats. While the crisis may have opened up the banking sector to new competitors on a scale not seen before, in several important respects it has also made retail banking a somewhat less attractive business proposition.

Prospects for key market segments

The key personal banking segments face lower growth prospects and/or intense competition. Both the mortgage and consumer credit segments are likely to grow more slowly during the coming years than during the years before the crisis. With wholesale funding less available, competition for retail deposits will be fierce. This will put pressure on lenders' interest margins and may limit the ability of new entrants to fund their growth in new market segments, most notably mortgages.

Stronger capital, liquidity and accounting requirements

Regulators are imposing tougher capital and liquidity requirements on banks as part of the reforms of the Basel capital adequacy framework. This is likely to reduce the structural profitability of banking, making it more capital-intensive and requiring banks to hold more lower-yielding assets. More generally, regulators are likely to be wary of banks earning the returns on equity they have enjoyed in the years before the crisis.

Consumer behaviour and pricing structures

In addition to the negative effects of the crisis, the new entrants also face the challenges of customer behaviour and pricing structures in retail banking. Despite all the moves to facilitate account switching, consumers remain instinctively reluctant to change their current accounts. Banks remain reliant on opaque and unpopular means of generating revenue from their current accounts, namely high overdraft charges and little or no interest paid on credit.

The failure of the UK Office of Fair Trading's court case against unauthorised overdraft charges and UK consumers' attachment to the misnomer of 'free banking', is likely to weaken the pressure on banks to move to a more equitable pricing structure (see Chapters 16 and 17 on consumer price perceptions and price management respectively). This leaves the new entrants with the challenge of offering PCAs on a profitable basis, without them relying on overdraft charges and negligible interest paid on credit balances as a means of generating revenue.

Strengths

Strength of brands

Whilst Metro faces the challenge of establishing itself as a new brand, a major strength of both Tesco and Virgin is the existing power of their brands as both are among the best-known consumer brand names in the UK. While the underlying strategies are a little different between the two companies, the strength of their brands has already enabled Tesco to expand successfully into adjacent sectors and Virgin to establish itself across a range of different sectors.

Tesco has diversified to varying degrees into petrol retailing, newspapers and magazines, health and beauty goods, kitchenware, household appliances, CDs, DVDs and online music downloads. The underlying model here is the supermarket as a 'one-stop shop'. This model extends the parameters of lateral diversification from the retailing of goods to the retailing of services. It is noteworthy that Tesco's ambitions to expand its services segment include Tesco Telecoms and Tesco.com/Tesco Direct, as well as Tesco Bank.

The strategy of Virgin is to enter and expand in consumer markets where it sees high prices and consumer dissatisfaction, bringing a fresh, unconventional challenging approach. The strength of its brand has allowed Virgin to operate across a range of structurally diverse consumer sectors, including air and rail travel, mobile telephony, health and financial services.

Innovation

Metro, Tesco and Virgin also bring to banking an innovative approach to products and services. This is already evident in their existing financial services businesses and their approach to customer service, for example via extended opening hours. Perhaps the nearest a retailer has ever come to literally retailing a financial service is Tesco's travel insurance. Members of the Tesco loyalty programme (Clubcard) can pick up a travel insurance pack in-store and take it to the checkout with the rest of their shopping. As soon as the insurance pack is scanned – along with the Clubcard to confirm the customer's identity – the customer is insured.

Virgin introduced the innovative One Account in partnership with RBS, combining a current account and a mortgage loan in a single product. Customers deposit their income and savings into the same account as their mortgage, so using their assets (on which they receive a lower interest rate) to reduce the balance on their mortgage (on which they pay a higher rate). The One Account also functions as a normal current account, which customers can use to make regular payments and cash withdrawals.

Metro Bank has sought to differentiate itself through its customer service ethos delivered via its branch network. Both academics and practitioners have questioned the continued relevance of the bank branch in the new digital banking world (King 2011). The core competencies of retail banking are credit scoring and customer relationship management, both of which can be carried out effectively without the need for bank branches. For a review of the decline of the bank branch in the UK up to 2013, see French, Leyshon and Meek (2013). However, for Metro Bank, its business model has as its central component the branch and the face-to-face service and advice that can be delivered in that environment. These service features are one of the innovations that new entrants could use to attract customers disillusioned by the impersonal service delivery of the large incumbent banks.

Existing customer relationships and infrastructure

Both Tesco and Virgin already have a substantial base of existing financial services customers to which they can offer new services. Tesco also has two additional resources at its disposal. First, it has the base of 16 million Clubcard holders. Second, it has its nationwide retail network through which to promote and support the offer of financial services. Given these resources, Tesco may be in a stronger starting position than Virgin to expand its financial services business. The retail network gives Tesco a potentially significant advantage in distribution. In comparison with other new entrants that have to rely more heavily on channels such as direct mail or advertising, Tesco stores offer a readily available and low-cost marketing channel for the display of product leaflets and other literature. They also offer a means of servicing existing customers, however, the extent of this success depends on how they are utilised as discussed in relation to weaknesses.

To support its expansion, Tesco Bank plans to develop its face-to-face proposition in store including branches, Travel Money bureaux and use of tills and this points to an ever-wider interaction between the parent retailer and its banking subsidiary. An important benefit is that the growth of the bank allows Tesco to internalise within the Group interchange payments that would otherwise flow externally. When Tesco Bank customers use Tesco ATMs, interchange is payable from Tesco Bank to the retail parent; when Tesco Bank credit cardholders use their cards in Tesco stores, interchange is payable from the retail parent to Tesco Bank.

There are also opportunities to build on customer loyalty and retention from across the Tesco group. Research commissioned by Tesco shows that 'retailing services' customers are its most valuable and most loyal. According to Tesco, customers who use two retailing services spend four times as much in store than those who don't use any services, customers with a Tesco credit card spend around 30 percent more with Tesco than 'lookalike' customers who do not have a Tesco credit card and customers with two retailing services (based on customers who have services from both Tesco Bank and Tesco Direct) are 25 percent less likely to 'lapse' over a 12-month period than 'lookalikes' without services.

Tesco defines 'lookalikes' as customers with the same life stage, share of spend, lifestyle and preferred store but who do not use a Tesco Retailing Service; 'lapse' is defined as customers who have dropped two or more share of spend categories over a 12-month period. The figures raise interesting questions about whether the most likely consumers of Tesco services are simply its most loyal shoppers or whether consumers of Tesco services subsequently become more active users of Tesco as a retailer. But clearly, the figures indicate a strong relationship between customers of Tesco as a retailer and Tesco as a service provider.

Weaknesses

Small size

Metro Bank is very small and both Virgin Money and Tesco Bank remain small in the overall context of UK personal banking, despite the size of their parent companies, familiarity of their parent brands and their presence in financial services for more than a decade. The current small size of Tesco Bank and Virgin Money relative to the market underlines the challenge they face in becoming mainstream players in full-service retail banking. Something is needed that involves much more than a continuation of their current organic growth. A massive expansion of their financial services activities will be required and in particular, with whole-sale funding much less available following the crisis, Virgin and Tesco will need to increase the size of their deposit bases by an order of magnitude. This is most likely to be achieved by a significant acquisition.

Low levels of customer awareness

Despite the strength of their brands, achieving a step change in their financial services activi-ties will require an uplift in the public's awareness and perception of Tesco and Virgin as providers of financial services. The awareness of Tesco Bank among Tesco customers has improved in recent years and there is now increased focus and impetus following full Tesco ownership of the bank. However, customer awareness remains well below that of the market leaders and is based on financial services that Tesco Bank has been providing for some time rather than new services such as current accounts and mortgages. Hence, there is a considerable task ahead in terms of raising awareness of any new products, such as personal current accounts.

Need for core skills

Having previously relied on partners, both Tesco Bank and Virgin Money now need to acquire and develop core banking skills in-house. The skills and expertise required may be very differ-ent from their existing businesses. Core skills needed to succeed in financial services include risk management, interest rate and liquidity management and regulatory compliance, with their importance underlined by the financial crisis. Compare these with the core skills in retailing: sourcing products, buying well, merchandising and fulfilment of the purchase by the consumer. These skills may transfer readily to other retail sectors, for example, supermarkets may use their superior buying power to secure competitive advantage over specialists in health and beauty retailing, but they transfer less easily to financial services.

Existing skills need to be applied in a commercial environment that is different – and that Tesco and Virgin want to be able to differentiate – from a traditional retail bank. For example, while Tesco may seek to combine the best of banking and retailing, financial services are not merchandised in the same way as tangible products sold in retail outlets. Only a limited number of financial services such as one-off travel insurance and foreign currency are purchased through a single transaction, at a set price in a similar way to a retail transaction. Core personal bank-ing services such as current accounts and mortgages involve the provision of an account on a long-term basis for the customer. Customers have to go through an application process, with the possibility of rejection and the pricing is more complex; often expressed as a percentage of the loan or deposit balance. The discounts, special offers and sales periods, central to retailing work less well when applied to financial services.

Indeed, whatever the aspirations of Metro, Tesco and Virgin to cut through the complexity of financial services, compliance requirements related to data protection, identity confirma-tion and money laundering often push in the other direction. The post-crisis period is likely to mean a tightening rather than a loosening of financial services regulation (as discussed in Chapter 1).

Delivery channels

A further challenge for Metro, Tesco and Virgin is their lack of a large branch network. Tesco has largely operated as a direct bank to date, but will it be possible for it to become a major provider of current accounts and mortgages without a physical network? These services can be managed and delivered through direct channels. However, the resilience of branches, despite long-standing predictions of the death of branch banking, underlines that many customers still like to use a physical outlet to conduct their banking.

However, apart from the common feature of physical proximity, bank branches are very different from retail stores. Shops are essentially outlets for the sale of goods. Customers come to browse and/or purchase specific items. Bank branches are sometimes described as a distribution channel, but this is in many ways a misleading description. Banks are not in the distribution business (other than perhaps for cash itself), they are principally places for the management of bank accounts. Customers may visit a branch to enquire about/apply for a banking service, but most branch visits are for carrying out transactions on existing accounts (mainly current and deposit accounts), such as paying-in cheques, paying-in or withdrawing cash or arranging more complex transactions that cannot be arranged remotely.

Conclusions

Before the financial crisis, both Tesco and Virgin had provided financial services for more than a decade. However, both were happy to operate as niche providers and they concentrated on a select range of products, operating through partnerships with existing banks and insurance companies. Neither showed an appetite for directly competing as full-service providers in retail banking. In the wake of the financial crisis, both now harbour ambitions to become full-service retail banks. But are the changes flowing from the financial crisis sufficient to justify such an expansion? Existing banks may be more unpopular, making non-banks more attractive, but there is a debit as well as credit side to the post-crisis investment case. Banking is set to be less profitable, making the market less attractive.

The biggest challenge for Metro Bank, Tesco Bank and Virgin Money, as full-service retail banks may be to grow quickly and profitably, while at the same time doing banking in a way that is markedly different from the mainstream. Tesco admits that one of the challenges it faces is the industry's 'standard economic model'. The hurdles to overcome for both PCAs and mortgages are high. The pricing of retail banking products in the UK has in some ways been analogous to the famous description of the art of taxation of Jean Baptiste Colbert, French economist and Minister of Finance under King Louis XIV of France 'The art of taxation consists in so plucking the goose as to obtain the largest possible amount of feathers with the smallest possible amount of hissing'.

The traditional banks remain reliant on opaque means of generating revenue from their PCAs, namely high overdraft charges and little or no interest paid on credit balances. Existing pricing structures are reinforced by the attachment of UK consumers to 'free' current account banking, 'free' credit cards and 'free' ATM withdrawals. In practice, this attachment to notionally 'free' banking services acts as a significant barrier to innovation and competition in pricing and it has resulted in significant cross-subsidies between different groups of banking customers.

Metro, Tesco and Virgin, therefore face the challenge of offering PCAs profitably without themselves relying on the same revenue models as existing providers. They also face the challenge of acquiring deposits without either offering unprofitable rates or tempting introductory rates that are then reduced over time. In light of their stated 'visions' for banking, high standards will be expected. Their services will be closely scrutinised by consumer and personal finance journalists, and ranked in the many comparison sites on the internet. Reputationally, Metro, Tesco and Virgin, are likely to face tougher customer standards than their existing bank competitors.

Notwithstanding, one of the key challenges for the existing 'players' in the retail banking market is that they have collectively lost the trust of their customers and indeed the wider community. Financial intermediation which occurs when those lending money to the banks (savers) implicitly agree with it then being lent out to borrowers, relies on the trust that their money will be available when they want it back. The great debate in banking thus needs to be how to restore the communities' trust in banks. The regulators have demanded more capital and liquidity and less leverage. This means that for customers, banking will become more (rather than less) expensive, there will be higher interest rates on loans and less availability of credit. Increased levels of financial literacy will be essential if financial services consumers are to be empowered to choose between the traditional providers and the new entrants.

There has been research into both irresponsible borrowing by consumers and irresponsible lending by providers (see Worthington and Durkin 2012), which have combined to produce co-destruction of value in retail banking. Banking regulators have stressed that these 'irresponsible' behaviours from both consumers and providers are no longer acceptable.

Looking forward, changes to the 'macro' environment of retail banking outlined may help to restore trust in the banks, but they will combine with existing structural forces to make it even more difficult for new entrants to make an impact in the market. Switching providers continues to be fraught with suspicion by customers, capital requirements make new entry expensive, credit is being rationed making lending less profitable and the housing market remains flat, perhaps because of fears of another financial crisis. New entrants, from whatever origins they emerge, will need both patience and luck if they are initially to survive and then prosper!

References

Financial Times 2013. 'Osborne speech: Reform of banking', February 4th, www.ft.com/cms/s/0/dc756e8c-6ec4–11e2-9ded-00144feab49a.html#axzz2v4xtmvf3 (accessed 5 March 2014).

French, S., Leyshon, A. and Meek, S. 2013. *The Changing Geography of British Bank and Building Society Branch Networks, 2003–2013*, The University of Nottingham, School of Geography.

Furash, E. E. 1993. Banking's critical cross-roads. *The Bankers Magazine*. March-April, pp. 20–26.

King, B. 2011. *Branch Today, Gone Tomorrow: the case for the death of branch banking*, Marshall Cavendish: Singapore.

Office of Fair Trading 2009. *Personal current accounts in the UK: A follow up report*, (available at www.oft.gov.uk

—— 2013a. 'OFT says major changes still needed in personal current account market, press release January 25, 2013', available at www.oft.com

—— 2013b. *Evaluating the impact of the 2008 OFT market study and UTCCR test case into personal current accounts*, available at www.oft.gov.uk

Worthington, S. and Welch, P. 2011. Banking without the banks. *International Journal of Bank Marketing*, 29(2), pp. 190–201.

Worthington, S. and Durkin, M. 2012. Co-destruction of value in context: Cases from retail banking. *The Marketing Review*, 12(3), pp. 291–307.

Part II

The financial services consumer and financial decision-making

3

Social and psychological influences on financial literacy

Bruce Huhmann

Introduction

Difficulty understanding and proficiently using financial services has been documented for consumers of all income levels in developed and emerging markets (for example, Al-Tamimi and Kalli 2009, Bolton et al. 2011, Cole et al. 2011, Fogel and Schneider 2011, Lusardi and Mitchell 2007, Nga et al. 2010, OECD 2005, Worthy et al. 2010, van Rooij et al. 2011). Difficulties have also been documented across a wide range of financial services (for example, Fogel and Schneider 2011, Powers et al. 2011, Tennyson 2011).

This difficulty has often been ascribed to a lack of financial literacy. However, the "financial literacy" term has been ill-defined and variously applied, which has hampered researchers' ability to improve consumers' financial decision-making. The term first became popular in the 1990s. The National Endowment for Financial Education and the Cooperative Extension System-United States Department of Agriculture cosponsored a *Financial Literacy for Youth Month* in January 1995. In academic literature, early "financial literacy" work (for example, Chen and Volpe 1998, Cutler 1997) spawned a body of research on consumer difficulties with financial concepts.

However, the realization that some consumers have difficulty grasping financial concepts predates the "financial literacy" term. For example, the school savings movement in the early 1900s sought to teach children effective money-management skills (Oberholtzer 1914). Lessons in budgeting and money management continued to appear in home economics and personal finance classes throughout the twentieth century. In the academic literature, Lorenz (1940) discussed consumer difficulty with understanding credit costs and recommended presenting them more concretely.

This chapter's purpose is to conceptualize financial literacy grounded in research on consumer cognition and identify influences on the development of financial literacy. This review and synthesis of financial literacy research and the consumer socialization, processing motivation and psychographic influences on its development should promote a theory-based foundation to addressing the recognized societal problems caused by poor consumer financial decisions. Poor consumer financial decisions negatively impact individual lives and national economies, as was evident in the housing crises in many nations during the recent recession. Financial management and responsibility for education, retirement, healthcare and long-term care are increasingly an individual rather than a collective undertaking. Thus, understanding financial literacy in the financial sector is vitally important.

Conceptualizing financial literacy

Construct definition is the first step to advancing research in a field. Financial literacy has no generally accepted definition (Remund 2010); the confusion in terminology stems from operationalizing "financial literacy" to fit readily available secondary data, the relative ease in measuring observable outcomes versus internal cognitive processes related to financial decision-making and the lack of a theoretical basis. Theory-based definitions of financial literacy and its components should help researchers communicate findings with each other and with financial service providers, regulators, advocacy groups and policymakers. Definitions should also aid efforts to understand internal psychological processes at work and improve them to the benefit of consumers and society.

Financial literacy is defined as the ability to comprehend financial information, optimize financial decisions and effectively manage financial resources. Table 3.1 compares it to a similar higher-order global construct: literacy. Both are continua whose level depends on capacity (both innate and learnt), prior knowledge and proficiency.

Next, the components of financial literacy – financial capacity, financial knowledge and financial proficiency – are examined from the broader theoretical perspectives of cognitive capacity, consumer knowledge and processing motivation, opportunity and ability.

Financial capacity

In *financial capacity*, one's capability is enhanced as learnt processing skills and heuristics allow more efficient use of one's limited, innate cognitive capacity in processing and comprehending financial information (see Table 3.1).

Table 3.1 A comparison of literacy to financial literacy

	Literacy	Financial literacy
Definition	Ability to effectively read and write printed and written material in a particular language.	Ability to comprehend financial information, optimize financial decisions and effectively manage financial resources.
Components		
Capacity	Capacity to successfully identify, understand and interpret printed and written materials associated with a particular language.	Capacity to successfully process and comprehend information about financial concepts, services and products. It is a function of limited, innate cognitive capacity and learnt processing skills or heuristics.
Prior knowledge	Prior knowledge of letters, language, vocabulary, sentence structure and grammar. Knowledge may be general or genre/situation-specific (e.g., lingo or jargon).	Prior objective knowledge of financial concepts, services and products. Knowledge may be general or domain-specific (e.g., loan, credit card, banking, health expenditure, investment, insurance, retirement planning).
Proficiency	Proficiency in communicating via and creating printed and written materials in a particular language.	Proficiency in optimizing financial decisions and managing financial resources. Includes proficiency in saving, budgeting, expenditure control and debt management.

Because cognitive capacity is limited, comprehension suffers when processing demand exceeds capacity (Hu et al. 2007). Financial services advertising and descriptions of terms often include non-diagnostic information that exhausts consumers' limited capacity. Impaired capacity leads to sub-optimal processing and decision-making. Financial decisions are often complex and the number of attributes to consider easily exceeds consumers' limited capacity. In addition, situational variables (for example, stress or distractions) temporarily limit capacity further (Estelami 2009, Huhmann and Bhattacharyya 2005).

Because cognitive capacity is innate, consumers are born with differing levels. Capacity constraints limit financial knowledge acquisition (Herd et al. 2012). To circumvent capacity constraints, consumers learn heuristics to focus on one or a few attributes identified in their existing financial knowledge as decision-making aids. This interaction of financial capacity and financial knowledge affects decision quality. For example, consumers may learn to more efficiently utilize limited capacity by focussing on a key attribute, then adjusting evaluations based on other attributes using *attribute anchoring*. Even financial advisors and stockbrokers, who have above-average financial knowledge, use attribute anchoring to simplify investment decisions (Estelami 2009, MacGregor et al. 1999). Heuristics are especially useful given financial services' many experience and credence attributes (Lim and Chung 2011).

Financial capacity can be enhanced even for consumers with less innate cognitive capacity. Consumers can learn skills to more efficiently utilize financial capacity, just as they can learn communication and mathematics skills to improve language and numerical capacities. In addition to heuristics that simplify and organize financial information, financial capacity improves by learning to: extract financial information from texts, charts, figures and graphs; accurately forecast expenses and returns based on probabilities; convert prices and yields from currency to percentages and back; recognize differences in numbers outside everyday experience; master financial terminology and jargon. Perfect efficiency is insurmountable (Willis 2008). However, each improvement advances one's capability to gather useful and accurate information, then process and comprehend it.

Financial knowledge

Financial knowledge is a consumer's prior objective knowledge of financial concepts, services and products accumulated in memory. It is a function of direct and indirect experience with financial materials, services and products moderated by financial capacity and motivation to process during an experience.

Financial knowledge involves memory of financial concepts and how financial services work. It includes general knowledge and knowledge specific to domains such as mortgages, mutual funds or credit cards (Hansen 2012). Chapter 8 provides a detailed study of mutual fund investors' knowledge calibration and behavioural biases. Because it can be viewed as a specific instance of the broader consumer objective knowledge construct (Alba and Hutchinson 1987), greater familiarity with financial services and more experience strengthen financial knowledge and correct misconceptions or erroneous beliefs.

However, correcting misconceptions and erroneous beliefs is more difficult than initially encoding information because new information that does not fit with prior knowledge may be distorted to make it congruent with existing knowledge and because prior knowledge is used to filter, comprehend, organize and encode new information that passes through constraints imposed by financial capacity (Huhmann and McQuitty 2009).

As cognitive capacity and memory closely relate, so too should financial capacity and knowledge. These constructs should interact, such that, when encountering financial information, additions or changes to financial knowledge depend upon financial capacity and motivation to process and learn new information. For example, despite large capacity, consumers should make poor financial decisions due to exposure to primarily inaccurate information; learning skills and techniques to improve financial capacity should increase the likelihood of adding financial knowledge. Greater financial knowledge should enhance capacity to process financial information through a feedback loop in which prior knowledge is used in comprehending new information (see Lee and Marlowe 2003).

Faced with a financial decision, one should access existing financial knowledge and new information readily available or located through an external search. Ability to adequately process and comprehend this new information depends upon financial capacity. Thus, financial capacity and knowledge should reinforce each other during decision-making to impact financial proficiency.

Financial proficiency

Financial proficiency is one's ability to effectively manage finances and optimize decisions. Research relates it to ability to save, budget and control spending, as well as competence in making rational, informed financial decisions (Nga et al. 2010, Perry and Morris 2005).

Financial proficiency is a function of financial knowledge and capacity. Research demonstrates that financial knowledge benefits financial proficiency (Hansen 2012, Hastings and Mitchell 2011, Hershey and Mowen 2000, Hilgert et al. 2003, Perry and Morris 2005, Shim et al. 2010). It also sharply increases among those with the highest cognitive ability (Lusardi et al. 2010).

Inadequate capacity or insufficient prior knowledge to comprehend and categorize new information for easy recall leads consumers to rely on incorrect conclusions, misconceptions or fallacious beliefs about financial products or concepts (for example, compound interest, back-end load mutual funds, finance charges, etc.) during decision-making. Conversely, financial decisions are optimized when consumers possess sufficient capacity and knowledge to process decision-related information. For example, more knowledgeable consumers made better decisions regarding Health Savings Account spending (Holtje 2012).

In addition to the insights into the relationships between financial literacy components, this chapter also identifies variables that should explain the development of financial literacy. The next sections explore these: consumer socialization, motivation to process and psychographic influences.

Consumer socialization

Enhancing financial capacity or learning new financial knowledge requires consumer socialization. Consumer socialization is the process by which consumers learn consumption-related attitudes, behaviours and skills. As shown in Figure 3.1, this learning can result from direct experience or indirect experience, through social interactions with others or observation of role models (Moschis and Churchill 1978).

Direct experience

Direct experience helps develop skills to efficiently use financial capacity. As consumers gain experience they become more capable processors of financial information, just as practicing mathematics or language aids numeric or verbal skills. For example, working enhances young adults' money management skills (Mortimer 2003). Greater experience leads consumers to develop more financial capacity-enhancing heuristics (Lee and Marlowe 2003).

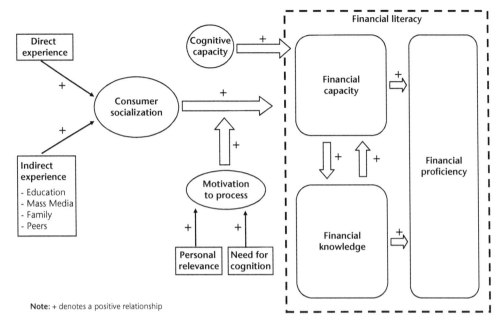

Figure 3.1 Consumer socialization and motivation to process on financial literacy

Direct experience improves familiarity, which increases efficient use of cognitive capacity by reducing cognitive effort requirements (see Alba and Hutchinson 1987). With cognitive effort reduced, likelihood of cognitive overloads declines, but likelihood of engaging in information search and processing rises (Hu et al. 2007). Familiarity with financial concepts should improve accuracy in encoding new financial knowledge, which benefits proficiency. Financial service experience reduces behavioural outcomes associated with poor financial literacy more than financial education (Hilgert et al. 2003, Peng et al. 2007). Greater financial asset experience leads consumers to use more sophisticated heuristics, which potentially enhances decision-making outcomes (Lee and Marlowe 2003).

In consumer behaviour, experience is an important source of prior knowledge, thus, financial services experience should enhance financial knowledge. Research detects a relationship between direct experience and financial knowledge (Al-Tamimi and Kalli 2009, Hilgert et al. 2003, Monticone 2010, Shim et al. 2010, Tennyson 2011).

One may gather sufficient direct experience over time for some financial services, such as credit cards. Unfortunately, the opportunity to obtain direct experience related to many financial services is limited because of their limited or one-time nature (for example, mortgages, pensions and long-term care). Thus, direct experience is inadequate as a consumer socialization agent to enhance financial literacy related to these infrequently-purchased, experience- or credence-attribute financial services (Franke et al. 2004, Lim and Chung 2011).

Indirect experience

Indirect experience also plays a role in developing financial literacy. It is obtained via communication with and observation of additional consumer socialization agents: educators, mass media, family and peers (Moschis and Churchill 1978).

Education

Lack of financial education negatively impacts financial literacy (Carlin 2012, Hilgert et al. 2003, Kehiaian 2012). Thus, financial education programmes (aka, financial literacy campaigns) have been touted as the answer to enhancing consumers' financial capacity and knowledge. As a result, governments encourage or mandate such programmes (for example, The UK's Personal Finance Education Group, the Financial Consumer Agency of Canada and the US Financial Literacy and Education Commission). Common target audiences include immigrants, women, renters, homebuyers, the unemployed, the bankrupt, small business owners and students (Fox et al. 2005, Hilgert et al. 2003, Kehiaian 2012). Some consumers (for example, white-collar professionals) are not targeted because they are assumed to be sufficiently well-educated as to avoid financial problems, despite pervasive financial difficulties (Brown and Taylor 2008, Estelami 2009, Willis 2008).

These programmes inconsistently improve financial literacy. Some comparisons of financial education programme graduates with untrained consumers find increased financial knowledge (Carlin 2012, Powers et al. 2011, Shim et al. 2010); others do not (Lusardi and Mitchell 2007, Mandell and Klein 2009). Sometimes, positive effects occur only for certain consumers (Cole et al. 2011) or certain types of financial education (Peng et al. 2007). These programmes may improve financial decision quality (see Lusardi and Mitchell 2007 for a review).

Financial education should be more effective if it differentiates between financial capacity and knowledge. The financial literacy of those who merely lack prior knowledge should improve by familiarizing themselves with financial concepts, products and services. For the remainder, their capacity-related inability to process and comprehend financial information should be addressed. A financial education programme seeking to teach consumers about mutual fund investing should first assess the target audience's financial capacity (for example, heuristics used to evaluate funds, such as past performance, management fees or assets under management), then design a financial literacy programme that enhances financial capacity, then financial knowledge.

A key focus of financial literacy research has been formal learnt knowledge and its delivery via financial education, yet consumers also learn financial capacity improving skills and acquire financial knowledge from the mass media, family and peers. Financial education programmes' inconsistent effectiveness explains why consumers report that their primary sources of financial knowledge, in addition to direct experience, are family, friends and the media, not these programmes (Hilgert et al. 2003).

Mass media

Mass media's editorial and advertising content also serve as consumer socialization agents. Amount of media exposure and consequently, number of advertisements viewed, increase vicarious learning (Moschis and Churchill 1978). Chapters 19 and 20 in this book describe the important socialization agent of financial services advertising.

Specifically focussing on consumer socialization via financial publication readership, research finds improved financial knowledge, information source selectivity and financial proficiency. Consumers in the top investment knowledge quartile are 1,245 percent more likely to use newspapers, 809 percent more likely to read financial magazines and books, 197 percent more likely to use financial information in the Internet and 124 percent more likely to consult personal financial advisors than bottom quartile consumers are to use these information sources. Conversely, they are 286 percent less likely to use advertising as an information source than bottom quartile consumers (van Rooij et al. 2011). Financial publication subscribers exhibit greater insurance knowledge than non-subscribers (Tennyson 2011) and newspaper readership improves financial proficiency (Moschis and Churchill 1978).

Family

Parents play a key role in shaping youths' financial literacy; they should initiate educating children about financial information processing and management early. Additionally, parents can act as co-obligors and actively advise children in use and management of financial services (Huhmann and McQuitty 2009, Limbu et al. 2012).

Examples of parents as financial literacy socialization agents are common. For example, youths are more proficient in risk diversification if their parents own stocks or have retirement or profit-sharing plans requiring allocation decisions. This is found even when differences in wealth are taken into account (Lusardi et al. 2010). Alternatively, youths whose families received public assistance while they were minors are 33 percent more likely to exhibit problematic financial behaviours than others (Worthy et al. 2010). As parental influence increases, credit card balance management becomes more responsible and usage frequency declines among youths (Limbu et al. 2012). Both direct instruction and vicarious learning from parents positively impact youths' financial knowledge and proficiency (Shim et al. 2010).

Parents have received the lion's share of research attention into the family's role in financial literacy socialization; other family members have largely been ignored. A potentially exciting avenue for future research is adult children's role in enhancing their aging parents' financial literacy.

Peers

Peer interactions about consumption matters increase awareness of buying processes and product availability, attributes and usage (Moschis and Churchill 1978). Peer observation and communication builds capacity-enhancing skills and financial knowledge, especially among consumers with little prior knowledge. For example, consumers in the bottom quartile on financial knowledge are 227 percent more likely to rely on friends, parents and acquaintances as an information source than those in the top quartile consumers (van Rooij et al. 2011).

Unfortunately, unless peers are good role models or information sources, they negatively impact financial literacy. Greater use of informal information sources (for example, family and peers) or industry salespeople is associated with lower insurance knowledge (Tennyson 2011) and word-of-mouth greatly influences consumer evaluations of financial services (Lim and Chung 2011).

Motivation to process

Motivation to process moderates consumer socialization's influence on financial literacy by affecting the degree to which experience and exposure to financial information is given attention, processed and encoded into long-term memory. For example, Wang (2012) finds greater knowledge of credit card disclosure statements among those who devoted more attention and processing effort. Motivation to process may be extrinsic (i.e., personal relevance of the information or experience) or intrinsic (i.e., one's need for cognition). Since both influence motivation to process, higher levels of one may somewhat compensate for lower levels of the other.

Personal relevance

Extrinsic motivation to process concerns two types of perceived personal relevance. First, *enduring involvement* is on-going interest in a product or topic. Second, *situational involvement* occurs when information is personally relevant to one's current decision or circumstance (Celsi and Olson 1988). When one needs a financial service, situational involvement increases motivation to process but may not satisfactorily boost financial literacy due to its temporary nature. However, ongoing factors boosting enduring involvement should benefit financial literacy. For example, Monticone (2010) found wealth motivated consumers to increase their financial knowledge. Personal relevance of retirement positively relates to financial knowledge about retirement planning and financial proficiency related to retirement preparedness (Hershey and Mowen 2000).

Declining financial literacy, despite government and industry financial education initiatives, demonstrates the important but often ignored role of personal relevance. Many interested in promoting financial literacy assume that any exposure to personal finance materials improves consumers' financial management behaviours (Hilgert et al. 2003). Familiarity aids financial literacy but only given sufficient processing effort. Exposure without processing limits one's ability to acquire and retain concepts.

Consumers process and retain only a fraction of the information to which they are exposed. Processing and acquisition increase when consumers are motivated to process. For example, consumers with highly negative debt experience process materials about budgeting and debt avoidance more than other consumers (Shahrabani 2012). Heuristics to improve financial capacity are developed as enduring involvement increases (Lee and Marlowe 2003).

Therefore, a one-size-fits-all approach to presenting financial information is as ineffective as a one-size-fits-all approach to advertising clothing. For example, students are uninterested in processing information about retirement strategies. Even if informed that government pensions would be discontinued, college students report no increased motivation to learn about saving for retirement (Powers et al. 2011). But if related to personally relevant topics (for example, financing university expenses), their greater attention and interest should translate into improved retention of financial concepts.

Need for cognition

Need for cognition (NFC) is intrinsic motivation to process. It represents one's propensity to engage in and prefer activities requiring considerable thought, regardless of personal relevance (Cacioppo and Petty 1982). With intrinsic motivation, the act of processing is enjoyable or personally rewarding to an individual.

As NFC increases, consumers are better able to evaluate financial information for inaccuracy or bias due to framing, weak arguments or extreme statements (Kuvaas and Kaufmann 2004, Martin et al. 2003, Price and Stone 2004). This is likely due to enhanced financial capacity and knowledge as NFC boosts motivation to process financial information. Higher NFC consumers develop more effective heuristics to enhance financial capacity (Lee and Marlowe 2003) and are more likely to read investment and financial media to increase their financial knowledge than lower NFC consumers (Martin et al. 2003).

Psychographic influences

Psychographic constructs (for example, values, lifestyle and personality) are under-researched in relation to consumer financial management (Huhmann and McQuitty 2009). This may be because much consumer financial management research has used secondary data sets (Brown and Taylor 2008, Lee and Hogarth 2000, Lusardi and Mitchell 2007, Hilgert et al. 2003). These externally-valid, readily-available datasets describe attitudes towards financial service issues and financial behaviour, but only indirectly investigate psychographics. This section briefly describes the influence on financial literacy of several psychographic constructs: locus of control, self-control/self-regulation, regulatory focus, materialism, learned helplessness, anxiety and self-efficacy.

Locus of control

Locus of control (LOC) is a personality trait that affects causal attributions. Internal LOC consumers expect that their actions generate predictable outcomes, whereas external LOC consumers expect that luck, fate or powerful others control outcomes or that great complexity makes outcomes unpredictable (Rotter 1966). External LOC emphasizes that financial well-being is out of one's hands (Falicov 2001, Reimanis and Posen 1980).

Internal LOC consumers are action-oriented and desire to master the skills needed to accomplish goals. In support, Perry and Morris (2005) found internal LOC consumers exhibit greater financial knowledge and proficiency than external LOC consumers.

Additionally, LOC should influence reliance on one's financial knowledge versus financial service providers' advice and expertise during decision-making. In support, research finds that internal LOC emphasizes taking responsibility for one's financial well-being and that effort is rewarded (Falicov 2001, Reimanis and Posen 1980). Internal LOC consumers are more likely to accept responsibility for their indebtedness than external LOC consumers (Livingstone and Lunt 1992).

Self-regulation and self-control

Most financial decisions by their nature involve intertemporal choices in which consumers weigh short-term costs/benefits against future costs/benefits (Fehr 2002). Developing financial literacy also involves intertemporal choices, because the benefits of improved financial literacy are in the future but the costs in time and effort to develop it must be borne first.

Consumers' self-regulation and self-control should also impact financial literacy through temporal discounting. *Temporal discounting* is the preference for smaller, immediate rewards over larger, delayed rewards (Loewenstein and Prelec 1992).

Self-regulation involves controlling impulses and substituting more appropriate consumption decisions for undesirable actions. After expending limited self-regulation resources, *ego-depletion* leads to stronger buying urges and greater unanticipated spending. It also results from physical or emotional exhaustion, competing cognitive demands, or competing temptations requiring self-regulation. In an ego-depleted state, consumers make suboptimal financial decisions regardless of financial capacity or knowledge. For example, experimental manipulation of ego-depletion reduces retirement plan participation intentions (Howlett et al. 2008).

Although both affect temporal discounting, ego-depletion is a transient state impacting financial proficiency, whereas self-control is an enduring trait with long-term consequences for financial literacy development. Self-control involves delaying gratification. Some consumers have *myopic self-control* with exaggerated emphasis on the present over the future. They succumb to impulse and choose immediate short-term pleasure at the expense of long-term costs. Myopic self-control is sometimes termed impatience (Hastings and Mitchell 2011). It leads to greater rather than optimal purchases of hedonic or leisure goods and less than optimal purchases of investment goods (Ainslie 1975, Mukhopadhyay and Johar 2005). Myopic self-control consumers devote insufficient effort to the utilitarian tasks of improving financial capacity and acquiring financial knowledge. They tend to be unprepared for durable repair expenses, use expensive quick-access credit sources (for example, payday loans) and have income shocks, excessive debt that they have difficulty repaying, low incomes, foregone voluntary pension contributions and few savings (Gathergood 2012, Hastings and Mitchell 2011, Kamleitner et al. 2012).

Conversely, *hyperopic self-control* consumers are markedly future-oriented. Such consumers purchase primarily utilitarian and investment goods but few hedonic, impulse or leisure goods. Hyperopic self-control should drive sufficient cognitive effort to the utilitarian tasks of improving financial capacity efficiency and acquiring financial knowledge. Hyperopic self-control consumers delay gratification to invest for the future. They borrow less, save more and experience better financial outcomes than other consumers. Future-oriented consumers tend to participate in retirement plans, especially when aware of participation's financial consequences (Howlett et al. 2008) and possess financial knowledge related to retirement and financial proficiency related to retirement preparedness (Hershey and Mowen 2000).

Regulatory focus

Regulatory focus theory posits that all goal-related behaviours, such as managing finances, are regulated by either a prevention or promotion focus. *Prevention-focussed* consumers seek security and loss avoidance; *promotion-focussed* consumers seek growth and gains (Higgins et al. 2001, Zhou and Pham 2004). Despite some financial gains, losses reinforce prevention-focussed consumers' initial regulatory focus due to their more painful emotional response to losses rather than pleasurable response to gains. Despite some financial losses, the stronger response to gains than to losses among promotion-focussed consumers reinforces their prior regulatory focus (Higgins et al. 2001). Consumers view stocks and trading accounts as promotion-focussed but mutual funds and retirement accounts as prevention-focussed (Zhou and Pham 2004).

When processing information, promotion-focussed consumers mentally access "ideals" (for example, aspirations, hopes and ideal outcomes/situations) and potential positive outcomes. They eagerly seek and favourably respond to affective aspects of persuasion, optimal interpretations and commonalities/relationships or abstract/global themes among diverse message items (Zhou and Pham 2004, Zhu and Meyers-Levy 2007). Thus, promotion-focussed consumers likely overtrade. Frequent stock trading tends to decrease performance (Barber and Odean 2000). They likely chase yields or performance by focussing on ideal outcomes, not risk; they focus more on potential benefits than costs. For example, promotion-focussed consumers spend more Health Savings Account funds on medical procedures than prevention-focussed consumers (Holtje 2012). However, promotion-focussed consumers should willingly use leverage, which may enhance gains or losses. They should underweight security-oriented financial products (for example, low-interest bank savings or insurance) and overweight growth-oriented products (for example, equities). Promotion-focussed consumers' stronger response to gains will reinforce existing financial capacity heuristics and skills and the adequacy of current financial knowledge.

Alternatively, prevention-focussed consumers should be concerned with insuring against loss and maintaining capital but less likely to use leverage to improve long-term financial positions. Prevention-focussed consumers access "oughts" (i.e., normative obligations, duties and responsibilities) and possible negative outcomes. They vigilantly seek and favourably respond to message substance, specifics and context-dependent interpretations (Zhou and Pham 2004, Zhu and Meyers-Levy 2007). One would expect prevention-focussed consumers to focus on financial products that minimize loss or risk (for example, insurance, low-risk low-return investments, fixed-income investments, fixed-rate mortgages, retirement savings and guaranteed annuities). Prevention-focussed consumers should reduce perceived risk by acquiring financial knowledge and avoid painful losses by developing financial proficiency.

Materialism

Materialism places importance on acquiring and using possessions to achieve happiness or to communicate status and success. Materialism strengthens beliefs that purchases create life trans-formations. These transformative beliefs include changes to the self and others' perceptions of the self, improving interpersonal relationships and enhanced pleasure, competence, capabilities or control over one's life.

Materialism should also motivate financial capacity and knowledge development by increas-ing enduring involvement in financial matters, however, it should impede financial proficiency. Higher materialism may cause financially-knowledgeable consumers who otherwise exhibit exceptional financial proficiency to overspend, deplete savings, overuse credit, be disinterested in budgeting, make more impulse purchases, have large difficult-to-manage debts and favourable attitudes towards borrowing (Fitzmaurice 2008, Hershey and Mowen 2000, Livingstone and Lunt 1992, Limbu et al. 2012, Richins 2011, Watson 2003).

Learned helplessness

Learned helplessness is the perception that events are uncontrollable (Abramson et al. 1978). This trait affects motivation to acquire financial knowledge or skills to more efficiently use financial capacity. Perceived lack of control associated with higher learned helplessness decreases motiva-tion to develop financial capacity or use prior knowledge during financial decision-making and external search behaviour, which harms financial knowledge acquisition (Motes 1982).

Interestingly, financial service providers may inadvertently increase consumers' learned help-lessness. For example, credit card agreements often include "universal default" clauses whereby issuers can raise consumers' interest rates automatically due to late payments on other cards or loans, or if an issuer believes a consumer is overly indebted, even without any late payments. Learned helplessness increases as consumers expect to suffer similar consequences regardless of financial service usage or attempts at financial management (Huhmann and McQuitty 2009).

Anxiety

Trait anxiety is one's likelihood of experiencing anxiety. Trait anxiety leads to lower-risk finan-cial decisions: lower investment of savings, greater holdings in interest-bearing accounts and greater likelihood of immediately selling stocks that have either increased or decreased in value (Gambetti and Giusberti 2012). Trait anxiety, which is universal across contexts, increases one's likelihood of experiencing financial anxiety.

Financial anxiety is situational and experienced in reaction to financial decision-making. It disposes consumers to avoid cognitive engagement with personal financial management, which hampers financial literacy development. It also slows response to and hampers processing of financial information. Financial anxiety is more common among lower rather than upper classes and decreases with age (Shapiro and Burchell 2012). Class and age differences are likely due to greater financial experience among upper classes and with age, therefore, experience should reduce financial anxiety to the benefit of financial capacity and knowledge.

Self-efficacy

Financial knowledge is objective knowledge. Some researchers include subjective perceptions about one's state of financial knowledge as part of financial knowledge (see Chapter 20 by Wang in this book). However, viewing subjective knowledge as separate highlights the role of self-efficacy or confidence (Alba and Hutchinson 1987) and knowledge calibration (see Chapter 8 of this book by Mishra and Kumar).

Self-efficacy is one's confidence or perceived ability to successfully perform a task. It grows with domain experience and familiarity. Financial decisions are complex, requiring considerable self-efficacy to optimally perform. Self-efficacy non-linearly relates to proficiency. Proficiency rises up to a certain self-efficacy level depending on the consumer's objective knowledge, then declines (Hu et al. 2007). This inverted U-shaped function's end-points are underconfidence and overconfidence.

The highest proficiency in financial decision-making occurs when a consumer has high financial knowledge and is neither underconfident nor overconfident. Such consumers have objective knowledge and correctly assess it. They tend not to rely on others who may not put their financial interests first. These consumers are less likely to rely on third-party experts and informal information sources (for example, peers and family) during insurance decision-making than underconfident consumers (Tennyson 2011).

Correct self-assessment of poor financial knowledge should encourage a consumer to seek help from others with greater financial literacy. More importantly, this should increase caution and external information search, which lessens negative financial outcomes despite poor financial literacy.

Underconfidence occurs when a consumer underestimates objective knowledge. To the detriment of financial outcomes, underconfident consumers unduly consider the input of others who may possess less financial knowledge, misunderstand their financial situation or are promoting other interests (for example, biased investment recommendation websites or blogs). Tennyson (2011) demonstrates this in the insurance domain.

Overconfidence occurs when a consumer's subjective self-assessment exceeds one's actual degree of knowledge, it is common worldwide (Buckland 2010, OECD 2005, Lusardi and Mitchell 2007). Overconfident decision-makers overestimate their knowledge and their previously successful heuristics while downplaying the current situation's details. They neither search for nor process all relevant information, they underestimate actual risks and overestimate their abilities (Hu et al. 2007). Unsurprisingly, overconfident consumers trade stocks more often than others to the detriment of net-worth accumulation (Grinblatt and Keloharju 2009, Zhou and Pham 2004).

Overconfidence about one's financial knowledge results in poor financial proficiency and suboptimal decisions (Hu et al. 2007, Willis 2008). It reduces seeking financial advice (Lusardi and Mitchell 2007), which should fill unacknowledged gaps in overconfident consumers' financial knowledge. Overconfidence might also decrease motivation to build financial capacity or knowledge, because overconfident consumers "already know it all".

Overconfidence is difficult to surmount. The *confirmation bias* is a self-reinforcing tendency to acquire and use information that fits existing beliefs (Jones and Sugden 2001). It leads overconfident consumers to ignore negative financial experiences and information that might alter their excessive self-efficacy perceptions.

Financial service marketers may help underconfident and overconfident consumers better process information and choose alternatives through matching self-efficacy to message framing. Underconfident consumers prefer concrete construals. They perceive concretely-framed messages as more relevant and process them more thoroughly. Alternatively, overconfident consumers prefer abstract construals, they perceive abstractly-framed messages as more relevant and process them more thoroughly (Wan and Rucker 2013).

Conclusion

Much information asymmetry is present in financial services. Financial services are complex, intangible experience or credence products. Providers possess specialized knowledge. But information asymmetry hinders consumers' ability to evaluate competing alternatives.

Citing bounded rationality, policymakers have typically responded with government regulation requiring greater information disclosure when promoting and selling financial services. Bounded rationality holds that limits on decision-making can be diminished by removing misleading message framing and increasing consumer knowledge, decision time, incentives to optimize decisions and the quantity and quality of available information (Simon 1997). Despite more and better quality information disclosures in marketing communications for financial services, research suggests that consumers may not read or process it as intended.

Although more information increases readership for search products, which can be evaluated prior to purchase, more information actually reduces advertising readership for experience products, such as financial services (Franke et al. 2004). Consumers exhibit fewer tendencies to read information about experience or credence attributes because they cannot verify information accuracy or relevance.

Since greater information disclosure requirements fail to reduce suboptimal financial decisions, financial literacy is important because it gives consumers a set of skills, heuristics, prior knowledge and proficiencies that helps to overcome the information asymmetry with financial service providers. As shown in this chapter, consumer socialization improves financial literacy through direct experience or indirect experience via communication with and observation of educators, mass media, family and peers. Although the need for cognition is beyond their control, policymakers, educators and marketers can improve motivation to process information during socialization by increasing the personal relevance of financial information. Without making financial information personally relevant or considering the target audience's financial capacity and prior knowledge, financial literacy campaigns will be ineffective. This chapter also describes factors that affect motivation to process financial information, develop capacity-enhancing skills and heuristics, acquire financial knowledge and use financial proficiency during decision-making (see Table 3.2).

Table 3.2 Summary of influences on financial literacy components

Influence	Financial capacity	Financial knowledge	Financial proficiency	Comment
Financial capacity		+	+	Enhances by increasing ability to process and comprehend financial information.
Financial knowledge	+		+	Enhances in the same domain (e.g., mutual funds).
Enduring involvement	+	+		Increases attention and processing during financial experiences or exposure to financial information.
High need for cognition	+	+		Greater information seeking, elaboration and structuring of complex financial concepts regardless of involvement.
Internal locus of control	+	+		Greater desire to master financial capacity-enhancing skills.

(continued)

Table 3.2 Summary of influences on financial literacy components *(continued)*

Influence	Financial capacity	Financial knowledge	Financial proficiency	Comment
Ego depletion			–	Leads to suboptimal financial decisions, such as foregoing retirement plan participation.
Myopic self-control	–	–		Too short-term-pleasure-oriented to devote time and effort to utilitarian task of financial literacy development.
Hyperopic self-control		+	+	Engage in utilitarian task of acquiring financial knowledge and improving proficiency to aid future financial outcomes.
Prevention regulatory focus		+	+	Acquire financial knowledge to reduce perceived risk and focus on financial proficiency to avoid painful losses.
Materialism	+	+	–	Transformative beliefs related to money and possessions prompt financial capacity and knowledge development, but interfere with their typically beneficial impact on proficiency.
Learned helplessness	–	–		External search and financial literacy growth seem pointless.
Financial anxiety	–	–		Slows/hampers information processing and decreases engagement with personal financial management activities.
Underconfidence	–	–	–	Doubt ability to comprehend financial information, successfully use prior knowledge or make good decisions.
Overconfidence	–	–	–	Overly sure of effectiveness of previously learnt heuristics and skills and sufficiency of knowledge and proficiency level.

Note: + enhances; – constrains

Social and psychological influences on financial literacy's impact on financial decision outcomes has received some attention (Huhmann and McQuitty 2009). However, more work is needed to establish the role of variables such as risk aversion, sensation seeking, social comparisons and self-monitoring; financial literacy research has primarily focussed on the rational component of decision-making. Consumer behaviour and psychology have identified the role of emotion in other decision-making domains; the relationship of emotion to financial literacy also requires investigation.

Research into financial literacy is a relatively recent phenomenon. This chapter uses consumer behaviour research to provide a theory-based structure for and antecedents to financial literacy. This chapter should be viewed as a starting point for additional research into the role of social and psychological influences on financial literacy. More insights await discovery.

References

Abramson, L.Y., Seligman, M.E. and Teasdale, J.D. 1978. Learned helplessness in humans: Critique and reformulation. *Journal of Abnormal Psychology*, 87(1), pp. 49–74.
Ainslie, G. 1975. Specious reward: A behavioral theory of impulsiveness and impulse control. *Psychology Bulletin*, 82(4), pp. 463–96.

Alba, J.W. and Hutchinson, J.W. 1987. Dimensions of consumer expertise. *Journal of Consumer Research*, 13(4), pp. 411–54.

Al-Tamimi, H.A.H. and Kalli, A.A.B 2009. Financial literacy and investment decisions of UAE investors. *Journal of Risk Finance*, 10(5), pp. 500–16.

Barber, B. and Odean, T. 2000. Trading is hazardous to your wealth: The common stock investment performance of individual investors. *Journal of Finance*, 55(2April), pp. 773–806.

Bolton, L.E., Bloom, P.N. and Cohen, J.B. 2011. Using loan plus lender literacy information to combat one-sided marketing of debt consolidation loans. *Journal of Marketing Research*, 48, pp. S51–S59.

Brown, S. and Taylor, K. 2008. Household debt and financial assets: Evidence from Germany, Great Britain and the USA. *Journal of the Royal Statistical Society*, 171(3), pp. 615–43.

Buckland, J. 2010. Are low-income Canadians financially literate? Placing financial literacy in the context of personal and structural constraints. *Adult Education Quarterly*, 60(4), pp. 357–76.

Cacioppo, J.T. and Petty, R.E. 1982. The need for cognition. *Journal of Personality and Social Psychology*, 42(1), pp. 116–31.

Carlin, B.I. 2012. Financial education and timely decision support: Lessons from Junior Achievement. *American Economic Review*, 102(3), pp. 305–8.

Celsi, R.L. and Olson, J. 1988. The role of involvement in attention and comprehension processes. *Journal of Consumer Research*, 15(2), pp. 210–24.

Chen, H. and Volpe, R.P. (1998). An analysis of personal financial literacy among college students. *Financial Services Review*, 7, pp. 107–28.

Cole, S., Sampson, T. and Zia, B. 2011. Prices or knowledge? What drives demand for financial services in emerging markets? *Journal of Finance*, 66(6), pp. 1933–67.

Cutler, N.E. 1997. The false alarm and blaring sirens of financial literacy: Middle-agers' knowledge of retirement. *Generations*, 21(2), pp. 34–40.

Estelami, H. 2009. Cognitive drivers of suboptimal financial decisions: Implications for financial literacy campaigns. *Journal of Financial Services Marketing*, 13(4), pp. 273–83.

Falicov, C.J. 2001. The cultural meanings of money: the case of Latinos and Anglo-Americans. *American Behavioral Scientist*, 45(2), pp. 313–28.

Fehr, E. 2002. Behavioural science: The economics of impatience. *Nature*, 415(6869), pp. 269–72.

Fitzmaurice, J. 2008. Splurge purchases and materialism. *Journal of Consumer Marketing*, 25(6), pp. 332–38.

Fogel, J. and Schneider, M. 2011. Credit card use: Disposable income and employment status. *Young Consumers*, 12(1), pp. 5–14.

Fox, J., Bartholomae, S. and Lee, J. 2005. Building the case for financial education. *Journal of Consumer Affairs*, 39(1), pp. 195–214.

Franke, G.R., Huhmann, B.A. and Mothersbaugh, D.L. 2004. Information content and consumer reader-ship of print ads: a comparison of search and experience products. *Journal of the Academy of Marketing Science*, 32(1), pp. 20–31.

Gambetti, E. and Giusberti, F. 2012. The effect of anger and anxiety traits on investment decisions. *Journal of Economic Psychology*. 33(6), pp. 1059–69.

Gathergood, J. 2012. Self-control, financial literacy and consumer over-indebtedness, *Journal of Economic Psychology*, 33(3), pp. 590–602.

Grinblatt, M. and Keloharju, M. 2009. Sensation seeking, overconfidence, and trading activity. *Journal of Finance*, 64(2), pp. 549–78.

Hansen, T. 2012. Understanding trust in financial services: The influence of financial healthiness, knowl-edge, and satisfaction. *Journal of Service Research*, 15(3), pp. 280–95.

Hastings, J.S. and Mitchell, O.S. 2011. How financial literacy and impatience shape retirement wealth and investment behaviors. *NBER Working Paper No. 16740*.

Herd, P., Holden, K. and Su, Y.T. 2012. The links between early-life cognition and schooling and late-life financial knowledge. *Journal of Consumer Affairs*, 46(3), pp. 411–35.

Hershey, D.A. and Mowen, J.C. 2000. Psychological determinants of financial preparedness for retirement. *The Gerontologist*, 40 (6), pp. 687–97.

Higgins, E.T., Friedman, R.S., Harlow, R.E., Idson, L.C., Ayduk, O.N. and Taylor, A. 2001. Achievement orientations from subjective histories of success: promotion pride versus prevention pride. *European Journal of Social Psychology*, 31, pp. 3–23.

Hilgert, M.A., Hogarth, J.M. and Beverly, S.G. 2003. Household financial management: the connection between knowledge and behavior. *Federal Reserve Bulletin*, 89(7), pp. 309–22.

Holtje, M.J. 2012. *Motivation and loss aversion in the Health Savings Account program*. Ph.D. University of Nebraska.

Howlett, E., Kees, J. and Kemp, E. 2008. The role of self-regulation, future orientation, and financial knowledge in long-term financial decisions. *Journal of Consumer Affairs*, 42(2), pp. 223–42.

Hu, J., Huhmann, B.A. and Hyman, M.R. 2007. The relationship between task complexity and information search: the role of self-efficacy. *Psychology & Marketing*, 24(3), pp. 253–70.

Huhmann, B.A. and Bhattacharyya, N. 2005. Does mutual fund advertising provide necessary investment information? *International Journal of Bank Marketing*, 23(4), pp. 296–313.

Huhmann, B.A. and McQuitty, S. 2009. A model of consumer financial numeracy. *International Journal of Bank Marketing*, 27(4), pp. 270–93.

Jones, M. and Sugden, R. 2001. Positive confirmation bias in the acquisition of information. *Theory and Decision*, 50(1), pp. 59–99.

Kamleitner, B., Hoelzl, E. and Kirchler, E. 2012. Credit use: Psychological perspectives on a multifaceted phenomenon. *International Journal of Psychology*, 47(1), pp. 1–27.

Kehiaian, S.E. 2012. Financial literacy and characteristics of Chapter 13 debtors. *International Journal of Business, Accounting, & Finance*. 6(1), pp. 142–55.

Kuvaas, B. and Kaufmann, G. 2004. Impact of mood, framing, and need for cognition on decision makers' recall and confidence. *Journal of Behavioral Decision Making*, 17(1), pp. 59–74.

Lee, J. and Hogarth, J.M. 2000. Relationships among information search activities when shopping for a credit card. *Journal of Consumer Affairs*, 34(2), pp. 330–60.

Lee, J. and Marlowe, J. 2003. How consumers choose a financial institution: Decision-making criteria and heuristics. *International Journal of Bank Marketing*, 21(2), pp. 53–71.

Lim, B.C. and Chung, C.M.Y. 2011. The impact of word-of-mouth communication on attribute evaluation. *Journal of Business Research*, 64(1), pp. 18–23.

Limbu, Y.B., Huhmann, B.A., and Xu, B. 2012. Are college students at greater risk of credit card abuse? Age, gender, materialism and parental influence on consumer response to Credit Cards. *Journal of Financial Services Marketing*, 17(2), pp. 148–62.

Livingstone, S.M. and Lunt, P.K. 1992. Predicting personal debt and debt repayment: Psychological, social and economic determinants. *Journal of Economic Psychology*, 13(1), pp. 111–34.

Loewenstein, G. and Prelec, D. 1992. *Choices Over Time*. New York: Russell Sage Foundation.

Lorenz, O.C. 1940. Consumer credit costs: What are they and who pays them. *Journal of Marketing*, 4(4), pp. 79–88.

Lusardi, A. and Mitchell, O.S. 2007. Financial literacy and retirement preparedness: evidence and implications for financial education programs. *Business Economics*, 42(1), pp. 35–44.

Lusardi, A., Mitchell, O.S. and Curto, V. 2010. Financial literacy among the young. *Journal of Consumer Affairs*, 44(2), pp. 258–380.

MacGregor, D.G., Slovic, P., Beny, M. and Evansky, H. (1999). Perception of financial risk: A survey study of advisors and planners. *Journal of Financial Planning*, 12(8), pp. 68–79.

Mandell, L. and Klein, L.S. 2009. The impact of financial literacy education on subsequent financial behaviour. *Journal of Financial Counseling & Planning*, 20(1), pp. 15–24.

Martin, B.A.S., Lang, B. and Wong, S. 2003. Conclusion explicitness in advertising: The moderating role of need for cognition (NFC) and argument quality (AQ) on persuasion. *Journal of Advertising*, 32(4), pp. 57–65.

Monticone, C. 2010. How much does wealth matter in the acquisition of financial literacy? *Journal of Consumer Affairs*, 44(2), pp. 403–22.

Mortimer, J.T. 2003. *Working and growing up in America*. Cambridge: Harvard University Press.

Moschis, G.P. and Churchill, G.A. 1978. Consumer socialization: A theoretical and empirical analysis. *Journal of Marketing Research*, 15(4), pp. 599–609.

Motes, W.H. 1982. A learned helplessness model of consumer behaviour. in R. Bush and S. Hunt, eds. *Marketing Theory: Philosophy of Science Perspectives*. Chicago: American Marketing Association, pp. 151–214.

Mukhopadhyay, A. and Johar, G.V. 2005. Where there is a will, is there a way? Effects of lay theories of self-control on setting and keeping resolutions. *Journal of Consumer Research*, 31(4), pp. 779–86.

Nga, J.K.H., Yong, L.H.L. and Sellappan, R.D. 2010. A study of financial awareness among youths. *Young Consumers*, 11(4), pp. 277–90.

Oberholtzer, S.L. 1914. School savings banks. *Bulletin*, 46 (620), Washington DC: United States Bureau of Education, Department of the Interior, pp. 1–187.

OECD. 2005. *Improving financial literacy: analysis of issues and policies*. Paris: Organization for Economic Co-Operation and Development.

Peng, T.-C.M., Bartholomae, S., Fox, J.J. and Cravener, G. 2007. The impact of personal finance education delivered in high school and college courses. *Journal of Family and Economic Issues*, 28, pp. 265–84.

Perry, V.G. and Morris, M.D. 2005. 'Who is in control? The role of self perception, knowledge, and income in explaining consumer financial behaviour. *Journal of Consumer Affairs*, 39(2), pp. 299–313.

Powers, M.L., Hobbs, J.M. and Ober, A. 2011. An empirical analysis of the effect of financial education on graduating business students' perceptions of their retirement planning familiarity, motivation, and preparedness. *Risk Management and Insurance Review*, 14(1), pp. 89–105.

Price, P.C. and Stone, E.R. 2004. Intuitive evaluation of likelihood judgment producers: Evidence for a confidence heuristic. *Journal of Behavioral Decision Making*, 17(1), pp. 39–57.

Reimanis, G. and Posen, C.F. 1980. Locus of control and anomie in Western and African cultures. *Journal of Social Psychology*, 112(2), pp. 181–89.

Remund, D.L. 2010. Financial literacy explicated: The case for a clearer definition in an increasingly complex economy. *Journal of Consumer Affairs*, 44(2), pp. 276–95.

Richins, M.L. 2011. Materialism, transformation expectations, and spending: Implications for credit use. *Journal of Public Policy & Marketing*, 30(2), pp. 141–56.

Rotter, J.B. 1966. Generalized expectancies of internal versus external control of reinforcements. *Psychological Monographs*, 80(609), whole issue.

Shahrabani, S. 2012. The effect of financial literacy and emotions on intent to control personal budget: A study among Israeli college students. *International Journal of Economics & Finance*, 4(9), pp. 156–63.

Shapiro, G.K. and Burchell, B.J. 2012. Measuring financial anxiety. *Journal of Neuroscience, Psychology, and Economics*, 5(2), pp. 92–103.

Shim, S., Barber, B.L., Card, N.A., Xiao, J.J. and Serido, J. 2010. Financial socialization of first-year college students: The roles of parents, work, and education. *Journal of Youth and Adolescence*, 39(12), pp. 1457–70.

Simon, H.A. 1997. *Models of Bounded Rationality*. Cambridge: MIT Press.

Tennyson, S. 2011. Consumers' insurance literacy: Evidence from survey data. *Financial Services Review*, 20, pp. 165–79.

van Rooij, M., Lusardi, A. and Alessie, R. 2011. Financial literacy and stock market participation. *Journal of Financial Economics*, 101 (2), pp. 449–72.

Wan, E.W. and Rucker, D.D. 2013. Confidence and construal framing: When confidence increases versus decreases information processing. *Journal of Consumer Research*, 39(5), pp. 977–92.

Wang, A. 2012. Socialization and processing effects on comprehension of credit card advertisement disclosures. *Journal of Financial Services Marketing*, 17(2), pp. 163–76.

Watson, J.J. 2003. The relationship of materialism to spending tendencies, saving, and debt. *Journal of Economic Psychology*, 24, pp. 723–39.

Willis, L.E. 2008. Against financial-literacy education. *Iowa Law Review*, 94(1), pp. 197–285.

Worthy, S.L, Jonkman, J. and Blinn-Pike, L. 2010. Sensation-seeking, risk-taking, and problematic financial behaviors of college students. *Journal of Family and Economic Issues*, 31, pp. 161–70.

Zhou, R. and Pham, M.T. 2004. Promotion and prevention across mental accounts: When financial products dictate consumers' investment goals. *Journal of Consumer Research*, 31(1), pp. 125–35.

Zhu, R. and Meyers-Levy, J. 2007. Exploring the cognitive mechanism that underlies regulatory focus effects. *Journal of Consumer Research*, 34(1), pp. 89–96.

4

Understanding how consumers make financial choices

A cross-disciplinary learning experience

Hazel Bateman, Jordan Louviere and Susan Thorp

Introduction

Every day, individuals must make dozens of choices. Most choices are inconsequential, such as choosing many fast-moving consumer goods like breakfast cereals or paper towels. Some are very consequential, such as the choice of mortgage type, allocating retirement savings across a menu of investment products and choosing whether or not to use retirement savings to buy a life annuity. What sets such financial choices apart from choices of fast-moving goods or day-to-day services (such as dry cleaning or garden maintenance) is significant uncertainty about the key factors underlying the consequences of the choices and the element of risk. Indeed, many major financial choices involve credence goods, where individuals can never know all the consequences (good or bad) of their choices in advance, which is also why they are seen as risky.

The purpose of this chapter is to describe and discuss three research case studies involving choices of retirement investment options, retirement benefit products (including life annuities) and mortgage type. In each case study, theory and methods from marketing, finance, economics and statistics are combined to develop a more complete understanding of consumer financial decision making. The chapter complements Chapters 6 and 7, both of which focus on different aspects of pension decisions and choices, in particular a qualitative understanding of factors affecting consumer decisions and the influence of specific product features (financial and non-financial) on decision processes.

What distinguishes these major financial choices from most, but not necessarily all, daily consumer decisions is that they have major wealth implications involving risk and uncertain consequences. The underlying services or products are complex to assess and require specific contextual knowledge (for example, a mortgagee's obligations on default) and some financial expertise (for example, understanding diversification) to be properly evaluated. Such products typically have multiple risks, may be irreversible, involve different time horizons, and can be subject to different regulations. Making the correct selection is particularly difficult as most financial choices have uncertain, non-independent payoffs, where the interplay among various risks affects the outcome (for example, investment, longevity and inflation risks all affect the outcome of pension provision). Any decision also will be affected by individuals' trust in institutions, product providers, regulators and government.

Two of the case studies specifically illustrate the complexity of market evolution effects. Unlike many consumer goods, retirement investment and life annuity products are relatively new to many consumer groups because they require individuals to take responsibility for the investment of their own funds (i.e., 401k products in the USA or pension/superannuation funds in Australia), a relatively new phenomenon in many economies. For example, successive governments in Australia have significantly changed various regulations and taxes applying to pension/superannuation funds, leading to frequent changes in product features. In the case of life annuities, few such products have been sold in Australia; for all practical purposes they are a "new" product to people entering retirement. Thus, Australia provides a rich context for the study of such financial choices. In contrast, a mortgage for a principal place of residence is a well-established product category. Even in such a well-established category, we show large differences in how individuals understand and evaluate products.

The usefulness of cross-disciplinary approaches is highlighted in several ways. In all three case studies we design and implement choice experiments in novel ways to help understand complex financial decisions. In the second and third case studies we show the importance of positioning the consumer in a hierarchy of decision states and in the first and second cases we also consider the implications of finance and economic theory (modern portfolio theory and expected utility theory) for choices to allow one to evaluate the quality of the decision context (particularly the effectiveness of information delivery) and the quality of individual decisions. Finally, in all cases we draw from many methods for modeling discrete micro-data to analyze experimental outcomes.

The remainder of the chapter is organized as follows. In the first case study we discuss rational consumer choices (i.e., what consumers should choose) and test several hypotheses about such choices for Australian retirement investment options. This case study emphasizes the importance of presentation format in product communication. This is followed by a second case study on Australian retirement benefit (including life annuity) choices focusing on using "choice-based measurement" methods to measure latent variables. In the final case study we describe and discuss what we call the Decision States Model and apply it to a pilot study of Australian mortgage choices. We show how classifying individuals into different decision states can provide interesting and important insights about how individuals consider and evaluate mortgage options. A novel feature of all three case studies is the integration of modes of analysis from marketing with standard models from economics and finance. We conclude the chapter with a discussion of general insights, limitations and potential future research directions.

A comparative evaluation of real-world investment risk presentations: combining a choice experiment and expected utility theory

Choosing a home loan should be easier than many other long-term financial decisions, most people have seen family and friends borrow for housing and can draw on social capital. Mortgages have similar, comparable features and repayment plans can be mapped against expected household income. Loan providers usually bear some or all of the default risk and because foreclosures or restructuring are costly, lenders tend to carefully evaluate borrower credit-worthiness, often giving advice about repayment plans. In a well-functioning market, borrower and lender are interested in mortgage contracts that are viable in the short and long term. In contrast, consumers make some major financial decisions, like retirement investing, with no past experience, or informal or peer advice.

An increasingly common decision confronting workers around the world is how to invest retirement savings. Many older workers began careers when publicly-provided social security and corporate-defined benefit plans dominated retirement provision, but pressures of population ageing and mobile workforces have seen migrations to defined contribution plans. Defined contribution plans leave critical decisions and their risks to individuals. Decisions about participation, contribution rates, investment options, product providers, insurance purchases and benefits are now the responsibility of ordinary people. Most risks are not shared with providers and retirement savings systems themselves are not yet mature, so few members have access to professional advice or can draw on experiences of friends and family to help them in choosing (Bernheim 2002). Indeed, retirement savings decisions probably are the most significant and complex financial decisions many individuals will ever make. For many superannuation/pension fund members, this may be their first brush with financial asset markets and consequently, with investment risk.

Standard economic theory assumes that not only are all investors aware, interested and capable, but they are also well-informed (in contrast to the Decision States Model presented in the third case study). Retirement savers are presumed to understand returns (compounding), inflation, asset price volatility, features of financial securities (for example, bond yields, coupons, equity dividends), have a thorough grasp of their own financial situation and preferences and the personal capacity to make decisions and carry through on them. Modern portfolio theory predicts that investors will choose a combination of assets that maximizes risk-adjusted returns, conditioning on each investor's risk aversion and wealth.

However, if the parameters of returns distributions are time-varying or poorly estimated, if uninsurable risks come into play, or preferences take non-standard forms, this choice can become complicated and it is increasingly appreciated that ordinary people are challenged by bounded rationality and bounded self-control (Mullainathan and Thaler 2000, Benartzi and Thaler 2001, Mitchell and Utkus 2006). Financial regulators usually assume investors are capable and engaged, needing only transparent information on risk and returns to make correct decisions. Indeed, a large body of literature in marketing and psychology has recognized decisions involving risk evaluations are not straightforward and are likely to be tilted by information framing (Agnew et al. 2008, Anagol and Gamble 2011, Brown et al. 2008, Vlaev et al. 2009).

In mandatory retirement savings systems, like Australia's Superannuation Guarantee, individuals at every phase of their working lives (and for many, during retirement as well) must choose an investment for their retirement contributions or make no choice and allow their savings to be invested at a superannuation/pension fund's discretion. Decisions are mandatory for individuals who: (1) have just become aware of the category "retirement savings plan" (or "superannuation" in our case), (2) are interested in the category but may not have the skills or information to make choices, and (3) may have the capability but prefer to delay or exit the "market". Retirement investment decisions confront individuals at every stage of decision-making, posing clear challenges to providers and regulators in the delivery of appropriate information.

How individuals assess investment risk is an important question. Over a working lifetime differences between investing in low return, risk-free bank accounts and investing in a portfolio of high-yielding risky assets can be in the order of 50 percent of wealth at retirement. Because governments increasingly compel individuals to make such decisions and live with the consequences, questions arise about the kinds of information that inform choices of investment options and how such allocation options should be structured.

Merging a theoretical framework into a choice experimental design

To answer these questions, we designed and implemented a choice experiment for a representative sample of Australian pension plan (superannuation fund) members. We asked participants to (hypothetically) allocate their entire current retirement savings and future contributions to one of three simple investment options in a series of choice sets.[1] The first option was a guaranteed bank account with a low real return (S), the second was a risky growth asset account with a higher expected return (R) and the third was a 50:50 mixed bank and growth account (M). We described these accounts to respondents in some detail; their task was to choose their most and least preferred options from each set (of three) in the experiment. These choices gave us a complete ranking of the three types of accounts for each individual in the experiment in each choice set. We were interested in responses to risk so we held the returns to each option constant and varied risk across choice sets (scenarios). Risk varied in two dimensions: the underlying volatility of risky returns and the way risk was described (or presented).

An important design issue in financial choice experiments is that researchers can rarely make clear judgments about the quality of respondent choices. For example, even if researchers could inventory each person's current financial position and their expectations, preferences and career prospects, computing an "optimal" retirement investment choice would be difficult and likely not robust. Consequently, we focus on testing hypotheses derived from fundamental and general predictions of theory and avoid specific or normative hypotheses associated with the choice experiment.

Each participant in this experiment received choice sets in which four levels of risky account volatility information varied between 12 percent per year and 28 percent per year. Table 4.1 shows the annual rate of return (above inflation) and volatility for the three investment options: bank account (safe – S), growth account (risky – R) and 50:50 mixed bank account and growth account (mixed – M) over the four levels of volatility from 12 percent (level 1) to 28 percent (level 4). The levels covered were not limited by historical experience in real financial asset markets. However, as explained below, we presented risk information in formats used by retirement plan providers, not as annual volatility.

Expected utility theory makes two general predictions about rational investment choices that can be used to evaluate account rankings. First, expected utility theory predicts that risk-averse respondents (having concave utility over wealth) will never choose the mixed option (M) as least preferred (which we refer to as type 1 inconsistency). If respondents are risk-averse, their choice of R or S options will always deliver lower utility than option M, regardless of underlying volatility, ruling out account rankings with M last. Second, if respondents preferred S to R at low levels of risk, they would not prefer R to S at higher levels of risk, ruling out some patterns of choices (type 2 inconsistency) (see Bateman et al. 2014b for proof).

This indicates that the choice experiment provides data to test whether respondents are conventionally rational (i.e., behave as predicted by expected utility theory) and to investigate the way risk presentations interact with this rationality test. To test the rationality hypothesis we had to present risk in several ways, reflecting standard formats used by financial service providers,[2]

Table 4.1 Variation in underlying risk of growth investment option

Level	Annual rates of return (above inflation)			Volatility	
	Safe	Risky	Mixed	Risky	Mixed
1	2%	4.5%	3.25%	12%	6%
2	2%	4.5%	3.25%	16%	8%
3	2%	4.5%	3.25%	20%	10%
4	2%	4.5%	3.25%	28%	14%

including range descriptions in text and diagram and probability tail and frequency descriptions. For example, for an R account with a volatility of 12 percent per year, respondents might read "There is a 9 in 10 chance of a return between -14% and +25% each year". For a frequency presentation, respondents would read "On average, negative returns occur 6 years out of every 20". In a sequence of choice sets, when the risk of the R account varied from 12 percent per year to 28 percent per year, the presentation style wording remained constant, but numbers changed to reflect higher or lower underlying risk. This lets us assess individuals' response to *risk level* separately from their response to *risk presentation*.[3]

In what follows we focus on comparing two presentations: a textual description of likely range of returns for each of the three accounts (P1) and a frequency description stating the expected number of years in 20 when returns would be negative in each account (P2). (Bateman et al. 2014b discuss all risk presentation formats.) We used these presentation formats because regulators were considering stipulating one of them to describe investment risk to Australian retirement savers at the time the choice experiment was conducted (Australian Prudential Regulatory Authority 2010, Australian Securities and Investment Commission 2012). Figure 4.1 shows a typical choice menu using presentation format (P1) when the underlying volatility of the risky asset was at 20 percent per year.

Failures of expected utility and the impact of risk presentation

We designed and implemented this experiment in 2010, collecting responses from 1199 randomly selected people who have at least one current retirement savings account and who were members of the Pureprofile web panel of more than 600,000 Australians. We also asked individuals questions about financial literacy and numeracy, wealth, income and demographics. "Irrational" choices (failure to conform to the expected utility theory predictions earlier noted) were common (i.e., 14 percent to 37 percent of the time depending on how we presented risk).

Features of options	Option A	Option B	Option C
Option type	100% bank account	50% bank account and 50% growth assets	100% growth assets
Average annual rate of return (above inflation)	2%	3.25%	4.5%
Level of investment risk	No risk	There is a 9 in 10 chance of a rate of return between -11.5% and 21%	There is a 9 in 10 chance of a rate of return between -25% and 40%

If these superannuation options were available for you to invest your money today

1. Which one of the three would you be **most likely** to choose?
    o   Option A
    o   Option B
    o   Option C
2. Which one of the three would you be **least likely** to choose?
    o   Option A
    o   Option B
    o   Option C

Figure 4.1   A representative choice task in the discrete choice experiment

Table 4.2 Rates of inconsistency with expected utility theory predictions

Format A "There is a 9 in 10 chance of a return between x% and y%."		Format B "On average, negative returns occur z years in every 20."	
Inconsistency		Inconsistency	
1	0.15	1	0.21
2	0.29	2	0.36

Table 4.2 shows the proportion of choices where respondents: (1) chose the mixed option (M) as worst (type 1 inconsistency),(2) failed to perceive increasing risk by switching to R (higher expected return) as volatility rose, or (3) switched to S (low real return account) as volatility declined (type 2 inconsistency). The overall level of inconsistency (1/5 to 1/3 of choices) and the rates of inconsistency varied substantially by presentation style. The range presentation (P1) produced the lowest rates of inconsistency (15 percent for type 1 and 29 percent for type 2), with much higher rates (21 percent for type 1 and 36 percent for type 2) for the presentation emphasizing the frequency of negative returns (P2). Multinomial logit modeling of inconsistent choice patterns on a range of personal covariates showed the inconsistencies were more common among the young and the less numerate.

Australian consumers must make this type of investment decision, so presenting salient information in the most comprehensible way is critically important for making sound choices. Our results favor range-based investment risk disclosure over frequency-based, loss-focused formats. Consistent with expected utility theory, when information about costs and benefits of growth asset investments are available and retirement savers can compare them with other investments using a comparable risk description, they are better equipped to make investment decisions. We also found that young, less-numerate people were more likely to need assistance in making investment decisions and should be a target for educational resources or personal advice.

These findings matter to regulators and providers of retirement products. Regulators worldwide are grappling with the best ways to present investment risk in an era of increasingly complex financial products and product providers are evaluating how to interpret these increasingly prescriptive regulations to the mass market.

Developing and applying "Choice-Based Measurement" methods to measure latent variables

The Decisions States Model (mentioned earlier and discussed in more detail in the next case study) warns that one should not assume that experimental subjects/survey respondents who make financial choices are already aware of the products or associated information, are interested in the choice options or are capable of making the choices required. As noted in this case example, widespread use of defaults, nudges and compulsion makes it more likely that complex financial "decisions" are being made by passive consumers or plan members who are not aware, interested or capable. Their choice outcomes may not reflect active choices and the defaults into which they then progress may not always be well-understood.[4] For example, Agnew et al. (2013) showed a common default option for retirement savings investments was understood by less than 40 percent of adults, despite a large majority of accounts being invested there. Consumers' understanding of common products (or even the products they use often) may be incorrect, particularly if nudges, defaults or compulsion play a role.

A clear idea of what subjects understand *ex ante* is crucial to designing any choice experiment and it is important to learn how well they understand the product or other attributes in such experiments. In particular, people may move through aware, interested and capable decision states as discussed in the next case example; they may form preferences and gain knowledge of products if they are involved or interested in the financial decisions in the choice experiment. However, involvement and interest are not directly observable so the purpose of this case is to show how one can proxy involvement by measuring the effort people make to understand features of products in choice experiments.

Pilot study of the retirement income landscape

On reaching retirement, members of defined contribution plans must decide what to do with their accumulated savings. Withdrawing a lump sum of wealth for further investment or consumption is a common option (in the US and Australia); far more popular than voluntarily taking out an annuity. Both countries operate private retirement savings schemes but few people convert retirement accumulations to lifetime annuities; around 1 percent of US 401(k) plan retirees purchase one (Employee Benefits Research Institute 2011) and in Australia only 100s of policies are sold annually in a market with several million retirees (Plan for Life 2012).[5] According to expected utility theory, not adequately insuring longevity risk can lead to large welfare losses (Davidoff et al. 2005).

This evidence seems to suggest that unpopularity of lifetime annuities is a reflection of consumer preferences and most annuity purchase decision research assumes ordinary people are capable of choosing retirement benefit products. However, a survey conducted before we designed the choice experiment in this section found minimal product awareness among consumers near to and entering retirement, low interest in retirement products and weak capability to understand key product features. Only one-third of 920 middle-aged respondents had heard of a life annuity (two-thirds were unaware) and only 20 percent and 8 percent respectively understood its longevity and income guarantee characteristics (few were capable). Respondents also had low awareness of other retirement income products like phased withdrawals. This is not surprising, as these are complex, once-in-a-lifetime products, unfamiliar to most pre-retirees and especially confusing to those with low financial literacy (Brown et al. 2012).

We explored these issues further by designing and implementing an experiment to assess the impacts of plan member awareness and specific product understanding on the quality of retirement benefit choices, particularly on demand for annuities (Bateman et al. 2014a). We recruited 854 people aged 50–64 from the Australian Pureprofile web panel, and asked them to allocate percentages of financial wealth at retirement to two retirement income streams: a liquid phased withdrawal account invested in risky assets and a life annuity. We varied four risk levels across these pairwise allocations (phased withdrawal versus life annuity) representing the risk of running out of funds in the phased withdrawal account before end of life and having to live on a reduced retirement income. In contrast, the annuity offered a guaranteed income stream for life but no bequest or liquid balance.

Based on the results of our pilot study of interest in and awareness of retirement income products, we did not assume respondents understood the products in the choice experiment. Instead, we offered them a simple explanation and comparison of the alternative products framed as answers to five questions and we labeled the products generically (see Table 4.3). We also asked a number of financial literacy and numeracy questions using objective and subjective measures, and asked about specific understanding of the mandatory retirement income system

Table 4.3 Description of retirement income products

	Product A: Get a guaranteed income	Product B: Withdraw a regular income
Who provides this product?	It is supplied by large life insurance firms. These firms have to meet strict government regulations to be allowed to sell this product.	It is supplied by superannuation funds. Your money is held in an account and invested in financial assets like shares and bonds.
How much income will I receive?	You will receive a fixed regular income.	You can decide how much of your balance to withdraw each year. Your account balance will fluctuate each year with financial markets. You will pay fees each year to the fund that manages your account.
How long do payments last?	You will receive the regular income for as long as you live, regardless of how long or short that is.	There is no guarantee you will have a lifetime income. How long payments last depends on investment returns, fees and your withdrawals.
What happens if I die?	If you die, payments stop.	If you die, remaining money in your account goes to your dependents or your estate.
Can I withdraw a lump sum for unforeseen events or changes of plans?	No. To purchase this product, you pay a lump sum to the insurance firm in exchange for the income stream and you cannot get it back. Your beneficiaries do not get the lump sum back if you die.	Yes. You can take all or a part of any remaining money out, but if you do it will not be available to pay you income in the future.

and retirement income products and demographics, health, life expectancy and retirement planning questions.

Table 4.3 contains descriptions of the retirement income products respondents were exposed to before the choice task. They received this information after the following introduction:

> In the next few questions we will ask you to complete 4 sets of choice tasks about 2 financial products. On leaving the workforce, most people need to use money from their superannuation and other savings to cover their spending. Industry and Government are looking for simple financial products to help Australians manage their superannuation and savings during retirement. The retirement income products we are going to show you are designed by large financial firms, like insurance companies and superannuation funds, to cover spending and manage financial risks in retirement.

The choice task asked people to choose a point on a continuum of 5 percentage point allocations to give to each product (from 0 percent to 100 percent) rather than forcing them to choose one product or the other. As they moved the slider (shown in Figure 4.2), we gave them information about changes to their likely retirement income path and they then chose their preferred combination of the two products.

Choices from the allocation task let us test if each person's sequence of retirement wealth allocations was consistent with the assumption of utility maximization. We could check whether they chose *no less* of the life annuity (product A) as the chance of exhausting all the money in

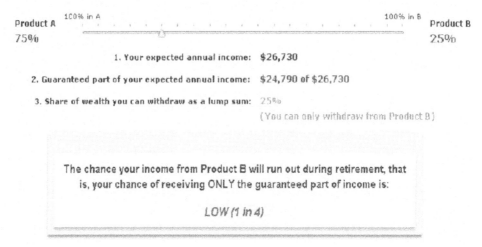

Figure 4.2 Illustrative product configurator for allocation task

their phased withdrawal (product B) increased. This tested whether respondents understood the main insurance feature of the annuity, namely, guaranteeing an income stream for life.

We measured this latent and unobservable "understanding" with three observables: involvement with the experiment, financial literacy and knowledge of retirement income products. We proxied financial literacy and commercial product knowledge by the proportion of correct answers to questions on these topics. We measured involvement with the experiment by scores from a short recall quiz testing knowledge of five common features of retirement products described in the allocation task.[6] The quiz scores measured respondents' involvement with the choice task via reading and understanding product information and showed if they could make an informed comparison between products. If a person could not recall key product features they were likely unaware, uninterested and incapable (i.e., not involved), and therefore less likely to choose consistently with utility theory.

Results showed that disengagement and lack of specific product knowledge lowered respondents' ability to respond well to risk information, making them more likely to violate theoretical predictions. Moreover, pre-existing financial literacy increased involvement (measured by recall quiz scores) but only involvement and numeracy predicted consistency. Financial literacy indicates awareness and interest, but understanding information specific to the decision at hand was the only capability builder. Elsewhere we found that structured communication and choice tasks can help retirement plan members learn the insurance features of income stream products, increasing their ability to perceive and manage retirement risk (see Bateman et al. 2014a).

Understanding and modeling financial product market evolution: using the Decision States Model to study the Australian mortgage market

This section presents and discusses a model of market evolution that relies on a large literature in academic marketing originating in advertising research that is variously known as a "hierarchy of effects" model or types of "consumer funnels" (Murray and Vogel 1997, Wijaya 2012, Kireyev et al. 2013). We call our version of this model the "Decision States Model" (DSM).

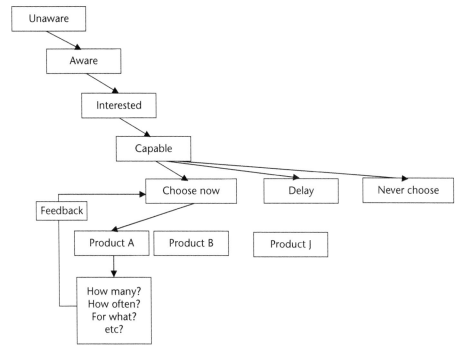

Figure 4.3   Decision States Model graphical framework

The DSM describes how individuals in a market pass through a series of discrete states, as shown in Figure 4.3. We propose that time in each state and the evolution of the individuals in each state (i.e., transition probabilities) are influenced by a variety of personal, market-related and informational factors (for example, education, skills levels, income, market maturity, number, types and features of product offerings, and types and sources of information).

The DSM is a stylized conceptual model of a product category and offerings in it. It characterizes any product (or service) market as a sequence of discrete states. Individuals move through these states to decide whether or not to make a choice in the market. Some product markets have low levels of product/service awareness (for example, voluntary life annuities). Prior to the launch of a new product category or a new product in a category, the vast majority of individuals are unaware of the category or products in it. Individuals persist in this unaware state until they become aware due to communications and information (for example, advertisements, friends and neighbors, web postings, social networks, etc.). In many product categories, some or even many individuals stay unaware for a long time, possibly a whole lifetime; in other product categories, individuals may quickly move from unaware to other states.

Once aware, individuals stay in that state until deciding whether benefits and problem solutions (more generally, usefulness and value of the category and the products in it) are of interest to them. Individuals typically become interested (or not) from product demonstrations, peer testimonials, reviews, advertisements, etc. Once an individual is interested, they often try to learn more (i.e., they engage in search and learning related to the category or products in it), but some individuals do not engage in search and learning, moving directly to deciding whether to choose. In any case, at some point individuals become sufficiently interested to consider choosing, then must decide whether they are capable of making a choice or not.

That is, even if interested, they may not be able to take advantage of, understand or use the category or products in it. Capability refers to constraints, barriers or other issues or problems that impact individual choice timing decisions. "Choice timing" means when or on what occasions one makes a choice. Constraints or barriers include affordability, education/skills or understanding sufficient to choose wisely, peer approval or disapproval, etc. Eventually, individuals decide whether and when to choose a category at all.

Individuals who are not capable will decide to delay choice (i.e., choose later or wait) or never choose (i.e., reject the category and its products). If deciding to choose now, they must decide which product(s) to choose; if they decide to delay, they must choose when to enter the market to choose; if never choosing, they entirely reject the category and its products. For some financial products like retirement investments, those who never choose are forced into default options.

We now describe and discuss a case study using the DSM to test hypotheses and develop insights about the mortgage market for principal place of residence in Australia. As in earlier case studies, we surveyed a sample of Australians aged 18 and over from the Pureprofile web panel. To qualify to participate, respondents had to have had a mortgage, currently have one, or anticipate having one in the next three to five years. We expected to see larger proportions of individuals in the more evolved decision states than a random sample of the entire population.

Implementing the Decision States Model

To define the decision states and classify respondents into them, we asked them several types of questions: (a) classifying themselves into each state, (b) experiences with and knowledge of several financial products, including mortgages, (c) importance of mortgage product features and if they had considered them, (d) knowledge and beliefs about mortgage product providers, (e) mortgage products and providers information sources, (f) financial literacy, product knowledge and numeracy and (g) personal and demographic questions. We discuss only a small subset of these survey measures. We used binary indicators (i.e., 0, 1 variables) to measure awareness, interest and capability, coded so that a "1" indicates more of each DSM construct. A complete list of the questions and indicator measures can be obtained from the authors on request.

We defined the first three constructs as follows. "Aware" was defined by six binary (agree, disagree) questions related to mortgages; agreements (coded "1") were summed to create a binary indicator that equals one if the sum is greater than four and zero if four or less. "Interest" was defined by three questions. We factor analyzed them and retained one factor, using the factor scores to create a binary indicator that equals 1 if the score is above the mean (standardized at zero), or zero if below the mean. "Capable" was defined by eight binary (yes, no) questions that we summed and used to create a single binary indicator that equals one if the sum is greater than four; otherwise, it equals zero. Respondents were asked to indicate all the products they would not choose due to personal circumstances.

The questions used to recruit study participants screened out those unaware of mortgage products. The nine DSM states are as follows: (1) unaware of mortgage products, (2) aware of mortgage products, (3) not interested in mortgages, (4) interested in mortgage products, (5) not capable of choosing mortgage products, (6) capable of choosing mortgage products, (7) has a mortgage (choose now), (8) currently without a mortgage but planning on one in the next 3–5 years (delay choice) and (9) will never choose a mortgage.

The screening criteria resulted in only four DSM states in this sample, such that we could classify all respondents uniquely into states 5, 6, 7 and 8. Respondent distribution in these states

Table 4.4 Distribution of membership by decision state class

DSM states	States	Membership frequency	Membership (%)
5	interested, not capable	18	4.4
6	interested, capable	24	5.9
7	choose now	192	47.1
8	delay	174	42.6
Total		408	100.0

is shown in Table 4.4. As expected, all respondents are aware and interested, but some are not capable (state 5) while others are capable (state 6).

We expect that the states can be discriminated by measures (covariates) from the survey for each respondent so we test if the states are systematically related to several measures of interest. We found states 5 and 6 are similar (both are aware and interested but differ on capability of choosing) and because both have few members we combine them in these tests. We first test if financial competence measures (numeracy, financial literacy and system knowledge) can discriminate the states. Results from multinomial logit estimation (not reported here) indicate that as a respondent's financial literacy score increases, they are less likely to be in state 8 relative to states 5 and 6 combined.

We asked twelve questions about potential barriers to getting a mortgage and tested whether the binary (yes, no) answers to these questions discriminate the classes. Questions and a summary of the estimation results are in Table 4.5, which shows several barrier questions are associated with state membership and discriminate between combined states 5 and 6 and states 7 and 8.

The results suggest that we should be able to discriminate the states on age and interest in mortgages. Multinomial logit estimation results suggest the following profile: states 5 and 6 are older (averaging over 55) compared to state 7 (averaging 40–44) and state 8 (averaging 30–34), they are more risk averse about investments (for example, index funds are risky),

Table 4.5 Barrier questions and estimation results for perceived mortgage barriers

Barriers	Statements: respondents agreed/disagreed	Estimation results	
		Class 7	Class 8
B1	I do not believe in having debts.	–	(–)
B2	I do not know enough about mortgage products to make good choices.	–	(+)
B3	I cannot afford a down payment.	(+)	(+)
B4	I cannot afford to pay the monthly or yearly payments.	–	–
B5	I do not have a credit history to qualify for a loan.	–	–
B6	I am personally opposed to loans on religious or moral grounds.	–	–
B7	I think that charging interest rates on loans is unethical.	–	–
B8	I cannot understand or fill out the application forms.	–	–
B9	I do not like asking a company to approve me for a loan.	–	–
B10	I think it's a bad time economically to take out a loan.	–	–
B11	I think it's a bad time for me personally to take out a loan.	–	–
B12	I do not need to borrow money to buy a home.	(–)	(–)
B13	I already have a home provided to me, so I don't need a loan.	(+)	(–)

more concerned about government interventions, less concerned about personal impacts of a 1 percent interest rate rise, less well-educated and more likely to be employed. Not surprisingly, this implies that states 5 and 6 are unlikely to be good targets for mortgage products as they are much older and perceive several barriers and problems with these products. This also implies considerable investment in education, information and communications if mortgage providers wish to target states 5 and 6. In contrast, states 7 and 8 are much younger, perceive few barriers and appear to be more knowledgeable; these are clear targets for mortgage products.

Limitations

There are two key limitations to the way we applied the DSM. First, this was an initial attempt to define indicator variables to measure the discrete states (constructs), so there naturally is scope for improvement and we will test some improvements in ongoing work. Second, screener questions used in the mortgage study eliminated some of the more interesting decision states, such as "unaware". One obvious way forward is to think critically about when and how to use such screener questions, as they can narrow the scope of the sample and the insights that can be obtained. Both limitations suggest a further overriding limitation, namely that we need a comprehensive set of indicators theoretically consistent with each decision state. These states are "latent" (i.e., cannot be observed directly), so one must develop measurement instruments that can do this reliably and accurately. Our results are promising, but there is much more work that can and should be done.

Conclusion

This chapter has described and discussed three research studies focused on financial decisions. The objective was to illustrate how a cross-disciplinary focus that combines marketing and finance can assist in understanding and analyzing financial choices. Having studied individual choices of financial products in several settings for several years, we have found a multi-disciplinary approach is necessary for effective research. Complex financial decisions now are almost unavoidable for workers and retirees in developed economies. Many of these decisions require detailed knowledge of the products, choice consequences can be long-term and sometimes irreversible and the outcomes typically are uncertain in several dimensions. Standard economic approaches assume people can, or will behave "as if" they can make fully informed, accurate and far-sighted decisions about such products and that they can and will make the long-term behavioral changes often needed to take full advantage of them. Standard economic models allow one to elucidate incentives and explain the behavior of sophisticated sectors of the market, but our work has consistently shown many decision-makers are not sufficiently motivated or equipped to fit this model.

The Decision States Model is a useful conceptual starting point for how consumers interact with credence goods in retail financial markets. It describes how consumers transit through discrete states of awareness, interest and capability leading to decisions to choose, delay or leave markets. Our DSM application for homeowner mortgage choices shows that groups close to the point of choosing can be discriminated with questions about problems or barriers to choosing, demographics such as age, work status and education, and skills and attitudes such as risk tolerance, expectations of financial prices and financial conditions. A key insight of the DSM is that many consumers are not in the capability state assumed by standard economic models. In turn, this suggests that those in evolutionary earlier states are unlikely to make choices consistent with expected utility theory; combining a theory model with DSM-based screening and clustering should lead to more robust tests of theory.

This point was clarified with the other two case examples (investment account choices for retirement savings and retirement benefit choices for pre-retirees). It is worth noting that financial decision-making is compulsory for many people in Australia. Compulsory programs such as the Australian retirement savings (superannuation) system include people who have not reached capability and may not even have an interest in these choices. Regulators confronting the low capability of many decision-makers have begun stipulating the form and content of disclosure documents to make them easier to comprehend. The first case study reports how we developed two simple choice restrictions implied by expected utility theory and tested retirement account rankings against them when respondents are randomly drawn from all stages of the decision states. This mimics the context of compulsory decision-making for retirement savings. When we interacted increasing levels of investment return volatility with different presentations for risk, we observed sensitivity to risk presentation. We found that more people made choices inconsistent with theoretical restrictions when we presented risk as a downside frequency rather than a range of returns. Naturally, more work is needed to determine whether there are one or more ways to frame such information that will produce more optimal decisions. But our results clearly show that several ways of framing this information clearly lead to suboptimal choices and points out the characteristic of the people more likely to make inconsistent choices.

The second case study highlighted a different aspect of the complementarity between the DSM and formal theoretical predictions. We studied a non-compulsory, complex financial decision, yet our survey results show few people were capable and most were not even aware of the financial products studied (i.e., life annuities). We provided specific and essential product information in the choice task and tested respondents' comprehension later. The results indicate that being fully involved with the information provision and developing capability increased compliance with basic risk management principles inferred from theory. The results also support the type of funneling implied by the DSM, as general financial literacy motivated more interest in specific product information, but only specific information (capability) directly improved choices.

The complementarity between the DSM described in the final case study and standard economic theory illustrated here is compelling. Applying tests of theory directly to random samples of individuals most likely will lead to noisy, negative results as some will not be capable. Using well-designed DSM applications to filter should help to choose samples where theory can reasonably be tested, while also informing researchers about general patterns of market evolution. Mapping decision states can direct policy interventions to those who face impediments due to lack of information, poor services, or regulation.

Future research directions

The limitations highlighted lead to one obvious future research direction, namely developing more theoretically consistent indicator variables for the latent states in the DSM. Other directions include developing empirical generalizations about relationships between people's characteristics and financial choices and relationships between decision state membership and variables of direct interest like financial numeracy and literacy, age, typical reliance on sources of information for financial decisions, etc. This line of research would seem to be in its infancy, so many potential contributions are possible.

Notes

1 The context of the experiment was the Australian retirement saving system. Under Australia's Superannuation Guarantee, all Australians who earn at least 8% of average earnings in a calendar year between

the ages of 18 and 70 participate in the mandatory retirement savings system. Members allocate their retirement savings to one or more accounts with a 'superannuation fund' or pension plan provider, many privately managed and all subject to regulation. Most adults are members of defined contribution, privately managed plans.

2 The relative merits of risk descriptions for retail clients are currently being debated by regulators concerned to ensure disclosures are standardized and comprehensible. For example, Australian regulators considered range graphs around an average return (Super System Review 2010) and an estimate of the expected frequency of negative returns over a twenty-year time period and settled on the latter (APRA 2010).

3 Notice that this is not a strict framing experiment since format P1 gave information about left and right quantiles of the returns distribution but format P2 gave information only about left quantiles.

4 In the Australian retirement savings system, for example, more than 90% of the workforce have accounts but rates of active decision-making appear to be much lower. Only around one third of members contribute more than the mandatory 9% of earnings and although workers can choose a provider for themselves, fewer than 5% do (ABS 2009, Super System Review 2010). While well-designed defaults can help unaware or uninterested individuals accumulate retirement savings, they also accommodate inertia and ignorance. Low interest is a concern to the industry and to policy-makers since it can inhibit competition in private financial markets (Super System Review 2010).

5 Academic research has not settled on a definitive explanation for the puzzling lack of demand for life annuities. See surveys in Brown (2008) and Benartzi et al. (2012).

6 This approach is informed by the idea of an Instructional Manipulation Check (IMC) as developed in Oppenheimer et al. (2009).

References

Agnew, J., Anderson, l., Bateman, H. and Thorp, S. (2013) Superannuation Knowledge and Plan Behaviour, *JASSA*, vol. 2013, no. 1, 45–50.

Agnew, J., Anderson, l., Gerlach, J.R. and Szykman, L. (2008) Who Chooses Annuities? An Experimental Investigation of the Role of Gender, Framing, and Defaults, *American Economic Review*, 98, 418–22.

Anagol, S. and Gamble, K.J. (2011) *Does presenting investment results asset by asset lower risk taking?* Working Paper, dePaul University. Available at http://ssrn.com/abstracts=1640791 (accessed 20 March 2013).

Australian Bureau of Statistics (ABS). (2009) *Employment Arrangements, Retirement and Superannuation, Australia*, Cat No. 6361.0. April to July 2007 (Re-issue), [pdf] Canberra, Australian Bureau of Statistics. Available at www.abs.gov.au/ausstats/abs@.nsf/mf/6361.0 (accessed 12 April 2013).

Australian Prudential Regulatory Authority (APRA). (2010) 'Good practice guidance – investment risk description', June 2010, [pdf] Sydney, Australian Prudential Regulation Authority. Available at www. apra.gov.au/Super/Documents/Ltr-IRD-29-June-FINAL-trustee.pdf (accessed 12 April 2013).

Australian Securities and Investment Commission (ASIC). (2012) 'Information Sheet 155 – Shorter PDSs: Complying with requirements for superannuation products and simple managed investment schemes', [pdf] Sydney, Australian Securities and Investment Commission. Available at www.asic.gov.au/asic/pdflib.nsf/LookupByFileName/info155-published-18-June-2012.pdf/$file/info155-published-18-June-2012.pdf (accessed 12 April 2013)

Bateman, H., Ecuest, C., Iskhakov, F., Louviere, J., Satchell, S. and Thorp, S. (2014a) 'Individual capability and Effort in Retirement Benefit Choice', UNSW Australia Business School Research Paper No. 2014ACTL07. Available at http://papers.srrn.com/s013/papers.cfm?.abstract_id=2494036.

Bateman, H., Eckert, C., Geweke, J., Louviere, J., Satchell, S. and Thorp, S. (2014b) Risk presentation and retirement portfolio choice, *Review of Finance*, in press. Available at http://papers.ssrn.com/sol3/papers.cfm?abstract_id=1776525.

Benartzi, S. and Thaler, R.H. (2001) 'Naive diversification strategies in defined contribution plans', *American Economic Review*, 91(1), 79–98.

Benartzi, S., Previtero, A. and Thaler, R.H. (2012) Annuitization Puzzles, *Journal of Economic Perspectives*, 25(4), 143–64.

Bernheim, B.D. (2002) Taxation and Saving, in A.J. Auerbach and M. Feldstein, (eds), *Handbook of Public Economics* 3: Elsevier, 1173–1249.

Brown, J.R. (2008) Understanding the Role of Annuities in Retirement Planning, in A. Lusardi, (ed), *Overcoming the Saving Slump*: University of Chicago Press, Chicago, IL, 178–206.

Brown, J.R., Kling, J.R., Mullainathan, S. and Wrobel, M.V. (2008) Why Don't People Insure Late-Life Consumption? A Framing Explanation of the Under-Annuitization Puzzle, *American Economic Review*, 98, 418–22.

—— (2012) Understanding the Role of Annuities in Retirement Planning, in A. Lusardi, (ed), *Overcoming the Saving Slump*: University of Chicago Press, Chicago, IL, 178–206.

Brown, J.R., Kling, Kapetyn, A., Luttmer, E.F.P. and Mitchell, O.S. (2013) *Complexity as a Barrier to Annuitization: Do Consumers Know How to Value Annuities? Pension Research Council Working Paper, WP2013–01*, Pension Research Council, University of Pennsylvania. Available at www.pensionre-searchcouncil.org/publications/document.php?file=1040 (accessed 20 March 2013).

Davidoff, T., Brown, J.R. and Diamond, P. (2005) Annuities and individual welfare, *American Economic Review*, 95(5), 1573–90.

Employee Benefits Research Institute (EBRI). (2011) *EBRI Databook on Employee Benefits, Employee Benefits Research Institute*, Washington DC. Available at www.ebri.org/publications/books/?fa=databook (accessed 20 March 2013).

Kireyev, P., Pauwels, K. and Gupta, S. (2013) 'Do Display Ads Influence Search? Attribution and Dynamics in Online Advertising', Working Paper No. 13–070, Harvard Business School. Available at www.hbs.edu/faculty/Publication%20Files/13–070.pdf (accessed 20 March 2013).

Mitchell, O.S. and Utkus, S. (2006) How Behavioral Finance can Inform Retirement Plan Design, *Journal of Applied Corporate Finance*, 18(1), 82–95.

Mullainathan, Sendhil and Thaler, Richard H., *Behavioral Economics* (September 2000) MIT Dept. of Economics Working Paper No. 00-27. Available at SSRN: http://ssrn.com/abstract=245828 or HYPERLINK "http://dx.doi.org/10.2139/ssrn.245828" \t "_blank" http://dx.doi.org/10.2139/ssrn.245828

Murray, K.B. and Vogel, C.M. (1997) Using a Hierarchy-of-Effects Approach to Gauge the Effectiveness of Corporate Social Responsibility to Generate Goodwill Toward Firm: Financial versus Nonfinancial Impacts, *Journal of Business Research*, 38, 141–59.

Oppenheimer, D.M., Meyvis, T. and Davidenko, N. (2009) Instructional Manipulation Checks: Detecting Satisficing to Increase Statistical Power, *Journal of Experimental Social Psychology*, 45, 867–72.

Plan For Life. (2012) *The Pension and Annuity Market Research Report: Plan for Life Actuaries and Researchers*, Mt. Waverly, Victoria.

Super System Review (2010) *Final Report, Part 1: Overview and Recommendations*, [pdf] Commonwealth of Australia, Canberra. Available at www.supersystemreview.gov.au/content/downloads/final_report/part_one/Final_Report_Part_1_Consolidated.pdf (accessed 20 March 2013).

Vlaev, I., Chater, N. and Stewart, N. (2009) Dimensionality of risk perception: Factors affecting consumer understanding and evaluation of financial risk, *Journal of Behavioral Finance*, 10, 158–81.

Wijaya, B.S. (2012) The Development of Hierarchy of Effects Model in Advertising, *International Research Journal of Business Studies*, 5(1), 73–85.

5

Household decisions on financial services

The role of the wife

Salvador Ruiz de Maya and Eva Tomaseti-Solano

Introduction

As the financial economy has expanded worldwide, financial institutions have increased the number of products they sell to households, such as mortgages, mutual funds, stock trading accounts, loans, insurance and various forms of savings and retirement products. The result has been a profound deepening of households' involvement in financial market activities (Fligstein and Goldstein 2012). For example, in credit markets, median household debt levels increased 179 percent from 1989 to 2007 as consumers took on an ever-wider array of credit card, home equity, mortgage, student and payday loans (Wolff 2007). Similarly, with respect to investment products, the percentage of households with stock equities or equity mutual funds increased in the decade before and after the turn of the twenty-first century and the frequency of transactions more than tripled in this time period (Kremp 2010).

The understanding of household financial decisions requires a review of family decision-making. Families represent two-thirds of households in the US, of which married couples and single parents with children account for more than 90 percent (Jacobsen and Mather 2012). However, after decades of study of family decision-making, it seems clear that when it comes to financial decisions, the disparity in gender roles may lead to families handling their finances less effectively. Survey data has shown that more than half of households' financial decision-making is shared equally between husband and wife (Barrington 2013). However, where one or the other spouse takes the lead role, the husband assumes control more than two-thirds of the time. The future, however, seems better, as married women are increasingly better educated than their husbands (Wang et al. 2013). Lloyds TSB (2013) points out that younger women have definitely taken a firm grip on the purse strings, moving from the traditional role of managing the day-to-day spending, to planning and selecting where money is kept for the long-term.

This chapter will focus on husband/wife family decisions, specifically, the changing influence of the wife in this joint decision-making unit. In order to better understand the increasing role of women in family decision-making, we will first review the literature on family financial decision-making. We will then examine how family decisions are related to risk aversion and analyze recent findings about these decisions through a meta-analysis.

Family decision-making

People prefer not to live alone, with the family being the most basic and important social unit that combines us into groups (Smith et al. 2010). The family constitutes an important decision-making unit as a result of the joint decisions and consumption acts carried out by its members (Boutilier 1993). The influence of each family member in the decision-making process has interested researchers for many years (Cotte and Wood 2004). Existing literature has covered family decision-making along with the negotiation processes and strategies that can explain family members' participation, as well as conflict resolution.

Decision-making in couples is a complex process which has been classified according to how couples implement each of the following four types of negotiation patterns: (1) joint and equal decision-making couples, where both partners play an equal part in the discussion and decision-making, (2) joint decision-making with one partner leading the couple in making decisions, with the leading partner sometimes discussing options with the other partner, but having a "delegated" authority to make decisions without much consultation, (3) independent decision-making couples, where decisions are made independently by one or both members, usually with little discussion between them, (4) no decision-making couples, where no decisions are made on assets and debts (Rowlingson and Joseph 2010). This typology has been widely used in research that characterizes decision authority as a spectrum ranging from the husband leading the decision to the wife leading the decision (for example, Ganesh 1997, Martínez and Polo 1999, Qualls 1982, Stafford et al. 1996).

However, how spouses negotiate their joint decisions can be better understood through the analysis of the reasons that explain the negotiation pattern in each situation. Three theories offer widely accepted explanations for most decisions within the family: Resource Theory, Bargaining Theory and Ideology Theory.

Resource Theory is related to traditional models that assume household decisions are based on pooled resources and common preferences (Jianakoplos and Bernasek 2008), the balance of power will be on the side of that partner who contributes the greatest resources to the marriage (Blood and Wolfe 1960). Traditionally, husbands had greater influence in purchase decisions because they had contributed a greater portion to the resources of the household. However, with increased level of education among females and a more equitable job market, changes in the decision-making process have occurred in favor of the increased role of wives in family decisions (Wang et al. 2013).

Bargaining Theory, based on bargaining models, proposes that household decisions depend on the relative bargaining power of the spouses (Jianakoplos and Bernasek 2008), which includes the respective ages of the spouses, education levels of each partner and the knowledge possessed by each partner concerning the product for which the decision is being made. As women have become more educated and provide more income for the family, their status in the decision process has increased. This has generated uncertainty about gender roles and responsibilities while the decision-making process has become more egalitarian (Belch and Willis 2002, Elder and Rudolph 2003).

Ideology Theory points to the importance of social norms in decision-making. Many choices, rather than being negotiated, are assumed to be the outcome of established customs. That is, the culture into which the spouses are socialized affects the sex-role orientation and topics about which partner, deliberately and for different reasons, renounces negotiation. Sex-role is based on gender and holds that men, because of their physical stature and their position in society, hold a dominant position while woman hold a subordinate position (Qualls 1987). In this sense, non-egalitarian and patriarchal societies foster less joint decision-making and more dominance by the husband (Ford et al. 1995). For traditional couples, spouses tend to conform to norms that prescribe involvement in gender-specific activities. For example, the wife administrates the finances that are necessary for the daily running of the household, whereas the husband controls the rest of the financial resources of the household and supervises the expenses made by the wife. On the contrary, culture can foster explicit negotiation processes, which may encourage couples to adopt more joint decisions (Dema-Moreno 2009, Vasantha Lakshmi and Sakthivel Murugan 2008). This higher power occurs more when the wife works outside the home, especially in a position of high occupational status, than when wives stay at home (Lee and Beatty 2002).

Negotiation and integration of spouses' preferences are the key elements behind the theories used to explain family decision-making but the stage of the family life cycle can also influence the negotiation process of the spouses. Wolgast's (1958) pioneering study on family decision-making showed that with advancing age, and perhaps increased length of marriage, joint decision-making declines. Latter findings have disputed this result. Webster and Rice (1996) found that as couples move toward the retirement years, significant marital power shifts in purchase decision-making take place among the more traditional and unequal-salaried couples, but not among equal-salaried couples. Also, when the husband retires, the role of the wife in the decision-making process has been found to increase even for traditional couples (Elder and Rudolph 2003).

Conflict resolution represents an additional perspective in the study of family decisions. The general tendency in family interactions includes the avoidance of conflict due to the cooperative nature of family decisions, sensitivity toward the other spouse's preferences, and the role of affection between husband and wife (Corfman and Lehmann 1987, Ruiz de Maya 1994). Conflict influences family decisions because each spouse is motivated to pursue his or her own utility (Su et al. 2008). Although spouses with stronger preferences may get their way by using strong influence behavior in a purchase decision (Qualls 1987, Su et al. 2003), husbands and wives may follow alternative sex roles, with husbands following goals having immediate personal consequences and wives focusing on harmonious relationships. When one spouse expresses strong preferences for specific product choices that differs from those of the other spouse, husbands are more likely to ultimately affect the decision (Ward 2006). The literature has identified conflict resolution strategies such as persuasion, negotiation, expert use, revenge or emotional influence (Makgosa and Kang 2009, Sheth 1974, Spiro 1983), of which the first two are the most frequently used in family decisions (Palan and Wilkes 1997).

Family financial decisions and risk aversion

An appropriate level of financial risk aversion is important to a household because of the relationship between willingness to take on risk in return for the potential for growing wealth. Trends in pensions have shown that for more individuals and households, financial management and risk-taking decisions are shifting away from professionals such as financial advisors and brokers (Hanna and Lindamood 2005). This is true especially for young people, who tend to use the Internet and other resources to obtain information on personal and household financial matters (please see Chapter 6 and related discussions on pension decision-making). Due to the shift away from professionals influencing household financial decisions and associated risk, it is relevant to analyze risk tolerance levels for married households; it would be especially interesting to examine how each spouse's individual risk tolerance contributes to that of the household as a decision unit.

Making successful investment choices is not a trivial accomplishment as such investments require knowledge of alternative rates of return and risk across different time horizons inherent in a variety of complex assets, combined with family-specific needs and goals about when the outcomes of these investments might be needed by the household. These investment decisions may well be among the most cognitively demanding that a family has to make (Smith et al. 2010).

Three subjective measures of household preferences affect households' financial decisions: rate of time preference, risk aversion and interest in financial matters. Rate of time preference reflects the amount of financial return an individual expects to obtain by postponing consumption and it is negatively related with age. While women are more patient than men, most of the variation in rates of time preference cannot be explained by individual characteristics (Donkers and Van Soest 1999). However, the variables which have been studied in depth in the literature on family decision-making are risk aversion and preferences for specific financial products.

Research on the effects of risk aversion on financial decision-making has shown that women play an important role on this decision dimension. According to bargaining models, if women are more risk-averse, then households should exhibit less financial risk taking as the bargaining power of the wife increases (Jianakoplos and Bernasek 2008). All other things being equal, wives are much less willing to take on financial risks than husbands and financial planners should try to quantify the risk tolerance levels of both the husband and the wife in prescribing financial advice. Risk aversion is also affected by demographic variables. For example, risk aversion increases with the age of the spouses, is positively related to the education level of the wife, but not affected by the husband's education level (Donkers and Van Soest 1999, Hanna and Lindamood 2005, Gilliam et al. 2011).

Research has shown that interest in financial matters increases with income, is greater for men than for women and has a strong positive effect on the home purchase decision (Donkers and Van Soest 1999). The participation of the husband in financial management of the household is positively related to his age and negatively related to the wife's level of education, pointing to the relevance of Bargaining Theory in understanding household financial decisions. The wife's level of education is positively associated with the household's quality of financial planning (Antonides 2011).

Research has also reported that the husband's influence is higher for decisions concerning financial products such as insurance (Bonfield 1978, Cosenza 1985, Jenkins 1979, Martínez and Polo 1999). For other financial products, there is disagreement concerning how spouses influence decision-making. For example, Jenkins (1979) found that husbands had greater influence for savings decisions while others have found that this decision is made jointly (Ford et al. 1995, Hopper 1995, Martínez and Polo 1999, Qualls 1982, Wolgast, 1958).

Economic decision-making is especially important in older ages, as individuals are increasingly asked to take greater control of their finances. They may, for example, need to adjust prior financial decisions relating to their household wealth and increase their focus on pensions and health care costs. Smith et al. (2010) carried out an investigation with a sample of couples aged over 50 years and obtained interesting findings. As in previous studies, they found that husbands were more likely to be the ones responding to financial questions than wives. This was particularly pronounced when the husband was much older than his wife. Higher education level of either spouse increased the probability of the husband being selected by the couple as the financial respondent. Education had a greater impact than age and the husband's education had a larger impact on him being selected as the financial respondent than that of the wife. The larger the fraction of family income from one spouse, the more likely it was for this spouse to be in charge of family finances.

The increasing relevance of women in household financial management and financial decisions

Macro changes in societies around the world have shown different patterns in the evolution of family composition patterns, values, norms and behaviors. Most of these changes have favored a more central role for women in both societies and families. For example, technological change in Western societies has allowed women to delay child bearing and earn significantly higher wages (Miller 2011). Cross-national research has also shown that increased female employment and educational homogamy (similar educational background) between partners are related to reduced poverty levels (Kollmeyer 2012). In this new context, women's role in households' financial decisions is therefore stronger and needs to be better understood.

The massive participation of women in the labor market is one of the most prominent social trends. It has also influenced financial and spending decisions (Dema-Moreno 2009, Belch and Willis 2002). If the wife contributes significantly to the household income, it is more likely that there is more equality in the amount of influence exerted in the decision-making process (Lee and Beatty 2002, Martínez and Polo 1999)

Although a review of the literature on household decisions concerning financial services shows evidence of the important role of women in financial decisions (Belch and Willis 2002, Ford et al. 1995, Razzouk et al. 2007, Webster and Rice 1996), there is no clear demonstration of this trend. To overcome this gap in the literature, in this chapter, we have searched for studies analyzing family financial decisions, then conducted a meta-analysis to summarize the findings.

Study method and data

We first developed a database of research studies on family financial decisions by searching for relevant studies through the most popular research databases such as ABI/Inform, Business Source Elite, Emerald, Proquest, the Association for Consumer Research database and Google Scholar. Authors of unpublished studies were also contacted. Candidates for inclusion were empirical studies that quantified the husband's or wife's influence in financial decision-making. A total of 26 studies over a 47-year time period involving 13,239 participants were identified (see Table 5.1).

This meta-analysis focuses on the magnitude of the effect of study variables (i.e. the change in influence as an independent variable changes). The literature has mainly used three types of measures to report the husband's and wife's influence in financial decisions. A number of these studies use a one-hundred-point scale, where the influence of each spouse is a percentage of the overall influence in the decision (Jenkins 1979, Ruiz de Maya 1994). Another group of studies have used internal scales of three and five points ranging from the husband dominating the decision to the wife dominating the decision (for example, Martínez and Polo 1999, Stafford and Ganesh 1996, Stafford et al. 1996). Finally, a third group uses independent items for each member (Belch and Willis 2002). In order to express all measures on a common scale, we transformed 3- and 5-point bipolar scales (husband decides – wife decides) as well as independent point scales into percentages (for example, a 3.5 mean of influence from a 5-point scale, where 1 = husband decides and 5 = wife, was coded as $100(3.5-1)/(5-1) = 62.5$ percent for the husband and as 37.5 percent for the wife). When the studies analyze influence in sub-decisions or decision stages, we averaged the results across key aspects of the decision (for example, when to buy or how much money to spend) or only considered spousal influence in the final decision stage.

We also coded eight independent variables. First, to account for the evolution of women's participation in family financial decisions and the impact of culture, we coded the year of

Table 5.1 List of studies with quantitative information on spouses' influence in financial decision-making

Authors (year)	Type of financial decisions			Average wife influence (%)
	Finances (bank, savings, financial services)	Insurances (life, house, others)	Retirement plan	
Belch and Willis (2002)		X		51[c]
Blood and Wolfe (1960)		X		37.50[a]
Bonfield (1978)		X		20.75[c]
Burns and DeVere (1981)		X		38.60[a]
Cosenza (1985)		X		41.45[a]
Davis and Rigaux (1974)	X	X		28.37[c]
Ford, LaTour and Henthirne (1995)	X	X		49.61[c]
Granbois (1962)		X		31.45[a]
Harcar and Spillan (2006)	X	X		35.86[b]
Hopper (1995)	X			35.20[b]
Jenkins (1979) (*)	X	X		29.24[b]
Kasulis and Hughes (1984)		X		30.65[a]
Martínez and Polo (1999)	X	X		37.97[c]
Na, Son and Marshall (1998) (*)		X		59.66[a]
Putnam and Davison (1987)	X			43.25[c]
Qualls (1982)	X	X		35.72[a]
Razzouk, Seitz and Capo (2007)	X	X		48.09[c]
Ruiz de Maya (1994) (*)	X		X	25.16[c]
Safilios-Rothschild (1969)		X		31.07[a]
Sharp and Mott (1956)		X		33.46[a]
Shukla (1987)	X	X		33.83[a]
Stafford and Ganesh (1996)		X		17.91[b]
Stafford, Ganesh and Garland (1996)		X		37.00[c]
Webster (1994)	X			46.46[c]
Webster and Rice (1996)	X			49.18[a]
Wolgast (1958)	X			56.43[a]

[a]Most of the data comes from a questionnaire which assessed the influence in a family decision to buy a product, i.e., a general question which did not refer to any aspect or stage of the decision-making.
[b]Mean score for the influence obtained through the average of sub-decisions.
[c]Mean score for the influence in the final decision stage out of other decision stages.
(*)Children also participated in the study

publication of the paper and the location of the study. Dummy variable coding was applied for the year of publication, such that we coded the period 1955–1985 as 0, and 1986–2007 as 1. The location of the sample was coded as North America/Australia, Asia, Latin America or Europe. We then coded other independent variables after reviewing the 26 studies found in the research database search. Variable selection was based on relevance to our research and data availability. We selected and coded the demographic characteristics of the samples in the 26 identified studies and associated methodological variables.

Based on the previous literature review, spouses' age and spouses' education are variables that may influence the wife's participation in financial decisions. The husband's age was coded as 1 if the average age in the sample was over 40 and 0 otherwise. The same coding method was applied to wife's age. Husband's education was coded as Low/Medium when less than 30 percent of the sample had college degrees or High when more than 50 percent of the sample graduated from high school and more than 30 percent of the sample had college degrees. Again, the same coding method was applied to the wife's education level. We coded age and education with the aim of obtaining two subsamples of similar size, given the constraints in the number of observations in the database.

When running meta-analysis, methodological variables are of interest because they can have a significant influence on the results while allowing for comparisons among the studies. More specifically, whether the spouse that responds to the questionnaire (as a single informant) and the scale used affect reported influence is largely an empirical question. We coded the informant as one of the spouses (in situations when the husband or the wife responded alone) and when the spouses responded together, the average of the spouses' responses were used (i.e., when the couple answered the questionnaire together). The scale was coded into three categories: 100 points (for studies that used this scale to report each spouse's decision influence), 3- or 5-point bipolar scales (ranging from the husband dominating decisions to the wife dominating the decisions), or 3–12-point scales (that assess the influence of only one of the family members' influence).

In order to establish which variables determine the relative influence of the wife on family financial decisions, we first completed a series of one-way ANOVAs. Data were weighted by the inverse of the variance of the wife's influence (weight = $p(1-p)/n$, where p is the wife's influence) to assign greater weight to the more precise studies (Sultan et al. 1990). Explained variance was assessed by the unadjusted R^2 in linear regressions.

Results

Results (see Figure 5.1) show a non-significant change in wife's participation related to time period, although in the expected direction ($F(1,76) = 1.378$; $p > .1$, adj $R^2 = .005$). However, the location of the sample has a significant impact. Wives' participation in family financial decisions varies geographically ($F(3,74) = 8.996$; $p < 0.001$, adj $R^2 = .238$). More specifically, while studies conducted in North America/Australia, Europe and Latin America result in non-significant differences in spousal influence on financial decisions, studies conducted in Asia reveal higher degrees of influence for wives when compared to studies conducted in North America/Australia, Europe and Latin America (Bonferroni test, $p < .05$ for the Asia-North America/Australia, Asia-Europe and Asia-Latin America post-hoc comparisons; similar results are obtained with the Kruskal-Wallis nonparametric test, weighting the cases by the inverse of the variance).

Additionally, the wife's influence is lower when the husband is aged over 40 years old ($F(1,38) = 6.168$; $p < 0.05$, adj $R^2 = .117$), and when the wife is aged over 40 ($F(1,42) = 3.453$; $p < 0.07$, adj $R^2 = .054$). Contrary to Antonides (2011), with higher levels of the husband's education and higher levels of the wife's education, the participation of the wife in family financial decisions decreases ($F(1,76) = 24.975$; $p < 0.001$, adj $R^2 = .237$; and $F(1,76) = 22.821$; $p < 0.001$, adj $R^2 = .221$). The effect of who provides the information on the wife's influence is also significant ($F(1,76) = 3.750$; $p < 0.06$, adj $R^2 = .034$), while there is no effect of the type of scale used to collect data on the wife's influence ($F(1,76) = 2.021$; $p > 0.1$, adj $R^2 = .013$).

The significant results found with the ANOVAs in previous analyses do not take into account collinearity (confounds) between predictors. We now use regression to analyze the changing role of wives in family financial decisions, including time (as a continuous variable) and geographic area, while accounting for covariates effects.

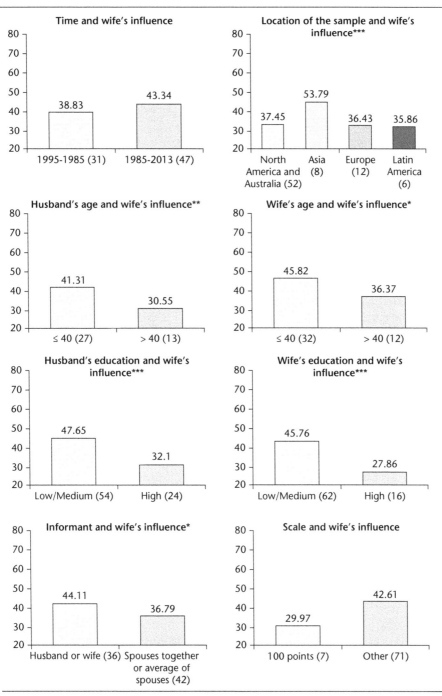

Note: Vertical axes represent percentage of wife's influence in family financial decisions; statistical significance assessed through ANOVAs.
*p < .1, **p < .05, ***p < .01

Figure 5.1   Determinants of wife's influence in family financial decisions (numbers in parentheses are cell sizes)

In running the regression analysis, three issues had to be considered. First, because deleting observations with missing values for spouses' age and education would have dropped the sample size, these variables were removed from the analyses. Second, while the use of multiple observations from a single manuscript is common practice in meta-analysis (Farley and Lehmann 1986, Szymanski and Henard 2001), it may result in correlated errors across observations. To control for this, we included dummy variables representing the studies. This allows us to determine whether some studies found an unusually large or small influence for either spouse. Third, collinearity exists among the predictor variables. In order to capture key results in a parsimonious model, we therefore employed a three-step procedure. First, we regressed all the independent variables and the dummy variables representing the studies on the influence of the wife. However, while in the ANOVAs we used a dummy variable to assess the effect of time, the centred continuous variable time (mean centred), was used in the regressions. Second, we dropped insignificant study dummies and re-ran the regressions. Third, we dropped variables that were not significant to obtain a more parsimonious model.

The regression analysis (Table 5.2) shows statistically significant overall results ($F(6,71) = 28.46$; $p < 0.001$; Adj. $R^2 = .681$). More specifically, it shows that wives' influence in family financial decisions has significantly increased over the period covered by the studies ($b = .004$ (standardized $b = .436$), $p < .001$) and with a significant effect of the location (continent where data were collected), and was higher both in North America/Australia ($b = .094$ (standardized $b = .313$), $p < 0.01$) and Asia ($b = .175$ (standardized $b = .539$), $p < 0.001$), compared with Europe. Considering methodological variables, the wife's influence is lower when it is reported by one of the spouses instead of a joint response ($b = -.082$ (standardized $b = -.243$), $p < 0.01$). The measurement scale used to capture the influence of each spouse does not exert any influence. Only one study reports significantly higher degrees of the wife's influence (Wolgast 1958, $b = .248$ (standardized $b = .411$), $p < 0.001$), and one study reports significantly lower levels of wife's influence (Stafford and Ganesh 1996, $b = -.322$ (standardized $b = .630$), $p < 0.001$).

Conclusions and managerial implications

Based on a database involving 13,239 participants from 26 empirical studies, we used meta-analysis to assess the evolution of the wife's influence in financial decision-making. Results show that the wife's influence depends on time and cultural context, as well as the spouses' ages

Table 5.2 Wife's influence in family decision making

Regression analyses. Unstandardized betas (std. errors)

Variable	Wife's influence
(Constant)	−8.283*
Time	.004*
Location of the sample: North America	.094*
Location of the sample: Asia	.175*
Informant: spouses together or average of spouses	−.082*
Wolgast (1958)	.248*
Stafford and Ganesh (1996)	−.322*
Adjusted R²	.681
n	78

*$p < .01$

and education levels, on methodological aspects of the study and the informant who reports spousal influence levels.

Although there is some indication in the literature for increasing influence of the wife in financial decisions in the last twenty years (Belch and Willis 2002, Ford et al. 1995, Razzouk et al. 2007, Webster and Rice 1996), our study confirms that this is indeed a real trend. Moreover, while some geographical areas show more balanced spouse participation in financial decisions (North America/Australia and Asia), the observations from Europe and Latin America reveal that husbands exert a stronger influence on those decisions.

Our findings are also consistent with previous literature concerning the effects of personal characteristics. Spouses' age and education are negatively related to the wife's participation in family financial decision-making. Concerning the former variable, Smith et al. (2010) show that as the husband's and wife's ages increase, the importance of economic decisions also increases, especially for men. Moreover, risk aversion also increases with age (Donkers and Van Soest 1999, Hanna and Landamood 2005, Gilliam et al. 2011). As the husbands become older they will see financial decisions as more important as they become more risk-averse, which will motivate them to take more responsibility in such decisions, thereby increasing their influence. A similar phenomenon occurs with respect to the spouses' education levels. Although previous research proposes a positive relationship between the wife's education level and her participation in financial decisions (Antonides 2011), we have found the opposite. This could be explained by the possibility that woman with higher levels of education usually have a partner with a similar level of education, taking into account that the husbands' education has a higher impact on family decisions than wives' (Smith et al. 2010), it may be that the husband's education determines the influence of both spouses on financial decisions.

At this point, we also have to acknowledge that our results depend on the representativeness of the 26 empirical studies used. Because not all cultures, countries, demographic variables and financial decisions were included in our sample, the results are limited. Furthermore, because of the different methodologies used in previous studies on this topic, some studies were not used for reasons such as not providing information about the wife's influence (for example, Dema-Moreno, 2009, Smith et al. 2010), showing strong incongruence between the spouses (for example, Antonides 2011), inaccuracy in the information they supplied (for example, Elder and Rudolph 2003), omitting crucial information to calculate the wife's influence (for example, Bobinski and Assar 1991), or including the influence of other people not directly related to the family, such as friends, relatives, neighbors, experts or sales persons (for example, Lee and Beatty 2002).

The implications of our findings for managers are straightforward. First, it is easier to understand family financial decisions once we know who participates in them and by how much. The analysis of how preferences are integrated will give highly valuable information to marketers of financial products. Second, from a marketing research perspective, the growing participation of the wife in family decisions and the fact that this reported influence depends on methodological issues such as the spouse being interviewed, confirm Kim and Lee's (1997) recommendation for using multiple informants in market research into family decision-making.

Acknowledgment

The authors thank the two editors for their helpful comments. This research was supported by grant ECO2012–35766 from the Spanish Ministry of Economy and Competitiveness and by the Fundación Séneca-Agencia de Ciencia y Tecnología de la Región de Murcia (Spain), under the II PCTRM 2007–10. The authors also thank the support provided by Fundación Cajamurcia.

References

Antonides, Gerrit (2011), "The Division of Household Tasks and Household Financial Management," *Journal of Psychology*, 219 (4), 198–208.

Barrington, Richard (2013), "Why Mothers Should Play a Bigger Role in Family Finances," *Forbes*, retrieved February 1, 2014, from www.forbes.com/sites/moneybuilder/2013/04/15/why-mothers-should-play-a-bigger-role-an-family-finances

Belch, Michael A. and Willis, Laura A. (2002), "Family Decision at the Turn of the Century: Has the Changing Structure of Households Impacted the Family Decision-Making Process?" *Journal of Consumer Behavior*, 2 (2), 111–24.

Blood, Jr., Robert, O. and Wolfe, Donald M. (1960), *Husbands & Wives. The Dynamics of Married Living*, The Free Press of Glencoe, Illinois.

Bobinski, George S. and Assar, Amardeep (1991), "Routine Financial Tasks Versus Investment Tasks: Gender-Related Division of Responsibility in Babyboomer Couples", *Gender and Consumer Behavior*, 1, 9–18.

Bonfield, Edward H. (1978), "Perception of Marital Roles in Decision Processes: Replication and Extension", *Advances in Consumer Research*, Vol. 5, ed. Kent Hunt, Ann Abor: Association for Consumer Research, 300–307.

Boutilier, Robert (1993), "Pulling the Fmily's Strings", *American Demographics*, 15 (8), 44–48.

Burns, Alvin C. and DeVere, Stephen P. (1981), "Four Situations and Their Perceived Effects on Husband and Wife Purchase Decision Making", *Advances in Consumer Research*, 8 (1), 736–41.

Corfman, Kim P. and Lehmann, Donald R. (1987), "Models of Cooperative Group Decision-Making and Relative Influence: An Experimental Investigation of Family Purchase Decisions", *Journal of Consumer Research*, 14 (June), 1–13.

Cosenza, Robert M. (1985), "Family Decision Making, Decision Dominance Structures Analysis: An Extension", *Journal of the Academy of the Marketing Science*, 13 (Winter), 91–103.

Cotte, June and Wood, Stacy (2004), "Families and Innovative Consumer Behavior: A Triadic Analysis of Sibling and Parental Influence", *Journal of Consumer Research*, 31, 78–86.

Davis, Harry L. and Rigaux, Benny P. (1974), "Perception of Marital Roles in Decision Processes", *Journal of Consumer Research*, 1 (June), 51–62.

Dema-Moreno, Sandra (2009), "Behind the Negotiations: Financial Decision-Making Processes in Spanish Dual-Income Couples," *Feminist Economics*, 15 (1), 27–56.

Donkers, Bas and Van Soest, Arthur (1999), "Subjective Measures of Household Preferences and Financial Decisions", *Journal of Economic Psychology*, 20, 613–42.

Elder, Harold W. and Rudolph, Patricia M. (2003), "Who Makes the Financial Decisions in the Households of Older Americans?" *Financial Services Review*, 12, 293–308.

Farley, John U. and Lehmann, Donald R. (1986), *Meta-Analysis in Marketing: Generalization of Response Models*, Lexington, MA: Lexington Books.

Fligstein, Neil and Goldstein, Adam (2012), "The Emergence of a Finance Culture in American Households, 1989–2007", Working Paper Series, Institute for Research on Labor and Employment, UC Berkeley.

Ford, John B., LaTour, Michael S. and Henthirne, Tony L. (1995), "Perception of Marital Roles in Purchasing Decision Processes: A Cross-Cultural Study", *Journal of the Academy of Marketing Science*, 23 (2), 120–31.

Ganesh, Gopala (1997), "Spousal Influence in Consumer Decisions: A Study of Cultural Assimilation", *Journal of Consumer Marketing*, 14 (2), 132–55.

Gilliam, John E., Grable, John E. and Hampton, Vickie L. (2011), "The Impact of Decision Power on Financial Risk Tolerance and Asset allocation", *Journal of Business & Economics Research*, 9 (5), 27–40.

Granbois, Donal Harry (1962), "A Study of the Family Decision-Making Process in the Purchase of Major Durable Household Goods", unpublished dissertation, Indiana University.

Hanna, Sherman D. and Lindamood, Suzanne (2005), "Risk Tolerance of Married Couples", paper presented at the *Academy of Financial Services Meeting*.

Harcar, Talha and Spillan, John E. (2006), "Exploring Latin American Family Decision-Making Using Correspondence Analysis", *Journal of World Business*, 41, 221–32.

Hopper, JoAnne Stilley (1995), "Family Financial Decision Making: Implications for Marketing Strategy", *Journal of Services Marketing*, 19 (1), 24–32.

Jacobsen, Linda A. and Mather, Mark (2012), "Household Change in The United States", *Population Bulletin* 67, no. 1.

Jenkins, Roger L. (1979), "The Influence of Children in Family Decision-Making: Parents' Perceptions", *Advances in Consumer Research*, Vol. 6, ed. William L. Wilkie, Ann Abor: Association for Consumer Research, 413–18.

Jianakoplos, Nancy Ammon and Bernasek, Alexandra (2008), "Family Financial Risk taking When the Wife Earns More", *Journal of Family and Economic Issues*, 29, 289–306.

Kasulis, Jack J. and Hughes, Marie Adele (1984), "Husband-Wife Influence in Selecting a Family Professional", *Journal of the Academy of Marketing Science*, 12 (2), 115–27.

Kim, Chankon and Lee, Hanjoon (1997), "Development of Family Triadic Measures for Children's Purchase Influence", *Journal of Marketing Research*, 34 (August), 307–21.

Kollmeyer, C. (2013), "Family Structure, Female Employment, and National Income Inequality: A Cross-National Study of 16 Western Countries." *European Sociological Review*, 29(4): 816–827.

Kremp, Phillippe (2010), "From Main Street to Wall Street? The determinants of stock-market participation and their evolution from 1995 to 2007", Working paper. Department of Sociology. Princeton University.

Lee, Christina K.C. and Beatty, Sharon E. (2002), "Family Structure and Influence in Family Decision Making", *Journal of Consumer Marketing*, 19 (1), 24–41.

Lloyds TSB (2013), "'Money Mummies' Are Taking Control of the Family Purse String," retrieved February 1, 2014, from www.lloydsbankinggroup.com/globalassets/documents/media/press-releases/lloyds-bank/2012/2809_mummies.pdf

Makgosa, Rina and Kang, Jikyeong (2009), "Conflict Resolution Strategies in Joint Purchase Decisions for Major Household Consumer Durables: A Cross-Cultural Investigation", *International Journal of Consumer Studies*, 33, 338–48.

Martínez, Eva and Polo, Yolanda (1999), "Determining Factors in Family Purchasing Behaviour: An Empirical Investigation", *Journal of Consumer Marketing*, 16 (5), 461–81.

Miller, Amalia R. (2011), "The Effects of Motherhood Timing on Career Path", *Journal of Population Economics*, 24, 1071–1100.

Na, W., Son, Y. and Marshall, R. (1998) "An empirical study of the purchase role structure in Korean families", *Psychology & Marketing*, 15(6), 563–76.

Palan, Kay M. and Wilkes, Robert E. (1997), "Adolescent-Parent Interaction in Family Decision Making", *Journal of Consumer Research*, 24, 159–69.

Putnam, Mandy and Davidson, William R. (1987), "Family Purchasing Behavior: II Family Roles by Product Category", in *Management Horizons Inc., a Division of Price Waterhouse*, Columbus, Ohio.

Qualls, William J. (1982), "Changing Sex Roles: Its Impact upon Family Decision Making", *Advances in Consumer Research*, Vol. 9, ed. Andrew Mitchell, Ann Abor: Association for Consumer Research, 267–70.

—— (1987), "Household Decision Behavior: The Impact of Husbands' and Wives' Sex Role Orientation", *Journal of Consumer Research*, 14, 264–79.

Razzouk, Nabil, Seitz, Victoria and Prodigalidad Capo, Karen (2007), "A Comparison of Consumer Decision-Making Behavior of Married and Cohabiting Couples", *Journal of Consumer Marketing*, 24 (5), 264–74.

Rowlingson, Karen and Joseph, Ricky (2010), "Assets and Debts Within Couples", *Institute of Applied Social Studies, University of Birmingham*.

Ruiz de Maya, Salvador (1994), "Relative Influence in Family Decision Making: The Measurement of Members Perception Agreement", unpublished dissertation, University of Murcia.

Safilios-Rothschild, Constantina (1969), "Family Sociology or Wives' Family Sociology? A Cross-Cultural Examination of Decision-Making", *Journal of Marriage and Family*, 31 (2), 290–301.

Sharp, Harry and Mott, Paul (1956), "Consumer Decisions in the Metropolitan Family", *The Journal of Marketing*, 21 (2), 149–56.

Sheth, Jagdish N. (1974), "A Theory of Family Buying Decisions", in *Model of Buyer Behavior: Conceptual, Quantitative, and Empirical*, ed. Jagdish N. Sheth, New York: Harper & Row, 17–23.

Shukla, Archana (1987), "Decision Making in Single- and Dual-Career Families in India", *Journal of Marriage and Family*, 49 (3), 621–29.

Smith, James P., McArdle, John J. and Willis, Robert (2010), "Financial Decision Making and Cognition in a Family Context", *The Economic Journal*, 120, 363–80.

Spiro, Rosann L. (1983), "Persuasion in Family Decision-Making", *Journal of Consumer Research*, 9, 393–402.

Stafford, Marla R. and Ganesh, Gopala K. (1996), "Perceived Spousal Influence in the Service Decision-Making Process: A Cross Cultural Investigation", *Journal of Applied Business Research*, 12 (4), 53–69.

Stafford, Marla R., Ganesh, Gopala K. and Garland, Barbara C. (1996), "Marital Influence in the Decision-Making Process for Services", *Journal of Services Marketing*, 10 (1), 6–21.

Su, Chenting, Fern, Edward F. and Ye, Keying (2003), "A Temporal Dynamic Model of Spousal Family Purchase-Decision Behavior", *Journal of Marketing Research*, 40, 268–81.

Su, Chenting, Zhou, Kevin Zheng, Zhou, Nan and Juan Li, Julie (2008), "Harmonizing Conflict in husband-Wife Purchase Decision Making: Perceived Fairness and Spousal Influence Dynamics", *Journal of the Academy Marketing Science*, 36, 378–94.

Sultan, Fareena., Farley, John U and Lehmann, Donald R. (1990), "A Meta-Analysis of Applications of Diffusion Models", *Journal of Marketing Research*, 27 (1), 70–77.

Szymanski, David M. and Henard, David H. (2001), "Customer Satisfaction: A Meta-Analysis of the Empirical Evidence", *Journal of the Academy of the Marketing Science*, 29 (1), 16–35.

Vasantha Lakshmi, Pinni and Sakthivel Murugan, M. (2008), "The Influence of Marital Roles on Product Purchase Decision Making", *Journal of Consumer Behavior*, 3 (1), 66–77.

Wang, Wendy, Parker, Kim and Taylor, Paul (2013), "Breadwinner Moms", Pew Research Center, www.pewsocialtrends.org

Ward, Cheryl B. (2006) "He Wants, She Wants: Gender, Category, and Disagreement in Spouse's Joint Decisions", *Advances in Consumer Research*, 33, 117–23.

Webster, Cynthia (1994) "Effects of Hispanic Ethnic Identification on Marital Roles in the Purchase Decision Process", *Journal of Consumer Research*, 21, 319–31.

Webster, Cynthia and Rice, Samantha (1996), "Equity Theory and the Power Structure in a Marital Relationship", *Advances in Consumer Research*, 23, 491–97.

Wolgast, Elizabeth (1958), "Do Husband or Wives Make the Purchasing Decisions?" *Journal of Marketing*, 23 (October), 151–58.

Wolff, Edward (2007), "Recent Trends in Household Wealth in the United States: Rising Debt and the Middle-Class Squeeze-an Update to 2007," Levy Institute Working Paper 589. Bard College.

6

What drives the purchase decision in pensions and long-term investment products in the UK?

Orla Gough and Roberta Adami

Introduction

The market for investment and personal pension products is in constant expansion, especially as a consequence of the UK government's drive to shift the burden of retirement income provision to individuals. Within employment schemes, many private-sector employers have already replaced defined benefit with defined contribution pension schemes to reduce costs and transfer financial risks to employees (Banks et al. 2005, Dobson and Horsfield 2009, Timmins 2010). Pensions are complex financial products and consumers may not fully appreciate the most relevant information to make an informed purchase decision. The UK's Financial Services Authority (FSA) and the Office of Fair Trading (OFT) have claimed that financial service providers make the decision-making process more complicated than it needs to be by excessive use of jargon and by presenting the costs related to purchasing a private pension in a way that makes it difficult for consumers to make straightforward comparisons (Adami and Gough 2008).

The decision to purchase pension products is, in most cases, a "once-in-a-lifetime" decision and as such allows little possibility of gaining knowledge through repeat purchases. The peculiar nature of purchasing a long term financial product such as a private pension (whereby the underlying financial and personal circumstances are highly likely to change over the investment period) renders the process especially difficult to evaluate for young individuals. For them, it is too early to tell, while pensioners, who are in a position to evaluate their investment, are likely to have faced very different conditions, not least, due to the ever-changing government pension provision for different age cohorts.

The amount an individual needs to save for retirement in 20 or 30 years' time depends on their expectations of their future earnings, health and life expectancy, as well as future government policies, investment returns, annuity rates and prices. Much of this information is not known and much of it can only be estimated. The uncertainty inherent in saving for retirement makes pensions quite different from any other product and service in terms of their intangibility (Lovelock 2007). Further, the financial services industry has been facing intense competition, both internally from traditional life companies but also from banks and non-financial firms such as retailers. The intensified competition highlights the critical importance of understanding consumer behaviour and the factors that influence the decision process.

This chapter covers the specific issues relating to the decision-making process within the financial services sector, specifically that of pensions. It draws on a survey of the drivers of the purchase decision as well as the distribution channels used for pensions and long-term investment products in the UK.

Consumers purchase decision-making in financial services

When faced with purchase decisions, consumers are equally likely to make rational decisions by buying products and services that maximize their utility as they are to buy impulsively and be influenced by family and friends, advertisers, role models, mood, situation and emotion. These factors form a comprehensive model of consumer behaviour that reflects the cognitive and emotional aspects of consumer decision-making. Individual consumers' choices have been found to be influenced by factors such as prior knowledge and experience, contingent brand choice and product complexity (Lee and Marlowe 2003). Further, consumers apply a variety of criteria in evaluating different purchase alternatives, which vary in importance and influence.

To rationalize the complexities involved in the choice of the purchase of a pension/investment product and the selection of the distribution channel, we employ the model of decision-making associated with consumer behaviour (Engel et al. 1990, Brassington and Pettitt 1997). The model identifies the stages of "Problem Recognition", "Information Search" and "Information Evaluation" as key preparatory stages to a "Choice", which leads to a purchase decision (Harrison et al. 2006, Kotler 2008). This model is based on the assumption that buyers will go through cognitive, affective and behavioural stages if there is involvement with a product category associated with a high degree of product differentiation. The model, however, is founded on a sequence of decisions that assume a rational consumer and does not cater for the role of different distribution routes. In practice customers are likely to pass through at least two choice levels: the choice of distribution route and the choice of service provider (a service brand). In Chapter 4, Bateman, Louviere and Thorp present an alternative Decision States Model that takes account of interest and capability in decision-making.

Decision-making may vary according to customer experience with the service. For example, first-time or infrequent customers of financial services often lack the required experiences to make informed decisions; thus they are likely to progress through at least two interrelated choice levels in their effort to select a service provider: a service category choice (the distribution route) and a service brand choice. Relational elements are also greatly valued by consumers when faced with a highly uncertain product outcome, as is the case with pension products.

Intangibility is the main distinguishing feature of financial services and products. At the pre-purchase stage, financial products such as pensions are difficult to evaluate, often due to lack of internal sources of information (such as knowledge of the product through past experience) and complexity of external sources of information, such as advertising and recommendations (Harrison 2000). In the case of complex services such as investment and pension products, there may even be a lack of need recognition by consumers. Accessible advice is often required before features and benefits of such services are understood. In a complex problem, customers are often less familiar with the different alternatives and circumstances surrounding the acquisition decision, hence they tend to go through more choice levels before deciding on a specific service provider.

Harrison introduced the second main discriminatory factor, which she termed "perceived knowledge", consisting of consumers' perceived knowledge and understanding of financial affairs, perceived confidence in dealing with financial matters and expressed level of interest (Harrison 1994). When buyers cannot easily evaluate the qualities and value of the service or capabilities of the service provider then brand reputation may serve as an important proxy for more detailed evaluations. Brand reputation and credibility of providers are more likely to lead to competitive advantage with services that are highly intangible and where customers' experience is of paramount importance (see Devlin 2001, de Chernatony and Cottam 2006). Chapter 14 provides a detailed discussion of the importance of branding in financial services.

Distribution channels

Within the pension and investment market, there are three main channels: Independent Financial Advisers (IFAs), direct sales force, also referred to as "tied agents", others, which include consumers purchasing directly from the service provider (often through their website) and bancassurance, the method of supplying insurance products to a bank's customer base through its distribution channels (Benoist 2002). In 2011 in the UK, there were around 20.8 million individual pension policies and 9.6 million endowment and investment policies in force (ABI, Quarterly Consumer Survey 2011). The distribution routes used for long-term investment and savings products are shown in Figure 6.1, comparing 2000 and 2011.

The vast majority of long-term investment and saving products were purchased through IFAs (78 percent, up from 72 percent in 2000), 9 percent were purchased from "Single Tie" providers (or Direct Salesforces, this figure declined from 20 percent in 2000 to 9 percent in 2011 and has been constantly declining for the last 20 years), while the remaining 13 percent of purchases were made through "Non-Intermediated" providers, up from 8 percent in 2000 (ABI 2011).

A report from Deloitte, published in 2012, suggests that the level of wealth is an important determinant of the type of intermediary used when purchasing a long-term investment product. The more "affluent" customers (those with cash savings higher than £50,000) are considerably more likely to purchase a long-term saving or investment product from an IFA than less wealthy customers. Power et al. (2012) estimated that 32 percent of those considered affluent customers purchased their savings/investment products from IFAs, while only around 14 percent of those with lower cash savings purchased a long-term investment through an IFA.

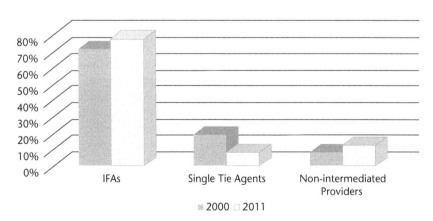

Figure 6.1 Distribution route for long-term investments and saving products

Source: Adapted from 'Quarterly Consumer Survey' (2011), Association of British Insurers (ABI), www.abi.org.uk

Drivers of purchase decisions

To better understand and explain the consumer difficulties involved in the purchase decision of a pension and long-term investment product and in choosing the most appropriate distribution route, we employ focus groups based on the framework of a decision-making model to investigate problem recognition, information search, evaluation tools and post-purchase assessment. The behavioural aspects of decision-making raised in the focus group interviews provided rich insights into the drivers that underline the initial problem recognition/awareness stage of the decision process and the important inter-relationship between the subsequent information search and choice of distribution channel.

We held nine sets of interviews, with focus groups that represent a sample of the UK population from different locations (Birmingham, Bristol and London). We grouped consumers by age and income so that they would discuss freely their financial affairs with people of similar socio-demographic characteristics. Four groups were comprised of individuals aged between 20 and 34 years with a personal annual income between £16,000 and £34,999 gross. In the other five groups we had respondents over 35 years of age, with annual gross personal income greater than £35,000. Industry data suggests that individuals earning less than £16,000 a year would not have enough disposal income to purchase private pension products, so were not targeted for the study.

All respondents selected were individuals who had purchased a personal pension in the past 12 months or were in the process of doing so at the time of the interview. We used a stratified random sample from the enquiries datasets of four financial services companies, which consisted of those who requested details of investment/pension products, and all had been offered a multi-distribution route. In total, 520 people were invited to participate in the focus groups; 102 accepted and 64 attended, with on average, 7 respondents in each focus group.

The discussion focussed on the key decision stages of problem recognition, information search, evaluation, choice and post-purchase evaluation. The data was analyzed using NUDIST software, which identifies specific words, themes or issues that commonly occurred within and across the discussion groups. The findings were studied within the framework of the classic decision-making model and content analysis was carried out by using quotes of recurrent and relevant statements made by respondents. All respondents were also asked to complete a financial literacy test to ascertain whether this was a significant variable. The composition of our sample is shown in Table 6.1.

We had an almost equal distribution in terms of gender in our sample (just over 51 percent male and 48.5 percent female) and an even distribution with regard to age groups, with a predominance of those between 30 and 49 of age. This can be justified as the majority of those with sufficient disposable income to invest in long-term financial products fall within the above age range. With regard to income, the majority of those interviewed were earning between £20,000 and £39,000 (40.6 percent of the respondents had incomes in the range of £20,000 to £29,000 per year) but also a significant minority (31.2 percent) of the sample earned more than £40,000.

The composition of our sample is in line with national statistics that show that the working age UK population is evenly distributed between men and women (49.6 percent men and 50.4 percent women), that their average and median ages are 38.6 and 37 respectively (ONS 2013), with a national average income in 2010 of £26,000 for those in full time work and £21,000 across the whole of the working population, including part-time workers (ONS 2010).

Problem recognition

The majority of respondents realized that state and occupational pensions would "not provide adequate post-retirement income" and believed that they would have to "put money away"

Table 6.1 Sample by age, gender and income

Age group	Male	Female	Total by age/Income
20–24	3	2	5
	(4.7%)	(3.1%)	(7.8%)
25–29	4	4	8
	(6.25%)	(6.2%)	(12.5%)
30–34	3	3	6
	(4.7%)	(4.7%)	(9.4%)
35–39	5	5	10
	(7.8%)	(7.8%)	(15.6%)
40–44	7	5	12
	(10.9%)	(7.8%)	(18.75%)
45–49	5	5	10
	(7.8%)	(7.8%)	(15.6%)
50+	6	7	13
	(9.4%)	(10.9%)	(20.3%)
Total	33	31	64
	(51.56%)	(48.44%)	(100%)
Income group			
£20–29k	12	14	26
	(18.7%)	(21.9%)	(40.6%)
£30–39k	9	9	18
	(14.1%)	(14.1%)	(28.1%)
£40k+	12	8	20
	(18.7%)	(12.5%)	(31.2%)

for their retirement. Trigger factors, leading to problem recognition are often experienced; common trigger examples given, were "children", "marriage" or "setting up a home with a long term partner". "Change of employment" was also mentioned in three focus groups, in particular when leaving a company with an occupational pension scheme for a company with no provision. This type of trigger factor was particularly common amongst males of all ages, but especially for those on lower income. Redundancy was also an important trigger, especially for men, as it meant that respondents had to re-address their finances. Other events such as divorce or death of a partner also caused respondents to re-assess decisions about their future. Older respondents, especially wealthier women, stated that often the death of their partner had been the "principal reason" for actively considering making provisions for their retirement.

Other triggers mentioned frequently were "the desire for a better pension", "the desire to retire early", "the negative experience of one or both retired parents" and "anxiety about government-reduced state retirement benefit". These were all considered important motivations to save money for retirement, especially for those on low income. Tax incentives of pension schemes were an appealing feature for those highly financially literate and on higher incomes.

Information search

Three main arrangements emerge from the interviews. If respondents had already contacted an IFA, the search was carried out entirely through them. Those who had made no prior contact with an IFA used the information search to evaluate the advisers, contacting, on average two providers for initial consultation. Other respondents initiated the search for a financial services company or IFA by phone or using the internet, following a recommendation from friends/colleagues or family members, usually, between 3 and 5 companies were contacted. At this stage of the process many felt the need for a "face-to-face" meeting with an adviser "to clarify and understand the details of a complex product". The need for personal contact diminished as respondents proceeded through the purchasing decision. At this stage of the information search many choose to use IFAs, to benefit from independent advice at a low cost, while a small percentage of respondents sought information from their local bank/building society, often prompted by a bank employee.

Evaluation

The two most important evaluation measurements of providers are based on historic fund performance and charges. The time scale on fund performance was generally 3, 5, 10 and 20 years, although more emphasis is placed on medium and long term performances (5, 10 and 20 years). Many IFAs display charts to illustrate their charges, perceived to be easier to evaluate than future performance. Consumers, particularly older women, place great emphasis on charges.

Those who could relate to previous experiences as financial services consumers would often use a combination of future performance and charges as evaluation tools. At this stage awareness of the brand becomes vital. The attributes most commonly cited were "long established" and "safe". Other highly-valued assessment tools were the quality of the documentation and the flexibility offered by the financial providers in terms of changing contribution levels in line with changes in life circumstances.

Purchase choice

There is a tendency to use "charges and fees" as a proxy for "value for money". Price comparison relates to pre-purchase evaluation. Respondents believed the purchase decision to be a long-term commitment and did not think they would change pension provider unless "extraordinary" events occurred. The awareness that the benefits would not emerge for years made it all the more difficult to judge the purchase decision. Those who purchased directly from the financial services providers felt more confident and expressed a more positive "retrospective" valuation as they perceived a higher degree of control over the decision-making process. The decision-making experience differed depending on the distribution route; using IFAs and direct product providers tends to reflect higher degrees of confidence and satisfaction.

Gender and age effects

The analysis suggests that women are more pro-active in the information search, however the evaluation is often carried out at the household level, while men are more likely to "search the internet" for product knowledge and reach a decision without consulting their spouse. Older groups tend to have an established relationship with an independent adviser, while younger groups are more inclined to use the internet/telephone/tied agent. Older groups are more anxious about the evaluation stage and keen to have guidance on their pension benefits from previous periods of employment. A significant percentage of younger respondents are not interested in "getting involved" in the decision-making, especially those on low incomes.

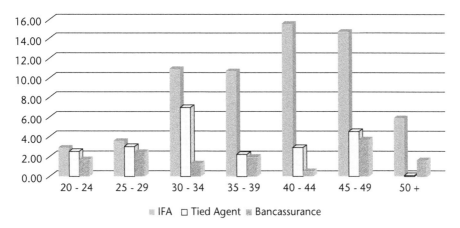

Figure 6.2   Distribution channel for pension products by age (values in percentages)

The distribution channels

Figures 6.2 to 6.4 show the distribution route chosen by participants according to their age, income and gender.

The predominant role of IFAs in the pension and savings market in the UK is illustrated in Figure 6.2, however there are marked differences between age cohorts. Most young respondents use IFAs and tied agents almost in equal measure, while a lower percentage of young respondents use bancassurers. Those aged 30 and over (by far the most likely group to invest in a private pension) choose IFAs in the vast majority of cases. The second most popular distribution route is Tied Agents, used particularly by 30–34 year olds, while bancassurance trails with maximum proportions of 3.8 percent amongst those aged between 45 and 49. These findings are partially in agreement with Ennew's (1992) who showed that interest in obtaining financial information through an Independent Adviser was greater amongst younger respondents, while it confirms the steady increase in popularity of this distribution channel from the early 1990s (Gough and Nurullah 2009).

Figure 6.3 shows that, while those on low and medium incomes opt in almost equal proportions for IFAs and Tied Agents, there is a clear preference amongst wealthier individuals for Independent Advisers. These results are firmly in line with literature showing that IFAs are

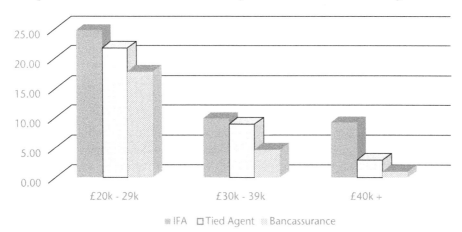

Figure 6.3   Distribution channel for pension products by income (values in percentages)

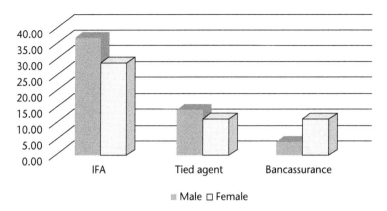

Figure 6.4 Distribution channel for pension products by gender (values in percentages)

the distribution route more frequently chosen by richer and older investors (Power et al. 2012, Hackethal et al. 2012). Finally, the results on gender are shown in Figure 6.4.

The results here suggest that although the vast majority of respondents overall choose IFAs, women are nearly four times more likely to use bancassurance than men. The higher propensity of women to choose bancassurance as an investment and pension distribution channel is also recognized by Webster (2004) and shows a lower inclination to shop around and collect information from independent sources than men. These results enrich the findings of the focus groups and confirm that both income and gender are very strongly related to the type of intermediary chosen.

Further, the findings of the study indicate a positive relationship between income and financial literacy. High income levels and financial literacy are important factors in determining whether customers are inclined to have an informed discussion on future fund performance and take the time to monitor it after the purchase. This finding indicates that those with greater levels of financial literacy are more proactive in searching financial information to try to overcome the existing information asymmetry between customers and financial services (as suggested in Chapter 3 by Huhmann). Those "high value" customers are less inclined to evaluate the product and intermediary on the basis of charges and more likely to choose IFAs as a distribution route. Respondents with less financial knowledge were more inclined to use bancassurance, the preferred choice of intermediary for young women on low incomes. The general agreement amongst respondents was that government should simplify the market and the way in which financial services companies operate. Many respondents, especially those on lower incomes, did not engage in the process, but felt that they had to go through it to avoid living in poverty after retirement.

Conclusions

Understanding consumers' decision-making when purchasing pension and long term saving products and establishing how decision-making affects the choice of distribution route is crucial to help financial providers to best target consumers with their products and services.

The findings of the empirical study in this chapter are based on the classic "purchase decision-making" model with the addition of the distribution channel choice. The analysis of problem recognition indicates that government provisions of retirement income are no longer considered sufficient by the majority of respondents. The need for purchase decisions is recognized long before seeking information on pension products. The insights on problem recognition are similar to those suggested by Rowlingson (2006), where individuals usually experienced a trigger factor during their life, such as change of job, redundancy or the birth of a child. The information search stage very often works as a proxy for selection of a distribution channel. Information search should provide useful insights to financial intermediaries offering pension and investment products in understanding the customers' needs. Search outcomes, however, are not straightforward. Our analysis shows considerable overlap and switching between channels at this stage. The IFA channel is by far the most popular distribution route and considered a more independent service.

Younger consumers are more likely to use the telephone or the internet to gather initial information. This is in part motivated by lack of trust of financial advisers and the belief that greater control can be exerted on the process. The two most important evaluation tools are the fund charges and the historic fund performance. However, most respondents voiced their concern that the investment outcomes would not be known until much later into the future, at retirement. Despite the uncertainty over fund performance it is very rare for those who do invest in private pensions to monitor the performance of the investment fund and equally uncommon to change private pension provider. Owing to the difficulties of choosing amongst many complex products, financial services customers value brand recognition as extremely important, as acknowledged by de Chernatony and Cottam (2006) and Taylor et al. (2007). The choice of a particular brand over another is often determined by reputation as well as the levels of charges and past performance.

IFAs play an important role in enhancing the level of understanding of the pension products and they are perceived to provide "good value for money" in recognition of the independent advice received in such a complex decision-making process. However, our findings indicate that there is still a need for more transparency in the commission paid to IFAs and the charges structure of pensions and pension-related products.

In terms of financial literacy, there is a positive relationship between income and financial literacy, customers with a higher degree of financial knowledge tend to evaluate products on the basis of past performance and to be less inclined to evaluate on charges. They are also more proactive in discussing the investment strategy and in monitoring the fund performance over time. Financial literacy plays an important role in the level of consumer engagement.

From the perspective of pension providers, the identification of specific consumer groups can enhance their ability to develop customized pension and investment products. Gender, income and level of financial literacy all greatly influence the type of distribution route chosen and the degree of consumer involvement in the purchase process. Low income individuals, especially women, are far less interested and less engaged in the purchase process and as a consequence bancassurance is more likely to be their preferred intermediary. The choice of product and distribution channel amongst these individuals is frequently the result of their bank cross-selling strategy rather than their own proactive search for the most suitable products.

As the market for private pensions and investment continues to grow, understanding the consumer's decision-making process is of significant interest to financial services firms. Products in this market like many others are available to consumers through multiple channels. Our research focusses on the UK, where we confirm the dominance of Independent Financial Advisers as the preferred distribution channel and provide an explanation of why most consumers choose this route, but we also offer clear indications of the characteristics of consumers in this market and of how they formulate their purchasing decisions.

The qualitative nature of our study does not allow us to generalize or extend our findings to other countries where regulatory systems and private pension markets may differ greatly from the UK. An example of how the regulatory framework does affect the development of the market for pensions and long-term investments products is bancassurance. Although the partnership between banks and insurance companies is highly developed in France and Spain, particularly for life-insurance products, bancassurance has enjoyed a far more limited growth in countries such as the US, UK and Japan, often hindered by regulatory barriers that limit the association between banking and insurance activities (Benoist 2002). It is also likely that the market for private pensions and long-term savings in the UK will experience important changes in view of the implementation of auto-enrollment in the workplace since October 2012. Although this new policy has been hailed as a success due to low percentages of workers opting out of auto-enrollment, its effects on private savings and ultimately on adequacy of retirement income are not clear yet.

References

Adami, R. and O. Gough, (2008) Pension reforms and saving for retirement: Comparing the United Kingdom and Italy. *Policy Studies* 29 (2): 119–135.

Association of British Insurers (ABI) Quarterly Consumer Survey (2011), *www.financiallibrary.co.uk/document_id=10736*

Banks, J., Blundell, R. and C. Emmerson (2005), The Balance between Defined Benefit, Defined Contribution and State Provision, *Journal of European Economic Association*, 3 (2–3), 466–476.

Benoist, G. (2002), Bancassurance: the New Challenges, *The Geneva Papers on Risk and Insurance*, 27 (3), 295–303.

Brassington, F. and S. Pettitt, (1997) *Principles of Marketing*. London: Pitman Publishing.

De Chernatony, L. and S. Cottam (née Drury), (2006) "Internal brand factors driving successful financial services brands", *European Journal of Marketing*, 40 (5/6): 611–633.

Devlin, J.F. (2001), Consumer Evaluation and Competitive Advantage in Retail Financial Services: A Research Agenda, *European Journal of Marketing*, 35 (5–6), 639–660.

Dobson, C. and S. Horsfield (2009) *Defined Contribution Pension Provision*, Department for Work and Pensions (DWP), Research Report No. 608.

Engel, J. F., Blackwell, R. D. and P. W. Miniard, (1990), *Consumer Behaviour*. Dryden: Hinsdale.

Ennew, C.T. (1992) Consumer Attitudes to Independent Financial Advice, *International Journal of Bank Marketing*, 10 (5): 4–12.

Gough, O. and M. Nurullah (2009) Understanding what Drives the Purchase Decision in Pension and Investment Products, *Journal of Financial Services Marketing*, 14 (2): 152–172.

Hackethal, A., Haliassos, M. and T. Jappelli (2012) Financial Advisors: A Case of Babysitters? *Journal of Banking and Finance*, 36 (2): 509–524.

Harrison, T. S. (1994), Mapping customer segments for personal financial services, *International Journal of Bank Marketing*, 12 (8): 17–25.

—— (2000) *Financial Services Marketing*. Prentice Hall, Wiltshire, UK.

Harrison, T., Waite, K. and P. White (2006) Analysis by paralysis: The pension purchase decision process, *International Journal of Bank Marketing*, 24 (1): 5–23.

Kotler, P. K. K. (2008) *Marketing Management*, 13th ed. Englewood Cliffs, NJ: Prentice-Hall.

Lee, J. and J. Marlowe (2003) How consumers choose a financial institution: Decision-Making criteria and heuristics, *International Journal of Bank Marketing* 21 (2): 53–71.

Lovelock, C. (2007) *Services Marketing: People, Technology, Strategy*, Pearson International Edition.

Office for National Statistics (2010) *Income Inequality Remains Stable*. 2010 News release.

—— (2013), *2011 Census: Population Estimates for the United Kingdom*, accessed on 12 December 2013.

Power, A., Cohen, S. and P. Evans, (2012) *Bridging the Advice Gap, Delivering Investment Products in a post-RDR World*, Deloitte Insights Report, Deloitte LLP, London.

Rowlingson, K. (2006), Living Poor to Die Rich'? Or 'Spending the Kids' Inheritance'? Attitudes to Assets and Inheritance in Later Life, *Journal of Social Policy*, 35, (2): 175–192.

Taylor, S. A., Hunter, G. L. and D. L. Lindberg, (2007) "Understanding (customer-based) Brand Equity in Financial Services", *Journal of Services Marketing*, 21 (4): 241–252.

Timmins, N. (2010) *Rising Threat to Defined Benefits Pension Schemes, Financial Times*, www.ft.com/cms/s/0/419caa5e-0533-11df-a85e-00144feabdc0.html#axzz2WHDynVYj

Webster, J. (2004). 'Digitalising Inequality: the cul-de-sac of Women's Work in European Services', *New Technology, Work and Employment*, 19 (3): 160–176.

7

Financial and non-financial attributes of pension fund structures

A customer perspective from the Netherlands

Nikos Kalogeras, Arvid O. I. Hoffmann and Dominik Mahr

Introduction

The environment in which financial services are distributed and marketed is becoming increasingly complex and challenging. After the recent turmoil in financial markets related to the 2008 financial crisis, the financial services sector in western economies has undergone drastic changes resulting in intense competition with rapid market entry of new service concepts and formats, consolidation and concentration, little growth and declined customer demand (Booz & Company 2011). In this new market place, the occurrence of committed and inherited relationships between customers and their financial services provider is becoming more important. Nowadays, customer retention and the ability to cross-sell products to existing customers are critical in the financial services industry (Estelami 2012).

Several strategies have been attempted to retain customers during the last decade. In order to increase customer loyalty and to maintain and increase customer retention rates, many financial services organizations have introduced innovative services. But after the global financial crisis, there is increasing customer dissatisfaction and distrust in the financial industry as a whole (Gritten 2011). Moreover, the technical complexity of financial services and the administrative charges for introducing innovative features do not allow market success for most of the newly developed services (Avlonitis et al. 2001). It has been argued that a more viable approach for financial services providers is to focus on less tangible and easy-to-imitate determinants of customer behavior such as evaluative judgments of perceived service quality and customer satisfaction (Worcester 1997, Bloemer et al. 1998). Such evaluative judgments may provide an effective, direct and meaningful measure of customers' preferences for complex financial services (Siskos and Grigoroudis 2002). Therefore, attention is centered on individual customers' preferences for aspects of complex financial services. Failure to identify customer preferences may result in low perceived quality of a service organization, as customers may feel that the marketed service of the organization does not capture their economic interests (Gustafsson et al. 2005). When this is the case, customer commitment is expected to decline.

The literature on relationship marketing reports extensively on the role of decision-makers' commitment. The greater the customer satisfaction and commitment to a service organization, the more the customer is inclined to continue and invest in this relationship (for example, Moorman et al. 1992, Gounaris 2003). This explains why service organizations are more concerned about gaining the commitment of their customers to the relationship rather than vice versa (Leek et al. 2002). However, as difficult/complex savings and investment decisions are increasingly becoming the responsibility of customers rather than of financial organizations (Richardson Agnew 2010), a challenge is presented for a more in-depth understanding of customer evaluative judgments (preferences) for the aspects of a complex financial offering.

Particularly, in the post-crisis era, the landscape of the financial services industry has changed dramatically. Many western economies (USA, EU) have witnessed a dramatic shift in pension coverage during the last twenty years. Indeed, policy-makers debate about the long-term solvency of pension funds and social security systems in light of the public debt crises that many of these economies are confronted with (Poterba et al. 2008). Customer dissatisfaction regarding the shift from defined benefit to defined contribution plans that offer portability but also involve investment decisions with personal responsibility may result in decreasing commitment of individuals and thus influence their participation in these programs (for example, Bertrand et al. 2006, Guiso et al. 2008). Therefore, a prominent decision context to examine customer preferences for a complex financial service is the pension fund industry, which is the focus of this chapter.

The research question addressed in this chapter is how customers evaluate the aspects that make up a pension fund's structural design, which are hypothesized to be important for customer commitment. Knowledge of customer preferences for the structural aspects of a pension fund may be crucial for re-designing pension fund programs and the enhancement of customer participation in these programs. Pension fund policies that provide customers with additional benefits (for example, increases in retirement savings, lower administrative costs) may enhance customer retention and therefore customer contribution to these pension fund programs. The empirical study of customer preferences for pension fund structural aspects, which may be directly linked to the degree that a pension fund provider is perceived to act as a market agent that captures their economic interests, is a challenging task.

We study customer preferences for two types of attributes (financial and non-financial) that make up the design of a pension fund program. These attributes are hypothesized to be important for customers' commitment to their pension fund provider. The empirical study concerns the preferences of customers from a major pension fund provider in the Netherlands. The empirical results demonstrate that customers prefer more financial attributes rather than non-financial attributes for the make-up of their pension fund structure.

The remainder of this chapter is organized as follows. First, we discuss the extant literature on how customers form preferences for financial service attributes. Second, we specify the methodology and the model used to study customer preferences for the design of pension fund programs. Third, we describe the study design in detail. Fourth, we present and discuss the results. Finally, we draw several concluding remarks.

Preferences for financial service attributes

When individuals decide to contribute to a savings or retirement plan, they have to make certain choices regarding their own portfolio allocation. This may be a challenging task because financial services entail high complexity due to their intangible nature and technical (financial) attributes (Easingwood and Mahajan 1989). Individual decision-makers may perceive the quality of a financial service in a subjective way and therefore cannot assess clearly all of its individual features and benefits, but rather evaluate the service holistically. Hence, individuals may not have well-defined portfolio preferences and accept default investment funds when trading (Benartzi and Thaler 2001). Recent evidence shows that most employees remain in a retirement default plan for a long time after their automatic enrollment in a pension system (Nessmith et al. 2007). As the power of this default bias is quite high, evidence suggests that it could be overcome only through committed attempts to encourage the active choice of individuals as driven by their preferences for several financial attributes of a pension fund program (Richardson Agnew 2010). Public and private financial institutions carry the responsibility to enhance the freedom of their customer preferences and help guide them toward welfare-promoting decisions and choices in a specific decision environment (Thaler and Sunstein 2003, 2008).

Indeed, the literature on constructed preferences argues that due to limited processing capacities, individual decision-makers often do not have well-defined preferences for the multiple attributes that make up a product's or service's structural design. Instead, preferences are often constructed on the spot by an adaptive decision-maker (for example, Bettman et al. 1998, Pennings and Smidts 2003). This might be an indication that contextual elements may have an influence on decision-makers' subjective, quality assessments of products/service attributes and therefore on their preference structure (Loewenstein 1992, Kalogeras 2010). Context specificity has traditionally been regarded as involving the decision-maker's response to the properties, characteristics and attributes of a decision task (for example, Simonson and Tversky 1992, Benarzi and Thaler 2001). This response may be reflected through the activation of an individual's cognitive heuristics (for example, a changing format/condition of a specific task context, the time for responding to this task). These heuristics may affect the subjective probability assessment of individuals (for example, preferences) and thereby their economic behavior (Barberis, 2003).

In the context of this chapter, we focus on the revealed economic behavior of pension fund customers. While several scholars (for example, Ramasamy and Yeung 2003, Gözbaşı and Çıtak 2010) have examined customer or investor preferences for the financial attributes (for example, average investment performance) of hedge or mutual funds, empirical research on customer preferences for pension funds' structural design is scarce to date. Past research mainly deals with individuals' risk preferences for single attributes such as the type of pension plan (for example, Society of Actuaries 2004, Gupta 2006, van Rooij et al. 2007) or examines individuals' attitudes and savings choices toward pensions and retirement planning (for example, Millar and Devonish 2009). In this chapter, we expand the extant literature by examining customer preferences for an enlarged set of attributes splintered in two classes: financial and non-financial.

Consistent with recent trends in the current decision environment regarding hedonic and social values that individuals may assign to different asset classes (for example, Derwall et al. 2005, Derwall et al. 2011, Hoffmann and Broekhuizen 2010, Vyvyan et al. 2007), we examine not only customer preferences for financial, but also for non-financial attributes. This line of thinking relies on academic work that deals with customer preferences and choice between the hedonic and utilitarian attributes of products (Hirschman and Holbrook 1982, Khan et al. 2004, Chernev 2004). Utilitarian attributes are described as "practical" and are associated with necessary functions in life (such as currency exchange), while hedonic attributes are associated with non-financial, pleasure-oriented, and experiential consumption (such as perceived elegance/style of an asset class) (Strahilevitz and Myers 1998, Mahr et al. 2013).

Past research in other categories of financial services (for example, mutual funds, insurance, mortgages) highlights the importance of both classes of attributes. For instance, Nilsson et al. (2010) examine the information search of mutual fund investors and support that socially responsible investors search more for social, ethical and environmental information rather than for "regular" financial (utilitarian) information, such as past financial returns and levels of risk. Mäenpää et al. (2006), Nilsson (2009) and Bauer and Smeets (2012), among others, provide evidence that other segments of mutual fund investors consider seriously during the pre- and post-purchase decision-making process criteria from two main classes: utilitarian (for example, return-oriented) and non-utilitarian (hedonic-oriented) benefits that are mostly related to ethical, social and environmental attributes of a fund. Recent findings on which class of attributes outperforms the other are mixed and seem to be dependent on the decision context, type of asset, and investors' background (Derwall et al. 2011). What is consistent across all of these studies is that the measurement of the importance that individuals (for example, customers of a financial service) assign to the attributes of a product/service appears to consist of a combination of cognitive and affective elements. The cognitive elements may relate mostly to the financial- or return-oriented attributes, whereas the affective elements relate mostly to hedonic attributes (Athanassopoulos 2000, Mäenpää et al. 2006, Al-Eisa and Alhemoud 2009).

Many studies in consumer financial decision-making reveal that the identification of the importance (utility) that customers assign to utilitarian and hedonic attributes of a product/service (in our context the attributes that make up a pension fund structure) may contribute to customers' loyalty and retention (Fornell 1992, Sharma and Patterson 2000, Hoffmann and Broekhuizen 2010), confidence (Anderson and Weitz 1989, Dwyer et al. 1987) and commitment (Moorman et al. 1992, Gounaris 2003, Burnham et al. 2003, Al-Eisa and Alhemoud 2009). The common presumption in such studies is that the prosperity and growth of a financial service provider in the retailing sector is based on customer commitment. A financial institution's quality might be perceived to be low when customers perceive that the attributes of its products/services do not capture their economic interests (Garbarino and Johnson 1999, Kalogeras et al. 2009, Al-Eisa and Alhemoud 2009). Financial service institutions that enjoy high commitment can develop a niche product/service that is highly desired by its investors (Anderson and Narus 1990).

In this study, we support the notion that the subjective utility (for example, preferences) that customers attach to particular financial and non-financial attributes of a pension fund structure signals the level of their commitment to their pension fund provider. Thus, we hypothesize that both classes (financial and non-financial) of attributes drive the overall utility that customers derive from their participation in a pension fund program.

Methodology and model

Recent research in investment behavior of market participants has put the human decision-making process in the spotlight (Smith 2003). Applied research in the areas of behavioral economics should confront models with more micro-level than macro-level data to investigate the drivers of behavior of individual market participants (for example, customers, investors, managers) (Heckman 2001). In the behavioral finance, marketing-finance and organizational sciences literature, the use of methodologies that are rooted in behavioral and experimental economics are emerging to study the relative importance (for example, subjective utility) that individual market participants assign to the attributes of a complex product/service or organization (Verhoef and Pennings 2012). A suitable methodological framework that allows the measurement and analysis of multi-attribute preferences should be employed.

Conjoint analysis is one such method that considers the elicitation of preference measurement parameters from the individual decision-makers' (subjects') holistic evaluative responses (overall utility) to different combinations of all the attributes. Conjoint analysis determines "the relative importance that people attach to salient attributes and the utilities they attach to the levels of attributes. Individuals are presented with stimuli that consist of combinations of attribute levels. They are asked to evaluate these stimuli in terms of their desirability" (Malhotra and Birks 2003: 684). For instance, Zinkhan and Zinkhan (1994) and Hooper (2001) employ conjoint analysis to examine the preferences of managers of multinational corporations for capital budgeting decisions, Moskowitz and Krieger (2001) assess customer preferences for combinations of various attribute-levels considered when they buy several financial products, Kalogeras et al. (2009) study the preferences of member-investors of a collective equity structure and Bauer and Smeets (2012) study the social preferences of mutual fund investors.

The use of conjoint analysis is grounded in the basic utility framework (Green and Srinivasan 1990) which assumes that decision-makers derive utility from the attributes of a product/service. In the context of this study, it is assumed that the levels of the financial and non-financial pension fund attributes contribute in an additive way to customers' overall utility (preference) as given in Equation 1:

$$\gamma_{jk} = \sum_{p=1}^{P}\sum_{l=1}^{L_p} x_{jklp}\beta_{jlp} + e_{jk} \tag{1}$$

where γ_{jk} is the preference of a customer j ($j = 1,\ldots, J$) for profile k ($k = 1,\ldots, K$) which represents a hypothetical pension fund profile; p ($p = 1,\ldots, P$) is an index for pension fund attributes, with P being the total number of attributes; l ($l = 1,\ldots, L_p$) is an index for attribute levels with L_p being the number of levels defined for attribute p; χ_{jklp} is a dummy variable that takes a value of 1 when level l of attribute p is selected in profile k for j and $\chi_{jklp} = 0$ otherwise; β_{jlp} is the utility that the customer j attaches to level l of attribute p, and e_{jk} is a normal error term with variance σ^2. Based on the structure of preferences (γ_{jk}), which is often defined in terms of a specific scale or metric and the value of the dummy variables (χ_{jklp}), the utility weights (β_{jlp}) can be estimated for each customer. We assume that individual customers add up the values (part-worths) for each attribute to assess the total value (sum of part-worths) for a combination of attributes that describes a pension fund profile.

To estimate the importance of each pension fund attribute, we calculate the relative importance weight (w_i) of each attribute. We do this by dividing the range in utility of one attribute by the sum of the ranges in utility for all attributes (Wilcox 2003).

Identification of attributes

To study customer preferences for pension fund attributes, we used a complementary combination of qualitative and quantitative research techniques. Such a research design provides accurate descriptions and evaluations of individual market participants' preferences because data on a specific topic is collected using independent methods that do not share any potential bias (Eisenhardt 1989). First, we conducted in-depth interviews with pension fund experts (scholars and practitioners). Next, we held focus-group discussions with customers of pension funds, the results of these discussions were used as input for the design of a conjoint data-gathering instrument. Finally, we examined empirically customer preferences for combinations of financial and non-financial attribute levels of a pension fund. Specifically, we conducted a large-scale survey (N = 912) to assess the preferences of customers of a large pension fund provider in the Netherlands.

Results of qualitative studies

To identify precisely the most relevant pension fund attributes, we conducted in-depth interviews with seventeen pension fund experts (for example, scholars at European universities and managers of a large pension fund provider in the Netherlands) and two focus group discussions with Dutch customers of pension fund services. Twelve customers were selected to provide a range of characteristics including, age, region, employment status and participated in each focus group session. The financial literacy of the customers who participated in the focus group discussions was quite high because most of them had a university education with a business/ economics profile.

Customers were asked to discuss the most prominent financial and non-financial attributes of a pension fund identified through the literature and in-depth interviews with experts. In each focus group session, respondents were provided with definitions and explanations for each attribute included in the pool of attributes identified in the previous steps of qualitative research. They were also motivated to express their own suggestions. We ensured that the attribute definitions were well understood by all customers before further discussion in the session. After each attribute definition was given, no special problems were encountered. Discussions identified five attributes, four financial attributes, each with three levels (i.e., alternatives) and one non-financial attribute with two levels. We summarize each of these attributes and their corresponding alternatives next. Table 7.1 provides an overview of these attributes and previous studies on which our choice is based.

Table 7.1 Financial and non-financial attributes of pension funds' structural design

Attribute[a]	Level	Previous studies
Financial Attributes		
Average Investment Performance[b]	4% 7% 10%	Grinblatt and Titman 1992, Carhart 1997, Srinivas, Whitehouse and Yermo 2000, Sapp and Tiwari 2004, Tapia 2008, Andonov et al. 2011
Coverage ratio[c]	90% 105% 120%	Bauer et al. 2006, van Rooij, Kool and Prast 2007, Mercer 2010, DNB 2010, Siegmann 2010
Administrative Expenses[d]	0.3% 0.9% 1.5%	Barber and Odean 2001, Wilcox 2003, Bateman and Mitchell 2004, Bikker and de Dreu 2006, Bauer, Cremers and Frehen 2010
Total Investment Portfolio[e]	< 500 million 500 million–10 billion > 10 billion	Chen et al. 2004, Bauer, Cremers and Frehen 2010, Andonov, Bauer and Cremers 2011, Dyck and Pomorski 2011
Non-Financial Attributes		
Socially Responsible Investing	Yes No	Kreander et al. 2005, Nilsson, Nordvall and Isberg 2010, Renneboog, Horst and Zhang 2011, Derwall et al. 2011, Bauer and Smeets 2012

[a]The attributes and respective levels (alternatives) were selected through the synthesis of a literature review, the consultation of experts from the academic and professional field, and focus group discussions with pension fund customers.
[b]The average investment performance indicates the average return on a yearly basis.
[c]Coverage Ratio of 100 percent implies that the value of the available assets of a pension fund is equal to the value of the nominal liabilities.
[d]In % of total pension fund assets
[e]In million Euros (€)

Average investment performance

Average investment performance is a long-term indicator of pension fund performance. Past studies on different types of funds (for example, mutual funds) suggest a positive relationship between past performance and future performance (for example, Grinblatt and Titman 1992, Carhart 1997, Sapp and Tiwari 2004). This finding is supported by Andonov et al. (2011) who report persistence in a pension fund's ability to deliver higher market timing and security selection returns. The funds that belong to the best performing quintile this year are more likely to remain among the best performing quintile the following year. Consistent with the studies referring to Dutch pension funds (for example, Tapia 2008, Srinivas et al. 2000), experts and customers agreed that the following three alternatives represent a realistic range of a pension fund's average annual performance: 4 percent, 7 percent and 10 percent. Experts supported that 7 percent is approximately the average investment performance of pension funds over the last 25 years. Accounting for 3 percent below and 3 percent above this average value, a good range to present low to high returns is provided. According to the experts, a good period to reflect economic trends is at least 25 years.

Coverage ratio

Customers seem to take into account the coverage ratio because they perceive that this ratio indicates the financial health of a pension fund. A coverage ratio refers to a fund's ability to cover debt obligations with its assets after all liabilities have been satisfied (Bauer et al. 2006). According to Dutch law, a coverage ratio of 105 percent is set as the minimum required level (DNB 2010). If a Dutch pension fund has a coverage ratio below this threshold, De Nederlandsche Bank (DNB) (The Dutch Central Bank) may intervene in the governance of the pension fund (van Rooij et al. 2007). Consistent with the data provided by DNB (2010), van Rooij et al. (2007), Mercer (2010) and Siegmann (2010), the previously-mentioned experts and focus group participants suggested that three alternatives correctly reflect a range of possible coverage ratios of pension funds in the Netherlands: 90 percent, 105 percent and 120 percent. The boundary of under- and overfunding is 150 percent as it is the coverage ratio required by the Dutch government (DNB 2010). According to the experts, it appears to be a good practice to use as the middle value; 90 percent is considered as a low coverage ratio and 120 percent as a high coverage ratio, both of which are realistic in representing true current or past situations.

Administrative expenses

Each pension fund incurs administrative expenses that often have a significant influence on pension benefits. The literature shows that there is a strong negative relationship between expenses and fund performance (for example, Bikker and de Dreu 2006, Bauer et al. 2010). Overall, individuals are not receptive to high administrative fees of different types of funds (for example, mutual funds) (Barber and Odean 2001, Wilcox 2003). According to the experts and participants in focus group discussions, the following alternatives represent a suitable range of the administrative costs of pension funds: 0.3 percent, 0.9 percent and 1.5 percent. These values are higher than what the literature suggests (for example, Bateman and Mitchell 2004, Bikker and de Dreu 2006). Experts explained that the introduction of a Dutch national act (*ontzaffing*) in 2006 led to lower state-bonds contributions to an investment portfolio. This in turn caused the need for making up more active investment portfolios that require higher investment expenses.

Total investment portfolio

Several scholars (for example, Chen et al. 2004, Bauer et al. 2010) suggest that the impact of scale (depending on the size) on a pension fund's performance is a crucial attribute. Dyck and Pomorski (2011) provide evidence about substantial positive scale economies in the asset management of DB pension plans. The ability to take advantage of larger economies of scale appears to depend on the governance structure of the fund (Bauer et al. 2010). Moreover, the study of Andonov et al. (2011) concludes that liquidity limitations cause diseconomies of scale in public asset classes such as equities, while economies of scale can be realized in alternative asset classes like real estate, private equity and pension funds, by asserting more bargaining power and resources for monitoring performance. Consistent with this logic, focus group participants and experts both agree that a "fund's total investment portfolio" is an important attribute that drives the utility of pension fund customers. The levels which were identified to use in the analysis are < 500 million, 500 million to 10 billion and > 10 billion Euros, which represent small, medium and large pension funds. Although these numbers are slightly different from what the literature suggests (for example, Chen et al. 2004, Dyck and Pomorski 2011), the in-depth interviews with experts clearly revealed that these numbers represent an equal division of Dutch pension funds between small, medium and large pension funds. The five biggest pension funds in the Netherlands have an investment portfolio of more than 10 billion Euros, while small pension funds are generally smaller than 500 million Euros.

Socially responsible investing (SRI)

Investing in a socially responsible way refers to "an investment approach in which social and personal values instead of financial considerations are the bases to integrate corporate social responsibility criteria into investment decisions" (Derwall et al. 2011, pp. 2137). Specifically, SRI may be also viewed as "an investment process that, in addition to the 'traditional' financial objective of investment, also uses social, ethical or environmental (SEE) criteria when individual and institutional investors make strategic decisions" (Nilsson et al. 2010). Despite the debate on whether SRI delivers higher investment returns (for example, Kreander et al. 2005), individuals may derive non-pecuniary benefits from this attribute (for example, Renneboog et al. 2011). Thus, individuals are expected to assign importance toward SRI (Derwall et al. 2011). Customers that participated in both focus group sessions expressed a preference for a pension fund that follows a socially responsible investment (SRI) behavior and strategy. Some experts recognized the importance of such an attribute and acknowledged that individuals may only be in favor of SRI if such a strategy does not lower their returns (see Chapter 33 for a more detailed discussion on SRI). Because a pension fund can choose (to some extent) to invest in a socially responsible way or not, and because it is difficult to assess SRI with numbers or in relative terms, the alternatives, "Yes" and "No", were suggested to be used in further analysis.

The choice of attributes as well as of alternatives (i.e., levels) associated with each attribute are consistent with past research. Table 7.1 presents the identified attributes and their corresponding levels but it also provides relevant literature sources from pensions and from other types of funds (for example, mutual, insurance, mortgages), that justify the choice of the selected attributes and their alternatives. In addition, the output of the focus group discussions was cross-validated through discussions with the experts (scholars and industry managers) that participated in the incipient phase of our qualitative research. All experts agreed that the selected attributes and their corresponding levels are actionable and represent well the most prominent choices regarding the aspects and corresponding options of pension fund structures in the Netherlands.

Conjoint design

The results of the qualitative (field) research as described before were used as inputs to the conjoint design described later. The number of attributes (five) allowed us to use a full profile conjoint design (Hair et al. 2005, Green and Rao 1971). Such a design implies that the product/service attributes are presented as complete profiles consisting of one level for each of the attributes. A 3 (Average Investment Performance) × 3 (Coverage Ratio) × 3 (Administrative Expenses) × 3 (Total Investment Portfolio) × 2 (Socially Responsible Investing) fractional-factorial main effect design generated a set of sixteen calibration profiles and holdout cases. We chose the fractional-factorial main-effects-only design to keep the number of profiles to be evaluated at a manageable level for respondents (Hair et al. 2005).

A pilot test consisting of fifteen interviews was conducted to assess the face validity and degree of comprehensiveness of the conjoint design task. Respondents indicated that the five attributes and their corresponding levels are easily communicable for realistic evaluation. Next, in the large-scale field study, 912 customers were asked to rate the calibration profiles of pension funds on a nine-point rating scale, which ranged from one (least preferred) to nine (most preferred). Profiles were presented to the customers through an online computer-assisted display. Care was taken to develop a user-friendly interface.

The sample participants consisted of 912 customers of a large pension fund provider in the Netherlands and the sample represented a diverse range of key demographics such as age, gender, occupation, education and financial literacy. Of the sample customers, 60 percent are male and 93.5 percent of them reported an employment status. We observe a relatively small frequency (18.8 percent) of young customers aged under 30 years old compared to middle-aged (age 30–45: 40.5 percent) and older-aged (age > 45: 40.7 percent) customers. Sixty-six percent of them reported that they have acquired a college/university degree, but only 18.8 percent have acquired any finance-related expertise.

Results and discussion

The results of the conjoint model are presented in Table 7.2. Prior to average part-worth estimates, we tested the level of association among the attributes and the goodness of fit measures. *Cramer's V* statistics indicate correlations below 0.6 for all attributes. Hence, we infer that all attributes used in the final conjoint design show low levels of association and measure different aspects and both goodness of fit indicators, *Pearson's Rho* (= 0.993) and *Kendall's Tau* (= 0.943), are above 0.9 and highly significant ($p < 0.001$).

The part-worth estimates show that all selected attributes are considered (although in varied ways) as important by the customers. For the financial attributes of coverage ratio, administrative expenses and total fund investment, customers selected the second levels as more preferred. That is, customers prefer a pension fund that has a coverage ratio equal to 105 percent, administrative expenses up to 0.9 percent (as a percentage of total fund expenses) and total size between 500 million and 10 billion Euros. For the financial attribute of average investment performance, customers prefer mostly the third level of 10 percent. This finding reveals the high aspirations and expectations of customers about the superior performance of their pension fund program. Finally, the conjoint results show that in the case of the non-financial attribute of socially responsible investing, customers prefer its first level. This implies that customers are in favor of an investment approach that also accounts for social and personal values and integrates corporate social responsibility criteria into pension fund investment styles.

Moreover, we calculated the pension fund attributes' relative importance, based on the range of the attributes' part-worth estimates (see Figure 7.1). Three financial attributes are the most

Table 7.2 Average part-worths (APWs) of pension fund attributes (N = 912)[a, b]

Attribute[a]	Level	APWs[c]
Financial Attributes		
Average Investment Performance[c]	4%	−0.223***
	7%	0.097***
	10%	0.126***
		(3)
Coverage ratio	90%	−0.324***
	105%	0.198***
	120%	0.127***
		(2)
Administrative Expenses	0.3%	0.042***
	0.9%	0.092***
	1.5%	−0.133***
		(2)
Total Investment Portfolio	< 500 million	−0.078***
	500 million–10 billion	0.043***
	> 10 billion	0.035***
		(2)
Non-Financial Attributes		
Socially Responsible Investing	Yes	0.106***
	No	−0.106***
		(1)

[a]Table 7.2 presents estimated part-worth results for the selected attributes that drive customers' overall utility of the pension fund's structural design (dependent variable) based on individual estimates. The levels that have a higher positive APW (value) are the most preferred ones.
[b]We tested the predictive validity for the individual part estimates by computing the Tucker coefficient in order to identify the degree of association between the predicted and the observed ratings of holdout pairs. The results showed that almost all individual part-worth predictive validity is satisfactory.
[c]A positive sign for the coefficient of an attribute indicates that this alternative is preferred (the highest in magnitude in case of 3 alternatives). For instance, for the coefficient of average investment performance, the 10% alternative is preferred to 7% and 4%.
***denotes *significance at $p < 0.001$*

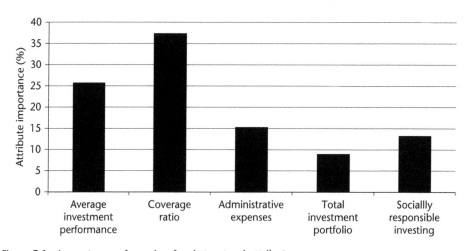

Figure 7.1 Importance of pension fund structural attributes

important. Customers attach high importance to the coverage ratio (37.0 percent), average past performance of the fund (25.7 percent), and administrative expenses (15.3 percent). The non-financial attribute of social responsibility is of moderate importance (12.2 percent) while the financial attribute of total investment portfolio has the lowest relative importance (9.0 percent).

These results indicate that customers consider the attributes regarding the fund's investment performance and ability to cover debt obligations with its assets as the most important attributes. The high importance that customers attach to the coverage ratio might be caused by the significant amount of media attention on this subject during the last few years (related to the 2008 financial crisis), as was mentioned by several pension experts. In addition, customers assign high importance to administrative expenses. This may be due to the fact that customers associate expenses and fund performance, which is also supported by several empirical studies (for example, Bikker and de Dreu 2006, Bauer et al. 2010). Customers are in favor of socially responsible investing while their strong preference for utilitarian outcomes is clear. These findings are in line with the notion that customers may derive non-pecuniary benefits from non-financial attributes and they are in favor of them only when their presence in a pension fund program does not lower their returns (Derwall et al. 2011). Finally, customers assign low importance to the total investment fund size because they may recognize that despite the advantages of economies of scale, large pension funds often tend to underperform due to liquidity limitations (Chen et al. 2004, Bauer et al. 2010). The ability to take advantage of larger economies of scale appears to depend on the governance structure of the fund. Andonov et al. (2011) conclude that the relationship between pension fund size and performance is not uniform and depends on the asset class and investment style.

Conclusions

A central finding in the relationship marketing literature is that the perceived quality of a product/service is the source of individual decision-makers' commitment (for example, Garbarino and Johnson 1999). Perceived quality can be conceptualized as the utility that customers derive from the services provided by a financial institution. The perceived quality will be high when customers believe that the financial service organization operates on behalf of their economic interests. In this chapter, we examined pension fund structural design based on a mixture of financial and non-financial attributes. To the best of our knowledge, the current study is the first one to empirically identify the relevance of these attributes for pension fund structural design from a customer perspective. The results show that customers desire mostly a pension fund program that has a high coverage ratio and average investment performance, a reasonable level of administrative expenses, a socially responsible investment style and a medium scale.

The findings of this study may have managerial implications for pension funds and other financial services organizations. For instance, the great importance that customers attach to coverage ratio and average investment performance of funds suggests that managers may concentrate their communications mainly on these two attributes. These two elements seem to substantially reinforce customers' commitment toward pension fund participation and willingness to contribute further to their enrolled plans. Such information may be used by managers when re-designing the structural features of a fund. Research in marketing and customer behavior shows the importance of the information revealed through individual preferences. Preferences are constructed, therefore, driven by variables that describe the decision context such as the competitive environment (Bettman et al. 1998, Pennings and Smidts 2003). Therefore, by relying on the revealed preferences of customers, fund managers may develop policies that satisfy the needs of customers and subsequently tailor services that are more preferred by customers than those offered by their competitors. This may solve issues related to customer retention and long-term solvency of fund providers.

The present study has some limitations and challenges that provide promising avenues for future research. For example, the findings are based on country-specific data. Although the policy trend and industry movement from defined benefit (DB) to defined contribution (DC) plans in the Dutch pension fund market have followed the pathway that US and several other western European pension systems have recently implemented, caution should be taken in generalizing these findings. Future research should account for specific decision context (for example, countries), characteristics and policy trends. In the context of the current study, we assumed homogeneity in customer behavior and did not account for behavioral variations across customer segments. Our sample characteristics show a variety of ages and financial literacy levels among our respondents and is therefore highly representative. Our analysis did not account for the fact that customers may make evaluative judgments about the selected attributes differently because of the diversity in their characteristics (for example, financial literacy) and other personality traits (for example, overconfidence). Future research should take into account customers' observed and unobserved (i.e., latent) heterogeneity. This is a challenging task, however; it means that one has to allow the average relative importance of attributes to differ across segments of customers.

Acknowledgments

We would like to express our special appreciation and thanks to the editors for their valuable comments and suggestions on an earlier version of this chapter. In addition, we would like to thank our MSc student assistants for helping with the data collection.

References

Al-Eisa, A.S. and Alhemoud, A.M. (2009). Using a Multiple-attribute Approach for Measuring Customer Satisfaction with Retail Banking Services in Kuwait. *International Journal of Bank Marketing*, 27(4), 294–314.

Anderson, E. and Narus, J.A. (1990). A Model of Distributor Firm and Manufacturer Firm Working Partnerships. *Journal of Marketing*, 54(1), 42–58.

Anderson, E. and Weitz, B. (1989). Determinants of Continuity in Conventional Industrial Dyads. *Marketing Science* 8(3), 310–23.

Andonov, A., Bauer, R.M.M.J. and Cremers, M.K.J. (2011). Can Large Pension Funds Beat the Market? Asset Allocation, Marketing Timing, Security Selection and the Limits of Liquidity, *ECCE Working Paper Series*. Retrieved from: papers.ssrn.com/sol3/papers.cfm?abstract_id=1885536&download=yes.

Athanassopoulos, A. (2000). Customer Satisfaction Cues to Support Market Segmentation and Explain Switching Behaviour. *Journal of Business Research*, 47(3), 191–207.

Avlonitis, G. J., Papastathopoulou, P. G. and Gounaris, S. P. (2001). An Empirically-based typology of product innovativeness for new financial services: Success and failure scenarios. *Journal of Product Innovation Management*, 18(5), 324–42.

Barber, B.M. and Odean, T. (2001). Boys will be Boys: Gender, Overconfidence and Common Stock Investment, *The Quarterly Journal of Economics*, 116 (1), 261–92.

Barberis, N. (2003). A Survey of Behavioural Finance. In Constantinides, G.M., Harris M. and Stulz, R. (Eds.), *Handbook of the Economics of Finance. Elsevier Science B.V.* 1051–1121.

Bateman, H. and Mitchell, O. S. (2004). New Evidence on Pension Plan Design and Administrative Expenses: The Australian Experience. *Journal of Pension Economics and Finance* 3, 63–76.

Bauer, R. and Smeets, P. (2012). 'Social Preferences and Investor Loyalty'. Working papers, European Centre of Corporate Engagement, Dept. of Finance, Maastricht University, the Netherlands.

Bauer, R., Hoevenaars, R. and Steenkamp, T. (2006). Asset Liability Management. In Clark, G., Munnel, A., Orszag, M., (Eds.), *The Oxford Handbook of Pensions and Retirement Income Oxford University Press*, 417–39.

Bauer, R.M.M.J., Cremers, M.K.J. and Frehen, R.G.P. (2010). 'Pension Fund Performance and Costs: Small is Beautiful'. Working paper, available at SSRN: Retrieved from: http://papers.ssrn.com/sol3/papers.cfm?abstract_id=965388

Benartzi, S. and Thaler, R.H. (2001). Naive Diversification Strategies in Defined Contribution Saving Plans. *American Economic Review*, 91(1), 79–98.

Bertrand, M., Mullainathan, S. and Shafir, E. (2006). Behavioural Economics and Marketing in Aid of Decision Making among the Poor. *Journal of Public Policy and Marketing*, 21(2), 8–23.

Bettman, R.J., Luce, M.F. and J.W. Payne (1998). Constructive Consumer Choice Processes. *Journal of Consumer Research*, 25(December), 187–217.

Bikker, J.A. and de Dreu, J. (2006). *Pension Fund Efficiency: The Impact of Scale, Governance and Plan Design*. DNB Working Paper, No. 109 / August 2006. Retrieved from www.jandedreu.nl/docs/DNB_WP_109.pdf

Bloemer, J., Ruyter, de K. and Peters, P. (1998). Investigating Drivers of Bank Loyalty: The Complex Relationship between Image, Service Quality and Satisfaction. *International Journal of Bank Marketing*, 16(7), 276–86.

Booz & Company. (2011). *2011 Financial Services Industry Perspective*, retrieved from www.booz.com/media/file/End_of_Year_Letter_2011_fs.pdf on March 13, 2014.

Burnham, T., Frels, J. and Mahajan, V. (2003). Consumer Switching Costs: A Typology, Antecedents and Consequences. *Journal of the Academy of Marketing Science*, 31(1), 109–26.

Carhart, M. (1997). On Persistence in Mutual Fund Performance, *Journal of Finance*, 51(5), 1681–1714.

Chen, J., Hong, H., Huang, M. and Kubik, J. (2004). Does Fund Size Erode Mutual Fund Performance? The Role of Liquidity and Organization. *American Economic Review* 94, 1276–1302.

Chernev, A. (2004). Goal-attribute Compatibility in Consumer Choice. *Journal of Consumer Psychology*, 14 (1/2), 141–50.

De Nederlandsche Bank (DNB) (2010). *Statistisch bulletin December 2010*. Retrieved on 8 January 2012 from www.dnb.nl/binaries/DNB%20sb%20dec_tcm46–244974.pdf

Derwall, J., Koedijk, K. and Ter Horst, J. (2011) A Tale of Values-driven and Profit-seeking Social Investors. *Journal of Banking & Finance*, 35, 2137–47.

Derwall, J., Guenster, N., Bauer, R. and Koedijk, K. (2005). The Eco-efficiency Premium Puzzle. *Financial Analysts Journal*, 61(2), 51–63.

Dwyer, R., Schurr, P. and Oh, S. (1987). Developing Buyer-Seller Relations. *Journal of Marketing*, 51(2), 11–28.

Dyck, A. and Pomorski, L. (2011). *Is Bigger Better? Size and Performance in Pension Plan Management*, Working Paper Rotman School of Management. Retrieved from www.rotman.utoronto.ca/pomorski/Is_Bigger_Better.pdf

Easingwood, C.J. and Mahajan, V. (1989). Positioning of Financial Services for Competitive Advantage. *Journal of Product Innovation Management*, 6(3), 207–19.

Eisenhardt, M.E. (1989). Building Theories fro Case Study Research. *The Academy of Management Review*, 14(4), 532–50.

Estelami, H. (2012). *Marketing Financial Services: Second Edition*. Indianapolis, IN: Dog Ear Publishing.

Fornell, C. (1992). A National Customer Satisfaction Barometer: The Swedish Experience. *Journal of Marketing*, 56(1), 6–21.

Garbarino, E. and Johnson, M.S. (1999). The Different Roles of Satisfaction, Trust, and Commitment in Customer Relationships. *Journal of Marketing*, 63(2), 70–87.

Gounaris (2003). S.P. Trust and Commitment Influences on Customer Retention: Insights from Business-to-Business Services. *Journal of Business*, 58(1), 126–40.

Gözbaþý, O. and Çýtak, L. (2010). An Evaluation of the Attributes Considered by Investment Professionals in Selecting Mutual Funds: The Case of Turkey. *International Research Journal of Finance and Economics* (36), 180–95.

Green, P.E. and Vithal, R.R. (1971) "Conjoint measurement for quantifying judgmental data." *Journal of Marketing research*: 355–363.

Green, P.H. and Srinivasan, V. (1990). Conjoint Analysis in Marketing: New Developments with Implications for Research and Practice. *Journal of Marketing*, 54(4): 3–19.

Gritten, A. (2011). New Insights into Consumer Confidence in Financial Services. *International Journal of Bank Marketing*, 29(2): 90–106.

Grinblatt, M. and Titman, S. (1992). The Persistence of Mutual Fund Performance. *Journal of Finance*, 47 (5), 1977–84.

Guiso, L., Sapienza, P. and Zingales, L. (2008). Trusting the Stock Market. *Journal of Finance*, 63(6), 2557–2600.

Gupta (2006). Pension Risk: Do Employees Care? *Pensions* 12(1), 4–11.

Gustafsson, A., Johnson, M.D. and Roos, I. (2005). The Effects of Customer Satisfaction, Relationship Commitment Dimensions, and Triggers on Customer Retention. *Journal of Marketing*, 69(4), 210–18.

Hair, J.F., Black, W.C., Babin, B.J. and Anderson, R.E. (2005). *Multivariate Data Analysis. A Global Perspective* (seventh edition). Pearson.

Heckman, J.J. (2001). Micro data, Heterogeneity, and the Evaluation of Public Policy. *Journal of Political Economy*, 109(94), 673–748.

Hirschman, E.C. and Holbrook, M.B. (1982). Hedonic Consumption: Emerging Concepts, Methods and Propositions. *Journal of Marketing*, 46(3), 92–101.

Hoffmann, A.O.I. and Broekhuizen, T.L.J. (2010). Understanding Investors' Decisions to Purchase Innovative Products: Drivers of Adoption Timing and Range. *International Journal of Research in Marketing*, 27(4), 342–55.

Hooper, V.J. (2001). *The Application of a Segmented Conjoint Methodology to International Capital Budgeting Decisions (Undated)*. Available at SSRN: http://ssrn.com/abstract=253759 or http://dx.doi.org/10.2139/ssrn.253759

Kalogeras, N. (2010). *Essays on Individual Decision Making*. The Netherlands: *Universitaire Pers Maastricht*.

Kalogeras, N., Pennings, J.M.E., van der Lans, I.A., Garcia, P. and Van Dijk, G. (2009). Understanding Heterogeneous Preferences of Cooperative Members, *Agribusiness: An International Journal*, 25(1), 90–111.

Khan, U., Dhar, R. and Wertenbroch, K (2004). A Behavioral Decision Theory Perspective on Hedonic and Utilitarian Choice. In *Inside Consumption: Frontiers of Research on Consumer Motives, Goals, and Desires* (Ed.) S. Ratneshwar & David Glen Mick, NY: Routledge 144–65.

Kreander, N., Gray, R.H., Power, D.M. and Sinclair, C.D. (2005). Evaluating the Performance of Ethical and Non-ethical Funds: A Matched Pair Analysis. *Journal of Business Finance and Accounting* 32(7), 1465–93.

Leek, S., Turnbull, P.J. and Naudé, P. (2002). Managing Business-to-Business Relationships: An Emerging Model. *Journal of Customer Behaviour*, 1(3), 357–75.

Loewenstein, G. (1992). The Fall and the Rise of Psychological Explanation in the Economics of Intertemporal Choice. In Lowenstein, G., Elster, J. (Eds.), *Choice Over Time*. NY: Russel Sage, 3–34.

Mäenpää, K., Kanto, A., Kuusela, H. and Pallab, P. (2006). More Hedonic versus Less Hedonic Consumption Behaviour in Advanced Internet Bank Services. *Journal of Financial Services Marketing*, 11(1), 4–16.

Mahr, D., Kalogeras, N. and Odekerken-Schröder, G. (2013). A Service Science Approach for Improving Healthy Food Experiences. *Journal of Service Management*, 24(4), 435–71.

Malhotra, N.K. and Birks, D.F. (2003). Marketing Research: An Applied Approach (2nd European edition). *Pearson Prentice Hall*.

Mercer, R. (2010). *Trends en Vergelijkingen Financiële Positie Pensioenfondsen (Trends in the Financials of Pension Funds)*. Retrieved on 8 January, 2012 from www.mercer.nl/articles/1391480

Millar, M. and Devonish, D. (2009). Attitudes, Savings Choices, Level of Knowledge and Investment Preferences of Employees toward Pensions and Retirement Planning: Survey Evidence from Barbados. *Pensions* 14(4), 299–317.

Moorman, C., Zaltman, G. and Deshpandé, R. (1992), "Relationships between Providers and Users of Market Research: The Dynamics of Trust within and Between Organizations," *Journal of Marketing Research*, 29(3), 314–28.

Moskowitz, H.R. and Krieger, B. (2001). Financial Products: Rapid, Iterative and Segmented Development by Conjoint Measurement and Self-authoring Iterative Procedures. *Journal of Financial Services Marketing*, 5(4), 343–55.

Nessmith, W.E., Utkus, S.P. and Young, J.A. (2007). *Measuring the Effectiveness of Automatic Enrollment*. Vanguard Center for Retirement Research, Volume 33.

Nilsson, J. (2009). Segmenting Socially Responsible Mutual Fund Investors: The Influence of Financial Return and Social Responsibility. *International Journal of Bank Marketing*, Vol. 27(1), 5–31.

Nilsson, J., Nordvall, A-C. and Isberg, S. (2010). The Information Search Process of Socially Responsible Investors. *Journal of Financial Services Marketing*, 15(1), 5–18.

Pennings, J.M.E. and Smidts, A. (2003). The Shape of Utility Functions and Organizational Behaviour. *Management Science*, 49(9), 1251–63.

Poterba, J.M., Venti, S.F. and Wise D.A. (2008). The Changing Landscape of Pensions in the United States. In *Overcoming the Saving Slump: How to Increase the Effectiveness of Financial Education and Saving Programs*, (Ed.) Lusardi, A., Chicago: University of Chicago Press, 17–46.

Ramasamy, B. and Yeung, M.C.H. (2003). "Evaluating mutual funds in an emerging market: factors that matter to financial advisors", *International Journal of Bank Marketing*, Vol. 21 Iss: 3, 122–36.

Renneboog, L., ter Horst and Zhang, C. (2011). Is Ethical Money Financially Smart? Nonfinancial Attributes and Money Flows of Socially Responsible Investment Funds. *Journal of Financial Intermediation*, 20(4), 562–88.

Richardson Agnew, J. (2010). Pension Participant Behaviour. In *Behavioural Finance, Investor, Corporations and Markets*, (Eds.) Baker, H. K. and Nofsinger, J.R., Hoboken, NJ: John Wiley & Sons Inc. 577–94.

Rooij, van M.C.J., Kool, C.J.M. and Prast, H.M. (2007). Risk-return Preferences in the Pension Domain: Are People Able to choose? *Journal of Public Economics*, 91(4): 701–22.

Sapp, T. and Tiwari, A. (2004). Does Stock Return Momentum Explain the Smart Money Effect? *Journal of Finance*, 59, 2605–22.

Sharma, N. and Patterson, P. (2000). Switching Costs, Alternative Attractiveness and Experience as Moderators of Relationship Commitment in Professional Consumer Services. *International Journal of Service Industry Management*, 11(5), 470–90.

Siegmann, A. (2010). Minimum Coverage Ratios for Defined-Benefit Pension Funds. *Journal of Pension Economics and Finance*, 10(3): 417–34.

Simonson, I. and Tversky, A. (1992). Choice in Context: Tradeoff Contrast and Extremeness Aversion. *Journal of Marketing Research* 29(3), 281–95.

Siskos Y. and Grigoroudis, E. (2002). Measuring Customer Satisfaction for Various Services Using Multicriteria Analysis. In D. Bouyssou, E. Jacquet-Lagrèze, P. Perny, R. Slowinski, D. Vanderpooten and P. Vincke, (Eds.), *Aiding Decisions with Multiple Criteria: Essays in Honor of Bernard Roy*, Kluwer Academic Publishers, Dordrecht, 457–82.

Smith, V.L. (2003). Constructivist and Ecological Rationality in Economics. *American Economic Review*, 93(3), 465–508.

Society of Actuaries (2004). Retirement Plan Preference Survey: Report of Findings. *Mathew Greenwald & Associates, Inc.*

Srinivas, P.S. Whitehouse, E. and Yermo, J. (2000). *Regulating Pension Funds, Structure, Perfromance and Invstments: A Cross-Country Evidence*. Washington D.C., *World Bank Social Protection Unit. Human Development Network*, paper 00/7, July 2000.

Strahilevitz, M.A. and Myers, J.G. (1998). Donations to Charity as Purchase Incentives: How Well They Work May Depend on What You Are Trying to Sell. *Journal of Consumer Research* 24, 434–46.

Tapia, W. (2008). Comparing Aggregate Investment Returns in Privately Managed Pension Funds. *OECD Working paper on Insurance and Private Pensions 22*. OECD, Paris.

Thaler, R.H. and Sunstein, C.R. (2003). Libertarian Paternalism. *American Economic Review*, 93(2): 175–79.

—— (2008). *Nudge: Improving Decisions about Health, Wealth, and Happiness*. Yale University Press.

Verhoef, P.C. and Pennings, J.M.E. (2012). The Marketing Finance Interface: An Organizational Perspective. In *The Handbook of Marketing and Finance*, Ganesan, S. and S. Bharadwaj (Eds.), Edward Elgar Publishing, 225–43.

Vyvyan, V., Ng, C. and Brimble, M. (2007). Socially Responsible Investing: The Green Attitudes and Grey Choices of Australian Investors. *Corporate Governance*, 15(2), 370–318.

Wilcox, R.T. (2003). Bargain Hunting or Star Gazing? Investor's Preferences for Stock Market Mutual Funds, *Journal of Business*, 76(4): 645–63.

Worcester, R.M. (1997), "Managing the Image of your Bank: the Glue that Binds", *International Journal of Bank Marketing*, 15(5), 146–52.

Zinkhan, F.C. and Zinkhan, G.M. (1994). An Application of Conjoint Analysis to Capital Budgeting: The Case of Innovative Land Management Systems, *Managerial Finance*, 20(7): 37–50.

8

Mutual fund investors' knowledge calibration and behavioral biases

Sanjay Kumar Mishra and Manoj Kumar

Introduction

The investment decision-making process of mutual fund investors (simply referred to as "investors") is irrational and biased because investors make investment decisions under certain constraints (Montier 2002). These constraints may be associated with the investor, such as their limited capability and commitment or come from the external environment, such as having access to limited information (Kornov and Thissen 2000, Simon 1990). Such constraints, directly or indirectly, are likely to impact the knowledge structure of investors by influencing their calibration of self-knowledge (Alba and Hutchinson 2000). Knowledge calibration refers to the correspondence between objective knowledge and subjective assessment of self-knowledge (Pillai and Hofacker 2007). Where the correspondence between objective knowledge and the subjective assessment of self-knowledge is high, the individual is described as well-calibrated, but poor correspondence implies miscalibration of self-knowledge. The empirical evidence suggests that miscalibration due to overconfidence in one's self-knowledge is a prevalent phenomenon and is recognized to be a stylized fact of the human cognition (Alba and Hutchinson 2000).

A clear understanding of knowledge miscalibration among investors is important to policy-makers and mutual fund (MF) managers. Knowledge miscalibration among investors lowers their financial capabilities (Dolan et al. 2012a) and may lead them to take inappropriate investment decisions due to irrationality and behavioral biases in their investment decision-making process. Therefore, policy-makers need to understand knowledge miscalibration prevalent among investors so as to plan policy interventions, which are directed at inculcating rational investment decision-making among investors. Similarly, MF managers need to understand knowledge miscalibration prevalent among investors so as to design appropriate MF products and effectively market them to suitable investors.

In spite of this, we have limited insights into the causes, manifestation and consequences of knowledge miscalibration. These insights are available from existing studies dispersed across multiple domains of literature, for example, psychology, consumer behavior and behavioral finance. So far, little effort has been made to synthesize these dispersed insights about knowledge miscalibration into meaningful implications for policy-makers and mutual fund managers.

The broad objective of this chapter is to provide a theoretical framework of knowledge calibration and behavioral biases among mutual fund investors. Specifically, the chapter answers the following questions: (1) What may lead to knowledge miscalibration among MF investors? (2) How does knowledge miscalibration manifest itself in the behavior of MF investors? (3) How does knowledge miscalibration influence the investment decision-making process of MF investors? (4) How does knowledge miscalibration influence the financial capability of MF investors? (5) What are the possible interventions that policy-makers and MF managers can make to favorably influence the decision of MF investors?

The rest of this chapter is organized as follows. First, the concept and causes of knowledge miscalibration among MF investors are explored. This is followed by a discussion of the manifestation of knowledge miscalibration in the behavior of MF investors. Then the influence of knowledge miscalibration on the investment decision-making process of mutual fund investors is discussed. In the next section, the influence of knowledge miscalibration on the financial capability of MF investors is summarized. In the penultimate section, the possible interventions that can be made by policy-makers and MF managers to favorably influence the decision of MF investors are suggested. Finally, the chapter concludes with a discussion of the possible directions for future research.

Concept of knowledge miscalibration among MF investors and its causes

Knowledge calibration refers to the correspondence between knowledge accuracy and the confidence with which knowledge is held (Pillai and Hofacker 2007). In the behavioral finance literature: (1) knowledge accuracy is determined by measuring the investor's objective knowledge (OK), i.e. the actual knowledge possessed by the investor (Mishra and Kumar 2011), (2) the confidence with which knowledge is held is determined by measuring the investor's subjective knowledge (SK), i.e. the investor's own perception of their knowledge (Mishra and Kumar 2011), (3) knowledge calibration is measured as the absolute difference between objective and subjective knowledge (Alba and Hutchinson 2000).

Investors who possess accurate knowledge regarding an investment product (high OK) and who are also highly confident in their knowledge (high SK) can be said to be well-calibrated; high OK with high SK leads to proper calibration of self-knowledge. An investor can be well-calibrated even when they possess inaccurate knowledge, but are realistic in their assessment of the low level of knowledge that they possess; low OK with low SK also leads to high calibration. Miscalibration results from the lack of correspondence between OK and SK. A low OK with a high SK leads to miscalibration arising from overconfidence. A high OK with a low SK leads to miscalibration arising from underconfidence (Pillai and Hofacker 2007). Figure 8.1 depicts this relationship between "objective knowledge", "subjective knowledge" and "calibration" within a 2 by 2 matrix.

Knowledge miscalibration arising from overconfidence or underconfidence may be enduring or situational in nature. The former reflects the permanent miscalibration of knowledge, whereas the latter reflects the miscalibration with respect to a specific investment situation. Empirical evidence suggests that generally a positive correlation exists between enduring miscalibration and situational miscalibration (West and Stanovich 1997). However, specific investment situations may trigger either a shift from enduring miscalibration toward improved calibration (Subbotin 1996) or a switch (from underconfidence to overconfidence or from overconfidence to underconfidence) (Plous 1995) depending upon the specific investment situation. For example, mutual fund investors, who are generally underconfident (enduring miscalibration)

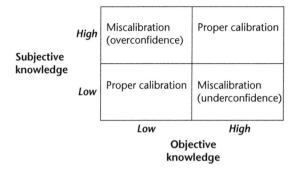

Figure 8.1 Subjective knowledge, objective knowledge and calibration matrix
Source: Pillai and Hofacker (2007). Reproduced with permission from Elsevier.

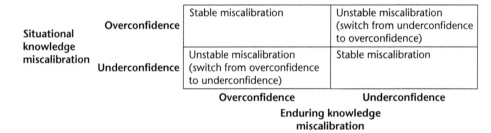

Figure 8.2 Interaction outcomes of enduring miscalibration and situational miscalibration for an individual MF investor

Source: Reprinted from The Lancet. Kishore Gopalakrishna Pillai and Charles Hofacker (2007) Calibration of consumer knowledge of the web. *International Journal of Research in Marketing* 18 Sep 2013, 24(3): 254–267. Reproduced with permission from Elsevier.

while making their decision individually (individual task) may become overconfident (situational miscalibration) when the same investment decision is being made in a group (Plous 1995). Figure 8.2 depicts the interaction between "enduring miscalibration" and "situational miscalibration" within a 2 by 2 matrix.

The literature on calibration suggests that (1) overconfidence is a prevalent phenomenon (Alba and Hutchinson 2000), (2) calibration may differ across individuals even when they belong to the same group, (3) certain groups/professionals (for example, weather forecasters and odds-makers[1]) are consistently better calibrated than others (for example, doctors) (Montier 2002). Researchers have offered several explanations for observed variability in calibration across individuals and across groups. The variability in calibration among individuals belonging to the same group may arise from differences in their cognitive abilities, personality variables and demographic variables (Winter 2003). However, the research on the exact nature of influence of these variables on an individual's knowledge calibration has so far not satisfactorily evolved.

Receiving immediate, regular and unambiguous feedback following a judgment (which enables validation and correction) consistently improves calibration (Montier 2002). For example, weather forecasters and odds-makers receive immediate, unambiguous feedback, which enables validation and correction, facilitating high calibration for both the groups. Calibration differences across professions arise due to the differences in their payoff matrix or loss functions

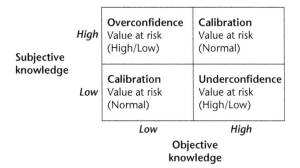

Figure 8.3 Subjective knowledge, objective knowledge and payoff matrix (value at risk) associated with calibration

(Pillai and Hofacker 2007). For example, doctors perceive the penalty for false negative as more devastating and therefore state their opinion with excessive conviction (i.e. confidence displayed is higher than the actual level of confidence) (Keren 1991). Figure 8.3 depicts the conjectured relationship between the "pay-offs" and possible "knowledge calibration" outcomes within a 2 by 2 matrix.

Knowledge miscalibration among mutual fund investors may mainly arise due to: (1) the characteristics of the product itself, (2) the characteristics of individual mutual fund investors, (3) the characteristics of the market, (4) situational factors. First, mutual funds are high credence products (Brady and Bourdeau 2005) wherein the investor has to predict the unknown realization of the market outcome at the time of investment; hence the investors are unlikely to receive regular and unambiguous feedback following the investment decision to enable them to calibrate their decision (Ronis and Yates 1987). Second, the existence of wide heterogeneity among individual mutual fund investors in terms of their cognitive abilities, personality characteristics and demographics is likely to distinctly influence the correspondence between subjective knowledge and objective knowledge (Spence 1996). Third, due to the existence of the sheer amount of information about mutual funds, which, though abundant, is often not organized and comprehensible (Mishra and Kumar 2011), investment in mutual funds is a complex decision process. Hence, calibration of knowledge is key to allowing investors to cope with incomplete but often abundant and imperfect information during their decision-making process. However, the difficulty of the task is likely to make investors prone to knowledge miscalibration (Fischhoff et al. 1977). Fourth, situational effects in decision-making are also likely to influence the calibration of knowledge (situational miscalibration). Gilovich et al. (1993) demonstrated that people tend to lose confidence in their prospects for success the closer they get to the moment of truth. Therefore, certain situational factors such as the complexity of task, payoff (outcome) associated with the task, individual versus group task, urgency of the task and peer pressure, etc., may influence the knowledge calibration of individual mutual fund investors.

Manifestation of knowledge miscalibration in the behavior of MF investors

Knowledge miscalibration may manifest itself in the form of numerous behavioral biases during the investment decision-making process of investors (Chiou et al. 2002). Table 8.1 summarizes the behavioral biases that mutual fund investors will be subjected to in the event that they are overconfident or underconfident during the investment decision-making process.

Table 8.1 Manifestation of knowledge miscalibration amongst investors

Miscalibration	Behavioural biases	Description	Source
1. Overconfidence	Self attribution bias	Self attribution bias refers to situations where good outcomes are attributed to skills, whilst bad outcomes are attributed to bad luck.	Gervais and Odean 2001
	Hindsight bias	Hindsight bias is the tendency of people to believe, after an event has occurred, that they predicted it before it happened. If people think they predicted the past better than they actually did, they may also believe that they can predict the future better than they actually can.	Barberis and Thaler 2003
	Confirmation bias	Confirmation bias refers to the desire to find information that agrees with one's existing view.	Montier 2002
	Illusion of control	A psychological error where an individual feels in control of a situation far more often than they are.	Montier 2002
	Unique invulnerability	The belief that "negative events and misfortunes will not happen to you".	Bodner et al. 2000
	Sensation seeking	A trait defined by the seeking of varied, novel, complex and intense sensations and experiences, and willingness to take financial risk for the sake of such experience.	Zuckerman 1994
2. Underconfidence	Illusion of risk shifting	A psychological error where an individual seeks risk avoidance by shifting the onus of decisions onto others even though the payoff associated with the poor decision is to be borne by the individual.	Mishra and Kumar 2012b
	Loss aversion	The disutility of giving up an object is greater than the utility associated with acquiring it. Hence the value function is concave for gains and convex for losses.	Kahneman et al. 1991
	Conservatism bias	A tendency to cling tenaciously to a view. Once the position has been stated most people find it very hard to move away from that view.	Montier 2002
	Ambiguity aversion	A behavioral bias where people are exceptionally afraid of financial situations involving ambiguity.	Montier 2002

Overconfidence among investors is prevalent and may manifest itself in the form of behavioral biases, for example, self-attribution bias (Barberis and Thaler 2003), hindsight bias (Barberis and Thaler 2003), confirmation bias (Montier 2002), illusion of control (Montier 2002), unique vulnerability (Bodner et al. 2000) and sensation seeking (Zuckerman 1994). Table 8.1 provides an explanation of each of these behavioral biases.

Overconfident investors are likely to: (1) attribute good performance of their investment portfolio to their own skills and bad performance of their investment portfolio to their bad luck (self-attribution bias), (2) exaggerate their ability to predict the macro/micro environment and financial market that impacts the future performance of their current investment portfolio (hindsight bias), (3) exaggerate their ability to control the factors that will influence the future performance of the current investment portfolio (illusion of control), (4) feel that their investment portfolio contains no unique risk (unique vulnerability), (5) seek information related to macro/micro environment and mutual fund attributes that confirms their view related to future risk and return associated with specific MF schemes (or portfolio) (confirmation bias), (6) seek pleasure by the fact that mutual fund investment is subject to market risk (sensation seeking).

Under-confidence among investors may manifest itself in the form of illusion of risk shifting (Mishra and Kumar 2011), loss aversion (Kahneman et al. 1991), conservatism bias (Montier 2002) and ambiguity aversion (Montier 2002). Table 8.1 provides an explanation of each of these behavioral biases.

Underconfident investors are likely to: (1) seek MF schemes with a predictable risk/return profile (for example, preference for index funds over active equity funds) (ambiguity aversion and illusion of risk shifting) and (2) assign more weight to downside risk in comparison to the upside return of the investment portfolio (for example, will have a preference for gilt funds over equity funds) (loss aversion and conservatism).

Though the interaction effect of these behavioral biases (i.e. multiplicative, additive or hierarchical) has not been empirically validated, it is expected that overconfident investors are likely to overestimate their knowledge, understate the risk, and exaggerate their ability to control the outcome of their investment decisions, and underconfident investors are likely to underestimate their knowledge, overstate the risk and avoid ambiguity (Montier 2002).

Knowledge miscalibration and the investment decision-making process of MF investors

In behavioral finance, the investment decision-making process has frequently been modeled as a multiple stage process: problem recognition, search for information, processing of information, choice of alternatives, purchase of the investment product and post purchase behavior (Mishra and Kumar 2012a). Considerable research on knowledge miscalibration has focused on various stages of the investment decision-making process, for example, information search behavior (Alba and Hutchinson, 2000), information processing behavior (Bloomfield et al. 2000, Fischhoff et al. 1977) and post purchase behavior (Barber and Odean 2000) of investors. It has been revealed that the investment decision-making process of mutual fund investors is likely to be distinctly influenced by knowledge miscalibration, and the influence of overconfidence on the investment decision-making process is likely to be distinct compared to that of underconfidence. Table 8.2 summarizes the influence of knowledge miscalibration on the investment decision-making process of mutual fund investors.

During the problem recognition stage, the stimuli among overconfident investors may stem from within, whereas stimuli among underconfident investors may come from

Table 8.2 Influence of knowledge miscalibration (overconfidence and underconfidence) on the investment decision making process of investors

Stages of Investment Decision Making Process	Overconfidence	Underconfidence	Source
Problem recognition	Stimuli may come mostly from within as this category of investors overreact to private information and under react to public information.	Stimuli may come from traditional or online marketing communication.	Daniel et al. 1998
Evoked set	Small	Large	Gronhaug 1973
Information search behavior	Inhibits information search.	Increases information search.	Alba and Hutchinson 2000
Information processing strategy	(1) Gives very high weight to highly unreliable attribute information. (2) Investors may not use adequate inference processing method. (3) Heavily rely on memory (prior experience) to support one of the possible answers.	(1) Gives very low weight to highly reliable attribute information. (2) Investors may not use adequate inference processing method. (3) Shifts the decision task onto others and susceptible to sales pressure.	Bloomfield et al. 2000, Fischhoff et al. 1977, Mishra and Kumar 2011
Selection	(1) Buy funds with high fees. (2) Chases past returns. (3) Invests in poorly diversified high risk portfolio. (4) Focus on actively managed funds.	(1) May hold index funds charging high fees. (2) Holds high front end load funds. (3) Preference for home bias.	Bailey et al. 2011, Elton et al. 2006
Regret aversion	High due to high extent of cognitive dissonance.	Low	Barber and Odean 2000
Switching behavior	More than what can be justified on rational grounds.	Low	Coval and Stafford 2007

traditional or online marketing communication of mutual fund companies. This is due to the fact that the overconfident investor is likely to overreact to private information and under react to public information (Daniel et al. 1998). The evoked set (i.e. the number of alternative mutual funds that are considered by an investor during the investment decision-making process) for the overconfident investor is smaller compared to that of the underconfident investor (Gronhaug 1973).

The goal of information search is usually to reduce uncertainty. Overconfidence among mutual fund investors is likely to inhibit information search and underconfidence will increase search (Alba and Hutchinson 2000); overconfident investors are likely to access fewer information sources as compared to underconfident investors (Jacoby et al. 2001) and are likely to rely more on internal search (i.e. memory and previous experience) than external search.

The miscalibration among investors, due to their inability to use an adequate inference processing method (Fischhoff et al. 1977), is likely to influence the way overconfident and underconfident investors process their information (Bloomfield et al. 2000). Overconfident investors are likely to give very high weight to highly unreliable attribute information (Bloomfield et al. 2000) such as mutual fund historical performance (Goetzmann and Peles 1997) and will rely heavily on memory (prior experience) to make their investment decisions. Underconfident investors will have a tendency to give very low weight to highly reliable information such as mutual fund fee (Sharpe 1996) and will seek others' advice to make their investment decisions. Therefore, due to knowledge miscalibration, overconfident investors behave irrationally and are likely to: (1) buy a fund with high fees, (2) chase past returns, (3) remain poorly diversified with a large loading on market risk and (4) focus on actively managed funds (Bailey et al. 2011). On the other hand, due to knowledge miscalibration, underconfident investors also behave irrationally and are likely to: (1) hold an index fund with high fees (Elton et al. 2006), (2) hold high front end load funds (Bailey et al. 2011) and (3) have a home bias[2] in their investment behavior (Bailey et al. 2011).

The post purchase behavior of mutual fund investors is likely to consist of post purchase satisfaction/regret and switching behavior. Overconfident investors will have a tendency for regret avoidance as they are likely to have an incredible degree of self-denial (Montier 2002). Hence, they are likely to face a high extent of cognitive dissonance (Barber and Odean 2000). Underconfident investors are less likely to be subject to post purchase regret due to their "illusion of risk shifting" (Mishra and Kumar 2012b), i.e. they will be subjected to the psychological error (illusion) that by shifting the onus for the decision onto others they have been able to shift the payoff associated with the poor decision onto others.

Researchers have widely discussed the trading behavior of overconfident investors (Coval and Stafford 2007). They have suggested that overconfident investors may self-attribute past good performance to themselves even though the performance of the investment was due to the overall market performance (Coval and Stafford 2007) and may overestimate the precision of their private information and eventually put too much weight on this information (Puetz and Ruenzi 2011). It is likely that overconfident mutual fund investors will have a higher tendency to switch among funds compared to a calibrated investor. Barber and Odean (2001) found that in their sample, men traded 45 percent more than women. They attributed this behavior to overconfidence among male investors. The switching behavior of underconfident investors is more likely to be driven by others' advice rather than self-assessment of their investment portfolio (Mishra and Kumar 2011).

Knowledge miscalibration and the "financial capability" of MF investors

Financial capability involves the knowledge and skill that it takes to make investment decisions to promote one's own long-term interests. Research papers and policy across the globe suggest that many individuals do not possess "sufficient" levels of financial capability (FSA 2008). Chapter 3, by Huhmann, discusses financial literacy and capability in detail. The behavioral finance literature suggests that the factors limiting one's financial capability are the lack of information and knowledge required to process the information and the prevalence of behavioral biases among individuals (FSA 2008). The second of these factors offers a predominant explanation for the prevalence of low levels of financial capability (Mandell 2004).

The behavioral finance literature suggests that knowledge miscalibration among MF investors is likely to lower their extent of financial vigilance and suppress contingency financial planning by them (Alba and Hutchinson 2000). Such impact of knowledge miscalibration is likely to influence significantly various aspects of their financial capability (Atkinson et al. 2006).

Table 8.3 Comparison of financial capability of calibrated and miscalibrated individual mutual fund investor

Aspects of financial capability*	Calibrated individual MF investor	Miscalibrated individual MF investor	Author
Keeping track	(1) Adequately track the performance of investment portfolio. (2) Reasonably estimate their accuracy of information related to investment portfolio.	(1) Inadequately track the performance of investment portfolio. (2) Overestimate/ underestimate their accuracy of information related to their investment portfolio.	Alba and Hutchinson 2000, Vallone et al. 1990
Meeting end needs	More likely to meet financial commitments.	Less likely to meet financial commitments.	Alba and Hutchinson 2000, Vallone et al. 1990
Planning ahead	(1) Reasonably estimate their preparedness to meet financial distress. (2) Reasonable level of preparedness to meet financial distress.	(1) Overestimate their preparedness to meet financial distress. (2) Low level of preparedness to meet financial distress.	
Choosing products	(1) Rely on the mix of internal search (memory) and external search. (2) Gives adequate weight to relevant attribute information.	(1) Biased towards internal search or external search. (2) Gives underweight/ overweight to relevant/ irrelevant attribute information.	Bloomfield et al. 2000
Staying informed	Reasonably estimate their informational preparedness to make informed choice.	Overestimate their informational preparedness to make informed choice.	Alba and Hutchinson 2000, Ganzach and Krantz 1991

*Source: Adapted from Atkinson et al. (2006).

Thus, financial capability of a miscalibrated MF investor is unlikely to be in line with what is expected of a rational mutual fund investor. Table 8.3 compares the financial capability of calibrated and miscalibrated mutual fund investors.

Implications for policy-makers

Knowledge miscalibration is likely to lead to a behavior distinct from what is anticipated using the traditional Mean Variance Model of Markowitz (1952). According to the traditional model, investors are assumed to be rational utility maximizers who consider expected return and risk of the investing avenues as the only crucial variables while making their investment decisions (Sharpe 1994, Tobin 1965). However, miscalibrated investors take irrational financial decisions and have lower financial capabilities (Dolan et al. 2012a). This in turn is likely to have an adverse impact on the performance of their investment portfolios (Bailey et al. 2011, Dolan et al. 2012a). Therefore, regulatory interventions are to be planned to inculcate rationality in the investors' investment decision-making process. Such interventions should focus on improving the investors' financial capability and minimizing their behavioral biases by reducing their knowledge and information constraints.

In India, the Security and Exchange Board of India (SEBI), the securities markets regulator, conducts investor education and awareness workshops directly, as well as through investor associations and market participants and also encourages market participants to conduct such workshops independently. The objective of such workshops is to change the minds (i.e. to reduce the level of miscalibration) of investors consistent with the standard economic model and theory of planned behavior (i.e. beliefs are likely to influence behavior) (Dolan et al. 2012a). Such workshops are mostly unsolicited from the perspective of investors and information and knowledge centric. Despite the wide acknowledgment of the importance of knowledge and information centric interventions in academic literature (NCAER 2011, Thaler and Sunstein 2008), the success of the workshops is limited due to the fact that: (1) unsolicited advice or imposed support is sometimes perceived as intrusive (Deelstra et al. 2003) and may not meet the desired objective of the program; (2) overconfident investors, due to their inherent characteristics, are unlikely to solicit advice (Meier and Sprenger 2008) and (3) behavioral biases are prevalent among investors (FSA 2008, Mandell 2004), which may impose a limit on the relevance of such workshops. The effectiveness of such workshops can be enhanced by conducting behavioral training during the programs that brings awareness of the over-/underconfidence among investors and help them behave in a way that improves their investment performance. For example, a passive index fund may be an appropriate investment option for overconfident investors to address their tendency to "trade and switch" more than the desired level.

The interventions to change the minds of investors need to be complemented by a change in the context (environment and situation) that limits the negative impact of knowledge miscalibration on financial capability of investors. Lessons from behavioral finance suggest that changing contexts can have a powerful effect on behavior (Dolan et al. 2012a). The irrationality in the behavior of the investor can be reduced through changes in the environment and how choices are presented to the investor (i.e. choice architecture) (Thaler and Sunstein 2008).

With ever-evolving information and communication technologies, scaling up of the interventions to change the context is becoming easy. A few such policy interventions in India include the use of default options to influence judgment and changing the incentive structure (Dolan et al. 2012a). Appropriate design of default options is likely to improve the financial capability of investors by influencing their choice architecture and focusing on more automatic processes of judgment and influence (Dolan et al. 2012a). In India, investors in the New Pension Scheme (NPS) are offered two investment choices during subscription to the scheme (i.e. active choice and auto choice). The default option (auto choice) offered is the "life cycle fund" where reallocation among asset classes is made, taking into consideration the life cycle stage of the investor. The objective of the default option in NPS is directed toward improving financial capability of the pension fund investor (those with knowledge and information constraints) through change in the context (i.e. designing default option). Similar policy interventions have been successfully applied in other countries (Madrian and Shea 2001) to influence the financial behavior of investors.

Another intervention designed by SEBI in India focuses on empowering mutual fund investors through transparency in payment and load commission and load structure (NCAER 2011). Reforms in the mutual fund industry in India have abolished the prevalence of entry load for all mutual fund schemes and investors are now allowed to pay commission separately to agents/advisors commensurate with the service provided to them (NCAER 2011). By changing the incentive structure, SEBI is intentionally promoting solicited/paid advice to investors, which is generally perceived as more helpful than unsolicited/unpaid advice (Deelstra et al. 2003).

Similar policy interventions have been also evident in other countries such as the UK (Collinson 2012) and Australia (Bowen 2011).

Dolan et al. (2012b) proposed other similar techniques under the mnemonic MINDSPACE that represent nine effects on the behavior operating largely on the automatic system: messenger, incentives, norms, defaults, salience, priming, affect, commitment and ego (Dolan et al. 2012a: 129). Policy-makers interested in improving the financial capability can explore the utility of similar influence techniques.

Implications for mutual fund managers

Based on calibration of self-knowledge by investors, mutual fund managers can classify them into the following four clusters (Bailey et al. 2011): overconfident, calibrated (high), calibrated (low) and underconfident. This allows them to design suitable interventions for each of the clusters. The extent of sensitivity of each cluster is likely to be significantly different with respect to fee, load, performance, liquidity and specific investment strategy. For example, Christoffersen and Musto (2002) found that money market mutual funds appear to raise fees to exploit over-confident investors who are insensitive to fees. However, not much empirical evidence exists with reference to the sensitivity of each cluster to the fundamental attributes of the mutual fund schemes. This is an interesting area in which future research studies can be planned.

Mutual fund managers may influence the behavior of miscalibrated investors by focusing on contextual changes. This approach is based on the proposition that knowledge miscalibration may lead investors to behave irrationally during their investment decision-making process. Therefore, the focus should be more on "changing behavior" without "changing the mind" (Dolan et al. 2012a). By focusing on change in the environment or choice architecture within the framework of MINDSPACE, MF managers can significantly influence the behavior of miscalibrated investors.

Evidence related to certain anomalies in the mutual fund market, such as persistence of low performing mutual funds (Harless and Peterson 1998) and preference for active funds over passive index funds (Lichtenstein et al. 1999) provide preliminary evidence that mutual fund managers are successfully able to influence the behavior of miscalibrated investors by focusing on motivation other than past risk adjusted returns (Harless and Peterson 1998). A few empirical studies conducted on the persistence of low-performing mutual funds suggest that funds with low performance face less elastic demand as they do not compete for performance sensitive sophisticated customers (Gil-Bazo and Ruiz-Verdu 2009) who have also been found to be better calibrated (Gort et al. 2008, Russo and Schoemaker 1992) and are likely to target unsophisticated (miscalibrated) investors, and low performance funds aggressively use influence techniques (elements of MINDSPACE) such as messenger and norms (depends more on the peer system and brokerage for their sales), incentive (offers more brokerage to brokers) (Gil-Bazo and Ruiz-Verdu 2009), which puts more effort on marketing (salience and priming) (Gil-Bazo and Ruiz-Verdu 2009) to consistently maintain the flow of funds.

Investors' preference for active funds over passive index funds (Lichtenstein et al. 1999), inspite of the fact that it is extremely difficult for active funds to achieve above market return over time (Malkiel 1995), suggests that mutual fund managers are successfully using influence techniques similar to that of low-performance funds to promote equity funds (mutual fund companies preference for active equity funds over passive index funds is clearly evident from the ratio of indexed funds to managed equity funds, which is extremely low in India and elsewhere in the world) among miscalibrated investors (Bailey et al. 2011).

Conclusion

Knowledge miscalibration may manifest itself in the form of numerous behavioral biases that are likely to lead to irrationality in the behavior of mutual fund investors during their investment decision-making processes (Chiou et al. 2002) and may adversely impact their financial capability (Mandell 2004). The rational mutual fund manager needs to take into consideration such behavioral biases of investors in order to design suitable MF products and to effectively market those schemes to investors. This chapter reflects on the evidence from earlier related work to provide a theoretical framework of knowledge calibration and behavioral biases among mutual fund investors.

Inspite of the evidence that miscalibration among investors is relatively stable (i.e. enduring miscalibration) (West and Stanovich 1997), specific investment situations may trigger a shift from enduring miscalibration (Plous 1995). This shift may be either toward improved calibration (Subbotin 1996) or switch (Plous 1995). An understanding of specific investment situations that lead to a shift from enduring miscalibration toward improved calibration has significant value for policy-makers in drawing strategies for changing behavior without changing the minds of MF investors. Future researchers may contribute toward this significant area of research. Insights are also needed to understand the process through which enduring and situational miscalibration combine to affect mutual fund investor behavior. However, this requires an understanding of the determinants of enduring and situational miscalibration. In addition to this, studies also need to investigate the situation in which preexisting levels of enduring miscalibration magnify or suppress situational miscalibration.

The discussion in the earlier sections of this chapter suggests that due to knowledge miscalibration, investors behave irrationally (Bailey et al. 2011). These irrationalities are distinctly evident in the behavior of overconfident and underconfident investors (Bailey et al. 2011, Elton et al. 2006). However, there is a dearth of literature quantifying the degree of this irrationality in the behavior of miscalibrated MF investors such as the degree of home biasness among underconfident investors (Bailey et al. 2011), poorly diversified investment portfolios of overconfident investors (Bailey et al. 2011) and other similar non-rational behavior. Further insights in these unexplored areas of research may be of significant value to policy-makers, regulators and the MF industry across the globe.

The preliminary evidence suggests that influence techniques (such as MINDSPACE) can be more effectively used on miscalibrated investors than calibrated investors and some of the elements are being used by regulators, policy-makers and mutual fund managers to influence the behavior of investors. However, the effectiveness of these influence techniques with respect to their intended purpose has not been well documented. Further research is needed to validate the effectiveness of these influence techniques among miscalibrated investors.

Finally, based on the calibration of knowledge, mutual fund managers can classify investors into the following four clusters (Bailey et al. 2011): overconfident, calibrated (high), calibrated (low) and underconfident. This allows them to design suitable interventions for each of the clusters as the extent of sensitivity of each cluster is likely to be significantly different with respect to fee, load, performance, liquidity and specific investment strategy, and the effectiveness of the influence techniques used by the mutual fund managers. However, this requires a mechanism through which mutual fund managers can predetermine the cluster in which a prospective mutual fund investor belongs. Evidence suggests that the variability in calibration among individuals belonging to the same group may arise from differences in their cognitive abilities, personality variables and demographic variables (Winter 2003). However, further evidence is required to map each of the cluster groups on the basis of personality and demographic variables.

Notes

1 Those who calculate and set betting odds based on the prediction of the result of a contest, such as a horserace or an election.
2 Home bias means the investor is likely to have an investment preference for (a) mutual fund companies based in the home country and (b) domestic funds relative to international funds.

References

Alba, J.W. and Hutchinson, J.W., 2000. Knowledge calibration: What consumers know and what they think they know. *Journal of Consumer Research*, 27(2), pp. 123–56.

Atkinson, A., McKay, S., Kempson, E. and Collard, S., 2006. *Levels of financial capability in the UK: Results of a baseline survey.* Bristol: University of Bristol.

Bailey, W., Kumar, A. and Ng, D., 2011. Behavioral biases of mutual fund investors. *Journal of financial economics*, 102(1), pp. 1–27.

Barber, B.M. and Odean, T., 2000. Trading is hazardous to your wealth: The common stock investment performance of individual investors. *Journal of Finance*, 55(2), pp. 773–806.

Barber, B. and Odean, T., 2001. Boys will be boys. *Quarterly Journal of Economics*, 116(1), pp. 261–92.

Barberis, N.C. and Thaler, R.H., 2003. A survey of behavioral finance. In: G. M. Constantinides, M. Harris and R.M. Stulz, ed. 2003. *Handbook of the economics of finance: Volume 1B, Financial Markets and Asset Pricing.* Elsevier North Holland, Chapter 18, pp. 1053–1128.

Bloomfield R., Libby, R. and Nelson, M., 2000. *Underreactions and overreactions: The influence of information reliability and portfolio formation rules.* Cornell University Working Paper.

Bodner, D., Cochran, C.D. and Blum, T., 2000. Unique invulnerability measurement in skydivers: Scale validation. *Psi Chi Journal of Undergraduate Research*, 5, pp. 104–8.

Bowen, C. 2011. *Future of financial advice: Information pack.* Technical report, Commonwealth of Australia.

Brady, M.K. and Bourdeau, B.L., 2005. The importance of brand cues in intangible service industries: An application to investment services. *Journal of Service Marketing* 19 (6), pp. 401–10.

Chiou, Jyh-Shen, Droge, C. and Hanvanich, S., 2002. Does customer knowledge affect how loyalty is formed? *Journal of Service Research*, 5 (2), pp. 113–24.

Christoffersen, S. and Musto, D., 2002. Demand curves and the pricing of money management. *Review of Financial Studies*, 15(5), pp. 1499–1524.

Collinson, P., 2012. FSA ban on commission-based-selling sparks "death of salesman" fears. *The Guardian*, December. Available at www.theguardian.com/business/2012/dec/30/fsa-ban-commission-selling-death (accessed 17 April 2014).

Coval, J. and Stafford, E., 2007. Asset firesales (and purchases) in equity markets. *Journal of Financial Economics*, 86(2), pp. 479–512.

Daniel, K., Hirshleifer, D. and Subrahmanyam, A., 1998. Investor psychology and security market under – and overreactions. *The Journal of Finance*, 53(6), pp. 1839–85.

Deelstra, J.T., Peeters, M.C.W., Schaufeli, W.B., Stroebe, W., Zijlstra, F.R.H. and Doornen, L.P. van, 2003. Receiving instrumental support at work: When help is not welcome. *Journal of Applied Psychology*, 88(2), pp. 324–31.

Dolan, P., Elliot, A., Metcalfe, R. and Vlaev, I., 2012a. Influencing financial behavior: From changing minds to changing contexts. *Journal of Behavioral Finance*, 13(2), pp. 126–42.

Dolan, P., Hallsworth, M., Halpern, D., King, D., Metcalfe, R. and Vlaev, I., 2012b. Influencing behavior: The Mindspace way. *Journal of Economic Psychology*, 33(1), pp. 264–77.

Elton, E.J., Gruber, M.J. and Blake, C.R., 2006. The adequacy of investment choices offered by 401(k) plans. *Journal of Public Economics*, 90(6–7), pp. 1299–1314.

Fischhoff, B., Slovic, P. and Lichtenstein, S., 1977. Knowing with certainty: The appropriateness of extreme confidence. *Journal of Experimental Psychology: Human Perception and Performance*, 3(4), pp. 552–64.

FSA, 2008. Financial capability: A behavioural economics perspective. Consumer Research, London: Financial Services Authority, 69.

Ganzach, Y. and Krantz, D.H., 1991. The psychology of moderate prediction: II: Leniency and uncertainty. *Organizational Behavior and Human Decision Processes*, 48(2), pp. 169–92.

Gervais, S. and Odean, T., 2001. Learning to be overconfident. *Review of Financial Studies*, 14(1), pp. 1–27.

Gil-Bazo, J. and Ruiz-Verdu, P., 2009. The relation between price and performance in the mutual fund industry. *Journal of Finance*, 64(5), pp. 2153–83.

Gilovich, T., Kerr, M. and Husted Medvec, V., 1993. Effect of temporal perspective on subjective confidence. *Journal of Personality and Social Psychology*, 64(4), pp. 552–60.

Goetzmann, W.N. and Peles, N., 1997. Cognitive dissonance and mutual fund investors. *Journal of Financial Research*, 20(2), pp. 145–58.

Gort, C., Wang, M. and Siegrist, M., 2008. Are pension fund managers overconfident? *Journal of Behavioral Finance*, 9(3), pp. 163–70.

Gronhaug, K., 1973. Some factors influencing the size of the buyer's evoked set. *European Journal of Marketing*, 7(3), pp. 232–41.

Harless, D.W. and Peterson, S.P., 1998. Investor behavior and the persistence of poorly-performing mutual funds. *Journal of Economic Behavior and Organization*, 37(3), pp. 257–76.

Jacoby, J., Morrin, M., Johar, G., Gurhan, Z., Kuss, A. and Mazursky, D., 2001. Training novice investors to become more experts: The role of information accessing strategy. *Journal of Psychology and Financial Markets*, 2(2), pp. 69–79.

Kahneman, D., Knetsch, J.L. and Thaler, R.H., 1991. Anomalies: The endowment effect, Loss Aversion, and Status quo bias. *The Journal of Economic Perspective*, 5(1), pp. 193–206.

Keren, G., 1991. Calibration of probability judgments: Conceptual and methodological issues. *Acta Psychologica*, 77(3), pp. 217–73.

Kornov, L. and Thissen, W.A.H., 2000. *Impact assessment and project appraisal.* 18(3), pp. 191–200.

Lichtenstein, D.R., Kaufmann, P.J. and Bhagat, S., 1999. Why consumer choose managed mutual funds over index funds: Hypotheses from consumer behavior. *The Journal of Consumer Affairs*, 33(1), pp. 187–205.

Madrian, B.C. and Shea, D.F., 2001. The power of suggestion: Inertia in 401(k) participation and savings behavior. *Quarterly Journal of Economics*, 116(4), pp. 1149–87.

Malkiel, B., 1995. Returns from investing in equity mutual funds 1971 to 1991. *Journal of Finance*, 50(2), pp. 549–72.

Mandell, L., 2004. *Financial literacy: Are we improving? Results of the 2004 national JumpStart survey.* Washington, DC: Jumpstart Coalition.

Markowitz, H., 1952. Portfolio selection. *Journal of Finance*, 7(1), pp. 77–91.

Meier, S. and Sprenger, C., 2008. *Discounting financial literacy: Time preferences and participation in financial education programs.* Federal Reserve Bank of Boston Public Policy Discussion Paper No. 3507.

Metcalfe, J., 1998. Cognitive optimism: Self-deception or memory-based processing heuristics. *Personality and Social Psychology Review*, 2(2), pp. 100–10.

Mishra, S.K. and Kumar, M., 2011. How mutual fund investors' objective and subjective knowledge impacts their information search and processing behaviour. *Journal of Financial Service Marketing*, 16(1), pp. 27–41.

——, 2012a. A comprehensive model of information search and processing behaviour of mutual fund investors. *Journal of Financial Service Marketing* 17(1), pp. 31–49.

——, 2012b. The impact of perceived purchase risk on investment behaviour of mutual fund investors. *Decision*, 39(2), pp. 3–20.

Montier, J., 2002. *Behavioral finance: Insights into irrational minds and markets.* Chichester: John Wiley & Sons Ltd.

NCAER, 2011. *How household save and invest: Evidence from NCAER household survey. National Council for Applied Economic Research.* Available at www.sebi.gov.in/cms/sebi_data/attachdocs/1326345117894.pdf (accessed 21 May 2013).

Pillai, K.G. and Hofacker, C., 2007. Calibration of consumer knowledge of the web. *International Journal of Research in Marketing*, 24(3), pp. 254–67.

Plous, S., 1995. A comparison of strategies for reducing interval overconfidence in group judgments. *Journal of Applied Psychology*, 80(4), pp. 443–54.

Puetz, A. and Ruenzi, S., 2011. Overconfidence among professional investors: Evidence from mutual fund managers. *Journal of Business Finance and Accounting*, 38(5–6), pp. 684–712.

Ronis, D.L. and Yates, J.F., 1987. Components of probability judgment accuracy: Individual consistency and effects of subject matter and assessment method. *Organizational Behavior and Human Decision Processes*, 40(2), pp. 193–218.

Russo, E. and Schoemaker, P., 1992. Managing overconfidence. *Sloan Management Review*, 33(2), pp. 7–17.

Sharpe, W.F., 1994. The Sharpe ratio. *Journal of Portfolio Management*, 21(1), pp. 49–58.

——, 1996. Mutual fund performance. *Journal of Business*, 39(1), pp. 119–38.

Simon, H.A., 1990. Invariants of human behavior. *Annual Review Psychology*, 41, pp. 1–20.

Spence, M.T., 1996. Problem–problem solver characteristics affecting the calibration of judgments. *Organizational Behavior and Human Decision Processes*, 67(3), pp. 271–79.

Subbotin, V., 1996. Outcome feedback effects on under and overconfident judgments (general knowledge tasks. *Organizational Behavior and Human Decision Processes*, 66(3), pp. 268–76.

Thaler, R.H. and Sunstein, C.R., 2008. *Nudge: Improving decisions about health, wealth, and happiness.* New Haven, CT: Yale University Press.

Tobin, J., 1965. The theory of portfolio selection. In F.H. Hahn and F.P.R. Brechling, ed. 1965. *The Theory of Interest Rates*. London: Macmillan, pp. 3–51.

Vallone, R.P., Griffin, D.W., Lin, S. and Ross, L., 1990. Overconfident prediction of future actions and outcomes by self and others. *Journal of Personality and Social Psychology*, 58(4), pp. 582–92.

West, R.F. and Stanovich, K.E., 1997. The domain specificity and generality of overconfidence: Individual differences in performance estimation bias. *Psychonomic Bulletin & Review*, 4(3), pp. 387–92.

Winter, S.G., 2003. Mistaken perceptions: Cases and consequences. *British Journal of Management* 14(1), pp. 39–44.

Zuckerman, M., 1994. *Behavioral expressions and biosocial bases of sensation seeking*. New York: Cambridge Press.

Part III

Managing financial services relationships and the customer experience

9

Financial services customer relationships

Meanings, motivations and manifestations

Annie Pei-I Yu and Tina Harrison

Introduction

The financial services industry has been recognized as a suitable context for relationship marketing. Financial services can be complex, customized and delivered over a continuous series of transactions (Ennew and Waite 2013, O'Loughlin and Szmigin 2006). Buyers are relatively unsophisticated; information asymmetries exist and buyers face uncertainty regarding technical outcomes due to credence qualities (Farquhar and Meidan 2010). There are alternative suppliers in the marketplace, in most cases the buyer controls selection of the service provider, switching and multiple subscriptions are possible for many types of financial products (Lees et al. 2007). Finally, there are frequently legal or contractual bonds between the parties, some that carry economic consequences (Harrison 2000).

In addition to these inherent characteristics, the financial services industries of many developed nations are also experiencing a highly dynamic and competitive marketing environment due to legislative drivers, technological developments and increased competition, not only between traditional players but also from new entrants (as shown in Chapter 2). In mature financial services markets, new customers are hard to find and new business tends to be won at the expense of competitors (Salazar et al. 2007). Moreover, the digital environment, while offering many advantages, is contributing to the dehumanization of the relationship, decreasing the physical and social proximity that financial institutions have relied on in the past to develop relationships (Brun et al. 2014). In response to this changing environment, understanding what relationships mean to consumers and how to develop them has become a key strategic focus for financial institutions in order to safeguard market positions and gain competitive advantage (Rajaobelina and Bergeron 2008, Giannakis and Harker 2014).

Set against this context, this chapter explores the meanings, motivations and manifestations of financial services customer relationships. The chapter begins with an overview of the definition and meaning of relationship marketing, in particular setting out the distinctions between transactional and relationship marketing views. The chapter then explores the rationale for relationship marketing from the financial institutions' perspective before moving on to discuss the meaning of relationships from the consumer perspective and consumers' motivations for relationship engagement. The final section of the chapter discusses the various manifestations of customer relationships, by exploring a range of relationship typologies from previous studies, acknowledging the multifarious, dynamic and contextual nature of relationships.

Definition of relationship marketing

Relationship marketing (RM) was first noted by Berry (1983: 25) as an approach aimed at "attracting, maintaining and ... enhancing customer relationships". Since then, there have been numerous definitions of relationship marketing put forth. Grönroos (2009) provides one of the most comprehensive definitions often cited. He suggests that the purpose of RM is to establish, maintain, enhance and commercialize customer relationships so that the objectives of the parties are met. This is achieved by the mutual exchange and fulfilment of promises.

Dann and Dann (2001) noted more than fifty definitions of relationship marketing in their review. A number of common elements are notable among the various definitions, which are echoed by Christopher et al. (2008). First, relationship marketing has been defined as focusing on the long-term and the building of long-term relationships, not only with customers but also with a variety of stakeholders in an effort to support long-term relationships with customers. This includes crucially the internal relationships with employees and external relationships with key constituents of the supply chain. Relationship marketing is also defined as focusing on the value of the long-term, in particular the lifetime value of the customer relationship. A relationship marketing approach allows short-term losses to be overlooked if the long-term potential is profitable. Finally, the definitions highlight that relationship marketing includes a focus on processes, systems and people in developing and maintaining relationships and generating value. These are crucial to support and maintain meaningful interactions with customers over time (Giannakis and Harker 2014).

Relationship marketing is often defined in the literature in relation to transactional marketing, alongside claims that it is inherently different from transactional marketing and represents a paradigm shift (Gummesson 1997). Transactional and relational marketing have been presented as polar extremes (Christopher et al. 1991, Payne et al. 1995). Transactional marketing emphasizes the short-term, single sale based on product features, limited or no customer service delivered at arm's length, compared to the long-term focus of relational marketing based on customer retention, built on customer value and supported by high contact and customer service (see Figure 9.1).

Carson et al. (2004) argue that transactional and relationship marketing have been treated in isolation, in theory and in practice, and that research has rarely considered how transactional and relationship marketing impact on each other in the development of customer relationships. Given that definitions of relationship marketing encompass recruitment and retention of customers, it would seem appropriate to consider the respective roles of transaction and relationship marketing holistically in the context of developing and managing customer relationships.

In their study, the authors highlight several key challenges facing the retail banking sector that impact on transaction and relationship marketing: the need to manage supply and demand, the need to control quality and productivity, the need to manage customer interactions and the need to manage customer expectations (Carson et al. 2004). They note that transactional marketing activity is most appropriate in recruiting customers or for marketing activities that are focused on the single sale or transaction event. They suggest that there is a greater alignment between the traditional marketing mix variables – product, distribution and pricing – with the

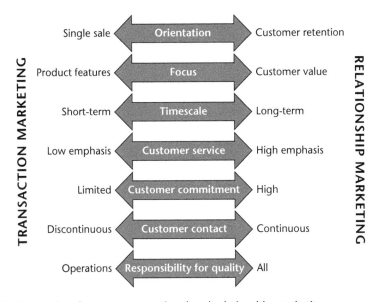

Figure 9.1 Comparison between transactional and relationship marketing
Source: Adapted from Christopher et al. (1991) and Payne et al. (1995).

activities of managing supply and demand and controlling productivity in support of transactional marketing activities.

In developing activity designed to retain customers the literature suggests that a relationship marketing approach is more appropriate, focused on the interactive relationship between two parties. Carson et al. (2004) suggest that the expanded services marketing mix variables – physical evidence, processes and people – are more aligned with the activities of managing customer interactions and expectations in relation to core relationship marketing activities. The importance of people and personal interaction has been noted by others as particularly important to the quality of the relationship in financial services (Rajaobelina and Bergeron 2008, Giannakis and Harker 2014). Promotion, communication and PR operate as support activities to transactional and relationship marketing.

Carson et al.'s (2004) research among retail banks showed that resource investment in marketing activities was unbalanced. Retail banks tended to under-invest in the core activities of transactional and relationship marketing, but over-invested in the support activities of promotion and communication.

A bias toward either an acquisition or a retention orientation can also have an impact on financial institutions' innovation performance. Arnould et al. (2011) find that a focus on customer acquisition positively enhances the diversity of customer knowledge development, which relates to a greater radical innovation performance, whereas a retention orientation enhances incremental innovation performance through increased depth of customer knowledge and supressed diversity of customer knowledge. Thus, in seeking simultaneously to recruit and retain customers, transactional and relationship marketing are both important, but they need to be approached in a balanced way and with organizational goals in mind (Carson et al. 2004). Notwithstanding, Farquhar and Panther (2008) identify a range of difficulties encountered by banks in attempting to balance acquisition and retention strategies and propose a framework of marketing activities that support acquisition and retention.

Rationale for relationship development: financial institution perspective

From the financial institution's perspective there are a number of motives for the retention of customers and benefits associated with the development of relationships. An underlying factor is the economic imperative (Athanassopoulou 2006). Long-term customers generally produce higher revenues and margins per customer than new customers (Maas and Graf 2008) and are more profitable than short-term customers (Reichheld and Sasser 1990, Van der Poel and Larivière 2004, Reinartz et al. 2008). This is because customers' economies generally improve over time.

A key economic outcome of long-term relationships is the prospect of cross-selling and up-selling. It is believed that long-term customers will buy more from the company (Shi et al. 2009, Kamakura et al. 2003, Paulin and Perrien 1998) and will spend more over time. Therefore, it is important to take a lifetime value perspective that considers the potential lifetime income from the customer relative to costs.

Using survival analysis to examine the retention and cross-selling potential for the investments and life assurance business, Salazar et al. (2007) demonstrated that if customers could be retained beyond a second purchase, the cross-sell potential increased significantly. Second purchases tended to be made around one year after the initial purchase by fewer than half of the customers. Thereafter, the proportion of customers making third and fourth purchases increased (60 percent made a subsequent purchase) and the timeframe in which purchases took place shortened (6 months instead of one year). Increasing the proportion of customers that made a second purchase would have a significant impact on subsequent cross-selling and the lifetime income from customers.

Not all long-term relationships are profitable though and there may be some short-term gains to be made from some customers in relation to certain types of financial transactions. Moreover, some types of customers or products are not immediately profitable but have the potential to be so at some future point (for example, student customers, mortgages and pensions). The financial institution therefore depends on retaining the customer over the long term in order to benefit financially from the relationship.

High acquisition costs offer one explanation of why customer profitability improves over time. The cost of customer acquisition has been estimated to be up to five times more than the cost of customer retention (Clutterbuck 1989, Liswood 1989). However, this is being questioned in the context of new online business models (see the discussion in Chapter 22 by Gandy on mobile payments). Where high set-up or acquisition costs exist, retaining customers over the long term allows these costs to be amortized over a longer timeframe. Another explanation for why long-term customers may cost less to serve than new customers is because they are more likely to be familiar with the company, its products and services and may make fewer requests or fewer demands on the time of employees (Augusto de Matos et al. 2009, Bejou et al. 1998). Customers who have been around long enough to learn a company's procedures and are familiar with the product line will receive greater value from the business relationship (Grayson et al. 2008, Reicheld and Teal 1996). There can even be opportunities for the co-creation of value (as discussed in detail by Michel in Chapter 13).

Long-term customers are less influenced by competitors' marketing activities (Kaltcheva and Parasuraman 2009, Colgate et al. 1996). Close relationships can act as a barrier to competitors' advances (Campbell and Frei 2010). As a result, long-term customers can be less price-sensitive (Kotler 2003). Moreover, building a long-term relationship with one family member allows for potential inter-generational relationships. Parental influence is a key factor influencing the choice of financial institution for young people and a key financial socializer (Kim et al. 2011).

It is assumed that building a relationship with one family member will have an impact on other members of the same family.

Finally, long-term customers can become the company's advocates by transmitting their positive experience, generating positive word-of-mouth and providing free and credible advertising for the institution (Zhang et al. 2010).

Understanding relationships from a consumer perspective

In addition to the benefits for financial providers already outlined, Alexander and Colgate (2000) note a growing base of literature that explores the benefits of relationship marketing for consumers. Indeed, the benefits for financial services providers, such as increased revenues, profits and competitive advantage, can only be achieved if consumers also perceive benefits from the relationship and are willing parties to the relationship (Gwinner et al. 1998); relationships are bi-directional. We cannot consider relationship marketing without acknowledging the perspective of the consumer. Relationship marketing implies an ongoing cooperative interaction between the firm and its customers and relies on the commitment of customers to continue to patronize one firm when faced with numerous possibilities. Relationship marketing is thus tempered by the consumer's motivation to reduce their choice set to be in a relationship with a firm (Sheth and Parvatiyar 1995).

Despite the importance of the consumer in understanding relationship marketing, the majority of research conducted into financial services relationship marketing has been conducted from the financial institution's perspective with the objective of understanding how to improve RM practice and increase cross-sales (see, for example, Ansell et al. 2007, Kamakura et al. 2004, Kamakura et al. 2003, Jarrar and Neely 2002, Krebsback 2000). By contrast, the consumer view of the financial services relationship has attracted much less attention in the literature, therefore, there is pressing need to explore consumer-financial services firm relationships from the perspective of the consumer.

Previous research has acknowledged that not all consumers desire to form relationships with organizations and not every consumer wishes the same degree or type of involvement with a service provider (O'Loughlin et al. 2004). Some customers deny the existence of or potential for any relationship with an organization and are content to engage in transactional behavior, others perceive themselves as engaging in relational behavior.

There is evidence to suggest that for some financial services contexts, consumers value their relationship and are willing to build a closer relationship with their financial services provider (Barnes 1994, Colgate and Alexander 1998). Research by Danaher et al. (2008) reveals that a third of respondents to a survey were seeking better relationships with their bank while another third were keen to form a relationship with their banking service provider. Consumers are most likely to want to form relationships when services are high in perceived risk or high in credence qualities, or when consumers are highly involved in the delivery of services (Barnes and Howlett 1998).

The concept of "consumer engagement" has emerged (van Doorn et al. 2011, Brodie et al. 2011) as an expanded domain of relationship marketing, indicating the nature of relationship behavior from the consumer's perspective. The concept particularly explores the interaction and emotional relationship between the consumer and the brand, the consumer and the firm, and the consumer and other consumers.

Consumer motives for relationship engagement

Understanding more about why consumers might wish to engage in a relationship with a service provider, particularly at an early stage of the relationship, may assist in developing more appropriate relationship management strategies. Consumer motives for developing or remaining in a relationship with a firm can relate to two basic reasons (Kumar and Pancras 2008): either they want to, or they have to. Wanting to stay might result from customer satisfaction and trust, whereas having to stay may result from the existence of exit barriers (Cannière et al. 2010) or the existence of no obvious alternatives. A refinement of these categories specific to bank loyalty is presented in Chapter 11 by El-Manstrly.

Sheth and Parvatiyar (1995: 256) suggest that the "fundamental axiom of relationship marketing is, or should be, that consumers like to reduce choices by engaging in an ongoing loyalty relationship with marketers". They go on to suggest that consumers engage in relational market behavior due to personal, social and institutional influences. Personal influences include a need to achieve greater efficiency in decision-making, to reduce the task of information processing, to achieve greater cognitive consistency in their decisions and to reduce perceived risks associated with future choices. Social influences arise from behavioral norms set by family members, the influence of peer groups or religious tenets. Institutional influences may arise from government mandates, employer influences or marketer induced policies.

Consumers who engage in a relationship may be motivated by the belief that they will attain certain benefits; motivations for relationship engagement can be explained by goal setting and goal attaining theory (Bagozzi 1995). Research has suggested that customers receive psychological benefits from close relationships (Gorelick 2010, Kammerer 2009, Sheth and Parvatiyar 1995, Berry 1995, Gwinner et al. 1998). In addition, there are social benefits such as familiarity, personal recognition and friendship (Nambisan and Baron 2009, Czepiel 1990, Buttle 1996), as well as economic benefits (Wendel and Dellaert 2009, Peterson 1995). Furthermore, customers can obtain customization benefits as service providers may tailor their services to meet customer specifications and requirements (Gelb et al. 2008). Customers can also enjoy confidence benefits which relate to the sense of reduced anxiety, faith in the trustworthiness of the service provider, reduced perceptions of anxiety and risk, and knowing what to expect (Colwell et al. 2009, Gwinner et al. 1998). Another source of advantage comes from special treatment which includes the ability of relational customers to skip queues and to receive special prices or offers (De Wulf et al. 2001, Michalski and Helmig 2008). The following sections explore some of the commonly cited motivations in more detail.

Economic motives

In the same way that financial institutions are motivated to develop relationships with customers to improve the bottom line, consumers also are motivated by economic benefits. For consumers, economic benefits include special deals, competitive interest rates, low transaction costs or service charges. These factors have appeared consistently as key criteria in bank selection research (Devlin and Gerrard 2005, Thwaites and Vere 1995). However, as noted by Estelami in Chapter 16, financial services' prices are not easily transparent for all products and consumers may struggle to appreciate the full economic implications.

It is assumed that customers exhibiting relational behavior are less price-sensitive, yet Dowling and Uncles (1997) argue that building up a relationship with a customer does not always lead to a less price-sensitive customer. Some retained customers may expect a price discount in exchange for their continued custom and loyalty. It is not unreasonable that long-standing customers may expect some reward for their longevity and commitment to the company.

There is some doubt as to whether consumers seeking to maximize economic needs do so out of a commitment to the organization. Economic needs have been identified as key factors motivating behavioral loyalty, suggesting that consumers may be willing to exit a relationship if a better offer is perceived to be presented by a competitor. However, understanding when and where economic needs arise allows financial institutions to respond appropriately. It also helps in understanding how to balance the transactional and relational dimensions.

Risk reduction motives

In consumer behavior theory, perceived risk and uncertainty are critical concerns in purchase decisions (Cox 1967, Dowling and Staelin 1994). In the context of financial services these concerns are compounded by the long-term nature of the product, information asymmetries and high financial consequences of making a poor decision. Risks include psychological risk, financial risk, performance risk and time risk. A key factor for consumers of financial services is the uncertainty of the future outcome of the financial decision; the performance risk. Consequently, consumers look for ways to avoid or minimize risk (Howcroft et al. 2007). Equally, risk avoidance can also explain why consumers are motivated to acquire particular types of financial products (such as insurance).

Financial services consumers may perceive a relationship developed over time with a financial institution as an outcome of risk reduction, especially for complex financial products. Barnes and Howlett (1998) suggest that consumers will more likely wish to form relationships when services are high in perceived risk, when credence qualities dominate and consumers are heavily dependent on the financial institution.

Previous research in the areas of brand loyalty, product loyalty and store loyalty has suggested that the "brand" can act as a risk reliever (Dawar and Parker 1994, Riley and de Chernatony 2000), also discussed by Farquhar and Robson in Chapter 14. Consumers may choose to be brand loyal in order to maintain cognitive consistency and psychological comfort (Hennig-Thurau et al. 2000). In the context of financial services, research has found that "bank reputation" (similar to brand) is a key factor for choosing a bank (Anderson 1976). Consumers may engage in a relationship because of the bank's reputation or brand image in order to reduce perceived risk. A key element of risk is trust: the greater the perceived trustworthiness of the institution the lower the perceived risk, therefore, trust building is important and is covered in detail in other chapters (see Chapters 10 and 30).

Simplifying information processing and decision-making

Sheth and Parvatiyar (1995) suggest that relational behavior is motivated by consumer desires to reduce the complexity of purchase decisions and achieve greater efficiency in decision-making. The inherent characteristics of financial services and the limits of consumer literacy (as discussed in Chapter 3 by Huhmann) serve to compound the complexity of financial services decision-making. Mishra and Kumar (in Chapter 8) illustrate the consequences arising from a miscalibration between actual, objective knowledge and perceived knowledge in decision-making. Even in cases where individuals are reasonably knowledgeable, consumers may find it difficult to access sufficient information on which to base an informed decision.

Information search for financial services is limited by information accessibility, validity and reliability of information and complexity of the product. Research into the mortgage purchase process (Lee and Hogarth 2000) highlights the limited amount of pre-purchase information searching conducted by consumers and reliance on few information sources, suggesting that purchase decisions in this context are far from informed. Paradoxically, it has been shown that the search process for more "straightforward" products may be more involved than for "complex" products (Weinberg 1997), due to greater access to information on such products and ability to understand it.

Faced with complex decision-making, consumers use heuristics to aid the task. Lee and Marlowe (2003) identified three heuristics used by consumers in the choice of a financial institution for a bank account: attribute-by-attribute decision-making, alternative-by-alternative decision-making and compensatory decision-making. Consumers with higher levels of product knowledge, experience and involvement and need for cognition tended to develop more clearly articulated decision criteria and were able to engage in more elaborate decision-making heuristics.

Relationships provide an opportunity for individuals to benefit from the learning accrued from the ongoing interaction and experience, in order to limit choices and simplify information processing. Future decision-making tasks can then be simplified by drawing on prior experiences and prior knowledge from memory (Sheth and Parvatiyar 1995). This is not possible for all types of financial services. Financial products vary enormously in their time horizons and frequency of purchase. Pensions and mortgages, for example, may be acquired only once in a lifetime for some consumers, hence opportunities for learning can be limited in such situations (as discussed by Gough and Adami in Chapter 6).

Product benefits or service treatment motives

Special product benefits or service treatment include a range of benefits which come in the form of first rate levels of service, preferential treatment, special operational conditions and time savings (Gwinner et al. 1998). In the context of financial services, consumers may engage in a relationship to acquire certain benefits such as quick access to services or easy access to other financial services from the same bank, or receive special treatment that most consumers do not get. Gwinner et al. (1998) argued that consumers who have already developed a relationship with a company may receive additional services or preferential treatment not normally obtained by non-regular customers.

Impact of motives on relationship engagement

Yu (2009) examined and compared the impact of six motives for relationship engagement on early-stage relationship development to ascertain whether there were any differences according to type of financial services product (savings account, mortgage or car insurance), consumer characteristics (according to level of involvement), and channel used (branch, telephone or internet). The rationale for the study was to understand the primary motivations that consumers have for engaging in a relationship with a financial services provider and the potential impact that this may have on the customer's subsequent relational behavior and implications for relationship management.

The research identified the existence of primary level motives and secondary level motives. The primary level motives for relationship engagement were the same regardless of financial services product sought. The top two motives for relationship engagement were identified as "simplifying purchase process" and "economic needs". The research found that secondary level motives differed according to financial product type. For mortgages "reducing perceived risk" featured as important, but not for savings and car insurance products. Differences were also found in terms of the least important motives for relationship engagement. In the case of savings and mortgages, "social-psychological needs" featured as the least important, whereas for car insurance consumers were least motivated by "obtaining special product benefits or service treatment". In the case of car insurance, this result might be explained by the fact that there is a legal obligation to have car insurance (at least to a certain level) and consumers often see it as a cost rather than an investment and seek to minimize the overall cost. Special product benefits and service treatment may be assumed to carry a higher price ticket.

Research by Bond and Stone (2004) among car insurance customers revealed that non-claimants were highly focused on price and price reduction. However, claimants were less focused on price as a single decision-criterion and were more likely to view it in relation to the bundle of benefits provided by the insurance policy. They were less motivated by economic benefits alone. This is interesting in considering the lifecycle of the insurance customer and how motives for relationship engagement may change over time, depending on the incidence of a claim.

Differences in motives for relationship engagement were also explored according to level of involvement. Involvement has been defined as the extent of personal relevance of the decision to the individual in terms of their basic values, goals, inherent needs, interests and self-concept (De Wulf et al. 2001, Mittal and Lee 1989, Zaichkowsky 1985), and has been shown to be an important factor in moderating consumers' decision-making processes (Kinard and Capella 2006).

Research has suggested that there is an association between product category involvement and the effectiveness of relationship marketing (for example, Berry 1995, Gordon 1998), although there seems to be a lack of consensus regarding the direction of the association. Some studies suggest that highly involved individuals are more likely to express a relationship with products or brands (Martin 1998, Quester and Lim 2003) and tend to be more loyal (De Wulf et al. 2001). However, others have expressed the opposite opinion.

Varki and Wong (2003) examined the impact of consumer involvement on consumers' willingness to engage in relationships with service providers and the effect that involvement has on consumers' expectations of relational efforts by the service provider. Research findings suggest that though there is not a huge difference in consumers' expectations between high-involved and low-involved consumers, high-involved consumers are more likely to engage in a relationship with services providers. In Yu's (2009) study, individuals expressing high purchasing involvement tended to be more concerned with "social-psychological needs" and "obtaining special product benefit or service treatment needs", whereas low involvement individuals were more concerned about "simplifying purchasing process".

With regard to channel used, Yu (2009) identified that individuals who mainly used face-to-face banking in branches tended to be motivated by: "social-psychological needs", "reducing risk needs", "obtaining special benefits", whereas individuals who preferred to use online banking expressed higher concerns for: "simplifying purchasing process". In general, users of branch-based channels, regardless of product used, seem to be motivated by the need for a more social/emotional relationship and risk reduction, whereas those using online methods were motivated by the need to keep costs low. The traditional physical channels provide opportunity for a social interaction that the internet lacks (Brun et al. 2014, Albesa 2007).

Financial services relationship typologies

The preceding discussion hints at the multidimensional, dynamic and contextual nature of relationships, the complexity of which has been acknowledged in the literature (O'Loughlin and Szmigin 2006). This is a potential explanation for seemingly conflicting results in studies of financial services relationships. For example, some studies suggest that relationships are based on inertia and convenience (O'Loughlin et al. 2004) rather than true loyalty and that transactional rather than relational behavior is the norm, whereas others have noted the importance of inter-actions and the impact on customer commitment (Howcroft and Durkin 2000).

The form of relationship can vary between different types of financial services consumers and across different types of financial services contexts or products. The same consumers may assume a different relationship approach according to different financial services contexts. Moreover, within the same context different consumers may adopt different forms of relational behavior.

Beckett et al. (2000) used the "ideal type" methodology to characterize financial services consumers and their behavior, recognizing that behavior is dependent on the context in which it occurs. Based on two key variables (customer confidence and involvement), financial services consumer behavior was grouped into one of four types: one resulting in no purchase and the remaining three that exhibit different tendencies toward relational behavior. "Repeat-passive" consumers exhibited high confidence but low involvement toward financial services. They exhibited behavioral loyalty that can be described as "passive". The apparent loyalty was due to one or more factors such as perceived lack of differentiation, motivation by convenience or inertia, or perception of high switching costs. However, a number of conditions were likely to prompt a switch from passive to active behavior, including lifecourse changes, sudden reduction in service quality and poor service recovery by the institution. This form of relational behavior is most likely to be exhibited for routine transaction-based relationships and subscription-based relationships such as bank accounts and credit cards.

'Relational-active' consumers exhibit high confidence and high involvement. These con-sumers are much more engaged and more knowledgeable about financial matters. This kind of behavior was most evident for financial products, which consumers feel confident in deal-ing with and knowledgeable about, particularly basic financial services with regular renewal terms (such as general insurance) and products with external search cues. Decision-making in these contexts typically occurred at arm's length, thus limiting the opportunities for an affective dimension to the relationship to develop and increasing the potential for relationship switching.

"Relational-dependent" consumers exhibited low confidence but high involvement. These consumers lacked control due to the complexity of the product. This type of relational behavior was most evident among the purchase of complex financial services such as investments and pensions. In such situations consumers tended to rely or depend on advice and expert sources, although differences were evident in the nature of advice sought according to socio-economic characteristics.

Dalziel et al. (2011) provide a multidimensional typology of customer relationships based on trust in relationship partner, relationship commitment, buyer-seller bonds and relationship ben-efits. Their qualitative analysis produced four relationship types: faltering, functional, perceptual and affective.

Faltering relationships can be described as "relationships on the edge". The relationships were either in the process of dissolution or continued despite high levels of customer dissatis-faction. Individuals felt trapped in the relationship. These relationships were characterised by a lack of trust, calculative commitment (based on economic concerns) rather than affective com-mitment (that is linked to true loyalty), and the feeling that they were not particularly valued or rewarded by the financial institution.

Functional relationships were characterized by calculative commitment and the perception that exiting the relationship was difficult and time-consuming. Consumers in functional rela-tionships did not seem to be motivated by relationship benefits; they tended to view benefits as one-off treats rather than part of the relationship-building efforts.

Perceptual relationships were characterized by distinctive perceptual bonds, meaning that individuals perceived a connection to the financial institution. In addition, trust was a key feature based on the competence and reliability of the bank staff. Individuals demonstrated calculative and affective commitment to the financial institution. The emotional attachment seemed to be based on the feeling that the bank made them feel special and was responsive to their needs.

Affective relationships were characterized by cognitive and affective trust, affective commitment and relationship benefits. Particular benefits included reducing customer risk and creating customer confidence, the consistency and reliability of the service interactions and the feeling that banks offered extras to their customers in appreciation of their banking relationship. The authors concluded that different forms of relationship are evident and that for a relationship to be successful it does not necessarily need to include an emotional dimension. Relationships can be built on satisfactory service experiences alone and that these types of relationship are not any less valuable. The implication of this is that financial services organizations need to develop different RM strategies for different RM types. The fit between customers' relational expectations and experiences is important.

This latter point was a key focus of Eriksson and Soderberg's (2010) research. The authors used intersubjectivity theory to conceptualize the different ways customers experience face-to-face interactions. They suggest that the perception of relationship depends on the symmetry of the way in which the customer and the provider mirror each other in an interaction. Based on qualitative research, four categories (which the authors refer to as metaphorical stories) emerged. The authors use the terminology What/Whom as a means of expressing what customers experience, in terms of how the customer approaches the provider and the customer's perception of how the provider approaches them.

The first category "it is like going to the dentist" (What-What) describes two parties interacting independently in a professional relationship. Customers feel they are respected and are confident that the other knows their job. Customers prefer to have a non-familiar relationship with a professional person. The second category "it is like I am unseen" (Whom-What) describes a lack of fit in the relationship. The customer expects a personal relationship but a non-familiar professional interaction is provided. This is a cause of frustration and dissatisfaction as these customers define their relationship as "non-existent".

The third category "it is just like prying" (What-Whom) describes a situation in which the customer expects a professional and distanced relationship but is met with familiarity. The customer views this as intruding and feels intimidated. This has an impact on their subsequent interaction with the bank. The final category "like someone I really know" (Whom-Whom) describes a situation in which the customer and provider are engaged in a familiar relationship willing to share stories and exchange personal information. The authors conclude that mutual relationships exist in only two of the four scenarios. Moreover, relationships are not simply defined by closeness or distance. Customers do not perceive all close interactions as relationships. Indeed, distance is sometimes desirable. Successful relationships exist when there is a fit between the parties in terms of their expectations and experience.

Conclusion

This chapter has reviewed the meaning, motivations and manifestations of relationship marketing, exploring relationship marketing from the firm and consumer perspective and the interactions between the two. The chapter began with an overview of the meaning and definition of relationship marketing and comparison between transactional and relationship marketing perspectives. It then provided an overview of the rationale for relationship development from the firm's perspective, followed by a discussion of consumer motivations for relationship engagement. The chapter ended with a discussion of relationship typologies.

The chapter has shown that research into financial services relationships has mostly been conducted from the point of view of the financial provider with the aim of understanding how to maximize revenue generation and manage relationships effectively. By contrast, there have been fewer studies conducted that have attempted to understand the relationship from the consumer perspective. Of the research that has been conducted, it is mostly qualitative and based on small-scale studies. The findings reveal that relationships are not homogeneous but are multidimensional, dynamic and contextual. It is possible that the same consumer may assume a different relationship position according to different financial services even with the same provider. The key for financial services providers is in understanding when a relationship is desired by consumers and what form that may take to ensure that the nature of relationship provided mirrors that expected by the consumer.

There are several suggestions for further research in this area. First, a more holistic study might be conducted that incorporates a wider set of relationship determinants from across the various studies and more quantitative analysis. Second, consumer engagement as a means of understanding relationship development is a useful angle. Whereas relationship marketing has tended to take a narrower perspective on the relationship or interaction between the consumer and the firm, consumer engagement takes into account a wider range of engagement aspects, such as engagement contexts, engagement objects, engagement phases and engagement levels (Brodie et al 2011). Finally, there is merit in exploring the concept of value co-creation (Vargo and Lusch 2008) in the context of relationship marketing, especially in relation to increasing self-service technology in banking.

References

Albesa, J. G. (2007). Interaction channel choice in a multichannel environment, an empirical study. *International Journal of Bank Marketing*, 25(7), 490–506.

Alexander, N. and Colgate, M. (2000). Retail financial services: transaction to relationship marketing, *European Journal of Marketing*, 34(8), 938–53.

Anderson Jr., W. T., III. Cox, E. P. C. and Fulcher, D. G. (1976). Bank selection decisions and market segmentation. *Journal of Marketing*, 40(1), 40–45.

Ansell, J., Harrison, T. and Archibald, T. (2007), "Identifying cross-selling opportunities using lifestage segmentation and survival analysis", *Marketing Intelligence and Planning*, 25 (4), 394–410.

Arnould, T. J., Fang, E. and Palmatier, R. W. (2011). The effects of customer acquisition and retnetion orientations on a firm's radical and incremental innovation performance. *Journal of the Academy of Marketing Science*, 39 (2), 234–51.

Athanassopoulou, P. (2006). Determining relationship quality in the development of business-to-business financial services. *Journal of Business-to-Business Marketing*, 13 (1), 87–120.

Augusto de Matos, C., Luiz Henrique, J. and de Rosa, F. (2009). Different roles of switching costs on the satisfaction-loyalty relationship. *International Journal of Bank Marketing*, 27 (7), 506–23.

Bagozzi, R. P. (1995). Reflections on relationship marketing in consumer markets. *Journal of the Academy of Marketing Science*, 23(4), 272–77.

Barnes, J. G. (1994). Close to the customer: but is it really a relationship? *Journal of Marketing Management*, 10, 561–70.

Barnes, J. G. and Howlett, D. M. (1998). Predictors of equity in relationships between financial services providers and retail customers. *International Journal of Bank Marketing*, 16(1), 15–23.

Beckett, A., Hewer, P. and Howcroft, B. (2000). An exposition of consumer behaviour in the financial services industry. *International Journal of Bank Marketing*, 18(1), 15–26.

Bejou, D. Ennew, C. and Palmer, A., (1998). Trust, ethics and relationship satisfaction. *International Journal of Bank Marketing*, 16, 4, 170–75.

Berry, L. L., (1983) "*Relationship Marketing*" in Berry, L.L., Shostack, G.L. and Upsay, G.D. (eds) *Emerging Perspectives on Services Marketing*. Chicago: American Marketing Association 8–25.

—— (1995) Relationship marketing of services-growing interest, emerging perspectives. *Journal of the Academy of Marketing Science*. 23(4), 236–45.

Bond, A. and Stone, M. (2004) "How the automotive insurance claims experience affects customer retention", *Journal of Financial Services Marketing*, 9(2), 160–71.

Brodie, R. J., Hollebeek, L., Juric, B. and Ilic, A. (2011). Customer engagement: conceptual domain, fundamental propositions, and implications for research. *Journal of Services Research*, 14(3), 252–71.

Brun, I., Rajaobelina, L. and Ricard, L. (2014). Online relationship quality: scale development and initial testing. *International Journal of Bank Marketing*, 32 (1), 5–27.

Buttle, F. (1996). *Relationship marketing. theory and practice*. London: Paul Chapman.

Campbell, D. and Frei, F. (2010) Cost Structure, Customer Profitability, and Retention Implications of Self-Service Distribution Channels: Evidence from Customer Behavior in an Online Banking Channel. *Management Science*. 56(1) 4–24.

Carson, D., Gilmore, A. and Walsh, S. (2004). Balancing transaction and relationship marketing in retail banking. *Journal of Marketing Management*, 20(3/4), 431–55.

Cannière, M., Pelsmacker, P. and Geuens, M. (2010) Relationship Quality and Purchase Intention and behavior: the moderating impact of relationship strength. *Journal of Business and Psychology*. 25(1), 87–98.

Christopher, M., Payne, A. F. T. and Ballantyne, D. (1991) *Relationship Marketing*. Oxford: Butterworth-Heinemann.

Christopher, M., Payne, A. and Ballantyne, D. (2008). *Relationship marketing creating stakeholder value*. Butterworth-Heinemann.

Clutterbuck, D. (1989). "Developing customer care training programmes", *Marketing Intelligence & Planning*, Vol. 7 issue 1/2 34–37.

Colgate, M. and Alexander, N. (1998). Banks, retailers and their customers: A relationship marketing perspective. *International Journal of Bank Marketing*, 16(4/5), 144–52.

Colgate, M., Stewart, K. and Kinsella, R. (1996). Customer defection: a study of the student market in Ireland. *International Journal of Bank Marketing*. 14 (3), 23–31.

Colwell, S., Hogarth-Scott, S., Depeng, J. and Joshi, A. (2009). Effects of organizational and serviceperson orientation on customer loyalty. *Management Decision*, 47 (10), 1489–1513.

Cox, D. F. (1967). *Risk taking and information handling in consumer behavior*, Cambridge: Harvard University Press.

Czepiel, J. (1990) Service encounters and service relationships: implications for research. *Journal of Business Research*. 20(1) 13–31.

Dalziel, N., Harris, F. and Laing, A. (2011). *A multidimensional typology of customer relationships: from faltering to affective*. 29 (5) 398–432.

Danaher, P. J., Conroy, D. M. and McColl-Kennedy, J. R. (2008). Who wants a relationship anyway? Conditions when consumers expect a relationship with their service provider. *Journal of Service Research*, 11(1), 43–62.

Dann, S. J. and Dann, S. M. (2001) *Strategic Internet Marketing*. John Wiley and Sons, Queensland.

Dawar, N. and Parker, P. (1994). Marketing universals: Consumers' use of brand name, price, physical appearance, and retailer. *Journal of Marketing*, 58(2), 81–95.

De Wulf, K., Odkerken-Schroder, G. and Iacobucci, D. (2001). Investments in consumer relationships: a cross-country and cross-industry exploration. *Journal of Marketing*. 65 (October), 35–50.

Devlin, J. and Gerrard, P. (2005). A study of customer choice criteria for multiple bank users. *Journal of Retailing and Consumer Services*, 12(4), 297–306.

van Doorn, J., Lemon, K. N., Mittal, V., Nass, S., Pick, D., Pirner, P. and Verhoef, P. C. (2010). *Customer engagement behaviors: theoretical foundations and research directions*. 13 (3), 253–66.

Dowling, G. R. and Staelin, R. (1994). A model of perceived risk and intended risk-handling activity. *Journal of Consumer Research*, 21(1), 119–34.

Dowling, G. R. and Uncles, M. (1997). Do customer loyalty programs really work? *Sloan Management Review*, 38(4), 71–82.

Ennew, C. and Waite, N. (2013). *Financial services marketing: an international guide*. 2nd edition, Abingdon, Oxon: Routledge.

Eriksson, K. and Soderberg, I-L. (2010). Customers' ways of making sense of a financial service relationship through intersubjective mirroring of others. *Journal of Financial Services Marketing*, 15, 99–111.

Farquhar, J. and Meidan, A. (2010). *Marketing of financial services*. 2nd ed, Basingstoke: Palgrave Macmillan.

Farquhar, J. D. and Panther, T. (2008). Acquiring and retaining customers in UK banks: An exploratory study. *Journal of Retailing and Consumer Services*, 15(1), 9–21.

Gelb, B., Geiger-Oneto, S. and Gelb, G. (2008). From knowing to doing: experience and flexibility make the difference. *Journal of Business Strategy* Vol. 29(5), 12–18.

Giannakis, D. and Harker, M. (2014). Strategic alignment between relationship marketing and human resource management in financial services organizations. *Journal of Strategic Marketing*, DOI: 10.1080/0965254X.2013.876082.

Gorelick, D. (2010). Customer benefits, now and forever. *American Printer* 127(3), 16.

Gordon, I. H. (1998). *Relationship Marketing*. John Wiley and Sons: Ontario.

Grayson, K., Johnson, D. and Chen, D. (2008). Is Firm Trust Essential in a Trusted Environment? How Trust in the Business Context Influences Customers. *Journal of Marketing Research*. 45(2), 241–56.

Grönroos, C. (2009). Marketing as promise management: regaining customer management for marketing. *Journal of Business and Industrial Marketing*. 24(5/6), 351–59.

Gummesson, E. (1997). Relationship marketing as a paradigm shift: Some conclusions from the 30r approach. *Management Decision*, 35(3/4), 267–72.

Gwinner, K. P., Gremler, D. D. and Bitner, M. J. (1998). Relational benefits in services industries: The customer's perspective. *Journal of the Academy of Marketing Science*, 26(2), 101–14.

Harrison, T. (2000). *Financial Services Marketing*. Harlow, England: Pearson Education.

Hennig-Thurau, T., Gwinner, K. P. and Gremler, D. D. (2000). Why customers build relationships with companies – and why not. In T. a. U. H. Hennig-Thurau (Ed.), *Relationship marketing: Competitive advantage through customer satisfaction and customer retention*. 369–91, Berlin, New York: Springer.

Howcroft, B. and Durkin, M. (2000). Reflections on bankcustomer interactions in the new millennium. *Journal of Financial Services Marketing*, 5(1), 9–20.

Howcroft, B., Hamilton, R. and Hewer, P. (2007). Customer involvement and interaction in retail banking: An examination of risk and confidence in the purchase of financial products. *Journal of Services Marketing*, 21(7), 481–91.

Jarrar, Y. F. and Neely, A. (2002). Cross-selling in the financial sector: customer profitability is key. *Journal of Targeting, Measurement and Analysis for Marketing*. 10(3) 282–96.

Kaltcheva, V. D. and Parasuraman, A. (2009). Personality-Relatedness and Reciprocity Framework in analysing retailer-consumer interaction. *Journal of Business Research*, 62(6), 601–8.

Kamakura, W. A., Kossar, B. S. and Wedel, M. (2004). Identifying innovators for the cross-selling of new products. *Management Science*. 50(8), 1120–33.

Kamakura, W. A., Wedel, M., De Rosa, M. and Mazzon, J. A. (2003). Cross-selling through database marketing: a mixed data factor analysis for data augmentation and prediction. *International Journal of Research in Marketing*. 60(3), 1–21.

Kammerer, D. (2009). The effects of customer benefit and regulation on environmental product innovation.: Empirical evidence from appliance manufacturers in Germany. *Ecological Economics*. Vol. 68 (8/9), 2285–95.

Kim, J, LaTaillade, J. and Kim, H. (2011). Family processes and adolescents' financial behaviours. *Journal of Family Economic Issues*, 32, 668–97.

Kinard, B. R. and Capella, M. L. (2006). Relationship marketing: The influence of consumer involvement on perceived service benefits. *Journal of Services Marketing*, 20(6/7), 359–68.

Kotler, P. (2003). Marketing Management, 11th Edition, Prentice Hall.

Krebsback, K. (2000). Banks new mantra: cross sell like crazy. *Bank Investment Consultant*. 10(8) 22–28.

Kumar, V. G. and Pancras, J. (2008). Cross-buying in retailing: drivers and consequences. *Journal of Retailing*, 84(1), 15–27.

Lee, J. and Hogarth, J. M. (2000). Consumer information search for home mortgages: who, what, how much and what else? *Financial Services Review*, 9, 277–93.

Lee, J. and Marlowe, J. (2003). How consumers choose a financial institution: decision-making criteria and heuristics. *International Journal of Bank Marketing*, 21(2), 53–71.

Lees, G., Garland, R. and Wright, M. (2007). Switching banks: old bank gone but not forgotten. *Journal of Financial Services Marketing*, 12, 146–56.

Liswood, L. (1989). "A new system for rating service quality", *Journal of Business Strategy*, Vol. 10, Issue 4, 42–45.

Maas, P. and Graf, A. (2008). Customer value analysis in financial services. *Journal of Financial Services Marketing* l. 13(2), 107–20.

Martin, C. L. (1998). Relationship marketing: A high-involvement product attribute approach. *Journal of Product and Brand Management*, 7(1), 6–26.

Michalski, S. and Helmig, B. (2008) What Do We Know About the Identity Salience Model of Relationship Marketing Success? *Journal of Relationship Marketing*. 7(1), 45–63.

Mittal, B. and Lee, M.-S. (1989). A causal model of consumer involvement. *Journal of Economic Psychology*, 10(3), 363–89.

Nambisan, S. and Baron, R. (2009) Virtual Customer Environments: Testing a Model of Voluntary Participation in Value Co-creation Activities. *Journal of Product Innovation Management*. 26(4), 388–406.

O'Loughlin, D. and Szmigin, I. (2006). Emerging perspectives on customer relationships, interactions and loyalty in Irish retail financial services. *Journal of Consumer Behaviour*, 5(2), 117–29.

O'Loughlin, D., Szmigin, I. and Turnbull, P. (2004). From relationships to experiences in retail financial services. *International Journal of Bank Marketing*, 22(7), 522–39.

Paulin, M. and Perrien, P. (1998). Relational norms and client retention: external effectiveness of commercial banking in Canada. *International Journal of Bank Marketing*. 16(1) 24–32.

Payne, A., Christopher, M. and Peck, H. (eds) (1995) *Relationship Marketing for Competitive Advantage: winning and keeping customers*. Oxford: Butterworth Heinemann.

Peterson, R. A. (1995). Relationship Marketing and the consumer. *Journal of the Academy of Marketing Science*. 23(4), 278–81.

Quester, P. and Lim, A. L. (2003). Product involvement/brand loyalty: Is there a link? *Journal of Product and Brand Management*, 12(1), 22–38.

Rajaobelina, L. and Bergeron, J. (2008). Antecedents and consequences of buyer-seller relationship quality in the financial services industry. *International Journal of Bank Marketing*, 27(5), 359–80.

Reichheld, F. F. and Sasser, W. E. (1990) "Zero defections: quality comes to services" *Harvard Business Review* Vol. 68(5), 105–11.

Reichheld, F. F. and Teal, T. (1996). *The loyalty effect the hidden force behind growth, profits, and lasting value*. Boston, Mass: Harvard Business School Press.

Reinartz, W., Thomas, J. and Bascoul, G. (2008). "Investigating cross-buying and customer loyalty." *Journal of Interactive Marketing* Vol. 22 (1), 5–20, 16p.

Riley, F. D. O. and de Chernatony, L. (2000). The service brand as relationships builder. *British Journal of Management*, 11(2), 137–50.

Salazar, M., Harrison, T. and Ansell, J. (2007). An approach for the identification of cross-selling and up-selling opportunities using a financial services customer database. *Journal of Financial Services Marketing*. 2, 115–31.

Sheth, J. N. and Parvatiyar, A. (1995). Relationship marketing in consumer markets. Antecedents and consequences. *Journal of the Academy of Marketing Science* 23(4), 255–72.

Shi, G., Shi, Y. K., Chan, A. and Wang, Y. (2009). Relationship strength in service industries. *International Journal of Market Research*. 51(5), 659–85.

Thwaites, D. and Vere, L. (1995). Bank selection criteria-a student perspective. *Journal of Marketing Management*, 11, 133–49.

Van der Poel, D. and Larivière, B. (2004). Investigating the role of product features in preventing customer churn, by using survival analysis and choice modelling: the case of financial services. *Expert Systems with Applications*. 27(2) 277–65.

Yu, A. P-I. (2009). "The impact of financial services type on consumer relationship engagement motives: an empirical investigation of retail banking consumers. Unpublished doctoral thesis". The University of Edinburgh.

Vargo, S. and Lusch, R. F. (2008). Service-dominant logic: continuing the evolution. *Journal of the Academy of Marketing Science*. 36, 1–10.

Varki, S. and Wong, S. (2003). Consumer involvement in relationship marketing of service. *Journal of Service Research*, 6(1), 83–91.

Weinberg, M. (1997). "Telemarketing of Financial Services-Eldorado or Mirage", The Marketors' City Lecture, The Worshipful Company of Marketers/City University Business School.

Wendel, S. and Dellaert, B. (2009). Situation-based shifts in consumer web site benefit importance: The joint role of cognition and affect. *Information and Management*. 46(1), 23–30.

Zaichkowsky, J. L. (1985). Measuring the involvement construct. *Journal of Consumer Research*, 12(3), 341–52.

Zhang, J., Dixit, A. and Friedmann, R. (2010). Customer loyalty and lifetime value: an empirical investigation of consumer packaged goods. *Journal of Marketing Theory & Practice*. 18(2) 127–39.

10

Trust and trustworthiness in retail financial services

An analytical framework and empirical evidence

Christine Ennew and Harjit Singh Sekhon

Introduction

Building long-term relationships has long been advocated as being one of the core activities of any business, no matter what its type or size. An effective relationship between any business and its customers is characterised by genuine commitment, which is rooted in the development of trust (Morgan and Hunt 1994). The idea that 'trust matters' is not novel and there is nothing new about its significance in business relationships. As a concept, trust is simple to recognise when it is present and just as simple to recognise when it is breached. Although the benefits of trust are many and varied, its presence requires that there is a basis on which one party gives trust and the other accepts it. Understanding the factors that drive trust and trustworthiness is important during the development and management of effective business relationships. The financial services sector is suffering from a crisis of trust and the reputations of providers have been badly damaged as a consequence (Hansen 2012). In this chapter we outline what it is to trust and explore the factors that enable financial services providers to demonstrate trustworthiness. This chapter complements Chapter 30.

Few conceptual or empirical studies of marketing relationships fail to discuss the construct of trust, but definitions and antecedents vary and lack coherence. Given the complexity of trust and its diverse disciplinary roots, this situation is perhaps unsurprising, and not entirely satisfactory. Drawing on theoretical insights from a variety of different disciplines, this chapter conceptualises the nature of trust in marketing relationships in general and explores the implications for organisations that seek to engender trust in their customers. The chapter begins by reviewing definitions of trust and identifying core themes within these definitions. Based on these key themes, it is argued that trust in marketing relationships can be seen as operating at two distinct levels, which are described as cognitive (lower level) and affective (higher level). Understanding the antecedents of consumer trust can provide important insights for financial services organisations as they seek to demonstrate trustworthiness to their customers. Empirical evidence from the UK is presented to substantiate the conceptual analysis.

Definitions of trust

Trust has long been established as a critical component of exchange relationships and as essential to the way that an organisation presents itself to its customers (see for example, Ben-Ner and Halldorsson 2010). Blois (1999) suggested that trust is superficially obvious but essentially complex. Given this, it is perhaps hardly surprising that there are a multitude of definitions of trust and a lack of coherence in the use of the words 'trust' and 'trustworthy'. In general, trust is a belief that is held by one party about the attitudes and behaviours of another party, thus it is multifaceted (Castaldo 2007), and context specific (Greenwood and Buren 2010). From a marketing perspective, trust would be a belief held by a customer about organisations or their representatives. In contrast, trustworthiness is a characteristic of one party which might lead another party to trust them (Blois 1999). In marketing terms, trustworthiness is an attribute of an organisation or its representatives that would lead customers to express trust. Any understanding of trustworthiness must be rooted in an understanding of trust and thus trust is the focus of the remainder of this section.

At the macro level trust can be seen as the basis for a stable collective existence, given that complete contracting is impossible and some degree of uncertainty is unavoidable in any transaction, trust provides a basis for social and economic exchange (Arrow 1974). In broad terms, trust has been identified as a means of promoting co-operation and reducing conflict in a variety of settings, including within work groups and between employees and managers across organisations (Rousseau et al. 1998), as well as serving as a governance mechanism for marketing relations (Doney and Cannon 1997). Indeed, Fukuyama (1995) equates the wellbeing of nations with the levels of trust that exist between and within its institutions. With such a diversity of perspectives on the role of trust, it is hardly surprising that there is a variety of different definitions of the construct, some of which are illustrated in Table 10.1. The list of definitions is designed to be indicative rather than exhaustive.

What is apparent from the definitions in Table 10.1 is that certain core themes are present, irrespective of the disciplinary origins of the definitions of trust (Rousseau et al. 1998, Sheppard and Sherman 1998): trust depends on the existence of risk, trust depends on interdependence between actors, trust is associated with vulnerability, trust involves confident expectations about future behaviour.

Central to almost all definitions of trust are the ideas of a willingness to be vulnerable and confident expectations (Rousseau et al. 1998). Vulnerability is a future construct that is founded on interdependence and risk; confident expectations relate to the ability of one party to predict how the target of trust will behave in the future. Although the relevance of individual vulnerability as a consequence of dependence on others and uncertainty about the future seems straightforward, the nature and meaning of the element of 'confident expectations' appears to be rather more open to debate.

In general, 'confident expectations' relate to the predictability of future behaviour that Sztompka (1999) describes as a bet on the future, but there seem to be some differences in the assessment of exactly what such predictability means. In part, this might reflect differences in the usage of particular words. For example, in some cases, the terms 'confidence' and 'reliance' are used interchangeably, in other cases they may be used jointly (see for example, Morgan and Hunt 1994). However, irrespective of the issue of semantics, it is apparent that the idea of predictability – knowing how a trusted party will behave – has a key role to play. Blois (1999) refers to this predictability as 'dependable habits' and suggests that the idea of predictability is essentially related to reliability. Similarly, Doney and Cannon (1997) make reference to credibility in the sense that an exchange partner's word can be relied upon. Wetzels et al. (1998) make use of the term 'honesty' to refer to the extent to which an exchange partner stands by their

Table 10.1 Some definitions of trust

Author	Source	Definition
Gambetta (1988: 217)	Social research	A particular level of the subjective probability with which an agent or group of agents will perform a particular action, both before he can monitor such action and in the context in which its effects are shown.
Anderson and Narus (1990: 45)	Channel marketing	The firm's believe that another company will perform actions that will result in positive outcomes for the firm, as well as take unexpected actions that would result in negative outcomes for the firm.
Moorman et al (1992: 315)	Services marketing	A willingness to rely on an exchange partner in whom one has confidence.
Morgan and Hunt (1994: 23)	Buyer-Seller relationships	When one party has confidence in an exchange partner's reliability and integrity.
McAllister (1995: 25)	Organizational theory	The extent to which a person is confident in, and willing to act on the basis of words, actions, and decisions of another.
Mayer et al (1995: 712)	Organizational theory	Willingness of one party to be vulnerable to the actions of another party based on the expectation that the other will perform a particular action important to the trustor, irrespective of the ability to monitor or control that other party.
Tyler and Kramer (1996: 5)	Organizational theory	Trust can be conceptualised as an orientation towards society and towards other that has social meaning beyond rational calculations.
Bhattacharya et al (1998: 462)	Strategy/ Economic theory	An expectancy of positive (or nonnegative) outcomes that one can receive based on the expected action of another party in an interaction characterized by uncertainty.
Lewicki et al (1998: 439)	Psychology	Confident positive expectations regarding another's conduct.
Sztompka (1999: 25)	Sociology	A bet about the future contingent actions of others.

word. A number of definitions of trust extend beyond this notion of predictability or reliability. Anderson and Narus (1990) refer to positive outcomes for the trustor while Wilson (1995) refers to the trustor's 'best interests'. Morgan and Hunt (1994) refer to integrity, which they relate to consistency, competence, honesty, fairness, responsibility, helpfulness and benevolence.

There seems to be general consensus that trust is based on elements of reliability and predictability in future behaviour. There also appears to be strong evidence to indicate that trust incorporates an element of benevolence or goodwill on the part of the trustee towards the trustor. Doney and Cannon (1997) consider trust as having dimensions of credibility and benevolence (although subsequent empirical evidence results in the two being combined into a single measure). Similarly, Sirdeshmukh et al. (2002) recognise the competence and benevolence aspects of trust while Wetzels et al. (1998) refer to honesty and benevolence. However, not all commentators accept the notion of the two dimensions to trust. In particular, Blois (1999: 199) comments that the reliability element alone does not constitute trust:

> What distinguishes trust from reliance is the expectation that the other party may take initiatives (or exercise discretion) to utilise new opportunities to our advantage, over and above what was either explicitly or implicitly promised.

Others, perhaps, take a less extreme position and propose the existence of different forms of trust. McAllister (1995), for example, draws a distinction between cognitive and affective trust. Cognitive trust is essentially based on some level of knowledge and belief about others; it represents a conscious choice on the part of an individual and is likely to be based on attributes such as the competence, reliability and dependability of exchange partners. In contrast, affective trust is essentially based on emotional ties in relationships and is likely to be structured around elements such as care and concern for others. In a similar vein, Darley (1998) distinguishes between a form of trust that is based on rewards and sanctions and one that is more idealised, honourable and personal. The former is essentially calculative, based on self-interest while the latter is non-calculative and may be thought of as being based on care and concern for the interests of the relationship partner.

Implicitly, the approaches adopted by McAllister (1995) and Darley (1998) are reflected in the marketing literature by, amongst others, Morgan and Hunt (1994) and Doney and Cannon (1997) and are based on the idea that different levels of trust may exist in relationships. Similar conceptualisations can be found in the organisational analysis literature. Lewicki and Bunker (1996), for example, refer to calculus-based trust, knowledge-based trust and identification-based trust, while Rousseau et al. (1998) make reference to calculus-based trust, relational trust and institutional trust. In contrast, the position adopted by Blois (1999) and Williamson (1993) suggests a single dimension to trust, but one that is more heavily rooted in interpersonal relationships, has a significant affective component and is essentially non-calculative. In order to resolve these different perspectives, it may be helpful to focus on the ways in which definitions of trust have developed from different disciplinary traditions and this issue is explored in more detail in the next section.

Perspectives on trust

Given the significance of trust in a range of different disciplines (including philosophy, economics, sociology and psychology), researchers in management and marketing have drawn heavily on these different traditions in developing business related conceptualisations. As a consequence, the construct of trust has been interpreted in a variety of ways.

In attempting to make sense of these different perspectives, Korczynski (2000) makes headway in explaining the apparent diversity by focussing attention on the bases on which trustors can be confident about the actions of trustees. He identifies four bases of confidence drawn from the perspectives of economics and sociology. Incentive or governance based trust is essentially a calculative construct. The basis for confidence lies in the governance structure of exchange; one party will not exploit another because it is not in their interest to do so. Reputation is seen as being a particular incentive that serves to discourage opportunistic behaviour. Personal relationship-based trust also incorporates a calculative element in which the sanction or incentive is based on interpersonal relationships but this is enhanced by the recognition of the value associated with information that one individual has with respect to another. A third basis for trust involves confidence-based on knowledge of the trustee's internal norms. This perspective does not rely on the economic or social interests of the trustee, but rather on an awareness of how individuals will behave based on knowledge of their values and norms. The final perspective on trust relies on confidence in the trustee that is based on institutional norms surrounding the relationships (for example, Giddens (1990, 1991) gives the example of trust as recognition that all individuals will honour the value of paper money).

Implicit in Korczynski's (2000) analysis is the existence of a calculative dimension and a non-calculative dimension to trust. Rousseau et al. (1998) also draw on a range of disciplines including economics, sociology and psychology to suggest another set of distinctions. Like Korczynski, they provide a similar interpretation of an institutional perspective on trust and indeed there seems to be widespread agreement about this particular perspective. It is in relation to other perspectives on trust that there seems to be more variation. According to Rousseau et al. (1998), calculus-based trust recognises the existence of potential sanctions for the breach of trust and credible information (for example, reputation) to support trust, such that the costs of breaching trust significantly outweigh the benefits. In contrast, relational trust is based on information that is unique to the relationship between trustor and trustee and includes an emotional element that is related to interpersonal care and concern.

Lewicki and Bunker (1996) identify three bases of trust. Again, the first level of trust is one that is calculus-based. The intermediate level is what they describe as knowledge-based trust, where confidence in future behaviour relies on interpersonal knowledge, a definition that is closely linked to Korczynski's concept of personal relationship-based trust. The final level of trust is described as identification-based trust and is based on mutual understanding of needs and wants. Again, this relates closely to Korcynski's concept of trust based on knowledge of internal norms and overlaps with elements of Rousseau et al.'s (1998) notion of relational trust. Further support for the proposition that trust has more than one dimension is provided by Benedicktus et al. (2010).

Given these perspectives on trust and the conceptualisations that have been used in marketing (drawing primarily from social psychology), we propose that trust in marketing relationships should be recognised as operating at two levels: cognitive (lower level) and affective (higher level).

Cognitive trust

Cognitive trust originates from rational choice models rooted in economics. It also overlaps with what Korczynski (2000) refers to as being more sociologically-based personal relations-based trust. In its cognitive form, trust serves as a foundation for market exchange in the absence of complete contracting. It implies that exchange partners will not behave in an opportunistic manner because it is not in their interests to do so, and is expected to manifest itself over time as a consequence of repeated interactions. Fundamentally, cognitive trust suggests that a trustee will be reliable and honest, they will do what they say they will do and have the capability to deliver on their promises.

Affective trust

Unlike cognitive trust, this type of trust is more complex with its roots in social psychology and it emphasises the significance of being concerned about the trustor's interests. Affective trust was described as relational by Rousseau et al. (1998) and aligns closely with Lewicki and Bunker's (1996) concept of identification-based trust and what Korczynski (2000) acknowledges as internal norms. This type of trust is about goodwill and the emotional connections which are the triggers for trust. These triggers can be the consequence of deep emotional links and the outcome of long-term investments in the relationship (Costigan et al. 1998) and thus as Castaldo (2007) posits it is 'mood felt'.

The aforementioned two forms of trust can be expected to exist in a hierarchical relationship, with cognitive trust leading to the affective form, although affective trust can emerge quickly (see Sekhon et al. 2013). Cognitive trust is the most basic level of trust and in marketing relationships it represents dependability, reliability and honesty. In its basic form it means that the customer believes the organisation will do what it says it will do. Affective trust is the higher form of trust and implies that consumers believe that the organisation shares their best interests and can reasonably be expected to engage in behaviour that results in positive outcomes for them.

Modelling trust and trustworthiness: a financial services perspective

The argument that trust supports market exchange is one of the central building blocks for an appreciation of trust in customer-organisation relationships, particularly so in a service context where the offering may possess high credence attributes. Financial services provide a case in point. The buying process is often confused by the variety and complexity of the products that are available, at least from a consumer perspective. Intrinsically, long-term savings and investment products are highly complex; the large number of variants of essentially the same product has the effect of adding to the layers of complexity that already exist. The difficulties associated with these products are further compounded by the inability of consumers to judge how well products will perform in the future, and in some cases, assessment may not be made for many years. For example, with many endowment products sold in the 1980s and 1990s in the UK, shortfalls in expected returns did not emerge for over a decade but as the products were sold as a means of repaying mortgages, the ultimate impact on consumer welfare was considerable.

Adding to the complexity, product performance depends on the skills of product providers (that the organisation should be able to manage) and the future of the economy (that is outside of organisational control). Moreover, the performance of similar product types may vary considerably according to the time period over which they are assessed and the timing of the initial purchase. As a result, inferior performance may be due to misfortune or poor timing rather than provider failure. These characteristics mean that it is exceptionally difficult for most retail customers to judge the quality of a product or a provider. Financial services are often described as being characterised by experience and credence qualities – their quality is best judged after purchase (experience qualities) – but even after purchase it may be difficult to assess whether realised quality is the result of a good product/provider or favourable economic circumstances (credence qualities). In making a purchase decision, consumers will have to rely on a range of factors including their past experience, the experience of others, specialist advice and most importantly, trust and confidence in the product provider.

Drawing on key features of the purchasing process, the conditions that make trust and trustworthiness important are clearly in evidence in relation to financial services. For example, risk, although relevant to most financial services in some way or another, will be most significant in relation to savings and investment products. Risk is inherent to the product but is compounded by consumers' typically low levels of interest/understanding and the impacts of uncontrollable factors. Another issue is vulnerability; since financial services can and do have a significant impact on the consumer's well-being, a poor performing product can have a significant impact on individual customers. Interdependence is another key feature; the nature of financial markets means that in general, individuals need the services of a specialist intermediary to deal with their financial needs. More significantly, product variety and complexity mean that the customer is dependent on a financial services organisation for advice and the more limited the customer's interest or understanding of financial services, the greater the dependence on a financial services provider or a financial adviser.

Of course, there are contractual safeguards to protect consumers as well, such as deposit insurance and consumer protection legislation; brand reputation imposes some constraints on opportunistic behaviour. Such safeguards are probably most powerful in relation to the more straightforward financial services (banking, savings, etc.) but even then they cannot cover every eventuality. As products become more complex (investments, pensions) and consumers become less interested, choices around purchase, product type and provider become fundamentally dependent on the consumer's willingness to trust and by implication, the trustworthiness of the provider. Such trust is beneficial to customer and provider for a number of reasons.

Trust has been found to reduce opportunism (Rindfleisch and Moorman 2003), increase customer loyalty (Agustin and Singh 2005, Buttle and Burton 2002), improve effective communication (Anderson and Narus 1990), increase customer satisfaction (Jyh-Shen and Droge 2006), increase customer commitment (Jap and Ganesan 2000), and has also been found to reduce perceived risk (Mayer et al. 1995). In general, findings from marketing research present a consistent picture with trust being shown to have a significant positive impact on consumer attitudes and behaviour.

Earlier, we argued that trust is essentially a belief held by an individual and may to varying degrees reflect that individual's personality and disposition (Blois 1999, Hansen 2012). The way organisations or other individuals can influence that belief is by signalling that they are trustworthy. Thus, the model we develop below takes trustworthiness as its focal construct (and as the main determinant of trust). In line with the discussion outlined in the previous section, trust is seen to have cognitive and affective components as well as being subject to variations at the level of the individual. The key for any organisation wishing to build trust with its customers is the ability to demonstrate that it is worthy of trust.

The essential issue then, is to identify the factors that will give rise to trustworthiness: what are the reputational and behavioural factors that result in organisations being perceived as trustworthy? Much of the research on trust has tended to focus on the consequences rather than the antecedents. Studies that do focus on antecedents tend to develop their conceptualisation around trust rather than trustworthiness despite a growing recognition of the significance of trustworthiness (Hardin 2002, Xie and Peng 2009). Thus, in attempting to identify the factors that give rise to perceptions of trustworthiness, we will draw on studies addressing trust as well as trustworthiness. Probably the most widely used perspective is that offered by Morgan and Hunt (1994) who suggest that shared values, communication and opportunistic behaviour are the key influences on trust in marketing relationships. These constructs are measured by the consumer's perceptions of what the organisation is or does. In contrast, Garbarino and Johnson (1999) adopt a general approach and identify attitudes towards the service (theatre performances) and satisfaction as antecedents to trust. Michell et al. (1998), although not specifically addressing the issue of antecedents, suggest that probity, equity, reliability and satisfaction are correlates, which may be managed by organisations in order to enhance the levels of trust in relationships with customers.

Doney and Cannon (1997) adopt a more process-driven conceptualisation of the determinants of trust. They highlight the roles of calculative processes, prediction processes, capability processes, intentionality processes and transference processes in the assessment of a trustee by a trustor, then identify specific supplier activities that contribute to those processes. For example, the predictive process is concerned with the ability of a trustor to predict the future behaviour of the trustee. This process is seen as being driven by factors such as length of the relationship with the organisation and its sales people, similarity and likeability of sales staff and frequency of contact.

Singh and Sirdeshmukh (2002) focus their analysis specifically on trustworthiness and identify operational competence, operational benevolence and problem-solving orientation as key indicators of the trustworthiness of managers and frontline staff. This perspective provides more specific indicators of managerial activities that may be used by organisations wishing to signal their trustworthiness. A problem-solving orientation involves, for example, the organisation or individual being willing to bend company policies to address consumer needs. Equally, operational benevolence represents the extent to which customers' best interests are understood and accommodated by the organisation. Palmer and Huo (2013), based on an assessment of published research, identify a number of factors that are consistent in the trust literature: ability, benevolence, integrity and predictability.

Drawing on the various factors that have been identified as influences on trust and trustworthiness, we propose a comprehensive conceptualisation of the nature and determinants of trustworthiness. This conceptualisation extends existing work in a number of ways. First, it identifies two distinct levels at which trust might exist: cognitive and affective. Second, it presents trustworthiness as a key antecedent of trust. Third it provides a more comprehensive analysis of the determinants of trustworthiness.

The model (see Figure 10.1) proposes that consumer trust in an organisation may be low level (i.e. cognitive) or high level (i.e. affective). In line with marketing studies that have reported close associations between these forms of trust (for example, Doney and Cannon 1997) it is suggested that cognitive trust can lead to affective trust. However, this is at variance with Williamson (1993) who would suggest that the two are contradictory.

Consumer trust is also related to individual characteristics, reflecting work in psychology which proposes that consumers may have different dispositions to trust. The other major determinant of trust is organisational trustworthiness that is related to expertise and competence, integrity and consistency in behaviour, effective communications, shared values and concern and benevolence. These drivers of trustworthiness will contribute to the development of both forms of trust but it is suggested that their impacts may be different for cognitive and affective trust.

Thus drawing on and synthesising existing research on trust and marketing relationships, a comprehensive set of proposed drivers of trustworthiness are identified.

Expertise and competence

For a trustee to be willing to accept vulnerability they have to be confident that the product provider has the ability to deliver its obligation(s) (Mayer et al. 1995), and promises. Ability is sometimes referred to as competence, while Doney and Cannon (1997) refer to it under the broad heading of the experience of the salesperson.

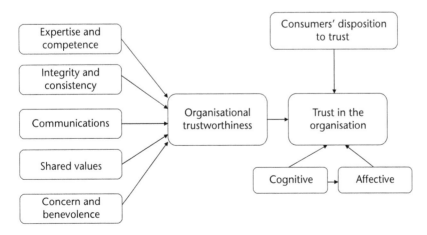

Figure 10.1 A model of trust in marketing relationships

For a consumer to recognise that a product provider is worthy of trust, they need confidence in the provider's ability to deliver. In the case of financial services, this relates to the ability of frontline staff to advise in a manner that is likely to yield the results that consumers seek. The consumer's willingness to be vulnerable will be dependent on assurances that the provider has the capability to deliver.

Integrity and consistency

Consistent behaviour over time contributes towards a financial services organisation's trustworthiness because it increases the predictability of future behaviours; reducing uncertainty and risk. Consistency in itself is not enough, there is also an important role for integrity. Integrity is related to the correctness in behaviour of the financial services provider. This is important because consumers of financial products must perceive that the product provider is honest and that they will do what they say they will do; consistent correct behaviour in the past will be one of the strongest indicators of consistent correct behaviour in the future.

Integrity (or its absence) in financial services is associated, for example, with a series of misselling cases that have impacted negatively on significant numbers of customers, resulting in the imposition of fines by regulators and have damaged the sector's reputation for trustworthiness (see Chapter 29 for a detailed analysis of misselling cases).

Communication

For Morgan and Hunt (1994) the flow of information is important for trustworthiness. When building trust, communication must not be interpreted as meaning a mundane exchange of information because the goal of effective communication should be to open up to each other (Solomon and Flores 2003) and to provide rich, frequent and meaningful communication. Taken together, the flow of information is an important enabler in building trust (Anderson and Narus 1990). Three aspects of communications are key: accuracy, explanation and openness (Whitener et al. 1998). Owing to the nature of financial services, accuracy may be of particular significance when evaluations need to be made of investment-type products that may not yield a return for 10–15 years, longer in the case of pension investments. Explanation and openness is also important when there may be shortfalls in returns designed to support other products, such as endowments so consumers can make informed decisions regarding various options, including the chance to purchase other products.

The outcome of clear communications is that consumers are informed about products, organisational changes and are updated during complex transactions. Given that communications may relate to the predictability or reliability of the service provider, it is essential that there is meaningful in-depth engagement in the process.

Shared values

The position of shared values in the trust literature is clear and there is a long tradition of research that highlights the importance of this broad construct (see for example, Kelman 1961). The idea that individuals and organisations might have shared values can be described in a number of different ways. For example, Doney and Cannon (1997) deal with shared values under the broad heading of similarity, but go on to position the narrative such that if a sales person shares the values of their consumers, it becomes simpler to predict future behaviour. Irrespective of precise terminology, the key feature of the construct of shared values is that it is concerned with similarity and identification between individuals and organisations. Where shared values exist then the probability is that it will lead to greater commitment and longevity (Morgan and Hunt 1994).

The creation of shared values with consumers is likely to be a product of the culture that exists within an organisation. The culture will, *inter alia*, reflect management beliefs/practices, which result in the development of trust internally and where an organisation is characterised by internal trust building, it will be better placed to build trust externally with customers. Research suggests that when building internal trust, the obstacles associated with its formation within the organisation may be greater than those associated with engendering trust externally (Galford and Drapeau 2003).

Benevolence

Benevolence is potentially a significant influence on trustworthiness (Sheppard and Sharman 1998) with three main dimensions: consideration and sensitivity, acting in protecting the interests of others and refraining from exploiting others. Together, this suggests that a financial services organisation that is able to demonstrate benevolence is showing that it will not exploit a consumer's vulnerability. Benevolent behaviour, for example, may go so far as to discourage the excessive consumption of certain debt-type products by those who may, in the long-term, be ill-equipped to afford them.

In the case of most financial services organisations benevolence is of particular relevance to the role of employees who are central given the highly intangible nature of the product offering. Thus, it is expected that employees will display a high degree of empathy with consumers. Bove and Johnson (2006) propose that benevolent behaviour on the part of the sales person is an antecedent of behavioural loyalty towards a sales person, leading to loyalty towards the service business.

Organisational trustworthiness is different from trust: it is a representation of behaviours past and present; an aspect of an organisation's reputation accumulated over time that may almost be viewed as a capital asset (Blois 2003). It is evident that trustworthy behaviour can impact positively on customer loyalty and retention; it can be of value in providing reassurance during periods of crisis. It may even be the case that regulators may be more favourably disposed where it is clear that a financial services organisation is genuinely trustworthy. Given that many financial services are characterised by a predominance of credence qualities, customer trust is a valuable but fragile commodity. Building and maintaining trust depends on an organisation being able to reassure its customers that it is indeed worthy of their trust. Such reassurance will come from past behaviours and active messaging, which demonstrate expertise and competence, integrity and consistency in behaviour, effective communications, shared values and concern and benevolence.

Evidence from empirical research

Empirical evidence on the evolution of trust and trustworthiness in the UK can be obtained from survey work undertaken by the Financial Services Research Forum.[1] Data tracking trust and trustworthiness over time were gathered from an exploratory study conducted in 2005, and full studies conducted in 2006, 2007, 2008 and 2009. In 2005, only information for financial services institutions (FSIs) was collected, but in 2006, 2007 and 2008, data was also collected for comparator institutions. Over the study periods, in total just over 13,000 units of data were gathered, thus providing one of the most robust and sophisticated datasets on trust and trustworthiness in the financial services sector in the UK.

The study period not only predates much of the recent crises of confidence in the financial services sector, it also includes the period during the height of the crises. A professional market research agency was employed and a CATI approach was used for data collection. In terms of survey participation, individuals were contacted by random selection from a commercial database. No incentives to take part in the survey were provided to sample members.

To ensure representativeness in terms of the type of institution and UK population, sample members were pre-screened before being asked to participate. The sampling method was not a panel data approach, as those sampled differed in each wave. The screening resulted in a sample that broadly reflected the density of the various types of financial services institutions in the UK and the UK population. The realised sample was split 56 percent male and 44 percent female. In terms of age groups, around 22 percent of the sample was under the age of 35 and the remainder of the sample was split broadly equally between the middle and older age groups. The sample achieved was revealing and relates to the dynamics of the market. For example, there were lower rates of penetration for mortgage and pension products amongst lower age groups, while in the case of credit cards and pure banking products penetration was fairly consistent across the age groups.

The measurement scales for the focal constructs relating to trust and trustworthiness were developed specifically for this study but drew heavily on pre-existing measurement approaches. The scale development process broadly followed the methodology suggested by Churchill (1979) with insights from Rossiter (2002), and a number of steps were undertaken to ensure that a robust set of measurement scales emerged (see Ennew et al. 2011 for more detail and the appendix for a listing of scale items).

The data was subjected to a confirmatory factor analysis using data from each of the waves, with 300 selected units from each round of data collection aggregated to create 1,500 units of data. The 300 cases for each wave were selected randomly using the random selection tool in SPSS.

The results from the confirmatory analysis (CFA) with n = 1500 for the key constructs show the following fit statistics: (χ^2 693.83, d.f 352, χ^2/d.f 2.12, RMSEA 0.063, CFI .956, PGFI .944, GFI .963) suggesting that the original eight constructs of the proposed model are acceptable (see Ennew et al. 2011).

We begin with descriptive statistics focussing on mean values for the key constructs. Figure 10.2 provides information on the evolution of trust over time based on the range of institutions considered in the study.

The analysis over time suggests a high degree of consistency in levels of customer trust in FSIs. Brokers and advisers are consistently the most trusted FSIs although they experienced a marginal decline in 2009 from the high of the previous year; life insurers tend to be the least trusted FSIs, along with credit card companies. Banks, building societies, general insurers, life insurers and investment companies all experienced a slight increase in 2009 while credit card companies deteriorated after an improvement in 2008. One-way analysis of variance suggests that the differences in overall trust across institution types are statistically significant. However, with 7 categories, many individual differences do not emerge as significant, with the exception of the broker/adviser category, which stands out as significantly better than most other types of FSI.

Further examination of the components of trust reveals some interesting patterns. Figures 10.3 and 10.4 examine the evolution of low level or cognitive trust (that measures the extent to which the institution does what it is supposed to do) and higher level or affective trust (that focusses on the extent to which the institution displays concern for the interests of its customers). One-way analysis of variance for these constructs broadly displays a pattern similar to that observed with overall trust.

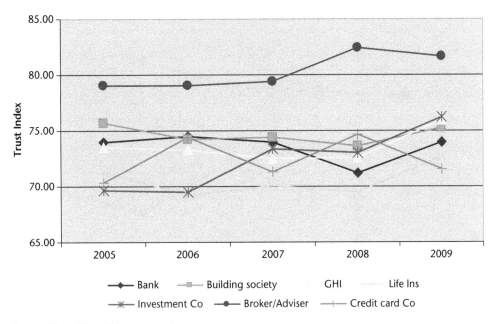

Figure 10.2 Overall trust over time

There is a high degree of consistency with the results for overall trust, as would be expected, but also some interesting variations. The strong position of brokers is clearly in evidence, but they appear to be affected by a drop in higher-level trust between 2008 and 2009. Credit card companies also appear to do particularly badly with respect to higher-level trust. Life insurers are the weakest institutions with respect to base-level trust but also show signs of

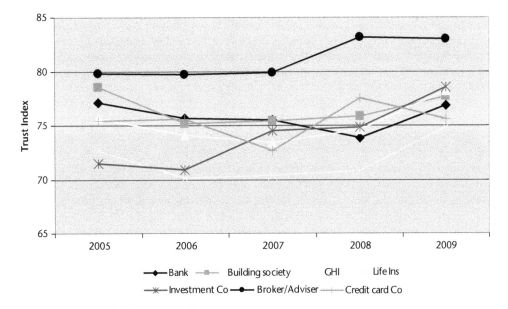

Figure 10.3 Base level trust over time

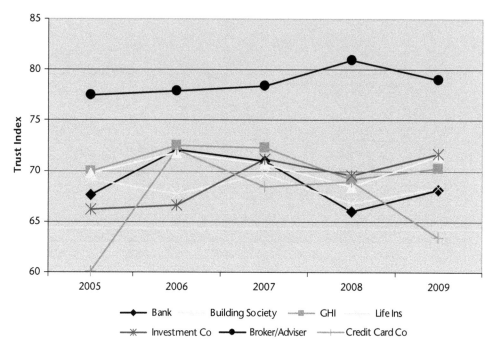

Figure 10.4 High level trust over time

improvement over time. In contrast, the picture is much more variable with respect to high-level trust where there seems to be rather less differentiation between institutions (with the exception of the favourable perceptions of brokers/advisers and the poorer perceptions of credit card providers) and weaker evidence of an improvement in comparison with 2008. A number of factors may explain this. First, the more idealised nature of high level trust may suggest that improvements across all institutions tend to take longer to materialise. Second, the strength of brokers/advisers probably reflects their perceived position as in some way independent, acting directly on behalf of customers. In contrast, the widely expressed concerns about the behaviour of credit card providers (particularly with respect to extending credit limits with little concern about ability to pay) may have contributed to their poor performance with respect to affective trust.

Figure 10.5 outlines the evolution of trustworthiness. Again, brokers show a high level of trustworthiness but also record a decline when compared with 2008. Other FSIs display a degree of stability with indications of a slight decline for credit card companies and a slight increase for other providers.

Figure 10.6 compares trust ratings for the financial services sector as a whole, with ratings for comparator institutions. These demonstrate that over the four-year period for which comparator data is available, the financial services sector has consistently recorded higher levels of trust than employers, supermarkets, mobile phone providers, the BBC and the NHS. The commercial institutions in this list are moving increasingly closer to financial institutions, but the BBC and the NHS remain significantly below financial services institutions, perhaps reflecting the fact that with financial services and commercial organisations, consumers choose between alternatives in a way that they do not with the BBC and the NHS.

Rather than estimating the full model outlined in Figure 10.1, we focus attention on the key relationships surrounding trustworthiness. A simple regression analysis of the determinants of

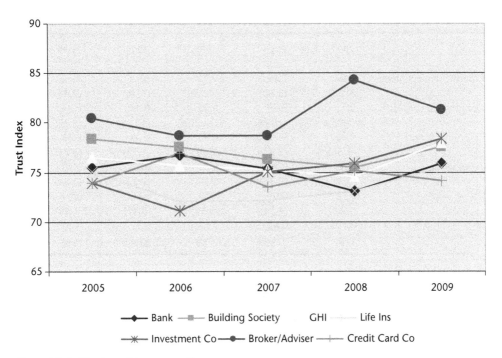

Figure 10.5 Trustworthiness over time

trustworthiness for the five rounds of data collection is presented in Table 10.2. As shown by the regression coefficients in Table 10.2, integrity and benevolence are consistently the factors that have most influence on consumer perceptions of the trustworthiness of financial institutions. In contrast, communications and shared values have only a marginal impact and in some cases are insignificant.

There is some variability in the coefficients associated with the various drivers of trust over the five-year period. In particular, there are indications that the impact of consumer perceptions

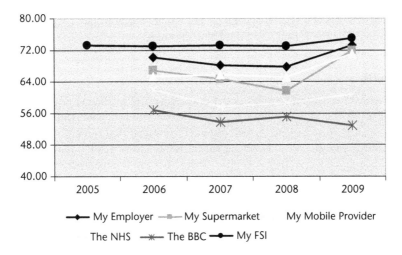

Figure 10.6 Comparative trust ratings over time

Table 10.2 An analysis of the determinants of trustworthiness by survey round

	2005 (Pilot)	2006	2007	2008	2009
Expertise and competence	0.07	0.09	0.15	0.12	0.20
	(2.55)	(3.28)	(4.94)	(4.46)	(7.45)
Integrity and consistency	0.33	0.39	0.36	0.47	0.34
	(9.83)	(13.66)	(12.20)	(15.29)	(11.99)
Communications	0.06	0.06	0.02	0.03	0.06
	(2.66)	(2.81)	(0.77)	(1.23)	(2.72)
Benevolence	0.32	0.21	0.24	0.23	0.25
	(8.79)	(7.35)	(7.61)	(7.73)	(8.27)
Shared values	0.12	0.09	0.08	0.10	0.03
	(4.68)	(4.56)	(3.35)	(5.10)	(1.60)
R^2	0.701	0.62	0.64	0.77	0.70
N	1767	3389	2783	2235	2685

(Figures in parentheses are t-statistics)

of a financial services provider's expertise and competence are increasing in importance, as shown by the increase in the regression coefficient during the five-year period.

Although there are signs that the drivers of trustworthiness vary over time, there is no systematic evidence that the relationship differs by institution type. The relationships outlined in Table 10.2 were re-estimated with the inclusion of institution-specific dummy variables but no significant effects were identified.

When examining the levels of trust and trustworthiness over time, it is clear that trust is at its highest when the specific provider has the opportunity to form a strong bond with the customer and explicitly act on their behalf, as in the case of financial advisors (brokers). This highlights the value of one-to-one relationships in developing a deeper sense of customer engagement. Clearly, the one-to-one approach will not be possible for all types of financial products or all types of customer. Building a reputation for trustworthiness will be more challenging where the relationship is at arm's length, as is the case with, say, a bank or a credit card provider. The variability in the data suggests that for some providers and for some customers, high levels of trustworthiness are present in the relationship and this reflects the importance of policy decisions that reflect the consumer's interest and values and communications that provide the necessary reassurance regarding the behaviour of the FSI and its staff.

Conclusions

Consumer trust has a key role to play in the development of marketing relationships and this is of particular significance in the financial services sector, not least because the products themselves are characterised as credence-based. Although consumer trust is fundamentally a property of the individual and may vary according to individual characteristics, the reputation that a financial services provider has for being trustworthy has a major impact on the extent to which consumers will be prepared to offer their trust. A key message for those involved in the marketing of financial services is the need to focus on activities that help to build trustworthiness. Although we have identified five key constructs around which such activity should be built, we are also conscious that the importance of the five constructs may be product, institutional and timing specific. Nevertheless, as is evident from the research reported in this chapter, the actual levels of trust, trustworthiness and their determinants remain remarkably stable over time.

In this study, it has been argued that trustworthiness plays a key role in the management of trust in customer relationships. We argue that trustworthiness will develop when financial service providers understand that expertise and competence, integrity and consistency, benevolence, shared values and communications play a key role in determining customers' evaluations of organisational trustworthiness and their subsequent willingness to trust. Building a reputation in relation to these attributes requires a focus on certain key business practices that relate to being customer orientated, being transparent and honest, and focussing on the reliable delivery of the right quality of products and services.

When there is a need to trust, there is a need to take on risk and accept vulnerability. The empirical evidence suggests that reassurances in relation to risk and vulnerability (trustworthiness) are most strongly influenced by the extent to which a financial services provider can demonstrate integrity and consistency, benevolence and more recently, expertise and competence.

Integrity and consistency is of particular significance because it can increase consumers' confidence in the predictability of the future behaviour of a financial services provider. Benevolent behaviour is important and depends on the ability to demonstrate that business policies are operated with a concern for the best interests of customers. These factors were shown to be consistently important throughout the time period covered by our analysis. In contrast, expertise and competence become more important over time. This quality requires the service provider to show it has the ability to do what it says it will, based on claims that are deliverable. This is a basic expectation that all consumers will have of financial services providers. In contrast, communications and shared values are less influential and their significance is more variable. Although communications concerns itself with the basic principle of sharing information and keeping consumers updated, shared values are about the extent to which there is similarity between the provider and the consumer, and the identification of behaviours that are aligned between the two.

In summary, the conceptual and empirical analysis outlined in this chapter highlights the significance of trust in the management of relationships between customers and financial services providers. From the perspective of the provider, the key consideration is engendering trust through the projection of trustworthiness. The evidence from a five-year period in the middle of the first decade of the twenty-first century suggests that the key drivers are integrity and consistency, benevolence, expertise and competence. The key message for financial services providers is that building effective customer relationships must be underpinned by business practices that enable customers to accept risk and vulnerability in purchase decisions, because they can be confident that their financial services provider behaves in an honest and predictable fashion, is concerned about their interests and has the ability to deliver on the promises it makes.

Note

1 Now the Centre for Risk, Banking and Financial Services, see www.nottingham.ac.uk/business/forum/publications.aspx

References

Agustin, C. and Singh, J. (2005) 'Curvilinear effects of consumer loyalty determinants in relational exchanges', *Journal of Marketing Research*, 42(1), pp. 96–108.

Anderson, J. and Narus, J. (1990) 'A model of distributor firm and manufacturer firm working partnerships', *Journal of Marketing*, 54 (January), pp. 42–58.

Arrow, K. (1974) *The Limits of Organization*, New York: Norton.

Benedicktus, R.L., Brady, M.K., Darke, P.R. and Voorhees, C.M. (2010) 'Conveying trustworthiness to online consumers: reactions to consensus, physical store presence, brand familiarity, and generalized suspicion', *Journal of Retailing*, 86(4), pp. 322–35.

Ben-Ner, A. and Halldorsson, F. (2010) 'Trusting and trustworthiness: what are they, how to measure them, and what effects them', *Journal of Economic Psychology*, 31, pp. 64–79.

Berry, L. (1995) 'Relationship marketing of services – growing interest, emerging perspectives', *Journal of the Academy of Marketing Science*, 23(4), pp. 236–45.

Blois, K. (1999) 'Trust in business to business relationships: an evaluation of its status', *Journal of Management Studies*, 36(2), pp. 197–215.

—— (2003) 'Is it commercially irresponsible to trust', *Journal of Business Ethics*. 45(3), pp. 183–93.

Bove, L. and Johnson, L. (2006) 'Customer loyalty to one service worker: should it be discouraged', *International Journal of Research in Marketing*, 23, pp. 79–91.

Buttle, F. and Burton, J. (2002) 'Does service failure influence customer loyalty?', *Journal of Consumer Behaviour*, 1, pp. 217–27.

Castaldo, S. (2007) *Trust in Marketing Relationships*, Edward Elgar Publishing Limited, Cheltenham, UK.

Churchill, G.A., Jr. (1979) "A Paradigm for Developing Better Measures of Marketing Constructs" *Journal of Marketing Research*, 16 (February), pp. 64–73.

Costigan, R.D., Ilter, S.S. and Berman, J.J. (1998) 'A multi-dimensional study of trust in organisations', *Journal of Management Issues*, 10(3), pp. 303–17.

Darley, J. (1998) 'Trust in organizations: frontiers of theory and research', *Business Ethics Quarterly*. 8(2), pp. 319–35.

Doney, P. and Cannon, J. (1997) 'An examination of the nature of trust in buyer-seller relationships', *Journal of Marketing*, 61(April), pp. 35–51.

Ennew, C. and Sekhon, H. (2003) 'The role of trust in the financial services sector: a marketing perspective', *Financial Services Research Forum*, Nottingham University Business School.

Ennew, C., Sekhon, H. and Kharouf, H. (2011) 'Trust in UK financial services: A longitudinal analysis', *Journal of Financial Services Marketing*, 16(1), pp. 65–75.

Fukuyama, F. (1995) *Trust: the social virtue and the creation of prosperity*, The Free Press, New York.

Galford, R. and Drapeau, A. (2003) 'The enemies of trust', *Harvard Business Review*, February, pp. 5–11.

Garbarino, E. and Johnson, M. (1999) 'The different roles of satisfaction, trust and commitment in customer relationships', *Journal of Marketing*. 63(April), pp. 70–87.

Giddens, A. (1990) *The Consequences of Modernity*. Polity Press, Cambridge.

—— (1991) *Modernity and Self Identity*. Stanford University Press, Stanford.

Greenwood, M. and Buren, H. (2010) 'Trust and stakeholder theory: trustworthiness in the organisation-stakeholder relationship', *Journal of Business Ethics*, 95, pp. 425–38.

Hansen, T. (2012) 'Understanding trust in financial services: The influences of financial healthiness, knowledge and satisfaction', *Journal of Service Research*. 15(3), 280–95. doi:10.1177/1094670512439105, Published online 1 May 2012.

Hardin, R. (2002), *Trust and Trustworthiness*. Sage Russell, New York.

Jap, S. and Ganesan, S. (2000) 'Control mechanisms and the relationship life cycle: implications for safeguarding specific investments and developing commitment', *Journal of Marketing Research*. 37(2), pp. 227–45.

Jyh-Shen, C. and Droge, C. (2006) 'Service quality, trust, specific asset investment, and expertise: direct and indirect effects in a satisfaction-loyalty framework', *Journal of the Academy of Marketing Science*, 34(4) pp. 613–47.

Kelman, H. (1961) 'Process of opinion change', *Public Opinion Quarterly*, 25(Spring), pp. 57–78.

Korczynski, M. (2000) 'The political economy of trust', *Journal of Management Studies*, 37(1), pp. 1–21.

Lewicki, R. and Bunker, B. (1996) 'Trust in relationships: a model of development and decline', In Bunker, B., Rubin, J. and Associates (eds.), *Conflict, cooperation, and justice*, pp. 133–73, Jossey-Bass, San Francisco.

Wetzels, M. Ko de Ruyter, Marcel van Birgelen (1998) "Marketing service relationships: the role of commitment", *Journal of Business and Industrial Marketing*, 13(4/5), pp. 406–423.

Mayer, R., Davis, J. and Schoorman, F. (1995) "An integrative model of organisational trust", *Academy of Management Journal*, 20, pp. 709–34.

McAllister, D. (1995) 'Affect and cognition based trust as foundations for interpersonal co-operation in organisations', *Academy of Management Journal*, 38(1), pp. 24–59.

Michell, P.C.N., Reast, J.D. and Lynch, J.E. (1998) 'Exploring The Foundations of Trust' *Journal of Marketing Management*, 14(1), pp. 159–72.

Morgan, R. and Hunt, S. (1994) 'The commitment trust theory of relationship marketing', *Journal of Marketing*, 58(July), pp. 20–38.

Palmer, A. and Huo, Q. (2013) "A study of trust over time within a social network mediated environment", *Journal of Marketing Management. 29*, (15/16), pp. 1816–1833.

Rindfleisch, A. and Moorman, C. (2003) 'Interfirm co-operation and customer orientation', *Journal of Marketing Research*, 40(4), pp. 421–36

Rossiter, J. (2002) The C-OAR-SE Procedure for Scale Development in Marketing. *International Journal of Research in Marketing*, 19, pp. 305–335.

Rousseau, D., Sitkin, S., Burt, R. and Camer, C. (1998) 'Not so different after all: a cross-discipline view of trust', *Academy of Management Review*, 23(3), pp. 393–404.

Sekhon, H., Roy, S., Shergill, G. and Pritchard, A. (2013) 'Modelling trust in service relationships: a transnational perspective', *Journal of Services Marketing*, 27(1), pp. 76–86.

Sheppard, B. and Sherman, D. (1998) 'The grammars of trust: a model and general implications', *Academy of Management Review*, 23(3), pp. 422–37.

Singh, J. and Sirdeshmukh, D. (2002) 'Agency and trust mechanisms in consumer satisfaction and loyalty judgments', *Journal of the Academy of Marketing Science*, 28(1), pp. 150–67

Sirdeshmukh, D., Singh, J. and Sabol, B. (2002) 'Consumer trust value and loyalty in relational exchanges', *Journal of Marketing*, 66(January), pp. 15–23.

Solomon, R. and Flores, F. (2003) *Building trust in business, politics and life*, Oxford University Press, Oxford.

Sztompka, P. (1999) *Trust: a sociological theory*, Cambridge University Press, Cambridge.

Wetzels, M., de Ruyter, K. and van Birgelen, M. (1998) 'Marketing service relationships: the role of commitment', *Journal of Business and Industrial Marketing*, 13(4/5), pp. 406–423.

Whitener, E., Brodt, S., Korsgaard, A. and Werner, J., (1998) 'Managers as initiators of trust: an exchange relationship framework for understanding managerial trustworthy behaviour', *Academy of Management Review*, 23(3), pp. 513–30.

Williamson, O. (1993) 'Calculativeness, trust and economic organisation', *Journal of Law and Economics*, 36, pp. 453–86.

Wilson, D. (1995) 'An integrated model of buyer-seller relationship', *Journal of the Academy of Marketing Science*, 23(4), pp. 335–45.

Xie, Y. and Peng, S. (2009) 'How to repair customer trust after negative publicity: the roles of competence, integrity, benevolence, and forgiveness', *Psychology and Marketing*, 26(7), pp. 572–89.

11

Should I stay or should I go?

The case of loyalty in the UK retail banking industry

Dahlia El-Manstrly

Introduction

The importance of loyal customers is well documented in marketing literature (for example, Jiang and Rosenbloom 2005, Reichheld 1996, Narayandas 1998). Loyal customers are assumed to spend more, buy more, resist competitors' offers and recommend the service provider (Gremler and Brown 1999). Anderson and Mittal (2000) suggest firms that focus on acquiring new customers, but are unable to retain them, are unlikely to see positive bottom-line results. In contrast, an increase in customer retention can positively impact on profitability, particularly for those firms in highly competitive markets such as financial services (Reichheld and Sasser 1990, Fornell and Wernerfelt 1987). Indeed, a mere two percent improvement in customer retention has been shown to impact on profitability through a ten percent reduction in overheads (Jamieson 1994).

Until the early 1970s, the UK financial services sectors were highly structured and based on specialist institutions with clear functional demarcation: banking, for example, was regarded as a very conservative industry (Trethowan and Scullion 1997, Llewellyn, 1990). Domestic and international competition tended to be limited; however, through deregulation, advances in technology and globalisation (Gardener et al. 1999, Ennew and Wait 2007, Lowe and Kuusisto 1999) there have been significant changes over the past few decades. Deregulation and technological advancement in particular have influenced consumer preferences and the intensity of competition, with more emphasis being placed on protecting profit. Consequently, creating and sustaining a loyal customer base is important and there is a need for financial institutions to determine the underpinning drivers of customer loyalty/disloyalty.

The purpose of this chapter is to identify the key drivers of customer loyalty within the UK retail banking industry. The unique contribution of this chapter to the loyalty literature is that it focusses on the actual rather than the perceived reasons for banking loyalty in order to provide better understanding of the "elusive phenomenon" (Oliver 1999). The chapter begins with a brief synthesis of the extant literature on the antecedents of customer loyalty. It then presents the findings from research using in-depth interviews to explore the antecedents of UK retail banking loyalty. The final section of the chapter discusses the theoretical and managerial implications, followed by concluding remarks. The chapter complements Chapter 9 by Yu and Harrison that explores the meanings, motivations and manifestations of financial services customer relationships.

The antecedents of customer loyalty

A review of 21 relevant studies into the antecedents of customer loyalty (see Table 11.1) reveals that over one-third (11 studies) identified customer satisfaction to be a key antecedent of customer loyalty (for example, Durvasula et al. 2004, Norquist et al. 2002), the same proportion again (11 studies) (for example, Khatibi et al. 2002, Durvasula et al. 2004) identified the importance of service quality as a determinant of loyalty. Within the service quality literature, the dominating perspective has been to assume that service quality and satisfaction are strongly related constructs. A further eight studies (for example, Lee and Cunningham 2001, Magin et al. 2003) indicated that switching costs play a significant role in driving passive loyalty, while six studies (for example, Bloemer et al. 1998, Al-Awadi 2002) revealed that corporate image, particularly in the banking context, influences loyalty. To a lesser extent the studies considered other factors such as customer value (for example, Buttle and Burton 2001, Durvasula et al. 2004, Ruyter and Bloemer 1999), positive mood (for example, Ruyter and Bloemer 1999), consumer knowledge or experience (for example, Wirtz and Mattila 2003), trust (for example, Morris et al. 1999) and commitment (for example, Kandampully 1998) as primary drivers of customer loyalty.

The antecedents of UK retail banking loyalty

The underlying concept of customer loyalty is well documented in the literature but the UK retail banking industry has received limited attention in terms of loyalty, despite its practical relevance. Therefore, in order to understand this phenomenon in more detail – in particular what loyalty means to banking customers and what drives loyalty – a series of in-depth interviews were conducted among UK retail banking customers to redress this imbalance and to "dig deeper", as Table 11.1 shows that there is apparently little consensus in the literature on what drives customer loyalty.

A qualitative approach was chosen for three reasons: the lack of previous qualitative investigations into loyalty, the opportunity to provide a greater understanding of the loyalty formation process from the customer's perspective and the desire to identify (rather than measure) the factors that influence customer loyalty and the relative importance of these factors.

According to theoretical sampling, individuals were selected to take part in the study based on meeting certain criteria relevant to the study. In particular, each respondent had to have a number of different banking services (products), different banking experiences and an experience of making a variety of decisions regarding the choice of specific banking provider. The sample was selected to take account of men and women from a variety of occupations. However, the final sample was slightly biased toward middle and upper middle-income customers. Lower income customers were underrepresented in the sample. Previous research (Gremler 1994) has shown that this socio-demographic group tends to use a limited range of financial services and consequently tends to possess a limited range of banking experiences. Upper income customers were also underrepresented, as access to this socio-demographic group is often more difficult to obtain.

Respondents included in the sample were recruited through the researcher's network of acquaintances and included former and current co-workers and their associates. In approaching the respondents, each individual was asked whether they would be willing to participate in a

Table 11.1 Literature review of the antecedents of customer loyalty

Author	Antecedents	Context
Chandrashekaran et al. (2007)	Satisfaction level and strength, length of the relationship, volume of business and favourability of prior experience.	B2B and B2C service industry
Grewal et al. (2007)	Perceived service quality, perceived control, physical environment and post-purchase perceived risk.	Health care
Gruen et al. (2007)	Customer to customer interaction.	Professional association meeting environment
Meyer-Waarden (2007)	Loyalty programmes.	Grocery
Roos and Gustafsson (2007)	Prejudice (negative attitudes), market factors personal/situational switching costs and critical incidents.	Telecom
Homburg and Fürst (2005)	Compliant satisfaction.	Wide range of manufacturing and services industries
Durvasula, et al. (2004)	Service quality, satisfaction and perceived value.	Life insurance
Wirtz and Mattila (2003)	Objective and subjective knowledge.	Chinese physician service
Magin et al. (2003)	Economic switching barriers relational switching barriers.	
Khatibi et al. (2002)	Overall service quality (e.g. channel of ordering, operating hours, fault reporting centre, response time and restoration time).	Telecom
Al-Awadi (2002)	Good management, image and customer services	Retail industry
Buttle and Burton (2001)	Satisfaction, transaction cost, perceived value, interpersonal relationship, variety seeking.	N/A
Clarke (2001)	Technology mediated channels.	UK Banks
Lee and Cunningham (2001)	Service quality and transaction/switching cost.	Banking and travel industry
Martensen et al. (2000)	Company image and perceived product quality.	Banks, internet, cable TV, soft drinks and fast food restaurants
Reichheld et al. (2000)	Customer satisfaction and word of mouth recommendations.	N/A
Ruyter and Bloemer (1999)	Value attainment and positive mood.	Education
Bloemer and Ruyter (1999)	Satisfaction positive emotions.	Delivery, railway, food and travel industry
Zeithaml et al. (1996)	Service quality.	Retailing, manufacturing, automobile and life insurance.
Gremler and Brown (1996)	Satisfaction, switching costs and interpersonal bonds.	Retail banking and dentistry
Ennew and Binks (1996)	Functional quality and technical quality	UK banking

45-minute interview on bank loyalty. All interviewees who were approached agreed to participate. All of the interviews were conducted over a six-week period.

On this basis, 29 individuals were recruited to take part in the interviews. Previous research has suggested that samples of 8–12 respondents are sufficient for generating themes in this type of qualitative work (Schouten 1991). Significant overlap and repetition in what respondents had to say about customer loyalty started to occur after about 20 interviews. Despite this, several more interviews were conducted to make sure that no new information had been missed, to be confident that theoretical saturation had been achieved. The final sample included 29 customers.

The interview began with a brief explanation of the purpose of the study, then to initiate discussion, interviewees were asked which financial service provider(s) they used and the services/products they held. Interviewees were asked to explain why they continued to use their main financial service provider and, when applicable, why they had switched to another provider. These interviews, which averaged 48 minutes in length, were mostly conducted in the interviewees' home or place of work.

With the permission of the interviewees, all interviews were recorded using a digital voice recorder in order to allow the interviewer to remain attentive and enhance the process flow, assist efficiency (no pauses while notes were taken) and capture the interviewees' actual comments. The audio files were subsequently transcribed using a transcription kit and saved as Word documents. The Word files were then imported into NVivo 2.0 for analysis. The resulting transcriptions amounted to more than 120 single-spaced pages of text.

After all the interviews had been conducted, the transcriptions were read and examined several times, with recurring thoughts or keywords highlighted. Segments of each transcript were then identified that included these highlighted terms. After several iterations through the data, the segments were organised into similar themes or categories. The most important/frequently mentioned drivers of loyalty formation emerged as satisfaction with the banking provider, perceived switching costs, lack of attractive alternatives, customer-perceived value, trusting the banking provider and perceiving the banking provider as an ethical institution.

Satisfaction

Respondents mainly mentioned satisfaction with their banking services as the most important reason for initiating and sustaining loyalty to their bank. Satisfaction is an overall evaluation of a customer's experiences with a service provider (Bitner and Hubbert 1993). Research shows that satisfaction is comprised of a utilitarian component, a judgment of how well the firm has met customers' expectations of performance, and a hedonic component, a feeling of (dis)pleasure arising from this evaluation (Han et al. 2008).

Customers described satisfaction in a variety of ways. For example, satisfaction with the banking services in general, satisfaction with service recovery procedures, satisfaction with the location and opening times. Some customers also reported that satisfaction with the service recovery process and doing things right first time was important. Banks that do not provide satisfactory services the first time, or fail to respond to service failures appropriately and quickly are less likely to build or sustain their customers' loyalty. Respondents' comments suggest that satisfaction with financial services provision is a minimum requirement for customer loyalty to establish.

The following comments illustrate how customer satisfaction with the services provided is necessary for initiating and sustaining loyalty.

> My bank is easy to get through…on the phone…It surprised me when someone picks up the phone because you expect to get this, press one for the other and up to ten for so and

so and then into another set of menus, and it really annoys me. I have been very impressed with that and it is definitely enough reason for me to stay with them.

(Female, aged 35, marketing manager)

I haven't had many problems with my bank and they have improved my sense of loyalty toward them by minimising problems. They work very hard trying to keep their customers quite happy. I expect decent service and that is what I had so far.

(Female, aged 51, professor)

I suppose if you shop around you can get better deals, I just leave it as it is. I am reasonably happy with my mortgage provider and the same for the current account and the savings. I am quite happy with them.

(Male, aged 59, fish vet)

Switching costs

The second most important reason described by interviewees for remaining with their bank is the costs they perceive they may incur if they switch their current bank. According to Burnham et al. (2003), switching costs are the perceived losses that customers will incur if they switch their existing provider. These losses could be procedural, financial or relational.

Many types of switching costs were mentioned by respondents as influential factors in remaining a customer of their current bank. Switching costs may contribute to passive or assumed loyalty, but customers may not feel loyal to the bank. Some of the switching costs are positive (such as relationship costs), whereas others are negative (such as financial costs). Six types of switching costs, including inertia, set-up costs, learning costs, perceived risk, relationship costs and financial costs, were identified as discussed in the following paragraphs.

Inertia

Inertia or apathy refers to a lack of desire or willingness to perform an action, and was the most frequently cited of the "switching costs" reasons customers remained with their bank, as illustrated by the following comments:

I considered switching, but inertia made me stay.

(Male, aged 47, teaching technician)

I just have not got rid of the dead wood. If I was more on the ball and I had more patience I would have put everything into one thing that works better for me, but I just let them drag on.

(Female, aged 41, mature student)

I am lazy with banking and I have been with the same bank for years because it is convenient and I can't bear to think of the hassle to change at all.

(Female, aged 58, chief technician)

Set-up costs

Set-up costs, refer to the hassle associated with switching and the time and effort required to change banking details. It emerged as the second most-mentioned factor impacting upon perceived switching costs and in turn loyalty, as illustrated in the following comments:

You always have to change direct debits, change accounts and it is a hassle. It is not easy. It is not that easy to change all your banking details of cheque books, cards and PIN numbers.

(Female, aged 53, departmental superintendent)

I don't know why I stayed. I think I couldn't be bothered with the hassle of changing I suppose. I never took the time to do it, I suppose.

(Female, aged 51, financial coordinator)

Every day of the week I consider leaving them. I stayed because I imagine they are all somehow the same, it's just the hassle of changing.

(Male, aged 50, research scientist)

Learning costs

Learning costs refer to the time and effort needed to acquire new skills, remember new banking details or become familiar with how to use a new banking system effectively.

You need to know how things work because they have different procedures, especially if you went to an online-only provider. Over the counter they are pretty much the same.

(Female, aged 50, computer advisor)

I never really had a desire to move bank because it was too much hassle to change sort codes and account numbers when I know them, and now the reason I stayed with TSB is that I can go to any TSB branch and they can pull up my file so there is no need to go into a specific branch the branch is wherever I am.

(Male, aged 49, professor)

Perceived risk

Perceived risk refers to the risk associated with something going wrong during the switching process or latterly with the new service, as illustrated by the following comments:

Because of the experience of our bank merging with another bank was so bad, we thought if we go somewhere else what if we have the same trouble.

(Female, aged 59, freelance writer)

I have so many direct debits....it would cause me too much problem to shift those because every time I deal with any large companies there are always major problems so that is why I still stay with my bank.

(Female, aged 46, university teacher)

Relationship costs

Relationship costs are the costs associated with losing a personal bond with the banking representative as well as losing recognition. The three comments provided below illustrate that relational bonds and recognition can make a customer stay despite knowing that other banks may be offering better deals:

> I have been with them since I was 18, I have not changed them, the services are the most important thing, whether it's through a branch system or telephone banking, the personal financial advisor is a very important thing within that branch system.
>
> *(Male, aged 59, management consultant)*

> Knowing the manager did influence my decision to stay with the bank at the time and I kept loyal to him rather than to the bank.
>
> *(Female, aged 58, chief technician)*

> Although other banks in the past were offering cash inducements to set up a current account, I have not moved because of my stupidly optimistic idea that sooner or later my bank will realise that I haven't moved and perhaps I am going to get some sort of recognition.
>
> *(Female, aged 42, research fellow)*

Financial costs

Financial costs (i.e. structural or sunk costs) are the economic costs that will be lost or incurred in switching from one provider to another. For example, interviewees mentioned losing money, discounts, rewards and special facilities. The following comments illustrate this theme:

> It did cross my mind to leave them but I would be out by £147 if I just said close the accounts, and that is why I stayed.
>
> *(Male, aged 51, technician)*

> My mortgage is like I am locked in for a period of years. I am just happy to go on with it as I cannot do anything about it at the moment.
>
> *(Female, aged 38, lecturer)*

In summary, respondents indicated that switching costs play a significant role in the development of their spurious loyalty to banking providers.

Attractiveness of alternatives

In addition to satisfaction and switching costs, customers perceive that there is little to differentiate the service offering available to them from other providers. In general, most customers do not perceive other banking providers as superior to their current bank. Apart from three customers who perceive their bank to be different, and for that reason have remained loyal, respondents mentioned perceived indifference as a reason for staying:

> I am quite sure, there is nothing very much now between the banks also because there is not a personal touch so I am quite sure they all pretty much the same. They all have internet banking; they all have telephone banking you are not speaking to any one in particular.
>
> *(Female, aged 59, freelance writer)*

> We don't see any other banks being that much better anyway, so it is nothing to do with loyalty or anything.
>
> *(Female, aged 43, doctor)*

I don't have huge loyalty to a big company like that; it is not like being loyal to a small organisation with personal service. No I think the feeling is that one is much the same as another, they're all big organisations and I don't feel there would be any benefits in moving.

(Female, aged 53, departmental superintendent)

Perceived value

According to Agustin and Singh (2005), value is the consumer's perception of the benefits enjoyed compared with the cost incurred in the maintenance of an ongoing exchange relationship. Perceived value takes into account the rate of interest, flexibility and good service, no current account fees and price and credit limits. Perceived value was mentioned as the main reason for staying with a banking provider. This is illustrated by the following comments:

The only reason I maintained my relationship with my bank is the theory or the feeling that I am getting a better rate of interest.

(Male, aged 39, lecturer)

If someone offers me a better deal I will probably change.

(Female, aged 55, computer advisor)

Trust

Only two customers mentioned trust as the main reason for their loyalty. Trust is the willingness to rely on an exchange partner in whom one has confidence (Moorman et al. 1992). Trust reduces perceived uncertainty and therefore perceived vulnerability in exchange relationships. In addition, Morgan and Hunt (1994) see trust as existing when one party has confidence in an exchange partner's reliability and integrity. The following comment illustrates perceived trust was the main reason for one customer to stay.

I don't know, it is like working with the doctor you trust, you go to the doctor he knows you, he knows better, you know that you can trust him, you tell him the problem, they tell you what is the best, they don't mess you around kind of filling this form, have you already talked to my secretary, so they just do it. I trust the XYZ.

(Male, aged 45, computer advisor)

Ethical behaviour

Four customers mentioned the ethics code of the bank as a determining factor in their loyalty. According to Mill (1998), ethics is intrinsically associated with the common "good" rather than a company's self-interest. However, ethical relativists (Crane and Matten 2004) argue that moral absolutes do not exist and the definition of what is moral is socially constructed. Ethics could mean different things to different people. The following comment illustrates the importance of ethical banking.

I think probably we would like to do more ethical banking and if the cooperative bank could offer the range of services that the other banks offer we would probably move.

(Female, aged 58, chief technician)

173

Conclusions

The primary purpose of this study was to offer a brief synthesis of the extant literature on conceptual and empirical issues relating to customer loyalty and its antecedents. In a context such as the financial services industry and in particular retail banking, competition is intense due to competitors offering similar financial products and low to moderate perceived switching costs. Retail banking providers need to work ever harder to retain their customers.

Banking providers are investing in different strategies such as improving customer satisfaction, providing better value products and increasing perceived switching costs. However, recent research has shown that although customer satisfaction is necessary, it is not sufficient to maintain and enhance loyalty.

The findings of this study suggest that banks will have to adopt effective strategies dependent upon the loyalty profile of their customer segment. More specifically, effective marketing strategies should not be limited to one or two drivers of loyalty. Effective marketing strategies need to consider the simultaneous impact of loyalty antecedents and the impact of product type (i.e. current account or mortgage) on loyalty formation. Management must continue to invest in providing good quality service offerings and should consider the role of satisfaction as well as other factors such as switching costs and perceived value in loyalty formation.

Factors such as corporate image were not mentioned at all by the sample as a determinable factor in banking loyalty, despite the findings of previous research. Factors such as trust did not feature as strongly as previous research would suggest: only one customer mentioned trust while commitment was not mentioned at all. The findings suggest that more research is needed in order to further our understanding of the relational aspects of loyalty. It may be that customers are influenced by different factors depending on whether they are the start of a relationship with their bank or seeking to deepen their loyalty. Chapter 9 explores relationships, in particular focussing on factors affecting early stage relationship development. Focusing on rational factors alone generates "passive" or "spurious" loyalty that is conditional and will change over time. However, focussing on the relational and rational factors ensures ultimate or active loyalty that is more sustainable.

References

Agustin, C. and Singh, J. (2005) Curvilinear Effects of Consumer Loyalty Determinants in Relational Exchanges. *Journal of Marketing Research*, 42(February), pp. 96–108.

Al-Awadi, A. (2002), "A proposed Model of Consumer Loyalty in the Retailing Sector Based on the Kuwaiti Experience", *Total Quality Management*, Vol. 13, No. 7, pp. 1035–46.

Anderson, E. and Mittal, V. (2000), "Strengthening the Satisfaction-Profit Chain", *Journal of Service Research*, Vol. 3, No. 2, pp. 107–20.

Bitner, M. J. and Hubbert, A.R. (1993), "Encounter Satisfaction versus Overall Satisfaction versus Quality", in The Service Quality Handbook, E.E. Scheuing and W.F. Christopher, eds. New York: American Management Association, pp. 72–94.

Bloemer, J., Ruyter, K. and Peeters, P. (1998), "Investigating Drivers of Bank Loyalty: The Complex Relationship between Image, Service Quality and Satisfaction", *International Journal of Bank Marketing*, Vol. 16, No. 7, pp. 276–86.

Burnham, T., Frels, J. and Mahajan, V. (2003), "Consumer Switching Costs: A Typology, Antecedents, and Consequences", *Journal of the Academy of Marketing Science*, Vol. 31, No. 2, pp. 109–26.

Buttle, F. and Burton, J. (2001), "Does Service Failure Influence Customer Loyalty?", *Journal of Consumer Behaviour*, Vol. 1, No. 3, pp. 217–27.

Chandrashekaran, M., Rotte, K., Tax, S. and Grewal, R. (2007) Satisfaction Strength and Customer Loyalty. *Journal of Marketing Research*, 44(February), pp. 153–163.

Clarke, I. (2001), *"Emerging value propositions for m commerce"*, *Journal of Business Strategies*, Vol. 18 No. 2, pp. 133–48.

Crane, A. and Matten, D. (2004). *Business Ethics: A European Perspective*. Oxford, UK: Oxford University Press.

Durvasula, S., Lysonski, S., Mehta, S. and Tang, B. (2004), "Forging Relationships with Services: The Antecedents that have an Impact on Behavioural Outcomes in the Life Insurance Industry", *Journal of Financial Services Marketing*, Vol. 8, No. 4, pp. 314–26.

Ennew, C. and Wait, N. (2007), *Marketing Financial Services: An International Guide to Principles and Practice*, Butterworth-Heinemann, Oxford.

Ennew, C.T. and Binks, M.R. (1996)., "Good and Bad Customers: The Benefits of Participating in The Banking Relationship", *International Journal of Bank Marketing*, Vol. 14 (2), pp. 5–13.

Fay, C. (1994), "Royalties from Loyalties", *Journal of Business Strategy*, Vol. 15, No. 2, pp. 47–51.

Fornell, C. and Wernerfelt, B. (1987), "Defensive Marketing Strategy by Customer Compliant Management", *Journal of Marketing Research*, Vol. 24, pp. 337–46.

Gardener, E., Howcroft, B. and Williams, J. (1999), "The New Retail Banking Revolution", *The Services Industries Journal*, Vol. 19, No. 2, pp. 83–100.

Gremler, D. (1994), "Word of Mouth about Service Providers: An Illustration of Theory Development in Marketing", in AMA Winter Educators' Conference Proceedings, Vol. 5, C.W. Park and D. Smith, eds. Chicago, IL: American Marketing Association, pp. 62–70.

Gremler, D. and Brown, S. (1999), "The Loyalty Ripple Effect: Appreciating the Full Value of Customers", *International Journal of Services Industry Management*, Vol. 10, No. 3, pp. 271–91.

Gremler, D. and Brown, S. (1996) Service Loyalty: Its nature, Importance, and Implications. In Edvardsson, B., Brown, S. and Johnston, R. (eds.) *Advancing Service Quality: A Globar Perspective*. Jamaica, NY: International Service Quality Association. pp. 171–80.

Grewal, D., Gopalkrisnan, R., Gotlieb, J. and Levy, M. (2007) Developing a Deeper Understanding of Post-Purchase Perceived Risk and Behavioural Intentions in a Service-Setting. *Journal of the Academy of Marketing Science*, 35, pp. 250–8.

Gruen, T., Summers, J. and Acito, F. (2000) Relationship Marketing Activities, Commitment, and Membership behaviours in Professional Associations. *Journal of Marketing*, 64(July), pp. 34–49.

Han, X., Kwortnik, R. J. and Wang, C. (2008), "Service Loyalty: An Integrative Model and Examination across Service Contexts", *Journal of Service Research*, Vol. 11, No. 1, pp. 22–42.

Homburg, C. and Fürst, A. (2005) How Organizational Complaint Handling Drives Customer Loyalty: an Analysis of the Mechanistic and the Organic Approach. *Journal of Marketing*, 65, pp. 95–114.

Jamieson, D. (1994), "Customer Retention: Focus or Failure", *Total Quality Management Magazine*, Vol. 6, No. 5, pp. 11–13.

Jiang, P. and Rosenbloom, B. (2005), "Customer Intention to Return Online: Price Perception, Attribute-Level Performance and Satisfaction Unfolding Over Time", *European Journal of Marketing*, Vol. 39, No. 1/2, pp. 150–74.

Kandampully, J. (1998), "Service Quality to Service Loyalty: A Relationship which Goes Beyond Customer Services", *Total Quality Management*, Vol. 9, No. 6, pp. 431–43.

Khatibi, A., Ismail, H. and Thyagarajan, V. (2002), "What Drives Customer Loyalty: An Analysis from the Telecommunications Industry", *Journal of Targeting, Measurement and Analysis for Marketing*, Vol. 11, No. 1, pp. 34–44.

Lee, M. and Cunningham, L. (2001), "A Cost/Benefit Approach to Understanding Service Loyalty", *Journal of Services Marketing*, Vol. 15, No. 2, pp. 113–30.

Llewellyn, D. T. (1990), *In the Future of Financial Systems and Services*, Macmillan Press, London.

Lowe, A. and Kuusisto, J. (1999), "The Institutional Stature of the Retail Bank: The Neglected Asset?", *International Journal of Bank Marketing*, Vol. 17, No. 4, pp. 171–81.

Magin, S., Algesheimer, R., Huber, F. and Herrmann, A. (2003), "The Impact of Brand Personality and Customer Satisfaction on Consumer's Loyalty: Theoretical Approach and Findings of a Causal Analytical Study in the Sector of Internet Service Providers", *Electronic Markets*, Vol. 13, No. 4, pp. 294–308.

Martensen, A., Dahlgaard, S.M.P., Dahlgaard, J.J., & Grønholdt, L. (2000). Modelling and measuring employee satisfaction and loyalty: A Danish pilot study. *Proceedings of the 3th International QMOD Conference: Quality Management and Organizational Development, Aarhus, Denmark, 20–22 August 2000* (pp. 310–324). Aarhus, Denmark: The Aarhus School of Business.

Meyer-Waarden, L. (2007) The Effects of Loyalty Programs on Customer Lifetime Duration and Share of Wallet. *Journal of Retailing*, 83, pp. 223–236.

Moorman, C., Zaltman, G. and Deshpandes, R. (1992), Relationships between Providers and Users of Marketing Research, the Dynamics of Trust within and between Organisations. *Journal of Marketing Research*, 29, pp. 314–29.

Morgan, R. and Hunt, S. (1994), "The Commitment-Trust Theory of Relationship Marketing", *Journal of Marketing*, Vol. 58, pp. 20–38.

Morris, S., Barnes, B. and Lynch, J. (1999), "Relationship Marketing Needs Total Quality Management", *Total Quality Management*, July, pp. 659–67.

Narayandas, D. (1998), "Measuring and Managing the Benefits of Customer Retention", *Journal of Service Research*, Vol. 1, No. 2, pp. 108–28.

Norquist, M., Gilbert, M., King, R., Brown, R. and Clark, P. (2002), "A Great Place to Shop, Work and Invest: Measuring and Managing the Service Profit Chain at Sears Canada", *Interactive Marketing*, Vol. 3, No. 3, pp. 225–61.

Oliver, R. (1999), "Whence Consumer Loyalty?", *Journal of Marketing*, Vol. 63 [Special Issue], pp. 33–44.

Reichheld, F. (1996), "Learning from Customer Defections", *Harvard Business Review*, Vol. 74, pp. 56–69.

Reichheld, F. and Sasser, W.E. (1990), "Zero defections: Quality Comes to Services," *Harvard Business Review*, Vol. 68, No. 5, pp. 105–11.

Roos, I. and Gustafsson, A. (2007), Understanding Frequent Switching Patterns: A Crucial Element in Managing Customer Relationships. *Journal of Service Research*, 10(1), pp. 93–108.

de Ruyter, K. and Bloemer, J. (1999), "Customer Loyalty in Extended Service Settings: The Interaction between Satisfaction, Value Attainment and Positive Mood", *International Journal of Service Industry Management*, Vol. 10, No. 3, pp. 320–36.

Schouten, J.W. (1991), "Selves in Transition: Symbolic Consumption in Personal Rites of Passage and Identity Reconstruction," *Journal of Consumer Research*, 17 (March), pp. 412–25.

Trethowan, J. and Scullion, G. (1997), "Strategic Response to Change in Retail Banking in the UK and the Irish Republic", *International Journal of Bank Marketing*, Vol. 15, No. 2, pp. 60–68.

Wirtz, J. and Mattila, A. (2003), "The Effects of Consumer Expertise on Evoked Set Size and Service Loyalty", *Journal of Services Marketing*, Vol. 17, No. 7, pp. 649–65.

Zeithaml, V., Berry, L. and Parasuraman, A. (1996), The Behavioral Consequences of Service Quality. *Journal of Marketing*, 60(2), pp. 31–46.

12

Financial services quality

People, processes and performance

Kent Eriksson

Introduction

Marketing research has had a significant impact in helping us understand the unique features of services. One of the most important distinguishing features of services is the lack of a physical dimension. Instead, services are characterized by interactive processes. The consumer of the service and the supplier of the service jointly create the service offering an experience as they interact. A service can thus be defined as "a process that leads to an outcome during partly simultaneous production and consumption processes" (Grönroos 2001: 150).

Quality in services is elusive. Often, services customers who have experienced high quality cannot articulate what element of the service makes it of high quality, but they know that they have experienced it. In other words, quality is elusive because it is perceived by the individual and therefore subject to personal and situational biases. Researchers have spent considerable time and effort in the pursuit of an increased understanding of service quality. To deliver services at a high quality can set one firm apart from the rest. The firm that consistently delivers services of high quality can outperform competitors, because they can attract and maintain customers and often also charge higher prices based on their superior quality (Bertini et al. 2012, Reichheld and Sasser 1990).

Financial services quality is a challenge to conceptualize and study, not only because quality is elusive, but also because financial services are elusive. Financial services can be defined as the transportation of value in space and time. For the financial services customer, this may mean that in order to make a decision now they are required to form an opinion about the quality of a service that may not be delivered for some time into the future. For example, the quality of a retirement savings fund can only be fully assessed after consumption at retirement, yet the decision to join a retirement saving plan may be made two or three decades before consumption. Notwithstanding, financial services firms aim to deliver high-quality services without either the customer or the financial services firm having a clear understanding of what it means or opportunity to fully assess it.

This chapter aims to present a framework for the understanding of financial services quality. In doing so, it will make it possible for financial service firms and customers to better understand what financial services quality is and how it develops. The chapter is structured so that it starts with a discussion of the unique characteristics of services in general, and financial services in particular, then follows a financial services quality development model. Finally, implications for financial services firms' use of service quality are presented.

Financial services quality as an interactive process

Services are characterized by the fact that they are intangible and that production of the service typically is conducted at the same time as it is consumed (Bitner and Brown 2008). One consequence of these conditions is that the customer is part of the service delivery: services are delivered in an interactive process with the customer (Grönroos 2001, Grönroos 2012). A customer who is knowledgeable, motivated and committed can take part in the interaction with the service provider to such an extent that the service customer effectively becomes a valuable co-producer of the service (Auh et al. 2007). The service production process is greatly enhanced by customer input, as the customer is the foremost expert on customer preferences. (Michel discusses customer co-creation processes in the context of financial services innovation in Chapter 13).

Services are largely people-based processes and as such involve interactions between people. As the customer interacts with the service provider, they come to know not only about the service offering, but also about the way that the service provider produces the offering. Often, customers interact repeatedly with a service provider then develop a relationship to the service provider and its staff. In such a relationship, the customer develops knowledge of production systems. For example, a bank customer may learn that some questions are best answered by a branch manager, whereas others can be answered through online banking. The customer may also learn that they need to use certain behaviors or language or present their financial information in a certain way in order to obtain approval for a particular financial services offering.

The interaction that takes place between a customer and a service provider is particularly important for the customer's perception of the service quality they receive. The reason for this is that quality is based on the customer's perception of the features of quality. These features can be identified as technical quality, referring to the quality of the outcome of the process and functional quality, referring to the quality of the process or service delivery (Grönroos 2001). The outcome is therefore what the customer receives at the end of the process and the process is the sum of all the interactions that take place along the way to the final outcome. Applied to financial services, the elusiveness of service quality becomes apparent. Consider a 40-year-old signing a contract for a retirement savings plan. The outcome of that service will not be possible to evaluate until well into retirement and the process may be difficult to evaluate because the performance of the fund manager, with whom the customer is likely to have limited or no interaction, is also difficult to evaluate.

The nature of the interactive process provides opportunities for learning. Before the customer has interacted with a service provider they may have some expectations of the service quality. As the interaction progresses, the customer's perception of the service quality may change due to increased knowledge of the offering provided by the service selling firm (Iyengar et al. 2007). For instance, services customers may perceive that they receive service of high quality from a provider, but if they become aware of an alternative provider offering better service, or, if they try another service provider's offering and find it to be superior, then the customer's perception of the quality of the initial provider will be perceived as being of less quality. In other words, service quality is perceived in relation to the customer's experiences and comparison of alternatives.

While service quality perceptions may be relatively stable for long time periods, they may also change dramatically due to specific situations (Iacobucci et al. 1995). For instance, a momentary stop in the online banking operations of a bank can cause a rapid decrease in perceived service quality. Customer perceptions of a service may also change when customers learn more about how to use the service (Fournier and Mick 1999). Therefore customers' quality perceptions are prone to change over time and financial services providers need to continuously gather information on the customer's financial services quality perception.

Financial services comprise a heterogeneous group of services, ranging from easily-evaluated services, such as payment transaction services, to those that are more difficult to evaluate, such as loans and financial advice. The difficulty associated with evaluating quality is heightened for more complex financial services. Another issue that complicates the way customers form perceptions of financial services quality is that interactions between customers and service providers are sometimes conducted through person-to-person meetings and sometimes using automated services or online systems. For instance, a bank customer may interact with the bank in personal meetings, telephone conversations, on the internet, mobile devices and at ATMs. The variability in distribution channels and service offerings makes it difficult to assess what customer service quality refers to.

Customer experience of using various distribution channels and various financial services has been found to be important in explaining customer perceptions of service quality (Carlson and Zmud 1999). As the customer interacts with a financial services provider, the customer's experience of distribution channels and financial services will change. As a result, the perceived service quality may change not only in terms of the overall assessed service quality, but also in terms of how differentiated the customer's perceived service quality is. For instance, a common finding is that customers differentiate service quality between the advisor (the person) and the financial services provider (firm) (Grayson et al. 2008).

Based on this, financial services quality can be viewed as the perceived quality of the outcome and process that the customer formulates through an ongoing interaction process with a financial services provider. Financial services quality also depends on the customer's experiences, knowledge and context. The financial services provider needs to see service quality as a continuous development process in relation to the customer (Grönroos and Ojasalo 2004).

The financial services quality process

Figure 12.1 shows that the service quality process can be broken down into three elements: quality experience, quality evaluation and quality production (Golder et al. 2012). These elements may not be particularly discrete in the minds of customers, but for financial services providers can be useful for the understanding and analysis of how to deliver financial services quality.

When an individual first becomes a customer of a financial services provider they will not have any prior experience of that provider. However, they may bring with them a history of

Figure 12.1   The financial service quality development process

experiences gained from being a customer of other financial services providers that contribute to forming some initial expectations and knowledge of the service they expect to receive; some of their past experiences may be relevant in forming their expectations. Over time, and through interactions, these expectations are likely to change with direct experience of the service quality. For example, in an advisory situation the customer will experience interactions with the advisor, the services offered, the way the offering matches the needs of the customer, etc. As the financial services provider interacts with the customer over an extended time period, it co-produces the customer's experiences. The experiences will result in the customer forming many perceptions of the interaction with the provider; among them the customer's overall perceived quality of the service. Quality experience, quality evaluation and quality production are three inter-connected elements that comprise the services quality process.

Financial services quality experience

Social learning theory emphasizes the importance of learning through experience (Wood and Bandura 1989). In modern marketing and business research, experience is often considered important for how individuals perceive situations. Experience is also important for the development of knowledge, as personal experience makes it easier to reflect on and compare those experiences with one's own other experiences (Wood and Bandura 1989).

The customer can experience financial services quality in many ways, due to three important characteristics of financial services: financial services delivered through many delivery channels, the service offering includes a considerable range of heterogeneity and financial services are often experienced as part of a long-term relationship with the financial services provider.

As financial services are delivered through many channels, customers may experience the service through a single channel or a mix of channels that they choose to use for different purposes. Many financial services providers that use multiple distribution channels have developed strategies for the management of the different channels. These strategies usually focus on how the channels work separately, and together, as an interface toward the customer. For example, in Chapter 23 Waite and Rowley discuss the management of the online service experience through the e-servicescape.

The customer's past experience of using a particular channel has been found to be important. For example, customers who have prior online experience have been found to use online financial services channels differently compared with customers who have no or little experience of online financial channels (Carlson and Zmud 1999). Moreover, research has shown that financial services customers need to learn to find a channel useful before they start to use it, or increase their use of it (Eriksson and Nilsson 2007). Despite differential channel usage among customers, Eriksson and Nilsson's (2007) research shows that financial services customers do not distinguish between different channels in terms of overall satisfaction with the bank. These findings from financial services research suggest that customers need to get used to a channel before they use it, but that they may evaluate the service offering of all delivery channels together. More research is needed in this area; particularly as mobile banking is emerging as a new distribution channel.

The variability of financial services concerns not only the number of financial services offered, but also variations in complexity. Financial services complexity ranges from an uncomplicated use of an ATM, to planning retirement savings. There is also a range of market segments served, from students, households, high net worth customers, small corporate customers, big corporate customers, organizations and institutions. The range of services offered has resulted in financial services providers organizing their operations according to market segments (Eriksson and Mattsson 1996). There are also financial service providers reflecting particular segments, such as community, online, corporate, agriculture and full-service banks.

Research has shown that financial services customers tend to have long-term relationships with financial services providers (Beckett et al. 2000). In such long-term relationships, the interaction process between the financial services provider and the customer frequently results in the development of social and business ties. These ties are particularly important and strong in business relationships (as discussed by Moles in Chapter 24). Trust is a key factor in the development of the relationship and can strengthen ties (as discussed by Hurley, Gong and Waqar in Chapter 30). Bonds can also be strengthened because the financial services provider offers a service arrangement that is difficult to switch to another financial services firm. For analytical purposes, therefore, relationships can be considered to be the result of interactions that have contributed to the formation and development of the relationship. While interactions within the relationship and the relationship itself are inseparable, individual interactions can change the relationship for the better or for worse.

For the customer's financial services quality experience, perceptions about the quality of the overall relationship as well as the individual interactions may co-exist. For instance, the customer may perceive that the overall relationship with the financial services provider is poor, but that the quality of an individual interaction is good. Interactions can be critical at times and can change the relationship dramatically. In banking, the loan application process is a particular service where a rejection or an approval may cause the customer to become more loyal or to terminate the relationship altogether.

The customer's perception of financial services quality depends on the nature of the service, service delivery channels and service relationship. To a large extent, these will interact. A customer who has previous experience of various channels and a good knowledge of financial services may perceive quality differently than a customer who has limited experience of the channels and poor knowledge of financial services. These are analytical distinctions that are useful for an increased understanding of financial services quality. However, the customer may not distinguish between these analytical dimensions as they conduct their financial services business.

The quality of the relationship is particularly important as the interactivity in the relationship can influence the customer's use of the service delivery channel and knowledge of how to use financial services (Lang and Colgate 2003). If a financial services provider can better describe how to use a channel, either online or in personal communications, then the customer will be better able to use the channel. The same holds for financial services. If the customer perceives financial services as more easily understandable, then they are better able to use them, without the financial services provider having to explain how they should be used.

The variability in financial services, channels and relationships leads to multiple customer experiences of financial services quality and consequently, customer perceptions of financial services quality. This exerts an impact on the ways in which customers evaluate quality and the processes by which financial institutions manage financial services quality.

Financial services quality evaluation

The experiences that customers have with a financial services provider will cause them to reflect on their experiences in one way or another. Experiences are delivered or co-created in the interactive service process, whereas evaluations concern how financial services quality is assessed and perceived.

In the interactions that the customer has with the financial services provider, the customer has some expectation of the service quality that will be delivered. This expectation serves as a benchmark for the customer, in the evaluation of the service quality. The expectations are formed through the interactions the customer has with the financial services provider in their relationship over time. However, the customer's expectations may shift due to experiences outside of the relationship. For instance, the use of an online system in another industry context may cause the customer to evaluate the features provided in online banking. The customer's context may therefore also be important when evaluations are made.

The customer's evaluation of quality is often what the customer feels is the quality that has been delivered. This is frequently not a structured process that results in an articulated statement of the extent to which expectations are met. Even though quality may be an important evaluation criterion for customers, they may not have a clear perception of what it means.

Quality evaluation forms when the customer evaluates the individual attributes of the service delivered. The expectations that a customer has can be categorized into "will expectations", "ideal expectations" and "should expectations". Will expectations refer to the attributes that the customer expects the financial service provider to have. Ideal expectations refer to the attributes that a customer would wish to be provided. Should expectations describe the attributes that the customer thinks the financial services provider ought to provide.

Will expectations are formed from the experiences that the customer has of the financial services firm and any other experiences that may influence the customer's perception of the service provider (Teas 1993, Golder et al. 2012). Will expectations can influence perceptions in that customers are biased to confirm what they already know or expect. Financial services offerings are often difficult to evaluate beforehand and in cases when a service is difficult to evaluate, customers tend to rely on their expectations of what they will receive.

Ideal expectations are what the customer perceives as the ideal attributes of a financial service. These ideal expectations depend on the ways in which the customer associates other experiences from within and outside of the financial services industry. For instance, a customer may have perceived exceptional quality at a travel agency; if the customer thinks that financial services firms ought to be able to act similarly to travel agents, then the experiences at the travel agency will contribute to the formation of the customer's ideal expectations of financial services quality. Expectations are what the customer perceives, so they may not necessarily have anything to do with whether travel agency services and financial services production are comparable. Expectations are all in the mind of the customer.

Should expectations are such that the customer expects that financial services ought to have certain attributes, as a minimum requirement. Should expectations can be seen as the lowest level of acceptable financial services quality perception. In terms of the experiences from which should expectations are formed, these are usually focused on what has been delivered in the past in financial services interactions. Should expectations also contain an element of value for money, in the sense that the customer pays for the service and expects that certain attributes ought to be present in the financial services offering or experience. If the customer does not receive what they feel they ought to, then this will cause the customer to have negative perceptions of the service quality regardless of the actual level of quality delivered.

The difference between will, ideal and should expectations is that the ideal expectations represent the highest expectations that the customer can imagine whereas should expectations represent the lowest or baseline expectations that the customer considers as acceptable. Will expectations are somewhere between and represent what the customer thinks they are likely to receive or experience. In the evaluation of financial services quality, the customer compares their perception of the quality of service experienced to their expectations. Expectations tend to be considered holistically, although some customers may differentiate between will, ideal and should expectations (Golder et al. 2012).

The gap between perceptions and expectations determines the extent to which customers are satisfied with the service quality. Customers will evaluate perceived service quality according to the extent that it exceeds, meets or falls short of expectations (Iyengar et al. 2007). Customers' evaluations are known to be asymmetrical, such that quality perceptions that fall short of expectations will cause a greater reaction in the customer than an evaluation that exceeds expectations (Mitra and Golder 2006).

The gap between perceptions and expectations is not static, it is a dynamic interaction over time; quality evaluations may change over time (Heinonen 2004, Mitra and Golder 2006). For example, a pension savings plan may be perceived as low quality if it performs poorly compared to the competition in the short term, but may prove to outperform the competition in the long term as retirement approaches. The customer's perceived quality of the fund is therefore likely to change over time.

From the viewpoint of the financial services provider, service quality evaluation processes are difficult to control because they depend on customers' expectations and experiences. The context in which evaluation takes place is also important. Perceptions are prone to change based on changing contexts; there is a need for financial services providers to monitor customers' contexts in order to monitor quality evaluations (Fournier and Mick 1999). For example, if the customer's financial situation changes or they start traveling or increase their online shopping, then that may influence their evaluation process of the financial services provider.

People and processes in financial service quality production

The third element in Golder et al.'s (2012) service quality process refers to how the service provider produces service quality; service quality production is the financial service provider's production of the service. However, the boundary between the financial services provider and the customer, in terms of production and consumption activities, may not be particularly clear.

The customer can be actively engaged in the co-production of services at various stages of the service quality production process (Lengnick-Hall 1996, Grönroos 2012). The financial services customer may take part in co-production by providing financial resources, information and even performing activities necessary for value creation by the financial services provider (Auh et al. 2007). In some cases, the financial services firm provides value by making it possible for customers to exchange with the financial services firm's resources in the form of financial market transactions, customer networking and service production system (Eriksson et al. 2007, Fjeldstad and Ketels 2006). Co-creation of value is explored in greater detail by Michel in Chapter 13.

Financial services operations are challenging because of the variety of services and multiple distribution channels. In particular, financial services face a difficult task in facilitating interdepartmental co-operation across their multiple distribution channels and heterogeneous market segments (Eriksson and Mattsson 2002, Eriksson and Mattsson 1996). Such interdepartmental co-operation has been found to be important for service production and customer perception of services (Dawes and Massey 2005, Hutt 1995, Luo et al. 2006). In practice, the ideal state of one coherent service interface is often difficult to achieve because of factors in the financial services provider's organization, the environment and the interactions with the customer.

Financial services providers are also under pressure to produce profit and shareholder value. In the effort to generate returns, one of the actions taken can be to work toward cost-reduction and increased efficiency in the internal operations of firms. In financial services operations, this may lead to an erosion of quality (Oliva and Sterman 2001). The reason being that short-term gains can be achieved by economizing on customer relationship development factors that are not directly related to the financial services delivery process. For example, hiring staff is usually more expensive than deploying automated services. Some financial services do not need to be delivered by staff and can instead be standardized and packaged; the handling of these services can be automated through online banking or other forms of technology and supported over the phone. The efforts that financial services firms make to cut costs have been found to have negative effects on the quality that customers perceive.

The reason quality becomes eroded is that staff who are under pressure, dissatisfied or consid- ering leaving the firm do not provide such good customer service as staff who are satisfied with their job (Dick 2008, Schneider and Bowen 1993). The efforts to make the operations of the financial services firms less costly often result in loss of human interactivity (Oliva and Sterman 2001). When staff are under pressure, the time available for each customer may be reduced. Human interactivity is also lost when financial services are offered online instead of in person. Interactivity is an important driver of customer perceptions of financial services quality because of the co-production of financial services. The quality enhancing effect of co-production is that not only does the customer gain a better understanding of how to use the resources that the financial services firm can offer, but also that the customer assumes some of the responsibility for service production (Oliva and Sterman 2001). The customer therefore becomes more forgiving in areas of poor service delivery.

The process of financial services quality production is a challenge because it involves cus- tomer interactions that are heterogeneous and occur through multiple distribution channels. The importance of personal interaction should not be overlooked. While reductions in staff may provide short-term financial gains, the loss in interactivity with customers may prove detrimen- tal to financial services quality.

Summary of the financial services quality process

While service quality is often an elusive perception held by customers, it can be considered as a process where quality is experienced, evaluated and produced. The service quality development process can be applied to financial services, but there is also the need to consider the unique features of financial services, such as multiple distribution channels, services heterogeneity and the complexity of some financial services.

In particular, financial services quality may be perceived through individual channels, for individual services, as well as across a range of channels and services together. Financial ser- vices may be experienced by a customer through an individual channel, but that experience may affect the customer's overall perception of the quality of the financial services provider. Financial services quality production is often tailored to separate channels and financial ser- vices, as well as different customer groups, which is why the customer may experience quality separately and differently from other customers. Evaluations of financial services quality are a different matter and are based on the relationship between expectations and perceptions of actual experience.

Measurement of service quality

One of the first wide-spread measurements developed to measure service quality was the SERVQUAL instrument developed by Parasuraman et al. (1988). SERVQUAL identifies five key dimensions that comprise service quality: reliability, responsiveness, assurance, empathy and tangibles. Customer evaluation of service quality is measured by calculating the scores for each dimension (using a 22-item scale) in relation to expectations of service quality and perceptions of actual experience. The difference between expectations and perceptions determines the customer's evaluation of quality. Despite its wide-spread use, SERVQUAL has been criticized (for a detailed review see Buttle 1996). Particular criticisms relate to the limitations of a single instrument across different industries, the need to take into account the context in which service quality is delivered, the difficulties of defining expectations and the extent to which expectations are stable over time and therefore accessible for measurement. In response to the latter point, Cronin and Taylor (1994) proposed the SERVPERF instrument based on perceptions only. Their research demonstrated that a perceptions-only model explains the greatest variation in service quality evaluation for consumers who are familiar with a service context.

Recent research on the measurement of service quality tends to focus on the "will", "ideal" and "should" expectations that customers may have and how these expectations are met by the service (Arasli et al. 2005).

Performance and service quality

Early studies of service quality suggested that increasing service quality could lead to increased business profitability and a reduction in customer defections. The argument put forward was that improvements in perceived quality together with loyalty and satisfaction were thought to be conducive to the development and maintenance of customer relationships (Reichheld and Sasser 1990). However, as Yu and Harrison illustrate in Chapter 9, the motivations customers have for engaging in relationships with financial services providers do not always relate to the quality of the service experience and relationships can be manifest in many ways.

Service quality does have performance implications, but it is not necessarily a performance measure in itself (Teas 1993). Firms may offer services of superior quality that are highly unprofitable. However, having services that are perceived as high quality may be an important means for building value in the customer relationship (Grönroos 2012, Heinonen 2004). Following its central role for customer relationship value creation, service quality is an integral part of marketing strategy and business development (Paltayian et al. 2012) and in the development of service productivity and brand equity (Rust and Huang 2012).

Service quality can thus have direct and indirect performance effects (Zeithaml 2000). The indirect effects can be divided into offensive indirect effects and defensive indirect effects. The offensive indirect effects are when quality increases market share, reputation and warrants a price premium for the financial services provider. The indirect defensive effects of quality are cost reductions, a stable volume of purchases because of customer retention and positive "word of mouth" about the service (Zeithaml 2000).

Customer satisfaction is a more widely-used performance measure that is also frequently included in balanced scorecards, along with accounting measures of performance (Cheng-Ru et al. 2011, Kaplan and Norton 2005). The reason may be that satisfaction is more linked to value for money, whereas quality is perceived to be more of a standard for service delivery (Iacobucci et al. 1995).

The process-driven nature of services should ideally be matched by research on how performance emerges as a result of the process. This is difficult to achieve in practice. Perhaps emerging advances in "big data" analysis on large customer datasets can produce quantitative prescriptions that would address such a problem. To date, qualitative research has provided the most practical methods for studying performance over the lifecycle (Heinonen 2004).

Conclusions

Both financial services firms and customers use the term "quality" to describe financial services. The understanding of what quality is, is a reflection of the interaction in the service encounter. The financial service encounter is of a special kind, because of the nature of the characteristics of financial services and the distribution channels involved. It appears that financial services quality as a term is useful for capturing the essence of the customer's relationship with the financial services provider, but there is still much need for research to fully understand this. For example, how does the customer perceive different distribution channels? Does the customer view them as separate services, or as an interface for all services? Is the quality of the relationship between the bank and the customer important? Does a customer who trusts the financial provider perceive quality differently from a customer who does not trust the financial provider? How does the nature of the service quality process change as people, technology, regulations and financial markets change?

For the customer, the implications are that they need to be aware that service delivery is a process. In that respect, they can put effort and information into the process in a constructive way. For instance, the customer can suggest improvements to the service delivery, point out where it does not work well and provide the firm with a chance to correct its errors. The more active the customer is the greater the chances are that they will receive something positive out of the service delivery.

Financial services firms would do well to monitor customer expectations on a continuous basis, during and after individual interactions. Monitoring can be done by administering surveys, in personal interactions, or through online communications. Following the recent financial crisis, financial services firms will increasingly be required to survey customers in order to comply with regulatory changes. This gives the financial services firm an opportunity to also monitor customer perceptions of service quality, in particular the "will", "ideal" and "should" expectations. Most financial services firms have large datasets on their customers' financial transactions. This is an underutilized resource that can be further developed to monitor behavior in relation to measurement of customer expectations (Heinonen and Strandvik 2009).

Financial services operations need to consider the effects on service quality of cost-cutting efforts to increase efficiency. Financial services quality benefits from the involvement of customers in co-production of services and erosion can be mitigated by increased efforts to interact with the customer. The work of skilled financial services staff is of course superior to most standardized or online service distribution channels. However, skilled staff may be costly to develop and maintain, so an alternative route may be needed. Financial services providers should maintain their employees and be selective in their recruitment efforts, as research has shown that dissatisfied staff deliver less satisfactory service than satisfied staff (Yavas et al. 2013).

Regardless of the definition of quality and the difficulties of identifying, measuring and delivering quality, customers know when they are satisfied with the quality they experience.

References

Arasli, H., Katircioglu, S. T. and Mehtap-Smadi, S. 2005. A comparison of service quality in the banking industry. *International Journal of Bank Marketing*, 23, 7, pp. 508–26.

Auh, S., Bell, S. J., Mcleod, C. S. and Shih, E. 2007. Co-production and customer loyalty in financial services. *Journal of Retailing*, 83, 3, pp. 359–70.

Beckett, A., Hewer, P. and Howcroft, B. 2000. An exposition of consumer behaviour in the financial services industry. *International Journal of Bank Marketing*, 18, 1, pp. 15–26.

Bertini, M., Wathieu, L. and Iyengar, S. S. 2012. The discriminating consumer: product proliferation and willingness to pay for quality. *Journal of Marketing Research*, 49, 1, pp. 39–49.

Bitner, M. J. and Brown, S. W. 2008. The service imperative. *Business Horizons*, 51, 1, pp. 39–46.

Buttle, F. 1996. SERVQUAL: review, critique, research agenda. *European Journal of Marketing*, 30, 1, pp. 8–32.

Carlson, J. R. and Zmud, R. W. 1999. Channel expansion theory and the experiential nature of media richness perceptions. *Academy of Management Journal*, 42, pp. 153–70.

Cheng-Ru, W., Chin-Tsai, L. and Pei-Hsuan, T. 2011. Financial service sector performance measurement model: AHP sensitivity analysis and balanced scorecard approach. *Service Industries Journal*, 31, 5, pp. 695–711.

Cronin J. R. J. J. and Taylor, S. A. 1994. SERVPERF Versus SERVQUAL: reconciling performance-based and perceptions-minus-expectations measurement of service quality. *Journal of Marketing*, 58, 1, pp. 125–31.

Dawes, P. L. and Massey, G. R. 2005. Antecedents of conflict in marketing's cross-functional relationship with sales. *European Journal of Marketing*, 39, 11/12, pp. 1327–44.

Dick, A. A. 2008. Demand estimation and consumer welfare in the banking industry. *Journal of Banking and Finance*, 32, 8, pp. 1661–76.

Eriksson, K. and Mattsson, J. 1996. Organising for market segmentation in banking: the impact from production technology and coherent bank norms. *Service Industries Journal*, 16, 1, pp. 35–46.

—— 2002. Managers' perception of relationship management in heterogeneous markets. *Industrial Marketing Management*, 31, 6, pp. 535–43.

Eriksson, K. and Nilsson, D. 2007. Determinants of continued use of self-service technology: the case of internet banking. *Technovation*. 27, pp. 159–67.

Eriksson, K., Fjeldstad, Ø. D. and Sasson, A. 2007. Knowledge of inter-customer relations as a source of value creation and commitment in financial service firm's intermediation. *Service Industries Journal*, 27, 5, pp. 563–82.

Fjeldstad, Ø. D. and Ketels, C. H. M. 2006. Competitive advantage and the value network configuration: making decisions at a Swedish life insurance company. *Long Range Planning*, 39, 2, pp. 109–31.

Fournier, S. and Mick, D. G. 1999. Rediscovering satisfaction. *Journal of Marketing*. 63, 4, pp. 5–23.

Golder, P. N., Mitra, D. and Moorman, C. 2012. What is quality? an integrative framework of processes and states. *Journal of Marketing*, 76, 4, pp. 1–23.

Grayson, K., Johnson, D. and Chen, D.-F. R. 2008. Is firm trust essential in a trusted environment? How trust in the business context influences customers. *Journal of Marketing Research*, 45, 2, pp. 241–56.

Grönroos, C. 2001. The perceived service quality concept – a mistake? *Managing Service Quality*, 11, 3, pp. 150–52.

—— 2012. Conceptualising value co-creation: A journey to the 1970s and back to the future. *Journal of Marketing Management*, 28, 13/14, pp. 1520–34.

Grönroos, C. and Ojasalo, K. 2004. Service productivity: towards a conceptualization of the transformation of inputs into economic results in services. *Journal of Business Research*, 57, 4, pp. 414–23.

Heinonen, K. 2004. Reconceptualizing customer perceived value: the value of time and place. *Managing Service Quality*, 14, 2, pp. 205–15.

Heinonen, K. and Strandvik, T. 2009. Monitoring value-in-use of e-service. *Journal of Service Management*, 20, 1, pp. 33–51.

Hutt, M. D. 1995. Cross-functional working relationships in marketing. *Journal of the Academy of Marketing Science*, 23, 4, pp. 351–57.

Iacobucci, D., Ostrom, A. and Grayson, K. 1995. Distinguishing service quality and customer satisfaction: the voice of the consumer. *Journal of Consumer Psychology*, 4, 3, pp. 277–303.

Iyengar, R., Ansari, A. and Gupta, S. 2007. A model of consumer learning for service quality and usage. *Journal of Marketing Research*, 44, 4, pp. 529–44.

Kaplan, R. S. and Norton, D. R. 2005. The Balanced Scorecard: measures that drive performance. *Harvard Business Review*, 83, 7/8, pp. 172–80.

Lang, B. and Colgate, M. 2003. Relationship quality, online banking and the information technology gap. *International Journal of Bank Marketing*, 21, 1, pp. 29–37.

Lengnick-Hall, C. A. 1996. Customer contributions to quality: a different view of the customer-oriented firm. *Academy of Management Review*, 21, 3, pp. 791–824.

Luo, X., Slotegraaf, R. J. and Pan, X. 2006. Cross-functional "coopetition": the simultaneous role of cooperation and competition within firms. *Journal of Marketing*, 70, 2, pp. 67–80.

Mitra, D. and Golder, P. N. 2006. How does objective quality affect perceived quality? short-term effects, long-term effects, and asymmetries. *Marketing Science*, 25, 3, pp. 230–47.

Oliva, R. and Sterman, J. D. 2001. Cutting corners and working overtime: quality erosion in the service industry. *Management Science*, 47, 7, p. 894.

Paltayian, G. N., Georgiou, A. C., Gotzamani, K. D. and Andronikidis, A. I. 2012. An integrated framework to improve quality and competitive positioning within the financial services context. *International Journal of Bank Marketing*, 30, 7, pp. 527–47.

Parasuraman, A., Zeithaml, V. A. and Berry, L. L. 1988. SERVQUAL: A multiple-item scale for measuring consumer perceptions of service quality. *Journal of Retailing*, 64, 1, pp. 12–40.

Reichheld, F. F. and Sasser, W. E. 1990. Zero defections: quality comes to services. *Harvard Business Review*, 69, 1, pp. 105–11.

Rust, R. T. and Huang, M.-H. 2012. Optimizing service productivity. *Journal of Marketing*, 76, 2, pp. 47–66.

Schneider, B. and Bowen, D. E. 1993. The service organization: Human resources management is crucial. *Organizational Dynamics*, 21, 4, pp. 39–52.

Teas, R. K. 1993. Expectations, performance evaluation, and consumers' perceptions of quality. *Journal of Marketing*, 57, 4, pp. 18–35.

Wood, R. and Bandura, A. 1989. Social cognitive theory of organizational management. *Academy of Management Review*, 14, 3, pp. 361–84.

Yavas, U., Babakus, E. and Karatepe, O. M. 2013. Does hope moderate the impact of job burnout on frontline bank employees' in-role and extra-role performances? *International Journal of Bank Marketing*, 31, 1, pp. 56–70.

Zeithaml, V. A. 2000. Service quality, profitability and the economic worth of customers: what we know and what we need to know. *Journal of the Academy of Marketing Science*. 28, pp. 67–85.

Part IV

Developing and managing the financial services offering

13

Financial services and innovation
A customer-centric approach

Stefan Michel

Introduction

The relevance of innovations in financial industries cannot be overestimated (Capozzi et al. 2007, Lyons et al. 2007). In the modern economy, markets, industries, firms and jobs all are being created and altered by innovations; customers' roles are being reconfigured as a result of radically new offerings.

But banks and insurance companies are rarely considered especially innovative. Only two banks – HSBC and Banco Santander – appear on a list of the world's fifty most innovative companies (Rehder and Levi 2011). Using Bank of America as the exception to prove the rule, Thomke (2003) argues that other financial service firms can and should apply the same rigor to their innovation as product manufacturers do. In a large quantitative panel study by McKinsey & Co., 54 percent of the 322 respondents asserted that innovation is more challenging for financial institutions than for companies in other sectors (Capozzi et al. 2007: 5). However, the reasons indicated for these challenges do not seem industry-specific, with the exception of regulatory and compliance constraints. In addition, insurance is different from banking in terms of complexity. A study by Siegel and Gale shows that insurance is the most complex industry in a set of twenty-five industries. Banking is ranked nineteenth on complexity (N.N. 2013: 24). Compounding the issue, traditional literature on innovation by service firms often provides a myopic view, focusing on incremental rather than disruptive service innovations.

This chapter seeks to contrast the more traditional, attribute-driven innovation approach (Devlin 1998, Vermeulen 2004, Rajatanavin and Speece 2004, Tipu 2011) with a radically customer-focused perspective. With this approach, it becomes possible to understand disruptive innovations in the financial sector according to a co-creation perspective (for example, Yunus 2003). In this perspective, the customer is always a co-creator of value (Vargo and Lusch 2004), so the focus shifts from traditional 'value-in-exchange' to 'value-in-use'. Moreover, an innovation is disruptive only if it significantly changes: (1) customers' roles (for example, budget manager, cash handler, investor, saver), (2) the way customers and providers integrate resources, or (3) the constellation by which value gets created (Michel et al. 2008a).

To present this argument, the chapter begins with a brief review of extant literature on innovation, supported by various examples from the financial services industry. This overview

Table 13.1 Categorization of financial services innovations

Innovation perspectives	Innovation categories	Financial services examples
Industrial logic innovations	Product/service innovation	• LIBOR mortgage • Reverse convertible securities • Square-meter household insurance • Consolidated 'relationship' statements • Online banking budget planner • 'Keep the change' program
	Process innovation	• Alerts, notifications, reminders via email/text message • Online payment
	Distribution innovation	• ATM banking • Mobile kiosk
Co-creation logic innovations	Changing the customer's role	• Phone banking • Online brokerage
	Changing the resource integration	• Microfinance • Help Point
	Disrupting the value constellation	• Credit score agencies • PayPal • Mobile banking

Source: Author.

provides students, researchers, practitioners and policy-makers with a comprehensive perspective and discussion of the key issues. Table 13.1 serves as a guiding framework for exploring, analyzing and categorizing financial services innovations (Oliveira and Von Hippel 2009, Avlonitis et al. 2001). The innovations in this table, spanning different countries and financial services markets, are at the heart of this chapter, which concludes with managerial implications and further research questions.

Industrial logic versus co-creation logic

At the core of any innovation is improved value creation. From a paradigmatic perspective, innovation can be studied according to two dominant logics. A goods-dominant logic (GDL) treats the customer as a recipient of value, which is created by the firm. This value, in turn, is considered 'value-in-exchange'; consequently the customer is studied mainly as a buyer of or payer for services and products. According to GDL, services and products are categories of 'goods' that differ mainly in terms of their tangibility.

In contrast, a service-dominant logic (SDL) proposes that value is always co-created with the customer. So the focus is 'value-in-use' and the customer is studied mainly as a user. According to SDL, the distinction between products and services is artificial because both categories are sought by customers if and when they require a service.

The two perspectives change the way innovation may be addressed. A traditional industrial logic, synonymous with the goods-dominant logic (Vargo and Lusch 2004, 2008), attributes value creation to the firm. In Porter's (1985) value chain approach, for example, firms gain a competitive advantage by creating more value in the course of their direct and indirect activities. Starting from this paradigm, principles developed in product innovation domains apply to service innovation, congruent with the heritage of service marketing, which developed on the basis of traditional distinctions between products and services (Fisk et al. 1993, Zeithaml et al. 2005). A customer orientation is integral to this view, but the predominant focus is on the offering of a 'new' service (for a review, see Paswan et al. 2009). As Vargo and Lusch (2006: 47) point out, in this tradition: 'Typically, service is treated as a kind of good (subset of product) that differs from other goods by lacking in certain qualities—tangibility, separability of production and consumption, standardizability, and inventorability.'

Applied to financial services, industrial logic innovations are primarily product and service innovations, complemented with process and distribution innovations (see Table 13.1). New financial products and services thus enter the market, such as an online budget planner that is dynamically linked to a customer's account transactions and assets. The workflow between the firm and the customer thus improves, perhaps through email alerts, and some touch points become automated. These innovations are important; some of them exert significant influences on costs, customer satisfaction and customer relationships. However, they retain a fundamental 'inside out' orientation. These industrial logic innovations create a better bank or insurance company.

Co-creation logic innovations instead create a better customer. The co-creation logic, also known as a service-dominant logic (Vargo and Lusch 2004, 2008), focuses not on the new offering but on improving customer value (Michel et al. 2008a, 2008b), in line with the two central propositions of the service-dominant logic (Vargo and Lusch 2008): the customer is always a co-creator of value and all social and economic actors are resource integrators. As Christensen et al. (2007: 2) put it: 'The customer simply has a job to be done and is seeking to "hire" the best product or service to do it'. Because customers are not passive recipients of value, but are active co-creators who integrate value from different sources, they are not interested in what the service is, that is, the value in exchange, but in what the service does in relation to their co-creation, reflecting the notion of value in use.

These two paradigmatic viewpoints are not mutually exclusive, nor do they necessarily signify two strategies. However, case research suggests that adopting an industrial logic is more likely to result in incremental innovations, whereas a co-creation logic likely provides opportunities for developing disruptive innovations (Michel et al. 2008a, 2008b).

Industrial logic innovations

Traditional typologies in financial services innovations (for example, Avlonitis et al. 2001: 327, Vermeulen 2004) can be broadly categorized as product/service innovations, process innovations and distribution innovations (see Table 13.1).

Product/service innovation

Banks and insurance firms often call their services 'products', which reflects their industrial logic mindset and further indicates a clearly-defined service offering, with a specified contract. Consider, for example, a LIBOR mortgage. Instead of a fixed interest rate for a specified period, homeowners can accept a mortgage whose rate is dynamically adjusted to the currency's reference London Interbank Offered Rate (LIBOR), to which the bank adds its margin. High yield reverse convertibles represent another example in investment markets: for a specified period, the investor receives a high yield (for example, 8 percent above the Treasury bill rate), but the repayment is tied to a basket of shares (for example, GE, Siemens and ABB). If one of these shares drops below a certain threshold level during the time of the contract, the investor receives repayment not in cash but in the lowest performing shares. Finally, in the insurance business, one company calculates premiums for household damage and loss policies based not on the value of the belongings (which is hard to estimate) but on the square meters of the residence (which is easy to calculate).

On the service side, popular innovations include consolidated relationship statements, which replaced separate statements for each bank account, and online budget planners that organize payments into spending categories and support budget comparisons. In another interesting innovation that helps customers increase their saving rates, 'keep the change' programs round up every debit card payment to the nearest dollar, then transfer the difference (between 1 and 99 cents) into customers' saving accounts.

Process innovation

Process innovations improve the workflow between the financial firm and the customer but do not change the underlying financial service offering or contract or distribution channel. For example, using email, SMS and other electronic channels to inform customers are widespread process innovations. The information shared can be directly related to the customer accounts, or it might contain indirectly related details, such as stock market news or special promotions and coupons for event offerings.

Process innovations in financial services firms are predominantly IT-driven. As the seminal articles by Hammer (Hammer 1990, Hammer and Champy 1993) predicted, the opportunity of new technology is not leveraged by making existing processes more efficient, but by rethinking and radically redesigning the processes within the firm. Given the amount and criticality of data in banking and insurance, it is no surprise that financial firms are much more affected by the technological revolution of the last two decades than other industries. As shown in Table 13.4 later, there is no indication that the need for process innovation will decline in the future (Capozzi et al. 2007: 4). The main driver for this, however, might be regulatory and compliance requirements, rather than technological progress or cost-saving implications.

Distribution innovation

In the widest sense, distribution innovations change the physical interaction between the firm and the customer. The most widely adopted innovation in this regard is ATM banking, whereby the bank clerk is replaced by an automated teller machine that provides a range of services. Another distribution innovation is mobile kiosks, which serve as 'mini-branches', whether to replace expensive, full-fledged branches or to reach very remote locations.

One study of 84 financial services firms in Greece showed that this type of innovation is the most profitable for a bank, compared with other types of innovations (Avlonitis et al. 2001). This is not that surprising given the transaction cost differences between face-to-face interactions and technology-supported encounters (see also Chapter 21 in this book).

Co-creation logic innovations

Changing the customer's role

Innovating the ways customers co-create value requires a thorough understanding of what customers do and the tasks they perform to 'get the job done' (Christensen et al. 2007). In most contexts, customers perform three distinct roles (see Sheth 2002, Sheth and Mittal 2004): users of a service or product, buyers who evaluate options and make purchase decisions and payers who provide financial resources.

In the insurance market, the user is the person needing coverage (for example, a teenage driver), the buyer is likely the parent who handles insurance decisions and the payer is the family or both parents. For a capital transaction in investment banking, the user is the CFO, whose job it is to complete the transaction; the buyer is a steering committee that includes the chair, CEO and CFO, and the payer is the shareholder who votes to fund the transaction during a General Assembly meeting.

In other cases, the same person performs all three roles: the terms user, buyer and payer refer not to distinct entities but to different co-creation roles. A customer may decide to open a bank account at a local bank (buyer), put money into the account (payer) and start using the features that the bank provides, such as checking accounts, an ATM and loyalty card points (user).

Two famous innovation examples changed customers' roles, namely, telephone banking and online brokerage. In their study of the introduction of phone banking in the United Kingdom by First Direct, Costanzo et al. (2003) distinguish a traditional financial service innovation approach from a more radical value innovation approach (Kim and Mauborgne 1999), in which the innovation is 'not more of the same' but a new way of banking. In 1998, First Direct had a customer satisfaction rating of 90 percent, while the Trustee Savings Bank (TSB) and Building Societies, its closest followers, reached only 65 percent and 59 percent, Barclays was at 43 percent. Its introduction of telephone banking entailed more than a process or service improvement, in that it changed the way the customers perform their necessary functions (discussed in further detail in Chapters 21 and 22). Other innovations in the same market include online banking (1997), direct car insurance (1985) and direct home insurance (1993) (Charitou and Markides 2003).

The Internet and the new economics of information (Evans and Wurster 1997) have deconstructed the traditional (industrial logic) value chain of banks, such that specialized players have redefined the roles of customers through particular innovations. Online brokerage represents an innovation in this category. Instead of covering the full equity brokerage value chain, companies such as Charles Schwab in the United States and Swissquote in Switzerland invite customers to perform much broader roles when trading. They remain responsible only for what investors cannot do themselves; establishing and maintaining platforms to trade shares on exchanges in New York, London, Frankfurt, etc.

Changing resource integration

Changing resource integration relates to the idea of a value constellation, which requires some introduction. A value constellation describes the interplay among actors and resources to co-create value (Lusch and Vargo 2006, Michel et al. 2008c, Normann and Ramirez 1993). A market exchange is not restricted to two parties but may include many and varied actors. The idea of a linear value chain (Porter 1985) gets extended to more complex value constellations (Normann 2001). In turn, innovative value constellations can be grouped into two categories. The more obvious are Internet-related applications, which have been truly discontinuous in the past decade or so. Perhaps somewhat less obvious are constellations that are not Internet-based but still bring together varied economic actors, such as Grameen Bank, an example of micro-finance (see Chapter 28 for an in-depth discussion of micro-finance) and Zurich's Help Point car insurance.

Grameen Bank was founded in Bangladesh by Muhammed Yunus, who received the Nobel Peace Prize in 2006 for his ongoing fight against poverty. A crucial ingredient of Grameen Bank's continued economic and humanitarian success was not its innovation of a new product or banking process, or even its new distribution model, in which representatives of the bank travel to rural villages. Such industrial logic innovations would not have been sustainable, because Grameen's customers lack essential resources. These mainly female entrepreneurs, with small-scale businesses, are generally illiterate and without any business training. But before extending loans to these entrepreneurs, Grameen Bank introduced resources to the villages, such as basic entrepreneurial training, financial responsibility, peer pressure, purpose and motivation, and help with buying and selling products. Perhaps most important, it created a community with a common purpose and high standards of accountability (Schiendorfer 2009, Yunus 2003). In this sense, Grameen Bank did not innovate a product, service or process. It has innovated the customer through a unique integration of monetary and non-monetary resources.

The second example of a new integration of resources comes from Zurich Insurance. Instead of requiring customers to bring their damaged cars to a repair shop then start the process of getting reimbursed, Zurich Insurance offers more than 120 Help Point locations in Switzerland, most within a 15-minute drive of policy-holders. At these Help Points, customers can have the damage fixed and receive a replacement car during the time of the repair. The customer pays nothing, other than a co-pay if their plan includes it. By incorporating repair service into the overall offer, not just repair payments, Zurich offers a premium service, but it can also save money by avoiding unjustified or inflated claims. Finally, it is able to collect more data about driving, vehicle safety and repair statistics.

Changing the value constellation

The previous section dealt with how innovations change resource exchanges within a value constellation. This section focuses on innovations that change the value constellation itself. Vargo et al. (2008) go so far as to argue that the proper unit of analysis for service innovations is not the service offering but the service system,[1] 'a configuration of resources including people, information, and technology, connected to other systems by value propositions'. As Table 13.1 indicates, innovations that change the value constellation, or service system, have been increasingly recognized, offering the 'powerful lesson … that companies aren't necessarily stuck with any given business environment. Instead, they can reconfigure their innovation ecosystems to suit their needs by asking what things can be separated, combined, relocated, added or subtracted' (Adner 2012, cited in Hayashi 2013: 41).

Credit score agencies (for example, Equifax, TransUnion, Experian) provide money-lenders, such as banks and credit card companies, comprehensive information about actual and potential customers. In return, the lenders report customers' payment history to the agencies. Customers can order their own summary reports and learn about how to improve their credit scores. This system improves the average efficiency of private credit application processes, due to its high standardization and collection of multisource information. It represents a clear change of the value constellation, rather than within it, because new actors participate in value creation.

PayPal, which was acquired by the online auction platform eBay in 2002, offers an online platform for small, peer-to-peer financial transactions and can therefore be categorized as a payment system innovation (Weichert 2007). By 2011, it operated in 190 countries, with more than 230 million members, of whom approximately 100 million were active. PayPal is not a bank, or a credit card company, or a merchant. It is positioned in the value constellation as a clearing system for smaller payments; in this system, eBay is the largest client. Thus, its growth strategy is to become a market leader in the newly created system for mobile payments, introducing the 'mobile wallet', which is not only a payment platform but also integrates rebates, coupons and virtual loyalty cards.

The third example in this category takes mobile payments even further. Kenya's M-Pesa system allows the transfer of money by text message. M-Pesa customers can deposit and withdraw money from a network of agents, including airtime resellers and retail outlets that sell mobile phone credits; they can transfer money to other users and non-users; and they can pay bills. The system processes 80 transactions per second, accounting for a massive sum of money. Estimates differ about exactly how much, but it may reach as much as 50 percent of Kenya's annual gross domestic product (Ryan 2013).

Managerial implications

The first part of this chapter focused on the 'what?' of innovation, using several examples that help distinguish between industrial and co-creation logic innovations. This second part of the chapter addresses the question of 'how?', that is, ways that managers of financial service organizations can manage innovations successfully.

Innovation process

It is common to describe the innovation process as a certain sequence of steps and activities. An early literature review by Avlonitis et al. (2001: 326) has revealed five distinct activities of the innovation process in financial services firms: idea generation and screening, business analysis and marketing strategy, technical development, testing, commercialization/launch.

According to an empirical study among small and medium-sized (SME) banks and insurance companies, a new service development process can be described by eight steps, of which only three are present in all of the 54 innovation projects studied (Vermeulen 2005: 438): idea generation (n = 54), concept development (n = 37), concept specifications (n = 54), IT specifications (n = 54), testing (n = 40), internal and external marketing (n = 42), launch (n = 46), evaluation (n = 8). While this study is limited to SME banks and insurance firms and focuses on product innovations, the list of steps serves as a basic framework for industrial logic innovations.

For co-creation logic innovations, the main difference is probably in the first step (idea generation) during which two questions need to be explored. What is the job the customer is trying to accomplish, and what is the best value constellation to achieve this?

Defining the 'job to be done' (Christensen et al. 2007) requires focusing on customer activities and not on the bank's offerings. Instead of thinking about 'a better mortgage' (bank offering), innovators explore how customers can be relieved and enabled in their co-creation. The relieving/enabling framework (Normann 2001, Michel and Brown 2005, Wikström and Normann 1994) helps to explore, identify and understand innovations related to customers' co-creation. Table 13.2 illustrates some applications in the financial services sector.

Overcoming barriers

Managing innovations in large companies (and many financial firms are very large and only growing larger through consolidation) requires identifying, understanding and overcoming the many hurdles that innovations face. In a longitudinal study with Dutch financial service providers, Vermeulen (2004) identifies four major barriers to innovation: functionally departmentalized structures, limited use of new product development (NPD) tools, conservative organizational culture, constraining information technology.

Innovations require contributions from several departments and functions within a bank in the design stage (for example, product management, IT, legal, marketing) and between

Table 13.2 Relieving/enabling framework applied to financial services

Customer's job to be done	Initial solution	Relieving innovation	Enabling innovation
Financing a house	Fixed-term mortgage over 30 years.	• Interest-only mortgage relieves the customer from paying principal. • Allowing the customer to use some pension fund assets relieves them in terms of monthly mortgage payments.	• LIBOR-linked mortgages enable the customer to optimize his/her overall financial portfolio. • Variable amortization terms enable the customer to manage cash flow better.
Settling a car accident claim	Customer gets damage assessed, has the car repaired, pays the bill and gets reimbursed by the insurer.	• The customer is relieved of any cash handling if the insurance firm pays the garage directly. • The customer is relieved of reporting the accident and proving the damage if the insurance representative settles the claim at the scene. • Customers are relieved of finding a garage, negotiating terms and paying the invoice if the insurance company offers Help Points.	• The customer is enabled to decide the best course of action if the insurance company issues a check that covers the damage, whether the customer has the car fixed or not.

the design and implementation stage. The tensions found by functionally departmentalized structures were mainly caused by misalignment, which in turn led to conflicts in priorities and resources. The study found that financial service providers are not used to project-based work and the use of 'product champions', which is common in fast-moving consumer goods companies, hence displayed limited use of NPD tools.

Managers perceived their culture as very conservative and not innovation-friendly. The main reason for this seems to be an inherent risk-aversion in financial services firms. Finally, while the IT landscape has changed since the time of the study, the problems of constrained information technology remain the same. First, there is a lack of IT resources. Second, the IT integration of several products into complex offerings is problematic. Third, the complexity of IT architectures makes it impossible for outsiders to judge what is possible and what is not (for an extended discussion on the role of technology, see Chapter 21).

In a field study among banks in Algeria, Cherchem (2012: 111) found that banks are not very successful at launching new products and services, the main reasons cited are: lack of market and customer insight, poor understanding of cost implications, poor communication processes and lack of training for front-line employees.

In a McKinsey & Co. survey (Capozzi et al. 2007), most respondents believed that innovation is more challenging for the financial service industry. However, except regulatory and compliance restrictions, this statement might result from a self-serving bias (i.e. an excuse for not being more innovative) rather than empirical facts. Many hurdles cited in Table 13.3 are common in other industries as well (n = 172, multiple answers possible).

These results, despite their limitations, highlight a few critical managerial implications, starting with the prerequisite of building a business case for an innovation portfolio.

Table 13.3 Strongest hurdles to innovation in financial service settings

Short-term financial success is expected in everything we do; innovations initiatives often result in short-term losses.	53%
The resources needed to pursue innovation initiatives aren't allocated because these resources are critical to short-term execution.	38%
Organizational mechanisms that would encourage the generation of new ideas and their execution don't exist in this industry.	36%
The industry is mature and as a result, opportunities to innovate are limited.	36%
The industry lacks insight into customer needs and behaviour.	31%
Leaders of financial services institutions generally do not value innovation.	18%
Regulation/regulatory pressure.	8%
Compliance restrictions.	2%
All others.	10%

Source: Adapted from Capozzi et al. (2007: 5).

Making a business case for an innovation portfolio

Like our classification (see Table 13.1), the McKinsey & Co. survey reported by Capozzi et al. (2007) distinguishes product, process, distribution and business model innovation (which overlaps with our concept of co-creation logic innovation). When asked which activities and investments are priorities, and which should be, the biggest gap arises with regard to business model innovation. Product innovation is the priority and it should remain in this position (see Table 13.4).

Faced with pressures for short-term results and a lack of resources, innovation champions work to build a business case for both industrial logic innovations, which tend to be incremental and co-creation logic innovations, which are disruptive. An applicable tool is the Balanced Scorecard by Kaplan and Norton (1992, 1993, 1996), to avoid too much focus on short-term results and prevent a failure to address the imperative of managing antecedents of financial success.

This company-wide, strategic view of innovation can also be incorporated into strategy maps (Kaplan and Norton 2004a, 2004b, 2004c), which connect learning and development, process improvement, customer satisfaction and loyalty to monetary results. In this context, innovation management should be treated not as an isolated project management task but as part of the overall company strategy for developing its capabilities.

Getting customer insights

A common obstacle to innovation, not only for financial services firms, is a lack of customer insights for generating effective new ideas. In a study among Algerian banks, the lack of market

Table 13.4 Importance of current and future innovation portfolios

	Current allocation of activities and resources (%)	*How important will each category be to your company's success over the next 3 years? (%)*
Product	34	40
Process	24	21
Distribution	14	14
Business model	13	25

Notes: n = 322. Percentage values do not add up to 100% because respondents could choose 'not applicable' or 'don't know' answers.
Source: Adapted from Capozzi et al. (2007: 4).

and customer insight was cited as the main obstacle to innovation (Cherchem 2012). In the global McKinsey study, employees and competitors are noted as the most frequent sources of innovation (according to 65 percent and 61 percent of respondents, respectively; Capozzi et al. 2007). Customer insights rank third, with only 38 percent frequency. In other words, approximately 62 percent of financial service leaders do not use customer insights as a frequent source of innovative ideas. Among the group of firms that does, 83 percent of them rely on customer segmentation (for example, customer relationship management systems), 68 percent use one-to-one interviews with customers, 66 percent use focus groups and 49 percent use observational techniques such as consumer ethnography (Schouten and McAlexander 1995).

Two points are important here. First, there is a crucial difference between customer data and customer insights. Customer data are facts; they cannot explain their own meaning. To innovate successfully, managers need a deeper understanding of what customers want. In recent years, firms have learned that in many cases, customers do not know what they want. Facebook is a good case in point. With about 1 billion users enrolled, it is clear that many 'want' Facebook. But who would have wanted Facebook, before it existed? Even if customers know what they want, they are often not able to articulate it (Jaworski and Kohli 2006: 100). Second, achieving a competitive advantage requires that the firm gain superior, unique, propriety data and insights about their customers, both current and potential.

Leadership matters

A study among 159 banks in the Southeast of the United States ranked a few identified success factors for innovation according to their importance. The result indicated that 'strategic leadership' is the most important factor, followed by 'change process features' and 'competitive intelligence'. In this study, 'management of technology' did not explain any variance over and above this criteria (Guimaraes et al. 2012: 48).

The most representative study (Capozzi et al. 2007) indicates some leadership shortcomings in greater detail. There are no clear incentives to innovate (72 percent of 322 respondents), no clear targets and metrics (71 percent), not enough experimenting (70 percent), no systematic funding (70 percent) and no external network in place to generate new ideas (67 percent). These factors relate directly to leadership and the similarity in their frequencies suggests the possibility of a clustering effect.

Some companies seem to have leadership for innovation. Others do not. Even self-reported leadership gaps acknowledge failures to invest in dedicated talents for innovation (64 percent), the lack of an effective organization and teams for innovation efforts (64 percent) and a missing innovation strategy developed by senior leaders (61 percent).

These findings also are supported by a large-scale, longitudinal study among 176 US-based retail banks. By following these banks over time and studying their Internet banking innovations, Yadav et al. (2007) confirm a hypothesized link between CEOs' attention focus and innovation outcomes. Specifically, banks whose CEOs attend to the future more are faster at detecting new technological opportunities. faster at developing initial products based on these technologies and superior at deploying these initial products. Their extensive study also revealed that firms whose CEOs attended more to the external environment detected new technological opportunities and developed initial products based on these technologies faster than did firms whose CEOs attended less to the external environment. There seems to be a strong link between what CEOs pay attention to and what their firms achieve in terms of specific innovation outcomes subsequently.

Although CEO attention is critical, a case study of Bank of America also indicates that a dedicated innovation unit, led by an innovation strategist, can help advance new ideas and accelerate the time to market. It formalizes the innovation process by breaking down functional barriers, challenging conventions and identifying organizational levers, such as contests and reward programs that foster a culture of innovation. In addition to coordinating tests and implementations of new concepts, this innovation unit can take responsibility for developing business cases and promoting promising ideas to decision makers (Rehder and Levi 2011, Thomke 2003).

Conclusions and directions for further research

Following a co-creation logic, this chapter has introduced a novel perspective to financial services innovation. We have compared this approach with the traditional and rather well researched approach, which follows an industrial logic. The co-creation logic helps financial service firms to study, reconsider and design innovation by changing the customer's role, changing the resource integration and changing the value constellation.

One important point needs to be mentioned here. Industrial logic innovations and co-creation logic innovations are not empirically distinct, but conceptually distinct. For example, the introduction of ATMs would be considered a 'distribution innovation' in an industrial logic view (what does the firm offer differently?), and a 'change of resource integration' in a co-creation logic (how does the customer 'get the job done' differently?). This is a different approach to innovation management and it requires further research.

Growing consensus among researchers implies that customers must be perceived as co-creators of value rather than as passive recipients of goods and services and yet the extant literature on service innovation fails to exploit the vast opportunities of this proposition fully. The co-creative role of the customer tends to be reduced to a co-designer role, with financial service firms seeking customers' input to create better offerings. Instead, a more promising avenue for research might be based on a different question: how can financial services firms innovate with regard to the co-creation role that the customer plays?

Both financial services firms and customers integrate resources, so service innovation requires the firm to rebuild and rearrange its resources to help customers who are integrating their own resources in novel ways. In this regard, three focal questions seem pertinent. How can financial services firms innovate to alter the three generic roles of customers: as users (co-creating value), buyers (making a buying decision) and payers (providing monetary feedback for exchange)?

With regard to customers' activities to 'get the job done', how can financial services firms relieve customers from activities they are not willing or are unable to perform, and how can they enable customers to perform those activities they prefer to do?

Finally, how can financial services firms create and redesign value constellations (i.e. the interplay across multiple actors and multiple resources that co-create values) for the benefit of the firm and its customers?

Note

1 In this chapter, the terms 'service system', 'ecosystem' and 'value constellation' are synonymous.

References

Adner, R. (2012) *The Wide Lens: A New Strategy for Innovation*, New York, Penguin.
Avlonitis, G. J., Papastathopoulou, P. G. and Gounaris, S. P. (2001). 'An Empirically Based Typology of Product Innovativeness for New Financial Services: Success and Failure Scenarios', *Journal of Product Innovation Management*, 18(5), 324–42.

Capozzi, M. M., Khanna, S. and Taraporevala, Z. (2007) 'Innovation in Financial Services: A McKinsey Global Survey', McKinsey Global Survey.

Charitou, C. D. and Markides, C. C. (2003) 'Responses to Disruptive Strategic Innovation', MIT Sloan Management Review, 55–64.

Cherchem, M. (2012). 'The Issue of Marketing Innovation in Financial Services: Case of the Banks and Insurance'. International Journal of Business and Management, 7(22), 109–14.

Christensen, C. M., Anthony, S. D., Berstell, G. and Nitterhouse, D. (2007) 'Finding the Right Job for Your Product', MIT Sloan Management Review, 48, 2–11.

Costanzo, L. A., Keasey, K. and Short, H. (2003) 'A Strategic Approach to the Study of Innovation in the Financial Services Industry: The Case of Telephone Banking', Journal of Marketing Management, 19, 259–81.

Devlin, J. F. (1998) 'Adding Value to Service Offerings: The Case of UK Retail Financial Services', European Journal of Marketing, 32, 1091–1108.

Evans, P. B. and Wurster, T. S. (1997) 'Strategy and the New Economics of Information', Harvard Business Review, 75, 71–83.

Fisk, R. P., Brown, S. W. and Bitner, M. J. (1993) 'Tracking the Evolution of the Service Marketing Literature', Journal of Retailing, 69, 61–103.

Guimaraes, T., Brandon, B. and Guimaraes, E. R. (2012). 'Empirically Testing Some Major Factors for Bank Innovation Success', Journal of Performance Management, 23, 34–46.

Hammer, M. (1990). 'Reengineering Work: Don't Automate, Obliterate', Harvard Business Review, 68 (July–August), 104–12.

Hammer, M. and Champy, J. (1993) Reengineering the Corporation: A Manifesto for Business Revolution. London: Brealey.

Hayashi, Alden M. (2013) 'The Inside and Outside View of Innovation', MIT Sloan Management Review 54, no. 3, 39–42.

Jaworski, B. J. and Kohli, A. K. (2006) 'Co-Creating the Voice of the Customer', In Lusch, R. F. and Vargo, S. L. (eds) The Service Dominant Logic of Marketing: Dialog, Debate, and Directions. New York, M.E. Sharpe.

Kaplan, R. S. and Norton, D. P. (1992) 'The Balanced Scorecard–Measures that Drive Performance', Harvard Business Review, 70, 71–79.

—— (1993) 'Putting the Balanced Scorecard to Work', Harvard Business Review, 71, 134–40.

—— (1996) 'Using the Balanced Scorecard as a Strategic Management System', Harvard Business Review, 74, 75–85.

—— (2004a) 'How Strategy Maps Frame an Organization's Objectives', Financial Executive, 20, 40–45.

—— (2004b) 'Strategy Maps', Strategic Finance, 85, 27–35.

—— (2004c) Strategy Maps: Converting Intangible Assets Into Tangible Outcomes. Boston, Harvard Business School Press.

Kim, W. C. and Mauborgne, R. (1999) 'Creating New Market Space', Harvard Business Review, 77, 83–93.

Lusch, R. F. and Vargo, S. L. (2006) 'Service-Dominant Logic: Reactions, Reflections, and Refinements', Journal of Marketing Theory, 6, 281–88.

Lyons, R. K., Chatman, J. A. and Joyce, C. K. (2007) 'Innovation in Services: Corporate Culture and Investment Banking', California Management Review, 50, 174–91.

Michel, S. and Brown, S. W. (2005) 'Market Offerings as Relievers and Enablers: Building On the Service Dominant Logic of Marketing'. Paper presented at the AMA Educators' Winter Conference, San Antonio TX.

Michel, S., Brown, S. W. and Gallan, A. S. (2008a) 'An Expanded and Strategic View of Discontinuous Innovations: Deploying a Service-Dominant Logic', Journal of the Academy of Marketing Science, 36, 54–66.

Michel, S., Brown, S. W. and Gallan, A. S. (2008b) 'Service-Logic Innovations: How to Innovate Customers, not Products', California Management Review, 50, 49–65.

Michel, S., Vargo, S. L. and Lusch, R. F. (2008c) 'Reconfiguration of the Conceptual Landscape: A Tribute to the Service Logic of Richard Normann', Journal of the Academy of Marketing Science, 36, 152–55.

N.N. (2013) Global Brand Simplicity Index: Siegel + Gale, http://simplicity.siegelgale.com/wp-content/uploads/2013/10/Global-Brand-Simplicity-Index-2013-eBook-spreads-FINAL.pdf (accessed 10 January 2014).

Normann, R. (2001) *Reframing Business: When the Map Changes the Landscape*. Chichester, Wiley.

Normann, R. and Ramirez, R. (1993) 'From Value Chain to Value Constellation: Designing Interactive Strategy', *Harvard Business Review*, 71, 65–77.

Oliveira, P. and Von Hippel, E. (2009) 'Users as Service Innovators: The Case of Banking Services', MIT Sloan School of Management Working Paper.

Paswan, A. K., D'Souza, D. and Zolfagharian, M. A. (2009). 'Toward a Contextually Anchored Service Innovation Typology', Decision Sciences, 40(3), 513–40.

Porter, M. E. (1985) *Competitive Advantage*. New York, The Free Press.

Rajatanavin, R. and Speece, M. (2004) 'The Sales Force as an Information Transfer Mechanism for New Service Development in the Thai Insurance Industry', *Journal of Financial Services Marketing*, 8, 244–58.

Rehder, P. and Levi, D. (2011) 'Innovation Excellence: What Bank Can Learn from Top Innovators in Other Industries'. www.accenture.com/Microsites/innovation-awards/2012/fs/Documents/pdf/Accenture-What-Banks-Can-Learn-from-Top-Innovators-in-Other-Industries.pdf

Ryan, P. (2013) 'Mobile Banking Lessons from the Developing World'. http://bankinnovation.net/2013/04/mobile-banking-lessons-from-the-developing-world

Schiendorfer, A. (2009) 'Consigning Poverty to the Museums. Interview with Muhammad Yunus, Founder of Grameen Bank', Bulletin, 55–57.

Schouten, J. W. and McAlexander, J. H. (1995) 'Subcultures of Consumption: An Ethnography of the New Bikers', *Journal of Consumer Research*, 22, 43–61.

Sheth, J. N. (2002) 'A Generic Concept of Customer Behaviour', *Journal of Customer Behaviour*, 1, 7–18.

Sheth, J. N. and Mittal, B. (2004) *Customer Behavior. A Managerial Perspective*. Mason, OH, South-Western, Thomson.

Thomke, S. (2003) 'R&D Comes to Services', *Harvard Business Review*, 71–79.

Tipu, S. A. A. (2011). 'Academic Publications on Innovation Management in Banks (1998–2008): A Research Note', *Innovation: Management, Policy & Practice*, 13(2), 236–60.

Vargo, S. L. and Lusch, R. F. (2004) 'Evolving to a New Dominant Logic for Marketing', *Journal of Marketing*, 68, 1–17.

—— (2006) 'Service-Dominant Logic: What It Is, What It Is Not, What It Might Be', In Lusch, R. F. and Vargo, S. L. (eds.) *The Service Dominant Logic of Marketing: Dialog, Debate, and Directions*. New York, M.E. Sharpe.

—— (2008) 'Service-Dominant Logic: Continuing the Evolution', *Journal of the Academy of Marketing Science*, 36, 1–10.

Vargo, S. L., Maglio, P. P. and Akaka, M. A. (2008) 'On Value and Value Co-Creation: A service Systems and Service Logic Perspective', *European Management Journal*, 26, 145–52.

Vermeulen, P. (2004) 'Managing Product Innovation in Financial Services Firms', *European Management Journal*, 22, 43–50.

Vermeulen, Patrick A. M. (2005) Uncovering Barriers to Complex Incremental Product Innovation in Small and Medium-Sized Financial Services Firms. *Journal of Small Business Management*, 43(4), 432–52.

Weichert, M. M. (2007) 'Payments Innovation: A Comparison of Banks and Non-Banks and How They Can Learn from Each Other', *Journal of Payments Strategy and Systems*, 2(3), 236–49.

Wikström, S. and Normann, R. (1994) *Knowledge and Value*. London; New York: Routledge.

Yadav, M. S., Prabhu, J. C. and Chandy, R. K. (2007) 'Managing the Future: CEO Attention and Innovation Outcomes', *Journal of Marketing*, 71, 84–101.

Yunus, M. (2003) *Banker to the Poor. Micro-Lending and the Battle against World Poverty*, New York, Public Affairs.

Zeithaml, V. A., Bitner, M. J. and Gremler, D. D. (2005) *Services Marketing*. New York et al., McGraw Hill.

14

A brave new world

Branding in financial services

Jillian Dawes Farquhar and Julie Robson

Introduction

The financial services sector worldwide still resonates from the global financial crisis of 2008 after which major brands suffered severe damage to their reputations. If the reckless lending practices of well-known brands were not enough, further revelations about money laundering, rate fixing and misselling continue to emerge. The news of these misdeeds has led to high levels of distrust among stakeholders of financial institutions (FIs). Many FIs are heavy investors in branding but, as a result of their own corporate misdeeds or those of their competitors, many brands have tarnished reputations. Although it may be tempting to blame this situation purely on malpractice, we argue that this is a good opportunity to assess branding in financial services as a whole. Were FI brands in a healthy position before the crises and on-going revelations? Did customers find the messages in the communication of brands consistent with their experience? Complaint columns, media analysis and financial blogs suggest that the customer experience was not always consistent with brand communications.

We would contend therefore that many FI branding attempts were not well conceived even before the crises revealed gaps between brand promise and experience. As FIs formulate new strategies so they can begin to regain the trust of their stakeholders, they also have the opportunity to revisit their brand strategies to realign them with changes in the marketplace and developments in marketing. To this end, this chapter proposes a model of financial services branding that addresses the issues faced by UK-based FIs and incorporates contemporary marketing thinking.

The chapter opens with an overview of the background to financial services and conventional approaches to branding. The next section reviews key branding constructs and recent contributions to branding and marketing. This review leads into a discussion and elaboration of a model for financial services branding that addresses the embedded and more recent challenges. The chapter concludes with theoretical and managerial implications and sets out areas for future research.

Background

Firms do not always behave as they should and can therefore find themselves in the position of having to take drastic action to rescue or to recover from damage inflicted on the brand. The media firm News International, for example, sacrificed one of its leading products, *The News of the World*, in an attempt to recover from the scandal of phone tapping in 2011. Siemens, the multi-national engineering firm, instituted a major overhaul of its structure, leadership, processes and culture to respond to accusations of systemic bribery in 2006. Although the financial world has encountered crises before, for example, the Wall Street Crash in 1929 and the Savings and Loan crisis of the 1990s, the events of 2008 onward connected unacceptable behaviors to specific brands.

Corporate misbehavior

During the financial crisis, a number of financial brands were lost or sustained significant damage. Lehman Brothers collapsed completely and U.S. government assistance was needed to support the insurer AIG and mortgage lenders Freddie Mac and Fannie Mae. Similar government bail-outs were needed in the UK for financial services brands Northern Rock, Royal Bank of Scotland (RBS) and Lloyds TSB. As many as thirteen countries were thought to have had a systemic banking crisis during that period (Laeven and Valencia 2010). As if not catastrophic enough, the crisis of 2008 has been followed by a series of revelations that banks and other FIs have engaged in a series of behaviors that have attracted considerable censure and huge financial penalties. Brands not directly involved in the 2008 crisis have been found to have mis-sold products (see Chapter 29 for an in-depth review), manipulated rates (for example, Barclays Bank and the Libor scandal), laundered the proceeds of criminal activity (HSBC) and paid excessive bonuses (most large brands), all of which have significantly undermined their brands and their reputations.

The degradation of brands in the financial services sector did not apply to all FIs. Global brands such as Amex and Citibank largely maintained their positions in global rankings, the Islamic banks stood apart from the traditional banks as ethical alternatives (see Chapter 26), retailers such as Marks & Spencer expanded their financial service portfolios, and non-bank financial service brands such as UK's Nationwide carefully distinguished themselves from high street banks. New entrants and non-bank alternatives also lined up to take on those customers who were sufficiently disenchanted with their FI to seek other providers, for example, Metrobank and Virgin (see Chapter 2 for a detailed discussion of new entrants). As a means of encouraging customers to switch and thus stimulate competition in the marketplace, an initiative to encourage customers to switch their bank was launched in the UK in 2013. At the time of writing the outcome of this initiative is not known. As the larger FIs are offering incentives to switch, it is likely that customers will switch from one high street provider to another in spite of the availability of better deals from alternative providers.

Branding financial services

In addition to the effect of the on-going crises on branding, there are deep-seated issues related to branding in financial services. First, there is the nature of the service offering. Financial services are intangible and therefore difficult to evaluate prior to purchase or even consumption. The products are often complex and infrequently purchased (for example, investments) or commoditized and difficult to differentiate (for example, motor insurance). The products are essentially a promise, where ownership is not transferred and reinstatement or payment is at a later date, which can be within a year or decades. In the absence of meaningful brands, customers will use such cues as price or brand to assist them in evaluating the purchase and its consumption. Banks sometimes attempt to use branding as a means of compartmentalizing the marketplace, for example, Churchill specializes in motor insurance. Can a single brand position be communicated across a diverse product range or should different brands be adopted for different product groupings?

Second, customers do not always adopt a comprehensive and considered approach when purchasing financial services. They lack interest in and have a limited understanding of financial services despite the central role that these services play in their everyday lives. Moreover, traditional consumer behavior models assume a rational and logical approach to decision-making, depicting the consumer as an information processor and problem solver (see, for example, Farquhar and Meidan 2010), in practice the consumer of financial services can be ill informed and surprisingly impulsive. Behavioral economists highlight the role of psychological and emotional factors in financial decision-making (for example, Tversky and Kahneman 1974), which bizarrely can lead consumers to act contrary to their best interests (Gehring 2013), for example, by remaining with a bank in spite of indifferent service or unexpected charges. Any attempts to encourage customers to switch their financial service provider usually involve an incentive or lower prices. These inducements are linked to the brand and accompanied by assurances of good customer service, but according to industry experts, have encouraged customers to focus primarily on price and not brand.

Third, the financial services sector is a crowded and noisy marketplace. Following deregulation in the UK from the1980s, the simple categories of banks, building societies and insurance companies faded to create financial services organizations offering a wide and overlapping range of products and services. Other countries, for example, the U.S., have undergone similar transformations (as illustrated in Chapter 1). Mergers and acquisitions followed, often resulting in rebranding, but a brand is a core asset and one that takes significant investment to build successfully. The act of rebranding can jettison this investment overnight and as brand and trust are entwined, it is a high-risk strategy. Following the financial crises, a number of FIs have rebranded to distance parts of their organization from the scandal. Notably AIG, who formed Chartis in 2009, then changed its name back to AIG in 2012 following repayment of its debt to the U.S. Government to symbolize the firm's recovery and a return to the values of its original brand.

We would argue that FI's branding strategies largely remain focused on links between the brand and marketing communications and as such undervalue the experience of customers and stakeholders. With current skepticism and mistrust, branding presents a greater challenge post crisis. What then do FIs want their brands to achieve? Is a brand a means of selling more products, a means of differentiating the offering or offering customers a particular experience? How does the customer engage with the brand, what is the nature of the relationship the customer wants with that brand and how may it be enacted? Finally, is the brand a means of shaping and creating marketing communications, is it a means of building relationships with customers/stakeholders and does it relate to a set of organizational values that drives the business?

FI branding is a recent development (de Chernatony and Harris 2000). At their beginning FIs employed brands as a symbol or sign to identify their premises or, in the case of the insurance fire marks, the premises they protected. As a result of subsequent investment in advertising, FIs have long been able to demonstrate high name awareness, but they have had little impact in terms of brand differentiation (Jones 1999). For example, in the 1920s Lloyds Bank were pioneers in film advertising (Winton 1982); in the 1970s and 1980s bank advertising featured more prominently on TV. Campaigns such as the TSB's 'The bank that likes to say yes' and the Midland Bank's 'Come and talk to the listening bank' created a brand image but often failed to represent the values and behaviors of the FIs themselves. The turning point for FIs in terms of branding came when they were no longer in competition with other FIs, but when new and different entrants, such as Marks & Spencer and Virgin, entered the market and a strong and meaningful brand proposition became important (see Chapter 2).

Branding

Classical descriptions of branding have often emphasized name, symbol and design as a means of communicating the values that a particular brand offers the marketplace (for example, Aaker 1991). The meaning of a particular brand has been defined as a mental picture or image in the customer's mind associated with the market offering (Berry 2000). From an organizational perspective, the brand is the visual, verbal and behavioral expression of the organization's unique business model (Knox and Bickerton 2003). For this image or expression to be realized, the brand should be salient, it should be able to create differentiation, it should be intense and arguably, the most important in this context, it should inspire trust. Owing to the nature of financial products as previously discussed, the role of trust in the purchase and consumption of financial services is pivotal.

Branding is an entity underpinned by multiple theoretical perspectives, which generates a range of concepts for practical and theoretical enquiry (Brodie et al. 2006). As well as familiar consumer-based concepts such as identity, logo, image, symbol, expression and personality, organizational concepts of positioning, cluster of values, vision, risk reduction and relational concepts that include promises, trust, commitment and experience (Brodie et al. 2006) all inform investigation in branding. Branding provides the means for building and sustaining relationships (Rust et al. 2004) so the antecedents and consequences of branding are analogous to those of relationship marketing (de Chernatony and McDonald 1998), namely, trust and commitment. A strong brand becomes a safe haven for customers, where they can visualize the offer more clearly and understand its value and benefits as well as appreciating any uncertainties and perceived risk associated in the consumption of the offer (Elliott and Yannopoulou 2007). Feeling that they are in a safe haven encourages customers to be loyal so that they are more likely to purchase more and engage in positive word of mouth about the brand (Chaudhuri and Holbrook 2001).

The strength of a brand of the focal firm in any network extends beyond the immediate customer groupings and can moderate relationships with partner firms and potentially impact on their performance (Morgan et al. 2007). The notion of a brand environment has been developed around the stakeholder theory (Farquhar 2011). Brands can evolve not only by intent on the part of the firm but also through the participating stakeholder network or community (for example, Muniz and O'Guinn 2001). It is the duty of brand managers to manage the evolution of their brands and relationships with stakeholders through the maintenance of brand values.

Brand values

The values that brands should aim to represent and share with customers need to be consistent with fostering the trust (Dall'Olmo Riley and de Chernatony 2000) that is so necessary in financial services consumption. Trust in financial services is a pivotal construct, it is discussed in depth in Chapters 10 and 30 in terms of the meaning and measurement of trust and trust building. In terms of branding, a consumer will trust a firm if they can infer that the firm is acting benevolently, in the best interests of the consumer and that there is an assumption of shared interests and values (Doney and Cannon 1997). Consumers will come to trust a firm if they have repeated positive experiences with the brand ultimately leading to confidence in the brand. If those experiences are not consistent or if the brand is undermined by corporate actions, then consumer confidence is eroded or lost.

The values that brands represent are often categorized as functional and emotional or symbolic (de Chernatony and Dall'Olmo Riley 1998). Functional values relate to the performance of the brand and an example might be house insurance cover paying for burst pipes and associated losses. The emotional values of the brand are associated with the consumer feeling positive about the brand and the brand experience. Emotional values will be dependent on the delivery of the brand's functional values. Both categories support the communication of the brand's value system through the customer experience (de Chernatony and Cottam 2006). Although this categorization of values has proved valuable in the past, some branding perspectives over-represent the functionalist aspect of the brand. Functional values are easily replicated and do not necessarily provide a firm platform for relationships and loyalty.

A more powerful interpretation of brands is that they act as vehicles of meaning (Kärreman and Rylander 2008) so that brands evoke associations and emotions, which the customer/employee/partner derives through experience with the brand. The employee may even be the primary client for the brand rather than the customer (Kärreman and Rylander 2008). The brand provides templates for action and conduct in interactions internally such as the building and maintenance of trust within the firm. Employees are therefore in a position to bring the brand values alive through interactions with other stakeholders. For this to happen, the onus is on management to enact the values of the brand at the highest level in the organization (de Chernatony and Cottam 2006).

The recognition that branding has a wider domain than that of customers has gained much ground and arguments have been developed for a brand having multiple stakeholders (see Farquhar 2011). According to Freeman (1984: 25), a stakeholder is 'any group or individual who can affect or is affected by the achievement of the organization's objective'. This definition extends the horizon of the firm and, we contend the brand, well beyond customer/employee/firm nexus. For an FI, the stakeholder network consists of governments, regulators, competitors, local communities, media and investors. The benefit of identifying and working within a stakeholder framework is that it enhances corporate strategy by recognizing and addressing the complexity of understanding the roles and interactions of firms and stakeholders (Freeman 1984). Each stakeholder brings knowledge to the relationship with the organization so shifting to a shared notion of interest and collaboration (Antonacopoulou and Meric 2005). Importantly for this debate, stakeholder theory has been linked to corporate social responsibility (for example, Neville et al. 2005).

Corporate reputation and corporate social responsibility (CSR)

The immediate relevance of CSR to the challenges facing FIs is that CSR increases trust in firms (Brammer and Pavelin 2006) and influences its corporate reputation (Lai et al. 2010). CSR has been portrayed as a multidimensional construct, which is composed of concern for shareholder/owners, stakeholders and the welfare of the community or state (Waldman et al. 2006). The normative framework, which governs a firm's CSR, is informed by the expectations of its stakeholder group (Maignan and Ferrell 2004). Many firms now have articulate and powerful NGOs and online communities as members of their stakeholder groups, which has put pressure on them to manage their reputations through transparent social responsibility (Bonini et al. 2009). Such are the positive effects of socially responsible behaviors and the negative effects of CSR violation that most firms not only pay careful attention to CSR issues, but also actively participate in CSR activities (Lai et al. 2010). For further reading, please see McDonald's integrative review of CSR in financial services in Chapter 32 and Nilsson's discussion of socially responsible investing in Chapter 33.

Corporate reputation, according to Neville et al. (2005), comprises a perception or assessment of a firm's behavior. This assessment comes about through a cognitive assimilation by the firm's stakeholders of a range of experiences with the firm. Having made the assessment, the firm's stakeholders then endow the focal firm with a potentially valuable resource: that of reputation. If a firm has a good reputation, it is better placed to withstand the effects of negative experiences and magnify the effects of positive experiences (Hillenbrand et al. 2013). A poor reputation offers none of these securities and potentially contributes to a degrading of what is likely to be a weak brand in the first place. The direct effect between CSR and corporate reputation offers firms with poor reputations an opportunity for rehabilitation or transformation through socially responsible behaviors.

Corporate initiatives in the area of reputation and responsibility enable the firm to promote such intangible assets to its stakeholders. These assets can be increased when the stakeholders themselves develop multidimensional relationships with the firm (Sen et al. 2006). Stakeholders may well make important decisions about resource allocation based on these relationships (Neville et al. 2005). Employees, for example, could decide to show greater initiative in their work, customers may decide to spend more on the focal firm's products and partner firms may decide to strengthen their relationship. The focal firm can boost the goodwill that is associated with being a good corporate citizen by incorporating their behaviors with their marketing initiatives (Sen et al. 2006). They can re-evaluate and possibly abandon some of the more conventional marketing practices, for example, a reliance on advertising and turn to alternative ways of interacting with their stakeholders.

Social media

Facebook has more than 901 million active users worldwide, which is an indication of the massive impact that social media has had on the way that we live. From a marketing perspective, social media create the potential for stimulating and memorable brand experiences provided that the interactions are meaningful (Hanna et al. 2011). Social media interactions should offer customers and arguably other stakeholders improved value, excellent service and an immediate relevance to their lives and their lifestyles. In this way, social media can provide firms with opportunities for creating value with their customers (Kietzmann et al. 2011). FIs have embraced social media as a means of strengthening relationships, in particular communicating with new and younger customers.

Postmodernist perspectives underlie social media, most significantly in undermining the control of managers. Brands instead are co-created through on-going interactions with their users (Neville et al. 2005). This shift away from being able to manage the brand is of major significance not only in financial services but in all other areas of business activity. Not only has ownership of the brand extended to users but each user infers distinctive and personal meanings from the same brand (Berthon et al. 2008). Through the construction of these highly individual meanings, each user has a unique and potentially intense experience with the brand. The user can then create content about that experience, which can then be built on (Asmussen et al. 2013, Hoffman et al. 2013) by Twitter followers or Facebook friends. Consistent with word-of-mouth research, poor brand experiences tend to be communicated most readily. The implications of social media, therefore, for branding and brand managers are profound. FIs have to acknowledge that user interactions or experiences endow their brands with meanings that they may not have planned or even desired. While they are unlikely to be able to control the entire range of media, such as appearances of their brand on social networking sites or YouTube, the role of brand managers is to monitor and respond quickly to any challenges to their offer (Tynan

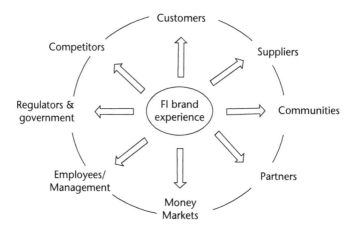

Figure 14.1 Brand environment for financial institutions

and McKechnie 2009). FIs need to ensure that they have appropriate structures, which support working within a socially-mediated environment.

The importance of social media on the brand environment makes an understanding of stakeholders in the extended environment of social media even more critical. In Figure 14.1 we depict the brand environment for a financial institution brand.

In Figure 14.1, there are eight stakeholders within the brand environment for a financial institution. All of these stakeholders have an experience with the focal brand, they are all connected through social or traditional media and they all have perceptions of the reputation of the focal firm. In addition to the customers and employees already mentioned as stakeholders, there are regulators, government, competitors, money markets and communities. Partners may act as distributors for financial services, for example, insurance and mortgages, by drawing them into the brand environment, they engage more fully with the brand experience rather than, for example, commission or other financial rewards. Money markets and suppliers provide the resources that support the FI in creating the brand experience but may engage more fully being part of that experience.

Service logic and brand experience

The themes of service logic (for example, Grönroos 2006, 2008) and service-dominant (SD) logic (Vargo and Lusch 2004, 2008) have made an important contribution to marketing thinking in focusing attention on value. Service and SD logic assert that service is articulated as a perspective on value creation rather than a category of marketing offering (Edvardsson et al. 2011), as exemplified in the traditional goods/service paradigm. The following extract, slightly adapted, summarizes service logic as follows:

> When using resources provided by the firm together with other resources and applying skills held by them, customers create value for themselves in their everyday practices. When creating interactive contacts with customers during their use of goods and services, the firm develops opportunities to co-create value with them and for them.
>
> *Grönroos 2008: 299*

A key principle in service and SD logic is value-in-use, this refers to the way in which customers, through processes of self-service, create value for themselves. This value is the outcome of synthesizing firm and customer resources. An important resource for the firm is the brand but the value of the brand is derived from the interactions, which stakeholders have with the firm. The firm needs to understand how customers create value from those interactions and to provide the necessary resources so that value can be created. Both brands and value-in-use are dynamic entities so customers and firms have to be receptive to learning about how best to synthesize resources (Lusch and Webster 2011). The firm learns about the customer experience so that it can design a co-creation experience around that (Payne et al. 2009) and to appreciate the resources the customer will bring to the value proposition in order to gain value-in-use The customer also learns how to apply specialized skills and knowledge as a fundamental unit of exchange (Vargo and Lusch 2004) or interaction (Grönroos 2008) so that they gain value-in-use.

A critical element or foundational premise of SD logic is that value can only be phenomenologically or experientially determined by the beneficiary or customer (Vargo and Lusch 2008). Consistent with service and SD logic, brand value is similarly co-created with all stakeholders and their collective perceived value (Vargo and Lusch 2004, 2008). The value of the brand is cumulatively built through processes that support the brand experience (Payne et al. 2009) and the onus is on the firm to create and maintain these processes so that value is repeatedly created with customers. As depicted in Figure 14.1, value is not created merely through the interaction between the customer and the firm but also through interaction between customers and other stakeholders (Arnould et al. 2006). Service and SD logic contribute two key dimensions to contemporary branding thought. First, value-in-use and brand experience are co-created through an integration of stakeholder resources. Second, service and SD logic assert that value is determined uniquely by the stakeholder, through on-going interactions with the brand.

The contributions from service and SD logic, corporate reputation and CSR and social media research lead to the proposition that brands are entities shared and created by stakeholders of the firm. While the firm may provide much of the financial resource for brands, it no longer has the degree of mastery of those brands that it had previously. In this new fluctuating brand environment, it is timely for the firm to appraise its branding strategies so that it can reap dividends rather than incur losses. Appraisals of this magnitude should take place at corporate level where the firm's brand champion shapes and drives strategy and resourcing, for example, the structure that underpins branding.

Branding architecture

Brand architecture refers to the structure within a firm that manages brands. This structure specifies the roles of the brand or brands and the nature of relationships between brands (Aaker and Joachimsthaler 2000). Brand architecture can be envisaged as a continuum, where the corporate brand lies at one end of the continuum and the individual product brand at the other (de Chernatony 2001). In a 'house of brands' architecture, each product has its own brand (Muzellec and Lambkin 2009). One reason a firm might choose to follow this particular structure is to avoid situations of cross contamination, for example, a product brand might fail but damage would be contained within that brand and not affect the firm's other brands or the corporate brand. Brand managers also justify the house of brands architecture on the basis that it allows them to maintain strong relationships with the product's particular groups of customers and to signal distinct specialist competencies to particular markets. Some FIs have experimented with this brand architecture but it is not a common strategy.

A little further along the brand architecture continuum lies the multi-corporate approach. With the multi-corporate style, a family of main brands rather than individual product brands is incorporated into an organization's brand architecture. Again, similar reasons are put forward by practitioners for a multi-corporate architecture such as a strong relationship franchise with different customer groups or distinct competencies to the marketplace (Muzellec and Lambkin 2009). There may be some evidence in support for multi-corporate brand architecture, for example, the Churchill brand may not have suffered as badly as the RBS corporate brand.[1]

For firms that select the architecture of corporate branding, which lies at the other end of the continuum, this structure allows for clearer definition enabling access not only to associations with the product but also to the organization itself (Aaker 2004). With this architectural approach, corporate identity and reputation are more clearly related to the corporate brand, thus establishing the external position of the firm in its marketplace and its brand environment. Internal meanings are more clearly articulated and embraced within the organizational culture thereby strengthening the corporate brand through an alignment of vision, culture and image (Hatch and Schultz 2003). With the corporate brand architecture, the role of employees, including senior management, is seen as crucially important in transmitting the brand values internally and externally (Balmer and Gray 2003).

With the clarity of brand experience being recognized at corporate level, senior management engage fully with the brand, its strategy and its integration with other corporate concerns, such as reputation. By adhering closely to values that are in tune with social responsibility, a firm is in a better position to deal with attacks on its brand (Kay 2006). By building a stronger brand, the brand environment becomes a community where stakeholders come together to co-create the brand. This strategy is supported by empirical research, which indicates that alternative conceptualizations of brand architecture such as the multi-corporate approach are not validated by consumer responses (see, for example, Devlin and McKechnie 2008). The evidence that consumers contribute to the development of a corporate brand and determine the levels of their own participation is extensive (McDonald et al. 2001), those brands that are ranked most highly in the various indices such as Interbrand all adopt the corporate brand approach, for example, Amex and HSBC.

In this section, we have evaluated elements that we argue would strengthen efforts by FIs to rebuild and maintain trust in their brand, which are summarized in Table 14.1. We now move onto a discussion of how these elements come together in the development of a model for contemporary branding in financial services.

The brand experience in financial services

The preceding review suggests that research advances in branding and marketing make important contributions to addressing branding challenges in the financial services sector. In this section, we develop a conceptual framework, which draws on these advances for a brave new world in financial services branding.

If a core purpose of a brand is to build and maintain trust, what does this signify for financial services brands? Financial services is a sector where trust in the provider of complex offerings, for example, retirement funding or health insurance, is of particular significance. FIs and other firms evince trustworthy behaviors through stakeholder encounters with the brand and the brand experience. The power of a brand is to act as a central organizing principle for an FI through an enactment of values and principles that guide strategies and behaviors internally so that they are aligned with the norms and expectations of stakeholders. When the reputation of a firm has been damaged through corporate misbehavior, stakeholders need to be involved in efforts that will eventually bring about the restoration of, or a significant improvement in, the reputation of the firm. We have argued that owing to the direct effects that CSR has on corporate reputation

Table 14.1 Summary table of branding literature

Element	Contribution to branding	Authors
Brand values	Foster trust, have emotional resonance, align experiences of stakeholders.	Dall'Olmo Riley and de Chernatony 2000, Kärreman and Rylander 2008
Corporate reputation and corporate social responsibility	Contributes to trust, recognizes the role of stakeholder, can enhance corporate reputation, consensus on norms.	Hillenbrand et al. 2013, Neville et al. 2005
Social media	Weakens firms' control of brand, facilitates relationships between stakeholders.	Neville et al. 2005, Hanna et al. 2011 Tynan and McKechnie 2009
Service logic	Emphasizes experiential assessment of value, organizational learning and integration of resources.	Grönroos 2006, 2008, Vargo and Lusch 2004, 2008
Architecture	Corporate branding is architecture most likely to resonate with customers (and stakeholders).	Aaker and Joachimsthaler 2000, Muzellec and Lambkin 2009, Devlin and McKechnie 2008

and the brand that FIs would benefit from engagement in 'actions that appear to further some social good, beyond the interests of the firm and that which is required by law' (McWilliams et al. 2006: 1). There are indications that FIs have responded to these calls. Barclays has developed a Citizenship plan, HSBC emphasizes its culturally diverse management team, First Direct continues to emphasize service reputation and personalization, Wells Fargo stresses responsible lending and Citibank promises conduct that is transparent, prudent and dependable.

For FIs, value creation, while offering long-term benefits to stakeholders, requires learning how to co-create value and its processes with customers and other stakeholders. As Payne et al. (2009) propose, the brand experience consists of a series of encounters, which the firm through learning manages in support of value creation. Encounters may be directly with the firm, through social media or with other members of the brand environment (see Figure 14.1) and again the onus is on the firm to learn about the dynamics of these multiple encounters. FIs offer a multiplicity of products, for example, an extensive range of home loan products with various product features, which many consumers may not fully understand until a problem occurs. Penalties for being overdrawn, late payments and other hidden charges destroy value (Farquhar 2013) and leave the customer feeling powerless. Moving to value co-creation is consistent with the changing business environment as envisaged, for example, by Cova and Dalli (2009) but some FIs will encounter a steep learning curve.

Culturally and structurally, FIs are not always well equipped to engage with stakeholders in such a way for value to be co-created as envisaged by its service and SD logic advocates. FI brand architecture may be unnecessarily complex with indications from empirical work pointing to corporate branding as a form of branding, which consumers appreciate and understand (Devlin and McKechnie 2008). On the other hand, it is possible that the multi-corporate brand architectures have insulated brands in the 'house of brands' from the damage sustained by other brands in the 'house'. Large conglomerates such as RBS demonstrate this type of branding architecture with such specialist brands as Ulster Bank for regional custom, Adam & Company for wealth management and plans to revive the brand of Williams and Glyn as a challenger bank. For FIs to concentrate on the stakeholder brand experience, they should re-appraise existing brand architectures.

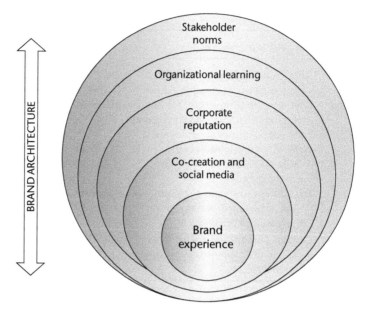

Figure 14.2 FI brand experience

While the literature suggests many avenues for FIs to address the challenges to their brands either deep-seated or as the outcome of the ongoing financial crises, they all require organizational learning, that is a change in the organization's knowledge that occurs as a function of experience (Argote 2013). The willingness to engage with a process of learning is likely to define which FIs enter the brave new world of a stakeholder brand experience. We have reviewed branding for financial services drawing contributions from marketing and management to develop a framework of brand experience in this sector (see Figure 14.2).

In Figure 14.2, the outermost circle consists of stakeholder norms, which FIs should absorb into the reconstruction of their corporate reputation. The theme of organizational learning has emerged in the review and discussion as being pivotal in co-creating the brand experience and there is corroboration for this assertion from Payne et al. (2009). With a corporate reputation that is closely aligned with stakeholder norms, the FI is in a stronger position to work on the brand experience. To understand the dynamics that the co-creation of the brand experience involves, a sound appreciation of how social media and service and SD logic can support this experience will be necessary. By concentrating on the co-creation of value, FIs can rethink the way that they interact with their customers. The brand architecture of the firm influences the brand experience and is represented as a constant but parallel theme. The closer that the brand experience is to the corporate brand, then the stronger the effect of the corporate reputation will be.

Conclusions

The purpose of this chapter has been to investigate financial services branding from two perspectives, first, the premise that branding strategies were overly focused on marketing communications and second, the need to rebuild and strengthen trust in the aftermath of the financial crises. As part of this review of branding, we have also drawn in contributions from strategic management and marketing such as service and SD logic and social media. We have developed a conceptual framework of branding in financial services, which presents branding as part of a brave new world for financial services. In this section, we discuss the theoretical and practical implications of our study and suggest further areas for research.

Theoretical implications

This study makes several contributions to branding theory in the marketing of financial services. First, it explicates the relevance of corporate reputation to the brand experience. Although there have been studies on corporate reputation, CSR and branding (for example, Lai et al. 2010), this framework extends theory here into the brand experience itself. Second, it recognizes organizational learning as being pivotal in aligning the brand experience in financial services with the re-appraisal of marketing evidenced in service and SD logic theory. Third, the study portrays social media as being a critical vehicle in the brand experience, in particular in the enabling of a unique brand experience, the loss of control of the brand as well as providing the means for communicating that brand experience. The only way of generating positive content is through ensuring a favorable brand experience. Fourth, service and SD logic offer the marketing of financial services an opportunity to re-appraise their marketing strategies, allowing them to move on from strategies that are no longer in line with stakeholder expectations. Finally, we make explicit connections between the brand architecture and the brand experience, where the corporate brand is more consistent with positive brand experiences within a stakeholder environment.

Managerial implications

The framework proposed in this chapter makes an explicit and direct link between corporate reputation and the brand experience. FIs therefore have to be aware that all activities carried out by the firm reflect and impact on the brand and the brand experience for its stakeholders. The brand is not managed exclusively through marketing communications but through stakeholder engagement with the brand over extended periods of time, in order to articulate the values of the brand. As part of revisiting or redefining their brand values, FIs should consider strengthening or in some cases recovering their corporate reputation through CSR and closer engagement with their stakeholder environment. Through the co-creation of value, the stakeholder and firm are drawn together so that the stakeholder gains influence over the way that value is created.

Service logic provides a firm base for evaluating not merely branding strategies but for sustainable marketing as a whole. With a focus on the creation of value, opportunities for clearer positions in the marketplace begin to open up, for example, FIs could embed themselves in local communities; they could strengthen associations with ethical trading or focus on premium accounts that offer real benefits.

Social media underlines a democratization of the marketplace, where brand managers form part of a brand community rather than managing the brand. Their new role has to be understood and re-evaluated so that social media content reflects the positive aspects of the brand experience.

As part of the re-appraisal of branding, FIs should review their brand architecture. There seems little reason in a global environment for distancing corporate brands from individual brand experiences and the closer the relationship between the firm and its brand may support a dynamic experience where value-in-use is facilitated. Multiple branding seems to confer minimal benefits.

Organizational learning underpins many of these changes and FIs will have to adapt and flex. Not all FI brands have suffered during this period. New entrants such as Metrobank, stalwarts such as building societies and brands with reputations built in other sectors have the opportunity to erode the market share of some of the bigger and more tarnished. Through building on their corporate reputation across sectors, for example, Marks & Spencer or Virgin, these brands are in a position to make further inroads into the financial services marketplace. It is quite possible that brands in the retail sector understand the brand experience more fully than some of the traditional FIs.

Further research

Emerging from this study, there are several areas for further research. Most importantly the conceptual link proposed between corporate reputation and brand experience requires some empirical support. While there are tentative links between service and SD logic and social media, this relationship offers considerable potential for further investigation. The discussion of brand architecture has emphasized its importance in managing brands but as yet there is little work into the association between brand architecture and the brand experience. Finally, the whole area of value co-creation and financial services is overdue for study and therein presents worthy potential work for scholars.

Note

1 RBS is selling off Direct Line of which Churchill is a part.

References

Aaker, D. (1991) *Managing Brand Equity*, New York: The Free Press.
—— (2004), 'Leveraging the corporate brand', *Californian Management Review*, 46(3), pp. 6–18.
Aaker, D. and Joachimsthaler, E. (2000) 'The brand relationship spectrum', *Californian Management Review*, 42(4), pp. 8–23.
Antonacopoulou, E. P. and Meric, J. (2005) A critique of stake-holder theory: management science or a sophisticated ideology of control? *Corporate Governance*, 5(2), pp. 22–33.
Argote, L. (2013) *Organizational Learning: Creating, Retaining and Transferring Knowledge*, New York: Springer.
Arnould, E., Price, L. and Malshie, A. (2006) 'Toward a cultural resource-based theory of the customer', In Lusch, R. F. and Vargo, S. L. (eds) *The service-dominant logic of marketing: dialog, debate, and directions*. Armonk, New York, pp. 320–33
Asmussen, B., Harridge-March, S., Occhiocupo, N. and Farquhar, J. (2013) 'The multi-layered nature of the internet-based democratization of brand management', *Journal of Business Research*, 66, 9, pp. 1473–83.
Balmer, J. and Gray, E. (2003) 'Corporate Brands: What are they? What of them?', *European Journal of Marketing*, 37(7/8), pp. 972–78.
Berry, L. (2000) 'Cultivating service brand equity', *Journal of the Academy of Marketing Science*, 28(1), pp. 128–37.
Berthon, P., Ewing, M. T. and Napoli, J. (2008) Brand management in small to medium-sized enterprises. *Journal of Small Business Management*, 46(1), pp. 27–45.
Bonini, S., Court, D. and Marchi, A. (2009) 'Rebuilding corporate reputations', *McKinsey Quarterly*, mckinsey.com/insights/corporate_social_responsibility/rebuilding_corporate_reputations (accessed 14/02/2013).
Brammer, S. and Pavelin, S. (2006) 'Corporate reputation and social performance: The importance of fit', *Journal of Management Studies*, 43(3), pp. 435–55.
Brodie, R. J., Glynn, M. S. and Little, V. (2006) 'The service brand and the service-dominant logic: missing fundamental premise or the need for stronger theory?' *Marketing Theory*, 6(3), pp. 363–79.

Chaudhuri, A. and Holbrook, M. (2001) 'The chain of effects from brand trust and brand affect to brand performance: The role of brand loyalty', *Journal of Marketing*, 65, 2, pp. 81–93.

Cova, B. and Dalli, D. (2009) 'Working consumers: The next step in marketing theory?' *Marketing Theory*, 9(3), pp. 315–39.

Dall'Olmo Riley, F. and de Chernatony, L. (2000) The service brand as relationships builder. *British Journal of Management*, 11, pp. 137–50.

de Chernatony, L. (1999) 'Brand management through narrowing the gap between brand identity and brand reputation', *Journal of Marketing Management*, 15(1–3), pp. 157–79.

—— (2001) *From Brand Vision to Brand Evaluation*, Oxford: Butterworth-Heinemann.

de Chernatony, L. and Cottam, S. (2006) 'Internal brand factors driving successful financial services brands', *European Journal of Marketing*, 40(5/6), pp. 611–33.

de Chernatony, L. and Dall'Olmo Riley, F. (1998) 'Defining a "Brand": beyond the literature with experts' interpretations', *Journal of Marketing Management*, 14(5), pp. 417–43.

de Chernatony, L. and Harris, F. (2000) 'The challenge of financial services branding: Majoring on category or brand values?' Open University Business School, August 2000.

de Chernatony, L. and McDonald, M. (1998) *Creating powerful brands*, 2nd edition, Butterworth-Heinemann: Oxford.

Devlin, J. and McKechnie, S. (2008) 'Consumer perceptions of brand architecture in financial services', *European Journal of Marketing*, 42(5/6), pp. 654–66.

Doney, P. and Cannon, J. (1997) 'An examination of the nature of trust in buyer-seller relationships', *Journal of Marketing*, 61, 2, pp. 35–51.

Edvardsson, B., Tronvoll, B. and Gruber, T. (2011) 'Expanding understanding of service exchange and value co-creation: a social construction approach', *Journal of the Academy of Marketing Science*, 39, 2, pp. 327–39.

Elliott, R. and Yannopoulou, N. (2007) 'The nature of trust in brands: a psychosocial model', *European Journal of Marketing*, 41(9/10), pp. 988–98.

Farquhar, J. (2011) 'Branding in financial services: a stakeholder perspective', *Journal of Strategic Marketing*, 19(1), pp. 43–56.

—— (2013) 'Selective demarketing: A value destruction perspective', In Bradley, N. and Blythe, J. (eds.), *Demarketing*, Abingdon: Routledge. pp. 117–37.

Farquhar, J. D. and Meidan, A. (2010), *Marketing of Financial Services* (2nd Edition), Basingstoke, Palgrave.

Freeman, R. E. (1984). Strategic management: A stakeholder approach. Boston: Pitman.

Gehring, N. (2013) 'Defining financial planning with the 4 factor decision model', *Journal of Financial Planning*, 1, 1, pp. 19–20.

Grönroos, C. (2006). Adopting a service logic for marketing. *Marketing theory*, 6(3), pp. 317–33.

Grönroos, C. (2008). Service logic revisited: who creates value? And who co-creates? *European Business Review*, 20(4), pp. 298–314.

Hanna, R., Rohm, A. and Crittenden, V. (2011) 'We're all connected: The power of the social media ecosystem', *Business Horizons*, 54(3), pp. 265–73.

Hatch, M-J. and Schultz, M. (2003) 'Bringing the corporation into corporate branding', *European Journal of Marketing*, 37(7/8), pp. 1041–64.

Hillenbrand, C., Money, K. and Ghobadian, A. (2013) 'Unpacking the mechanism by which corporate responsibility impacts stakeholder relationships', *British Journal of Management*, 24, 1, pp. 127–46.

Hoffman, D., Novak, T. and Stein, R. (2013) 'The digital consumer', in Belk, R. and Llamas, R. (eds.), *The Routledge Companion to Digital Consumption*, Abingdon: Routledge, pp. 28–38.

Jones, J. (1999) 'The future of banking: Implications of branding and loyalty', *Journal of Financial Services Marketing* 3, 1, pp. 53–66.

Kärreman, D. and Rylander, A. (2008) Managing meaning through branding—The case of a consulting firm. *Organization Studies*, 29(1), pp. 103–25.

Kay, M. (2006) 'Strong brands and corporate brands', *European Journal of Marketing*, 40(7/8), pp. 742–60.

Kietzmann, J., Hermkens, K., McCarthy, I. and Silvestre, B. (2011) 'Social media? Get serious! Understanding the functional building blocks of social media', *Business Horizons*, 54, 3, pp. 241–51.

Knox, S. and Bickerton, D. (2003) 'The six conventions of corporate branding', *European Journal of Marketing*, 37(7/8), pp. 998–1016.

Laeven, L. and Valencia, F. (2010) 'Resolution of banking crises: the good, the bad, and the ugly', *IMF Working Paper*, WP/10/146.

Lai, C.-S., Chiu, C.-J., Yang, C.-F. and Pai, D.-C. (2010) 'The effects of corporate social responsibility on brand performance: the mediating effect of industrial brand equity and corporate reputation', *Journal of Business Ethics*, 95, 3, pp. 457–69.

Lusch, R. F. and Webster, F. E. (2011) A stakeholder-unifying, co-creation philosophy for marketing. *Journal of Macromarketing*, 31(2), pp. 129–34.

Maignan, I. and Ferrell, O. (2004) 'Corporate social responsibility and marketing: an integrative framework', *Journal of the Academy of Marketing Science*, 32(1), pp. 3–19.

McDonald, M. H., de Chernatony, L. and Harris, F. (2001) Corporate marketing and service brands – Moving beyond the fast-moving consumer goods model. *European Journal of Marketing*, 35(3/4), pp. 335–52.

McWilliams, A., Siegel, D. and Wright, P. (2006) 'Corporate social responsibility: strategic implications', *Journal of Management Studies*, 43(1), pp. 1–18.

Morgan, F., Deeter-Schmelz, D. and Moberg, C. R. (2007) Branding implications of partner firm-focal firm relationships in business-to-business service networks. *Journal of Business & Industrial Marketing*, 22(6), pp. 372–82.

Muniz Jr, A. M. and O'guinn, T. C. (2001) Brand community. *Journal of consumer research*, 27(4), pp. 412–432.

Muzellec, L. and Lambkin, M. (2009) 'Corporate branding and brand architecture: a conceptual framework', *Marketing Theory*, 9(1), pp. 39–54.

Neville, B., Bell, S. and Mengü, B. (2005) 'Corporate reputation, stakeholders and the social performance-financial performance relationship', *European Journal of Marketing*, 39({9/10}), pp. 1184–98.

Payne, A., Storbacka, K., Frow, P. and Knox, S. (2009) 'Co-creating brands: diagnosing and designing the relationship experience', *Journal of Business Research*, 62(3), pp. 379–89.

Rust, R. T., Zeithaml, V. A. and Lemon, K. N. (2004) Customer-centered brand management. *Harvard Business Review*, 82(9), pp. 110–20.

Sen, S., Bhattacharya, C. B. and Korschun, D. (2006) The role of corporate social responsibility in strengthening multiple stakeholder relationships: a field experiment. *Journal of the Academy of Marketing Science*, 34(2), pp. 158–66.

Tversky, A. and Kahneman, D. (1974) 'Judgment under uncertainty: heuristics and biases', *Science*, 185, 4157, pp. 1124–31.

Tynan, C. and McKechnie, S. (2009) 'Experience marketing: a review and reassessment', *Journal of Marketing Management*, 25(5–6), pp. 501–17.

Vargo, S. L. and Lusch, R. F. (2004) Evolving to a new dominant logic for marketing. *Journal of Marketing*, 68(1), pp. 1–17.

Vargo, S. L. and Lusch, R. F. (2008) Service-dominant logic: continuing the evolution. *Journal of the Academy of Marketing Science*, 36(1), pp. 1–10.

Waldman, D., de Luque, M., Washburn, N. and House, R. (2006) 'Cultural and leadership predictors of corporate social responsibility values of top management: a GLOBE study of 15 countries', *Journal of International Business Studies*, 37, 6, pp. 823–37.

Winton, J. R. (1982). *Lloyds 1918–69*. Oxford: Oxford University Press.

15

The many deaths of a financial services offering

David R. Harness and Tina Harness

Introduction

One of the most powerful concepts in marketing is that of the product life cycle (PLC), which portrays a product going through various stages akin to a biological life. These stages include birth, growth, maturity, decline and finally death (Kotler 1965). Products do not simply die, instead, they have to be managed out of existence, which requires that organizations plan and resource the removal activity. As an activity it is perhaps 'unloved' by product managers and academic theorists (Hise et al. 1984, Greenley 1994, Harness and Harness 2013) and rarely discussed in text books and in academic journals, yet it has a significant role to play in enabling organizations to achieve a range of commercial objectives (Friedman and Krausz 1986). Central to this is that the act of elimination is understood, that it becomes a part of the normal planning and management of offerings and that organizations set objectives when implementing it to gain benefits beyond the act of ceasing production.

Eliminating a financial service offering is seen as a challenging activity. The regulatory controls and contractual obligations inherent to many financial service offerings, combined with product intangibility, IT-based production and on-going usage, and customer relationship concerns, place the customer at the centre of an elimination activity. This requires that financial service organizations gain the permission of the customer before they can eliminate certain types of offerings. Elimination in this sector ultimately alters how customers own and use an offering. This, when combined with the structural constraints formed by regulatory and contractual obligations, has a significant impact on the elimination decision process and the manner in which it is conducted.

This chapter outlines and discusses the practices, processes and critical influences that shape the way financial service organizations eliminate offerings. It provides an overview of what financial services offerings are, what customer core financial needs are and the operating environment faced by financial services organizations when contemplating product elimination. The elimination process is overviewed, highlighting the impact of critical influences on the ability to gain success. The chapter concludes by arguing why product elimination, as a subject and as a functional activity, should be given the same credence as other activities related to the management of offerings. Finally, the chapter suggests areas where further research, specifically from the perspective of the customer, will add to our understanding of financial services product elimination.

The financial services historic context

The product strategy of financial institutions has been shaped over the years by a number of interconnected forces. The deregulation in the 1980s changed forever the structure of the industry and the nature and intensity of competition faced by each provider (Ennew and Wright 1990). It enabled the traditional suppliers – retail banks, building societies and insurance organizations – to expand their product portfolios into what had previously been seen as the preserve of a specific business type. It was also a period marked by the decline in the 'mutual movement' as building societies became publically listed companies, shifting their business models to promote market share and profitability to satisfy the demands of their new institutional stakeholders (Ennew and Wright 2007). The trading conditions and operating environment were defined by a booming housing market, the growth of consumerism and availability of cheap finance. The ability to make profit increased the attractiveness of the sector to new players, such as overseas credit card suppliers, for example, MBNA entered the UK market in 1993, and non-financial services type organizations such as supermarkets, for example, Tesco and Sainsbury's, and utility corporations (Thwaites and Glaister 1992, Waite 2001). Chapter 2 provides a more in-depth and detailed discussion of new entrants to the sector and the implications this has on competition.

In order to compete, the enlarged sector engaged in widespread product proliferation, adopted multiple distribution channels, embraced the opportunities provided by IT and undertook aggressive acquisition and merger activity in the pursuit of scale economies. This resulted in the creation of 'one stop' financial service providers with multiple, duplicated and diverse product ranges, which did not always fit the needs of specific customer groups.

A financial service industries (FSI) product is service-based, significantly intangible, supplier and customer co-produced, co-owned and dependent on IT for its creation, management and distribution. FSI products answer five types of customers' needs as summarized in Table 15.1.

The product provides the basis for financial services organizations to compete, engage with customers and make profit (or loss). The fact that the sector has witnessed widespread proliferation of offerings is not surprising. It reflects the relatively low cost of producing new offering variants, utilizing existing IT systems, short time length from design to launch and stable customer core needs. It has enabled the sector to react quickly to market changes and capture opportunities gained from harnessing customer data to innovate through segmentation, and adopt new delivery technologies.

Overview of financial services product elimination

Product life cycle theory, while indicating that an offering will die, provides only limited insight into how this stage is accomplished. The idea that offerings are simply switched off has long since been seen as an over simplification of reality (Avlonitis and James 1982). Instead, the end stage of a product life is underpinned by a set of interlinking and complex activities. These can be summarized as recognition of elimination need, evaluation of offering to identify alternatives to elimination, strategy selection, implementation and post elimination evaluation. The process through which an offering goes on to be eliminated and what takes place at each stage is dependent on a range of internal and external forces. These interact to determine the nature of the elimination activity influencing its level of complexity, managerial effort required, time length of the activity, and impact on customers. The outcome of the process should be that an

Table 15.1 Overview of customer core financial services needs linked to product solutions

Customer core need	Product/Service solution
Liquidity and money transfer, the need to access cash and make payments.	Current accounts, ATM, over the counter withdrawal, debit cards, prepayment cards, web and smart phone based.
Asset security to protect money from theft and from depreciation (savings and investments).	Saving accounts, ISAs, investment tools, pensions, etc.
Borrowing to facilitate purchase of offerings.	Credit cards, overdrafts, unsecured loans, mortgages, hire purchase agreements.
Financial advice, high product complexity makes customers reliant on advice from suppliers to understand how offering answer their needs and perform.	Customers may seek advice from their FSI supplier, from independent sources and increasingly through web-based comparison sites.
Insurance determined by a customer's perception of risk, i.e. that an event might happen against what they are willing or able to pay to protect their financial well-being.	Car insurance, health insurance, disability insurance, life insurance.

Source: Adapted from Yorke (1982) and Stevenson (1989).

offering ceases to exist. Within the financial services context this means that production, on-going customer support and legacy liability is terminated.

Three reasons have been identified which make this difficult. First, the freedom to eliminate products is severely constrained by contractual and legislative controls that determine how a product functions and the extent to which its functioning can be altered (Harrison 2000). Second, the simultaneous nature of production/consumption (Ennew and Waite 2007, Lovelock and Wirtz 2011), shared ownership (Howcroft and Durkin 2000) and on-going usage (Bowen and Schneider 1988), means that elimination requires a change in the customer's usage relationship with an offering (Stewart 1998). Third, because consumers' core financial needs tend to be relatively stable, it could drive customers to consider competitors and therefore, is not good for business (Harness and Marr 2002, Homberg et al. 2010). Because of these conditions, and the intangible nature of the offering, two forms of product elimination have developed in the sector (Harness and MacKay 1997). First, full elimination in which the offering ceases to exist as an outcome of being eliminated. Second, partial elimination in which an offering is altered at an attribute level (benefits) or at a functional level (how used) so the ability to purchase is limited to either some or all (new) customer types or a combination of each.

Financial services product elimination framework

The idea that financial services product elimination is based on one set of processes fails to present a true picture. The stages involved and what each stage achieves is determined by the role of the offering in the organization's portfolio, regulatory and contractual constraints and the product's design/core function. In combination these promote complexity. Not every product will be subjected to a multi-staged elimination process. For example, a one-year fixed interest rate investment account will have inbuilt termination. At the end of its programmed life, a customer's funds will be returned to them, or automatically rolled over into another offering, with the outcome that the product ceases to exist. Other offerings will go through a number of stages similar to that outlined in Figure 15.1.

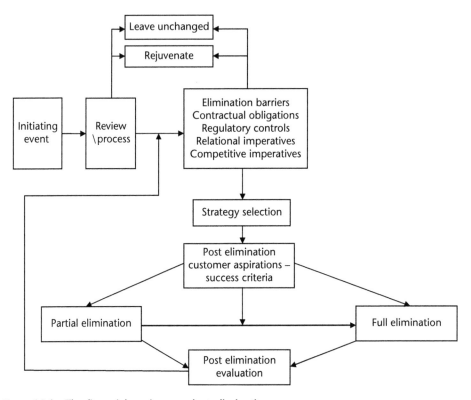

Figure 15.1 The financial services product elimination process
Source: Adapted from Harness (2004).

The starting point for elimination is that the organization recognizes something has changed, internally or externally, which questions a product or product range viability. This will trigger a review in which various options other than to eliminate will be considered (Oghojafor et al. 2012). If elimination is deemed necessary then the challenge for the organization is to select an implementation strategy, set objectives to guide the removal process and define what post termination success outcomes can be sought specifically linked to future customers' aspirations. Post elimination evaluation differs between full and partial elimination. For full elimination, it provides an opportunity for the organization to reflect on the process in order to identify ways and means to improve it. For partial elimination the question for the organization is what to do next, whether to leave the offering to continue to function in a limited capacity or review it prior to deciding whether to continue its withdrawal until it can be fully eliminated. The different elimination processes that can be used are discussed in the following section.

Initiating event

Knowledge of the reasons financial service products become elimination candidates is extensive. Some eighty-two 'drivers' of elimination have been identified, caused by internal operational factors, changing business needs and on-going flux in the external operating environment. These have been summarized into eight core themes (Harness 2003) in Figure 15.2.

While presented as individual themes, the reality is that offerings tend to be eliminated for a number of reasons. Drivers in related themes may combine. For example, within the 'personnel'

Figure 15.2 Eight themes summarizing the causes of financial services product elimination

theme, the effectiveness of the sales force can be impacted by the need to undertake compliance training and the level of complexity of an offering (time-consuming and difficult to sell) may make a specific offering unviable (Argouslidis and McLean 2001). Drivers in unrelated themes may also combine. For example, within the 'strategic related theme' is the impact of mergers and acquisitions on an organization's product portfolio. This would include duplication of offerings, incompatibility of IT systems or different views of risk, which may work as individual factors or combine together to question a product or product line viability. This means that the causes of elimination can come from a wide and sometimes disparate range of interlinked factors, which make identifying the cause complicated. This has implications for how organizations monitor the range of factors that can impact product viability. A starting point though is to understand broadly, at a theme level, which are most likely to result in product review.

Research has shown that product performance is the principle driver of product elimination. This is not surprising, the product is the primary link to the customer; it generates income and provides the means to compete. However, the sector has struggled since the 1980s with the challenges and opportunities created from intense structural and competitive change. To increase competitive ability the sector proliferated products and delivery channels, resulting in often complex and confusing offerings, which were hard to sell and maintain (Snow and Walker 1990). These offerings were launched with little thought about which core customer needs they would satisfy or how they would complement the existing portfolio. This period also saw the advent of customer relationship marketing (CRM) (see Chapter 11), which promoted activities to retain customers identified as having medium to long-term economic value to the organization. The deregulation of the 1980s encouraged the retail banks, building societies and insurance companies to move into each other's product areas. Customers became sales targets for their cross and up-selling activities, with success being measured by the number of offerings held and usage levels. This meant that the historic attitude of letting customer accounts remain dormant, for example, was seen as an unnecessary tie up of marketing effort and not supportive of CRM based activities.

The 'cost management related' theme contains a range of factors, which uniquely impact on the financial service sector. In physical goods the majority of costs relate to production – raw materials, production line, distribution, etc. – and elimination removes these costs. Partial elimination leaves the financial services offering still in existence requiring on-going support and resource, which will continue to be consumed for as long as the product exists. Even when full elimination is conducted (i.e. the offering ceases to have an existence), the organization may not see a reduction in its cost infrastructure. Financial service offerings' production platforms (IT, distribution channels and human actors) tend to be shared, what is eliminated is often simultaneously replaced with a new version. Elimination at a product category level (for example, selling the mortgage book to another supplier) may allow the organization to reduce head count to gain significant cost reductions. Instead, what elimination does is to allow suppliers to achieve better cost control by limiting the number of new customers buying an offering, reducing add-on benefits that makes servicing and customer support more simple and less costly.

The financial services crisis, which began in 2008, has resulted in a radically altered sector (see Chapter 1 for a more detailed discussion) to overcome the problems caused by sub-prime lending (Hall 2009) and global economic recession. The changes in the UK included part nationalization of banking groups (for example, LloydsTSB, Royal Bank of Scotland). The unprecedented level of mergers and acquisition (for example, Santander Bank UK was established through the acquisition of Abbey National, Bradford & Bingley and Alliance & Leicester). These structural changes amplify the need for the organizations to achieve significant operating cost reduction and lower risk exposure (Harness and Harness 2013).

The 'information and new technology related', 'operational based' and 'personnel (sales-force)' themes are strongly interrelated. For example, 'information and new technology' relates to how the product is produced and managed whereas 'operational based' is the application of an organization's information technology capability to develop delivery channels (for example, web based, phone apps) or rationalize existing ones such as call centres. The role technology plays in financial services is increasing across all aspects of the business implying that its importance as a driver will increase. There are a number of dimensions to this. First, technology has enabled organizations to capture and leverage customer information to provide the means to differentiate its users. This is foundational to developing bespoke offerings, selecting or deselecting customers and aligning offerings to fit new segments. Second, how customers want to access their offerings is changing and moving away from bank branch to online. For example, the use of phone 'apps' to conduct certain financial activities is highly attractive because it provides accessibility, immediacy, convenience and portability (see Chapter 22). As organizations seek to fully exploit the opportunities that banking apps can provide, it is likely to drive changes to their product portfolio and service provision. This may lead to fewer and simpler offerings for customers, blurring the lines that separated, for example, a savings offering and a checking account. Third, the growth of online comparison sites make it easier for customers to see the relative performance of their offering compared to those supplied by their own organization and alternative suppliers. This higher level of transparency is likely to encourage suppliers to remove offerings that question competitiveness and to become more proactive in managing customers to ensure their satisfaction.

The 'personnel theme' takes account of the importance of employees' interfacing with customers. It drives elimination because of the costs involved in training to ensure compliance. Technology such as web-based delivery removes direct human interaction. The 'external operating environment' theme reflects the impact of regulatory change, population demographics, emergent business opportunities and entry of new players into the market. The relevance of this category is highly influenced by prevailing economic conditions. See Chapter 2 for a detailed discussion of new entrants.

The drivers outlined in Figure 15.2 do not automatically result in the elimination of an offering. Elimination depends on a range of factors, from how pressing the need for elimination is, what the consequences of action or inaction are and how they were identified. In this sense the drivers in Figure 15.2 act as a trigger to review and inform how such a review will be conducted.

The review process

The review process is a set of evaluations about the offering, which results in one of four decisions: to leave it unchanged, to rejuvenate it, to eliminate it (Hise and McGinnis 1975, Avlonitis et al. 2000) or to partially eliminate it (Harness and Marr 2004). Understanding of how to review candidates for elimination has been researched extensively. Avlonitis and James (1982) summarized critical influences on the review process into five areas. These include market reaction, financial implications, range of policy considerations (potential to create portfolio gaps), creating managerial capacity and enabling new product development. Although originally developed from studies into the removal of physical goods, their relevance to financial services is high. Other factors such as the extent to which offerings satisfy compliance requirements, corporate sales objectives, profit aspirations and customer requirements were identified as having specific resonance for UK financial services (Argouslidis 2007a, 2007b, Papastathopoulou et al. 2012). To this Harness (2004) added the ability to generate future sales and adaptability to enable delivery through emerging platforms such as web based, tablets and banking apps.

The factors used to determine the outcome of the review process will be unique to the organization. The importance of each criterion to an elimination event will depend on organization size, resource base, financial importance of the product relative to other offerings, number of customers affected, influence of current market and economic forces. For example, prior to 2008 the mortgage market had grown by expanding the sub-prime segment: a segment that ultimately proved highly vulnerable to changes in the economic cycle. The level of exposure of many western banks to this segment had become obscured, making the level of risk unknown and is perceived to be a major contributory factor to the banking crises. The response of the UK banks to this was swift. It reduced the number of mortgage products at market, specifically those available to sub-prime customers. The review process where the decision was taken to withdraw mortgages would have been ad hoc and created in response to the unfolding crises.

Ad hoc reviews compared to on-going product reviews account for the majority of elimination decisions (Harness and Harness 2013). An ad hoc review does not mean lacking in rigour as such reviews take account of a range of information sources, examine availability of alternative courses of action, evaluate different elimination strategies (Argouslidis 2007b, Gounaris et al. 2006) and determine post removal success objectives (Harness and Harness 2013). Ad hoc review enables the organization to respond flexibly to emerging events increasing the ability to act quickly (Muir and Reynolds 2011) to prevent further financial loss, reduce exposure to risk and mitigate competitor action.

225

Influences on the selection of elimination strategy

The review process may conclude that the offering has to be eliminated. In selecting an elimination strategy the organization has to address two questions. First, to what extent can the functioning of the offering be altered so it can be closed (i.e. remove on-going liability and customer support)? Second, what is the best strategy to accomplish elimination? The idea of constraints on the ability to eliminate an offering is not unique to the financial services industry (see, for example, the work of Hise 1977, Avlonitis and Hart 1985, Gupta et al. 1987) and it does impact on freedom of action. Figure 15.3 summarizes the key constraints identified. The two posing significant challenges are regulatory control and contractual obligations.

Regulatory control requires organizations to comply with the relevant codes of conduct in line with various acts of parliament (for example, in the UK the Financial Services Act 1986 and subsequent revisions). Contractual obligations define the agreements between each party as to how a product functions and under what circumstances this can be changed. It depends on the type of offering and the basis of the agreement between the parties, and defines when customer permission is needed before an offering can be altered. When faced with either regulatory or contractual obligations organizations are likely to have to negotiate with their customers to implement full elimination.

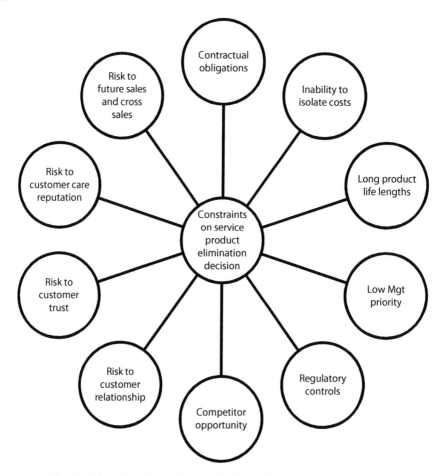

Figure 15.3 Constraints on implementing product elimination

Other barriers also exert a powerful influence on the decision to eliminate and the choice of withdrawal strategy. These can be divided into two broad areas. First, the intangible nature of the offering, its means of production, difficulty of apportioning actual cost, long life length combined with managerial reluctance may reduce the urgency of terminating a product. These conditions rely on the effects of natural customer churn and mortality to erode the offering's user base to a point when it ceases to exist. Second, removing an offering can create opportunities for competitors to capture market share. This is either because a gap is made in the market or that dissatisfaction encourages customers to look to alternative suppliers.

Implementation of elimination

To overcome elimination constraints a range of different removal strategies have evolved in the sector. At this stage it is worth reviewing what product elimination in a financial services context is. The original conceptualization of elimination came from physical goods manufacturers. Manufacturing companies' product line decisions are dominated by the physicality of production, i.e. use of raw materials, tooling production lines, warehousing, distribution, etc. The decision to cease production has been shown to result in the selection of one of five processes: run out, phase out immediately, drop from a standard range and reintroduce as a special, drop immediately and sell out (Hart 1991). These strategies are underpinned by the organization's intent to cease production in the most cost- and time-efficient way. The exception is the drop from the standard range and reintroduce as a special, used to support customers with offerings that have long life lengths and which would provide sufficient financial or relational reward to make 'one offs'. Elimination is designed to fully remove or redeploy the means (production line) and attributes (raw materials, stocks of finished goods, etc.) of production so that no new units of an offering are produced. In this context, full elimination describes a set of activities to ensure that an offering's production is terminated and intent that this is the eventual outcome of the activity.

For example, phase out immediately allows the organization to cease production after it has satisfied existing contracts, depleted raw materials, etc. Financial services have different production means and attributes. Production is based on the combination of the organization's IT systems and employees, customer interaction and is influenced by delivery format (branch vs. internet). Production attributes (i.e. the raw materials of a financial service offering) are determined by the availability of finance and level of acceptable risk exposure; these impact on the type of strategies that can be used to eliminate an offering. It also means that the notion of full elimination has to be modified to take account of the barriers, the production mechanism and the nature of the offerings.

To overcome the challenges posed by such factors, two forms of product elimination have evolved in the sector. The first, akin to the notion of elimination in the manufacturing sector, is termed 'full elimination' (Harness and MacKay 1997). The intent guiding selection of this removal strategy is that the offering will cease to be produced and all liability associated with it will be terminated; the offering will cease to exist. The nature of production and product intangibility for simple financial services offerings, such as basic savings accounts, makes implementing this strategy relatively straightforward.

Second, partial elimination is used for all product types to negate the constraints faced by the organization in achieving full elimination. Partial elimination differs from full elimination in a number of important respects. Critically, the supplier will still have to provide on-going support and meet any liability in relation to the product that arises. The change can be described as elimination because offering availability, usage or function will be altered in some way. This may

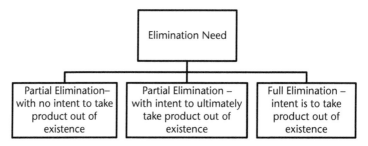

Figure 15.4 Relationship between cause of elimination and use of partial and full elimination

include ceasing sales to all or some types of new customers, removing product attributes while leaving the core function untouched, removing the ability of existing users to purchase additional units or extend usage of the offering. The intent concept determines how this removal process is managed and the ultimate outcome.

Offerings with considerable life lengths, such as pensions, tend to be subject to stringent controls; partial elimination could be based on the supplier choosing not to take new business, though the functioning of the offering will remain unchanged. The intent to fully eliminate the offering in this case will be low because ultimately human mortality will result in its termination. Intent may not exist if the business case for keeping customers in a partially eliminated offering is strong. This happens when new product development is frequently used to acquire new customers, or when the offering has a finite life, such as personal loans or fixed term interest rates for saving offerings (see Figure 15.4). Where the intent to fully eliminate exists, the use of a partial removal strategy secures time to plan the withdrawal process. This may include negotiating with customers to get agreement to transfer them to other offerings or to identify a third party organization willing to buy the product and its associated customers.

Types of elimination strategies

Harness (2003) identified that the majority of elimination actions fall into the partial elimination category, though this is closely followed by full elimination. These can be translated into processes that result in either full or partial elimination (Harness and Harness 2004). Figure 15.5 summarises five strategies for implementing full elimination.

Of the five full elimination strategies, only the first was found to have extensive use in research. The desire to retain customers, even when the need to eliminate is strong, is evident in this strategy. The strategies which sold customers to competitors or terminated their relationship were found to be used infrequently. This indicates that maintaining customer relationships is important to how full elimination is conducted. This is echoed in the strategies used for partial elimination (see Table 15.2) where the first three strategies essentially hide from current users that the offering has been altered. The primary objective is to retain customers within the product offering, either permanently or until the constraints denying the ability to fully implement are removed. The ability to effectively hide the elimination action seems unique to services offerings, reflecting the nature of production, intangibility and stable customer core needs. The elimination of manufactured offerings becomes obvious to the customer when they seek to replace it (i.e. when it is fully consumed, worn out, or becomes obsolete). It this case it is in the best interests of the manufacturer to encourage customers to buy the replacement or alternative offering. This is made easier because production and consumption are separate with product ownership being transferred at point of purchase to the customer. These conditions make the customer external

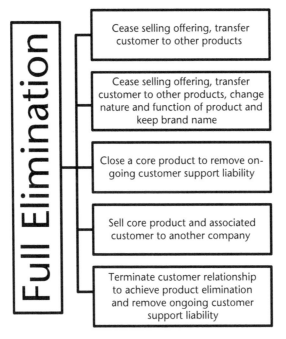

Figure 15.5 Full elimination strategies

Source: Adapted from Harness and Harness (2004).

to the organization and thus less influential in how the activity is conducted. In financial services, retaining customers in an offering can provide commercial advantages while negating the problems caused by constraints imposed by regulatory and contractual obligations. This reinforces the advantages of keeping the removal activity hidden to reduce the potential for customer discontent.

The second set of partial elimination strategies are designed to encourage customers to migrate to an alternative offering. These strategies shown in Table 15.2 encourage customers to want to move to other offerings by making them more attractive or by reducing benefits of the existing offering. This can seemingly be used with a degree of finesse by balancing the two elements to control the speed of migration of customers out of the offering. Again, the value

Table 15.2 Partial elimination strategies

Partial elimination strategies
Product removed from new sales, existing owners untouched
New sales of product terminated, unchanged for existing customers.
New sales of product terminated, unchanged for existing customers, relaunched later as 'new'.
Withdraw from general sales, sell only to specific new customer segments.
Product made less attractive to existing customers to encourage migration
New sales of product terminated, usage limited for existing users.
Merge similar products, retain existing name.
Reduce product attributes, core function left unchanged.
Merge a number of products together and renamed.

Source: Adapted from Harness and Harness (2004).

of maintaining positive customer relationships can be seen with these strategies, though they tend to be used once the decision for full elimination has been taken. For example, customers in a savings account may notice their interest rate is reduced making it less attractive compared with newly launched offerings in the market. This will encourage some customers to automatically migrate, while others, because of inertia (Stewart 1998), will remain in the offering. Over time, with the interaction of customer mortality and natural churn, the number of users will decrease, resulting in the offering operating at a loss, thus initiating full elimination. Customer migration at this stage may be forced or accomplished through account closure i.e. terminating the customer relationship.

An aspect that has been implicit within the discussion is the idea that the organization is often managing the event to gain wider outcomes than merely the removal of a troublesome offering. The existence of customer and competitor linked constraints serves to reinforce this. The impact this has on the management of the elimination process is twofold. First, the process itself has to be understood so desired outcomes can be built into it. For example, if the objective is to retain customers, success is determined by the percentage held post partial elimination. This requires that the operational details of the process are defined, for example, when and how best to communicate with customers and that the costs of elimination, timescale and who has responsibility for each element are fixed. The trigger for changing the intent from partial to full elimination may need to be established by a mixture of hard measures, such as cost of servicing small customer numbers and soft measures such as benefits of maintaining a customer relationship. It is clear that if critical success factors are not identified during the review stage and built into the elimination process, the ability of the organization to realize its post elimination commercial objectives will be undermined (Harness and Harness 2013). Financial services organizations are influenced by the nature of the initiating problem and range of constraints faced when selecting an elimination strategy. For many types of offering this means that the process of taking a fully-marketed and serviced offering to one that ceases to exist is potentially a highly risky and complex activity. The process would appear, prima facie, linear and sequential – initiating event, selection of strategy, implementation, post-elimination evaluation – though in reality this is an over simplification.

Product elimination success

Many types of financial service offerings continue to exist after being subjected to partial elimination. The framework outlined in Figure 15.1 highlights that elimination is a set of interrelated processes that begins with some form of initiating event, takes the offerings through a number of evaluation and decision stages, and selects a means to accomplish a desired end outcome (full or partial). It has an implementation stage that can be based on the simple deletion of a line of computer code instantaneously taking an offering out of existence. It may require considerable coordination of a range of activities over many years. Financial services organizations exist as profit making entities and as such costs, timescales, resource utilization, market opportunities and ability to make profit will influence any change process undertaken. Success can be broadly defined as the achievement of the goals an organization sets in conducting a planned activity. Success, therefore, plays a significant part in shaping the removal action. To take account of this, three distinct success constructs have been developed (Harness and Marr 2004).

Financial services offerings are terminated for a range of reasons (see Figure 15.2). These force the organization to make a response ranging from do nothing, rejuvenate or fully or partially eliminate. Therefore, the first product elimination success construct is related to the extent to which the organization can remove the need or driver of elimination. An elimination candidate consumes managerial, employee and support resources and may harm the ability of the organization to achieve other commercial objectives. Removing such drivers therefore, has a benefit to the organization, which provides a measure of success. The second success construct is related to how the activity is implemented. Product withdrawal requires that a planned and managed process is undertaken to ensure coordination between interrelated activities and sequences that enable an offering to reach a specific condition, for example, transferring customers to an alternative offering is dependent on the product being created and that users are informed. This has been termed process elimination success (Harness and Marr 2001). The third success construct is dependent on the ability to manage the elimination process to gain a specified end stage outcome. This includes post elimination objectives determined by the level of existence sought, impact on customer, and competitive related issues. The impact on customers is perhaps the most significant of these outcomes as it relates to the ability of the organization to continue to gain economic benefit from their relationship with those individuals (Martin 2002, Harness and Harness 2013).

The range and types of success measures have been grouped into one of four themes. Operationally a high level of overlap and interlinking will exist between themes and their associated measures. The themes indicate that elimination can provide a range of positive benefits for an organization, despite elimination being seen as essentially a negative activity. The four themes and their associated measures are outlined in Table 15.3. The first three themes focus on how elimination provides internal business benefits. This reflects the intangible nature of offerings, production attributes (availability of liquidity), production means (human and electronic), and operational requirements imposed by compliance with regulatory and control obligations. The fourth theme takes account of a number of factors. Foundational to this is that customers provide revenue streams, purchase offerings and are often protected by contractual and regulatory obligations. Partial elimination, although required by the existence of these obligations, serves the purpose of keeping customers within the organization despite the need to change the usage or ownership relationship of an offering.

The capacity to gain success is related to the ability to plan the removal activity. This is determined by the criticality of the elimination driver, the proactivity of the product management function and the quality of evaluation data. It is also based on the extent to which an organization has practice and experience of conducting elimination. The challenges of partially eliminating a simple savings account to enable the simultaneous launch of a new version are considerably less than those posed in removing complex offerings. Complex offerings require open-ended customer support and that the organization maintains production capability and the ability to fulfil related liabilities, for example, a health care insurance supplier may have to pay out for conditions related to an insured period that arise many years after the product has been sold. This suggests that organizations need to learn from how they manage the elimination process through some form of post elimination review that can be used to improve the planning of further deletion activity.

Elimination and customer relationships

Underpinning the Customer Relationship Management (CRM) concept is an acceptance that some customers are more valuable than others and thus should be retained by the organization. Financial service elimination is accomplished by altering the ownership and usage experience of the customers because of shared production, product intangibility, contemporaneous and on-going consumption, long product life, regulatory controls and contractual obligations, all of which make the customer central to the removal process. The CRM aspect stems from the

Table 15.3 Product elimination success measures

Success themes	Success measures
Management- and sales effort-related	Reduces product portfolio confusion.
	Improves sales forces effectiveness.
	Improves management effectiveness.
	Strategic planning enabler.
	Ensure compliance with regulatory requirements.
	Creates capacity to launch new offerings.
	Remove a training requirement.
Physical and financial resource-related	Release resources.
	Increase capacity in production and delivery platforms.
	Improved financial structure.
	Eliminate to budget.
	Eliminate to time plan.
Product portfolio-related	Increased product portfolio performance.
	Increase product area profitability.
	Decrease risk (failure/financial exposure).
	Increased sales.
	Improved competitive position.
	Reduce product duplication.
	Enables simultaneous elimination and NPD activity.
	Improves service quality.
	Improves the balance of sales portfolios.
	Remove unprofitable customers.
	Remove exposure to risk/loss.
Customer-related	Customer retention.
	Customer satisfaction.
	Reduced customer confusion.
	Enable customer elimination.
	Removes causes of customer dissatisfaction.
	Maintain customer purchasing relationships.
	Maintain positive PR.

Source: Adapted from Harness and Harness (2013).

ability to impact, through elimination, how the customer views the organization, and conse-quently, their purchasing motivation (Harness and Harness 2004). As a CRM tool it can be used in three distinct ways. First, by relying on partial elimination strategies, the act and thus the impact on the customer remains neutral; i.e. hidden from them so they feel no tangible change in ownership and usage. Second, by making the customer feel that they are in a worse position post elimination may increase their negative view of the organization and encourage them to look to other suppliers. Third, by using elimination as an opportunity to communicate with customers and to offer them product and services with better terms and conditions the organi-zation could strengthen their purchasing relationship. Organizations have to be mindful that all three options potentially carry negative consequences that can damage their long-term reputa-tion. For example, leaving customers in an offering that provides poor performance compared to others in the portfolio may bolster profit, but raises questions of business ethics and whether the company has the best interests of the customer at heart. The process of making customers want to exit a product or the organization could unleash negative word of mouth and, when coupled with the power of social media, could impact many current and future customers' purchasing decisions. Despite the importance of end stage product management on customer relationships, this is an area where much more research is needed before our understanding can be considered complete.

Conclusions

The end stage of a product life provides challenges and opportunities for an organization beyond that suggested by adherence to product life cycle theory (PLC). PLC was conceptualized as a way to view the life of an offering holistically. This seems to have determined where research effort has been placed, for example, studies on NPD and product rejuvenation are plentiful whereas those focused on product end stage are relatively scarce. It also reflects where product managers view their priorities and interests. Without a developed understanding of product end stage management, an organization denies itself the opportunity to use this, at least in service supplier environments, to gain benefits over and above removing a troublesome offering. This chapter goes some way to proving the case for product elimination to be seen as mainstream and as a critical part of product management theory and practice. The fact that an offering has to be eliminated is not necessarily an admission of failure, in reality it is a normal part of an offering's overall functioning.

End stage product management has the potential in the financial services sector to be a highly complex activity. Complexity stems from the existence and interaction of a number of factors. These include product type, criticality of initiating event, levels of constraints, post elimination aspirations and product life lengths. These influence the type of elimination activity that can be conducted, specifically the number of stages involved, level of activity, which exists concurrent with the normal day-to-day function of a product portfolio. Complexity poses two specific challenges for organizations. First, it requires that end stage product management is conducted proactively. As this chapter has indicated, this has not always been the case. Product intangibility and shared IT based production results in difficulties in apportioning actual cost and has caused organizations to keep offerings in existence, thus running contrary to good commercial practices and impeding the ability to delete them. Second, because product type, function, constraints faced, and reasons for being terminated differs, each elimination action will present unique challenges for decision makers. The greater an elimination action is underpinned by inherent complexity, the harder it will be to gain customer related aspirations. The process outlined in Figure 15.1 provides a useful guide, but does not remove the need for organizations to blueprint the different types of elimination actions they conduct. In doing this an understanding of how to plan and implement each elimination event will be enhanced and the ability to proactively seek opportunities to enrich customer experience and relationships can be identified. This is necessary because elimination in this sector is intrinsically linked to managing the product ownership and usage relationship of the customer.

This chapter has presented a robust body of work on financial services product elimination. Some of what is presented intuitively makes sense and certainly echoes the findings of empirical based studies conducted in the physical goods domain, yet our understanding of financial services elimination comes from few empirical studies. Although much has been gained from these studies into the practices, process and influencing factors on financial services elimination, the organizational perspective on these studies and the overall lack of research suggest that our understanding of financial services product elimination is only partial. For example, despite accepting that customers play a critical influencing role in product removal, we know little about how it impacts them. This is identified as a critical knowledge gap. A study by

Homberg et al. (2010) in a business to business setting noted that customers experience psychological and economic costs as a result of product elimination, which challenges inter-firm relationships.

Research effort in financial services elimination should be focused in two distinct but related areas. First, identifying and understanding the impact of elimination on customer perceptions and willingness to remain loyal to an organization; linking more clearly the range of elimination strategies that exist in order to consider how they impact on customer perception and how this can be influenced by communication activity, timescales, etc. This is an important first step in being able to manage to achieve specific outcomes. Other issues to be taken into account are connected to how elimination changes customer perception of risk, and the length of time that such effects might have on future purchasing intention. What would be seen as fair and ethical practice must be considered and how customers could be encouraged to provide positive word of mouth from gaining a positive product elimination experience. Second, based on this understanding, to identify how this might reshape the management practice and process of product elimination. From this, a more holistic understanding of product elimination, which incorporates organization and customer perspectives can emerge.

References

Argouslidis, P. C. (2007a) 'The evaluation stage in the elimination decision making: process: evidence from the UK financial services sector', *Journal of Services Marketing*, 21(2), pp. 122–36.

—— (2007b) 'Problem situations triggering line pruning in financial services: Evidence from the UK'. *The International Journal of Bank Marketing*, 25(6), pp. 372–93.

Argouslidis, P. C. and McLean, F. (2001a) 'Financial service elimination: objectives and problem situations', *Journal of Financial Services Marketing*, 15(3), pp. 227–37.

Avlonitis, G. and Hart, S. (1985) 'A typology of product elimination decisions: some preliminary results', *Marketing into the 1990's and Beyond*, pp. 644–61. Strathclyde University Working Paper.

Avlonitis, G. and James, B. (1982) 'Some dangerous axioms of product elimination decision making', *European Journal of Marketing*, 16, pp. 36–48.

Avlonitis, G., Hart, S. and Tzokas, N. X. (2000) 'An analysis of product deletion scenarios', *Journal of Product Innovation Management*, 17(1), pp. 41–56.

Bowen, D. E. and Schneider, B. (1988) 'Services Marketing and Management: Implications for Organizational Behavior'. In B. M. Shaw and L. L. Cummings (eds.), *Research in Organizational Behavior*, Greenwich, Conn.: JAI Press.

Ennew, C.T. and Waite, M. (2007) *Financial Services Marketing*. Butterworth-Heinemann, Oxford.

Ennew, C. T. and Wright, M. (1990) 'Retail banks and organizational change: evidence from the UK', *International Journal of Bank Marketing*, 8(1), pp. 4–9.

—— (2007) '*Financial Services Marketing*', Oxford: Butterworth-Heinemann.

Friedman, H. H. and Krausz, J. (1986) 'A portfolio theory approach to solve the product elimination problem', *The Mid Atlantic Journal of Business*, 24(2), pp. 43–49.

Gounaris, S. P., Avlonitis, G. and Papastathopoulou, P. G. (2006) 'Uncovering the keys to successful service elimination: Project Servdrop', *The Journal of Services Marketing*, 21(1), pp. 24–26.

Greenley, G. E. (1994) 'A comparative study of product launch and elimination decisions in UK and US companies', *European Journal of Marketing*, 28(2), pp. 5–29.

Gupta, Y. P. (1987) 'Technical paper: a theoretical model for product elimination decisions', *International Journal of Operation and Product Management*, 7(3), pp. 59–69.

Hall, M. J. B. (2009) 'The sub-prime crisis, the credit crunch and bank "Failure": an assessment of the UK authorities' response', *Journal of Financial Regulation and Compliance*, 17(4), pp. 427–52.

Harness, D. (2003) 'The end stage of a financial service product', *Journal of Financial Services Marketing*. 7(3), pp. 220–29.

—— 'Product elimination: a financial services model', *International Journal of Bank Marketing*, 22(3), pp. 161–79.

Harness, D. and Harness, T. (2004) 'The new Customer Relationship Management tool – product elimination', *The Services Industries Journal*. 24(2), pp. 67–80.

—— (2013) 'Product elimination for post-downsizing success', *Journal of General Management*, 38(2), pp. 39–60.

Harness, D. and MacKay, S. (1997) 'Product deletion: a financial services perspective', *International Journal of Bank Marketing*, 15(1), pp. 2–12.

Harness, D. and Marr, N. E. (2001) 'Strategies for eliminating a financial services product', *Journal of Product and Brand Management*. 10(7), pp. 423–36.

—— (2002) 'What caused the banks products to die? a New Zealand perspective', *Australian Marketing Journal*. 10(2), pp. 44–54.

—— (2004) 'A comparison of product elimination success factors in the UK banking, building society and insurance sectors', *International Journal of Bank Marketing*. 22(3), pp. 126–43.

Harrison, T. (2000) *Financial Services Marketing*, London: Prentice Hall.

Hart, S. J. (1991) 'Implementing product withdrawal: a cross-sectional analysis', *Marketing Education Group (MEG) Conference Proceedings*, Cardiff Business School, pp. 1329–49.

Hise, R.T. (1977) *Product/Service Strategy*, Petrocello/Charter, New York, NY. pp. 245–79.

Hise, R. T. and McGinnis, M. A. (1975) 'Product elimination: practices policies and ethics', *Business Horizons*, 18(June), pp. 25–32.

Hise, R. T., Parasuraman, A. and Viswanathan, R. (1984) 'Product elimination: the neglected management responsibility', *The Journal of Business Strategy*, 14(4), pp. 56–63.

Homberg, C. Fürst, A. and Prigge, J. (2010) 'A customer perspective on product eliminations: how the removal of products affects customers and business relationships', *Journal of the Academy of Marketing Science*, 38(1), pp. 531–49.

Howcroft, B. and Durkin, M. (2000) 'Reflections on bank-customer interactions in the new Millennium', *Journal of Financial Services Marketing*, 5(1), pp. 9–20.

Kotler, P. (1965) 'Phasing out weak products', *Harvard Business Review*, March/April, pp. 107–118.

Lovelock, C. and Wirtz, J. (2011) *Services Marketing, People, Technology, Strategy*, (7th edition), London: Prentice Hall.

Martin, M. A. (2002) 'Consumer responses to discontinuance of favorite products: an exploratory study', *Advances in Consumer Research*, 29, pp. 249–50.

Muir, J. and Reynolds, N. (2011) 'Product deletion: a critical overview and empirical insight into this process', *Journal of General Management*, 37(1), pp. 5–30.

Oghojafor, B. E. A. Aduloju, S. A. and Olowokudejo, F. F. (2012) 'Product elimination: the nigerian insurance industry experience', *International Journal of Business Administration*, 3(2), pp. 174–83.

Papastathopoulou, P, Gounaris, S. P. and Avlonitis, G. J. (2012) 'The service elimination decision-making during the service life cycle: some empirical evidence', *European Journal of Marketing*, 46(6), pp. 844–74.

Snow, K. and Walker, G. D. (1990) 'Product deletion and renewal in financial services: A Canadian case study.' Birmingham Polytechnic working paper series, pp. 1–9.

Stevenson, B. D. (1989) *Marketing Financial Services to Corporate Clients*, Cambridge: Woodhead, Faulkner.

Stewart, K. (1998) 'An exploration of customer exit in retail banking', *International Journal of Bank Marketing*, 16(1), pp. 6–14.

Thwaites, D. and Glaister, K. (1992) 'Strategic responses to environmental turbulence', *International Journal of Bank Marketing*, 10(3), pp. 33–40.

Waite, N. (2001) 'New entrants in the financial services sector: the case of kwik-fit insurance services', *International Journal of Bank Marketing*, 19(5), pp. 213–16.

Yorke, D. A. (1982) 'The definition of market segments for Banking Services', *European Journal of Marketing*, 16(3), pp. 14–22.

Part V
Financial services pricing strategies

16

Consumer perceptions of financial services prices

Hooman Estelami

Introduction

In this chapter we will discuss how consumers form their perceptions of financial services prices. We will first highlight the role that customer perceptions of financial services prices play in customer engagement with financial services organizations. We will then discuss the unique characteristics of financial services prices, which can make them difficult for consumers to evaluate. A discussion of cognitive processes through which financial services price perceptions are formed will be then presented. In this discussion we will draw from research findings in psychology, marketing and behavioral economics, focusing on what is known about how consumers evaluate financial services prices and the heuristics that they often use to conduct such evaluations. The chapter will conclude with a discussion of public policy measures and improved marketing practices that may aid consumers in making informed decisions related to financial services prices.

Significance of price perception formation for financial services organizations

For most financial services organizations, the pricing decision is one of the main issues that management need to address. This is because price has a series of effects that go beyond its direct financial impact on the company (Farquhar and Meidan 2010, Harrison 2006). Price serves as the sole source of revenue for financial services organizations. In other words, unlike other marketing mix elements such as advertising and distribution, which represent costs to the financial services provider, revenue recuperation to cover these costs is only possible through price (Oyelere and Turner 2000). Price can also represent the positioning of the company with respect to its competitors and serve as a signal to the industry as to where a financial services organization is positioned. In addition, in financial services markets where product and service quality may be difficult to measure, price can often serve as an indicator of quality and has a significant impact on customer perceptions of the financial services provider (Estelami 2008, Rao 2005). For these reasons it is critical to ensure that the prices being charged provide for profitable operations are consistent with company goals, while projecting the correct marketing signals to potential and existing customers.

One of the unique aspects of price that differentiates it from other marketing mix elements is its numeric nature, which makes it easily comparable across competitors. The fact that price is communicated in transactional settings makes it one of the more visible components of a company's competitive strategy. When compared to other marketing mix elements such as sales force allocation, channel incentives and advertising budgets, which are not are not visible to competitors and customers in the marketplace, the visibility of price makes it an easily identifiable market signal. The result of this is that changes in price can result in quick shifts in market share and the loss or gain of customers. These losses and gains can transpire more quickly for price changes than changes of similar magnitude in other marketing mix variables (Janakiraman et al. 2006).

In the context of financial services, price serves a unique role beyond its typical roles in many other markets. This is because for most financial services, quality is highly elusive. For example, it is often difficult for policyholders to determine the level of quality associated with an insurance policy. This is because most policyholders never have to file a claim and as a result many never experience the full spectrum of services associated with an insurance provider. In such cases customers often rely on price as an indicator of quality assuming that a higher-priced insurer provides superior service compared to a lower-priced one. The elusive nature of quality is widely present in a range of financial services, such as financial advisory services, banking and most insurance markets. The inability to quantify quality often encourages consumers in these markets to rely on price as an indicator of quality. For this reason, regulators and public policy advocates often criticize the true embedded value in some financial services and question the ability of consumers to arrive at an economically sound assessment of financial services offers. Many of the concerns raised in the public domain regarding the motivations and actions of financial services organizations in the years leading to the financial crisis can be traced to aggressive and deceptive pricing practices. In the years following the financial crisis much more attention is being given to the need to raise consumers' financial literacy levels (see Chapter 3 in this book), ensuring trust in the banking sector (see Chapter 30) and expanding the reach and affordability of financial services (see Chapter 35). It is therefore essential to understand not only the financial impact of a given price but also the unique perceptual impact that it has on customers and the public. This is an especially important concern in light of the fact that, in contrast with goods markets for which a large volume of pricing research exists, for financial services the amount of research conducted on pricing practices and market responses resulting from them is considerably limited.

Unique characteristics of pricing financial services

In recent years, the financial services sector has been the centre of attention by regulators, public policy advocates and consumer protection lobbyists who have questioned the trustworthiness of industry practices, and the leadership style of some of the large global financial services organizations (Bennett and Kottasz 2012, Ennew et al. 2011, Norton 2010). At the heart of many financial services transactions is an underlying sense of trust by the customer that the financial services provider will act in the best interest of its customers. This concept – often referred to as fiduciary responsibility – requires financial services professionals to balance their personal financial goals and give greater priority to the intended customer benefits made possible through their services. For example, in the securities brokerage business, it is assumed (and in some markets, required by regulations) that a broker initiates trades on a client's portfolio based on sound economic criteria rather than their own incentive to maximize brokerage commissions. A natural conflict of interest arises; a broker may increase their own commission income by increasing the number of trades but at the same time these trades may not be in the best interest of the client.

The potential for conflicts of interest makes trust a central construct in most financial services transactions as it affects the customer's perceptions of fairness associated with a financial services provider (Harrison 2003). The accumulation of decisions made with self-interest by a financial services provider can result in hardship for its customers, public distrust and the overall questioning of its marketing practices (see Chapter 30). In contrast, financial services providers that work in the best interest of their customers can benefit financially from the developed trust. They can demand a premium for what they offer and as a result in some cases can transform trusting relationships into highly profitable ones (Dimitriadis 2010, Dimitradis et al. 2011). This premium represents profit opportunities for those financial services providers who intend to work ethically and can result in a direct relationship between pricing practices and management policies for financial services firms (please consult the discussion of company related factors in pricing policies discussed in Chapter 17).

One of the other unique aspects of financial services that affects their pricing is intangibility. Although for many manufactured goods standard product testing procedures exist to quantify the level of product quality in lab and field settings, such approaches, which rely on quantifying tangible measures of quality, do not exist for financial services (Ehrlich and Fanelli 2012). For example, for manufactured goods, product durability tests can be applied to determine manufacturing quality. Such opportunities are not available for financial services due to the absence of tangible and measurable physical attributes. It is difficult, if not impossible, to determine whether a particular investment product will yield good returns in the long run, as the financial results of an investment may not be apparent for many years after the initial outlay of funds. As a result, the marketplace for financial services does not readily have access to objective product quality information that may be available in many other markets through organizations such as JD Power and Associates, CNet, Consumer Reports, or regulatory bodies. Under these circumstances price itself becomes an indicator of financial service quality and is representing not only the financial sacrifice that customers have to accept, but also signaling – correctly or not – the quality of the financial service offering.

The external market environment also has a tremendous impact on the price perceptions associated with many categories of financial services. Whether a particular price is considered acceptable or not may depend on the state of the financial markets. In the US, the prime interest rate is used as a reference point for rates charged for a range of short-term credit products and in the UK the base rate serves a similar reference role. For example, the interest rate paid on a credit product may be viewed as excessive if the reference rate significantly drops. That is because short-term interest rates charged for credit transactions such as revolving lines of credit are correlated with prime and base rates. Unless the lender proactively adjusts interest rates to reflect reference rate fluctuations, its offering for the price of its credit products (as measured by charged interest rates) would be out of sync with the market. Shifts in the market's reference interest rates can also influence perceptions of attractiveness of investment products, which are often benchmarked against risk-free investment options available in the financial markets. The process of pricing certain categories of financial services may therefore require constant assessment of market conditions, to adjust and refine prices with the objective of ensuring relative balance with key financial market indicators.

Another central characteristic of price in the context of financial services is that customers often do not have a great deal of insight into the features and benefits of many financial services. This is because financial services are not transacted at a high level of frequency and customers often do not receive a great amount of exposure to information related to their prices and other attributes. This reduces the level of price memory that is associated with a financial service, and customers often cannot recall the price that they may have paid for a financial service, though they may currently subscribe to it. The consumer challenges in evaluating financial services are further complicated in new financial services contexts where no prior consumer exposure exists (Nejad and Estelami 2012). In addition to the infrequent nature of financial services transactions, which contributes to the weak memory traces, the unexciting nature of financial services further reduces customer interest andso reduces the amount of customer attention given to financial services transactions. This further weakens the memory traces related to price and results in price knowledge levels that are considerably lower for financial services categories than other categories of goods and services (Estelami 2005).

An additional challenge in the pricing of financial services is that profitability can be difficult to quantify on a per-customer basis. The nature of financial services transactions is such that customers interact with the financial services provider over an extended period of time and through many transactions. The variability around the frequency of these transactions, as well as the depth of each individual transaction, makes it difficult to assess the cost associated with serving each customer (please see Chapter 17 for a discussion of the challenges of costing and pricing financial transactions). Some transactions may be highly profitable for the financial services organization, others may be time-consuming and costly. In addition, the fact that a considerable proportion of the costs of operating a financial services organization are fixed costs makes the process of allocating such costs across transactions and across customers an analytically difficult task. As a result, quantifying the profitability associated with an individual customer may be difficult to achieve. Given that costs are a major consideration in establishing prices, the use of traditional cost-based pricing practices in the specific context of financial services can become challenging and as a result other approaches to pricing may be called for.

Drivers of financial services price perceptions

In this section we will discuss the rational economic view of how financial services prices should be objectively evaluated by consumers. We will then contrast this rational view with what is known in terms of cognitive short-cuts (heuristics) that consumers take in evaluating financial services prices. The impact of these heuristic approaches on price perception formation and on the practice of pricing financial services will also be discussed. It is important to note that the heuristics discussed in this section account for the majority of financial services decisions, but do not include the entire inventory of heuristics that may apply to financial decisions.

One of the unique features of pricing financial services is the multidimensionality of price. The common view of pricing in many goods and services markets is that price is a unidimensional construct; in financial services price often consists of multiple dimensions. For example, the price of a manufactured good such as a shoe or a computer is typically a single number. Potential buyers can easily compare offers based on the product features and price. In contrast, financial services prices typically consist of several numbers. For example, the price of a checking account may consist of a monthly maintenance fee, fees for writing checks, overdraft fees and money transfer fees. Additional restrictions and requirements such as minimum balances that would need to be maintained in order to receive specific price discounts may also need to be considered. The added complexity resulting from the multidimensionality of price can result in significant cognitive demands for consumers.

Complex mathematical operations are at the heart of financial services prices (Estelami 2003a, Huhmann and McQuitty 2009). In the bank pricing example previously mentioned, the bank account holder may need to consider the number of checks they write every month, the frequency of money transfers expected every month and the possibility of needing to use the overdraft line of credit before determining what the likely net price for the bank services would be. Similarly, when purchasing an insurance policy, a potential policyholder needs to know the underlying risk being covered by the policy as well as the likely claim amount associated with incidents being covered. From an expected outcome framework, the product of these two figures would represent the expected value of the insurance policy to the policyholders. However, not only is it a challenge for one to gain access to underlying risk information, for example, in the form of actuarial tables showing the probability of various claim amounts, but also the task of conducting the required arithmetic can be a challenge for most individuals. Often, the economic perspective of price, which requires formal financial computations, risk projections and numeric processing, cannot be exercised by most individuals facing financial services prices.

Research has shown that the increased level of cognitive demands associated with financial services prices can directly result in physiological stress, as measured by indicators such as increased heart rate, rising blood pressure and elevated levels of oxygen consumption (Dehaene 1992). In addition, as the number of price dimensions increase and as the complexity of arithmetic operations required to compute the price increases, as expected, the ability of consumers to evaluate the price significantly drops. For example, in a study using trained finance professionals, it was found that if multiplication was used as the required computation in a complex price instead of addition, significant increase in the length of time to evaluate the price can be observed (Estelami 2003b, 1999). The mental arithmetic requirements needed for evaluating financial services prices can inhibit objective evaluation of offers. This clearly represents concerns regarding the ability of the population of consumers being able to correctly evaluate the economic sacrifices associated financial services offers present to them. The net effect of price complexity in financial services is the use of simplifying cognitive short-cuts – also referred to as heuristics – which helps consumers cope with the complex prices being presented to them in financial services markets. These heuristics help consumers evaluate their options more quickly, though at times with systematic inaccuracies.

Effects of numeric presentation of price dimensions

Research in pricing has shown that the numeric format in which a price of an offer is presented can influence the perceptions of the offer. For example, the price of a $200 item can be viewed as more attractive if it is slightly modified to $199. Though from an economic point of view both prices are substantively equivalent, from a perceptual view this change in format can make the latter price presentation appear more attractive. The left to right processing of digits by the human brain biases consumer perceptions when the first digit encountered in the latter price is the number 1, whereas in the former price it is the number 2 and thereby signals a higher price level (Schindler and Kirby 1997). Therefore, $199 will be perceived as a lower price because it is in the $100 range, whereas the former is in the $200 range, though the two amounts are nearly equivalent.

Similar to the effect observed for goods markets where prices that are slightly below threshold levels are viewed as less expensive, price dimensions that are formatted as such also generate more positive responses in financial services decisions. For example, in a credit transaction, setting monthly payments at $199 will generate more positive responses than $200. However, research has shown that the numeric format effects are far more profound in the multi-dimensional pricing environment of financial services. This is because financial services price dimensions often need to be used in computational tasks in order to evaluate the net price. For example, in a credit transaction where monthly payments across multiple months exist, objective evaluation of the total cash layout requires the use of multiplication (of monthly payments by the number of months). The format in which the price dimensions are communicated can inhibit or facilitate the required arithmetic. For example, if the price is communicated as $200 for 20 months, it would be much easier for a consumer to conduct the multiplication, compared to a price such as $169 a month for 24 months. The computational response time associated with the latter is in the order of 10 times longer than the corresponding response time for the former price presentation (Estelami 2003b, 1999). As a result, the numeric price format can have a direct influence on how price perceptions are formed and whether accurate computational tasks are carried out by consumers.

Effects of hyperbolic discounting

Many financial transactions relate to receiving or payment of funds over time. For example, an investment product requires the outlay of current funds in anticipation of returns to be received at a future point in time. In such transactions, an individual's perspective on how much future returns are acceptable when considering the current outlay would drive his investment decision. Traditional economic theory would suggest that money today is more valuable than money tomorrow, a concept commonly referred to as the time value of money. Although this view is commonly agreed on, in practice it is not as rigorously exercised in financial services decisions of consumers (Lowenstein and Thaler 1989). Therefore, the tradeoffs made between present and future spending that consumers consider acceptable varies significantly from prescriptive economic thinking. For example, the discount rates that consumers use in order to weigh present outlay of investments against future returns vary from the interest rates exercised in financial markets. These differences are systematic and highly predictable and the patterns of response are referred to as hyperbolic discounting by behavioral economists (Ainslie 1991, Mazur 1987). According to hyperbolic discounting, individuals are believed to use excessively high discount rates in valuing immediate consumption needs, while very low discount rates – far below those of financial markets – are applied for decisions related to consumption anticipated in the distant future.

The impact of hyperbolic discounting on financial services decisions may be a natural gravitation toward present consumption and ignorance about matters related to planning a financial future. For example, a consumer may be willing to pay a high interest rate on a credit card to purchase a discretionary item today but not value future consumption needs (for example, during retirement years) and as a result may decide not to contribute sufficiently to their retirement funds or personal savings. One of the fundamental drivers of hyperbolic discounting is the lack of impulse control, a phenomenon observable in human and animal behavior. Consumption decisions made by animals such as mice and monkeys in laboratory settings where immediate rewards and future consumption are balanced using systematic manipulation of efforts and the timing of rewards show hyperbolic discount patterns that resemble human financial decisions (Ainslie 1991, Burnham 2005). This phenomenon suggests that the underlying neurological hardwiring of the human brain is restricted in many similar ways that animal consumption decisions are driven.

The pricing effect of hyperbolic discounting in financial services markets is often apparent for financial products that engage in the trade-off between present and future flow of funds. For example, tax return service providers have recognized that consumers often overvalue immediate access to their tax returns. As a result, many tax filing companies provide the option to their clients of receiving funds immediately upon the filing of the taxes, in the form of accelerated tax returns. In some cases the accelerated returns may be considerably smaller in value than what the client would receive had they waited several weeks for the tax return to be processed by the tax authorities. In those cases, the implied discount rates in the transaction are often very high and in some studies have been found to far exceed the interest rates charged for high-risk credit card transactions. Other financial services, where pricing practices may be affected by hyperbolic discount patterns, include investment services, insurance and mortgages. In all of these categories of financial services, many consumers may overestimate the value of immediate flow of funds and underestimate distant flows. The discount rates and the means by which these trade-offs are made would need to be determined through formal market research and can help guide pricing decisions.

Effects of short-term memory overload

Limitations surrounding human memory capacity and information retention ability play a significant role in how price perceptions for financial services are formed. In attempting to understand how consumers process these prices it is essential to recognize the role of short-term and long-term memory. The human memory system consists of separate memory banks. Long-term memory retains factual information such as one's home address, name and date of birth. Long-term memory is able to retain a large amount of information for very long periods of time, and in some studies has been shown to have no capacity or duration limit. In contrast, short-term memory retains information only for about 10 seconds and can store roughly 7 pieces of information (Hitch 1978, Miller 1956, Vanhuele et al. 2006). The way short-term and long-term memory interact determines how information is processed and retained, including price information.

Short-term memory plays a special role in the processing of financial services prices. This is because financial services prices are typically highly complex. In order for consumers to evaluate financial services prices they would need to process the array of price dimensions being presented to them and in many cases conduct mental computations involving the various price dimensions. Short-term memory is heavily utilized in conducting mental computations as well as in the cognitive assessment of complex decision scenarios.

For example, in evaluating a typical mortgage product, a consumer may need to examine nearly a dozen product attributes even for a single mortgage provider. Given that a typical mortgage product may have many price attributes (for example, interest rate, penalty fees, closing costs, etc.) a large number of attributes need to be examined. In the context of deciding among multiple mortgage providers, the number of attributes that need to be examined multiplies, resulting in a massive number of information items that have to be considered by the consumer. In such scenarios, it is not difficult to imagine the information overload that occurs and the consumer may simplify his task by only focusing on a subset of these attributes at any one point. This strategy is a result of limitations in short-term memory capacity, which constrain the number of items of information being processed at any given point in time to 7. Similarly, when facing a financial decision where payments are extended over multiple time periods, the consumer would need to conduct mental multiplication in order to multiply the monthly payments by the number of payments in order to determine the total cash layout. Such mental calculations heavily utilize short-term memory, for example, to carry digits from single-digit multiplication operations, to conduct mental addition and to carry out other numeric transformations needed to complete computational sub-tasks that would produce the multiplication result of the two numbers.

The net effect of short-term memory limitations on consumer financial decisions manifests in a variety of forms. One effect is increased physiological stress when facing financial services prices that strain short-term memory limitations. Financial services prices that require complex arithmetic tasks (for example, multiplication and division) create higher levels of physiological stress than those that require simpler arithmetic tasks (for example, addition and subtraction). Often the former take longer for consumers to evaluate and are associated with slower response times in laboratory settings (Estelami 2003b). Another manifestation of short-term memory limitations is that consumers may opt to simplify their decision by not carrying out the required mental computations altogether. This, in many ways, represents the abandoning of the evaluation process and the transition toward sub-optimal decision-making. For example, when choosing between a series of mortgage products, the homebuyer may decide to only focus on interest rate and not pay much attention to other attributes of the mortgage products being presented in the various choices present. A study by Lee and Marlowe (2003) in the context of retail bank decisions showed that when making decisions about which financial institution to use, many consumers compare their choices attribute-by-attribute, rather than holistically, by focusing on the retail location first, then on secondary attributes such as rates and customer services. The result of such a simplification process can be catastrophic from a consumer perspective as it would lead to a poorly thought-out decision and in the case of banking products, which are long-term in nature and involve large outlay of funds, the resulting decisions may be economically harmful in the long-term.

Effects of long-term memory limitations

In addition to the inhibiting effect of short-term memory on the consumer's ability to process financial services prices, long-term memory limitations can also have detrimental effects on price perceptions. When exposed to prices of financial services, consumers have the opportunity to learn the price information and to retain this information in long-term memory for future decision-making. Increased levels of such exposure to prices can enhance long-term memory traces and improve the accuracy of consumer memory for prices. As outlined earlier, long-term memory can have unlimited capacity and retain information for very long time periods. However, retrieving this information can be a challenge and studies suggest that price memory is weak in most markets, financial or otherwise (Estelami 2005, Turley and Cabannis 1995, Kinsey and McAlister 1980).

Research on price memory in goods markets has shown that consumers do not retain accurate knowledge of prices. For example, studies in consumer packaged goods markets show that roughly half of all consumers are unaware of the exact prices for products that they regularly purchase (Estelami et al. 2001). Therefore, even in the simple context of goods markets, where price is often a single number, consumers fail to recall prices accurately. As can be expected, the problem becomes considerably more profound when dealing with financial services prices that are multidimensional and complex. The fact that the price of a financial service consists of multiple numbers implies that consumers would need to remember not only a single price dimension but also all the price dimensions associated with the financial service offer, in order to accurately recall the price at a future point in time. This can be a highly challenging task and as a result most consumers do not recall financial prices well.

Consumer memory for financial services prices is further hampered by the fact that the attractiveness of a financial service may vary not just because of the price itself but also by its relative position with respect to the external environment in which the financial service is offered. For example, credit products and investment products are often evaluated in comparison to financial market interest rates, such as the prime rate or ten-year Treasury rates. As a result, the interest charged for a credit product cannot be evaluated in isolation by itself and must be assessed in the context of comparable financial market rates. This makes the task of assessing and remembering the price further complicated, it is no longer sufficiently diagnostic for decision-making. The fluctuations in market interest rates in the external environment make it more difficult to focus on the price, as prices too often have to be adjusted based on fluctuations in external benchmarks, in order to remain competitive. The volatility in prices resulting from constant price adjustments by financial services providers needed to reflect changing market conditions makes the task of memorizing financial services prices more difficult.

Long-term memory for financial services prices is further hampered by the fact that the frequency of purchase associated with most financial services transactions is low. Many financial services are purchased infrequently and the length of time between purchase occasions may be in the order of years. For example, one may examine the prices for an automobile insurance policy once per year or decide on a mortgage product once every several years. This is in contrast with most other markets where purchase frequencies are much higher and transactions occur on a much more regular basis. The infrequent exposure to price and the infrequent incidence of decisions in financial services reduces the likelihood of price information being retained in long-term memory. As a result, long-term memory for financial services prices has been shown to be significantly lower than long-term memory for other forms of services or goods (Estelami 2005).

Effects of risk misperceptions

Because many financial services focus on the management of risk, consumer perceptions of risk can have a significant effect on how they evaluate the prices of certain categories of financial services. For example, an insurance product is intended to protect the policyholder from specific risks. How the policyholder views such risks, as reflected in the perception of the probability of likelihood of the event occurring, will guide the policyholder's level of need for the policy and as a result influence her price sensitivity. If the event is perceived as highly likely, higher prices are likely to be tolerated.

The way individuals perceive risk can affect how prices of financial services that have risk management as the core of their offering are perceived. Risk perceptions are known to be systematically inaccurate, such that individuals often overestimate or underestimate risk. For example, in a national survey where respondents were asked to express their perception of the likelihood of various life hazards, it was found that risk perceptions can be biased systematically (Slovic et al. 1977). Rare events, such as deaths by vitamin poisoning or venomous bites were found to be significantly overestimated by the public. In contrast, much more frequent events such as deaths resulting from heart attacks were underestimated.

The reasons for overestimation of unlikely events and the underestimation of likely ones are believed to be variations in media exposure of such events, as well as mental filtering effects (Bazerman and Moore 2008, March 1988). Media exposure for rare events often elevates the level of the public's attention to those events. The media coverage of rare events, as reflected, by the amount of new programming, is disproportionately high compared to the underlying probability of such events taking place. As a result, the memory traces associated with rare events overemphasizes their significance, thereby elevating the perceptions of such risks. Furthermore, for frequent events, individuals tend to discount the prominence of a particular risk because they may unconsciously view themselves to also be at risk but would like to deny such a possibility in order to reduce cognitive dissonance. Attribution strategies can be used to enable filtering, for example, by attributing death resulting from a heart attack to an individual's genetic background, rather than diet and exercise that are more controllable and mandate one to accept more personal responsibility.

Significant pricing complications arise due to consumers' lack of access to risk information. Because for most risk categories probability tables are not publicly available in the form of actual tables that insurance companies often utilize in pricing their policies, the typical consumer unfortunately has to rely on their perceptions of risk when evaluating prices for risk-based financial services such as insurance and investment products. This creates opportunities for some financial services firms to capitalize on consumer ignorance, while maximizing their own profits. For example, certain categories of insurance products covering risks that are low in probability experience high margins, for the simple fact that consumers overestimate the risk, while the underlying risk is low and does not represent significant costs to the insurer. Much needs to be done to better inform the public on risk levels and to prevent the selling of risk-based financial solutions at prices that may be considered by some as excessive and abusive.

Consumer coping strategies

In this section we will discuss how consumers cope with the effects outlined in the previous section as they relate to financial services prices. The coping strategies discussed enable consumers to function and operate with the complexities presented to them in the form of financial services prices. We will discuss three of the more commonly recognized coping strategies. These strategies help reduce the cognitive stress associated with evaluating financial services prices, while at the same time contributing to inaccuracies in price perceptions. It is important to recognize the existence of these coping strategies and to recognize the degree by which they can influence price related decisions in financial services.

Attribute anchoring

The multidimensionality of financial services prices, in conjunction with short-term memory limitations often encourage consumers to simplify their decisions by not paying attention to all the presented price dimensions but to focus on only a subset of the price dimensions and often a single dimension. This process is referred to as anchoring; the focus on an individual price dimension dominates (anchors) the perception that is generated for that price and little adjustment is subsequently made to reflect the magnitude of other dimensions of the price (Morwitz et al. 1998). For example, in evaluating a mortgage product a home-buyer may anchor on the interest rate, focusing on its value and pay only minor attention to other aspects of the price such as prepayment penalties and closing costs. The net effect of this process is that homebuyers may gravitate toward mortgage products with low interest rates and be willing – unknowingly – to pay higher amounts for attributes such as closing costs and prepayment penalties on which they are not focused. The insufficient adjustment made for the values associated with the remaining price dimensions creates contexts that can result in suboptimal price decisions, whereby the objective net price – taking into account all the price dimensions – may be higher than the consumer perceives it to be.

In the context of credit transactions, it has been shown that consumers often use an anchoring process as well. For example, with payments that are distributed over multiple periods of time, it has been shown that consumers anchor their decisions on the monthly payments (Estelami 1997). As a result, they may not pay sufficient attention to the frequency of payments and therefore become biased toward financial offers that reflect low monthly payments, not recognizing the total outlay of funds. This strategy helps the consumer avoid the cumbersome task of conducting the required mental multiplication and can clearly generate decision outcomes that are not optimal. Low monthly payments may be perceived as attractive, however, when considering the frequency of payments it may also represent a large total outlay of cash, which the consumer may not recognize.

The pricing effect of the anchoring phenomenon has also been recognized in price decisions related to investment products. For example, in determining what price to sell the security possessed in an investment portfolio, investors often anchor their decisions on the price originally paid for the investment. At first glance this decision strategy may seem reasonable; the rational economic view of such decisions is that one should focus on the long-term prospects of any investment rather than its original price at the time of purchase. Investments that are likely to devalue over time should be divested from despite experiencing prices that are below their original purchase price in order to prevent further losses. In the long-term, investors' tendency to hold on to stocks that are trading at prices below their purchase price leads to investment portfolios that are heavily populated by securities that decline in value. This phenomenon is so frequently observed in financial market decisions that it has been labeled as 'keeping losers and selling winners' (Barber and Odean 2000). The selling of winners occurs when investors decide to sell a stock because its market price exceeds the original purchase price. An investor may choose to sell such a stock in order to realize the gain in value in the form of selling profits, not recognizing that the stock may rise further in value. Anchoring price-related buy and sell decisions on the originally paid price for security can simplify such financial decisions but in the long term can have a detrimental impact on investment returns. This phenomenon has been observed in all investors, professional or not and is evident regardless of seniority and level of investment experience (Barber and Odean 2008, Hastie and Dawes 2009).

Studies have shown that anchoring phenomena can occur across the population, even with highly financially savvy decision-makers. For example, in a classic study involving experienced stockbrokers, it was found that in buy and sell decisions related to securities, brokers simplify their decisions by focusing on asset returns as an anchor and modifying their decisions slightly to reflect risk (Slovic 1969). As a result, their decisions are heavily weighted on asset returns, and do not sufficiently take into account the risks of the securities. Subsequent studies have shown that this effect can be replicated even with highly seasoned investors and therefore highlights the degree to which the anchoring process may influence price-related decisions for the average investor (Barber and Odean 2000).

Mental accounting

Many financial decisions relate to budgeting and the allocation of funds for expenditures spread over extended periods of time or across spending categories. The breaking down of spending into time-dependent or category-dependent categories can result in a simplification strategy referred to as mental accounting (Soman 2001, Thaler 1985). Through this process, consumers categorize expenses into different mental accounts and thereby simplify their financial decisions. The categorization process associates each financial expense with a specific mental account. For example, a mental account may exist related to expenditures on a daily basis and another mental account may relate to expenses on a monthly basis. Spending on meals may be considered a daily expense whereas paying rent may be considered a monthly expense. Furthermore, where funds are to be spent or where they are sourced from can affect spending behavior.

The mental accounting process can directly influence price sensitivity in financial services. Financial transactions that are associated with specific mental accounts can be perceived as more or less expensive depending on which mental account the consumer associates them with. An insurance company may choose to quote its price on a daily basis – for example, as 50 cents a day – rather than on its yearly equivalent, which is almost $200. The former presentation encourages consumers to associate the price with a daily mental account whereas the latter would be associated with a yearly mental account. It has been shown that consumers are less price-sensitive to shorter-term mental accounts such as daily expenditures and more sensitive when amounts are quoted in the larger yearly format. As a result, the 50-cent-per-day presentation will generate more favorable price perceptions.

Mental accounts are often used in the context of financial services decisions. For example, when receiving tax returns at the end of a tax year most individuals treat the receipt of the tax return amounts as found money. They categorize the tax return in a mental account associated with unexpected gains. The spending behavior associated with such mental accounts is often impulsive and unplanned and as a result, monies received in this form are frequently spent on unnecessary discretionary items (Burnham 2005).

From a financial services pricing perspective, mental accounting can have positive and negative price perception effects. Consumers may perceive the price of the financial service as more attractive if it is presented in the context of a short-term mental account, such as a daily or weekly expenditure. Similarly, money received that is framed as an unexpected gain may be more easily spent than money that is part of the planned fiscal and budgetary process of an individual. Recognizing that the mental budgeting process is a simplification strategy and can lead to suboptimal financial decisions has motivated public policy advocates to pursue legislation, which may prevent consumers from making financial decisions that are suboptimal. For example, with tax returns in the United States, new regulations are under discussion to mandate tax returns not be provided as a lump sum, which may be treated as 'found money', but dispersed over extended periods of time to prevent impulse spending decisions.

Price-quality cue utilization

Research in pricing has long established that consumers can simplify their purchase decisions by using price as an indicator of product quality (Rao 2005). This is often a strategy utilized in contexts where the objective quality measures are not readily available. For example, the quality of mechanical repair services or insurance products may not be immediately evident. Often, long-term use of the service may be needed in order to experience its true objective quality. In such cases, consumers tend to rely on other pieces of information that they may consider indicators of quality. For example, brand-name or price can be used as indicators of quality.

For commoditized financial services where quality is largely unobservable, use of price as an indicator of quality is commonplace. For example, insurance and investment services are difficult to assess in terms of their quality levels. In insurance, the majority of policyholders will never experience the claims process and as a result will never have the opportunity to personally assess the quality of the full spectrum of services provided by the insurer. Similarly for investment services the long-term returns from the advice provided by an investment advisor may not be apparent for many years after the investment decision has been made. In such categories of financial services the diagnostic value of price increases, making it a driver of perceived quality.

The use of the price as an indicator of quality in financial services can result in market responses that are the opposite of what traditional economic theory would predict. Traditional economic thinking considers the demand for a product or service to be a downward sloping function, whereby higher prices are associated with lower levels of market demand. However, the use of the price-quality cue in financial services would suggest that higher prices would be viewed more positively by consumers and as a result can generate higher levels of sales. This is one of the reasons many financial services categories, despite the commoditized nature of the products, experience significant levels of price variation from one competitor to the next. From a pricing perspective, it is essential to question the extent by which price is used as a measure of quality by potential buyers and to integrate this understanding into the pricing process. This may result in price levels higher than what one would typically expect and at the same time help prevent price wars in the marketplace.

Conclusion

This chapter has focused on identifying the primary drivers of consumer perceptions of financial services prices. As is evident from the coverage provided, there is common agreement among researchers and practitioners that consumers are relatively limited in their ability to process prices of financial services offers. These consumer limitations are unfortunately at times misused and abused by financial services providers who choose to capitalize on them through specific pricing practices. Consumers' inability to understand financial services prices can result in financial decisions that are harmful to the financial well-being of individual consumers and in some cases to society at large. Pricing practices that capitalize on these limitations can, at the same time, represent noticeable profit opportunities for financial services providers. It is in this dilemma that financial services professionals need to determine where they stand. The pursuit of profits in its extreme form may translate into significant compromises in ethical and moral values and in some cases the violation of established regulations. It is hoped that the presentation of the material in this chapter encourages pricing practitioners in financial services organizations to adopt consumer-friendly approaches in how they communicate prices to existing and potential customers.

The vulnerability of consumers in evaluating financial services prices has, over the years, given rise to the creation and implementation of regulations related to pricing. For example, in the United States, the Truth in Lending Act mandates that credit transactions should be communicated in easily understandable forms to consumers. It requires that providers of credit products communicate the price of credit transaction in the form of an annual percentage rate (APR). This requirement helps reduce the amount of confusion that may result from the consumer examining complex multidimensional credit terms and simplifies the consumer's task to the inspection of a single price dimension: the APR. Similar regulations have come to life in recent years around the world, in managing the communication of price information in the markets for credit cards, investment services and insurance. The intent of these regulations is to simplify price-related financial decisions so that consumers can better understand the terms and conditions related to financial services price offers presented to them. Although these regulations help consumers in most occasions, much still needs to be done: consumer vulnerability, limited education on financial matters and poor discipline in financial decision-making continue to harm the public.

One could argue, as some scholars have, that regulations by themselves may not suffice in protecting consumers from misperceptions related to financial services prices. Much also has to be done by educators and financial literacy advocates. A well-informed public that is educated on financial matters is less likely to inaccurately perceive financial services prices. Education on financial decision-making can help individuals dissect the decision elements related to financial products, including those related to price. It is critical that the public be exposed to financial literacy initiatives on a regular basis. This exposure can be a part of basic educational requirements provided to children and young adults and incorporated as a standard component of the education system. Unfortunately, the primary education systems in most countries today fail to provide this essential tool to their students.

A more assertive perspective would extend the scope of responsibility to the management of financial services organizations who make pricing decisions. Pricing practices do not exist in isolation and are often exercised with the awareness and approval of senior management. For this reason, financial services organizations of the future, in responding to public demand for more transparent pricing, will need to modify their marketing and management philosophies to better reflect the need for clarity in prices. As business models evolve, the benchmarks by which management success is evaluated and rewarded may need to shift away from focusing only on measures of profitability and market share and include other measures that reflect the clarity and transparency of customer transactions. The financial crisis of the last decade highlighted the significance of the need for clarity in pricing practices exercised by the industry. In responding to ongoing public distrust following the financial crisis, the financial services industry needs to adopt more consumer-friendly practices in communicating prices. Leadership in this direction would not only help consumers make informed price-related financial decisions, but would help re-establish public trust, and provide organizations who take the lead in this direction with a competitive advantage.

References

Ainslie, G. (1991), 'Deviation of rational economic behavior from hyperbolic discounting', *American Economic Review*, 81(2), pp. 334–48.

Barber, B. and Odean, T. (2008), 'All the glitters: the effect of attention and news on the buying behavior of individual and institutional investors', *The Review of Financial Studies*, 21(2), pp. 785–818.

Barber, B. and Odean, T (2000), 'Trading is hazardous to your wealth: the common stock investment performance of individual investors', *Journal of Finance*, 55(2), pp. 773–806.

Bazerman, M. and Moore, D. (2008), *Judgment in Managerial Decision Making*. New York: Wiley

Bennett, R. and Kottasz, R. (2012), 'Public attitudes towards the UK banking industry following the global financial crisis', *International Journal of Bank Marketing*, 30(2), pp. 138–47.

Burnham, T. (2005), *Mean Markets and Lizard Brains*. New York: John Wiley & Sons.

Dehaene, S. (1992), 'Varieties of numerical abilities,' *Cognition*, 44(1), pp. 1–42.

Dimitriadis, S. (2010), 'Testing perceived relational benefits as satisfaction and behavioral outcome drivers', *International Journal of Bank Marketing*, 28(4), pp. 297–313.

Dimitriadis, S., Kouremenos, A. and Kyrezis, N. (2011), 'Trust-based segmentation,' *International Journal of Bank Marketing*, 29(1), pp. 5–31.

Ehrlich, E. and Fanelli, D. (2012), *The Financial Services Marketing Handbook: Tactics and Techniques that Produce Results*. Bloomberg Financial. Sussex: John Wiley & Sons.

Ennew, C., Sekhon, H. and Kharouf, H. (2011), 'Trust in UK financial services: a longitudinal analysis', *Journal of Financial Services Marketing*, 16(1), pp. 65–75.

Estelami, H. (2008), 'Consumer use of the price-quality cue in financial services', *Journal of Product and Brand Management*, 17(3), pp. 197–208.

—— (2005), 'A cross-category examination of consumer price awareness in financial and non-financial services', *Journal of Financial Services Marketing*, 13(3), pp. 56–72.

—— (2003a), 'The strategic implication of a multi-dimensional pricing environment', *Journal of Product and Brand Management*, 12(4), pp. 322–34.

—— (2003b), 'The effect of price presentation tactics on consumer evaluation effort of multi-dimensional prices', *Journal of Marketing Theory and Practice*, 11(2), pp. 1–16.

—— (1999), 'The computational effect of price ending in multi-dimensional price advertising', *Journal of Product and Brand Management*, 8(3), pp. 244–56.

—— (1997), 'Consumer perceptions of multi-dimensional prices', In Brucks, M. and MacInnis, D.J. (eds.) *Advances in Consumer Research*, 24. Provo, UT: Association for Consumer Research, pp. 392–99.

Estelami, H., Lehmann, D.R. and Holden, A.C. (2001), 'Macro-economic determinants of consumer price knowledge: a meta-analysis of four decades of research', *International Journal of Research in Marketing*, 18 (5), pp. 341–55.

Farquhar, J. and Meidan, A. (2010), *Marketing Financial Services*. 2nd edition. London: Palgrave MacMillan.

Harrison, T. (2006), *Financial Services Marketing*. London: Financial Times Management.

—— (2003), 'Why trust is important in customer relationships and how to achieve it', *Journal of Financial Services Marketing*, 7(3), pp. 206–9.

Hastie, R. and Dawes, R. (2009), *Rational choice in an uncertain world: the psychology of judgment and decision making*. New York: Sage.

Hitch, G. (1978), 'The role of short-term memory in mental arithmetic', *Cognitive Science*, 12(2), pp. 89–97

Huhmann, B. and McQuitty, S. (2009), 'A Model of Consumer Financial Numeracy' *International Journal of Bank Marketing*, 27(4), pp. 270–93.

Janakiraman, N., Meyer, R.J. and Morales, A.C. (2006), 'Spillover effects: how consumers respond to unexpected changes in prices and quality', *Journal of Consumer Research*, 33(3), pp. 361–72.

Kinsey, J. and McAlister, R. (1980), 'Consumer knowledge of the costs of open-end credit', *Journal of Consumer Affairs*, 15(2), pp. 249–70.

Lee, J. and Marlowe, J. (2003), 'How consumers choose a financial institution: decision making criteria and heuristics', *International Journal of Bank Marketing*, 21(2/3), pp. 53–71.

Lowenstein, G. and Thaler, R. (1989), 'Anomalies: intertemporal choices', *Journal of Economic Perspective*, 3(4), pp. 181–93.

March, J. (1988), 'Variable risk preferences and adaptive aspirations', *Journal of Economic Behavior and Organization*, 9(1), pp. 5–24.

Mazur, J. E. (1987), 'An adjustment procedure for studying delayed reinforcement', In Commons, M.L., Mazur, J.E., Nevins, J.A. and Rachlin, H. (eds.) *Quantitative Analysis of Behavior: The Effect of Delay and of Intervening Events on Reinforcement Value*. Hillsdale, NJ: Ballinger.

Miller, G. A. (1956), 'The magical number seven, plus or minus two: some limits on our capacity for processing information', *Psychological Review*, 63(1), pp. 81–97.

Morwitz, V. G., Greenleaf, E. and Johnson, E. (1998), 'Divide and prosper: consumers' reactions to partitioned prices', *Journal of Marketing Research*, 35(4), pp. 453–63.

Nejad, M. and Estelami, H. (2012), 'Pricing financial services innovations', *Journal of Financial Services Marketing*, 17(2), pp. 120–34.

Norton, S. D. (2010), 'A comparative analysis of US policy initiatives and their implications in a credit crisis: the depression era of the 1920s in a twenty-first century context', *Journal of Financial Services Marketing*, 14(4), pp. 328–45.

Oyelere, P. B. and Turner, J. D. (2000), 'A survey of transfer pricing practices in UK banks and building societies', *European Business Review*, 12(2), p. 93–99.

Rao, A. R. (2005), 'The quality of price as a quality cue', *Journal of Marketing Research*, 42(4), pp. 401–9.

Schindler, R. M. and Kirby, N. (1997), 'Patterns of rightmost digits used in advertised prices: implications for nine-ending effects', *Journal of Consumer Research*, 24(3), pp. 192–201.

Soman, D. (2001), 'The mental accounting of sunk time costs: why time is not like money', *Journal of Behavioral Decision Making*, 14(2), pp. 169–85.

Slovic, P. (1969) 'Analyzing the expert judges: a descriptive study of a stockbroker's decision processes', *Journal of Applied Psychology*, 53(2), pp. 255–63.

Slovic, P., Fischhoff, B., Lichtenstein, S., Corrigan, B. and Combs, B. (1977), 'Preference for insuring against probable small losses', *Journal of Risk and Insurance*, 44(2), pp. 237–58.

Thaler, R. (1985), 'Mental accounting and consumer choice', *Marketing Science*, 4(3), pp. 199–214.

Turley, L.W. and R.F. Cabannis (1995), 'Price knowledge for services: an empirical investigation', *Journal of Professional Services Marketing*, 12(1), pp. 39–52.

Vanhuele, M., Laurent, G. and Dreze, X. (2006), 'Consumers' immediate memory for prices', *Journal of Consumer Research*, 33(2), pp. 163–74.

17

Price management in financial services

George J. Avlonitis and Kostis Indounas

Introduction

A review of the literature on financial services pricing reveals that a number of authors have underlined the importance of pricing for financial services providers:

> The price component of any marketing mix has a number of important roles to fulfill. First, and perhaps most importantly, it affects revenue and therefore profitability. Second, it is a competitive tool that can be used to exploit market opportunities and, third, it contributes to the image created for the product within the marketing mix. In broad terms, the role of pricing in a marketing context is to determine a price, which will produce the desired level of sales in order to meet the objectives of the business strategy.
>
> *Hughes 1990: 112*

Similarly, Farquhar and Meidan (2010) have argued that pricing is the only element of the marketing mix that generates revenues for the firm, while all the others are cost driven. In line with the above arguments, Oyelere and Turner (2000) and Estelami (2012) point out that price is the most flexible element of the marketing strategy, in that pricing decisions can be implemented relatively quickly in comparison with the other elements of marketing strategy. A financial services provider can easily make and implement a decision to alter its prices, whereas the decision to change an existing channel of distribution or promotional campaign may necessitate a longer period of time (Avlonitis and Indounas 2007).

The importance of pricing strategy for financial institutions is further intensified by the fact that price competition has increased among these institutions in recent years within a number of countries (Estelami 2012). Moreover, empirical studies have shown that more and more customers turn to price in order to choose among competing alternatives (for example, Santonen 2007), while other studies have indicated that perceived problems with pricing have the strongest impact on defection rates (Colgate and Hedge 2001).

Despite the importance of pricing financial services, pricing has been argued to be the most neglected element of the marketing mix of financial services organizations (Estelami 2012). This situation has led many financial service providers to rely on simplified pricing formulas that do not reflect the real cost or value of their services. For instance, Howcroft and Lavis (1989: 3) suggest that:

> Traditionally retail banking has tended not to regard pricing as part of a general strategic process. This phenomenon results from a basic lack of knowledge of the essential cross-profit characteristics of products and customers. Consequently, purely qualitative considerations such as customer convenience, efficiency and speed of service, etc., became central at the expense of pricing considerations.

Within the same context, Farquhar and Meidan (2010) suggest that pricing strategy in financial institutions is not always well developed.

Based on the above arguments, this chapter investigates the pricing strategy of financial services providers. The emphasis is placed on incorporating the latest literature from theoretical and empirical points of view and presenting as many real examples and cases as possible. The chapter is divided into four main topics. The unique characteristics of financial services pricing are discussed in the first section of the chapter, while the main company and market related factors that affect price decision making are analyzed in the second section. The pricing process (i.e., pricing objectives, pricing methods and pricing policies) that financial institutions may follow is presented in the third section and the pricing strategy of new financial services is discussed in the fourth section of the chapter.

The current chapter is related to Chapter 16 by Estelami, which focuses on how consumers perceive and evaluate the prices offered by financial institutions. In particular, this perception and evaluation along with other customers' characteristics are considered to affect financial services pricing significantly and are discussed in this chapter. The importance of these characteristics is also reflected in the customer-based pricing methods, which are also presented in this chapter. The current chapter is also linked to Chapter 18 by Wei et al. on price bundling; price bundling is considered to be a pricing policy and is also highlighted in this chapter.

Unique characteristics of financial services pricing

Determining prices for financial services is a complex issue that has some differences in comparison with pricing other types of services or even physical products (Nejad and Estelami 2012). First, when it comes to the banking sector specifically, pricing has traditionally led to cross-subsidization that can be identified at three distinct levels: (a) the strategic level where the corporate sector is cross-subsidized at the expense of the retail sector, (b) the business level where borrowers are cross-subsidized at the expense of depositors and (c) the marketing level where cross-subsidization exists within specific service categories such as credit cards (Farquhar and Meidan 2010). For instance, a customer that pays their credit card balance in full within a pre-determined period of time (usually one month) is not charged any fee and is cross-subsidized by those customers who prefer to pay only a portion of this balance within this period and are therefore charged a fee (interest rate). The other side of this example is that the customer who pays in full is also cross-subsidizing others who do not pay in full.

Second, due to the complex nature of financial services and the fact that most financial services share the same costs, it is hard to determine the unit cost of a specific service. For instance, what is the cost of an individual house loan or personal loan? What is the cost of motor insurance or a specialized mutual fund? The result of this difficulty in determining the real cost of financial services, is that final prices do not always reflect actual costs (Ehrlich and Fanelli 2012).

Third, the role of risk is increased when pricing financial services. The demographic, psychographic and behavioral characteristics of an individual customer results in determining their risk profile, which in turns affects the final price that will be levied. The impact of personal risk is a crucial factor in determining the vast majority of insurance, investment and banking related services (Estelami 2012).

Fourth, the broader political and economic environment in which a financial institution operates is of paramount importance in designing its pricing strategy. Government intervention in terms of determining interest rates and imposing specific laws, along with the impact of economic variables such as the level of GDP, income and labor cost have a significant impact on the final price of financial services such as loans and savings accounts (Farquhar and Meidan 2010, Kotler and Armstrong 2012).

Factors that influence financial services pricing

A review of the existing literature reveals the existence of a limited number of empirical studies that endeavor to examine the main factors that affect financial services pricing. Meidan and Chin (1995) examined the pricing practices of 45 building societies in the UK and concluded that costs and competitors' prices were the main factors that triggered their pricing decisions.

Furthermore, Avlonitis and Indounas (2006) investigated the pricing behavior of 17 banks and 29 insurance companies operating in Greece and found that the banks were influenced by the economy's macroeconomic indices (for example, interest rates), as might be expected. Moreover, they were influenced by their marketing objectives and strategies and endeavored to incorporate their pricing strategy into their overall marketing strategy. Additionally, insurance companies were mainly influenced by company related factors, namely, their cost base, the applications and uniqueness of their services, without, however, disregarding the conditions surrounding their political and social environment.

A review of the existing literature also reveals that the main factors that are expected to affect price decision-making may be classified into two categories: company-related factors (for example, service cost, corporate culture) and market-related factors (for example, competitors' and customers' characteristics). Each one of these factors will be discussed in more detail.

Company related factors

As Table 17.1 reveals, company-related factors can be divided into organizational characteristics and service characteristics.

Table 17.1 Company-related factors that affect financial services pricing

Organizational characteristics
Corporate objectives and strategies
Corporate culture
Company's position in the market
Company size
Marketing objectives and strategies

Service characteristics
Service type
Service cost
Service risk
Service quality
Other service characteristics

Organizational characteristics

Various organizational characteristics affect pricing decisions, including corporate objectives and strategies, corporate culture, the company's position in the market, company size and marketing objectives and strategies. Pricing decisions should be in line with the overall corporate objectives and strategies (Indounas and Roth, 2012). Such objectives and strategies may include profit maximization, return on investment (ROI), market share increase, penetration in a new market, market development and the effort to convey a premium image among others. For instance, HSBC has built a prestigious image for its offerings in the various countries that it operates and tries to differentiate itself from its competitors on factors such as establishing a strong global brand name and ensuring the safety of deposits for its customers. Its pricing strategy is in line with this premium image as its prices are in many cases higher (for example, lower interest rates in savings accounts) than the competition.

Company goals may change over time. Initially, a company may set a low price in order to penetrate a new market. Once it becomes well established, it may change its objectives and bring them in line with those objectives pursued in other markets.

Corporate culture is another issue that affects price determination. For example, those financial services providers that are market-oriented place an emphasis on incorporating market inputs (such as customers' needs and competitive prices and potential reactions) in their pricing process and provide their marketing department an increased role in the strategy development process. Other financial services providers such as leading US banks (for example, J.P. Morgan, Bank of America) may rely on cross-functional collaboration when setting prices, whereas others may be based solely on top management's decisions. Similarly, there are companies that have formalized their whole pricing effort through assigning specific responsibilities and standardizing routine activities. On the other hand, other financial services providers may place their emphasis on leaving some kind of flexibility in this effort (Indounas 2009, Palmer 2008).

A company's position in the market may be one of the following: leader (the largest market share), challenger (the second or third largest market share), follower or niche player (targeting small specialized market segments). Each one of these positions in the market is associated with specific corporate strategies, which have an impact on the pricing strategy. For instance, leaders endeavor to protect their existing clientele basis through confrontation strategies, while challengers and followers try to gain market share through leapfrogging strategies (Kotler and Armstrong 2012, Walker et al. 2006).

To this end, a leading bank or insurance company is expected to demonstrate the pricing method of price leadership, on the basis of which it sets the rules of the game and determines the general level of prices in the market. In most of the cases, challengers and followers have no other option but to adopt these prices or any other price initiative made by the market leader. Niche players have some degree of freedom in setting their prices given the fact that they mainly target small market segments with specialized needs, which other companies may avoid to cater. For instance, in the case of the UK banking system, Barclays, HSBC, Lloyds are the main leading banks that set the rules of the game when it comes to the market's average prices, while banks such as Harrods Bank and Sainsbury's Bank are considered to be niche players that target small and specialized customer segments.

Company size affects price decision-making in that pricing in smaller companies is more or less a top management decision, while in larger companies pricing decisions are the outcome of inter-functional collaboration (Monroe 2003). As a firm grows larger, the development and maintenance of close and personal relationships with customers becomes more difficult. Stated differently, unlike in larger firms, organizational individuals at the customer interface in smaller firms hold a greater opportunity, flexibility and authority to thoroughly discover the requirements of their customers and to tailor their offerings accordingly (Argouslidis and Indounas 2010). Thus, developing relationship pricing systems where prices are also in accordance with the needs of customers might be easier for smaller financial services providers (for example, small co-operative banks in many European countries).

Price cannot be isolated from the other elements of the marketing mix, reflecting the need for a coherent marketing strategy (Estelami 2012). The product, distribution and communication strategy affects the pricing strategy. For instance, a differentiated type of car insurance that offers added value (for example, after sales service) will permit a higher price. An advertising campaign that promotes bargains will inevitably affect the final price of this service, leaving no other option but to levy a low price. The selection of distribution channels will determine the agents' profit margins and consequently, the service's final price. Moreover, the cost of providing financial services is different between different distribution channels such as traditional branches, automated teller machines (ATMs), internet banking and mobile banking. A company that enters a new market may select to mass penetrate this market or to penetrate a niche of it. The final decision will influence which price to set.

Service characteristics

Service characteristics include service type, service cost, service risk and service quality. The financial services sector offers a wide variety of services with different characteristics that affect price decision making. For instance, insurance companies such as the ING Group, which is a Dutch global provider of financial services, have established specialized departments called underwriting and actuarial, the suggestions of which are of paramount importance when setting the final price. On the other hand, pricing decisions within banks are part of a broader marketing strategy that is mainly formulated by the relevant business units that are responsible for each service category such as the credit cards unit, personal banking and corporate banking (Papastathopoulou et al. 2001).

The cost of any financial service figures prominently in the pricing process as it sets the basis for the final price (Palmer 2008). Given the cost differentials across different countries, a frequent practice among global firms is to levy prices with wide price gaps. Costs can be divided into variable and fixed costs: the former change according to the level of production, while the latter remain stable irrespective of the final outcome of production.

A common problem for many financial service providers is how to manage their costs given the difficulty in allocating fixed costs among the different services that they offer in each market. For instance, how are the marketing department's salaries reflected in the services offered by mutual funds providers such as Morgan Stanley or Credit Suisse? Similarly, how is depreciation of a specific machine incorporated into the final price of a service offered by an insurance company such as Allianz? This problem leads many firms to determine in advance the total volume that they believe they will achieve, then allocate fixed costs on the basis of this volume. However, this practice often results in over or under estimation of the real price of a service (Indounas 2006). This problem is further intensified by the fact that many financial services share the same costs.

In order to overcome the above difficulty, a different method for calculating costs is required. To this end, the Activity Based Costing (ABC) system has started to be used extensively over the last years by many global firms. The ABC is an alternative accounting technique, which endeavors to identify the direct costs relating to a specific service (Hung 2011, Ibrahim and Saheem 2013).

Service risk is a crucial factor that determines financial services pricing (Ehrlich and Fanelli 2012). The role of risk can be perceived from the financial institutions' and the customers' point of view. From the institutions' perspective, the higher the risk that a customer presents for the financial institution the higher the final price they will pay. In the insurance sector, for example, the final price of a life insurance policy will be determined by the risk profile of a customer in terms of their medical history, age, sex and place of residence, among others. Insurance companies such as the American International Group in the US have established risk scores for different categories of customers on the basis of their demographic, psychographic and behavioral profile and, with the aid of historical data that have been formulated by specialized departments (such as underwriters and actuaries), they formulate the necessary price level (i.e., fee) for different insurance services. The higher the risk, the higher the insurance rates that customers will pay. Similarly, banks determine the final price (i.e., interest rates) for services such as loans on the basis of the level of risk related to specific customers.

From the customer perspective, the higher the level of risk that a customer is willing to accept in order to gain access to a financial service the higher the financial benefits that he will expect to receive. For instance, a customer who has chosen to invest in high risk types of mutual funds or other investment related services will expect a higher interest rate at the end of their investment. Similarly, higher return volatility translates into higher expectations of overall returns in the long run.

When a financial institution offers a high-quality service in the market, it would impose a high price. Companies such as the Citigroup or HSBC have traditionally used this approach in an effort to create an exclusive image for their services. This is a two-way relationship in that the price is often used by customers as a cue in order to judge the quality of the service, especially in such cases where the customer lacks any other cues (for example, previous experience with the service, word of mouth) to evaluate quality (Tse 2001). For instance, when choosing among competing types of investment related services, a customer who does not possess any technical knowledge may use price (i.e., level of interest rates) as an indicator to judge the quality of the alternative offerings. Empirical studies have also found a positive relationship between price and quality in the financial services sector (Estelami 2008, Kangis and Passa 1997).

Estelami and De Maeyer (2010) used an experimental design in order to study the divided pricing effects on financial service quality expectations. Divided pricing, according to these authors, refers to the situation where 'instead of pricing a product using a single number (for example, $200), prices can also be presented to consumers in more complex divided forms consisting of multiple dimensions (for example, $20 a month per 10 months)' (Estelami and De Maeyer 2010: 20–21). After investigating the cognitive effects that occur because of dividing the price into multiple payments, they concluded that divided pricing has varying effects on consumer expectations of service quality, depending on firm reputation and the underlying risk associated with the financial service.

A number of other service characteristics may also influence the final price of a financial service, leading to higher than the average market prices: (1) differentiation in terms of a strong brand name, reputation, after sales service, technical or functional superiority from the customers' point of view, (2) innovativeness in terms of satisfying a unique need that existing financial services cannot capture, (3) value in that the benefits associated with the financial service are higher than the costs, (4) customization in terms of the ability to be tailor made to customers' individual needs and characteristics, (5) availability in terms of the fact that the more difficult it is to find a financial service, the higher its price is expected to be, (6) automation in terms of the fact that banking services provided through ATMs, internet banking and phone banking have a lower price than services offered through traditional outlets.

Table 17.2 Market-related factors that affect financial services pricing

Micro-environment related characteristics
Customers' characteristics Competitors' characteristics The Porter's five forces Other characteristics
Macro-environment related characteristics
Political environment Social environment Economical environment Technological environment

Market-related factors

As Table 17.2 shows, the market-related factors that affect the price of a financial service are divided into two categories: characteristics related to the financial institution's micro-environment and characteristics related to the financial institution's macro-environment. Each one of these characteristics is examined in detail in the following sections.

Micro-environment related characteristics

The main influences on price in the micro-environment are customer characteristics and competitor characteristics. Customers' characteristics affect the final price of financial services because they determine their willingness to pay for a specific service and, thus, set a ceiling to the final price (Meidan 1996). A review of the existing literature reveals the lack of a widely-accepted definition regarding the meaning of price from the customer's point of view. Diamantopoulos (1991) defined price as an agreement between the seller and the buyer concerning what each is to receive. This concept of 'agreement' or 'mutual benefit' can be summarized in the following formula:

$$\text{Price} = \frac{\text{Monetary sacrifice by the buyer}}{\text{Sacrifice in terms of the quantity of goods given by the supplier}}$$

Based on this formula, price is a function of the money given by the buyer and the quantity of goods given by the supplier. Within this context, there seems to be some kind of sacrifice for both parties. The extent to which the final price will be accepted by both parties and an exchange between them will take place depends on whether their sacrifices coincide.

This definition suggests that price is an agreement and assumes that consumers know what the price is and understand what they are paying. However, what was made clear in Chapter 16 is that this is not always the case in financial services. In particular, it was highlighted that consumers are relatively limited in their ability to process and evaluate the prices that financial institutions offer.

A number of empirical studies have attempted to examine the impact of factors such as price awareness, price sensititivity, perceived value and perceived quality on customers' evaluations of financial services' prices, while other studies have focused on the investigation of the cognitive process that customers use in order to evaluate these prices, the ability of customers to retain prices in their memory and their reactions to multidimensional prices and discounts (for example, Estelami 2008, Estelami and De Maeyer 2010). Chapter 16 discusses in much more detail how consumers perceive and evaluate the prices offered by financial services providers and sheds light on these issues.

Individual demographic characteristics such as age, income, marital status, financial status and education also influence the final prices of financial services providers. Different types of savings accounts target different customer profiles (for example, the unemployed, students and older individuals with a pension) and offer different interest rates. Similarly, affluent customers in personal or private banking sectors may also receive better interest rates in their usual savings accounts. Customers' psychological characteristics such as their lifestyle also have an impact on the final prices of some financial services. Specific types of credit cards (for example, gold or bronze ones) are characterized by high interest rates and annual fees and target price insensitive customers that seek status and exclusivity. Additionally, behavioral characteristics such as loyalty and previous collaboration with the financial institution, exert an influence on final prices; loyal customers, for example, may negotiate a better interest rate for their savings accounts.

Competition is another key factor in financial services pricing (Estelami 2012). Taking into consideration competitive prices is of paramount importance if effective price decision-making is to be made. The intensive competition in many markets and the lack of real differentiation among alternative offerings leaves no other option but to monitor closely competitors' prices and price similar to them.

Apart from prices, competitors' potential actions are another important input in financial services price decision making. For instance, how will a competitor react to a price initiative (i.e., price decrease or increase) of a company? Will it retaliate or will it prefer to keep its existing prices? Reviewing competitors' behavior in the past is sometimes a useful guide to answering these questions. Discussions with competitors' key customers or industry experts may be another solution. By and large, competitors' response will depend on their belief as to whether this price initiative is expected to be permanent or temporary.

The Porter's five forces model (Porter 1980) is another tool used to analyze a company's micro-environment. These forces refer to the threat of new competitors entering into the market, the bargaining power of suppliers, the bargaining power of buyers, the threat from substitutes and the intensity of rivalry among existing companies.

Regarding the threat of new competitors entering into the market, the factors that influence the ease of such entrance include the economies of scale that existing companies in the market have managed to achieve, their cost advantages, the level of their service differentiation and their accessibility to existing distribution channels. The lower this threat, the higher the ability of existing companies to set the rules of the game and determine the market average level of prices to their own benefit.

The bargaining power of suppliers also influences the final price of a financial service. Factors that determine suppliers' power relate to their number, the degree of their service differentiation, their ability to integrate vertically and the ease by which customers can substitute their suppliers' products.

In line with suppliers' bargaining power, buyer bargaining power in an industry is affected by the number of buyers, the degree to which buyers are aware of the companies' costs, the level of their price sensitivity and their possibility to vertically integrate. An increased bargaining power of buyers is expected to lead to price discounts. By and large, such power is a characteristic of business-to-business rather than consumer financial markets.

The threat from substitutes also influences the final price of a financial service. The reason is that the higher the ability of customers to turn to substitute financial services, the higher the possibility of price wars among existing competitors.

The intensity of competition may vary across different markets as the number of competitors may differ. A global financial services firm may face different levels of competition in each country that it operates. Along with the number of competitors, the degree to which their offerings are considered as differentiated by customers will determine the intensity of rivalry in an industry. A strong competitive environment will lead many companies to adopt the existing market level of prices and adjust their prices to this level.

In the case of the banking industry in the US, despite the regulatory and capital requirements of starting a new bank, ultimately the barriers to entry are relatively low. While it is nearly impossible for new banks to enter the industry offering the trust and full range of services as a major bank, it is easy to open up a smaller bank operating on a regional level, or an internet-only bank.

Regarding the bargaining power of suppliers, capital is the primary resource of any bank and there are four major suppliers: customer deposits, mortgages and loans, mortgage-backed securities and loans from other financial institutions. The power of suppliers is different in different US states and can be characterized as medium to high.

With reference to the bargaining power of buyers, individual corporate customers have more power than retail customers. However, the internet has greatly increased the power of the retail customer since it has increased the ease and reduced the cost for these customers to compare the prices of opening/holding accounts as well as the rates offered at various banks.

As far as the threat from substitutes is concerned, the industry does not suffer any real threat of substitutes related to deposits or withdrawals. However, insurances, mutual funds and fixed income securities are some of the many banking services that are also offered by non-banking companies.

Regarding the intensity of competition, the banking industry is considered to be highly competitive as customers have difficulty in perceiving real differences among competing alternatives. We are likely to see further consolidation in the banking industry due to acquisitions and mergers.

The insurance market in the US is a vast, nationwide market and companies compete intensively for a share of it. Some insurance companies stress their low prices, others customer service and others whatever gives them an edge in the marketplace. Insurance companies such as Geico and Progressive have been especially aggressive in touting cost savings. Other companies such as State Farm and Allstate certainly compete on price but they stress service after an accident. Life insurance companies do the same thing. There are even companies that specialize in comparing policies for customers. Competition drives down excess profits and means better, cheaper options for consumers.

Apart from the above characteristics, a number of other characteristics affect the nature of a company's micro-environment and consequently, its price decision making (Avlonitis and Indounas 2004), such as the level of concentration in the market, the market size, market growth, existing profit margins in the market and the barriers to entry. For example, a high level of concentration in the market will lead to the dominance of a few companies that will set the rules of the game and pursue price leadership strategies. A small market in terms of competitors' total turnover imposes competitive pressures that lead to a downward pressure on prices. In terms of market growth, markets that have reached their maturity or decline stages are characterized by a downward pressure on prices. With regard to profit margins in the market, industries with low profit margins may force companies operating in them to impose low prices. Finally, high barriers to entry (for example, due to significant investments, legal constraints, oppositions from customers or employees, potential negative effects on corporate image) will affect the intensity of competition and, thus, the general level of market prices.

Macro-environment related characteristics

A financial service provider's macro-environment includes the political-legal, economic, social and technological environment (Farquhar and Meidan 2010). Regarding the political environment, government intervention at the national and international level is a crucial factor in financial services pricing. More specifically, the Euribor that is determined by the European Central Bank affects the interest rates that are determined by the Central Bank of each country, which in turn has an impact on the price of financial services.

As far as the economic environment is concerned, macroeconomic variables such as interest rates, exchange rates, inflation, GDP, income, government deficits among different countries have a crucial impact on the final prices of financial services firms. Significant discrepancies exist among different countries (for example, Japan or UK and most African countries) regarding labor relations, which have a direct impact on labor cost and consequently, final prices.

With reference to the social environment, cross-cultural differences among countries affect the use of specific pricing policies. High prices are regarded as an indicator of high quality in western developed countries contrary to less-developed countries, which might view high prices as taking advantage of the customer (Kotabe and Helsen 2010). Moreover, more and more customers nowadays seek more sophisticated financial services (for example, bancassurance, complex investment related services).

When it comes to the technological environment, technology has transformed the financial services industry and has permitted the introduction of new financial services that incorporate technological advantages (for example, mobile banking, internet banking) and reduce the charges and fees associated with traditional offline services. Furthermore, specialized search engines give customers the ability to search for the best price among a number of globally competing financial institutions.

The pricing process in financial services markets

The pricing process that a financial services firm may follow in order to set its prices consists of the formulation of pricing objectives, pricing methods and pricing policies (for example, Indounas 2009). Each one of these elements will now be discussed in more detail.

Pricing objectives

According to Indounas (2009), pricing objectives provide directions for general action. Most companies seem to formulate their pricing strategies by having a variety of objectives in mind given the complexity that characterizes pricing decisions. In terms of their nature, pricing objectives can be either quantitative or qualitative. The former may be measured more directly and are related to profits, market share, sales or other financial indices such as liquidity or ROA. They are expressed in financial terms or through the form of a ratio (for example, return on assets). The latter cannot be measured easily and describe the relationship between the company and its customers (for example, determination of fair prices for them), competition (for example, price stability in the market), distributors (for example, determination of prices that appeal to their needs) or even the market itself (for example, market development).

The adoption of specific pricing objectives may facilitate the adoption of other pricing objectives. For instance, acquiring new customers or avoiding offensive pricing practices such as price wars may improve the company's financial position in the long term. Similarly, customer relationship management objectives may improve the company's profitability and prosperity.

In other words, there seems to be a hierarchy of pricing objectives where achieving certain objectives can further lead to the achievement of other objectives. However, pricing objectives may also be in conflict with each other. Profit maximization, for example, may impose difficulties in stabilizing the competitive climate in a market, while an emphasis on sales maximization is expected to decrease profit margins.

As in the case of factors that affect price decision-making, the empirical studies that examine the pricing objectives of financial institutions are also limited. In particular, the empirical study that was conducted by Meidan and Chin (1995) in 45 UK building societies found that the most important pricing objectives among the companies in their sample were profit margin related objectives, while less emphasis was given to market share related objectives.

Another study carried out by Avlonitis et al. (2005) found that the insurance companies in their sample endeavored to satisfy their final customers' and distributors' needs, in order to develop their market by charging 'fair' and differentiated prices. On the other hand, banks were mainly guided by quantitative pricing objectives and more specifically by achieving satisfactory profits and return on their investments.

Pricing methods

Pricing methods describe the specific formulae used in order to reach a service's final price (Avlonitis and Indounas 2006). These formulae might range from highly sophisticated methods (for example, break-even analysis) to simple methods (for example, pricing according to the market's average prices). Moreover, the complexity of pricing decisions imposes the need to adopt more than one pricing method. For instance, a particular pricing method might be used in everyday pricing decisions, while another method may be adopted in special circumstances.

Table 17.3 presents a number of pricing methods and formulae that can be used by a financial services firm when levying prices. Given the fact that cost, competition and customers' characteristics are the main factors triggering price setting, these methods may fall into the

Table 17.3 Pricing methods followed by financial services providers

Cost-based methods	
Cost-plus pricing	Price = Unit cost + Profit margin (% of unit cost)
Target return pricing	$Price = \dfrac{[invested\ capital + (invested\ capital * ROI)]}{Forecasted\ level\ of\ sales}$
Break even analysis	$Break\ even\ quantity = \dfrac{total\ fixed\ costs}{Price - variable\ cost}$

Competition-based	
Pricing similar to competitive prices	
Pricing above competitive prices	
Pricing below competitive prices	
Price leadership	

Customer-based	
Perceived value pricing	

relevant categories, namely, cost-based, competition-based and customer based methods (for example, Avlonitis and Indounas 2006, Farquhar and Meidan 2010). Each one of them is analyzed below.

Cost-based pricing methods

Cost-based pricing methods include cost-plus pricing, target return pricing and break-even analysis. Cost-plus pricing requires the imposition of a profit margin (expressed as a percentage) on a financial service's unit cost. For instance, if the cost of offering an annual car insurance (including fixed, variable costs and the estimation of the driver's risk profile) is €350 and a gross profit margin of 10% is required, the final price will be determined at €385. Although straight-forward in its use, the main drawback of the method in question is that it disregards market conditions (Monroe 2003) and as previously noted, it is not always easy to calculate the unit cost especially for those financial services that share the same costs.

Target return pricing is based on the assumption that a desired return on investment (ROI) is required for selling a specific service. For instance, in the case of the insurance company described in the previous section, if the invested capital for offering this type of car insurance is €500,000, the desired return on investment is 20% and the forecasted level of sales is 3,000 units, the final price will be €200. The main disadvantage of this method is that, as in the case of cost-plus pricing, the market conditions tend to be disregarded. Moreover, there seems to be a vicious circle when price is based on the forecasted level of sales and the final price of a service inevitably affects total sales (Meidan 1996).

The break-even point for a final service is the point where total revenue received equals total costs. A break-even point in terms of quantity or sales is typically calculated in order for a business to determine whether it would be profitable to sell a proposed service. If the service can be sold at a price higher than the one related to the break-even point, then the firm will make a profit, while if the service is sold at a price below this point, the firm will make a loss.

In the case of the above insurance company, if the total fixed costs are €60,000, the variable costs for offering an annual medical insurance are €5,000 and a proposed price is €5,500, the break-even quantity should be 120 units, which means that the company should sell this service to at least 120 customers and achieve, thus, at least €660,000 sales in order not to have a loss. If the company can sell its service to more than 120 customers, then it will have a profit. The break-even analysis pricing method relies on: (a) the determination of prices through a cross-functional collaboration where different departments such as finance and marketing provide cost and market related data respectively and (b) a scenario analysis on the basis of which the impact of different prices on finding that minimum level of quantity or sales that are required in order to have neither profits nor loses is evaluated. To this end, contrary to the two previous cost-based pricing methods, market conditions are taken into account to a greater extent. The reason for that is that the effect of any proposed price on the level of quantity or sales requires thorough examination of market-related data such as customers' attitudes to different price levels and expected competitive reactions (Nagle et al. 2010).

Competition-based pricing methods

These methods rely on the market's average prices. The ability for a financial services firm to levy a price above these prices is a function of the intensity of competition in the market and the degree of its service differentiation (Ehrlich and Fanelli 2012). If customers perceive that this differentiation is real, they would be willing to accept a higher price.

On the other hand, a lower price might be justified by the company's corporate strategy, dictating, for instance, mass penetration in the market or targeting a niche market that is price sensitive. It may be also the best alternative when the company has managed to achieve significant cost advantages over its rivals, which permit the offering of lower prices than the competitors'.

Apart from this distinction of pricing similar, above or below the market's average prices, a financial services firm, which is the market leader, may also adopt the method of price leadership (Monroe 2003). This scenario may be the case in oligopolistic markets where a small minority of companies (or even one company) may have managed to dominate the market due to cost or technological advantages or even due to differentiated offerings. For instance, the international banking industry is characterized by the dominance of a few large companies, which set the rules of the game, leaving no other alternative for smaller companies than to follow their price initiatives. The decision to be a price leader may also be made, not by the company itself but rather by its competitors that may decide to follow its prices.

Customer-based pricing methods

In order to follow this method, the value that customers attach to the financial service needs to be examined. Formal marketing research is required in order to estimate the value associated with a financial service. Value represents the relationship between the costs and benefits associated with consuming a financial service (Farquhar and Meidan 2010). However, apart from the monetary cost, other types of costs include the psychological, effort and journey time cost. On the basis of this method, every characteristic of the service is translated into benefits and is priced accordingly. The more benefits associated with a service, the higher its value and, thus, the higher its final price. For instance, an annual fiduciary deposit may be offered at a standard interest rate by a bank with the only requirement not to withdraw the initial capital before the expiry date. However, if such a requirement does not exist or if the customer has the ability to get his interest on a monthly basis rather than waiting for the end of the first year, the total value that the customer experiences in terms of the benefits offered is higher. In this situation, the bank is expected to increase its price accordingly by offering a lower interest rate.

A study conducted by Avlonitis and Indounas (2006) among 17 banks and 29 insurance companies operating in Greece, revealed that the most widely-used pricing method by both types of companies was pricing according to the market average prices due to the intense competition that they were facing in their markets. By contrast, the least used method was the target return pricing method, mainly due to the perceived difficulty related to its practical implementation.

Pricing policies

Pricing policies refer to the way that the final price is presented to customers. Thus, after reaching a price through adopting a specific pricing method, a pricing policy will aid the company to levy the specific price offered to customers. The basic pricing policies that can be followed by a financial services provider are list pricing, differentiated pricing, negotiated pricing, discount pricing, price bundling and commission based pricing (for example, Avlonitis and Indounas 2007, Ehrlich and Fanelli 2012, Estelami 2012, Nejad and Estelami 2012). Each one of these policies is analyzed in the following sections and presented in Table 17.4.

Table 17.4 Pricing policies followed by financial services providers

List pricing
Differentiated pricing
Negotiated pricing
Discount pricing
Price bundling
Commission based pricing

List pricing policy relies on setting one price without differentiating it across the different market segments that the company may target. Its basic advantage is the ease associated with its practical implementation. For instance, most banks have pre-determined interest rates for the different types of savings accounts or loans that they offer in the market. Similarly, an investment company has set standard commissions on its different categories of mutual funds or bonds (Ehrlich and Fanelli 2012).

Differerentiated pricing relates to offering different prices to different categories of customers and is used extensively by financial services providers (Calomiris and Pornrojnangkool 2009). By and large, price differentiation relies on the customers' demographic, psychographic and behavioral profile. For example, a bank may offer a better interest rate for a fiduciary deposit to a customer that has a long-lasting relationship with the bank. Similarly, an insurance company will set a higher price for a private medical insurance to an older customer than a younger one, due to higher levels of risk.

The extreme case of differentiated pricing is negotiated pricing (Avlonitis and Indounas 2007). This policy is used extensively in business-to-business contexts such as corporate banking where each individual customer is set a different price on the basis of their personal characteristics and buying behavior. Prices for business loans, for example, will be set on the basis of the unique needs and characteristics of each business client that desires such a type of loan.

Price discounts are used by financial institutions in order to gain short-term benefits such as temporary sales increases. A bank may choose to offer a specific type of credit card at no fee for a short period of time (for example, one month) in order to attract new customers. Similarly, a mutual fund may be offered at a very low commission for a specific period of time in order to expand the existing clientele basis. A specific form of discount pricing is loss-leader pricing, where one service is offered at a very low price (close to its cost) in order to attract customers and entice them to buy other services at higher prices. Financial providers have traditionally used this policy in the field of student-related services (Hughes 1990).

A financial services provider may offer a bundle of services, which would not be purchased individually. Chapter 18 on price bundling discusses in much more detail the role of the specific pricing policy in financial services markets through providing many examples on how financial institutions may profit from its adoption. For instance, banks offer a variety of services simultaneously when opening a new savings account (for example, debit card, credit card at a premium rate, internet banking). The basic advantage for the customer is that they receive a lower price than if they obtained all these services individually. The advantage for the firm is that it can combine high and low profit services and services that share the same costs and are managed more effectively.

In addition to the above policies, a financial services firm may also use the policy of commission-based pricing. This policy is used in all types of investment related services in that a customer pays a fee when buying or selling this service. The financial institution may also impose an annual fee for managing this service. Similarly, insurance companies reward their agents and distributors with a commission that is calculated on the final price that a customer should pay.

Pricing new financial services

Financial markets have witnessed the introduction of many new innovations in recent years. One of the most difficult decisions facing a financial institution is how to price a new service in its market (Nejad and Estelami 2012). Certainly, the pricing process that was described in the previous section can be equally applied in the case of new financial services. However, there are also some pricing strategies that can be particularly useful in the case of new services. All classic marketing and pricing textbooks describe three basic strategies for pricing a new product or service: skimming pricing (i.e., a high initial price), penetration pricing (i.e., a low initial price) and pricing similar to competitive prices (for example, Monroe 2003, Nagle et al. 2010, Palmer 2008).

Skimming pricing relates to a high initial price in order to achieve maximum short-term financial results. Its basic principle is to gain the highest possible price from each market segment; beginning with the highest value segments and moving on to the lower value ones. This strategy is the preferred option in the case of an innovative, high quality, differentiated service, which conveys a prestigious image and gives the company the opportunity to cover the costs of developing the new service and reduce the high initial price in the future. Competitors should not be able to enter the market easily and undercut the high initial price, while a significant number of customers should exist in the market and be willing to sacrifice low price for high quality.

On the other hand, penetration pricing relates to a low initial price and is the preferred alternative when a company offers undifferentiated services, targeting price sensitive customers, especially in a mass scale. Moreover, this strategy aims at enticing new customers to try the new service, achieving satisfactory market share and discouraging the entrance of new competitors in the market. Furthermore, the strategy in question may be the preferred option when the company has the ability to reduce the unit cost as volume increases. Finally, pricing similar to competitors is the preferred option in the case of a market characterized by intensive competition and lack of differentiation among competing services.

Nejad and Estelami (2012) examined the optimal pricing strategy for financial innovations through a simulation based approach. They demonstrated that when high degrees of price sensitivity exist and a short time horizon for competitive entry is expected, a low initial price is the optimal strategy. On the other hand, when price sensitivity is low and the expected time horizon for competitive entry is long, a high initial price would be the best choice for a financial institution.

Conclusion

The aim of this chapter was to analyze how financial institutions price the services that they render in their markets. The chapter focused on four main topics that relate to the unique characteristics of financial services pricing, the fundamental factors that affect price decision-making, the pricing process that can be used and the way new financial services in particular are priced. Regarding the unique characteristics of financial services pricing, the increased role of the risk and the broader macro-environment along with the fact that it is difficult to estimate the unit cost were highlighted. The cross-subsidization phenomenon across different customers was discussed. With reference to the factors that affect price decision-making, it was pointed out that they may fall into two large categories, namely, company related factors and market related factors. The former include organizational and service characteristics while the latter consist of the company's micro- and macro-environment. As far as the pricing process is concerned, the pricing objectives, methods and policies that a financial services provider may follow were presented. When it comes to new financial services pricing, the three alternative pricing strategies, namely, skimming pricing, penetration pricing and pricing similar to competitors were analyzed.

What was also pointed out in this chapter, were the limited number of empirical studies that have been conducted in the field of financial services pricing. To this end, there are prominent research directions for the future. For instance, future research could investigate how the use of technology and modern information systems may affect pricing decisions. Customers' price awareness may be increased even more due to the role of the internet, while the application of CRM techniques due to the abundance of customers' personal data may permit financial institutions to offer tailor-made services and customized prices. Furthermore, does online pricing entail challenges that offline pricing is not associated with? A contingency approach to studying financial services pricing may be another fruitful future research direction. For example, how does the pricing process differ across different cultural or national contexts? Are specific company and market related factors more important in large or small financial services providers? How pricing decisions are actually made in insurance companies versus banks or investment brokers. The examination of these issues may contribute significantly to the existing literature, whereas it may also help managers responsible for setting prices for financial services to make pricing decisions more profitably and effectively.

References

Argouslidis, P. and Indounas, K., 2010. Exploring the role of relationship pricing in industrial export settings: empirical evidence from the UK. *Industrial Marketing Management*, 39(3), pp. 460–72.

Avlonitis, G. and Indounas, K., 2004. The impact of market structure on pricing objectives of service firms. *Journal of Product and Brand Management*, 13(5), pp. 343–58.

——, 2006. How are prices set? An exploratory investigation in the Greek services sector. *Journal of Product and Brand Management*, 15(3), pp. 203–13.

——, 2007. An empirical examination of the pricing policies and their antecedents in the services sector. *European Journal of Marketing*, 41(7/8), pp. 740–64.

Avlonitis, G., Indounas, K. and Gounaris, S., 2005. Pricing objectives over the service life cycle: some empirical evidence. *European Journal of Marketing*, 39(5/6), pp. 696–714.

Calomiris, C.W. and Pornrojnangkool, T., 2009. Relationship banking and the pricing of financial services. *Journal of Financial Services Research*, 35, pp. 189–224.

Colgate, M. and Hedge, R., 2001. An investigation into the switching process in retail banking services. *International Journal of Bank Marketing*, 19(4/5), pp. 201–12.

Diamantopoulos, D., 1991. Pricing theory and evidence: a literature review. In M.J. Baker, ed. *Perspectives on marketing management*. Sussex: John Wiley & Sons, pp. 61–193.

Ehrlich, E. and Fanelli, D., 2012. *The financial services marketing handbook: tactics and techniques that produce results*. 2nd ed. Bloomberg Financial. Sussex: John Wiley & Sons.

Estelami, H., 2008. Consumer use of the price-quality cue in financial services. *Journal of Product and Brand Management*, 17(3), pp. 197–208.

——, 2012. *Marketing financial services*. 2nd ed. Indianapolis: Dog Ear Publishing.

Estelami, H. and De Maeyer, P., 2010. An exploratory study of divided pricing effects on financial service quality expectations. *Journal of Financial Services Marketing*, 15(1), pp. 19–31.

Farquhar, J. and Meidan, A., 2010. *Marketing financial services*. 2nd ed. London: Palgrave MacMillan.

Howcroft, B. and Lavis, J.C., 1989. Pricing in retail banking. *International Journal of Bank Marketing*, 7(1), pp. 3–7.

Hughes, M., 1990. Pricing. In C. Ennew, T. Watkins and M. Wright. *Marketing financial services*. Oxford: Heinemann Professional Publishing, Ch. 6.

Hung, S.J., 2011. An integrated system of activity-based quality optimization and economic incentive schemes for a global supply chain. *International Journal of Production Research*, 49(24), pp. 7337–59.

Ibrahim, M.E. and Saheem, W.H., 2013. Managers' motivational antecedents to support activity-based costing systems. *Journal of Applied Business Research*, 29(3), pp. 935–43.

Indounas, K. 2006. Making effective pricing decisions. *Business Horizons*, 49(5), pp. 415–24.

——, 2009. Successful industrial service pricing. *Journal of Business and Industrial Marketing*, 24(2), pp. 86–97.

Indounas, K. and Roth, S., 2012. Antecedents and consequences of strategic price management: An analysis in the New Zealand industrial service context. *Australasian Marketing Journal*, 20(2), pp. 113–21.

Kangis, P. and Passa, V., 1997. Awareness of service charges and its influence on customer expectations and perceptions of quality in banking. *Journal of Services Marketing*, 11(2), pp. 105–17.

Kotabe, M. and Helsen, K., 2010. *Global marketing management*. 5th ed. New Jersey: John Wiley & Sons.

Kotler, P. and Armstrong, G., 2012. *Principles of marketing*. 14th ed. Cloth: Prentice Hall.

Meidan, C.A., 1996. *Marketing financial services*. London: MacMillan Business.

Meidan, C.A. and Chin, A.C., 1995. Mortgage-pricing determinants: a comparative investigation of national, regional and local building societies. *International Journal of Bank Marketing*, 13(3), pp. 3–11.

Monroe, K.B., 2003. *Making profitable decisions*. Irwin: Mc-Graw Hill.

Nagle, T.T., Hogan, J. and Zale, J., 2010. *The strategy and tactics of pricing: A guide to growing more profitably*. 5th ed. New Jersey: Prentice Hall.

Nejad, M. and Estelami, H., 2012. Pricing financial services innovations. *Journal of Financial Services Marketing*, 17(2), pp. 120–34.

Oyelere, P.B. and Turner, J.D., 2000. A survey of transfer pricing practices in UK banks and building societies. *European Business Review*, 12(2), pp. 93–99.

Palmer, A., 2008. *Principles of services marketing*. London: McGraw-Hill.

Papastathopoulou, P., Avlonitis, G. and Indounas, K., 2001. The initial stages of new service development: a case study from the Greek banking sector. *Journal of Financial Services Marketing*, 6(2), pp. 147–61.

Porter, M., 1980. *Competitive strategy*. New York: Free Press.

Santonen, T., 2007. Price sensitivity as an indicator of customer defection in retail banking. *International Journal of Bank Marketing*, 25(1), pp. 39–55.

Tse, A.C.B., 2001. How much more are consumers willing to pay for a higher level of a service? A preliminary survey. *Journal of Services Marketing*, 15(1), pp. 11–17.

Walker, O.C., Boyd, Jr. H.W., Mullins, J. and Larreche, J.C., 2006. 6th ed. *Marketing strategy: a decision-focused approach*. Irwin: McGraw Hill.

18

Price bundling

A smart pricing strategy for banking

Wei Ke, Georg Wuebker and Jens Baumgarten

Introduction

In September 2011, Bank of America, squeezed by the debit interchange fee cap introduced by the Durbin Amendment of the Dodd-Frank Wall Street Reform and Consumer Protection Act, announced its intention to impose a $5 monthly fee to its debit card users (Rauch 2011). This brute force change in debit card pricing gave rise to a grassroots campaign (Lopez 2011), which quickly gained traction through social networks and caught the attention of mainstream media. Bank of America was not the only bank involved in this "debit fee fiasco"; Wells Fargo, JP Morgan Chase, Regions, SunTrust, Citibank and PNC all reportedly planned to introduce a $3–$5 monthly fee to their debit card users. As public backlash grew, a consumer protest movement called "Bank Transfer Day" (Pfeifer and Reckard 2011) sprang up and called for voluntary switches from retail banks to not-for-profit credit unions by 5 November 2011. The result was that on 1 November 2011, Bank of America announced that it would cancel its plan to charge its debit card users and the other banks backed off at around the same time (Sidel 2011). In January 2012, Bank of America CEO, Brian Moynihan, acknowledged in the fourth quarter earnings call that the "debit fee fiasco" resulted in a 20 percent jump in account closings at Bank of America (Kim 2012). Meanwhile, the National Association of Federal Credit Union reported a 700 percent increase in new account openings at affiliated credit unions in October 2011, compared with the same period the previous year (FOXBusiness, 2011).

The reason imposing a debit card fee caused so much consumer backlash is simple: Bank of America and its peers in the banking industry made it so easy for their customers to realise that they were worse off after the fee hike. Regardless of the theoretical frameworks on bounded rationality, pricing psychology, or choice behaviours, when the only thing that changes for the debit card is the price – while all the non-price features would remain the same as before – it would take minimal mental accounting for a customer to realise that they are going to be in a state much worse off than before. None of the banks were offering to replace the debit cards in the customers' wallets with a new one. If one could argue that banks did not know enough about the theories of consumer pricing psychology, there was certainly no excuse for them not to draw lessons from a similar incident that happened only a few weeks before in a similarly consumer-facing industry. Netflix drew consumer ire by announcing its intention to drop DVD rental from its standard monthly plan while maintaining the plan's monthly fee at the current level (Titlow 2011). The reason for the public backlash is simple: Netflix made it easy for its customers to realise that they were worse off when the only thing that changed in the new plan was the service level without a corresponding change in pricing.

How should banks price their products? What would they have to do when they want to change the pricing of their existing products? Banks today already face a tough macroeconomic environment with high levels of consumer debt and historically low interest rates, stricter regulatory scrutiny (for example, Dodd-Frank, SEPA, MiFID II, Basel III, to name a few), an increasingly competitive marketplace and a mistrustful and price sensitive customer base. How can banks cope with these negative market factors through smarter pricing?

If the episode of "debit fee fiasco" is any guide, the answer does not lie in changing the price alone, but in how we should re-package or adjust the values of a banking product as it is being re-priced. In other words, the answer lies in Price Bundling. It would not be hard to imagine that Bank of America's customers might react just a bit more favourably when it instead decided to introduce a new cheque/current account with the increased debit card fee already included in the monthly maintenance fee; some of its customers would like it so much that they would willingly pay for it.

A renowned case for price bundling outside the banking world comes from the software giant Microsoft. By smartly combining its applications or software into the "Office" bundle, Microsoft extended the quasi-monopoly of Word to Excel, Access and PowerPoint. The "Office" bundle became so successful that it was able to dominate with a market share of over 90 percent. What can banks learn there?

In this chapter we will discuss why price bundling is an effective pricing strategy for bank products and explain how to successfully implement price bundles. The next section gives an overview of price bundling for banking and lists its various forms. The following section addresses the rationale for price bundling, explores why price bundling is a way to increase profits, explains the advantages of bundling from the bank's and the customer's perspectives and discusses how bundling can be a win-win proposition that benefits both the bank and its customers. Unfortunately, the advantages of price bundling are not always so easily achievable and therefore we use the subsequent section to describe a customer-centric process banks should take to successfully implement price bundling. Finally, in the last section, we discuss several organisational change management considerations to ensure the successful implementation of a bundling strategy.

Price bundling in banking

Price bundling is not in itself a new concept to banks, especially in the retail banking business. Simply put, price bundling is about combining multiple banking product or service features into a bundle and imposing a maintenance fee for the entire bundle.[1] The end result of bundling is a banking solution that hopefully satisfies the financial needs of a customer. The right bundling leads to higher customer and frontline banker acceptance; ideally, it should also lead to a higher profit to the bank. Banks would normally construct such bundles by using a core product (for example, a cheque/current account) as the lead feature, coupled with auxiliary products (for example, a credit card or travel insurance) or services (for example, concierge service or notary public). For example, NatWest, a UK retail bank, offers three packaged accounts under the Select brand and a premium Black account. These current accounts offer different types of insurance (for example, travel, mobile phone and car breakdown cover), discounts on leisure activities, identity theft assistance, concierge service, etc. Figure 18.1 illustrates a list of typical product or service options in a banking bundle.

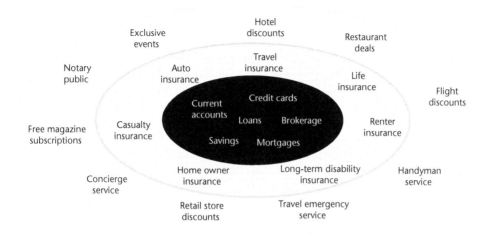

Figure 18.1 Optional elements in a banking bundle

A core banking product can itself be a bundle, this adds much flexibility to the way banking bundles can be constructed. For example, a cheque/current account is typically configured by bundling such products and services as online/mobile banking access, salary direct deposit, overdraft protection, electronic bill payments, etc.

Price bundling can take many forms in practice. Stremersch and Tellis (2002), and more recently, Venkatesh and Mahajan (2009) provide good surveys and syntheses of the academic literature on general forms of bundling. There are two key underlying dimensions that can be used to classify the various forms of bundling strategies: bundling focus (product/price bundling) and bundling form (pure/mixed). To complement the literature on pre-configured bundles, Hitt and Chen (2005) studied "customised bundling" which allows customers to create their own bundles by combining individual product/service features. They demonstrated through a stylised model that customised bundling is appropriate for budget constrained customers who value only a relatively small set of offered products.

All of the applicable forms for banking have good analogies in other industries. Five common examples are mixed bundles, non-linear price bundling, targeted bundles, channel-based bundles and family plans (see Figure 18.2).

Innovative bundling	Mixed bundling	Non-linear price bundling	Targeted bundles	Channel based bundles	Family plans
Global best practices	McDonald's	BahnCard	Apple Student Discount	Hilton Hotel Chain	Verizon Wireless ShareEverything
Banking best practices	Credit Suisse Bonviva	Deutsche Bank Savings Accounts	Postbank Card for Lawyers	HSBC vs. First Direct	VolksbankFamily Loyalty Bonus

Figure 18.2 Forms of price bundling

Mixed bundles are pre-configured bundles with stand-alone add-on options for purchase. At a McDonald's restaurant, one can purchase an Extra Value Meal (i.e. pre-configured bundles containing a specific type of burger or sandwich bundled with fries and a soft drink) and stand-alone add-ons such as an ice cream sundae or a milkshake. Similarly, Credit Suisse offers Bonviva banking bundles that consist of current accounts, credit/debit cards and savings accounts in one package, while also allowing a customer to open other stand-alone banking or investment accounts.

Non-linear price bundles leverage non-linear price structures and consist of price discounts on the same level of offered product features or services. Deutsche Bahn's BahnCard programme combines varying degrees of discounts on future train travel and on other services such as car-sharing for three levels of annual membership fees. For different monthly maintenance fees that a customer would pay up-front, Deustche Bank offers different interest rate bonuses for its savings accounts as well as different discounts or waivers on incidental fees (for example, ATM withdrawals, overdrafts, etc.) for its current accounts.

Targeted bundles cater to a specific customer segment. Computer and consumer electronics giant Apple offers product packages specifically configured for students and assigns sales representatives to university campuses to serve this key demographic. Similarly, Postbank of Germany offers financial product packages that meet specific needs of certain professions, for example, lawyers.

Channel-based bundles are bundles that differ by distribution channel. Depending on the booking channel (i.e. hilton.com, a discount travel website, a brick and mortar travel agency, etc.), the Hilton hotel chain offers rooms that combine with different amenities such as breakfast and spa discounts, often at a different room rate. Similarly, HSBC offers more attractive rates but more restricted access for its online/telephone-only First Direct product suite, compared to its branch-based product suite.

Family plans represent the ultimate bundle that links all products and services across a group of customers (often members of the same household) through a common pricing structure or currency. Verizon Wireless, one of the largest mobile service providers in the US, offers a ShareEverything plan that allows the sharing of mobile data allowances across devices (for example, smartphones, tablets and wifi hotspots) owned by different family members, all for a simple monthly fee. Through its Family Loyalty Bonus scheme, Volksbank of Germany allows customers who belong to the same household to pay one monthly fee for all banking services and to build up reward points and bonuses in the same pool.

In this chapter, we will only focus on two basic, stylised forms of bundling to explain the concept: pure price bundling and mixed bundling.

The rationale for price bundling

Why is price bundling a way to increase profits? What are the advantages of bundling from the bank's perspective, as well as from the customer's perspective? Can price bundling be a win-win proposition that benefits both the bank and its customers?

As initially pointed out by Adams and Yellen (1976) and later revisited by Wuebker (1998) and Simon and Wuebker (1999), price bundling transfers the untapped willingness-to-pay from one product to another product. We use a stylised example to illustrate this concept. We refer the reader to Salinger (1995) for a more general example. Suppose a bank wants to bundle its current account product with another product such as a credit card. Suppose through market research, the bank has identified four customer segments based on their differing willingness-to-pay in terms of a monthly maintenance fee for these products (the current account and the credit card) respectively. Without loss of generality, we simplify the case to one customer representing each of the four segments.

Table 18.1 shows the revealed willingness-to-pay ("WTP") from market research. In the standard definition of willingness-to-pay, a customer would agree to a purchase when the price is lower than or equal to their willingness-to-pay.

To further simplify the case, we assume the costs of offering these products are zero, so revenue optimisation and profit optimisation are equivalent and would reach the same optimal price point. What are some of the ways the bank can bundle (or not bundle) its products? What is the revenue-optimal price point for each of the two products in each bundling scenario?

There are three possible ways of bundling the two products, as summarised in Table 18.2: not bundle at all and sell the two products individually ("no price bundle"), bundle the current account and the credit card together and offer the bundle as the only option for the customers ("pure price bundling"), sell the bundle as well as the two individual products ("mixed price bundling").

It turns out that not bundling at all is a clear loser in terms of total profit, while mixed bundling is able to do a bit better than pure bundling. Let us take a closer look at each option to understand why this is the case.

No price bundle: the optimal price in this scenario (from evaluating all possible pricing scenarios) is $8.00 for the current account and $8.50 for the credit card. At these prices, exactly two units of the current account and two units of the credit card are sold by comparing the prices with the willingness-to-pay of each customer for the corresponding product. The total resulting profit is ($8.00 × 2: customers 1 & 2) + ($8.50 × 2: customers 3 & 4) = $33.00. Figure 18.3 gives a graphical representation of the demand outcome under the optimal prices.

Pure price bundling: in this scenario, the bank only sells a single bundle consisting of both the current account and the credit card. The optimal price for pure price bundling turns out to be $10.50 and all four customers would buy the bundle. Consequently, the profit is now

Table 18.1 Willingness-to-pay by segment for current account, credit card and the bundle

Customer segment	Willingness-to-pay in monthly maintenance fee		
	Current account	Credit card	Bundle (current account + credit card)
1	$9.00	$1.50	$10.50
2	$8.00	$5.00	$13.00
3	$4.50	$8.50	$13.00
4	$2.50	$9.00	$11.50

Table 18.2 Revenue-optimal scenarios

Pricing Strategy	Optimal Prices			Demand			Profit
	Current account	Credit card	Bundle	Current account	Credit card	Bundle	
No price bundle	$8.00	$8.50	–	2	2	–	$33.00
Pure price bundling	–	–	$10.50	–	–	4	$42.00
Mixed price bundling	$9.00	$9.00	$13.00	1	1	2	$44.00

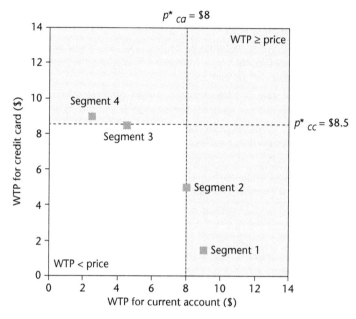

Figure 18.3 Optimal pricing for the "no price bundle" scenario

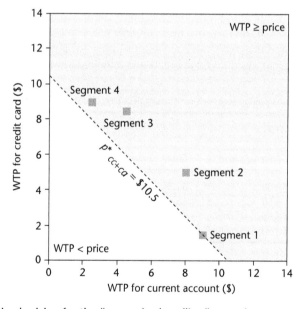

Figure 18.4 Optimal pricing for the "pure price bundling" scenario

$10.50 × 4 = $42.00, or an increase of 27.3% over the "no price bundle" scenario. Figure 18.4 gives a graphical representation of the demand outcome under the optimal prices.

Mixed price bundling: this type of bundling is more profitable than "pure price bundling". Pricing optimally at $9.00 for the current account, $9.00 for the credit card and $13.00 for the current account and credit card bundle would increase profits by 33.3% over the "no price

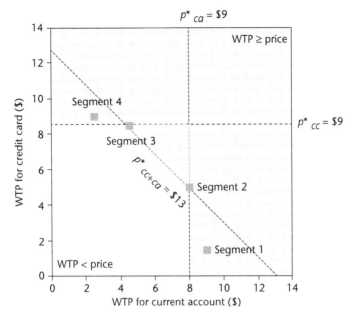

Figure 18.5 Optimal pricing for the "mixed price bundling" scenario

bundle" scenario and 4.8% over the "pure price bundling" scenario. Total profit in mixed price bundling is ($9.00 × 1, customer 1) + ($9.00 × 1, customer 4) + ($13.00 × 2, customer 2 & 3) = $44.00. Figure 18.5 gives a graphical representation of the demand outcome under the optimal prices.

Customers with willingness-to-pay in the rectangles X and Y will become buyers of one of the two products.

The reason price bundling works is because customer willingness-to-pay can be aggregated in a way that allows the excess (positive) consumer surplus from one product to be transferred to compensate for the deficit (negative) consumer surplus in another product. We define "consumer surplus" as the difference between the customer willingness-to-pay and the retail price for a product or service. Through price bundling, there is opportunity to build up the excess consumer surpluses from the products that have them to make up for the deficit consumer surpluses in the other products, while still ensuring the overall willingness-to-pay for the entire bundle to be greater than the retail price of the bundle. Customers would thus purchase the bundle even though their individual willingness-to-pay for some of the products in the bundle (i.e. those products with a deficit consumer surplus) could be lower than the corresponding retail price. Even better, there may be room to further increase the price and profit if there is excess consumer surplus for the bundle under current pricing. This is the reason "mixed price bundling" in our example is able to achieve additional profit increase over "pure price bundling".

Besides the much improved profit, price bundling also reduces the complexity in managing the customers based on their purchase type (Schmalensee 1984). When the products are sold separately in the "no price bundle" scenario, there are four customer types based on a total combination of buyers versus non-buyers for current accounts versus credit cards. In the "pure price bundling" scenario, the bank only needs to worry about two customer types, based on whether they buy or not buy the bundle.

Mixed price bundling, on the other hand, creates extra complexity when it comes to customer purchase types because now we would have to deal with bundle buyers, single product buyers and non-buyers all at the same time. In a more positive light, however, it does allow us to categorise the customer types in a precise manner. Ultimately, the decision of whether to adopt "mixed price bundling" or "pure price bundling" rests on the outcome of a trade-off analysis between the added profit and the cost in managing the increased complexity in customer purchase dynamics. In our case here, the additional $2 in profit for "mixed price bundling" over "pure price bundling" may not be worth the trouble of the increased complexity in the product portfolio; in other cases, "mixed price bundling" may win hands down. This trade-off must be carefully examined in each case. We also refer the reader to work by Prasad et al. (2010) who used a stylised model to argue that mixed bundling would be more profitable for a portfolio of products that were neither low in marginal costs nor high in network externality. Recent work by Derdenger and Kumar (2013) used an empirical model to evaluate the performance of no bundling, pure bundling and mixed bundling. The authors found that mixed bundling dominates pure price bundling due to the effects of inter-temporal substitution as well as a greater level of flexibility offered to the customers from a mixed bundling arrangement. They also found that bundling in general serves as a substitute to network effects, when the bundled products or services are sold in two market types but are complementary to each other (for example, video game consoles and video games) and is better used when such effects are weaker.

There are several advantages for banks to adopt price bundling. Price bundling is a powerful method for profit improvement. Pricing pressure has increased considerably over the last few years on account of the growing competition from online banks. This is especially true for core products, such as cheque/current accounts and savings. By bundling these products with higher margin products or services, banks can improve their financial situation tremendously.

Price bundling leads to higher cross-selling and thus increased sales overall; this is because it gives customers additional incentives (by way of transferal of excess consumer surplus) to buy certain products or features that they would otherwise not buy on an individual basis. In our example in Table 18.2, the "no price bundle" scenario achieves the sales of 2 units for each of the two products, whereas the "pure price bundling" scenario achieves the sales of 4 units of the bundle (hence 4 units for each of the two products). Increased cross-selling means a deeper customer relationship and therefore a more loyal and usually more profitable customer (as discussed by Yu and Harrison in Chapter 9).

Price bundling lets banks mitigate price competition because the bundled products are not always directly comparable with competitive offerings, this makes direct price comparison difficult in the customer's mind. At the same time, bundling provides an opportunity for banks to transform into solution-oriented system providers and thus shifts the competition from the individual product level (many) to the system level (few).

Price bundling (only "pure price bundling") may also help reduce costs and sales complexity. Banks can realise synergy on cost and complexity and pass it on to their customers in the form of lower prices. One example that demonstrates this is actually in the automotive industry: Daimler Chrysler used bundling to reduce the number of possible combinations of optional equipment components. This lowered production costs and enabled Chrysler to reduce the price of the respective models by around 10 percent. The lower prices helped the car manufacturer to tap into new segments and significantly increase revenue and profit. Banks too can achieve similar synergy through price bundling, due to the fact that bundled products are sold by design in the same process as opposed to different discrete processes and thus personnel and transaction costs can be saved.

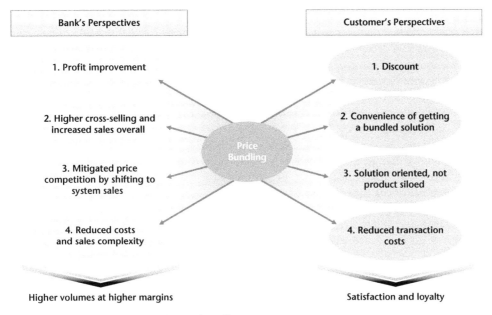

Figure 18.6 The advantages of price bundling

Let us not forget about the customer's perspective. Price bundling has several advantages for customers, cost advantages being the most obvious. Enabling customers to purchase everything from one bank at a lower price leads to increased customer satisfaction and loyalty in a solution-oriented approach to financial services, as well as an increased sense of comfort and convenience from the "one stop shop" purchase experience. Figure 18.6 summarises the main advantages of price bundling from both the bank's and the customer's perspectives.

Creating and implementing successful bundles

The advantages of price bundling, as shown in the previous section, are not always so easily achievable. If banks want to use price bundling as a strategy to grow profitably, they would have to follow a customer-centric process.

Step 1: understand your customers and design bundles to satisfy their needs

The key success factor for price bundling rests on a good balance between the bank's interests against those of the customers. From the bank's perspective, it may be a good idea to combine attractive, high demand, "must have" products or services with unattractive, low demand ones, in order to increase the sales of the latter (as we have demonstrated in the example previously). It is here that banks can learn a lot from other industries (for example, Microsoft Office or McDonald's Value Meals). If the bundle contains too many unattractive products or services, customers may opt out and try to buy the attractive products separately. For example, if McDonald's were to offer coffee as part of a Value Meal bundle that already contains a burger, fries and a soda, the customers would likely stop buying the bundle altogether and just buy the burger (the lead product) separately. It is therefore crucial to have an optimal mix between the attractive products and the unattractive ones in a bundle.

To achieve this, banks must strive to understand the needs and the behaviours of their customers and clearly define target customer segments. Building bundles that allow customers to immediately tell which is intended for whom is vital to the success of the bundling strategy. The telecommunications industry serves as a benchmark. In June 2012, Verizon Wireless, the largest US wireless carrier, switched its mobile phone plans from ones that differentiate on talking minutes to ones that differentiate on data usage and device connections (Albanesius 2012). Verizon recognised that the arrival of smartphones has changed the way its customers use the mobile phone service. Internet data usage and the ability to link multiple devices under the same phone plan are what drive customer needs today, instead of talking minutes of the pre-smartphone days. As a result, the new Verizon phone plan ("Share Everything Plan") allows its customers to select the total amount of data they wish to download each month, while bundling in unlimited talk time in every plan.

When creating bundles, it is important to explore the emotional linkage between the bank and the customer as this increases customer loyalty and decreases the feeling that the product offerings at the current bank are easily substitutable with those of a different bank. The reader will recall from Figure 18.1 a typical list of products or services a bank has at its disposal for constructing bundles. Often, the individual features of the core products can be similar due to commoditisation (for example, all cheque/current accounts tend to have direct deposit and bill payment functions). Even auxiliary services such as concierge services and travel insurance, etc., can be indistinguishable from the competition. In the absence of product concepts that shift existing paradigms (for example, Apple iPhone), what fundamentally allows a bank to differentiate itself from its competitors would come from how these various product/service building blocks are configured and combined into a bundle.

Step 2: construct and evaluate bundle options

Candidate bundles can be constructed and evaluated through customer research as well as internal expert judgment. A good starting point is for the product managers to list all potential bundle features (products and services that make up a bundle) in a brainstorming session or a workshop setting. It is important to have a good mix of attractive, high demand features and unattractive, low demand features in the list. At this point, the notion of feature "attractiveness" is primarily based on the judgments of the product managers. We could use focus groups or a mini quantitative survey to validate whether the "attractiveness assumptions" are correct. These exercises are also useful to help us shorten the feature list by taking out features that are simply too unattractive (refer again to the McDonald's burger-coffee bundling scenario we described earlier).

The ultimate measure of feature attractiveness is through feature-level willingness-to-pay. A more attractive feature should command a higher willingness-to-pay and as such is by definition more valuable than a less attractive one. There are several methods we can employ to measure feature-level willingness-to-pay, each having its advantages and disadvantages. For a more academic treatment of the subject, we refer the reader to the survey article on measuring willingness-to-pay by Breidert et al. (2006). The authors proposed a classification framework for methods that measure willingness-to-pay. Revealed preference can be measured by market data and from experiments (such as laboratory experiments, field experiments and auctions). Stated preference can be measured using direct questioning (such as expert judgments and customer surveys) and indirect questioning (such as the use of conjoint analysis and discrete choice analysis).

To complement the literature, Jedidi et al. (2003) proposed a general empirical methodology, through the use of computationally intensive Markov Chain Monte Carlo method ("MCMC"), to measure heterogeneity in reservation prices for bundles.

In practice, we often find that financial institutions tend to conduct field experiments in a sporadic manner, if at all, in order to observe revealed preferences for willingness-to-pay. Historical data points that capture the outcome of uncontrolled "natural" experiments are usually biased and should not be used as the sole source of measure for willingness-to-pay. The stated preference approach has the advantage of being forward-looking by allowing researchers and practitioners to prime respondents into a scenario that they may not have experienced historically. In addition, it leverages experimental design principles to ensure the efficient, balanced capture of willingness-to-pay preferences. They are, however, not without their own drawbacks. We discuss three stated preference methods in detail.

Direct questioning in a customer survey

The simplest method is to directly ask the customers how much they are willing to pay for each feature and the combined bundle. However, this method has several drawbacks. Direct price questioning tends to artificially increase price awareness. It is also a real possibility for a few "smarter" respondents to game the survey process. The end result for both is a lower-than-actual price for each of the surveyed features. Direct price questioning may be useful as part of the mini quantitative survey to help validate feature attractiveness and shorten the initial long list of bundling features.

Choice-based conjoint analysis

Marketing research shows that choice-based conjoint is a much better method in understanding how customers trade off (often in a hidden, latent manner) the bundled features in a purchase decision. A typical choice-based conjoint exercise consists of a series of simulated shopping scenarios that the survey respondents would have to evaluate. In each scenario, several bundle options, constructed from the short list of features obtained previously, are shown based on orthogonal experimental design principles. All bundle options should also have a price tag, for example, monthly maintenance fee for the entire bundle. The survey respondent could also select no purchase if they do not like any of the presented options. A well designed conjoint exercise would present bundle options in such a way that a clear winner is not immediately obvious, this would then force the survey respondent to make trade-offs between several options based on an evaluation of feature attractiveness against bundle pricing. Figure 18.7 shows a sample choice-based conjoint exercise.

An algorithm is then used to estimate the utility of each bundle feature. Feature utility corresponds to the perceived value of the feature; normally it has a positive sign. Price, on the other hand, would have a negative utility associated with it. Linking the positive utility of a feature against the negative utility of a price allows us to compute the break-even utility value as expressed in price, a much more accurate approach to measure feature-level willingness-to-pay. Utilities can be estimated simplistically at the segment or population level using classic methods like Maximum Likelihood Estimation on a Multinomial Logit functional form (Train 2009); they can also be estimated at the individual respondent level using the Hierarchical Bayesian algorithm (Allenby and Rossi 2006). The latter method would give a lot more flexibility in discovering individual differences on feature attractiveness and willingness-to-pay, these

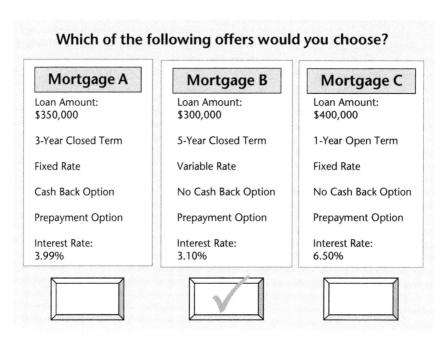

Figure 18.7 A sample choice-based conjoint exercise

individual differences then form the basis for discovered customer segmentation. Utility values are ultimately fed into a market demand simulator to help forecast demand of a given line-up of bundles.

Choice-based conjoint does have a drawback. Only a limited set of features can be used and reliably measured due to both computational restrictions and consumer psychology. Even with an orthogonal design, adding more features would in general increase the complexity of the design of the conjoint exercise and increase computational burden in utility estimation later on. Consumer psychology also indicates that a typical customer can only account for a limited number of features (typically a maximum of six features on average for bank products) in making purchase decisions. Having to consider more features would increase choice difficulty, which research such as the seminal work by Iyengar and Lepper (2000) shows would lead to the customer simply giving up on making any choice, hence default to no purchase.

Expert judgment

A third methodology to measure feature-level willingness-to-pay is expert judgment. This method does not rely on customer surveys and is therefore the least expensive to execute. The idea behind expert judgment is the recognition that stakeholders at a bank or a financial institution would already have sufficient insights and knowledge of market reaction in different price scenarios. Typically, 10–15 experts from different departments of the bank (for example, sales, product management, pricing management, etc.) would come together in a workshop and do a structured, multi-step exercise where they would individually estimate the customer willingness-to-pay for different bundle options. The individual estimations are fed into a computer simulation model and the results are then discussed. It is common to have discrepancies in the estimates and this is why discussion is one of the key steps in this method.

Participants exchange the reasons for their estimations, which in consecutive rounds gradually improve until consensus is reached.

From our experience in working on small bundling issues, expert judgment results can come close to the findings of more complex methods, as long as the right people – those who have direct knowledge or interaction with the customers, such as frontline sales staff, marketing, and product management – are included in the workshop. However, to construct more complex bundles, sophisticated methods such as choice-based conjoint analysis are more appropriate.

Step 3: optimise and finalise the bundles

The methods we mentioned in the previous step to help construct and evaluate bundles all contain a market demand simulator as a key output. The simulator allows us to play with what-if scenarios on the feature configuration and pricing of a bundle line-up in order to forecast the market demand of this line-up. Attaching a nonlinear constrained optimisation algorithm to the simulator would then, in theory, give us the ability to find the optimal pricing or feature combination in an automated and scientific way. Our experience shows, however, that we should not rely solely on the automated output of the optimisation algorithm. At the end of the day, bundle optimisation is an exercise that balances science with art. Feature attractiveness is a subjective measure and so is willingness-to-pay for the overall bundle and the features therein. What tends to work well in practice is to: (1) use the insights we have gathered from the research methods in the previous step on feature attractiveness and willingness-to-pay to manually construct a few candidate bundle line-ups, (2) input those line-ups into the market demand simulator, (3) use the optimisation engine to find the best profit-maximising price (subject to business rules and constraints) for each candidate bundle line-up and (4) pick the best performing bundle line-up as the champion to go forward with.

Let us also not forget pricing psychology. Purchase decisions are often triggered by the situation in which the customer finds themselves. If the debit fee fiasco is simply a bad episode of underestimating the power of consumer pricing psychology that banks would rather forget, there are quite a few well-documented psychological biases that could work in a bank's favour. The famous experiment by Ariely (2008) on the digital and print subscription options of the Economist magazine was recently verified on the streets of Milan using banking analogies by our colleague Trevisan (2013). Figure 18.8 illustrates Trevisan's experiment: two groups

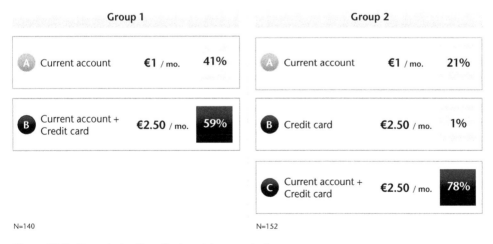

Figure 18.8　Bounded rationality in pricing psychology

283

of randomly selected pedestrians were invited to a choice exercise. Group 1 was given two options: (A) a current account that would cost €1 per month or (B) a current account plus credit card bundle that would cost €2.5 per month. Group 2 was given the same two options as Group 1 plus a new stand-alone credit card option that would cost the same €2.5 per month as the current account plus credit card bundle. The stand-alone credit card option was inserted between the other two options. The result of the experiment showed that 59 percent of Group 1 chose the bundle in option B. Not surprisingly, practically no one (only 1 percent) in Group 2 picked the new stand-alone credit card option because for the same price one could get the more feature-rich current account plus credit card bundle. What was surprising, however, was that 78 percent of Group 2 chose the bundle (compared to 59 percent of Group 1 who did the same). In essence, the presence of the new stand-alone credit card option allowed a customer to more easily realise (by way of reduced effort on mental accounting) that the current account plus credit card bundle was a good deal and thereby increased the appeal of the otherwise more expensive bundle option. For a more comprehensive treatment of consumer perceptions of financial services prices, we refer the reader to Chapter 16.

There are two other bundling-related behavioural research results worth noting. Gilbride et al. (2008) have studied the framing effect in mixed price bundling and found that the way prices are presented or framed in a bundle line-up could give customers more incentives to purchase bundles than stand-alone products/features, or vice versa. Soman and Gourville (2001) found that price bundling could lead to the decoupling of transaction costs and the value benefits of the purchased product/service bundle and subsequently influence the likelihood to use a paid-for product/service in the bundle.

Behavioural and psychological biases on the part of the consumers lead to concerns of "mis-selling", a subject explored at length in Chapter 29. Bundling, by design, obfuscates a clear understanding of the pricing of each product or service feature that collectively makes up the bundle. If a bundle contains complex financial products, such as both a loan and credit insurance, there is legitimate concern that a consumer may be persuaded to get the bundle without fully understanding the financial implications thereof. As a result, regulators, in such countries as the US or Canada, have put in place rules that strictly forbid the bundling of loans with insurance products and the use of price discounts to favour the sale of such a bundle.

Once the bundles are set, let us revisit the question of whether to adopt pure price bundling or mixed price bundling. As the reader will recall, our case studies in the previous section have shown that mixed price bundling, where both bundles and individual stand-alone features are offered, could mean more profit than pure price bundling, where only bundles are sold. The question, as we have discussed, is whether the increased complexity in handling and managing the product portfolio under the mixed price bundling configuration would outweigh the financial benefits (for example, improved profit) and the added flexibility (through individual stand-alone features) in the bundle line-up. The answer to this question merits a strategic discussion at the CEO or executive level, whose support will help align and clarify the bundling objectives.

Step 4: deploy value communication tools to sell the bundles

A good bundle line-up is only half the story; how to communicate the value of the bundles and to empower frontline sales in selling the bundles is equally important. A chic-looking, intuitive tool that can be hosted online or on a mobile device is a good start. Our experience shows that account finder tools play a big role in helping customers understand the value of the bundled features, purchase would often follow after value is well understood. Through the tool, customers are given the opportunity to indicate their financial needs, and are then presented

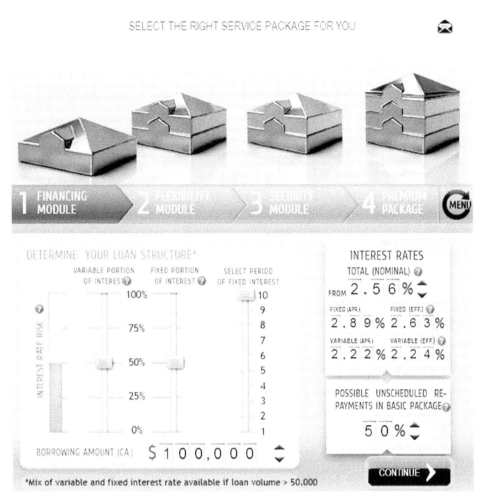

Figure 18.9 Mortgage finder

with a bundle recommendation (along with its pricing). It is also possible to allow them to further customise the features of an initial bundle recommendation. An example of one such tool for mortgages is shown in Figure 18.9.

It is crucial for the tool to be designed in a way that allows instant feedback, as the customer adjusts the answers to the needs-probing questions. An instant pricing change as a result of a small tweak to the answer of a needs-probing question helps the customer see the value of such a change in the language of price, the most direct and effective way of communicating the values of the features that make up a bundle. Figure 18.10 shows a calculator for the house bank rewards system where adding or subtracting a product would instantly be reflected in the amount of discounts a customer would enjoy in the form of monthly fees.

Key success factors for price bundling

Mastering price bundling is critical for a bank to achieve financial success and create a loyal and happy customer base. Optimal bundling, at the same time, is a daunting result to achieve.

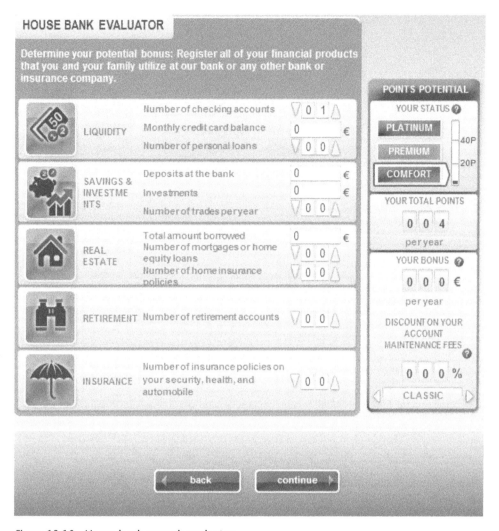

Figure 18.10 House bank rewards evaluator

We have seen many banks lack the knowledge to control the complex bundling process, including clarification of objectives, selection of products, identification of willingness-to-pay and segment sizes, simulation and optimisation of the relevant product/service combinations, etc. Our experience shows that the key success factors for price bundling include: CEO support to help align and clarify bundling objectives, a customer centric mentality that focuses on understanding what your customers need and what they value, sophistication in using best fit research and analytical methods to acquire customer intelligence, smart needs-fulfilling bundle designs that optimally leverage customer pricing psychology and willingness-to-pay and effective communication of bundle values and empowerment of frontline bankers by implementing value communication tools at the point-of-sale.

We refer the reader to Chapter 17 for a more detailed discussion on the company-related and market-related factors that influence price management for financial services. Examples of our work in Europe and North America provide further evidence of the benefits of price bundling (see Table 18.3).

Table 18.3 Economic benefits of bundling

Company	Market challenge	Impact of bundling
Retail bank	Declining profitability from current accounts.	65% customers up-sold to packaged current accounts.
Regional retail bank	Declining revenue from credit cards.	Increased profit by 30% by linking and motivating credit card and current account usage.
Savings bank	Diversification of retail product portfolio.	Average earnings per account increased by €11 by introducing a packaged current account.
Regional savings bank	Volatility of balances in savings portfolio.	Increased profit by €1.5 million by linking savings and current account and introducing tiered interest rates.
Large private bank	Competition from niche providers.	Increased profit by CHF 40 million by rewarding customers with higher rates of interest based on product holding.
Money remitter	Commoditization of product line.	Increased profit of core service by 40%.
Payment processor	Consistent downward pressure on transaction fees from clients.	Increased profit by $75 million by offering packaged services with transaction thresholds.

Conclusions

Price bundling transfers the untapped willingness-to-pay from one product to another. If used correctly, bundling can lead to win-win situations for both the financial institutions and the customers. Our objective for this chapter is to provide an overview of the common forms of price bundling, including pure bundling and mixed bundling, and their applications in financial services. We examined the arguments for price bundling as a powerful method to improve profit, induce a higher cross-selling rate, mitigate price competition and in the case of pure price bundling, reduce costs and sales complexity. To create and implement successful bundles, we recommend following a four-step customer-centric process that begins with a better understanding of the needs of the customers and ends with the deployment of value communication tools that help facilitate the sale of the constructed bundles. Ultimately, the key to successful bundling relies on organisational change management.

Price bundling is an active subject for both academic researchers and practitioners today. In recent years, exciting development of the emerging channels, such as mobile banking, has enabled financial institutions to experiment with new product and service bundles in a more rapid and targeted manner. Data captured through digital interactions with the customers, often characterised as "big data" offer new avenues and opportunities for future empirical, theoretical and interdisciplinary work on bundling. We encourage the reader to continue exploring the bundling research through these new developments.

Note

1 Here the maintenance fee is a leading price metric to which a customer pays the most attention. There could still be other fees associated with account usage, but they would typically go up or down based on how high the maintenance fee is.

References

Adams, W. J. and Yellen, J. L. (1976). Commodity Bundling and the Burden of Monopoly. *The Quarterly Journal of Economics, 90*(3), 475–98.

Albanesius, C. (2012, Jun 12). Verizon Unveils 'Share Everything' Data Plans, *PC Magazine*. Retrieved from www.pcmag.com/article2/0,2817,2405671,00.asp

Allenby, G. M. and Rossi, P. E. (2006). Hierarchical Bayes Models. In R. Grover and M. Vriens (Eds.), *The Handbook of Marketing Research*: Sage Publications.

Ariely, D. (2008). *Predictably Irrational*. USA: HarperCollins.

Breidert, C., Hahsler, M. and Reutterer, T. (2006). A Review of Methods for Measuring Willingness-to-Pay. *Innovative Marketing*, *2*(4).

Derdenger, T. and Kumar, V. (2013). The Dynamic Effects of Bundling as a Product Strategy. *Marketing Science*.

FOXBusiness. (2011, Nov 7). Credit Unions Feel Boost from Bank Transfer Day, *FOXBusiness*. Retrieved from www.foxbusiness.com/personal-finance/2011/11/07/credit-unions-feel-boost-from-bank-transfer-day

Gilbride, T. J., Guiltinan, J. P. and Urbany, J. E. (2008). Framing effects in mixed price bundling. *Marketing Letters*, *19*(2), 125–39.

Hitt, L. M. and Chen, P.-Y. (2005). Bundling with Customer Self-Selection: A Simple Approach to Bundling Low-Marginal-Cost Goods. *Management Science*, *51*(10), 1481–93.

Iyengar, S. S. and Lepper, M. R. (2000). When Choice is Demotivating: Can One Desire Too Much of a Good Thing? *Journal of Personality and Social Psychology*, *79*(6), 995–1006.

Jedidi, K., Jagpal, S. and Manchanda, P. (2003). Measuring Heterogeneous Reservation Prices for Product Bundles. *Marketing Science*, *22*(1), 107–30.

Kim, S. (2012, Jan 23). BofA Debit Fee Plan Led to 20% Jump in Closed Accounts, *ABC News*. Retrieved from http://abcnews.go.com/blogs/business/2012/01/bofa-debit-fee-plan-led-to-20-jump-in-closed-accounts

Lopez, L. (2011, Oct 31). This 22-Year-Old Is Leading A Huge Campaign Against Bank Of America, *Business Insider*. Retrieved from www.businessinsider.com/molly-katchpole-petition-leads-ordinary-mans-fight-against-bank-of-america-debit-fees-2011-10

Pfeifer, S. and Reckard, E. S. (2011, Nov 4). One Facebook Post Becomes National Movement to Abandon Big Banks, *Los Angeles Times*. Retrieved from http://articles.latimes.com/2011/nov/04/business/la-fi-bank-transfer-20111105

Prasad, A., Venkatesh, R. and Mahajan, V. (2010). Optimal Bundling of Technological Products with Network Externality. *Management Science*, *56*(12), 2224–36.

Rauch, J. (2011, Sep 29). Bank of America to Charge Debit Card Use Fee, *Reuters*. Retrieved from www.reuters.com/article/2011/09/29/us-bankofamerica-debit-idUSTRE78S4GQ20110929

Salinger, M. A. (1995). A Graphical Analysis of Bundling. *The Journal of Business*, *68*(1), 85–98.

Schmalensee, R. (1984). Gaussian Demand and Commodity Bundling. *The Journal of Business*, *57*(1), S211–S230.

Sidel, R. (2011, Nov 1). Retreat From Debit-Card Fees Continues, *The Wall Street Journal*. Retrieved from http://online.wsj.com/article/SB10001424052970203707504577010291984996510.html

Simon, H. and Wuebker, G. (1999). Bundling – A Powerful Method to Better Exploit Profit Potential. In R. Fuerderer, A. Herrmann & G. Wuebker (Eds.), *Optimal Bundling: Marketing Strategies for Improving Economic Performance*: Springer.

Soman, D. and Gourville, J. T. (2001). Transaction Decoupling: How Price Bundling Affects the Decision to Consume. *Journal of Marketing Research*, *38*(1), 30–44.

Stremersch, S. and Tellis, G. J. (2002). Strategic Bundling of Products and Prices: A New Synthesis for Marketing. *Journal of Marketing*, *66*(1), 55–72.

Titlow, J. P. (2011, Oct 10). Customer Backlash Forces Netflix to Drop 'Qwikster' DVD Plan, *ReadWrite*. Retrieved from http://readwrite.com/2011/10/10/netflix_drops_qwikster_dvd_plan

Train, K. (2009). *Discrete Choice Methods with Simulation* (2nd ed.): Cambridge University Press.

Trevisan, E. (2013). *The Irrational Consumer: Applying Behavioural Economics to Your Business Strategy*: Ashgate Publishing.

Venkatesh, R. and Mahajan, V. (2009). Design and Pricing of Product Bundles: A Review of Normative Guidelines and Practical Approaches. In V. R. Rao (Ed.), *Handbook of Pricing Research in Marketing* (pp. 232–57). Northampton, MA: Edward Elgar Publishing Company.

Wuebker, G. (1998). *Preisbündelung. Formen, Theorie, Messung und Umsetzung*. University of Mainz, Wiesbaden: Gabler.

Part VI

Communicating and promoting financial services

19

The neglected art (and science) of financial services advertising

Karen Robson and Leyland Pitt

Introduction

Financial services are a central component of most of our lives: we keep our money in banks, we acquire insurance policies for our homes, cars, and lives, we invest money for our retirements and we use credit to make large purchases. Due to the reach and significance of financial services, financial services advertising is big business.

Despite the importance of advertising for financial services, it is not without its challenges. Because financial services offerings are largely intangible, financial services marketers look for ways to make them more real to a vast array of customers. To do this, they utilize a wide spectrum of media, ranging from print, radio and television, to online, mobile commerce and social media. They struggle to differentiate what are essentially commodity offerings from those of their competitors by designing appealing messages, and finding ways of targeting their messages at unique market segments untapped by others. This happens in a business environment characterized by economic turmoil, by radical shifts in society and cultures, by changes in legislation, and by a bewildering array of new technologies. These are certainly not trivial issues.

This chapter considers some of the many issues that financial services advertisers face, and suggests some ways in which these challenges can be overcome. First, the chapter examines the characteristics of financial services that make advertising not only more difficult, but also more necessary; these include intangibility, simultaneity, heterogeneity and perishability. These, and other characteristics present enormous challenges to the advertising of financial services, but also offer immense opportunities for innovativeness and creativity.

Next, the chapter presents an overview of the extent of financial services advertising, including the magnitude of the phenomenon and trends and practices. Then it considers the basic effects that advertising can achieve. While many laypeople and even practitioners believe that the purpose of advertising is to increase sales, advertising experts and scholars are generally of the opinion that all advertising can really do is to inform/create awareness, persuade, and remind. If financial services advertisers bear this in mind, they can set realistic objectives for advertising strategies and campaigns, and can also measure performance against these objectives in a direct and rational fashion.

Then, the chapter turns to the creation of advertising messages, and the selection of advertising media. At a time when significant changes are occurring in media (television networks are struggling, print is dying, and a plethora of new media are emerging), financial services advertisers need to seriously reconsider not only the messages they create, but also the media they will choose to disperse these messages. Finally, the chapter considers changes and challenges in financial services advertising

Advertising: what it is and what can it do?

Advertising is one-way, paid-for communication through mass media by an identifiable sponsor, directed at making the target audience aware of something, persuading it of something or reminding it of something (Barton 1950). A brief look at this simple definition is worthwhile. Advertising is one-way, which makes it different from personal selling (which is two-way). It is also paid for, which makes it different from publicity (which is, strictly speaking, free). It uses mass media, such as the press, radio, television and billboards, and currently a variety of online tools. The sponsor of an advertising message is identifiable, which makes advertising different from propaganda, in which it can be more difficult or impossible to identify the sponsor. There is a target audience and advertising can do three things to this audience.

First, advertising can make potential customers aware of something of which they were previously unaware. It can therefore inform the customer of a new or improved financial service such as a new credit card, a change in interest rates or the opening of a new branch of a bank, etc. Second, advertising can persuade customers to do something. For example, it can motivate customers to request further information (such as enquiring about a new credit card by phone), sample a financial services offering (such as a small number of free stock trades), or visit a new branch.

Third, advertising can also remind customers of a service, and the financial services firm behind it. Many people wonder why well-known, established brands are still advertised and why they continue to do so. The reason is that if customers are not reminded of the brand they may actually forget about it. A financial services brand such as HSBC, known to most of Asia, Western Europe and North America, still emphasizes that it is the bank that understands different global markets and cultures. Financial services advertisers can also impact sales by reminding consumers of occasions, for instance, "Don't forget your travel insurance", "Your tax return is due by the end of April – use H&R Block" or American Express's past use of "Don't leave home without it".

Characteristics of financial services advertising

What makes services different from goods? Or, in other words, what unique characteristics do services possess that goods do not? What makes our purchases of banking distinct from our purchases of items such as soft drinks? To begin to understand the characteristics of financial services advertising that make it special, reviewing what makes services (more generally) unique is a good starting point. These characteristics include intangibility, simultaneity, heterogeneity and perishability.

The first of these, intangibility, is the most fundamental difference between goods and services: whereas you can see, touch and hold a product, you cannot do these with a service. Services are performances or experiences, rather than things. Because services are intangible, service providers and customers alike are faced with unique issues in selling and purchasing services. First of all, service providers have nothing to show customers to allow them to feel the quality or test the service.

To overcome the issue of intangibility, service providers give customers evidence of what they are purchasing. For example, advertisements and testimonials feature individuals and families similar to the customer who have purchased the service, and illustrate the benefits they have enjoyed from it. For customers, intangibility means that they are unable to see what they are purchasing, and will have very little, if anything, to show for the exchange. As a result, the testimony of others (word of mouth) becomes more valuable than in the case of goods.

In addition, the ambiance and certain tangible elements of the service setting (including such things as employee uniforms, service counters and surrounding furniture) can contribute to a sense of security and trust. Indeed, the "trusted advisor" has always been paramount in consumer decisions regarding financial services (Gill 2008) (Chapter 10 discusses trust and trustworthiness in relation to different types of financial services provider). Furthermore, in the wake of the global financial crisis, consumers have become increasingly skeptical and distrusting of financial service providers (Mattila et al. 2010), and as such the importance of establishing a sense of security and trust has become even more important (as discussed in Chapter 30).

Simultaneity refers to the fact that with services, production and consumption often occur at the same time, whereas with goods, production and consumption do not tend to happen simultaneously. In order to open a new bank account, consumers must go to a bank to obtain the account; moreover, at the same time that the bank teller produces the service, consumers are consuming it.

Interestingly, the issue of simultaneity leads to the need to manage the customer as a part-time employee, in a sense. To illustrate, consider using the services of an accountant to have one's income tax return completed. A client in this situation needs to keep records, invoices and accounts, sign forms, and file returns. If a client fails to do this, an accountant would not be able to provide an adequate service. Viewed this way, not only does a customer come inside a service factory and do some work, in many cases the quality of the service is almost as dependent on the customer as it is on the service provider. The customer can therefore be seen as a co-producer in service firms, and is in a substantial sense a "part-time employee". In addition, because services are produced and consumed simultaneously, the provider can customise the service; in fact, there is an opportunity to create something unique for each customer.

The next aspect that makes services unique from goods is heterogeneity. Because services are intangible, and are produced and consumed simultaneously by people, it means that one cannot set up production lines to deliver an identical service each time. Services tend to have the characteristic of heterogeneity; in other words, they vary in output. In the case of financial services, for example, the experience of banking will vary from customer to customer. One impact that heterogeneity has is that quality is more difficult to control with services: by the time a customer has received poor service, it is already too late. However, heterogeneity is a matter of degrees: more people-based services tend to possess a higher degree of heterogeneity than technology-based services.

Finally, services are perishable. Because goods are produced before they are consumed, they can be stored until needed. Services cannot, as they are produced and consumed simultaneously. For example, financial consulting firms have consultants' time that dies the moment it is not used; insurance companies have unused capital reserves. To understand and minimize the effects of service perishability, astute services marketers manage two things: supply and demand. Managing supply in a service setting requires organising all those factors of service production that affect the customer's ability to acquire and use the service (for example, hours of operation, staffing at peak time). Managing demand requires the services marketing mix, such as advertising, to stimulate or dampen demand.

Financial services themselves have four additional elements that the authors of this chapter argue further set them apart as services, and create additional challenges for the financial services advertiser. First of all, financial services are highly complex. Unless you are trained in finance or accounting, financial services are not easy to understand as they require significant knowledge about financial calculations. (The impact of knowledge on consumer financial decision-making is discussed in detail in Chapter 8) For example, understanding financial services requires understanding of interest rates, discounted cash flows and taxation, which require specialized training. On top of these calculations, the complexity of financial services is further increased by the presence of "legalese" language that most customers do not understand, and probably do not care to.

Second, financial services are dull. No one gets excited about a mortgage or about retirement benefits, only what they lead to such as a nice house or a better retirement. Likewise, life insurance and car insurance are uninteresting to most people and, in certain cases, represent a legal obligation. Financial services in general are boring. As a result, marketers face an additional challenge in engaging consumers, and in educating consumers about the complexities described above. It may be considerably more difficult for a financial service provider than an entertainment service provider to spark interest in consumers to begin with.

Third, financial services are usually "grudge" purchases. Consumers do not want to spend money on financial services, but they have to. That is, it is simply not realistic to keep all of one's money outside of financial institutions, or to go one's entire life without purchasing insurance. Thus, while consumers need financial services, many purchase them begrudgingly. Viewed this way, financial services are a necessary evil, which means that service providers are faced with consumers who, from the beginning, are not likely to be pleased about having to make their purchase.

Finally, financial services demand a significant proportion of many consumers' budgets. In fact, financial services such as mortgages and retirement packages are among the most expensive things we purchase in life. Because financial services are so expensive, the service (and payment) can linger over many years. For example, mortgages are often issued in 30-year terms, and saving for retirement begins (for many people) decades before an individual leaves the work force. Having reviewed what makes services in general, and financial services in particular, unique, we now take a closer look at financial services advertising.

Financial services advertising: an overview

Companies operating in the financial services arena are faced with the formidable task of advertising their intangible, dull and expensive services to consumers. Furthermore, when financial services firms are successful in persuading consumers to purchase their services, consumers do so reluctantly. Despite the fact that financial services are some of the most important elements of modern life, financial services firms face tremendous obstacles when connecting with consumers. As a result, advertising is particularly important to financial services firms. Despite this, research from the UK shows that financial services firms waste more advertising opportunity than any other industry (Greenyer 2004). In particular, Greenyer (2004) found that the UK retail banking sector, and the UK credit card sector, waste a great deal of advertising opportunity. These results have been supported by Gill (2008), who argues that, in particular, opportunities for online marketing of financial services have been untapped.

Not surprisingly, the importance of marketing financial services is reflected in the amount of money financial services firms spend on advertising. A 2012 report by Kantar Media reports that in 2011, spending on financial services marketing in the United States alone totalled over

$10 billion. In contrast, total spending on restaurant advertising in the United States was less than $6 billion in 2011 (Kantar Media 2012b). As with other industries, financial services firms reduced their spending on marketing immediately after the financial crisis (Lee et al. 2012). For example, financial services media spending in the United States (excluding spending on internet advertisements) fell from $9.7 billion in 2008 to $8.2billion in 2009 (Kantar Media 2012a). Within this drop in spending on marketing, national banks and investment firms saw the main reductions in spending on advertising. However, spending on marketing has risen again to above pre-crisis levels, with no signs of slowing down in the years to come.

Spending by financial services category

Financial services providers include banks, credit card issuers, investment firms, brokerages and insurance companies. Each of these types of companies contributes a different proportion to the overall spending on financial services marketing. Insurance companies, including life insurance, home and personal property insurance, auto insurance, as well as insurance brokers and agencies contributed almost 37 percent of the total spending to financial services marketing in 2011, in the United States. Credit card companies contributed roughly 16 percent of the total spending, followed by commercial banks (13 percent) and investment companies (11 percent) (Kantar Media 2012a).

Among consumer banks, the Bank of America vastly outspent its competitors on advertising in 2011, spending $1.4 billion. This number is almost double the amount spent by the next two highest spenders, Ally Financial and Capital One Financial Corporation, which spent $87 and $84 billion respectively. The leader in media spending within credit card companies in the United States is JP Morgan Chase and Company, which spent over $360 million in 2011. Other credit card companies with significant marketing budgets include Capital One Financial Corp, which spent $245 million in 2011, and American Express Corp, which spent $233 million in 2011. All of the top 8 spenders on marketing spent on average over $100 million each on media spending in 2011, while all other credit card companies allocated less than $15 million each to their media spending (Kantar Media 2012a).

Financial services advertising: selecting media

Marketers in the financial services sector have a myriad of options as to the media they use to connect with current and potential customers. Marketers can choose traditional media, such as television, radio and print ads, or non-traditional media, such as advertising on mobile phones, digital billboards, or on webisodes. In what follows, we explore these various options and review how financial service firms are using them.

Online advertising

Financial services are not excluded from the general trend towards Internet advertising; for example, in the UK, the number of consumers who bank online grew by almost 17 million in the decade from 1998–2008 (Gill 2008). Mobile advertising of financial services often comes in conjunction with mobile banking, in which a consumer is connected to a bank through a mobile device such as a smartphone, personal digital assistant, or cell phone (Laukkanen and Kiviniemi 2010).

Mobile banking is a particularly important way of reaching consumers of financial services, as it creates significant value for consumers through increased feelings of control, increased time savings, and access to real time information (Laukkanen and Lauronen 2005). As a result, marketers (especially those in the financial services sector) need to embrace mobile communications platforms (Laukkanen and Kiviniemi 2010, Riivari 2005, Laukkanen and Lauronen 2005).

Gupta (2013) argues that the best way for marketers to communicate via mobile platforms is not through banner ads, or pop up ads, but rather through mobile apps themselves. Mobile apps, according to Gupta, will trump more traditional advertisements partly because consumers do not perceive apps to be forms of advertising. Instead, Gupta argues that consumers view them as functional components of their mobile devices. Furthermore, banner or pop up ads can be perceived by users as irritating.

Further support for using smartphone apps comes from the finding that smartphone users spend an average of 82 percent of their mobile minutes using apps, compared to only 18 percent with web browsers. In addition, smartphone users download an average of 40 apps onto their devices (Gupta 2013). Clearly, the potential for marketing to consumers via apps is significant. Not surprisingly, mobile ad spending in the finance sector has been increasing rapidly (Kuchinskas 2012). This increase places spending on mobile ads by financial services companies higher than spending by telecommunications, automotive, or retailing sectors.

Television advertising

Television advertisements have long been popular with marketers, including those in financial services, for many reasons. Television has the ability to reach large numbers of current and potential customers, which has obvious benefits in terms of generating awareness. Indeed, given the benefits to mass marketing, it is not surprising that Kantar Media (2012a) reports that the main advertising medium used by financial services marketers is Cable and Network television. However, the effectiveness of television advertisements is difficult to determine, and television can be prohibitively expensive.

Marketers interested in advertising on television need to consider the program and channel as the two more important factors in their decision-making: does a particular program available on a particular channel present an opportunity to reach the right audience? However, marketers need to think about additional factors in their decision-making, including the time of day, cost of advertising, the duration of the ad, the frequency that the ad is shown, and the position that the ad takes within a commercial break.

Print advertising

Print advertising, such as ads in newspapers, magazines and fliers, is another popular medium for communicating to consumers about financial services. Newspapers, for example, are timely and can be used to target specific neighbourhoods or areas. Magazines have similar benefits; however, the advertisements may be less timely depending on the frequency with which magazine issues are published. Newspaper and magazine advertisements suffer some drawbacks; the impact of such advertisements is difficult to track.

Cross-media effects

Marketers do not typically use one type of medium at a time, instead, they generally use a combination of print, television, online and other forms of media (Nichols 2013). When this happens, the question arises as to whether the different media interact with each other. The answer, according to most marketing experts, is yes, they do! Pfeiffer and Zinnbauer (2010) argue that traditional media are useful in the early stages of an advertising campaign, but that it is necessary to use online advertising later on in order to drive activity.

Nichols (2013) reveals that despite using multiple media forms to connect with customers, marketers often measure the performance of each of their marketing activities as if they work independently of one another. This practice, known as swim-lane measurement, can result in over or under estimating the impact of different advertising media. For instance, Nichols (2013) reports that when looking at social media ad revenue in isolation, the impact of social media ads is significantly underestimated. In contrast, when looking at paid search ads in isolation, the impact of such ads is overestimated.

Financial services advertising: communicating messages

Consumers harbour negative attitudes towards financial service firms, are skeptical about advertising from financial service providers, and use words such as "greedy", "opportunistic" and "impersonal" to describe financial institutions (Mattila et al. 2010). Indeed, especially since the global financial crisis, financial services companies have been faced with the task of rebuilding consumer trust (see Chapter 30 for a fuller discussion on this topic).

Research suggests that including messaging about corporate social responsibility can mitigate against consumer perceptions of deception and dishonesty (Mattila et al. 2010), although financial services firms still have a long way to go in restoring their image (see Chapter 32 for a detailed discussion of corporate social responsibility). In the face of skeptical consumers, some researchers suggest that financial service advertisers should focus their messaging on restoring their image, rather than on providing information about goods and services (Mattila et al. 2010).

Historically, not all financial services firms have been focused on conveying information about their corporate social responsibility efforts. In an analysis of the different types of appeals made in advertising of financial services in various countries, Albers-Miller and Straughan (2000) found that appeals to quality were very common in the USA, Israel, France, Chile, Finland and Taiwan, and moderately common in a number of other countries. The second most important appeal was found to be financial value (Albers-Miller and Straughan 2000). More recently, Lee et al. (2011) found that appeals to value and atmospherics have been popular in advertising of financial services.

When communicating messages, financial service advertisers must remember to tailor ads to the desired target market. Lawson et al. (2007) highlighted in their study that despite increasingly targeting women, financial services print advertisements did not tailor their ads differently to women than to men. Because women respond differently to advertising appeals than men, the lack of ad tailoring potentially reduces the effectiveness of ads.

As with marketers in other industries, marketers of financial services are faced with consumers who are increasingly developing their own advertisements (Steyn et al. 2010, Berthon et al. 2008). Although there is no evidence to suggest that consumers prefer consumer generated ads over agency created ads, the fact remains that financial services firms are no longer the sole source of advertisements about services they offer. One of the results of this is a loss of control over messaging: at a time when consumer trust of financial services providers is low, financial services marketers may have cause for concern over consumers generating their own messages. In addition, there is evidence to suggest that popularity of consumer generated ads among ones peers may affect the likability of ads (Berthon et al. 2008).

Advertising's role in financial services marketing communication strategy

One way of developing a reasoned approach to marketing communication strategy is to use what consumer psychologists have called 'hierarchy of effects' models, and then to consider what the various forms of marketing communication can do to achieve maximum communication effectiveness. Hierarchy of effects models are attempts to describe the mental steps customers go through from the time they first begin to think about a particular need or want, until the time they satisfy this need or want through purchase, and even on to the time after purchase and consumption when they re-evaluate their purchase and consumption decision. The steps that a consumer purchasing a life insurance policy might go through, and the key tasks that the seller would have to perform are summarized in Table 19.1.

The steps above typically include recognising the need, seeking information and developing product specifications (what might satisfy the need?), evaluating the alternatives in terms of goods and suppliers, making the purchase, and evaluating the purchase after the time. As can be seen from the third column in Table 19.1, the communication tasks facing the financial services marketer differ down the hierarchy, or as the buyer moves through the various stages. In the beginning, the marketer's tasks tend to revolve around making customers aware of needs, or encouraging them to recognize needs. Customers then need to be given information, so that they can better understand the characteristics of the product that will best satisfy their need. This must be done on quite a large base in order for the financial services marketer to have

Table 19.1 What do we want to achieve in marketing communication? The case of a life insurance policy

New customer/ prospect buying phase	A consumer and a life insurance policy	Key advertiser/seller communications objectives and tasks		Relative communication effectiveness
		Financial services advertiser will strive to:	Financial services seller will be:	Low High
1. Need recognition	"I need to provide for my family when I'm no longer here"	Generate awareness	Prospecting	
2. Developing product specifications	"I can only afford to pay X per month, and what if I am injured?"	Enable feature comprehension	Opening relationship, qualifying prospect	
3. Search for and evaluation of suppliers	"Who are the life insurance companies?"	Generate leads	Qualifying prospect	
4. Evaluation	"Which life insurance offering best suits my needs?""	Enable performance comprehension	Presenting sales message	
5. Supplier selection	"I'll buy that one"	Negotiate terms/ Customise offer	Closing sale	Advertising Personal Selling
6. Purchase feedback	"Have I made the right decision?"	Reassure	Servicing account	

Source: Adapted from Berthone et al. (1996).

access to sufficient customers. Next, buyers' choices need to be narrowed down, and they can then move to actual purchase. Finally, once purchase has occurred, buyers need to be assured that they have made the right decision so that they can make a similar one in the future when the need arises again.

The processes form a useful framework for financial services marketers, because they show that to perform the tasks at each stage of the process, the marketer must accomplish defined purposes. This is shown from a personal selling perspective in column 4 in Table 19.1. A life insurance salesperson typically prospects (finds enough customers who might have a need for life insurance), qualifies (ranks prospects in terms of likelihood of purchase), presents information in the form of a sales message so that the prospect can be moved towards a decision; closes the sale by signing a deal or getting the prospect to purchase a life insurance policy, and then follows up to offer reassurance that a good deal has indeed been done and to identify opportunities for future business (see Chapter 34 for a detailed discussion of the ethics of the selling process).

As can be seen from the last two columns in Table 19.1, one-way and two-way communication (advertising and personal selling respectively) vary considerably in terms of their effectiveness in the phases of the decision hierarchy. Generally, advertising is at its most effective in the early stages of the decision-making process and personal selling at its best towards the end of the process. Advertising is very effective at making many people aware of a need and at informing them of the existence of a financial services offering that might satisfy it. It is much less effective at actually getting the customer to buy the offering ("doing the deal"), or at offering personal reassurance that the customer has made the right decision.

Personal selling is an inefficient way of attempting to make a lot of customers aware of a need in a short time and at low cost. Particularly if the market is large, as it is for many financial services offerings, it would be prohibitively expensive to use a large sales force merely to make customers aware of a need and the offering that might satisfy it. However, personal selling is a very effective way of convincing individual customers that they should sign on the dotted line, and at visiting them after the purchase to determine whether everything is satisfactory. The final point to note in Table 19.1 is that effective marketing communication is integrated: the best marketing communication strategies will use tools such as advertising where they are most effective (for example, generating awareness), and personal selling where it works best (closing the sale). Of course, other media forms have emerged, such as the Internet and social media, which allow for even more integration.

Financial services advertising: how powerful is it?

Just how influential is the advertising that permeates so much of our everyday life? Many people might answer that it is a strong force, as marketers would not appear to spend so much time and money on it if it were not. Others see advertising as a very powerful, almost sinister influence that can get gullible customers to buy things they do not want, do not need and cannot afford. In reality, the impact of advertising is actually very weak, because the communication effect of a single company or brand becomes diluted in a crowded marketplace.

To illustrate the point, the total amount spent on advertising in the US in 2010 was around $131 billion (Bloomberg News 2011). With a US population of around 300 million at the time, we can conclude that the average American was exposed to $443 worth of advertising that year. Now let us consider this effect in the context of one of the bigger financial services advertising budgets, such as the $734 million spent by the insurance giant, Berkshire Hathaway, the largest financial services advertiser in the US in 2010. Using the same method results in an average ad exposure of \$2.45 per head for this organization. In other words, the largest financial services advertiser's \$2.45 worth of advertising per consumer is competing against a total \$443 worth of advertising exposure.

This paints a grim picture of the power of advertising in financial services. However, before dismissing advertising as relatively powerless, two points should be made. First of all, many advertising executives would argue that their messages are much more focused than this and are targeted not at the average customer but at the ones who really matter, which would mean that the net effect would be far greater on the individual. This point is worth noting. A second point is that if the financial services advertising spend is so low by comparison, it must be spent wisely. The message should be tested well, media should be carefully chosen and managed, and the effects of advertising must not only be measurable, but be measured. With these points in mind, the power of advertising appears much greater.

Financial services advertising: key decisions

Most financial services advertising decisions fall into three sets of key activities: setting advertising objectives, determining the message and media and setting the advertising budget. As such, these are the most important advertising decisions a financial services marketer needs to make.

Advertising objectives

Before embarking on an advertising initiative, financial services marketers need to consider what the objectives will be: what is the advertising meant to achieve? This helps to determine whether the advertising worked. If we were to ask most advertisers what the objectives of their advertising campaigns are, the answer would almost certainly be "to increase revenues (or sales)".

However, most advertising does not have a direct effect on revenues. This is because advertising is only one of a number of variables (good offering, right price, availability and so on) that affect sales and its effect on sales is usually so indirect as to be unmeasurable.

The things advertising can do (as already stated) are inform, persuade and remind. By thinking of financial services advertising objectives in this sense, it is possible to define advertising objectives that are realistic, measurable and important. By informing, advertising achieves changes in awareness. These changes are realistic (if more people are not more aware of the offering as a result of a campaign, the advertising has probably not worked), important (customers have to be aware before they can move through the decision process) and measurable (only 20 percent of customers were aware of the new offering before the advertising campaign, and now 80 percent are). Similarly persuasion is important, realistic and measurable (for example, how many people tried the free offering, visited the new branch while the campaign was on, logged onto the website for more information?), as is the ability of advertising to remind (or example, what is the first brand of credit card that springs to mind? And the second?).

What to say and where to say it: a look at message and media

Most large financial services firms employ the services of an advertising agency: a firm that specialises in broadcast communication. The agency is given the responsibility for crafting the creative message, selecting the media (print, radio, television, etc.) in which it will be conveyed, and timing the messages. This is generally an effective arrangement, for most financial services firms prefer not to permanently employ the expensive yet considerable talents and skills that a large advertising agency is able to bring to the table. In addition, most firms prefer to leave the marketing communication to specialists. The evidence also suggests that advertising works best when the firm selects a good agency and trusts them to design the best campaign for them, even when it appears to be risky.

Perhaps the best example of this is that given by Bob Townsend in his book *Up the Organisation*. Townsend, Chief Executive Officer of Avis Car Rental, considered the slogan, "We're number 2. We try harder", to be risky and possibly lead to Avis being perceived as inferior. However, he stuck with the agreement made with the agency that he would let them do the creative work, and let the campaign proceed. Today, though, it is remembered as one of the most successful positioning campaigns in history.

This does not mean that a financial services firm should give the agency free rein to do as it pleases without some involvement from its side. The astute financial services marketer will be critical, and have a reasonable understanding of what media are available, what they cost, and what the advantages and limitations of each are. However, the intelligent financial services marketer will also not do the agency's work for them. If the firm likes the ad, it should simply pay for it and let it run. If it does not like the campaign, it should tell the agency and suggest they start again. It should not agonise over small print, the angle of a photo shoot, or the smile on the face of a model: that is what the firm is paying the ad agency for!

The advertising budget: how much to spend?

One of the difficult decisions that financial services marketers face is how much to spend on advertising. Some even hope there may be some kind of magic formula out there that will tell them how much to invest, but each advertising campaign is different.

Two problems confuse the question of how much to spend. First, the utility of advertising is not linear, but S-shaped. In simple terms this means that spending below a certain amount is entirely wasted: it is so small that it does not get noticed and therefore makes no difference. At the other extreme, one can also spend too much: beyond a certain point, additional advertising has no positive effect on awareness, persuasion or remembering, let alone sales. Second, advertising has what is termed a residual effect, which is difficult to quantify in simple accounting terms. It is not the kind of expenditure that is spent in one year, with the benefits being reaped the same year. If the advertising works, the benefits may last for a very long time. For example, CitiBank's slogan "The Citi never sleeps" is still remembered more than thirty years after it was first created by the firm's ad agency.

How, then, are advertising budgets determined? Usually they are set as an arbitrary percentage of sales, say 5 or 10 percent. Accountants approve of this method because it is simple, and with spreadsheets, one can do all kinds of "what-if" calculations. The problem with the approach is that it has little logic attached to it. First, the percentage chosen is arbitrary (based on random choice or personal whim, rather than any reason or system). Second, it can lead to gross overspending, or substantial underspending.

The best way to determine a financial services advertising budget is neither easy nor precise, but it is certainly better than picking an arbitrary number. It involves a look once more at the objectives set for the advertising. Then the firm needs to carefully consider what has to be done to achieve those objectives, in terms of the number of individuals that need to be reached with the message, and the frequency by which they should be exposed to it. Next, the cost of this in terms of message creation and, of course, the media budget, must be calculated. That will be the advertising budget. If that kind of money is not available, overambitious objectives might have to be cut, or better ways of achieving them found.

Financial services advertising: current and future research

Past research has looked at a number of important issues in financial services advertising, including differences in advertising appeals in various countries (Albers-Miller and Straughan 2000), differences in pre- and post-recession advertising (Lee et al. 2011), as well as the role of consumer generated advertising of financial services (Steyn et al. 2010). Overall, however, there remain a number of important research questions for advertisers of financial services, ultimately we argue that financial services advertising is an understudied area that presents significant opportunity for future research.

Given the increase in internet use and mobile advertising, research should explore the effectiveness of online advertising, including mobile apps, in greater detail. The trend towards internet banking and mobile app use shows no signs of slowing down, if these media are to become increasingly important for marketers of financial services, research should seek to learn more about this area. In addition, researchers would do well to assess the effectiveness of other traditional forms of advertising in comparison to online advertising.

Whether financial service firms have been successful in restoring their image after the financial crisis remains to be seen. If financial services firms have not been successful in restoring their image, research should look into how best to achieve this.

Most of the research reviewed in this chapter was conducted in the United States and the United Kingdom. Researchers would do well to investigate the state of financial services advertising globally. Cross-cultural differences in advertising, and global advertising campaigns, would be worthwhile to study.

Conclusion

This chapter began with a review of the characteristics of financial services, which include broad characteristics (intangibility, simultaneity, heterogeneity and perishability) as well as characteristics specific to financial services (that is, financial services are complex, dull, grudge purchases and expensive). These characteristics pose challenges for providers of financial services, but also present opportunities for innovation and personalized service, as well as for creative advertising.

However, part of the challenge is in connecting with consumers and in generating awareness of financial services, which can be accomplished by advertising. Financial service firms spend immense amounts of money on advertising, with insurance companies and credit card companies being the largest spenders. Financial service firms can choose from a number of different media forms, including print, radio, outdoor advertising, television and mobile advertising. The most common media for advertising is television, although mobile ad spending is rapidly increasing. When choosing media types for advertising, it is also important to bear in mind that cross-media effects may occur, as one mode of advertising may impact another.

The content of financial services advertising has changed in recent times due to the impact of the global financial crisis (Ahn et al. 2011). In the years since the crisis, financial services companies have been increasingly perceived as untrustworthy or dishonest and have adopted a more direct, assertive approach to their messaging.

The hierarchy of effects model describes the cognitive process and steps that consumers go through when they think about a particular need or want, which includes need recognition, developing product specifications, search for financial services providers, evaluation, provider selection and finally purchase feedback. As these illustrate the steps that a consumer goes through when considering a purchase, they provide a useful framework for financial services marketers in considering marketing communication in general and advertising in particular.

Setting a budget for advertising is one of the most difficult decisions that financial services marketers face. However, taking a close look at the objectives prior to setting the budget is recommended. Ultimately, the things that advertising can do are inform, persuade and remind. Financial services marketers are well advised to consider these three potential outcomes, and to consider what objectives they have in mind before embarking on an advertising initiative.

This chapter concludes with a call for researchers to investigate financial services advertising in a number of areas. The ubiquity of mobile phones and increased use of online advertising warrants additional study, as does advertising across different cultures. In addition, the progress that financial service firms have made in reducing their image as dishonest remains to be assessed.

References

Ahn, H., Song, Y. and Sung, Y. (2011). When the going gets tough, ads become straightforward but multi-appealed: The influence of the recession on financial services advertising appeals. *Journal of Financial Services Marketing, 16(3/4)*, 230–43.

Albers-Miller, N. D. and Straughan, R. D. (2000). Financial services advertising in eight non-English speaking countries. *International Journal of Bank Marketing, 18*(7), 347–58.

Barton, R. *Advertising Handbook* (Englewood Cliffs, NJ: Prentice Hall, 1950), 928.

Berthon, P., Pitt, L. and Campbell, C. (2008). Ad Lib: When customers create the ad. *California Management Review 50*, 6–30.

Berthon, P.R., Pitt, L.F. and Watson, R.T. (1996). The World Wide Web as an Advertising Medium: Towards an Understanding of Conversion Efficiency. *Journal of Advertising Research*, Vol. 36, 1 (January/February) (Special 60th Anniversary Edition), 43–53.

Bloomberg News. (2011). *US Advertising Spending Rose 6.5 percent in 2010*. Available at www.bloomberg. com/news/2011-03-17/u-s-advertising-spending-rose-6-5-in-2010-led-by-television-internet.html

Gill, C. (2008). Restoring consumer confidence in financial services. *International Journal of Bank Marketing, 26*(2), 148–52.

Greenyer, A. (2004). The impact of different media channels on consumers and the wastage of potential advertising opportunities through existing customer communications. *Journal of Financial Services Marketing 8*(3): 279–90.

Gupta, S. (2013). For Mobile Devices, Think Apps, Not Ads. *Harvard Business Review*.

Kantar Media. (2012a). *Financial-Services Report*. Available at: www.iabcanada.com/wp-content/ uploads/2012/07/Kantar-Media_Financial-Services-Canada-IAB-Report_Jan-24-2013.pdf

—— (2012b). *Kantar Media Reports U.S. Advertising Expenditures Increased 3 Percent in 2012*. Available at http:// kantarmediana.com/sites/default/files/kantareditor/Kantar-Media-Reports-US-Ad-Expenditures-Increased-three-percent-in-2012.pdf

Kuchinskas, S. (9 May 2012) "Financial Mobile Ad Spend Up 314 percent," *ClickZ*.

Laukkanen, T. and Kiviniemi, V. (2010). The role of information in mobile banking resistance. *International Journal of Bank Marketing, 28*(5), 372–88.

Laukkanen, T. and Lauronen, J. (2005). Consumer value creation in mobile banking services. *International Journal of Mobile Communications, 3*(4), 325–38.

Lawson, D., Borgman, R. and Brotherton, T. (2007). A content analysis of financial services magazine print ads: Are they reaching women? *Journal of Financial Services Marketing, 12*(1), 17–29.

Lee, T. D., Chung, W. and Taylor, R. E. (2011). A strategic response to the financial crisis: an empirical analysis of financial services advertising before and during the financial crisis. *Journal of Services Marketing, 25*(3), 150–64.

Mattila, A., Hanks, L. and Kim, E. (2010). The impact of company type and corporate social responsibility messaging on consumer perceptions. *Journal Of Financial Services Marketing*, 15(2), 126–35. doi:10.1057/ fsm.2010.10

Nichols, W. (2013). Advertising Analytics 2.0. *Harvard Business Review*.

Pfeiffer, M. and Zinnbauer, M. (2010). Can old media enhance new media? How traditional advertising pays off for an online social network. *Journal of Advertising Research, 50*(1), 42.

Riivari, J. (2005). Mobile banking: a powerful new marketing and CRM tool for financial services companies all over Europe. *Journal of Financial Services Marketing, 10*(1), 11–20.

Steyn, P., Wallström, Å. and Pitt, L. (2010). Consumer-generated content and source effects in financial services advertising: An experimental study. *Journal of Financial Services Marketing, 15*(1), 49–61.

20

An AMO model for communicating and promoting financial services

Alex Wang

Introduction

Processing financial services communications effectively may help both consumers and financial marketers since financial information acquisition and processing are important for consumers to make informed financial decisions. Acquiring and processing financial services communications requires the necessary ability, motivation and opportunity to do so. This chapter discusses the Ability, Motivation and Opportunity (AMO) Model (Greenwald and Leavitt 1984, Hallahan 2000, MacInnis and Jaworski 1989, Petty and Cacioppo 1979, 1981, 1986) and presents relevant research findings based on the individual variables in the context of financial services communications.

Financial ability is a function of cognitive capacity that impacts on skills in processing financial services communications. Motivation is an activated state of involvement in processing financial services communications. Opportunity refers to the executional characteristics, such as media characteristics, that facilitate information processing in financial services communications. The three intertwined variables influence how consumers select and process financial services communications since these three variables may not only direct the attention that consumers devote to processing financial services communications but may also influence how consumers perceive financial services communications. Understanding the roles of these variables and their relationships in processing financial services communications may help financial marketers set realistic objectives, design financial services communications strategically and execute effective media plans to measure performance against their marketing communication objectives.

The first relationship discussed in this chapter is between ability and motivation to process financial services communications. Although this relationship has been examined in the Elaboration Likelihood Model (ELM) (Petty and Cacioppo 1986), this stream of research has not been applied extensively to the area of financial services communications and is still not well understood. Although financial marketers look for ways to enhance consumers' opportunities to process financial services communications via different media, consumers' levels of motivation could influence how they process such communications. Digital and mobile media such as the Internet and mobile devices are gaining popularity (Zarem 2008). The second relationship discussed in this chapter is the interaction between motivation and opportunity to process financial services communications.

Due to different channel characteristics that can influence the delivery of financial services communications, consumers may formulate preferences in using different media to process financial services communications. A consumer's ability to process financial services communications is highly related to their knowledge of financial concepts, products or services (Alba and Hutchinson 1987, 2000, Hallahan 2000, Wang 2006, 2009a, 2011a, 2012a, 2012b). Due to consumers' abilities and opportunities to process financial services communications, knowledge and opportunity may interact to influence the processing of financial services communications. This is the third relationship discussed in this chapter. This chapter then discusses practical implications of the research based on the three relationships examined. The practical implications may help financial marketers design financial services communications and execute media plans effectively. This chapter also complements Chapter 14 on branding and Chapter 19 that explores various methods of advertising and communication.

AMO model in the context of financial services communications

Elaboration of a specific financial services communication usually has sequential effects on accepting or rejecting the communication, forming or changing attitudes based on the communication and acting on the communication (Andrews 1988, Greenwald and Leavitt 1984, Hallahan 2000, MacInnis and Jaworski 1989, Petty and Cacioppo 1979, 1981, 1986). Three variables have been suggested as important antecedents to information processing and elaboration of financial services communications: ability, motivation, and opportunity (Wang 2009a, 2009b, 2011a, 2012a, 2012b). Figure 20.1 illustrates the relevant constructs related to the three variables.

In the first part of Figure 20.1, motivation and ability to process financial services communications could serve as mediating factors that influence the opportunity to process financial services communications. The levels of processing, influenced by opportunity, motivation and ability, could influence attitude formation, whereas the effects of opportunity to process financial services communications on attitudes toward financial services communications and

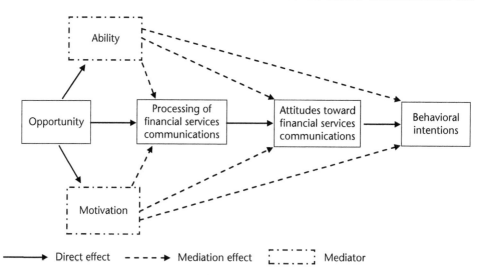

Figure 20.1 Ability, motivation and opportunity to process financial services communications

behavioral intentions could also be mediated by motivation and ability to process financial services communications. Overall, attitudes toward financial services communications could have direct effects on behavioral intentions. This section discusses the three variables and presents relevant research findings based on the individual variables in the context of financial services communications.

Ability to process

Ability here refers to a consumer's ability in interpreting messages in financial services communications (Wang 2009a, 2011a, 2012a, 2012b). Consumers who are able to process financial services communications could comprehend a financial services communication more efficiently than consumers who are unable to understand the financial services communication. Financial ability is related to financial knowledge that is learned, represented, and stored in memory (Alba and Hutchinson 1987, 2000, Wang 2006, 2009a, 2011a, 2012a, 2012b). Financial knowledge can be retrieved, used, and updated to make analogy, inference, reasoning, and elaboration regarding financial services communications (Alba and Hutchinson 1987, 2000, Wang 2006, 2009a, 2011a, 2012a, 2012b).

Knowledgeable consumers may engage in more than superficial processing because of their ability to understand financial services communications (Alba and Hutchinson 1987, 2000). As a result, higher levels of financial knowledge could improve processing and elaboration of financial services communications (Wang 2009a, 2011a, 2012a, 2012b). In the same line of reasoning, the bias invoked by knowledgeable consumers could also be attributed to counter arguments to specific messages in financial services communications (Wang 2012a). Therefore, knowledgeable consumers could also resist attitude change in response to the messages in financial services communications (Alba and Hutchinson 1987, 2000, Petty and Cacioppo 1979, 1981, 1986, Wang 2012a).

Financial knowledge has several important dimensions: objective financial knowledge, subjective financial knowledge and financial experience/familiarity (Friestad and Wright 1994, 1995, Alba and Hutchinson 1987, 2000). Objective financial knowledge is accurately stored financial information, whereas subjective financial knowledge is a belief about that state of financial knowledge (Bettman and Park 1980, Park and Lessig 1981). Although subjective and objective financial knowledge are different, both are influenced and enhanced by financial experience and familiarity and financial education (Wang 2009a, 2011a, 2011b, 2011c, 2012a, 2012b). Subjective financial knowledge can be thought of as a degree of confidence, whereas objective financial knowledge refers only to what a consumer actually knows (Alba and Hutchinson 1987, 2000). Mishra and Kumar, in Chapter 8, examine in detail objective and subjective knowledge in relation to mutual fund investors' knowledge calibration.

Consumers with higher levels of objective financial knowledge usually have developed more complex schemata with well-formulated processing criteria (Marks and Olson 1981). When consumers with higher levels of objective financial knowledge process financial services communications, less cognitive effort is required and relevant objective financial knowledge can be activated automatically, resulting in the availability of evaluation criteria and rules for processing financial services communications (Campbell and Kirmani 2000). Following these arguments, Wang (2011a, 2012b) examined how objective financial knowledge influenced processing and comprehension of financial services communications. Using specific questions to measure investors' levels of objective financial knowledge, the results revealed that investors with higher levels of objective financial knowledge comprehended the financial services communications more than investors with lower levels of objective financial knowledge.

Hilgert et al. (2003) examined the effects of objective financial knowledge on financial behavior in terms of cash-flow management, credit management, saving and investments. Their results revealed that financial knowledge in a specific area was positively correlated with a financial practice in the specific area. They also found that consumers who scored highest on questions relating to credit management, saving and investing exhibited good credit management, saving behaviors and investing habits. Conversely, studies found that the less financially literate were less likely to manage debt (Norvilitis et al. 2006, Wang 2011b), to plan for retirement (Lusardi and Mitchell 2007, 2008, Wang 2011c), to accumulate wealth (Stango and Zinman 2009, Wang 2009a, 2011b, 2011c), to participate in the stock market (Christelis et al. 2010, Wang 2009a), to understand basic financial concepts related to bonds, stocks, and mutual funds (Hilgert et al. 2003, Wang 2009a, 2012b) and to comprehend investment disclosures (Wang 2011a, 2012a, 2012b).

In general, subjective financial knowledge may not affect how many elaborative thoughts consumers could generate (Wang 2006; Wang 2009a). Since subjective financial knowledge is usually influenced by consumers' self-confidence (Alba and Hutchinson 1987, 2000, Friestad and Wright 1994, 1995), consumers may not generate accurate comprehension of financial services communications. On the contrary, consumers with higher levels of objective financial knowledge seem to be able to generate positive comprehension and financial behaviors. Consumers' true financial knowledge rather than confidence and experiences could be a key component for financial literacy. Nonetheless, objective financial knowledge may enhance subjective financial knowledge and vice versa. This is because subjective and objective financial knowledge are both influenced by financial experiences.

While ability to process financial services communications can contribute to financial literacy, the structures of financial knowledge could help consumers accumulate financial literacy in different degrees. In Chapter 3, Huhmann defines financial literacy as a global construct including capacity, comprehension, prior knowledge and proficiency. Financial literacy could be influenced by objective financial knowledge and experiences mostly (Wang 2013). Similar to the correlation between subjective and objective financial knowledge, there could be a correspondence between financial literacy and ability to process financial services communications.

A stream of research has uncovered negative sides of financial literacy (Wang 2013). Less financially literate are less likely to understand terms and conditions of consumer loans and mortgages, to search for cheaper mortgages (Moore 2003) and to understand investment disclosures (Wang 2011a, 2012a, 2012b). Consumers with higher financial literacy tend to plan for retirement and have an emergency fund (Lusardi 2010). They also are less likely to engage in credit card behavior that generates high interest payments and fees (Lusardi 2010, Wang 2011b). In essence, financial literacy could have the greatest effect on eliciting responsible financial behaviors (Perry and Morris, 2005).

Motivation to process

Motivation to process indicates a level of activated state of involvement in processing financial services communications. A consumer needs to first attend to the messages of a financial services communication and then process the messages. This conceptual origin of emphasizing motivation to process a financial services communication can be traced to the Elaboration Likelihood Model (ELM) and the Heuristic-Systematic Model (HSM) (Chaiken 1987, Chaiken et al. 1989, Chaiken et al. 1996, Petty and Cacioppo 1986). The heightened involvement may facilitate a motivated predisposition to allocate cognitive resources to process the messages in a financial services communication (Wang 2009b, 2011d).

Involvement may be activated by the level of relevancy consumers attribute to a financial services communication (Wang 2006a, 2009b, 2011d, 2012a). In the same vein, the heightening status of involvement could be based on message or personal factors (Wang 2006a, 2009b, 2011d, 2012a). Thus, research has suggested that involvement may be best applied to the context of financial services communications when it is associated with personal involvement or is associated within a particular domain in message involvement (Wang 2009b, 2011d, 2012a).

Although personal and message involvement can facilitate information processing of a financial services communication differently, these two different types of involvement fundamentally act as activators for motivation to process a financial services communication. Research has examined how message involvement affected college students' comprehension of credit card advertisement disclosures and revealed that college students' message involvement with the disclosures positively influenced their comprehension of the disclosures (Wang 2012a). The findings suggest that consumers who are involved more in processing specific messages in a financial services communication may be more likely to create the memorial representation of the messages. Consequently, consumers may be more likely to use the memorial representation of the messages to effectively use the financial services communication.

In essence, lower levels of cognitive capacity facilitate lower levels of message involvement to process the messages in a financial services communication. The higher levels of cognitive capacity generate higher levels of message involvement to process the messages in a financial services communication. When deeper processing of the messages in a financial services communication is activated, consumers increase the amount of attention to process the messages in the financial services communication and expand greater cognitive efforts to comprehend the messages in the financial services communication.

A term often associated with motivation to process is engagement. Wang (2006a, 2009b, 2011d) has defined engagement as a possible driver of involvement. Engagement may be a driver of message or personal involvement since it can be determined by either contextual or media characteristics. For example, research has traditionally considered perceived need for relevant information as a primary antecedent of message involvement (Burnkrant and Sawyer 1983, Wang 2006a). The higher degree of interactivity enabled by digital media can also enhance message involvement (Wang 2009b, 2011e, 2011f). Engagement initiated by either contextual relevance or interactivity becomes an important driver of personal or message involvement since engagement can be a precondition to involvement that influences the information processing of financial services communications (Wang 2009b, 2011d, 2011e).

In the context of financial services communications, contextual relevance focuses on the extent to which relevant messages in financial services communications are framed and presented based on surrounding contexts (Wang 2011d). For example, a financial marketer may place an advertisement next to an article discussing best ways to secure a personal loan by comparing offers from different financial institutions in a magazine. In this case, the advertisement related to the article (surrounding context) may engage readers due to the surrounding context that assimilates information relevance. While readers are reading the article, the advertisement may activate consumer attention and initiate engagement with the advertisement due to contextual relevance.

Research examined whether a financial marketer's advertisement placed next to investment information (the contextual relevance effect) would generate stronger message involvement, recall, and attitude than an advertisement that was placed next to the same investment information and not about finance (Wang 2011d). The results revealed that the contextual relevance effect created by the financial services advertisement and the surrounding context increased the perceived contextual relevance among consumers. Message involvement, recall and attitude toward the financial services advertisement were all enhanced. More importantly, the engagement effect on attitude toward the financial services advertisement was mediated by message involvement. These findings not only provide evidence to support the relationship between engagement and message involvement but also demonstrate the importance of contextual relevance as a metric for effective financial services communications.

In addition to the mediating effect, motivation to process activated by personal involvement could also moderate the effects of exposure and cognitive processing on outcomes such as comprehension of a financial services communication (Wang 2009b). Consumers with higher levels of personal involvement can pose favorable outcomes in terms of gaining attention and elaboration of a financial services communication. When consumers are personally motivated to process a financial services communication, their cognitive structure could guide the interpretation and integration of any messages in the financial services communication. Consumers' levels of personal involvement could influence how they perceive a financial services communication and assess evaluative dimensions of the financial services communication.

Opportunity to process

Opportunity to process focuses on how financial marketers strategically use executional factors to facilitate information processing of financial services communications. Executional factors such as media integration could enhance financial marketers' abilities in delivering financial services communications (Kanso and Nelson 2004, Trappey and Woodside 2005, Wang 2006a, 2006b, 2009b, 2011e, Wang and Nelson 2006, Wouters and Wetzels 2006). Media integration of financial services communications aims to leverage the convergence of different media to provide more opportunities for consumers to process financial services communications (Wang 2009b, 2011e). In essence, using media integration to deliver financial services communications may establish a set of exposures that increase consumers' opportunities to process the financial services communications (Wang 2009b, 2011e).

Research on message repetition has provided theoretical foundations that support the media integration effect on information processing of financial services communications (Wang 2009b, 2011e). When financial services communications are presented in multiple media, consumers may consider messages in various financial services communications as independent pieces of information and process them based on different orientations. The message repetition effect can elevate the accessibility of messages about products or services in financial services communications by providing at least two additional processing opportunities (Bettinghaus and Cody 1994, Wang 2009b, 2011e).

Message repetition could also contribute to positive perceptions of financial services communications since multiple exposures to the financial services communications can increase consumers' familiarity with the financial services communications (Moorthy and Hawkins 2005, Wang 2009b, 2011e). Research has shown that the effects of media integration positively enhanced attitudes toward the television spot, perceived media engagement, and brand attitudes (Wang 2011e). Moreover, perceived engagement mediated the effect of attitude toward the television spot on brand attitude (Wang 2011e).

Financial marketers have more opportunities to expose consumers to the messages in a financial services communication via a magazine tablet edition that has the ability to combine elements of print and digital media (Zarem 2008, Wang 2011f). A financial services communication in a magazine tablet edition can offer eye-catching and overlaying content with sound and animation that may exploit consumers' sensory traits (Shaw 2004, Galin 2013, Wang 2011f). The various presentation modalities work as the sensory medium through which the messages in a financial service communication can be communicated via a magazine tablet edition (Wang 2011f). For example, audio-visual cues may be more engaging and meaningful than visual-only cues in a financial services communication delivered by a magazine tablet edition (Wang 2011f, Wang and Muehling 2010).

In essence, the important user characteristic to enhance opportunity to process a financial services communication is the degree of engagement experienced during reviewing a financial services communication in a magazine tablet edition (Galin 2013, Ryan and Jones 2009, Wang 2011f). Because the unifying principle behind engagement is interactivity in which messages in a financial services communication are presented in interactive formats (Lemonnier 2008, Rosenkransa 2010, Wang 2011f), the opportunity to process a financial services communication could be enhanced by message repetition, media integration, message strategies and utilization of new media. Enhancing consumers' opportunities to process financial service communications enables consumers to gain accessibility of the information important to their financial dealings. Consequently, consumers can make informed decisions and manage their finances effectively.

Implications for financial marketers

In addition to the mediating effects illustrated in Figure 20.1, there are also possible moderating effects among opportunity, motivation and ability to process financial services communications. These moderating effects could potentially change the ways that financial marketers design financial services communications and execute media plans. The purpose of this section is to provide financial marketers with ideas that could help them to design financial services communications strategically and execute effective media plans based on the possible moderating effects.

Financial marketers can measure and categorize consumers' levels of motivation and ability to process financial services communication in three different ways. First, financial marketers can conduct surveys to analyze their customers' interests, experiences and levels of financial knowledge to categorize their levels of motivation and ability to process financial services communications. Financial marketers can use data mining techniques to analyze their customers' financial behaviors to categorize their levels of motivation and ability to process financial services communications. Financial marketers can also use customers' browsing history on their websites to analyze the magnitude and intensity of information processing and categorize their levels of motivation and ability to process financial services communications.

The literature reviews suggest that the processes and outcomes of financial services communications are interactive and depend on consumers' opportunity, ability and motivation to process financial services communications. These three intertwined variables influence how consumers select, process and perceive financial services communications. Based on different levels of motivation and ability to process financial services communications, financial marketers can provide consumers with different levels of opportunity to process financial services communications. Financial marketers can also execute different message characteristics in financial services communications to appeal to consumers with different levels of motivation and ability to process financial services communications. This section further discusses specific message and media strategies based on the correlations between the intertwined variables.

Integrating motivation into opportunity to process

Research has suggested that personal involvement is a motivation factor that can influence opportunity to process financial services communications because lower and higher levels of personal involvement can reduce or augment the need for more opportunities to process financial services communications (Wang 2009b). For example, investors who perceive higher levels of personal involvement with a financial subject discussed in a financial blog could exhibit higher media engagement by following the financial blog's suggestions to process more financial services communications on other websites after learning about the subject via the financial blog. In this case, the personal importance associated with the financial subject could augment the opportunities to process financial services communications related to the financial subject.

Based on the above arguments, Wang (2009b) has examined the possible interaction effects between personal involvement and opportunity to process financial services communications on perceived media engagement and brand attitude by testing a financial institution's integrated financial services communications. The opportunity to process financial services communications was executed by media integration of a financial institution's integrated financial services communications including a television commercial that invited consumers to visit the financial institution's website for more financial services communications. Among the participants with lower levels of personal involvement, the participants in the condition with media integration did not perceive stronger media engagement and brand attitudes than the participants in the condition without media integration. Among the participants with higher levels of personal involvement, the participants in the condition with media integration perceived stronger media engagement and brand attitudes than the participants in the condition without media integration.

The findings suggest that the need for more opportunities to process financial services communications could be contingent upon consumers' levels of personal involvement. Consumers with lower or higher levels of personal involvement could respond to opportunities to process financial services communications differently. In other words, the benefits of having more opportunities to process financial services communications could not be warranted for all consumers. The manifestation of the opportunity effect requires higher levels of personal involvement since higher levels of motivation to process financial services communications can motivate consumers to process more financial services communications. Based on the above findings and arguments, Table 20.1 illustrates possible executional strategies regarding different levels of opportunity and motivation to process financial services communications.

Table 20.1 Executional strategy on motivation and opportunity to process

Motivation	Opportunity	
	Fewer	More
Lower	Using vivid and attention-getting visuals and simplified messages to persuade consumers to process messages in financial services communications delivered by multiple media.	Using incentives and attention-getting messages to prime consumers to process different sources of financial services communications. Web addresses could be provided in the financial services communications.
Higher	Focusing on using message repetition effects of financial services communications to encourage consumers to process more financial services communications delivered by multiple media.	Providing consumers with various financial services communications via various media. The interactivity and other engagement factors could also be considered in the overall media plans.

In essence, higher levels of personal involvement could cause a shift of attention to media integration of financial services communications and augment perceived media engagement initiated by media integration of financial services communications. Brand attitude could also be enhanced among consumers with higher levels of motivation and opportunity to process financial services communications. On the contrary, consumers with lower levels of personal involvement could disregard financial services communications delivered by multiple media because they could consider extra financial services communications via media integration unnecessary or redundant. Thus, media integration of financial services communications may not work as well for consumers who have lower levels of personal involvement.

Social media could enhance the interaction between financial services brands and consumers. The interactive functions could also enhance message involvement and engagement so that financial services brands could increase the levels of motivation and opportunity to process financial services communications delivered by social media (Wang 2011d, 2011e). Consumers could also express their opinions via financial blogs and social networking sites. In this case, their levels of motivation to process could strengthen other consumers' opportunities to process financial services communications.

Collaborating ability with opportunity to process

It is important to understand possible collaborating strategies based on ability and opportunity to process financial services communications since the collaborating strategies could facilitate processing of financial services communications. One of the collaborating strategies is to enhance the source effects of financial services communications by creating information consistency and consensus as opportunity enhancement strategies that correspond to consumers' levels of ability to process financial services communications. Information consistency focuses on the extent to which a financial marketer communicates consistent messages in multiple financial services communications. Information consensus focuses on whether financial services communications from various financial marketers reach an agreement about what the financial services communications communicate to consumers.

Rosplock (2008, 2010) has suggested that one of the top characteristics sought in a financial advisor is trustworthiness. In this case, a financial advisor's consistent recommendations could be an important factor in building trustworthiness and reflecting financial expertise since one essential consideration in whether a consumer would follow a financial advisor's recommendations involves a financial advisor's overall ability to make effective recommendations consistently. A consumer may also conduct his or her own research from other sources to confirm a financial advisor's recommendations. If a consensus is reached between the consumer's own research and the financial advisor's recommendations, the consumer could be more inclined to follow the recommendations.

Chapter 30 has presented a framework for understanding and restoring trust in universal banks. One of the relevant topics discussed is alignment of interests. This is consistent with the effects of information consistency on building trustworthiness. The relationship between consumers and financial advisors can be considered as the relationship between trustors and trustees. If no alignment of interests can be reached between consumers and financial advisors, distrust could influence the relationship negatively. Financial advisors need to manage their financial services communications effectively and consistently to avoid any distrust that could influence their relationships with their customers negatively.

The above arguments are supported by attribution theory, suggesting that a consumer such as an investor can make an external attribution that assigns causality to an outside source such as a financial advisor (Heider 1958). A financial advisor's recommendation is a form of financial services communications that an investor can use in facilitating the attribution process. Kelley (1967, 1973) has advanced Heider's (1958) theory by considering distinctiveness, consistency and consensus as three factors that may affect the formation of attribution. These three factors collaborate with levels of ability to process financial services communications to influence processing of financial services communications.

Consumers' levels of ability to process financial services communications could collaborate with information consistency and consensus as opportunity enhancement strategies to process financial services communications. Either information consistency or consensus requires multiple financial services communications to occur. Information consistency and consensus also rely on message repetition effects to become visible. Consumers with higher levels of ability could require credible sources manifested by information consensus from various financial services communications in the attribution process. Consumers such as investors with higher levels of ability may be willing to take more risks (Wang 2006) so that they may be more interested in recommendations that present certain levels of discrepancy in anticipation of better returns.

Consumers with lower levels of ability to process, however, could be more inclined to process financial services communications that feature information distinctiveness and consistency. Since ability may be correlated to message involvement as a motivation factor (Petty and Cacioppo 1979, 1981, 1986) this type of consumer may have neither ability nor motivation to process financial services communications from multiple sources. Due to incapability of using category-based processing, consumers with lower levels of ability may search for peripheral cues to process financial services communications. Thus, consumers with lower levels of ability to process financial services communications could focus on information distinctiveness and consistency of financial services communications to process financial services communications.

In essence, information distinctiveness and consistency could serve as peripheral cues for consumers with lower levels of ability to process financial services communications. Financial marketers need to maintain information consistency in their financial services communications to communicate with consumers with lower levels of ability. Consumers with different levels of ability could also attribute their processing of financial services communications to peer or expert recommendations to process financial services communications (Wang 2005, 2008). The increased reliance on financial services communications with endorsements based on rapport or credibility could also be important for consumers with fewer opportunities to process financial services communications if they have the ability and motivation to process multiple financial services communications.

Research has suggested that integrating financial advertising and publicity about a product or service could be a great strategy to form information consistency or consensus in response to consumers' gradual progress of sophisticated interaction with media (Wang 2006b, Wang and Nelson 2006). This similar message repetition strategy could be an effective way to communicate financial services communications to consumers with lower levels of ability but more opportunities to process financial services communications. Since varying messages in advertising and publicity about a financial product or service could also be an effective technique in enhancing trust and information utility (Wang 2006b, Wang and Nelson 2006), consumers with lower levels of ability could process financial services communications from two different communication forms with consistency or consensus and form favorable perceptions of financial services communications.

In the context of social media, consumers who are highly involved in using social media could strengthen the opportunity to process financial services communications. This is because

Table 20.2 Executional strategy on ability and opportunity to process

Ability	Opportunity	
	Fewer	*More*
Lower	Executing information consistent with peripheral cues to communicate key benefits of products or services in financial services communications.	Using a synergetic effect of advertising and publicity to execute financial services communications that may prime different orientations of processing.
Higher	Executing information consistent with peer or expert recommendations to enhance source credibility in financial services communications.	Using various financial services communications via various media that contain information consensus or discrepancy to facilitate deeper engagement and processing.

consumers who are highly involved in using social media could have higher levels of proficiency in searching and processing financial services communications. When consumers are able to search and process financial services communications via social media, they not only have more opportunities to process financial services communications but also have more opportunities to use the communications. Consumers who are highly involved in using social media could also share their opinions via financial blogs and social networking sites to generate opportunities for other consumers to process financial services communications. Table 20.2 illustrates possible executional strategies regarding different levels of ability and opportunity to process financial services communications.

Cooperating motivation and ability to process

Consumers usually react to financial services communications differently based on calibrations of ability and motivation to process financial services communications. The ELM framework suggests that knowledgeable and motivated consumers are likely to allocate more cognitive capacity to process financial services communications. For example, research has found that consumers' levels of ability to process information would influence their processing of financial disclosures because consumers with higher levels of cognitive capability would activate higher levels of message involvement with the financial disclosures (Wang 2012b).

On one hand, this finding suggests that knowledgeable consumers could be motivated to operate more extensive processing of financial disclosures. On the other hand, consumers with lower levels of ability and motivation to process financial services communications could look for peripheral cues in financial services communications to form temporary attitudes toward specific messages in financial services communications (Petty and Cacioppo 1986). Owing to consumers' lower levels of ability and motivation to process financial services communications, this type of consumer may focus on processing messages that formulate feature analysis, categorization and elementary meaning analysis in financial services communications (Alba and Hutchinson 1987).

Consumers with higher levels of ability but lower levels of motivation to process financial services communications could potentially present some challenges for financial marketers. First, the lower levels of motivation to process and the higher levels of ability to process financial services communications could prevent consumers from wanting to process financial services communications. When this type of consumer tries to process financial services communications, they have higher levels of ability to process financial services communications analytically by applying decision criteria readily available from memory (Bettman and Sujan 1987). Consequently, this type of consumer could either ignore or reject any messages in financial services communications.

Research, for example, has examined college students' experiences of using a credit card and found that experiences in using a credit card could have an inverse and negative effect on comprehension of the financial disclosures related to a credit card advertisement (Wang 2012a). This suggests that consumers who consider themselves as having a degree of ability in using a credit card could tend to think that they do not need to process financial services communications such as financial disclosures. Alternatively, these consumers could simply ignore financial disclosures due to higher levels of confidence in using a credit card. Either situation could be exacerbated by lower levels of motivation to process financial services communications.

In the same vein, disconfirmation could also emerge when knowledgeable consumers' evaluations of financial services communications indicate discrepancies due to their counter-arguments (Alba and Hutchinson 2000, Chang 2004, Wang 2009a). In reasoning out the discrepancies, knowledgeable consumers could generate more external-based elaborative thoughts in relation to internal-based elaborative thoughts (Wang 2006). Disconfirmation could also emerge when confident consumers evaluate financial services communications due to their subjective preferences (Alba and Hutchinson 2000). Consumers with higher levels of financial subjective knowledge could generate more internal-based elaborative thoughts in relation to external-based elaborative thoughts (Chang 2004). Strategically selecting selling points to include in financial services communications that appeal to knowledgeable and confident consumers could be the most important task for financial marketers to communicate and promote their products or services to these types of consumers. Moreover, understanding the reference points of these consumers could enhance the effectiveness of financial services communications.

Consumers with lower levels of ability but higher levels of motivation to process financial services communications could be ideal consumers for financial marketers since incentives can be provided in financial services communications for favorable processing. Although this type of consumer could also focus on processing messages that formulate feature analysis, categorization, and elementary meaning analysis in financial services communications (Alba and Hutchinson 1987, 2000), higher levels of motivation could facilitate information processing of financial services communications that feature appealing and simplified messages in financial services communications. Based on the above findings and arguments, Table 20.3 illustrates possible message strategies based on calibrations of ability and motivation to process financial services communications.

Conclusion

Following the 2008 financial crisis, consumers and financial marketers all have opportunities to reconsider their positions about their financial future. It is imperative for consumers and financial marketers to understand the important role that financial services communications play in facilitating learning of financial matters and making financial decisions. This chapter argues that understanding the variables that enhance or inhibit processing of financial services communications could help financial marketers communicate to consumers more effectively. The first step is for financial marketers to understand consumers' levels of ability, motivation and opportunity to process financial services communications.

Table 20.3 Message strategy on motivation and ability to process

Motivation	Ability	
	Lower	Higher
Lower	1. Using peripheral cues.	1. Using peripheral cues.
	2. Using simplified messages.	2. Providing incentives.
Higher	1. Using vivid and attention-getting visuals.	1. Using credible messages.
	2. Using priming and framing.	2. Gathering information consensus.
	3. Creating message consistency.	3. Using strong arguments.
		4. Providing details.
		5. Advocating important benefits.

Consumers' levels of ability, motivation and opportunity to process financial services communications present different challenges for financial marketers. Levels of ability to process financial services communications are dependent on financial knowledge. The structures of financial knowledge that facilitate financial literacy can change how consumers process and react to financial services communications. Levels of motivation to process financial services communications are manifested by levels of personal or message involvement with financial services communications. Levels of opportunity to process financial services communications are dependent on the approach to the execution of different media. In general, enhancing consumers' levels of ability, motivation and opportunity to process financial services communications can enhance message involvement, media engagement and comprehension of financial service communications. Moreover, attitudes toward financial services communications and behavioral intentions could be predictive.

The second step is for financial marketers to understand the relationships among consumers' levels of ability, motivation and opportunity to process financial services communications. The correlations among the three variables could present more insightful perspectives in designing and delivering financial services communications. On one hand, engagement may become a driver of personal or message involvement to collaborate with ability and opportunity to facilitate processing of financial services communications. On the other hand, information cues such as consistency and consensus in financial services communications, executed based on message, communication and opportunity enhancement strategies could be useful for financial marketers to effectively communicate and promote financial products or services to consumers with different levels of ability to process financial services communications.

In essence, there is no one way for financial marketers to serve customers and communicate to consumers via financial services communications. In the same vein, there is no one way for financial marketers to design financial services communications and execute media plans that disseminate financial services communications. The important task is for financial marketers to identify and categorize consumers based on their levels of ability, motivation and opportunity to process financial services communications. Using qualitative and quantitative research, financial marketers could potentially generate different segments of consumers that would react to different message strategies positively. These positive message strategies rely on identifying appealing selling points, attracting attention, enhancing message involvement and augmenting media engagement. Consequently, financial marketers could enhance the effectiveness of financial services communications designed to reinforce or change financial attitudes and behaviors.

References

Alba, J. and Hutchinson, J. W., 1987. Dimension of consumer expertise. *Journal of Consumer Research*, 13(4), pp. 411–54.

——, 2000. Knowledge calibration: What consumers know and what they think they know. *Journal of Consumer Research*, 27(2), pp. 123–56.

Andrews, J. C., 1988. Motivation, ability, and opportunity to process information: Conceptual and experimental manipulation issues. In: M. J. Houston, ed. *Advances in Consumer Research*, Provo, UT: Association for Consumer Research, pp. 219–24.

Bettinghaus, E. P. and Cody, M. J. 1994. *Persuasive communication*, 5th ed., Wadsworth Publishing.

Bettman, J. R. and Park, C. W., 1980. Effects of prior knowledge and experience and phase of the choice process on consumer decision processes: A protocol analysis. *Journal of Consumer Research*, 7(3), pp. 234–48.

Burnkrant, R. E. and Sawyer, A. G., 1983. Effects of involvement and message content on information processing intensity. In: R. J. Harris, ed. *Information Processing Research in Advertising*, Hillsdale, NJ: Lawrence Erlbaum, pp. 43–64.

Campbell, M. C. and Kirmani, A., 2000. Consumers' use of persuasion knowledge: The effects of accessibility and cognitive capacity on perceptions of an influence agent. *Journal of Consumer Research*, 27(1), pp. 69–83.

Chaiken, S., 1987. The heuristic model of persuasion. In: M. P. Zanna, J. M. Olson and C. P. Herman, eds. *Social influence: The Ontario Symposium*, Hillsdale, NJ: Erlbaum, pp. 3–39.

Chaiken, S., Liberman, A. and Eagly, A. H., 1989. Heuristic and systematic information processing within and beyond the persuasion context. In: J. S. Uleman and J. A. Bargh, eds. *Unintended thought*, New York: Guilford Press, pp. 212–52.

Chaiken, S., Wood, W. and Eagly, A. H., 1996. Principles of persuasion. In: E. T. Higgins and A. Kruglanski, eds. *Social psychology: Handbook of basic mechanisms and processes.* New York: Guilford Press, pp. 553–78.

Chang, C., 2004. The interplay of product class knowledge and trial experience in attitude formation. *Journal of Advertising*, 33(1), pp. 83–92.

Christelis, D., Jappelli, T. and Padula, M., 2010. Cognitive abilities and portfolio choice. *European Economic Review*, 54(1), pp. 18–38.

Friestad, M. and Wright, P., 1994. The persuasion knowledge model: How people cope with persuasion attempts. *Journal of Consumer Research*, 21(1), pp. 1–31.

——, 1995. Persuasion knowledge: Lay people's and researchers' beliefs about the psychology of advertising. *Journal of Consumer Research*, 22(1), pp. 62–74.

Galin, M., 2013. *Magazine tablet editions' top interactive ads. How marketers got readers to get more info, open sites and download apps.* Available at http://adage.com/article/media/top-interactive-ads-magazines-tablet-editions/240326 (accessed 18 April 2013).

Greenwald, A. G. and Leavitt, C., 1984. Audience involvement in advertising: Four levels. *Journal of Consumer Research*, 11(2), pp. 25–42.

Hallahan, K., 2000. Enhancing motivation, ability, and opportunity to process public relations messages. *Public Relations Review*, 26(4), pp. 463–80.

Heider, F., 1958. *The Psychology of Interpersonal Relations*, Wiley, NY.

Hilgert, M. A., Hogarth, J. M. and Beverly, S., 2003. Household financial management: The connection between knowledge and behavior. *Federal Reserve Bulletin*, 89(7), pp. 309–22.

Kanso, A. and Nelson, R. A., 2004. Internet and magazine advertising: Integrated partnerships or not? *Journal of Advertising Research*, 44(4), pp. 317–26.

Kelley, H. H., 1967. Attribution Theory in social psychology. In: D. Levine, ed. *Nebraska Symposium on Motivation*, Lincoln: University of Nebraska Press, pp. 192–341.

——, 1973. The processes of causal attribution. *American Psychologist*, 28(2), pp. 107–28.

Lemonnier, J., 2008. Rich Media. *Ad Age*, 79(11), pp. 48.

Lusardi, A., 2010. *Americans' financial capability*, February 26, http://fcic-static.law.stanford.edu/cdn_media/fcic-testimony/2010-0226-Lusardi.pdf

Lusardi, A. and Mitchell, O. S., 2007. Baby boomer retirement Security: The role of planning, financial literacy, and housing wealth. *Journal of Monetary Economics*, 54(1), pp. 205–24.

——, 2008. Planning and Financial Literacy: How Do Women Fare? *American Economic Review*, 98(2), pp. 413–17.

MacInnis, D. J. and Jaworski, B. J., 1989. Information processing from advertisements: Toward an integrative framework. *Journal of Marketing*, 53(4), pp. 1–23.

Marks, L. J. and Olson, J. C., 1981. Toward a cognitive structure conceptualization of product familiarity. In K. B. Monroe, ed. *Advances in Consumer Research*, Ann Arbor, MI: Association for Consumer Research, pp. 178–83.

Moore, D., 2003. *Survey of financial literacy in Washington State: Knowledge, behavior, attitudes, and experiences*. Technical Report n. 03–39, Social and Economic Sciences Research Center, Washington State University.

Moorthy, S. and Hawkins, S. A., 2005. Advertising repetition and quality perceptions. *Journal of Business Research*, 58(3), pp. 354–60.

Moreau, C. P., Lehmann, D. R. and Markman, A. B., 2001. Entrenched knowledge structures and consumer response to new products. *Journal of Marketing Research*, 38(1), pp. 14–29.

Norvilitis, J. M., Osberg, T.M., Young, P., Merwin, M. M., Roehling, P. V. and Kamas, M. M., 2006. Personality factors, money attitudes, financial knowledge, and credit-card debt in college students. *Journal of Applied Social Psychology*, 36(6), pp. 1395–1413.

Park, C. W. and Lessig, C. P., 1981. Familiarity and its impact on consumer decision biases and heuristics. *Journal of Consumer Research*, 8(2), pp. 223–30.

Perry, V. G. and Morris, M. D., 2005. Who is in control? The role of self-perception, knowledge, and income in explaining consumer financial behavior. *Journal of Consumer Affairs*, 39(2), pp. 299–313.

Petty, R. E. and Cacioppo, J. T., 1979. Issue involvement can increase or decrease persuasion by enhancing message-relevant cognitive responses. *Journal of Personality and Social Psychology*, 37(10), pp. 1915–26.

——, 1981. *Attitudes and Persuasion: Classic and Contemporary approaches*, Dubuque, IA: William C. Brown.

——, 1986. *Communication and Persuasion. Central and Peripheral Routes to Persuasion*, New York, NY: Springer-Verlag.

Rosenkransa, G., 2010. Maximizing user interactivity through banner ad design. *Journal of Promotion Management*, 16(3), pp. 265–87.

Rosplock, K., 2006. *Women and wealth*. Research Report, Gen-Spring Family Offices. Available at www.genspring.com/documents/RESEARCH-Women-and-Wealth-Summaryof-Key-Findings.pdf (accessed 20 April 2013).

——, 2008. *Wealth alignment study*. Research Report, Gen-Spring Family Offices. Available at www.genspring.com/documents/RESEARCH-Wealth-Alignment-Study-Summary-of-Key-Findings.pdf (accessed 20 April 2013).

Rosplock, K., 2010. Gender matters: Men's and women's perceptions of wealth are mostly aligned. *Journal of Wealth Management*, 12(4), pp. 15–30.

Ryan, D. and Jones, C., 2009. *Understanding digital marketing: Marketing strategies for engaging the digital generation*. London: Kogan Page.

Shaw, R., 2004. *Evolution of rich media*. Available at www.imediaconnection.com/content/2618.imc (accessed 18 April 2013).

Stango, V. and Zinman, J., 2009. Exponential growth bias and household finance. *Journal of Finance*, 64(6), pp. 2807–49.

Trappey, R. J. and Woodside, A. G., 2005. Consumer responses to interactive advertising campaigns coupling short-message-service direct marketing and TV commercials. *Journal of Advertising Research*, 45(4), pp. 382–401.

Wang, A., 2005. The effects of expert and consumer endorsements on audience response. *Journal of Advertising Research*, 45(4), pp. 402–12.

——, 2006a. Ad engagement: A driver of message involvement on message effects. *Journal of Advertising Research*, 46(4), pp. 355–68.

——, 2006b. When synergy in marketing communication online enhances audience response. *Journal of Advertising Research*, 46(2), pp. 160–70.

——, 2008. Consensus and disagreement between online peer and expert recommendations. *International Journal of Internet Marketing and Advertising*, 4(4), pp. 328–49.

——, 2009a. Interplay of investors' financial knowledge and risk taking. *Journal of Behavioral Finance*, 10(4), pp. 204–13.

——, 2009b. Cross-channel integration of advertising: Does personal involvement matter? *Management Research News*, 32(9), pp. 858–73.

——, 2011a. The effects of investment knowledge and visual communications on comprehension of investment disclosures. *Journal of Financial Services Marketing*, 16(2), pp. 125–38.

——, 2011b. Effects of gender, ethnicity and work on college students' credit card debt: Implications for wealth advisors. *Journal of Wealth Management*, 14(2), pp. 85–100.

——, 2011c. Younger generations' investing behaviors in mutual funds: Does Gender Matter? *Journal of Wealth Management*, 13(4), pp. 13–23.

——, 2011d. The contextual relevance effect on financial advertising. *Journal of Financial Services Marketing*, 16(1), pp. 50–64.

——, 2011e. Branding over Internet and TV advertising. *Journal of Promotion Management*, 17(3), pp. 275–90.

——, 2011f. The effectiveness of mobile magazine: Implications for mobile marketers. *International Journal of Mobile Marketing*, 6(1), pp. 63–76.

——, 2012a. Socialization and processing effects on comprehension of credit card advertisement disclosures. *Journal of Financial Services Marketing*, 17(2), pp. 163–76.

——, 2012b. The effects of knowledge, gender and age on comprehension of investment disclosures. *Journal of Wealth Management*, 15(3), pp. 9–19.

——, 2013. *Financial Communications: Information Processing, Media Integration and Ethical Considerations*, New York, NY: Palgrave Macmillan.

Wang, A. and Muehling, D. D., 2010. The effects of audio-visual and visual-only cues on consumers' responses to co-branded advertising. *Journal of Marketing Communications*, 16(5), pp. 307–24.

Wang, S. A., 2006. The effects of audience knowledge on message processing of editorial Content. *Journal of Marketing Communications*, 12(4), pp. 281–96.

Wang, S. A. and Nelson, R.A., 2006. The effects of identical vs. varied advertising and publicity messages on consumer response. *Journal of Marketing Communications*, 12(2), pp. 109–23.

Wouters, J. and Wetzels, M., 2006. Recall effect of short message service as a complementary marketing communications instrument. *Journal of Advertising Research*, 46(2), pp. 209–16.

Zarem, J. E., 2008. *The state of digital magazine delivery*. Available at www.foliomag.com/2008/state-digital-magazine-delivery-2008 (accessed 18 April 2013).

Part VII
Distribution and delivery of financial services

21

The role of technology in financial services distribution and delivery

Fernando Jaramillo

Introduction

> *[The] physical movement of goods from producers to consumers…was perhaps…the essence of marketing in its elemental state.*
>
> *(Bartels 1988: 215)*

The perennial question in logistics and distribution is finding effective and efficient ways for distributing products to customers. Bartels (1988) asserts that from the 1960s to the 1980s product distribution research transitioned from basic cost studies to investigating inter-organizational behaviors among channel members to research on distribution management strategies. The emphasis on physical products later changed to a focus on customer service and services quality (Parasuraman et al. 1988, Zeithaml et al. 1996). However, in both product and service situations, earlier examinations of distribution and delivery systems assumed a physical interaction with the customer.

Technology has redefined the structure of financial services markets by altering the ways in which organizations interact with their customers and build relationships with them (Breidbach et al. 2013). Technology creates a virtual world made of information that enables a new marketplace "where products and services exist as digital information and can be delivered through information-based channels" (Rayport and Sviokla 1995: 75). In retail banking, customers are shifting from traditional branches towards alternative delivery channels like internet banking, mobile banking, and phone banking. Similar changes are observed in the insurance industry where insurers are shifting from traditional channels towards low-cost distribution alternatives like call centers, mobile, and internet based offerings. Verma (2012) posits that insurance companies have increased partnerships with banks and other affinity groups to leverage from the distribution systems of their partners. Verma (2012) also talks about the emergence of bancassurance products.

The World Retail Banking Report (WRBR) (2012) shows that 70 percent to 90 percent of customers worldwide believe that internet banking is an important channel for them (Lassignardie and Desmares 2012). WRBR shows that 40 percent to 75 percent of customers rank mobile channels and the phone as important. In addition, the report shows that over 50 percent of customers worldwide used mobile banking in 2011 and predicts a 60 percent usage rate by 2015 (Lassignardie and Desmares 2012).

A survey of 1,000 U.S. adults by the American Bankers Association (ABA) (2012) found that customers rate the internet as their favorite channel for conducting their banking business, but the popularity of mobile banking is gaining ground among 'millennials' (those born between the 1980s and early 2000s). Thirty-nine percent of the respondents in the ABA survey indicated that the internet is the method most often used to manage their bank accounts, compared to 18 percent that used a brick-and-mortar branch. Research by the Pew Research Center (Fox 2013) also demonstrates a significant increase in both internet banking and mobile banking in the U.S.

Service distribution and delivery technologies like internet, mobile, and telephone banking can benefit financial institutions by providing opportunities to serve the customer at significantly lower costs (Ahmad and Buttle 2002). For instance, Sahoo and Swain (2012) report that transaction costs using traditional tellers average 1 Re in India, which are significantly higher than ATM (0.45 Re), phone banking (0.35 Re), debit cards (0.20 Re) or internet transaction costs (0.20 Re). Similarly, Ahmad and Buttle (2002) report that the cost of running a checking (current) account in the UK using a call center is about a third of the cost of using a branch bank.

The World Economic Forum (WEF) (2012) posits that traditional distribution models are inadequate for low-income countries because accounts are small and the number of customer transactions is limited. The WEF report concludes that current branch networks in emerging markets cannot reach large segments of the population and thus calls for large-scale and lower-cost distribution alternatives that require less capital investment. Partnering with other financial and non-financial institutions is critical for accessing mass market consumers. For example, Banco Postal in Brazil has developed agreements with a select group of partners to deliver bank products in post offices. In Colombia, Multibanca Colpatria collects loan payments from customers through utility bills run by an electric utility company.

Technology also creates opportunities for delivering financial services to unattended markets. Berger and Nakata (2013) recently showed that information communication technologies (ICTs) help a financial institution serve consumers at the "Base of the Pyramid" (BOP) in five sub-Saharan African Countries. BOP customers gained access to a wide range of financial products including savings, remittances, cash withdraws and loans through mobile banks, point-of-service systems, and m-banking. Innovative ICTs thus have positive implications for poverty alleviation and economic development. The use of technology and other strategies for reaching the poor are discussed in Chapter 35.

This chapter offers an in-depth review of the financial services distribution and delivery literature and proposes future research opportunities. The chapter also talks about research examining the impact of technology on the firm and the customer. This review of the literature demonstrates that technology offers new service distribution and delivery alternatives that can benefit the firm and the customer. The chapter complements Chapters 22 and 23 in this section that focus in more detail on mobile technology and the e-experience delivered via the online environment.

Self-service technologies, internet and mobile banking

This section centers around the notion that technology can improve customer service levels by providing new and more efficient forms of service delivery that enable firms to respond to customer needs with greater agility. Alternative channels provide financial institutions with opportunities to enhance their customer value proposition and achieve higher levels of customer satisfaction. However, as shown below, empirical research linking service-technologies with customer outcomes has rendered mixed results. For instance, Proenca and Rodriguez's (2011) study of banking customers in Portugal found that customers who rely on self-service technology are less likely to complain about banking services than non-users of self-service technology. However, their study also shows that there were no significant differences between users and non-users of self-service technology on customer satisfaction, propensity to change banks, and repurchase intentions.

The "good side" of self-service technologies

Research recognizes that self-service technologies offer many advantages to customers like convenience, interactivity, connectivity, and the ability to customize (Brun et al. 2014). Walker et al. (2002) assert that technology can provide customers with services that they want and when they want them. Technology enables a faster, more reliable, and more convenient service. For example, smartphone applications from Chase and Bank of America allow their customers to take a picture of a check and then deposit the money in their checking or savings account. Greater convenience can potentially lead to increased customer satisfaction and customer value (Meuter et al. 2000).

Meuter et al.'s (2000) seminal study posits that technology allows firms to customize their service offers while providing customers with the convenience of consuming service when needed. Meuter et al. (2000) examined 459 incidents involving satisfactory self-service technology encounters. The study found that customers were satisfied in conditions where the technology helped them address an urgent and difficult situation triggered by an external environmental factor, such as getting cash after a car accident when all the banks are closed. High satisfaction also resulted in conditions where customers viewed the service as a better alternative to the traditional interpersonal method of service delivery. Some of the factors associated with a better alternative evaluation are: ease of use, time and money savings, and having the product/service when and where they are needed. Satisfying events are related to positive behaviors like word of mouth and repurchase intentions.

Consumers using self-service technologies like internet and mobile banking have greater access to products and services and can save their time by not having to visit a retail outlet or relate with a service employee. A study of young consumers in Turkey shows that consumers associate internet banking with attributes such as "easy to use", "less restriction on users", "easy to access" and "seeing banking alternatives more easily" (Calisir and Gumussoy 2008: 218). The study also shows that young consumers view ATM and phone banking as providing them with "time saving" benefits.

Findings from a survey of 18,000 customers in 35 countries in the World Retail Banking Report (2012) indicates the percentage of customers reporting a positive experience with Internet banking is higher than traditional branch banks in North America (63 percent versus 62 percent), Central Europe (56 percent versus 49 percent) and Western Europe (49 percent versus 43 percent).

The "bad side" of self-service technologies

Research recognizes the advantages of self-service technologies but also demonstrates that self-service technologies can create a distance between the customer and their service providers. Brun et al. (2014: 5) view self-service technologies as a "double-edged sword" for financial institutions that is responsible for the technological dehumanization of the customer-vendor relationship. Calisir and Gumussoy (2008) also report that young customers believe that self-service technologies restrict social relations. They posit that self-service technologies are ineffective alternatives for serving customers that seek specialized and advisory services that require experts to "engage intimately with the customer" (Calisir and Gumussoy 2008: 219).

As Marr and Prendergast (1993: 9) assert, "a preference for humans in banking is a global reason for not using self-service technology". Technology does not provide customers with the enjoyment that they may receive from personally going to their financial institution to conduct business. Black et al. (2001) found that some consumers refrain from using the Internet for financial transactions because it does not provide them with opportunities to socialize. When technology is imposed on the customer or when it fails, technology use can also result in feelings of frustration, intimidation, and technology-induced hostility (Walker et al. 2002). Providing customers with information and guidance about the benefits of self-serving technology can help financial institutions overcome a person's natural resistance towards adopting new service delivery alternatives (Laukkanen and Kiviniemi 2010).

Meuter et al. (2000) examined 364 incidents involving customer dissatisfaction. Dissatisfaction was primarily driven by technological failure, process failures, and product design failures. Similarly, Marr and Prendergast (1993) report that ATM users are concerned about machines not working, being unsafe or running out of cash. Technological failures often occur due to unclear directions about using a product and the inability to discuss a situation with a customer service representative (Meuter et al. 2000). When things go wrong, individuals will likely attribute the failure to the technology. Dissatisfaction negatively affects word of mouth and future purchase intentions.

These findings indicate that effective channel mix strategies require a thorough analysis of customer preferences in terms of perceived benefits and perceived costs of various competing and complementary distribution alternatives.

Insurance channels

The insurance industry relies on a combination of distribution channels that include both traditional agent-led channels as well as alternative contact channels like internet, company-led, bank-led, and bancassurance. Dumm and Hoyt (2002) assert that insurers use multiple channels to balance the needs of consumers and distribution costs. They posit that higher price insurance products require greater service and personalized dealings which are effectively offered via independent agency channels. Conversely, cost effective channels are a better fit for insurance with a low level of complexity.

Forman and Gron (2009) identify two technological innovations that affected insurance distributions and enabled multichannel offers. The first innovation in the 1970s and 1980s is the adoption of mainframe computer technologies that enabled instantaneous information exchanges between insurance companies and agents. A second innovation is related to the adoption and growth of internet offerings. Technological advances have resulted in today's multichannel offerings to customers.

The World Insurance Report (2013: 31) shows that "multi-distribution initiatives are a critical part of insurers' strategies to retain customers and keep them loyal – and ultimately to grow revenues". This report shows that customers prefer the internet or mobile applications for comparing policies and services, assessing information, and finding the best rates. Report findings demonstrate that the availability of online channels is critical for the industry because it is an important driver of insurer selection. Online channels explain 22 percent of the customer selection of life insurers and 26 percent of the selection of non-life insurance. However, the report also concludes that customers still have a stronger preference for agents and brokers for gaining trust in their insurers (the role of agents and brokers in the formation of trust is clearly evident in the study discussed in Chapter 10).

An investigation of insurer channels in Taiwan discusses the emergence of bank-insurance partnerships and increased sales from bancassurance channels (Chang et al. 2011). The growth of bancassurance sales has been driven by both reduced delivery costs and the benefits of one-stop shopping of complementary bank and insurance products.

New channel adoption

This section talks about the technology acceptance model (Venkatesh and Davis 2000), and the technology readiness model (for example, Parasuraman 2000) in explaining new channel adoption. The section also summarizes empirical evidence from the financial services literature in support of the technology acceptance (TAM) and technology readiness models (TRM). The section builds upon the TAM and TRM models by incorporating precepts from the online consumer behavior literature. For instance, it talks about the role of perceived risk, perceived control, and shopping enjoyment in increasing technology acceptance.

The Technology Acceptance Model (TAM)

TAM relies on precepts from the theory of reasoned action which posits that behavioral intentions are driven by both the attitude towards an action as well as subjective norms (Ajzen and Fishbein 1980). Individual attitudes are the degree to which a person has a favorable or unfavorable evaluation towards an object. Subjective norms pertain to a person's perception about what their reference group thinks they should do. Montazemi and Saremi's (2013) meta-analysis shows that social influence plays an important role in motivating consumers to adopt internet banking products.

TAM also posits that attitudes towards technology adoption are explained by perceived usefulness, perceived ease of use, and trust. TAM has received ample empirical support which has been summarized in meta-analytic studies (for example, Schepers and Wetzels 2007, Wu et al. 2011). TAM has been applied to a variety of financial services contexts such as internet banking adoption (for example, Yousafzai and Yani-de-Soriano 2012) and use of ATMs (for example, Proenca and Rodriguez 2011).

A recent meta-analysis that investigates initial use intention of internet banking brings additional support to the TAM model (Montazemi and Saremi 2013). Meta-analytic findings from 26 studies conducted in 14 countries demonstrate that use intention of internet banking is preceded by: (1) trust in the internet bank, (2) trust in the physical bank, (3) perceived usefulness of the internet bank, and (4) perceived ease of use of the internet bank (Montazemi and Saremi 2013). The meta-analysis also shows that social influence also affects intention to use through a mediating process that involves trust and ease of use.

Individual-level factors like consumers' propensity to trust as well and consumers' innovativeness had a significant indirect effect on intention to use. Another important finding of this meta-analysis is that structural assurances like safety nets, guarantees, and security regulations provide a sense of security which affects both customers' trust in the internet bank as well as intention to use. Security and ease of use are positively correlated with brand awareness, brand image, and brand loyalty (Al-Hawari 2011).

A well supported notion in the self-service technology (SST) literature is that customers are reluctant to adopt new technologies unless motivated to do so. New channel adoption is driven by both hedonic (for example, enjoyment) as well as utilitarian (for example, convenience) motives. For instance, Byun and Feinberg (2007) showed that enjoyment, usefulness, and ease of use were related to customer attitudes and intentions to use mobile banking services in South Korea.

Convenience

Customers are more willing to adopt new channel options when they think that the service offering is convenient (Collier and Kimes 2012). Convenience is defined as "the perceived time and effort required to finding and facilitating the use of an SST" (Collier and Kimes 2012: 40) and is conceived as a multi-dimensional construct composed of ease of use as well as time and effort savings perceptions.

Convenience affects customer perceptions of the efficiency and the effectiveness of service transactions and eventually leads to higher satisfaction and trust in the service provider (Collier and Kimes 2012). Convenience perceptions are positively related to internet banking adoption and retention (for example, Gerrard and Cunningham 2003, Khare et al. 2012). Gerrard and Cunningham (2003) asked internet banking consumers to indicate what influenced their service adoption decision. In all cases an aspect of convenience was mentioned: "I can do most of my banking business either from home or work"; "I do not have to spend time going to a branch or an ATM"; "When I have used my branch in the past, I have had to queue up; now I do not even think about queuing" and "Even if the bank is 'closed', I can still do my banking business" (Gerrard and Cunningham 2003: 20).

Convenience perceptions affect customer beliefs that self-service technologies are superior to traditional banking channels: "Internet banking is a convenient way to manage my finances" (Tan and Teo 2000: 16). Karimi (2013) notes: "Whether you're checking your bank accounts, transferring funds, or making a payment, online banking is a convenient way to manage your basic transactions. More banks and credit unions are offering online banking options as a convenience to customers, and now it's easier than ever to keep track of your finances."

Similarly, Keaveney (1995) shows that inconvenience is an important determinant of customer switching behavior in service industries. In Keaveney's (1995: 74) study, customers felt inconvenienced by aspects like "the service provider's location, hours of operation, waiting time for service, or waiting time to get an appointment". Alternative channels like internet or telephone financial services should thus help financial institutions reduce perceptions of an inconvenient service.

Customer characteristics

Technology adoption in financial services is also influenced by individual customer differences like technology readiness and customer demographics (for example, Yousafzai and Yani-de-Soriano 2012). Technology adoption is positively related to education level (for example, Nasri 2011, Proenca and Rodriguez 2011), which is often related to income and a greater need for financial products and services. Also, males are also more inclined to be early adopters of new financial services technologies (for example, Akinci et al. 2004, Khare et al. 2012). The large majority of new technology adopters are also young (for example, Khare et al. 2012, Nasri 2011). Technology driven channels consequently will play a fundamental role in attracting the new generation of consumers.

Risk perceptions

Adoption of innovative channels of financial services delivery is also influenced by perceived risk (Black et al. 2001). Tan and Teo (2000) show that perceived risk affects attitudes towards technology in financial services and the subsequent use of traditional channels like bank tellers. Perceived risk evaluations include a cost dimension and a probability dimension (Littler and Melanthiou 2006). The cost dimension consists of the person's assessment of the amount that would be lost due to an unfavorable act while the probability aspect refers to the perceived likelihood of the act.

Littler and Melanthiou (2006) identified four types of perceived risk that are relevant to internet banking (IB) customers: (1) security risk, (2) time risk, (3) financial risk and (4) performance risk. Their study showed that customers are concerned about hackers and risk inherent to unauthorized access to their accounts. In terms of time risk, some customers refrain from using internet banking applications because they do not want to waste their time in learning how to perform a task online. Financial risk refers to the expected possibility of losing money: "I mean imagine one day you go to the ATM to withdraw some money and to your surprise you find out there is no money in your account" (Littler and Melanthiou 2006: 438). Finally, customers were concerned about product performance uncertainty: "Obviously what they tell you is that it is secure, but then again you always question that and ask whether that is really true" (Littler and Melanthiou 2006: 439). Littler and Melanthiou (2006) show that the preferred strategy for managing customer perceived risk is an offering of money back guarantee assurance that promises reimbursement of risk related costs. The notion that perceived risk is an important driver of the adoption of internet banking has received worldwide empirical support (for example, Nasri 2011).

Risk perceptions are also affected by the possibility of security breaches. Service providers should be cautious about gaining more information than is necessary from customers and be careful about keeping this information secure. Malhotra and Malhotra (2011) posit that security breaches of financial information (for example, credit card or bank account numbers) and customer information (for example, social security numbers) have a financial cost to the customer and also affect trust in the service provider. Events involving hacking and stealing customer and financial information from up to 110 million customers from Target in the U.S. highlight the importance of preserving information security (CNN Money, Isidore 2014).

Technology Readiness Model (TRM)

Researchers have also relied on precepts from TRM to explain new product and channel adoption. Technology readiness represents "people's propensity to embrace and use new technologies for accomplishing goals in home life and work" (Parasuraman 2000: 308). TRM posits that individual level variables are related to technology adoption. As Parasuraman (2000) asserts, individuals simultaneously hold favorable and unfavorable opinions about technology. Consumers' opinions about technology are critical as they explain consumers' adoption and use of financial service technologies (for example, Ratchford and Barnhart 2012)

Optimism and innovativeness are linked to higher adoption while insecurity and discomfort reduce technology adoption (for example, Parasuraman 2000, Son and Han 2011). Findings from Ratchford and Barnhart (2012) demonstrate that technology readiness is an individual personal disposition towards technology, and that this disposition includes optimism, innovativeness, insecurity, and discomfort aspects. Personal disposition towards technology is related to various behaviors like moving money between bank accounts online, applying for a credit card online, or using an online bank that did not have a brick and mortar location (Ratchford and Barnhart 2012: 1214).

TRM also suggests that usage rates are positively related to satisfaction and eventually retention (for example, Son and Han 2011). TRM has been used to explain both past use and intentions to use in various technology-based services including ATM use and telephone banking (for example, Parasuraman 2000). The TRM also plays an important role in explaining variance in customer responses to bankers' actions (Yousafzai and Yani-de-Soriano 2012).

Customers' coping strategies

When deciding to adopt a new product, customers evaluate a mix of positive benefits as well as negative aspects of the new product. Mick and Fournier (1998) identified eight *paradoxes of technology* that explain positive and negative feelings from customers that occur simultaneously. Their study found that technology can lead to eight opposed perceptions: (1) engaging/disengaging, (2) assimilation/isolation, (3) fulfills/creates needs, (4) efficiency/inefficiency, (5) competence/incompetence, (6) new/obsolete, (7) freedom/enslavement and (8) control/chaos.

Technology paradoxes provoke conflict and uncertainty that trigger anxiety and stress and then a behavioral coping strategy response (Mick and Fournier 1998). Coping strategies occur at the pre-acquisition stage or at the consumption stage of the buying process (Mick and Fournier 1998). Customer coping strategies include avoiding strategies like refusal and delay as well as confronting strategies like extended decision making and pre-test (Cui et al. 2009, Mick and Fournier 1998). Cui et al. (2009) show that avoidance strategies have a negative effect on beliefs that the product is useful, easy to use, and fun. They also found that confronting strategies have a positive impact on product beliefs.

In remote service transactions, customers can experience mixed feelings about a service (Paluch and Blut 2013). A separation/customer integration paradox occurs when customers simultaneously express a desire to be a part of the remote service and a desire not to be integrated into the service delivery process (Paluch and Blut 2013). Paluch and Blut (2013) showed that the optimal level of process integration in terms of customer quality and satisfaction perceptions is contingent on whether the service was initiated by the customer or the provider. They found that customers should be involved only when the service provider initiates the service. Involvement is detrimental when the service is initiated by the customer. These findings have important implications for service delivery strategy.

Conclusions and directions for future research

This review of the literature shows that customer decisions to adopt new technologies in distribution and service delivery are highly complex. Extant research has relied on various frameworks like the technology acceptance model (TAM), the technology readiness model (TRM), the market orientation perspective, as well as precepts from the coping strategies perspective. However, as rational individuals, customers are looking for ways of maximizing the value they receive from service vendors. They are comparing existing alternatives with new offerings and deciding on what is best for them. They search for offerings that are useful and convenient to them. They refrain from adopting technologies that are difficult to use, risky or untrustworthy. As Evanschitzky et al. (2012) show, customers are looking for a service that is advantageous and provided by a market-oriented firm who cares about them.

This chapter has reviewed extant research into technology use in financial services. In doing so, it identifies a number of fruitful avenues for further research enquiry. For example, research linking consumers' use of technology with customer satisfaction and firm performance is lacking. Research investigating factors that moderate relationships explained in the TAM/TRM models is also sparse. Self-service technologies in financial distribution and delivery provide firms with opportunities to strengthen customer relationships by giving customers efficient and effective services that are faster, better, and less costly. However, as Zhu et al. (2013) assert, users of self-service technologies can experience service failures which result in dissatisfaction and lost sales. Customers facing service failures can engage in customer recovery efforts (CRE). Zhu et al. (2013) show that CRE is positively related to: (1) customer beliefs that the service failure is due to their own error (internal attribution), (2) the degree to which they think that they have control over the service technology (perceived control) and (3) the degree to which a customer thinks that the service technology is interactive and provides sufficient information for recovery. Our review of the literature shows that research on customer recovery efforts related to technological failures in financial services is lacking and is worthy of further attention.

Empirical studies provide mixed results about the benefits of alternative distribution offerings to customers. For example, a study involving 18 retail banks operating in Turkey from 1990 to 2008 shows that internet banking had a negative impact on bank profitability two years after the adoption (Onay and Ozoz 2013). The study reports that the interest income to total assets ratio was 37 percent prior to adoption and only 16 percent after the adoption. Yet, an analysis of 105 banks in Italy from 1993 to 2002 reports that internet offerings are positively related to ROA (Ciciretti et al. 2009). In their study, internet banks had higher ROA compared to banks that did not offer internet-banking to customers (0.993 percent and 0.842 percent respectively). A meta-analytic study could estimate the average impact of internet adoption on performance and explore for potential moderating factors.

As Ramdas et al. (2013) posit, radical delivery of services innovations are rare. Ramdas et al. (2013) propose a framework for innovation in service delivery that focuses on four dimensions: (1) the structure of the service provider and customer interactions, (2) the scope of the service boundary, (3) the allocation of service tasks and (4) the delivery location. This framework could be used to investigate the impact of radical channel innovations on the customer and the organization. Chapter 13 in this book also proposes a customer-centric approach to new financial services innovations.

Modifying the scope of boundaries allows financial institutions to offer complementary services that are attractive to corporate customers. Using business-to-business portals that its major clients had with suppliers, Citigroup created a platform that reconciled purchase orders and invoices which allows suppliers to receive advance credit from Citigroup (Ramdas et al. 2013). TD Ameritrade altered the traditional manual trading operations by means of automatic electronic trading. Automatic electronic trading benefits investment banks and customers by reducing trading costs and the possibility of transaction errors. SafeSave from Bangladesh altered the traditional model where customers approach a bank for transactions. Bank agents at SafeSafe visit clients' homes and businesses to collect deposits and offer withdrawals (Ramdas et al. 2013). Rabobank agents decide on the best way to approach and serve their clients by working in the customer's office, at home, or in the office. Academic research examining how radical delivery of service innovations affects customer attitudes, perceptions of value, and behavioral intentions is warranted.

An important share of the profitability of financial institutions comes from service fees charged to their clients (Marceau 2013). Gounaris et al. (2010) posit that internet customers are less loyal because the internet provides them with greater opportunities to compare service characteristics and pricing. Clients from vendors offering financial services over the internet may thus be more sensitive to price increases than those using traditional sales channels.

Research investigating customer response to pricing of internet financial services and their impact on perceptions of quality, satisfaction and purchase intentions is needed.

The adoption of innovative financial services technologies in developing countries lags behind that of developed countries (Akinci et al. 2004). Lower penetration rates are attributed to the telecommunication infrastructure, an inhibitive policy environment, as well as political interference of governments in the financial sector (Agu 2012). However, empirical studies examining the adoption of financial service technologies in developed countries have shown that customer adoption decisions are driven by factors like security, privacy, reliability, and trust (for example, Agu 2012, Nasri 2011, Rotchanakitumnuai and Speece 2003) which are also found in the developed world. Multi-country research investigating the moderating role of cultural and social preferences as well as economic constraints and environmental factors on relationships explained by the technology acceptance or the technology readiness model is lacking.

Significant differences between rural and urban customers in terms of technology use are expected in developing countries (for example, Donner 2008). Research examining how urban versus rural consumer differences affect preferences for financial service delivery is also needed.

Studies examining consumers' coping strategies have relied on Mick and Fournier's (1998) typology which distinguishes between confronting and avoidance coping strategies. However, as Moschis (2007) asserts, in addition to these strategies customers also employ non-consumption coping strategies like seeking social support or engaging in positive thinking. Moschis (2007) proposes a comprehensive model to examine consumer stress and coping mechanisms. This model could be tested using a financial services setting to enhance our understanding of channel adoption and stress coping mechanisms.

Technology has significantly altered the interactions between service providers and their customers and the distribution of financial services. A disadvantage of technology centers around the concerns of dehumanization of the customer-vendor relationship (Brun et al. 2014). However, newer technologies may also help enhance social interactions. Blasco-Arcas et al. (2011) argue that technology can support social connectivity through various technological innovations like video conferencing, network connectivity software, and interactive television which facilitate bidirectional exchanges of information among users and resemble face-to-face contacts. Further research exploring when the technology dehumanization hypothesis holds is warranted.

Serving customers requires providing them with multiple competing and complementary distribution offers. Multichannel strategies enable firms to offer their customers a full service provision. As discussed in Chapter 9, such strategies are likely conducive to customer relationship building.

References

Agu, E. (2012). 'A qualitative study of the problems and prospects of online banking in developing economies – case of Nigeria'. *Journal of Internet Banking and Commerce*, 17(3), pp. 1–20.

Ahmad, R. and Buttle, F. (2002). 'Retaining telephone banking customers at Frontier Bank'. *International Journal of Bank Marketing*, 20(1), pp. 5–16.

Ajzen, I. and Fishbein, M. (1980). *Understanding attitudes and predicting social behavior*. Englewood Cliffs, N.J.: Prentice-Hall.

Akinci, S., Aksoy, S. and Atilgan, E. (2004). 'Adoption of Internet banking among sophisticated consumer segments in an advanced developing country'. *International Journal of Bank Marketing*, 22(3), pp. 212–32.

Al-Hawari, M. A. (2011). 'Do online services contribute to establishing brand equity within the retail banking context?' *Journal of Relationship Marketing*, 10(3), pp. 145–66.

American Bankers Association (2012). *ABA Survey: popularity of mobile banking jumps*, October 9th 2012. www.aba.com/Press/Pages/100912PreferredBankingMethods.aspx (accessed 8th April 2014).

Bartels, R. (1988). *The history of marketing thought, third edition*. Columbus, OH: Publishing Horizons.

Breidbach, C. F., Kolb, D. G. and Srinvasan, A. (2013). 'Connectivity in service systems: Does technology-enablement impact the ability of a service system to co-create value?' *Journal of Service Research*, 16(3), pp. 428–41.

Berger, E. and Nakata, C. (2013). 'Implementing technologies for financial service innovations in the base of the pyramid markets'. *Journal of Product Innovation Management*, 30(6), pp. 1199–1211.

Black, N. J., Lockett, A., Winklhofer, H. and Ennew, C. (2001). 'The adoption of internet financial services: a qualitative study'. *International Journal of Retail & Distribution Management*, 29(8), pp. 390–98.

Blasco-Arcas, L., Aznar-Baranda, J. I., Hernández-Ortega, B. and Ruiz-Mas, J. (2011). 'IPTV as a service distribution channel'. *Industrial Management & Data Systems*, 111(9), pp. 1381–98.

Brun, L., Rajaobelina, L. and Line, R. (2014). 'Online relationship quality: scale development and initial testing'. *International Journal of Bank Marketing*, 32(1), pp. 5–27.

Byun, S. and Feinberg, R. A. (2007). 'Understanding consumer acceptance of mobile technology for financial service delivery'. *AMA Winter Educators' Conference Proceedings*, pp. 81–82.

Calisir, F. and Gumussoy, C. A. (2008). 'Internet banking versus other banking channels: Young consumer's view'. *International Journal of Information Management*, 28(3), pp. 215–21.

Chang, P. R., Peng, J. L. and Fan, C. K. (2011). 'A comparison of bancassurance and traditional insurer sales channels'. *The Geneva Papers*, 36(1), pp. 76–93.

Ciciretti, R., Hasan, I. and Zazzara, C. (2009). 'Do internet activities add value? Evidence from the traditional banks'. *Journal of Financial Services Research*, 35(1), pp. 81–98.

Collier, J. E. and Kimes, S. E. (2012). 'Only if it is convenient: Understanding how convenience influences self-service technology evaluation'. *Journal of Services Research*, 16(1), pp. 39–51.

Cui, G., Bao, W. and Chan, T. S. (2009). 'Customers' adoption of new technology products: the role of coping strategies'. *Journal of Consumer Marketing*, 26(2), pp. 110–20.

Donner, J. (2008). 'Research approaches to mobile use in the developing world: A review of the literature'. *The Information Society*, 24(3), pp. 140–59.

Dumm, R. E. and Hoyt, R. E. (2002). 'Insurance distribution channels: Markets in Transition'. Paper presented at the 38th Annual Seminar of the International Insurance Society in Singapore, July 7.

Evanschitzky, H., Eisend, M., Calantone, R. J. and Jiang, Y. (2012). 'Success factors of product innovation: An updated meta-analysis'. *Journal of Product Innovation Management*, 29(1), pp. 21–37.

Forman, C. and Gron, A. (2009). 'Vertical integration and information technology investment in the insurance industry'. *The Journal of Law, Economics, & Organization*, 27(1), pp. 180–218.

Fox, Susannah (2013). *51% of U.S. Adults Bank Online*. Pew Research Internet Project. Pew Research Center, August 7, 2013. http://pewinternet.org/Reports/2013/Online-banking.aspx

Gerrard, P. and Cunningham, J. B. (2003). 'The diffusion of internet banking among Singapore consumers'. *International Journal of Bank Marketing*, 21(1), pp. 16–28.

Gounaris, S., Dimitriadis, S. and Stathakopoulos, V. (2010). 'An examination of the effects of service quality and satisfaction on consumers' behavioral intentions in e-shopping'. *Journal of Services Research*, 24(2), pp. 142–56.

Isidore, C. (2014). 'Target: Hacking hit up to 110 million customers'. CNN Money http://money.cnn.com/2014/01/10/news/companies/target-hacking (accessed 8th April 2014).

Karimi, S. (2013). 'Online banking tips to keep your accounts secure'. U.S. News, February 26, http://money.usnews.com/money/blogs/my-money/2013/02/26/online-banking-tips-to-keep-your-accounts-secure (accessed 8th April 2014).

Khare, A. Mishra, A. and Singh, A. B. (2012). 'Indian consumers' attitude towards trust and convenience dimensions of internet banking'. *International Journal of Services and Operations Management*, 11(1), pp. 107–22.

Keaveney, S. M. (1995). 'Customer switching behavior in service industries: an exploratory study'. *Journal of Marketing*, 59(2), pp. 71–82.

Lassignardie, J. and Desmares, P. (2012). *World retail banking report 2012*. www.capgemini.com/resources/world-retail-banking-report-2012, Capgemini and Efma.

Laukkanen, T. and Kiviniemi, V. (2010). 'The role of information in mobile banking resistance'. *International Journal of Bank Marketing*, 28(5), pp. 372–88.

Littler, D. and Melanthiou, D. (2006). 'Consumer perceptions of risk and uncertainty and the implications for behavior towards innovative retail services: The case of Internet Banking'. *Journal of Retailing and Consumer Services*, 13(6), pp. 431–43.

Malhotra, A. and Malhotra, C. K. (2011). 'Evaluating customer information breaches as service failures: An event study approach'. *Journal of Service Research*, 14(1), p. 44–59.

Marr, N. E. and Gerard P. Prendergast. (1993). 'Consumer adoption of self-service technologies in retail bank-ing: Is expert opinion supported by consumer research?' *International Journal of Bank Marketing*, 11, pp. 3–10.

Marceau, G. (2013). 'Online banking in France'. *International Business Research*, 6(2), pp. 1–7.

Meuter, M.L., Ostrom, A.L., Roundtree, R. I. and Jo Bitner, M. (2000). 'Self-service technologies: Understanding customer satisfaction with technology-based service encounters'. *Journal of Marketing*, 64(July), pp. 50–64.

Mick, D. G. and Fournier, S. (1998). 'Paradoxes of technology: consumer cognizance, emotions, and coping strategies'. *Journal of Consumer Research*, 25(September), pp. 123–43.

Montazemi, A. R. and Saremi, H. Q. (2013). 'Factors affecting internet banking pre-usage expectation formation'. *46th Hawaii International Conference on System Sciences*, pp. 4666–75.

Moschis, G. P. (2007). 'Stress and consumer behavior'. *Journal of the Academy of Marketing Science*, 35(3), pp. 430–44.

Nasri, W. (2011). 'Factors influencing the adoption of internet banking in Tunisia'. *International Journal of Business and Management*, 6(8), pp. 143–60.

Onay, C. and Ozoz, E. (2013). 'The impact of internet-banking on brick and mortar branches: The case of Turkey'. *Journal of Financial Services Research*, 44, pp. 187–204.

Paluch, S. and Blut, M. (2013). 'Service separation and customer satisfaction: Assessing the service separation/customer integration paradox'. *Journal of Service Research*, 16(3), pp. 415–27.

Parasuraman, A. (2000). 'Technology readiness index'. *Journal of Service Research*, 2(4), pp. 307–20.

Parasuraman, A. Zeithaml, V. A. and Berry, L. (1988). SERVQUAL: A multiple-item scale for Measuring consumer perceptions of service quality. *Journal of Retailing*, 64(1), pp. 12–20.

Proenca, J.F. and Rodriguez, M. A. (2011). 'A comparison of users and non-users of banking self-service technology in Portugal'. *Managing Service Quality*, 21(2), pp. 192–210.

Ramdas, K.T, Teisberg, E. and Tucker, A. (2013). 'Ways to reinvent service delivery'. *Harvard Business Review*, 90(12), pp. 98–106.

Ratchford, M. and Barnhart, M. (2012). 'Development and validation of the technology adoption propen-sity (TAP) index'. *Journal of Business Research*, 65(8), pp. 1209–15.

Rayport, J. F. and Sviokla, J. J. (1995). 'Exploiting the virtual value chain'. *Harvard Business Review*, 73 (November-December), pp. 75–85.

Rotchanakitumnuai, S. and Speece, M. (2003). 'Barriers to Internet banking adoption: a qualitative study among corporate consumers in Thailand'. *International Journal of Bank Marketing*, 21(6/7), pp. 312–23.

Sahoo, R. K. and Swain, S. C. (2012). 'Study of perceived value and performance of e-banking in India with a special reference to Punjab National Bank'. *Industrial Journal of Management & Social Sciences*, 5(1), pp. 64–75.

Schepers, J. and Wetzels, M. (2007). 'A meta-analysis of the technology acceptance model: Investigating subjective norm and moderation effects'. *Information & Management*, 44(1), pp. 90–103.

Son, M. and Han, K. (2011). 'Beyond the technology adoption: Technology readiness effects on post-adoption behavior'. *Journal of Business Research*, 64(11), pp. 1178–82.

Tan, M. and Teo, T. S. H. (2000). 'Factors influencing the adoption of internet banking'. *Journal of the Association for Information Systems*, 1(5), pp. 1–42.

Venkatesh, V. and Davis, F. D. (2000). 'A Theoretical extension of the technology acceptance model: Four longitudinal field studies'. *Management Science*, 46(2), pp. 186–204.

Verma, S. (2012). *Trends in insurance channels 2012*. Capgemini. www.slideshare.net/fullscreen/capgemini/trends-in-insurance-channels-2012/16

Walker, R. H., Craig-Lees, M., Hecker, R. and Francis, H. (2002). 'Technology-enabled service deliv-ery'. *International Journal of Service Industry Management*, 13(1), pp. 91–106.

World Economic Forum. (2012). *Redefining the Emerging Market Opportunity: Driving Growth through Financial Services Innovation*. New York, NY.

World Insurance Report (2013). www.capgemini.com/wir13 *Capgemini and Efma*.

Wu, K., Zhao, Y., Zhu, Q., Tan, X. and Zheng, H. (2011). 'A meta-analysis of the impact of trust on technology acceptance model: Investigation of moderating influence on subject and context type'. *International Journal of Information Management*, 31(6), pp. 572–81.

Yousafzai, S. and Yani-de-Soriano, M. (2012). 'Understanding customer-specific factors underpinning internet bank adoption'. *International Journal of Bank Marketing*, 30(1), pp. 60–81.

Zeithaml, V. A., Berry, L. and Parasuraman, A. (1996). 'The behavioral consequences of service quality'. *Journal of Marketing*, 60 (April), pp. 31–46.

Zhu, Z., Nakata, C., Sivakumar, K. and Grewal, D. (2013). 'Fix it or leave it? Customer recovery from self-service technology failures'. *Journal of Retailing*, 89(1), pp. 15–29.

22

Mobile banking, a business models approach

Anthony Gandy

Introduction

Mobile banking is a subject of much research and discussion, in both academia and the banking industry. While the focus of most academic research has been on customers and potential users, it is worth also reviewing mobile banking from the business perspective of banks. Such a review would indicate that mobile banking services (and mobile payments) potentially form part of a trend to deconstruct banking services, a process which challenges the fundamental justifications for building large banks and integrating financial services. This chapter considers the threats to traditional banking presented through mobile banking services, especially in the context of the potential impact that payment-only models could have to the personal current (checking) account, which is a vital 'anchor' product for large scale banking groups.

Much of the research undertaken on the growing use of mobile banking technologies has focused on the consumer adoption decision and has asked why customers are increasingly using these technologies and what obstacles prevent adoption. The initial success of mobile banking was limited, especially when the services used a simple Short Message Service (SMS) structure. However, as the technology has developed, Laukkanen and Pasanen (2008: 88) note that mobile banking began to meet different needs and offered a different value proposition compared to traditional electronic banking. Further studies have focused on adoption and have examined differences in adoption rates, by age groups (Koenig-Lewis et al. 2010), the effects of gender (Riquelme and Rios 2010) and regional differences in adoption (Cruz et al. 2010, Püschel et al. 2010). Other studies have evaluated how effectively banks have used information channels to overcome resistance to adoption (Laukkanen and Kiviniemi 2010) and the specific advantages of mobile banking in poor and under-banked economies (Hinson 2011).

There are fewer papers, however, which have focused on the strategies of banks and the business models which they adopt. Hinson (2011) discusses how mobile banking models in poorer nations could be structured. Earlier, Rilvari (2005) considered how the new channel could enhance the customer relationship strategies of banks in Europe. In this chapter we examine what mobile banking is and consider how different models of innovation adoption could impact the established business models of the large scale integrated financial services companies which dominate retail banking. According to Chatterjee (2013: 97), 'a business model is a configuration (activity systems) of what the business does (activities) and what it invests in (resources) based on the logic that drives the profits for a specific business'.

Banks potentially face a disruptive event in the delivery of retail financial services and may see their activity system disaggregated and key resources undermined. In this case the resource is their relationship with their existing customers which banks wish to retain through integrated financial services, and the activity system is the delivery channels which reflect this vision; payment-only mobile services represent a threat to this system.

The focus of this chapter is on large scale banks and financial services companies, though this category is made up of a number of subcategories. First, there are the large scale concentrically diversified banks which offer a range of products and services along the lines of the 'bancassurance' model (financial groups which offer a range of banking and insurance products to primarily the retail market). Second, there is the 'universal' banking model (where a bank operates in all fields of banking, from savings to mortgages to corporate banking). There are many other terms such as 'allfinanz' and 'composite insurers', the latter being insurance groups which offer both life and general insurance products and often contain reinsurance arms.

We term these established enterprises as the integrated 'aggregated' model, as their competitive stance is to offer a wide range of products through a full range of delivery channels – not to be confused with 'aggregation services' which emulate such an approach through consolidating multiple service providers' accounts into a consolidated individualised customer portal. These integrated aggregated firms represent the main banking groups known across a wide range of markets and product lines. Companies in this group vary greatly; they include Barclays and Lloyds Banking Group in the UK, JP Morgan Chase and Bank of America in the US, BNP Paribas and Credit Agricole in France and Santander and Bankia in Spain, to name just a few examples. Notably, these groups may not 'manufacture' every product in their portfolio, but in general offer a full range of financial services through their own capabilities or through partnership with others.

These firms contrast with a second set of institutions which are using mobile solutions as a way of entering the sector. They also fall into a number of subgroups, the first being specialist start up firms focusing on a single banking service, at the same time there are larger firms which have diversified into the banking sector. In both cases we look at firms which are primarily focused on one banking product offering: mobile payments. We describe these as the 'disaggregated' model.

Mobile banking: the threat of payment-only services

Effectively there are two potential visions for what mobile banking services actually are: those mobile services which form a portal to a substantial part of a bank's product range, including access to current (checking) account services, payments, savings, card products, potentially borrowing facilities, insurance products and investments; and those offerings which disaggregate the services and focus on one function; the prime example being payment-only mobile facilities.

The difference is critical as banks have faced a new level of competition from disaggregated banking providers, and not just in the mobile sphere. As outlined below, the model for large scale banking and financial services groups has been one where anchor products are used to retain customers to allow further products to be sold to them to build a bundled relationship with customers. This model is being challenged by price comparison services (such as the UK's Big 4 price comparison services: *Compare the Market, Confused, Go Compare* and *Money Supermarket*) and peer to-peer lenders (such as the US's *Lending Club* and *Prosper*) like never before. Services such as peer-to-peer and price comparison services use new technologies to offer customers an opportunity to disaggregate or 'deconstruct' (Li 2001) their relationships with individual firms, and to re-aggregate them through alternative providers. Mobile banking has the potential to further deconstruct the integrated banking model, if it allows rivals to develop market share in the specific subset of payments-only services. Indeed, it appears that there is a strong momentum to develop new payment vehicles which focus on payments only, often integrating online and mobile payments capabilities.

According to Knowledge@Wharton/Ernst and Young (2013), in 2001 there was one mobile payment application in use globally. It is estimated that by 2013 there were 150 mobile payment services in operation and another 90 in development. The focus on electronic mobile payment systems represents something of a disaggregation of their services. While established banking groups are certainly represented in the groups introducing these payment services, so too are a new generation of rivals.

For some companies mobile payments represent a unique diversification opportunity. For others however, mobile payments represent an extension of their roles as e-commerce enablers and online payment agents. It is not surprising that PayPal offers mobile payment apps on the major smartphone platforms. The use of PayPal's apps is highly focused on servicing its traditional online market, such as making a payment for an eBay purchase when a bidder is surfing via their tablet or smartphone. Notably, despite PayPal processing $27bn of payments via their mobile apps in 2013, the firm has very little presence in the offline, high-street payment market (Garcinga 2014).

However, as new entrant firms develop online volumes, it provides the potential for economies of scale which can then be deployed in the physical world of high-street payments. One problem faced by these new entrants is how to bridge the gap between the tools used for online payments and the tools more traditionally used for high street payments, however, a variety of technologies from in-store Quick Response (QR) codes to Near Field Communications (NFC) are helping online payments firms open up their networks to physical world shoppers (Lunden 2013).

Further, new entrants to the sector, without the sunk costs that the established players have and the path-dependencies which often go with sunk costs, have the opportunity to utilize other payment capabilities that begin to overlap with banking facilities. For example, PayPal has introduced a service in the US, *Mobile Check Capture*, which allows customers to pay checks into their PayPal accounts using their mobile phones (O'Grady 2010). The customer writes the check and photographs it, and it is cleared via the image. It is not a full banking service, but payments-only models are a potential real threat to banks.

There is also the possibility that some payment services providers could integrate their services with a more radical interpretation of what money actually is. Notably, PayPal president David Marcus raised concerns that Bitcoin, was potentially a useful store of value (Shankland 2013). While not a prospect Marcus supported at the moment, there is an extreme model where a mobile payment service could be created which eschewed any link to the banking system through some form of cryptocurrency.

There are many variations on the online/mobile payments model. It is not just established players who are looking at the mobile market; new entrants are trying to develop viable models as well. ThinkLink's *FaceCash* system is another variation which uses the subscriber's mobile phone to display a bar code and (for security) a photograph of the subscriber. Subscribers give their mobile phones to the retailer, who scans the bar code. Subscribers cannot spend more than the balance of their *FaceCash* account, which gives *FaceCash* many of the attributes of a prepaid card. Like prepaid cards, subscribers do not need to have bank accounts and their *FaceCash* accounts can be topped up by third parties.

Of even more direct concern to banks is the role that mobile network operators can play. Safaricom/Vodafone's *M-PESA* service is an astonishing technological success. Launched in Kenya (Hughes and Lonie 2007), it offers banking and payment services to the unbanked and has spread throughout Africa. It is widely viewed not only as a cheap way of making person-to-person payments at a distance (such as in income repatriation or transfer payments), but is also often seen as safer to use than cash. It is interesting to think of a technology which has come from a developing country into the developed economies, where there is potentially a greater concern for established banks regarding mobile payments. In developed countries, established banks are often concerned that there is an opportunity for mobile network operators to extend their involvement in payment markets by the mobile networks using their billing facility to offer customers a payment method and even a credit facility. Customers could pay for services on the high-street using NFC technology or QR codes by adding the payment for a product or a service to their monthly mobile bill. This enables them to use their mobile billing accounts as a form of credit card; not only would this allow mobile network providers to move into the payments business, but also it could potentially offer an economic model via charging for credit facilities. While this threat has been recognized for many years, it has yet to come to pass.

Mobile banking models for aggregated financial services groups

The aggregated business model

A key issue for banks would be if the introduction of mobile banking led to any form of disaggregation or deconstruction of the value bundle they offer customers. An integrated approach to financial services lies at the very heart of most major retail banking groups. Large scale banking groups have become wedded to a concentrically-diversified model which aims to not only exploit economies of scale, but also to exploit economies of scope. Economies of scope as described by Panzar and Willig (1975) have become recognised as a key way in which institutions can achieve competitive advantage, as outlined by Porter (1980) and others. Concentrically diversified firms manage multiple products which are based around a core market, technology or capability. They gain advantage from developing, making and selling a number of different but related products and services that together will deliver competitive advantage.

The original works on economies of scope focused quite clearly on the cost benefits of the model and this has been further explored in the realm of financial services. Producing and offering multiple products through a single financial services entity, it has been argued that economies of scope can result in lower costs. Abheek (2004) claimed that, in the UK, the Swiss Re company believed that an insurance policy (presumably general insurance) sold through a bank had distribution costs of only 25 percent of the cost of selling the same policy through a separate direct sales force. If such claims are true there is a clear competitive advantage. Elsas et al. (2010) have found that there are real advantages in diversification for banks which are based on the way in which financial services are produced. As institutions in other industries become more specialised, banks become more diversified and operating advantages become more evident.

According to Vennet (2002: 254) 'conglomerates are more revenue efficient than their specialized competitors and the degree of both cost and profit efficiency is higher in universal banks than in non-universal banks'. Aguirre et al. (2008) found banking systems which allow universal banks to exist were in general more efficient than banking systems regulated so that only functionally discreet banks could exist. Tangible efficiencies and lowered per-product prices in bundled financial products have been noted by other researchers (see Fields et al. 2004 and Okeahalam 2008).

Of course, such arguments are now disputed, especially where the costs and benefits accrued merely relate to the banking groups and ignore wider economic and social costs. Laeven and Levine (2007) identified a valuation discount for diversified banking groups leading to concern that there are agency issues with a complex institution, and this concern has clearly grown since the financial crisis. The social cost of supporting complex financial services groups which have enormous scale and are interwoven with every financial activity in an economy is potentially very great and the mood is very much against enabling giant integrated groups to grow any further; indeed most policy makers would reverse the trend if they could (as discussed in Chapter 1).

The benefits of scope economies to aggregated groups themselves have also been questioned. Even before the financial crisis, corporate finance researchers seemed to hold a very different opinion to bank researchers. Rajan et al. (2000) suggested that diverse divisions within a firm can lead to inefficient allocation of resources and investments, and lower firm values. Berger and Ofek (1996) found that diversified firms have values that are 13–15 percent below the sum of the imputed values of their segments.

However, the benefits of scope economies are still seen as important, and bank researchers have widened the benefits from the areas of cost and portfolio risk to also include revenue advantages. The original concept of economies of scope was very much based on the idea that producing and distributing two closely associated products in tandem would be more efficient than two separate firms making and selling the products. Berger et al. (1987) extended the concept as it applied to the banking and finance sector. They outlined both cost-based benefits and revenue advantages, where the key advantages for the concentrically diversified model were shared fixed costs, improved customer insight, risk reduction (through spreading of customer revenues across different product types), reduction in customer service costs, such as managing change of addresses and other activities for multiple products simultaneously.

The French Association for Credit Institutions has defined bancassurance very much as a revenue enhancement strategy. It is 'a business strategy – mostly initiated by banks – that aims at associating banking and insurance activities within the same group, with a view to offering these services to common customers who, today, are mainly personal customers' (Staikouras 2006: 125).

The proposition is simple: banks have an established relationship with customers. This gives them four key advantages when selling insurance products. First, the bank can develop in-depth information on the customer's life stage and circumstances and make intelligent offers based on this understanding. Second, the customer's bank is likely to be trusted by the customer and seen as an obvious source of financial products of all types. While intuitively this argument may seem less strong now following the various financial crises which have occurred, research still shows that while distrust of the financial system is low, many people still give greater credence to their own provider of services (Ennew 2012: 2). Third, the bank can offer attractive terms to the customer because it can view profitability at a relationship level and potentially offer discounts based on this higher-level view, and also because it can gain a cost advantage by selling to a known customer and avoiding the extra costs of marketing to unknown customers and having to perform complex verification procedures. Finally, and building on the previous points, the bank can directly link baskets of products and bundle them together, for example adding life, buildings and contents insurance to a mortgage sale, though this form of bundling has become controversial as it is sometimes seen as poor value for the customer. It is this model which is at the core of the large scale diversified banking group. It is represented in the organisational structure of the banks, their customer intelligence frameworks and their distribution channel choices.

What is described above is a business model. Amit and Zott (2001) conceptualised business model analysis using the 'NICE' framework where the design themes consist of Novelty, Lock-in, Complementarities and Efficiency. Established large scale banking groups using the bancassurance or universal models have, in general, looked to deliver elements of all four factors where possible, but the key areas of advantage are Lock-in, Complementarities and Efficiency.

Novelty is often hard to deliver for an extended period of time. Banking is a networked business where interfaces between customers and banks and between banks and other banks have to have a high degree of commonality in order to make operational systems, especially payments and asset transfers, work correctly. While it is possible to offer temporary novel inducements to customers and indeed mobile banking has potentially offered a brief period with some novelty, large scale banks have primarily focused on offering customers an integrated service which delivers a high level of complementarity between products and services. The customer purchasing into the combination of products and services, is effectively locked-in to the service.

Lock-in, through offering complementarities and efficiency in operations has been the central creed for large scale banks and financial services groups. The bancassurance and universal banking models are based on the opportunity to cross-sell complementary products from insurance to banking customers. The universal banking model offers all banking services to their customer base, including their corporate customers, creating complementary sales and lock-in opportunities to both retail and corporate customers.

This form of concentric-diversification requires that financial services groups build customer loyalty and extend their share-of-wallet in order to sell a bundle of services. Nagata et al. (2004: 2) state that there are two benefits from financial conglomeration which are 'cost reduction and revenue enhancement' through bundling. Koderisch et al. (2007) argue that banks can benefit from 'bundling' through exploiting the 'credence' established through the anchor product and then leveraging the relationship by using cues from customers to offer an extended product line even beyond financial services. It is bundling products which enables competitive advantage and is also the outcome of competitive advantage as the large firms have fully bought into the concept. The concept of bundling is explored in further detail in Chapter 18.

Aggregated models: customer management and channel strategies

To operationalize the aggregated model, banks and financial services groups have used two primary tools. First, there is the use of customer relationship management toolkits which enable cross-selling to customers through knowledge of the customers' financial activities coupled to a model of the customers' life stages. Second, large scale institutions have looked to leverage their investment in channels and channel technologies, offering a comprehensive range of channels to both target customers and to enable customers to access their services in the manner most convenient to them.

There has been an enormous investment in customer relationship technologies aimed at managing the customer relationship with a view of cross-selling to them (Rust et al. 2004). Krasnikov et al. (2009) found that commercial banks in the US which had invested in CRM saw a decline in cost efficiency but an increase in profit efficiency. This investment has been coupled by a drive by major banks to offer a wider range of convenient distribution channels so as to exploit the customer knowledge at the point of contact to cross sell product to them; CRM and channel strategy have become interwoven.

Channels can be categorised through a number of different matrices. Xue et al. (2007) classified the channels used in retail banking according to whether they were physical or virtual, and also based on whether they are provided in a self-service mode or provided through employees. In general, it appears that the trend has been for channel demand to move from employee serviced channels toward self-service channels and from physical channels to virtual channels. In this process banks have removed staff from as many interactions with customers as possible, where those transactions are for service activities and typically not for sales opportunities. Salmen and Muir (2003) describe this as a change from the 'bring principle' to the 'fetch principle'. Nevertheless, while customers drive more transactions themselves, it is not meant to be at the expense of offering deep relationships and maintaining cross-selling advantages. However, there is the possibility that such moves have normalised banking transactions as 'fetch' products driven by the customer, potentially allowing in new rivals.

Mobile banking and the aggregated model

As described above established large scale banks operate using some form of aggregation model where they aim to bring together multiple services to the customer through multiple delivery channels. Traditional branches represented a unified experience, where customers visited to inquire about and purchase new financial solutions and to use services they had already subscribed to. The key anchor product for this model was and continues to be the personal current (checking) account, the banking service which incorporates access to the payment system through tools such as cheque (check) books, debit cards and ATMs. The personal current account is effectively a portal to transaction services and other banking services which can be accessed on the high street and managed in branches over the telephone or through the Internet. This makes the interpretation of what mobile banking actually represents very important. Is mobile banking a portal to customers' banking services, or is it a disaggregation of the banking relationship where payments are dealt with outside of the established multi-product banking 'wrapper'?

Laukkanen and Pasanen (2008: 87) synthesise a number of definitions, finding that mobile banking is a portal to a bank's services which can be viewed as a subset of its electronic banking services. They then note common features including payments and account balance facilities. Such a definition allows for both the concept of a portal into the bank and for separated payment services as the functionality outlined is somewhat limited. Lee et al. (2003) argued that banks recognized the need to offer mobile banking as there was a very high value in customers' minds associated with the benefits of having mobile access to bank accounts. This would support the need for banks to offer this portal as part of their comprehensive service offering.

In the current market place we can see banks both offering portal-led approaches, which fit with their internally aggregated model and payment-only approaches, competing with the new generation of payment services which are competing for both online and high street transactions. Portal-led approaches can simply be the presentation of the standard web banking services geared for either a mobile or tablet screen. It could also mean offering an application which fits into the 'app' ecosystem of today's mobile devices.

However, banks must also consider whether these portal services need to be fully integrated with high-street and person-to-person payment frameworks or whether these are a different category altogether. What banks cannot do is ignore the mobile payments space as it could undermine their own payments businesses. It would be a problem for banks if payment capabilities become separated from the traditional bundle of interwoven products as they may no longer control payments which are a core facility of the personal current account, the most important anchor product available to banks.

At one stage the loss of control over payments may not have been seen as a major issue. Certainly this has been the case during periods of rapid asset growth. In these circumstances, banks can become somewhat ambivalent about the fees they earn from payments which are very small and usually represent a financial return substantially lower than potential returns available on lending products. According to the consulting group McKinsey (De Ploey and Denecker 2006), in 2002 European banks spent 300bn per annum processing payments, a third of all their expenditure. However, payments only contributed 24 percent to revenues and returned just 9 percent of profits. The cost–income ratio of the payments business is 90 percent, while for many of the most efficient retail banks the overall cost–income ratio is now below 50 percent.

This argument now seems less robust. Following the global financial crisis, retaining payments income has become crucial. The Boston Consulting Group (2009) estimates payment services to represent 30–50 percent of bank revenues (which does seem to be remarkable) and views it as one of the more attractive businesses within banking. However, it is not just revenues which are of importance in offering payment services. Payments are the embedded anchor for personal current accounts. Payment flows provide information and relationships core to both the retention strategy of banks and the cross-sell/up-sell opportunities which make the aggregated banking model work. From the customer's point of view, payments have a particularly important role in their relationship with financial services providers. According to Hasan et al. (2012: 165) 'Effective payment services are also important in helping banks to establish long-term relationships with their customers'.

Regulation has made the economic arguments for not losing control over the payments space even more important. First, banks are being given new goals by regulators, to achieve higher liquidity ratios based on the Basel Committee's new short-term Liquidity Coverage Ratio and the longer-term Net Stable Funding Ratio. Cash balances provide some value in achieving these ratios in an efficient manner, especially if they then help to persuade the customer to use time-deposits, which tend to be very 'sticky' forms of liquidity and can help banks achieve their liquidity ratios.

In addition, since the financial crisis, it is now more apparent that the previously regarded low 9 percent return on capital available to payments operations is actually now highly valuable, not least because it requires relatively low levels of regulatory capital, increasing the relative return compared to some other forms of bank activity. Thus, the payments business is now looking much more financially appealing and, in addition, greatly contributes to the efficient management of the banks' treasury operations. Payments are no longer just about retention and cross selling. The move by new entrants into the current (checking) accounts and payments space, discussed by Worthington in Chapter 2, poses a real threat to traditional banks. It would therefore seem dangerous for banks to cede payments territory to a new generation of rivals offering payment services only.

Not surprisingly then, established large scale banks are offering not just portal services but are also competing in the payment-specific mobile services space. Clearly the aim will and should be to merge these in the minds of customers so as to wrap the customer into the bank and make payments a core anchor for the rest of the service offering. Efforts to achieve this can be seen around the globe. In the UK, Barclay's Pingit Service and Royal Bank of Scotland's Monetise-based 'Pay your Contacts' have long been launched. In Turkey, banks such as DenizBank with its *fastPay* service and Turkiye Is Bankasi's *IsCEP* service allow either person-to-person or payment through the use of QR codes for consumer purchases. Banks are fighting back, though there is a risk that new players, especially those which have already gained strength in other areas of payment processing, could begin to add to the disaggregation/deconstruction of banking services before banks have completely defended the space.

Conclusion

Established banks are now in the process of making mobile payments a mainstream transactional channel, and a core element of the bank customer relationship. This is despite the fact that the payment element of current accounts is being contested by others, and some of these rivals are potentially significant. The aggregated model most banks use is justified through the exploitation of established customer relationships as a resource for cross-selling other products, and relies on the retention value of anchor products. Mobile payments-only services are one of many threats banks face from disaggregated/deconstructed new rivals. Given that third party aggregation services exist which can bring together multiple financial services through a portal populated by customers themselves, it is not impossible that deconstructed services could be re-aggregated for customer convenience without the need for a traditional bank intermediary.

While the threat represented by any single model may be low and banks can intercept each deconstructed model with an emulation of their own (and of course many banks actively compete in the mobile payment space), the overall threat is potentially cumulative. While peer-to-peer and price comparison services are the realm of innovative new enterprises, the mobile payments sector is attracting major corporations from the information technology and mobile network operator markets, as well as the new generation of online payment enterprises which have already embedded themselves in the electronic payments industry.

The most effective defence for banks is to exploit their established retail and interbank payment networks. The key for mobile-to-bank account payment and transfer schemes is to link a telephone number to bank account details. Banks already run systems (often through a centralized payment service) which control bank account-to-bank account payments. It would be possible to build a robust secure database which would match telephone numbers to account numbers via these established interbank networks. An example of this approach is the UK's Paym service where the database providing the mobile number-to-bank account details is the responsibility of the Payments Council, the established coordinator of UK retail and interbank payments. Such a process, while it may not seem that different to schemes run by non-banks, would allow all established banks that belong to the central payments scheme an opportunity to leverage joint economies of scale and the network advantages of the established payment network.

References

Aguirre, M.S., Lee, T.K. and Pantos, T.D., 2008. Universal versus functional banking systems: the structure conduct performance hypothesis revisited. *Journal of Banking Regulation* 10 (1), pp. 46–67.

Abheek, B., 2004. Bancassurance: New concept catching up fast in India. *The Chartered Accountant*. 52 (12), pp. 1348–51.

Amit, R. and Zott, C., 2001. Value Creation in E-Business. *Strategic Management Journal*, 22 (6/7), pp. 493–520.

Berger, P.G. and Ofek, E., 1996. Bustup takeovers of value-destroying diversified firms. *Journal of Finance*, 51(4), pp. 1175–1200.

Berger, A.N., Hanweck, G.A. and Humphrey, D.B., 1987. Competitive viability in banking scale, scope, and product mix economies, *Journal of Monetary Economics*, 20, pp. 501–20.

Boston Consulting Group, 2009. Global payments 2009: weathering the storm. *Boston Consulting Group Report*. March 2009.

Chatterjee, S., 2013. Simple Rules for Designing Business Models. *California Management Review*, 55(2), pp. 97–124.

Cruz, P., Neto, L. B. F., Muñoz-Gallego, P. and Laukkanen, T., 2010. Mobile banking rollout in emerging markets: evidence from Brazil. *International Journal of Bank Marketing*, 28(5) pp. 342–71.

Elsas, R., Hackethal, A., Holzhäuser, M., 2010. The anatomy of bank diversification. *Journal of Banking and Finance*, 34, pp. 1274–87.

Ennew, C., 2012. Trust: trends and analysis. *Financial Services Research Forum Research Note*, University of Nottingham, September 2012.

Fields, L.P., Fraser, D.R. and Kolari, J.W., 2004. *What's different about Bancassurance? evidence of wealth gains to banks and insurance companies*. Working Paper, Texas A&M University.

Hasan, I., Schmiedel, H. and Song, L., 2012. Returns to retail banking and payments. *Journal of Financial Services Research*, 41(3), pp. 163–95.

Hinson, R.E., 2011. Banking the poor: The role of mobiles. *Journal of Financial Services Marketing*, 15(4), pp. 320–33.

Hughes, N. and Lonie, S., 2007. M-PESA: mobile money for the "unbanked" turning cellphones into 24-hour tellers in Kenya. *Innovations: Technology, Governance, Globalization*, 2.1–2, pp. 63–81.

Knowledge@Wharton/Ernst and Young, 2013. *Mobile Banking: Financial Services Meet the Electronic Wallet*. Wharton School, University of Pennsylvania, online http://kw.wharton.upenn.edu/ey-global-banking/mobile-banking

Koderisch, M., Wuebker, G., Baumgarten, J. and Baillie, J., 2007. Bundling in banking – A powerful strategy to increase profits. *Journal of Financial Services Marketing*, 11(3), pp. 268–76.

Koenig-Lewis, N., Palmer, A. and Moll, A., 2010. Predicting young consumers' take up of mobile banking services. *International Journal of Bank Marketing*, 28(5), pp. 410–32.

Krasnikov, A., Jayachandran, S. and Kumar, V., 2009. The impact of customer relationship management implementation on cost and profit efficiencies: evidence from the U.S. commercial banking industry. *Journal of Marketing*, 73(6), pp. 61–76.

Laeven, L. and Levine, R., 2007. Is there a diversification discount in financial conglomerates? *Journal of Financial Economics*, 85, pp. 331–67.

Laukkanen, T. and Kiviniemi, V., 2010. The role of information in mobile banking resistance. *International Journal of Bank Marketing*, 28(5), pp. 372–88.

Laukkanen, T. and Pasanen, M., 2008. Mobile banking innovators and early adopters: How they differ from other online users? *Journal of Financial Services Marketing*, 13(2), pp. 86–94.

Lee, M. S. Y., McGoldrick, P. F., Keeling, K. A. and Doherty, J., 2003. Using ZMET to explore barriers to the adoption of 3G mobile banking services', *International Journal of Retail & Distribution Management*, 31(6), pp. 340–48.

Li, F., 2001. The Internet and the Deconstruction of the Integrated Banking Model. *British Journal of Management*, 12, pp. 307–322.

Lunden, I., 2013. With payment code, PayPal taps QR codes and existing hardware for large retailer mobile payments, *Techcrunch, Oct 8, 2013* Available at http://techcrunch.com/2013/10/08/with-payment-code-paypal-taps-qr-codes-and-existing-hardware-for-retail-mobile-payments (accessed 02/02/2014).

Nagata, T., Maeda, Y. and Imahigashi, H., 2004. Economies of Scope in Financial Conglomerates: Analysis of a Revenue Side. *Financial Services Agency Research Review* 1, pp. 1–20.

O'Grady, J. D., 2010. *New PayPal Mobile feature: photograph a check and deposit it (updated)*. The Apple Core [blog], 7 October 2010. Available at www.zdnet.com/blog/apple/new-paypal-mobile-feature-photograph-a-check-and-deposit-it-updated/8342 (accessed 01/02/2014).

Okeahalam, C., 2008. Does Bancassurance Reduce the Price of Financial Service Products? *Journal of Financial Services Research* 33 (3), pp. 147–62.

De Ploey, W. H. F. and Denecker, O. P. M., 2006. How Europe's banks should prepare for payments reform. *McKinsey Quarterly*, February.

Panzar, J. and Willig, R., 1975. Economies of scale and economies of scope in multi-output production. *Economic Discussions*, Paper No. 33, Bell Laboratories.

Porter, M.E., 1980. *Competitive Strategy: Techniques for Analyzing Industries and Competitors*. Free Press.

Püschel, J., Mazzon, J. A. and Hernandez, J. M. C., 2010. Mobile banking: proposition of an integrated adoption intention framework. *International Journal of Bank Marketing*, 28(5), pp. 389–409.

Rajan, R., Servaes, H. and Zingales, L., 2000. The cost of diversity: The diversification discount and inefficient investment. *Journal of Finance*, 55(1), pp. 35–80.

Rilvari, J., 2005. Mobile banking: a powerful new marketing and CRM tool for financial services companies all over Europe, *Journal of Financial Services Marketing*, 10(1), p. 11–20.

Riquelme, H. E. and Rios, R. E., 2010. The moderating effect of gender in the adoption of mobile banking. *International Journal of Bank Marketing*, 28(5), pp. 328–41.

Rust, R.T., Ambler, T., Carpenter, G.S., Kumar, V. and Srivastava, R.K., 2004. Measuring marketing productivity: current knowledge and future directions. *Journal of Marketing*, 68, pp. 76–89.

Salmen, S. M. and Muir, A., 2003. Electronic customer care: the innovative path to e-loyalty. *Journal of Financial Services Marketing*, 8 (2), pp. 133–44.

Shankland, S., 2013. *PayPal president David Marcus: Bitcoin is good, NFC is bad*. CNET, 10 December 2013. Available at http://news.cnet.com/8301–1023_3-57615080-93/paypal-president-david-marcus-bitcoin-is-good-nfc-is-bad (accessed 01/02/2014).

Staikouras, S. K., 2006. Business opportunities and market realities in financial conglomerates. The International Association for the Study of Insurance Economics. *The Geneva Papers*, Number 31, pp. 124–48.

Vennet, R.V., 2002. Cost and profit efficiency of financial conglomerates and universal banks in Europe. *Journal of Money, Credit and Banking* 34 (1), pp. 254–82.

Xue, M., Hitt, L. M. and Harker, P. T., 2007. Customer efficiency, channel usage, and firm performance in retail banking. *Manufacturing & Service Operations Management*, 9 (4), pp. 535–58.

23

E-servicescapes in online banking

Towards an integrated conceptual model of the stimuli contributing to the online banking experience

Kathryn Waite and Jennifer Rowley

Introduction

The website is an important channel through which customers interact with and receive service from their bank. Within retail banking the distribution channel has a dual function, not only enabling consumption of the service but also acting as a signal of service quality. For example, high street branches were traditionally the main channel for retail banking products; the physical presence and premium location of a branch network acted as a tangible, search attribute, one that provided the consumer with an indication of a high level of resources, which, in turn, communicated security (Lockett and Littler 1997). Similarly, when discussing online banking, the website has been considered to act as a tangible search attribute (Aladwani 2001, Mukherjee and Nath 2003). Several researchers have emphasised that good quality e-technology is particularly important in encouraging consumers to adopt online banking (Joseph et al. 1999, Chou and Chou 2000, Jayawardhena 2004, Ibrahim et al. 2006). Hence, in order to attract and retain customers, banks need to monitor and manage the online banking interface, which forms the basis of the e-banking experience.

This chapter argues the case for developing a more integrated approach to understanding and theorising the user/consumer experience of online banking and draws on the concept of the "Servicescape" (Bitner 1992). We use "e-servicescape" as a synonym for terms such as the virtual servicescape (Mari and Poggesi 2013, Vilnai-Yavetz and Yates 2006), online servicescapes (Harris and Goode 2010), e-scape (Koernig 2003), cyberscape (Williams and Dargel 2004) and cybermarketscapes (Venkatesh 1998). It is proposed that e-services, in general, are self-service environments, which means they are environments in which "there is no interaction between customers and employees" (Bitner 1992: 59). Therefore, the website or other virtual service platform with which the user interacts constitutes the online banking e-servicescape. In this chapter, we present a typology of the specific components of the online environment; our analysis is complementary to Chapter 21 in which Jaramillo examines technology adoption at an organisational and individual level.

Our chapter begins by presenting the theoretical foundations and precedents that inform our proposed e-servicescape. Specifically, we introduce Bitner's original physical Servicescape framework. Next, we review existing e-servicescape frameworks and prior research on web atmospherics, e-service and e-banking quality as a basis for the proposal of an integrated conceptual model of the e-servicescape. This is then used as a framework within which to discuss the nature of the online banking e-servicescape. The chapter concludes with recommendations for practice and for further theoretical and empirical research on the online banking e-servicescape.

Theoretical foundations and precedents

The term "atmospherics" is often accredited to Kotler (1974: 50), and was defined by him as "the conscious designing of space to create certain effects in buyers". Kotler suggested that elements of the service environment, such as brightness, shapes, scents, music and colour can be modified in order to provoke emotional effects that will affect purchase intentions. Atmospherics elements can be tangible (i.e. buildings, carpets, signage) or intangible (colour, scent, music, temperature) (Hoffman and Turley 2002). Atmospherics research tends to focus on one or two environmental stimuli, or cues, and their effect on internal (for example, emotions) and behavioural responses (Hooper et al. 2013).

The Servicescape concept (Bitner 1992) is a framework that groups atmospheric elements into a taxonomy. Bitner (1992) proposed that the Servicescape, sometimes referred to as the service environment, comprises three dimensions: ambient conditions, spatial layout and functionality, and signs, symbols and artifacts. Ambient conditions are background characteristics such as temperature, music and odour. Spatial layout and functionality refers to elements that deliver the service experience, such as the way equipment and furnishings are arranged and the ability of these items to facilitate performance and goal outcome. Signs, symbols and artifacts are items that serve as explicit and implicit signals for the user of the Servicescape, such as the style of the décor and rules of behaviour. These three dimensions contribute to the Servicescape and are perceived by both customers and employees.

Bitner (1992) argues that the atmospheric groupings within the Servicescape influence not only customer purchase intentions but also employee actions and that both groups may respond cognitively, emotionally and physiologically to the environment. She proposes a range of internal responses in each of these categories and consequent behaviours, and views the components of the Servicescape as being controllable by the firm, arguably to a greater extent than the person-based service delivery characteristic of physical service environments. Hence, Bitner offers the Servicescape framework as a tool through which organisations can utilise the physical surroundings in their service settings to achieve both marketing and strategic goals.

The theoretical underpinning of the Servicescape derives from the work of Mehrabian and Russell (1974) in the environmental psychology literature. This proposes the stimulus-organism-response (S-O-R) paradigm, in which stimuli (S) from the environment are posited to affect people's internal evaluations (O), which in turn influence behavioural responses (R). The three emotional states, pleasure/displeasure, arousal/non-arousal and dominance/submissiveness (PAD) mediate responses to the environment, which take the shape of approach or avoidance behaviours. Approach is the desire to remain in a store and to explore its offerings, whilst avoidance is associated with a desire to terminate any engagement with a store or service. However, as Mari and Poggesi (2013) suggest, much of the later research on the Servicescape seeks to explore the impact of the Servicescape on quality perceptions and customer loyalty (for example, Baker et al. 2002, Harris and Ezeh 2008).

Understanding the e-servicescape

Research in internet marketing has focussed on the elements of a website that encourage visitors to stay (stickiness) and to transact. Studies have been carried out into the effect of navigation (for example, Dailey 2004, Griffith 2005), colour (for example, Mandel and Johnson 2002, Gorn et al. 2004), images (for example, Ekhaml 1996) and website aesthetic appeal (Zeithaml et al. 2002, Grewal et al. 2004). These have tended to focus on one or two atmospheric elements. Whilst studying a limited number of cues at any one time may allow for tighter experimental design and more concrete research outcomes, it may not accord with the way in which people experience online environments. According to Gestalt psychologists, consumers form overall impressions of consumption objects and integrate information and evaluations of specific features (Zimmer and Golden 1988, Mattila and Wirtz 2001). In addition, in online environments, cues may be more difficult to isolate (Demangeot and Broderick 2010). Wells et al. (2011: 390) provide evidence that supports a more holistic approach and report in their experimental work that an individual's perceptions of quality for a particular website element increases when all other dimensions are high quality even when the manipulation of the particular element remains unchanged; they identify this as a "halo effect" between dimensions.

Only a few authors have adopted a holistic and integrated perspective to the conceptualisation or investigation of the e-servicescape, or the factors that contribute to the online service environment. Table 23.1 presents the dimensions of the most significant studies and aligns these dimensions against those contained in Bitner's (1992) Servicescape framework. Harris and Goode (2010) study a variety of websites, whilst Jeon and Jeong (2009) and Hopkins et al. (2009) have adapted Bitner's (1992) framework of the environmental dimensions of the physical servicescape. In contrast, rather than adapting the Servicescape framework, Demangeot and Broderick (2010) identify the attributes of the retail web environment from an extensive literature review of prior studies in the services marketing, information systems, experiential and environmental psychology disciplines. In Table 23.1, the dimensions proposed in each study are identified together with the items within each dimension. The Demangeot and Broderick (2010) "exploration" dimension is mapped over both "spatial layout and functionality" and "signs, symbols and artifacts". The following paragraphs will critically discuss each dimension of the Servicescape as it has been adapted to the online context and will draw on this analysis to suggest a re-formulation.

Ambient conditions

Bitner (1992: 66) identifies ambient conditions as "background characteristics of the environment" that "affect the five senses" and in some cases "may be totally imperceptible"; she specifies "temperature, lighting, noise, music and scent". In their formulation of the e-servicescape, Jeon and Jeong (2009) propose that in the context of a website, ambient conditions would include items such as colour, quality photos, a virtual tour, music/sound effects and animation effects. It appears that there is confusion between an *ambient* element and an *aesthetic* element. Jeon and Jeong (2009: 4) clearly consider ambient conditions to relate to the aesthetic or visual aspects of the website and hypothesise that "ambient/aesthetic conditions positively affect perceived e-servicescape. A blending of the ambient and the aesthetic is apparent in the e-servicescape framework proposed by Harris and Goode (2010: 231), who write: "online aesthetic appeal refers to the online ambient conditions and to the extent to which consumers interpret the Servicescape as attractive or alluring". Hopkins et al. (2009) also confuse ambient

Table 23.1 Comparing servicescape and e-servicescape models

Model	Model dimensions		
Servicescape (Bitner 1992)	Ambient conditions • Temperature • Air quality • Noise • Music • Odour	Spatial layout and functionality • Layout • Equipment • Furnishings	Signs, symbols and artifacts • Signage • Personal artifacts • Style of décor
E-servicescape Hopkins et al. (2009)	Ambient conditions • Aesthetic appeal • Atmospherics appeal	Spatial layout and functionality • Navigability • Ease of use	Signs, symbols and artifacts • Information content • Information quality
E-servicescape (Harris and Goode 2010)	Aesthetic appeal • Originality of design • Visual appeal • Entertainment value	Layout and functionality • Usability • Relevance of information • Customization • Interactivity	Financial security • Perceived security • Ease of payment
Environmental attributes (Demangeot and Broderick 2010)		Sense-making • Page clarity • Site architecture Exploration • Market informativeness • Non-marketer informativeness • Visual impact • Experiential intensity	
Environmental dimensions of E-servicescape (Jeon and Jeong 2009)	Ambient conditions • Colour • Quality photos • Virtual tour • Music/sound effects Animation effects	Design aspects • Overall structure/layout • Use of space Functional aspects • Interaction with website owner • Saved time • Convenience • Information adequacy	Search aids and slogans • Keywords • Metatags • Slogans

conditions with aesthetic elements. We argue that these formulations ignore Bitner's proposal that ambient conditions should form a *background*. In addition, the linking of ambient conditions with aesthetics shows a limited understanding of the role of visual aesthetics within computer science. Gait (1985: 714) argues that aesthetics are "important in making interfaces understandable, memorable and appealing to computer users". Thus, aesthetics are more than background features; they are prominent features of website design. Examples of visual aesthetics are "font definitions, type-setting conventions, color combinations, graphics design considerations, high resolution for viewscreens and the shapes of windows" (Gait 1985: 714). A stronger case can be made for aligning aesthetic items with the Servicescape dimension of spatial layout and functionality, which contains elements whose arrangement, according to Bitner (1992: 66), should "facilitate performance and the accomplishment of goals".

This leaves us with the problem of what should comprise ambient conditions within the e-servicescape? We propose that items comprising ambient conditions should include speed of connectivity, website availability and provision of a secure connection. We define speed of connectivity as the time it takes to connect or load up web pages; this will be device specific, and may not be directly within an organisation's control but will be integral to the e-servicescape as perceived by the customer. We define website availability as the website being present at the Uniform Resource Locator (URL) and not having been removed, withdrawn for site maintenance or not accessible from a mobile phone. Provision of a secure connection, we propose, is the organisation's use of Hypertext Transfer Protocol Secure (HTTPS) to protect the consumer from having their communications intercepted by third parties.

Ambient conditions are online service characteristics that are background to the core experience and are "sensed" by the consumer. A link can be made between ambient conditions and the concept of "must-be" quality expectations found within the Kano classification model (Kano et al. 1984). Zhang and von Dran (2001: 12) write that must-be or basic quality "is the minimum acceptable to the consumer and encompasses things customers take for granted and do not think about – their presence goes unnoticed, but their absence will generate complaints". Their empirical work supports our proposition in its classification as basic quality expectations of an "indication of system loading/responding time" and "stability of website availability" (can always access website).

Spatial layout and functionality

Bitner (1992) specifies that spatial layout and functionality refers to those items that are necessary in order for the consumer to achieve their intended goal. Bitner (1992) defines functionality as the ability of physical items (such as machinery and equipment) to deliver the service and defines spatial layout as the way in which those physical items are arranged. We argue that those items related to effective online information provision should be grouped within spatial layout and functionality. Huizingh (2000: 124) states that "providing information is the basic goal of a web site", even if the ultimate goal is a transaction, information provision is the first stage. Rust and Lemon (2001: 85) argue that the internet "by *its very nature* is a network of technology exchanging intangible information" (emphasis added). Functionality items would include the content/information quality such as currency, relevance, understandability, validity, reliability and trustworthiness. We also include within functionality those items that act as tools within the website. This list includes, but is not limited to, items such as navigation tools (including search engines, menus, hyperlinks); identity-based tools (including password-inputting, CAPTCHA (i.e. the typing in of a computer-generated word), pre-population of identity details, personalisation and recommendations) and transaction tools (including shopping baskets, checkouts, product comparison, customer reviews and payment gateways).

Spatial layout refers to the arrangement of the above functional items and includes the sizing of fonts, the ordering of information, white space, frames, menus, panes and dialogue boxes. In formulating this list, we draw broadly on the perspective offered by visual aesthetics, which studies how the manipulation of such elements influences information usability and appeal.

Table 23.1 indicates that other authors also include information provision within spatial layout and functionality. For example, Demangeot and Broderick (2010: 216) use the label "sense-making attributes" to group together "page clarity" and "site architecture" which "enable shoppers to grasp the content and organisation of the pages (or scenes) presented to them, as well as the interconnections between individual pages". However, in their formulation of the e-servicescape they group functional attributes relating to information provision within a separate heading of "exploration" and state that these items "suggest abundance to the shopper and invite deeper examination". Demangeot and Broderick (2010: 127) also include "visual impact" which is the "attention-grabbing, aesthetic, visual diversity of individual web pages" within the exploration dimension. They operationalise this concept by measuring the appeal of the visual design and site aesthetics to the consumer. In addition, they formulate the construct of "experiential intensity" which is defined as "the ability of the site to produce an involving shopping experience" (p. 127) and operationalise this construct through measures of the extent to which the website replicates the experience of offline shopping.

Whilst the choice of the term "exploration" is grounded in the theories of psychology and is thus congruent with the S-O-R theoretical model underpinning of Bitner's (1992) framework, there is a weakness in that the measurement and operationalisation of the constructs is at the level of individual user perceptions. This introduces subjectivity and intangibility and a level of abstraction that results in limited understanding of which specific attributes of the website stimulate the given response. Chiou et al. (2010) argue that a focus on user perceptions does not provide the necessary internal evaluation, which is important in evaluating the consistency between a company's overall strategy and website design.

Elsewhere, there is also a tendency for authors to move from lower order items to higher order outcomes. For example, Jeon and Jeong (2009) do not discuss "spatial layout" but locate items such as the structure of the website, the use of space and navigational functions within "design aspects". They formulate "functionality" as a separate dimension and, whilst acknowledging the importance of information adequacy, they also list outcomes from website use, i.e. "saved time" and "convenience". Hopkins et al. (2009) include perceptions of "navigability" and "ease of use". Harris and Goode (2010: 233) also argue for the "centrality of information relevance", but their formulation of the e-servicescape lists within layout and functionality the concepts of "usability", "relevance of information", "customisation" and "interactivity". They do not address spatial layout. This movement from website features to outcomes fails to provide concrete guidance as to what should be present on the website in order to deliver these consumer goals. The introduction of abstraction through using higher-order constructs obscures the necessary detailing of those items that comprise the e-servicescape.

Signs, symbols and artifacts

When considering signs, symbols and artifacts (SSA) prior work fails to fully engage with Bitner's (1992) framework, as shown in Table 23.1. Hopkins et al. (2009: 29) propose that the "counterpart to this dimension is the information component of the website", as this is the component that acts like a sign by guiding the customer through service delivery. Jeon and Jeong (2009) reframe SSA as "search aids and slogans". They also include within their formulation, company name and logo but they extend the concept of signage to include the use of "meta-tags" and "keywords" within web pages that are used for search engine optimisation. We question the degree to which "meta-tags" and "keywords" are explicitly perceived by the customer. Harris and Goode (2010) do not specifically address SSA but include within their framework the dimension of "financial security". They state that this is measured by perceived site security and ease of payment. We argue that security perceptions will be formed by the use of SSA, such as trust marks within the site, and that ease of payment will also be facilitated by signage to direct the consumer.

Bitner argues that the role of signage is multi-faceted and encompasses labelling, directional indicators, communication of rules and "communicating firm image" and also includes other objects that act as cues to "the meaning of place and norms and expectations of behaviour

Table 23.2 Reformulated e-servicescape

E-servicescape dimensions		
Ambient conditions	Spatial layout and functionality	Signs, symbols and artifacts
• Speed of connectivity	• Font and font size	• Symbols of brand identity
• Website availability	• Use of white space	• Signs of trustworthiness
• Secure connection	• Frame sizes	• Visual design artifacts
	• Pane sizes	• Aural design artifacts
	• Dialogue boxes	• Affiliate artifacts
	• Menus	
	• Information order	
	• Content/information quality	
	• Navigation tools	
	• Identity based tools	
	• Transaction tools	

in the place" Bitner (1992: 66). Following Bitner's (1992) framework we list within this dimension signs, symbols and artifacts that communicate website provenance, differentiate the service offering and communicate norms and expectations of provider behaviour such as trustworthiness. Hence, the e-servicescape SSA dimension includes, but is not limited to, the following items:

• Symbols of brand identity (colour, sonic logo, visual logos, brand logo).
• Signs of trustworthiness (trust marks, security certification, guarantees, customer reviews).
• Visual design artifacts (colour, images, animation).
• Aural design artifacts (music, sound effects).
• Affiliate artifacts (commercial content, advertising).

Based on the preceding discussion, our proposed e-servicescape framework is presented in Table 23.2.

Towards an e-servicescape for online banking

Drawing on empirical research into online banking, this chapter will now apply the e-servicescape framework to the online banking context. Online banking is an established method of distribution. For example, Pew Research reports that in the US, "online banking is a relatively common activity: 61% of adult internet users do it, making it about as popular an activity as using social networking sites" (Zickuhr and Smith 2012: 12). However, the theory that examines online banking is limited in its theoretical underpinning and also in it focus. In a critical literature review, Waite (2009) identifies that existing research into online banking mainly utilises three theories: diffusion of innovation theory (Rogers 1995), expectation-disconfirmation theory (i.e. SERVQUAL, Parasuraman et al. 1988, 1991) and the user-intention perspective (i.e. TAM., Davis et al. 1989). In addition, Klaus and Nguyen (2013: 429) argue that a limitation of online banking research is the continued focus on the "customer perspective rather than the firm's strategic viewpoint". The development and application of the e-servicescape to this context addresses these research gaps and contributes to the formulation of the online banking strategy.

Ambient conditions

Ambient conditions are those which underpin the core online experience (i.e. speed of connectivity, website availability and the presence of a secure connection, etc.). An examination of the online banking research supports this formulation. In terms of the online banking literature, Waite (2009) finds that these attributes are placed within the dimensions of "accessibility" and "reliability" in online banking quality studies. Congruent with this formulation, Yang et al. (2004: 1165) identify a measurement dimension which they label "security", which encompasses a "low risk associated with online transactions, safeguarding personal information and safety in completing online transactions". In terms of website availability, Jayawardhena (2004: 202) identifies a dimension that reflects customers' expectations of "the freedom of e-banking at a time of their own choosing with no time restrictions". Li and Worthington (2004: 7) find that "electronic connectivity explains some 29 percent of the variation of Internet banking adoption". Technical failures in the banking system result in customers being unable to access their money or undertake transactions; the distress and inconvenience caused indicates the extent to which connectivity is "taken for granted" until it is no longer present (Financial Times 2012, BBC 2013).

Spatial layout and functionality

This element is focussed on those attributes that deliver the service outcomes. We argue for the primacy of information provision within this element. This focus is supported by Lovelock (1991: 15) who identifies financial services as an information processing service "that does not require the customer's physical presence from an operational perspective". Online banking researchers indicate that customers expect banks to provide accurate and up to date information, not only about the services that the bank offers but also accurate and timely updates as to the transactions that have taken place within their account (Jun and Cai 2001, Joseph et al. 2005, Bauer et al. 2005, Maenpaa 2006).

Effective information exchange is not only about the accuracy and reliability of content but also about the format in which that information is presented. Walker (2011), in an investigation into bank website design, finds that the positioning of logos, main menus, white space and other webpage elements all improved the webpage scanning behaviour of study participants. In addition, Laukkanen (2007: 793) highlights the importance of clear visual display especially in the case of mobile phone banking so as to reduce "feelings of uncertainty in service consumption".

In order to protect funds from theft and fraud, bank websites utilise identity-based tools. The importance of these tools for information-seeking tasks as opposed to transaction-based tasks has been questioned by Waite and Harrison (2004). There is disagreement over the extent to which pre-population of online forms is desirable, because such practices, whilst introducing user convenience, also increase user doubts as to the security of personal data (Briggs et al. 2004). The design of identity-based tools is also subject to a device effect. For example, Laukkanen (2007: 793) finds that for mobile phone banking, consumers' expectations are that "the data input method needs to be simplified ... in situations where a large amount of data are entered. When paying bills electronically the customer usually needs to enter passwords and access codes in order to log into the service ... this increases the burden on the customer, especially when the service is used via a mobile phone". It appears that the functionality of identity-based tools varies according to task scenario and according to the device that is being used to access online banking. There is a need for empirical work to examine this phenomenon.

Navigation tools such as search engines, menus, links to other tools and a logical layout are items core to website quality (McKinney et al. 2002) and have been measured within several online banking quality studies (Jayawardhena 2004, Waite 2006). These items are also listed as measures of the "ease of use" construct within those studies informed by the Technology Adoption Model (Davis et al. 1989). Findings show that customers consistently rank these items as important. For example, Jayawardhena (2004) finds that the statement relating to navigation has the highest factor score within the web-interface dimension of online banking service quality. Broderick and Vachirapornpuk (2002) find that difficult navigation is linked to switching behaviour and negative word of mouth about online banks.

Transaction tools in the context of online banking include the ability to make money transfers between accounts or between the customer's bank and another organisation for bill payment. Research indicates that customers expect these tools to be present (Joseph et al. 2005). There should also be the facility to purchase financial products such as insurance or currency exchange (Bauer et al. 2005). However, for some product categories (for example, pensions) the ability to purchase online remains limited due to the specialised extended nature of the supply chain (Harrison et al. 2006). There is a need for research that investigates how customers respond to the presence or absence of transaction functionality within the online banking e-servicescape, in respect of specific product types.

Signs, symbols and artifacts

This element focusses on those elements which are used as signals and which communicate to the customer the nature of the service which they have received or are about to receive. Consumer risk perceptions have been identified as a barrier to online banking use (Curran and Meuter 2005) and there has been considerable focus on those SSAs that communicate the trustworthiness of the online banking website and also the trustworthiness of the bank itself. For example, Yousafzai et al. (2005) propose a model for trust-building that lists various SSAs as antecedents to trusting intentions, including giving customers clear and obvious access to security policies, access to privacy policies, providing guarantees regarding liability, statements about regulatory compliance, third-party verifications as to security and privacy, customer testimonials, professional website design and consistency in branding. Their research, whilst finding significant differences between four banks along these dimensions, provides support for security policy, privacy policy, legal statements and professional website design as statistically significant predictors of trusting intention.

There are differences in research findings regarding visual design artifacts such as animations and aural design artifacts. Bauer et al. (2005: 171) argue that the dimension of "enjoyment and entertainment … is a relevant criterion for assessing the quality of bank portals" and propose the inclusion of animation and multimedia elements. However, Joseph et al. (2005) find that music and visual appearance is perceived as having a low importance in service delivery performance and this is reinforced in later research by Walker (2011: 231), who finds that "graphics in general and animation in particular feature low in users' lists of website evaluation criteria". There is evidence that customer preferences vary according to age and personality type as research by Maenpaa et al. (2006: 5) finds that hedonic consumers prefer entertaining auxiliary features on bank websites and that as a segment these consumers tend to be younger and with lower disposable incomes.

Affiliate artifacts are listed within SSA. Several financial institutions operate affiliate campaigns whereby they receive website visitors as a result of referral from other websites and may display branding and other information within the e-servicescape. Affiliate marketing is a fast growing method of customer acquisition and business development (Fox and Wareham 2007). This practice is particularly prevalent within the insurance marketplace, with 72 percent of consumers who shopped around for car insurance using at least one price comparison website (PCW) (OFT 2011). The biggest affiliate marketers are brands in their own right (for example, the UK-based price comparison website www.comparethemarket.com). Whilst it can be argued that PCWs are a functionality that provide economic value for the consumer (Laffey and Gandy 2009), the PCW sector is gaining a poor image for lack of basic website security (Martin 2013), misleading advertising claims (McMillan 2014), intrusive data collection techniques (Edwards 2007) and failing to accurately compare like with like in the rank of results (Read 2013). In November 2013, the UK Financial Conduct Authority announced that it was to begin a thematic review into insurance PCWs to examine the clarity and fairness of the information provided (FCA 2013). Surprisingly, there has been little empirical research that explores this topic despite the practices being so ubiquitous and contentious (Mariussen et al. 2010). Brear and Barnes (2008) examine the application of affiliate marketing within three financial services markets and find that affiliate marketing needs to be implemented in a much more contingent manner. However, there remains a clear research gap for examination regarding the presence of this artifact within the online banking e-servicescape from the customer perspective (Gregori and Daniele 2011).

Tensions within the online banking e-servicescape

The preceding sections have drawn on extant research in order to illustrate how each of the dimensions within the proposed e-servicescape framework might operate in the context of online banking. This section develops the discussion further by introducing two key dilemmas that arise when considering how the framework might be applied to specific contexts and systems. The first dilemma concerns the paradoxical choice between the elements of the e-servicescape, whilst the second dilemma concerns how the dimensions of the proposed e-servicescape might influence different aspects of online banking, within the different contexts of the various clusters of products that may be offered online.

Paradoxical choice

There has been discussion in the wider online literature of paradoxical choices within website design. Mick and Fournier (1998) coin the term "technological paradox" where the provision of one website attribute reduces the efficacy of another. It is proposed that potential conflicts reside within those items in the spatial layout and functionality (SLF) dimension and the signs, symbols and artifacts (SSA) dimension, and how these might impact upon ambient conditions.

One example of a potential conflict would be the provision of identity verification tools within the SLF dimension that might reduce accessibility. Namely, logging into a secure connection might increase the time it takes to access the online banking service. Thus, a secure website might be considered as a less accessible website. Equally, a highly accessible website that does not require a consumer to log on might be viewed as insecure and risky. For example, Smyth (2010) found that the Barclays' online banking system was vulnerable to online fraud due to the neglect of security in favour of usability. Specifically, the identity authentication process was simplified to require only four pieces of customer data.

A second example of potential conflict is that consumers could perceive an aesthetically pleasing website as being inaccessible and unreliable. For example, the time needed to download graphics and other interactive features to support SSA might reduce speed of access, if the customer does not have the necessary software to display graphics then the reliability of the website might also be reduced. On the other hand, a consumer might perceive a website that is highly accessible and reliable due to limited aesthetic attributes as one that is not pleasurable to use.

A research approach that might be employed in addressing these tensions within the e-servicescape is Task-Technology Fit Theory (Goodhue and Thompson 1995). Following this approach, a financial services organisation might seek to measure the degree to which items within SLF and SSA facilitate task-specific performance. For example, research into online banking by Waite and Harrison (2002) shows that customers have different requirements of a website when undertaking information search compared with the requirements associated with accessing an account for transaction purposes.

Product context

Financial services products can be grouped according to the way in which they meet consumer needs and the extent to which they are short- or long-term products (see Table 23.3). Short-term products tend to result in patterns of more frequent customer interaction with the online channel, for example, in checking a balance in the case of current (cheque) accounts, savings accounts and credit cards. In the context of car insurance, interaction would occur annually when renewing the policy and even less frequently with regard to making a claim. It can be argued that in these instances customers might place greater importance on ambient conditions and SLF to facilitate goal-directed behaviours. Longer-term products tend to result in less-frequent patterns of interaction (Ennew and Waite 2007) due to the infrequency of purchase and the deferred nature of the product benefits; on the other hand, these are considered higher-risk products (Harrison 2000). In these product groupings greater importance might be placed on SLF meeting information needs to minimise pre-purchase risk and also on SSA to signal brand strength and reputation.

The first product to be offered through electronic channels was the current account (Harrison 2000). However, a wider range of products have become available online as the channels have become more established. Despite this diversification and growth of online products, the majority of the extant literature concerning the provision of online financial services has focussed on online current accounts and there is a paucity of research that examines how the elements of the e-servicescape might influence the different product clusters that form part of the online banking offer. Reviewing the literature, we find only three studies that have focussed on specific product categories other than online banking and none of these focussed specifically on the Servicescape concept.

Harrison et al (2006) examine pension provider websites and find that customers place importance on search engine tools, calculation tools and timely and relevant information, which would be classed under the SLF dimension of the e-servicescape. However, their review of online provision shows that pension websites tend to focus on symbols of brand identity and strength and provided links to affiliates, which would be classed under the SSA dimension of the e-servicescape.

Table 23.3 Exemplars of financial services product groupings

Financial need	Short-term products	Long-term products
Cash accessibility	Current account	N/A
Asset accumulation	Savings account	Pension
Deferred payment	Credit card	Mortgage
Risk management	Car insurance	Life insurance

Source: Adapted from Ennew and Waite (2007).

Coughlan et al. (2001) examine online mortgage provision. They find inconsistency between the in-branch, hybrid and internet-only application processes; this finding highlights an opportunity to use the Servicescape concept as an analytical tool. They also find that mortgage provider websites present information in a manner which is hard to understand and not appropriate to meet the demands of the online registration process. In addition, they find that the poor navigation flow of the websites means that customers engaged in self-service activities do not have any feedback as to their progress. This research indicates that in this context there is a need for a focus on SLF. Research by Lim et al. (2009) looks at the relationship between quality perceptions and trust in the context of online car insurance. They distinguish between information quality (which contains items related to SLF) and web system quality (which contains items related to ambient conditions). They find that information quality has a significant impact on purchase intention and recommend that automobile insurers focus on this more than web system quality.

Banks may have several e-servicescapes to design and maintain, they need to decide whether these multiple instantiations of e-servicescapes are components of an integrated overarching e-servicescape, or best regarded as distinct servicescapes, with different functionalities, design, styles, audiences and purposes. Research indicates that effective information provision is an important element of the online banking e-servicescape across a range of product contexts (i.e Coughlan et al. 2001, Harrison et al. 2006). This suggests that banking organisations should focus on the SLF aspects of the e-servicescape. A detailed discussion of the factors influencing the effectiveness of financial services communications is provided by Wang in Chapter 25.

Towards an online banking e-servicescape research agenda

In the case of an online service offering, the role of the website or e-servicescape as a tangible extrinsic cue is critical. Wells et al. (2011) write that since "the e-commerce channel remains limited in conveying experiential attributes compared to the physical store", then elements of the website need to be managed in order to signal to the customer the quality of the product about to be received. Indeed Bitner (1992) describes how elements within the Servicescape provide cues about the level of service that can be expected and the professionalism of the provider. Whilst there has been a considerable body of research concerning online banking, there has been no evidence of application of the e-servicescape to online banking. This paucity of research on the e-servicescape is borne out by Mari and Poggesi's (2013) systematic review of research into servicescape cues and customer behaviour. Although they identify twenty-seven empirical or theoretical articles on aspects of the e-servicescape, none of these relate to banking or financial services. We propose that research is needed in the areas of marketing strategy, technology management and consumer behaviour (Figure 23.1).

Marketing strategy

Multiple organisations

There is a need for research into how the e-servicescape varies between banking organisations. The online banking environment plays a critical role as the source of cues that customers have available to assist them in forming a judgement about the service (Demangeot and Broderick 2007); it is important to isolate those elements that comprise the e-servicescape. Bitner (1992: 67) explains how the identification of these elements contributes to "careful and creative management of the Servicescape" which will "contribute to the achievement of both external marketing goals and internal organizational goals". We suggest that it is the way in which the

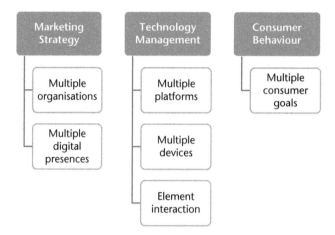

Figure 23.1   E-Servicescape research needs

Servicescape can reflect both organizational strategy and customer response to that strategy that makes it such a useful tool. Bitner (1992: 67) identifies three strategic roles that the Servicescape fulfils. First it acts as a "visual metaphor" for the service offering and in doing so communicates the "relative quality of the service". Second, it acts as a "facilitator…by either aiding or hindering the ability of customers and employees to carry out their respective activities". Third, it acts as a "differentiator in signalling the intended market segment, positioning the organization and conveying distinctiveness from competitors". She suggests that by "examining how the Servicescape is designed and managed in other industries" organisations can "gain strategic insights". There has been limited research that compares and contrasts the e-servicescape of banking organisations within or between national marketplaces and there is a need for more detailed exploration of multi-channel practice both across cultures and industries (Klaus and Nguyen 2013).

Multiple digital presences

There is a need to examine how the importance of elements of the e-servicescape might vary across multiple digital presences for an organisation. Banks may have multiple web presences, including sometimes more than one website, or elements of their website that are intended for different constituencies, i.e. current account customers, mortgage customers and insurance customers. Online banking and website research in general does not delve very far into the differential e-servicescapes that might be experienced whilst moving between service offerings contained within an organisation's website.

Technology management

Multiple platforms

Online platforms through which the online service experience is delivered are continually evolving in ways that affect how bank customers expect to engage with their bank. Specifically, with the advent of social media, organisations and brands now have not only an "official" presence through their website, but also a number of social media presences on platforms such as Facebook and Twitter. These platforms are used not only for marketing communications but also for customer service activities such as complaint resolution. Patricio et al. (2003: 471) found that "in a multi-channel context, customer satisfaction with internet services depends not only on the performance of this channel in isolation but also on how it contributes to satisfaction with the overall service offering". It is important that the service offering is consistent with an overall strategy of engagement. Adapting and updating the seminal Servicescape concept for the digital environment helps practitioners to better understand and manage a portfolio of channels.

Multiple devices

In addition, very little attention has been directed towards the array of devices through which consumers may experience e-servicescapes. Many of these devices are mobile, but have varying screen sizes, apps and internet access points. Further, mobile devices have been seen as devices in which the physical and social contexts impact on consumer information searching, use and decision-making behaviours (Houliez 2010). However, despite the acknowledgement that both mobile technologies and social media provide opportunities for consumers to share, communicate and collaborate in e-servicescapes, very scant attention has been paid to this changing aspect of the e-servicescape.

Element interaction

Research is needed into the interaction between different elements within the e-servicescape. Cebi (2013: 1030) argues that "none of the proposed approaches for the evaluation of websites considers the interactions among design parameters". There is evidence from practice of a "trade-off" being made between different aspects of the e-servicescape. There is a need for a deeper understanding of the interaction between e-servicescape dimensions and also of the overall importance of the dimension to the overall performance of the banking website.

Consumer behaviour

Multiple consumer goals

There is a need to examine how the importance of elements of the e-servicescape might vary according to different online consumer goals. Online banking research has tended to focus on transaction tasks to the exclusion of other tasks such as information seeking (Devlin and Yeung 2003, Lassar et al 2005: 183). Banks might find it useful to reflect on the types of behaviours that they are seeking to cultivate from users through the design of their e-servicescape. Within a particular service offering, users may undertake a range of tasks and the differences between tasks may also moderate the impact of various e-servicescape features. For example, the e-servicescape needs to support users in the completion of an array of tasks, ranging from the mundane and "every day", such as checking a balance, to the less frequent, but routine, such as setting up a direct debit, to the more unusual and challenging tasks, such as reporting a lost debit card, signing up for a current account, or taking out a major loan. The bank is seeking different behaviours in these different contexts and therefore different stimuli may be more or less effective in encouraging such behaviours.

Conclusion

Bitner (1992) argues that the Servicescape has a boundary spanning role that draws cross-functional teams from across the firm including marketing, facilities management and human resources. She sees this as the strength of the concept. This chapter proposes a conceptual e-servicescape framework and comments on its specific application in the online banking context. The proposed e-servicescape framework provides a clear differentiation between stimuli and user responses, which tend to be inter-woven in the dominant research paradigm based on e-service quality and TAM.

In addition, the framework provides a contextualisation for previous and future studies on the impact of specific aspects of the e-servicescape, known as web atmospherics. This framework contextualises both practice and research into the online banking experience. In particular, it seeks to counter the current emphasis in online experience research, theory and practice on the use of service quality dominated theoretical and measurement and evaluation perspectives of banking websites.

We invite other researchers and practitioners to draw on this framework to contribute to a broader and more integrated evaluation of the online banking environment. This chapter highlights several gaps in understanding and we propose three research areas: marketing strategy, technology management and consumer behaviour.

References

Aladwani, A. (2001). "Online Banking: A Field Study of Drivers, Development Challenges and Expectations", *International Journal of Information Management*, Vol. 12, No. 3, pp. 213–25.

Baker, J., Parasuraman, A., Grewal, D. and Voss, G. B. (2002). "The Influence of Multiple Store Environment Cues on Perceived Merchandise Value and Patronage Intentions", *Journal of Marketing*, Vol. 66 No. 2, pp. 120–41.

Bauer, H. H., Hammerschmidt, M. and Falk, T. (2005). "Measuring the Service Quality of E-Banking Portals", *International Journal of Bank Marketing*, Vol. 23, No. 2, pp. 153–75.

BBC (2013). "RBS Must Do Better After Payment Fault Says Boss", *BBC News*, 3 December 2013, Available online at www.bbc.co.uk/news/business-25193884 (accessed 7 January 2014).

Bitner, M. J. (1992). "Servicescapes: the Impact of Physical Surroundings on Customers and Employees", *The Journal of Marketing*, Vol 56, No 2, pp. 57–71.

Brear, D. and Barnes, S. (2008). "Assessing the Value of Online Affiliate Marketing in the UK Financial Services Industry", *International Journal of Electronic Finance*, Vol 2, No 1, pp. 1–17.

Briggs, P., Simpson, B. and De Angeli, A. (2004). "Personalisation and Trust: A Reciprocal Relationship?", *Designing Personalised User Experiences in e Commerce*, Human-Computer Interaction Series Vol 5, pp. 39–55, Springer.

Broderick, A. J. and Vachirapornpuk, S. (2002). "Service Quality in Internet Banking: the Importance of Customer Role", *Marketing Intelligence and Planning*, Vol. 20, No. 6, pp. 327–35.

Cebi, S. (2013). "Determining Importance Degrees of Website Design Parameters Based on Interactions and Types of Websites", *Decision Support Systems*, Vol 54, pp. 1030–43.

Chiou, W. C., Lin, C. C. and Perng, C. (2010). "A Strategic Framework for Website Evaluation Based on a Review of the Literature from 1995–2006", *Information & Management*, Vol 47, No 5, 282–90.

Chou, D.C. and Chou, A.Y. (2000). "A Guide to the Internet Revolution in Banking", *Information Systems Management*, Vol. 17, No. 2, pp. 51–57.

Coughlan, J., Macredie, R. D. and Patel, N. (2001). Understanding the consumption process through in-branch and e-mortgage service channels: a first time buyer perspective. *International Journal of Bank Marketing*, 29(2), pp. 148–67.

Curran, J.M. and Meuter, M.L. (2005). "Self-Service Technology Adoption: Comparing Three Technologies", *Journal of Services Marketing*, Vol. 19, No. 2, pp. 103–13.

Dailey, L. (2004). "Navigational Web Atmospherics: Explaining the Influence of Restrictive Navigation Cues", *Journal of Business Research*, Vol. 57, No. 7, pp. 795–803.

Davis, F. D., Bagozzi, R. P. and Warshaw, P. R. (1989). "User Acceptance of Computer Technology: A Comparison of Two Theoretical Models", *Management Science*, Vol. 35, No. 8, pp. 982–1003.

Demangeot, C. and Broderick, A. J. (2010). "Consumer Perceptions of Online Shopping Environments: A Gestalt Approach", *Psychology & Marketing*, Vol. 27, No. 2, pp. 117–40.

Demangeot, C. and Broderick, A. J. (2007). Conceptualising consumer behaviour in online shopping environments. *International Journal of Retailing and Distribution Management*, 35 (11), pp. 878–94.

Devlin, J. F. and Yeung, M. (2003). "Insights into Customer Motivations for Switching to Internet Banking", *International Review of Retail, Distribution and Consumer Research*, Vol. 13, No. 4, pp. 375–92.

Edwards, K. (2007). "Affiliate Marketing Finally Goes Mainstream", *Marketing Week*, Vol. 30, No. 35, 27.

Ekhaml, L. T. (1996). "Make Your Presence Known on the Web! Tips for Writing and Publishing Web Documents", *School Library Media Activities Monthly*, Vol. 12, No. 10, pp. 33–35.

Ennew, C. and Waite, N. (2007). *Financial Services Marketing*. Routledge.

Financial Conduct Authority (FCA) (2013). *The FCA Launches Review into Price Comparison Websites*, Available online at www.fca.org.uk/news/the-fca-launches-review-into-price-comparison-websites (accessed 7 January 2014).

Financial Times (2012). "The Upgrade that Downed the Royal Bank of Scotland", *Financial Times*, June 25 2012, Available online at www.ft.com/cms/s/0/4ecdb67c-beb9–11e1-b24b-00144feabdc0.html#axzz2aGk31UQ2 (accessed 27/7/13).

Fox, P. and Wareham, J. (2007, January). "Controlling Your Brand: Contractual Restrictions Placed by Internet Retailers on Affiliate Marketing Activities in Spain", In Conference proceedings of the 20th Bled eConference, Bled, Slovenia, pp. 125–42.

Gait, J. (1985). "An Aspect of Aesthetics in Human-Computer Communications: Pretty Windows", *IEEE Transactions on Software Engineering*, Vol SE-II, No 8 August, pp. 714–17.

Goodhue, D. L. and Thompson, R. L. (1995). "Task-technology Fit and Individual Performance" *MIS quarterly*, pp. 213–36.

Gorn, G. J., Chattopadhyay, A., Sengupta, J. and Tripathi, S. (2004). "Waiting for the Web: How Screen Color Affects Time Perception", *Journal of Marketing Research*, Vol 41, No 2, pp. 215–25.

Gregori, N. and Daniele, R. (2011). "Affiliate Marketing in Tourism: Determinants of Consumers' Trust", *Information and Communications Technologies in Tourism*, in R. Law, M. Fuchs & F. Ricci (eds) Proceedings of the International Conference in Innsbruck, Austria, January 26–28, pp. 559–71.

Grewal, D., Lindsey-Mullikin, J. and Munger, J. (2004). "Loyalty in E-Tailing: A Conceptual Framework", *Journal of Relationship Marketing*, Vol. 2, No. 3–4, pp. 31–49.

Griffith, D. A. (2005). "An Examination of the Influences of Store Layout in Online Retailing", *Journal of Business Research*, Vol 58, No. 10, pp. 1391–96.

Harris, L. C. and Ezeh, C. (2008). "Servicescape and Loyalty Intentions: An Empirical Investigation", *European Journal of Marketing*, Vol. 42, No. 3/4, pp. 390–422.

Harris, L. C. and Goode, M. M. (2010). "Online Servicescapes, trust, and purchase intentions", *Journal of Services Marketing*, Vol. 24, No. 3, pp. 230–43.

Harrison, T. (2000). *Financial Services Marketing*. Essex: Pearson Education.

Harrison, T., Waite, K. and Hunter, G. L. (2006), "The Internet, Information and Empowerment," *European Journal of Marketing*, Vol 40, No 9/10, pp. 972–93.

Hoffman, K. D. and Turley, L. W. (2002). "Atmospherics, Service Encounters and Consumer Decision Making: An Integrative Perspective", *Journal of Marketing Theory and Practice*, Vol 10, No 3, pp. 33–47.

Hooper, D., Coughlan, J. and Mullen, M. R. (2013). "The Servicescape as an Antecedent to Service Quality and Behavioral Intentions", *Journal of Services Marketing*, Vol 27, No. 4, pp. 271–80.

Hopkins, C. D., Grove, S. J., Raymond, M. A. and LaForge, M. C. (2009). "Designing the e-Servicescape: Implications for Online Retailers", *Journal of Internet Commerce*, Vol 8, No. 1–2, pp. 23–43.

Houliez, C. (2010). "When Non-Store Meets In-Store: Mobile Communications Technology, servicescapes, and the Production of Servicespace", *Journal of Customer Behaviour*, Vol 9, No. 2, pp. 201–20.

Huizingh, E. (2000). "The Content and Design of Web Sites: An Empirical Study," *Information and Management*, Vol. 37, No. 3, pp. 123–34.

Ibrahim, E. E., Joseph, M. and Ibeh, K. I. N. (2006). "Customers' Perception of Electronic Service Delivery in the UK Retail Banking Sector", *International Journal of Bank Marketing*, Vol. 24, No. 7, pp. 475–93.

Jayawardhena, C. (2004). "Measurement of Service Quality in Internet Banking: The Development of an Instrument", *Journal of Marketing Management*, Vol. 20, No. 1/2, pp. 185–207.

Jeon, M. M. and Jeong, M. (2009). "A Conceptual Framework to Measure E-Servicescape on a B&B Website", (August 1, 2009) International CHRIE Conference-Refereed Track Paper 14, http://scholarworks.umass,edu/refereed/Sessions/Saturday/14

Joseph, M., McClure, C. and Joseph, B. (1999). "Service Quality in the Banking Sector: the Impact of Technology on Service Delivery", *International Journal of Bank Marketing*, Vol. 17, No. 4, pp. 182–91.

Joseph, M., Sekhon, Y., Stone, G. and Tinson, J. (2005). "An Exploratory Study on the Use of Banking Technology in the UK", *International Journal of Bank Marketing*, Vol. 23, No. 5, pp. 397–413.

Jun, M. and Cai, S. (2001), "The Key Determinants of Internet Banking Service Quality: A Content Analysis", *International Journal of Bank Marketing*, Vol. 19, No. 7, pp. 276–91.

Kano, N., Nobuhiku S., Fumio T. and Shinichi T. (1984). "Attractive Quality and Must-Be Quality", *Journal of the Japanese Society for Quality Control* (in Japanese), Vol 14, No 2, pp. 39–48.

Klaus, P. and Nguyen, B. (2013). "Exploring the Role of the Online Customer Experience in Firms' Multi-Channel Strategy: An Empirical Analysis of the Retail Banking Services Sector", *Journal of Strategic Marketing*, (ahead-of-print), pp. 1–14.

Koernig, S.K. (2003). "E-scapes: The Electronic Physical Environment and Service Intangibility", *Psychology and Marketing*, Vol 20, No 2, pp. 151–67.

Kotler, P. (1974). "Atmospherics as a Marketing Tool", *Journal of Retailing*, Vol 49, No 4, pp. 46–64.

Laffey, D. and Gandy, A. (2009). "Comparison Websites in UK Retail Financial Services" *Journal of Financial Services Marketing*, Vol 14, No 2, pp. 173–86.

Lassar, W. M., Manolis, C. and Lassar, S. S. (2005). "The Relationship Between Consumer Innovativeness, Personal Characteristics, and Online Banking Adoption", *International Journal of Bank Marketing*, Vol. 23, No. 2, pp. 176–99.

Laukkanen, T. (2007). "Customer Preferred Channel Attributes in Multi-Channel Electronic Banking", *International Journal of Retail and Distribution Management*, Vol. 35, No. 5, pp. 393–412.

Li, S. and Worthington, A.C. (2004). "The Relationship Between the Adoption of Internet Banking and Electronic Connectivity: – An International Comparison", Discussion Paper No 176 – May 2004, Queensland University of Technology, Brisbane, Australia.

Lim, S. H., Lee, S., Hur, Y. and Koh, C. E. (2009). "Role of trust in adoption of online auto insurance". *Journal of Computer Information Systems*, Vol 5, No 2, pp. 151–59.

Lockett, A. and Littler, D., (1997). "The Adoption of Direct Banking Services", *Journal of Marketing Management*, Vol. 13, No. 8, pp. 791–811.

Lovelock, C. (1991). *Services Marketing*, 2nd Edition, Prentice-Hall, Englewood Cliffs.

Maenpaa, K. (2006). "Clustering the Consumers on the Basis of their Perceptions of the Internet Banking Services", *Internet Research*, Vol. 16, No. 3, pp. 304–22.

Maenpaa, K., Kanto, A., Kuusela, J. and Paul, P. (2006). "More Hedonic Versus Less Hedonic Consumption Behaviour in Advanced Internet Bank Services", *Journal of Financial Services Marketing*, Vol. 11, No. 1, pp. 4–16.

Mandel, N. and Johnson, E. J. (2002). "When Web Pages Influence Choice: Effects of Visual Primes on Experts and Novices". *Journal of Consumer Research*, Vol. 29, No. 2, pp. 235–45.

Mari, M. and Poggesi, S. (2013). "Servicescape Cues and Customer Behavior: a Systematic Literature Review and Research Agenda". *The Service Industries Journal*, Vol. 33, No. 2, pp. 171–99.

Mariussen, M, Daniele, R. and Bowie, D. (2010). "Unintended Consequences in the Evolution of Affiliate Marketing Networks: A Complexity Approach", *Service Industries Journal*, Vol 30, No 10, pp. 1707–22.

Martin, A. (2013). "Simply Getting a Quote From a Price Comparison Site May have Handed Your Details to Theives: Experts Say Lack of Basic Security Puts Millions At Risk of Fraud", *Mail Online*, 23 December 2013, Available online at www.dailymail.co.uk/news/article-2528140/Simply-getting-quote-price-comparison-site-hand-details-thieves-Experts-say-lack-basic-security-puts-millions-risk-fraud.html (accessed 7 January 2014).

Mattila, A. S. and Wirtz, J. (2001). "Congruency of Scent and Music as a Driver of In-Store Evaluations and Behavior", *Journal of Retailing*, Vol. 77, No. 2, pp. 273–89.

McKinney, V., Yoon, K. and Zahedi, F. M. (2002). "The Measurement of Web-Customer Satisfaction: An Expectation and Disconfirmation Approach", *Information Systems Research*, Vol. 13, No. 3, pp. 296–315.

McMillan P. (2014). "FCA Raises Concerns Over Moneysupermarket.com Adverts", *Money Marketing*, 2 January 2014, Available online www.moneymarketing.co.uk/news-and-analysis/regulation/fca-raises-concerns-over-moneysupermarketcom-adverts/2004719.article (accessed January 7 2014)

Mehrabian, A. and Russell, J. A. (1974). *An Approach to Environmental Psychology*. the MIT Press.

Mick, D. G. and Fournier, S. (1998). "Paradoxes of Technology: Consumer Cognizance, Emotions, and Coping Strategies", *Journal of Consumer Research*, Vol. 25, No. 2, pp.123–43.

Mukherjee, A. and Nath, P. (2003). "A Model of Trust in Online Relationship Banking", *International Journal of Bank Marketing*, Vol. 21, No. 1, pp. 5–15.

OFT (2011) *Private Motor Insurance: Summary of Responses to the OFT's Call for Evidence*, December 2011, Crown Copyright. Available online at www.oft.gov.uk/shared_oft/market-studies/private-motor-insurance/Motor_Insurance.pdf (accessed 28 July 2013).

Parasuraman, A., Berry, L. L. and Zeithaml, V. A. (1988). "SERVQUAL: A Multiple-Item Scale for Measuring Customer Perceptions of Service Quality", *Journal of Retailing*, Vol. 64, No. 1, pp. 12–40.

—— (1991). "Understanding Customer Expectations of Service", *Sloan Management Review*, Vol. 32, No. 3, pp. 39–48.

Patricio, L, Fisk, R.P. and Falcao e Cunha, J. (2003), "Improving Satisfaction With Bank Service Offerings: Measuring the Contribution of Each Delivery Channel", *Managing Service Quality*, Vol. 13, No. 6, pp. 471–82.

Read, S. (2013). "Comparison Sites Need to Be More Transparent About their Offers", *The Independent*, 20 December 2014, Available online at www.independent.co.uk/money/spend-save/simon-read-comparison-sites-need-to-be-forced-to-be-more-transparent-about-their-offers-9018584.html (accessed 7 January 2014).

Rogers, E. M. (1995). *Diffusions of Innovation*, 4th Edition, The Free Press, New York, NY.

Rust, R.T. and Lemon, K.N. (2001). "E-Service and the Consumer", *International Journal of Electronic Commerce*, Vol 5, No. 3, pp. 85–101.

Smyth, B. (2010). "Privacy vs. Usability: A Failure of Barclays Online Banking?", School of Computer Science Technical Report CSR-10-05, University of Birmingham. Available online at www.bensmyth.com/publications/2010-attacking-Barclays-online-banking (accessed 27/7/13).

Venkatesh, A. (1998). "Cybermarketscapes and consumer freedoms and identities", *European Journal of Marketing*, Vol. 32, No. 7/8, pp. 664–76.

Vilnai-Yavetz, I. and Rafaeli, A. (2006). "Aesthetics and Professionalism of Virtual Landscapes", *Journal of Service Research*, Vol. 8, No. 3, pp. 245–59.

Waite, K. (2006). "Task Scenario Effects on Bank Web Site Expectations", *Internet Research*, Vol. 16, No. 1, pp. 7–22.

—— (2009). *An Exploration Of Normative And Predictive Expectations Of Bank Web Site Features: A Tale Of Two Task Scenarios*, PhD Thesis, University of Edinburgh

Waite, K. and Harrison, T. (2002). "Consumer Expectations Of Online Information Provided By Bank Websites". *Journal of Financial Services Marketing*, Vol. 6, No. 4, pp. 309–22.

Waite, K. and Harrison, T. (2004). "Online Banking Information: What We Want and What We Get", *Qualitative Market Research: An International Journal*, Vol 7, No. 1, pp. 67–79.

Walker, P.R. (2011) *How Does Website Design In The E-Banking Sector Affect Consumer Attitudes And Behaviour?* PhD Thesis, University of Northumbria at Newcastle.

Wells, J.D., Valacich, J.S. and Hess, T.J. (2011). "What Signals are you sending? How Website Quality Influences Perceptions of Product Quality and Purchase Intentions?", *MIS Quarterly*, Vol 35, No2, pp. 373–96.

Williams, R. and Dargel, M. (2004). "From Servicescape To "Cyberscape". *Marketing Intelligence & Planning*, Vol. 22, No. 3, pp. 310–20.

Yang, Z., Jun, M. and Peterson, R.T. (2004). "Measuring Customer Perceived Online Service Quality", *International Journal of Operations and Production Management*, Vol. 24, No. 11, pp. 1149–74.

Yousafzai, S. Y., Pallister, J.G. and Foxall, G.R. (2005). "Strategies for Building and Communicating Trust in Electronic Banking: A Field Experiment", *Psychology and Marketing*, Vol. 22, No. 2, pp. 181–201.

Zeithaml, V.A., Parasuraman, A. and Malhotra, A. (2002). "Service Quality Delivery Through Websites: A Critical Review of Extant Knowledge", *Journal of the Academy of Marketing Science*, Vol. 30, No. 4, pp. 362–75.

Zhang, P. and von Dran, G. M. (2001). "User Expectations and Rankings of Quality Factors in Different Web Site Domains", *International Journal Of Electronic Commerce*, Vol. 6, No. 2, pp. 9–33.

Zickuhr, K. and Smith, A. (2012). *Digital Differences. Pew Internet & American Life Project*, Available online at http://pewinternet.org/Reports/2012/Digital-differences.aspx (accessed 29 July 2013).

Zimmer, M. R. and Golden, L. L. (1988). "Impressions of Retail Stores: A Content Analysis of Consumer Images", *Journal of Retailing*, Vol 64, No 3, pp. 265–93.

Part VIII

Corporate financial services marketing

24

Relationships and the business-to-business marketing of financial services

Peter Moles

Introduction

This chapter examines the business-to-business (B2B) marketing relationships between financial services firms and business users of their products and services. As such, it complements Chapter 9 on personal customer relationships. It should be noted that B2B marketing has received less research attention than business-to-consumer (B2C) marketing. There are a number of possible reasons to explain this relative neglect: lack of access to data, the complexities of the relationships, the lack of apparent uniformity in the service offering and the diverse nature of the businesses involved.

The chapter starts by first providing some background on the different financial firms involved, namely banks, asset management firms, and insurance companies, and the marketing challenges they face. This overview highlights that B2B marketing involves satisfying the product and service needs of knowledgeable professionals and their advisors. It identifies the following themes in the literature: the antecedents that influence the entrance and exit decisions for business purchases and relationships, the determinants of the length and duration of those relationships, and core service marketing issues, such as trust, communication, and commitment that affect value perceptions of the service offering.

Overview of business-to-business marketing relationships

Marketing relationships for financial services firms that cater to the needs of other businesses have a number of characteristics in common with marketing relationships for consumers, but at the same time they have certain distinct differences. A key difference is that consumer products and services tend to be generic and mass marketed and individually small in value in relation to the size of the seller's business; on the other hand, business products are customised, tailored to the customer, and large in value. In addition, whereas consumers are generally considered as unsophisticated, ill-informed and subject to a variety of cognitive biases, on the other hand, selling to businesses involves dealing with professionals who are seen as sophisticated and well-informed in their decision-making (Korniotis and Kumar 2010). Furthermore, there are likely to be fewer informational differences between buyers and sellers concerning the value of the product offering (Nath and Mukherjee 2012). Consequently, B2B marketing can be considered distinct from consumer marketing from the point of view of both academic research and business practices.

Research in this area has focused on particular types of financial institutions and their relationships with their business customers. While we may refer to B2B marketing of financial services as a unified process, in practice it takes place between: (i) banks and large and small industrial and commercial firms, (ii) asset managers and plan sponsors of pension funds, (iii) insurers and corporates and other financial service firms. The key differentiators of B2B from business-to-consumer (B2C) marketing relate to the type of services being offered, the nature of the relationship between the two parties and the fact that B2B uses customised products and services.

Most large banks have both retail and corporate divisions and hence engage both in B2B and B2C marketing. In the B2C case, they offer standardised products to individuals, and to micro and small enterprises. Marketing processes typically will be standardised and run generically across the target group. In the corporate division, which deals with B2B relationships, tailored and individualised services are sold to small and medium-sized enterprises (SMEs) and large corporations. Typically, a relationship manager (account or client manager) looks after the relationship between the bank and the corporate customer and this is an important B2B distinguishing feature, as it personalises the relationship between provider and client (Guo et al. 2013).

In a similar way, investment management firms offer specific products to individual investors in the form of pooled funds, such as mutual funds or open-ended investment companies (OEICs), or other managed investments. These will be standardised products and will be mass marketed to consumers. On the other hand, the B2B marketing relationships between plan sponsors and investment management firms involve tailored products and services, such as providing individualised portfolios designed to meet the particular investment objectives of the corporate client (Goyal and Wahal 2008). In this case, customising is such that no two corporate clients will necessarily have the same portfolio objectives, constraints, and composition. As with banks, client executives will manage the ongoing relationship between the fund management firm and their corporate clients. The marketing of insurance follows the same pattern, with standard products for consumers, but customisation for business clients.

In the B2B marketing context, the above products and services are characterised by interactive, longer-term relationships that may last years but are nevertheless subject to challenge and termination by one or other party (Gambini and Zazzaro 2013). To establish a relationship, sellers of financial services, such as banks, asset management firms, and insurance companies, typically compete to provide a range of corporate finance, investment services and insurance products to industrial and commercial firms, be they multinational, large, or small and medium-sized enterprises (SMEs), and to other financial services firms. If successful in winning business, these various types of financial services firms experience differences in the strengths of the relationships that bind the buyer and seller together.

For banks, once a relationship is established it is likely to persist for a considerable time because of the high costs of changing banks. For example, Ongena and Smith (2001) indicate a median banking relationship of four years in their study based on a sample of listed Norwegian firms. Elyasiani and Goldberg (2004) find that the average length of a relationship for SMEs is 7.77 years and state that this is longer than the relationship with other financial institutions. Peltoniemi (2007) found an average duration of a bank relationship of 9.08 years.

On the other hand, the relationships for investment firms and insurance companies appear to be less durable. Buyers in these areas are more willing to switch providers based on assessing the benefits and performance as the cost of changing suppliers in these cases is seen as considerably lower.

A further key feature that distinguishes B2B marketing in financial services compared to the consumer market is the high knowledge level and sophistication of buyers. Unlike retail consumers who are largely uninformed purchasers, corporate buyers will have a high degree of understanding of the quality and value of the services they are commissioning. To ensure value for money and select the most appropriate provider, at the start of the process of establishing a relationship, the buyer is likely to set up a "beauty contest" where suitably selected firms are asked to bid on the service to be provided. So in establishing a relationship, businesses are likely to look at a range of potential providers in terms of the factors that make them attractive partners. Furthermore, in the case of pension plan sponsors in particular, they may engage a consultant to advise on this process, who will also select the short-listed bidders.

Consequently, identifying the significance and strengths of the determinants and antecedents to the decision has been a key research interest in this area. However it is perhaps because the B2B marketing process is more complex and relationship-dependent that there is less research on this aspect of financial services marketing than on marketing to consumers. The literature in this area is not large but it highlights some of the real complexities involved. To give an idea of the multifaceted nature of the issues in the B2B context, Theron and Terblanche (2010) identify no less than 23 dimensions of relationship marketing in the literature: attractiveness of alternatives, power, bonding, commitment, communication, competence, conflict, cooperation, coordination, customisation, dependence, empathy, goal compatibility/congruence, opportunistic behaviour, reciprocity, relationship benefits, relationship-specific investment, satisfaction, service quality, shared values, switching costs, trust, and uncertainty.

Purchase, retention and termination

While Theron and Terblanche (2010) find many potential dimensions, researchers looking at B2B relationships have sought to understand the determinants involved in the purchase, retention and termination decisions as key stages in the management of a customer relationship. Underlying these key relationship decisions are the economics of distrust due to the asymmetric information that exists between the buyer and the seller but which, on the other hand, are mitigated by the benefits of a long-term commitment (Freixas and Rochet 1997). Research on services marketing views mutual commitment as the base for building relationships and brand loyalty. A key factor of this commitment is the building of a partnering relationship between the provider and the customer and for this reason most of the research has focused on the antecedents and determinants that affect the relationship.

As Camarero (2007) points out, financial services is a context in which managers emphasize relational and service quality strategies. Within this literature, commitment is seen as either affective or calculative, or a combination of both. Affective commitment can be thought of as the psychological benefits derived from the relationship. On the other hand, calculative commitment implies a rational evaluation of the value of the service since "committed customers continue a relationship, provided the costs associated with leaving the partner are higher than the expected benefits of switching." (Yanamandram and White 2010: 571) As Iyer and Bejou (2008) suggest, developing customer relationships is challenging, given the special characteristics of services and the complexities of determining expectations. They highlight the important fact that users of services go beyond the evaluation of service quality and that perceptions of the service include a wide variety of dimensions, many of which are quite subjective. They argue that building loyalty is necessary to ensure repeat business or to maintain a relationship. They point out that a single bad experience of the service can have a tremendous negative impact, especially if the causes are within the control of the provider. As Wong et al. (2008) point out, in financial services and in the insurance industry in particular, there are often few objective measures for determining service quality.

The next sections discuss B2B relationships from the perspective of the three broad categories of B2B financial services: banking, investment management services, and insurance.

Banking relationships

The majority of research in B2B financial services relationships has been conducted in relation to corporate customers and their banks. A key issue in the literature on banking B2B relationships has looked at the antecedents in the building of a relationship. For instance, Guo et al. (2010), looking at the newly deregulated Chinese banking market, identify six antecedents that influence the affective and calculative commitment of corporate customers. These can be split into objective criteria, namely interdependence and the service portfolio, and more subjective criteria, such as shared values, trust, service quality, and customer orientation. Ongena et al. (2011) look at the factors that influence firms' choice of banks. They find that bank reputation is an important decision factor for maintaining a particular bank relationship. On the other hand, they find that firms that put an emphasis on the price of bank services are both more likely to terminate relationships and reduce the number of services. Presumably such firms are more calculative in their approach to their banks.

In a survey of Canadian treasury officers that examines a range of factors that influence bank choice, Rosenblatt et al (1988) found that after taking into account criteria such as efficiency (ranked 1st in the study) and reliability of service (ranked 2nd place), they ranked qualitative factors such as responsiveness of contact person (3rd), quality of accounts manager (10th), good relationship with contact person (11th) and consistency in contact person (13th) above objective factors such as expertise in cash management (16th), knowledge of the company (18th), availability of credit (23rd), and quick turnaround of loan applications (29th). Interestingly, a long-standing relationship only ranked 23rd and good salesmanship was ranked last in 31st place. The authors concluded that service quality and the quality of their contacts at the bank were the principal decision criteria. Given the significant changes that have taken place in banking since this study, it is surprising that researchers have not revisited this topic in more detail. What we do find – and this will be discussed later – are a number of studies that examine particular aspects of the banking relationship, in particular elements such as commitment and trust.

In the corporate banking market, we can distinguish two types of lending processes: asset or transaction-based and relationship-based (Carey et al. 1998). The former is removed from the borrower and mostly relies on hard information. Relationship-based lending on the other hand relies more on soft information. Udell (2008), in a survey of commercial lending, finds that relationship lending depends on soft, i.e. non-quantifiable, information whereas other ways of lending depend on hard, quantifiable, information. An interesting issue, therefore, is to what extent the lending relationship allows the creation of soft information.

The role of the personal relationship manager is key to the creation of soft information. However, Tyler and Stanley (2001) highlight the near crisis in the banker-corporate customer relationship that has marginalised the role of the personal relationship manager. They argue that if banks seek to sustain this relationship they need to put the relationship manager at the centre of service arrangements and delivery. As will be discussed below, the benefits of a relationship not only apply to banks but also apply to banks' B2B customers in that a better knowledge of customers with whom they have a relationship translates into better loan terms.

Looking at bank selection, Yavas et al. (2004) identify three latent constructs that influence SMEs' choices. Both the search dimension that precedes the purchase decision and the experience and quality judgements about the provider gained after entering into a relationship with the provider are fairly objective criteria as they include factors such as the interest rate, collateral, and fees for the service. On the other hand, the credence dimension looks to attributes such as integrity, competence, and knowledge, which are harder to evaluate.

Intangibility of banking relationships

The studies here highlight the importance of intangible factors in the bank-corporate customer relationship, such as trust and integrity. Interestingly, this is very similar to the findings for B2C customer relationships in banking. For instance, Dalziel et al. (2011) identify four key relationship components for banks' retail consumers: trust, commitment, buyer-seller bonds and the benefits of the relationship.

Clearly in marketing financial services, intangible factors are important and can be explained due to the fact that a key element of the bank B2B relationship is dealing with the information asymmetry between the provider and the consumer of the services. When looking at both collateral and the borrower lender relationship, Brick and Palia (2007) document a positive 21 basis point interest rate reduction effect for the borrower-lender relationship for a one standard deviation increase in its length, which acts as a proxy for relationship quality.

Certainly at the bank level, there appear to be substantial benefits from an established relationship, as Engelberg et al. (2012) find when analysing the cost of bank loans. They identify significant benefits from better information flow and monitoring. They report that firm-bank personal connections shift the loan terms significantly in favour of the borrower through substantially lower interest rates, fewer covenants and larger loans. They further argue that personal relationships are a factor that allow the bank to excel in difficult to evaluate and problematic situations.

These results concur with Uchida et al. (2012) finding that loan officers lending to SMEs are responsible for producing important soft information. Their study indicates that this is more important for small banks. Whether this is due to the lack of quantitative data or the ease of establishing a relationship is not known, but it does suggest that a relationship orientation. Peltoniemi (2007) in a study using data from a single Finnish bank finds that the length of the relationship lowers the cost of credit and that this is particularly the case for high-risk firms.

The role of relationships also seems to matter even in what economists might consider to be anonymous markets, such as interbank lending. For example, Cocco et al. (2009) identify three conditions that lead to banks establishing relationships with other banks: (1) banks with large reserve imbalances are able to pay a lower interest rate, (2) smaller banks and banks with more non-performing loans and which, as a consequence, have limited access to the interbank market need to rely on relationships for funding, (3) banks establishing relationships with banks with less correlated borrowing needs, allowing funding reciprocity. They suggest that established relationships allow banks to reduce the cost of managing liquidity risk in the presence of market frictions, such as transaction and information costs. Using an in-depth interview approach, Guo et al. (2013) find that banks, by entering into a long-term relationship with their corporate clients, were able to manage the credit risk involved and increased their revenues, thereby creating more profit and increasing shareholder value.

On the other hand, Gambini and Zazzaro (2013) find that for SMEs which have long-lasting bank relationships, this adversely affects the ability of small bank-relationship firms to grow compared to similar bank-independent firms. However, the relationship has a positive mitigating effect for medium-to-large firms. They argue that the beneficial effects of relationship lending are, for small firms, offset by the negative effect of capture, risk and externalities. Looking at the same issue, Farinha and Santos (2002) find that SMEs initially borrow from one bank but that firms will increase the number of relationships conditional on growth opportunities and poor performance. They attribute this to small firms' concerns about hold-up costs and the unwillingness of the existing relationship bank to increase its exposure.

Based on a study that integrated market orientation, relationship marketing, and services marketing, Camarero (2007) suggests that relationship activities – customization, personalization, communication, and personal relationships – are the key drivers of performance. Market orientation provides an organizational focus to addressing the future needs of customers. Camarero argues that relationship and service quality are the direct results of banks and other financial institutions adopting a market orientated approach. Service quality is the necessary consequence of building and sustaining relationships.

Cultural factors

An interesting proposition, that remains to be fully tested, is that the findings concerning the determinants of B2B financial services relationships might be culturally-driven. Dash et al. (2009), using a cross-cultural sample from Canada and India, find that B2B bank relationships are based on the specific cultural context in which they take place. In their sample, they find that Indian society, with its low individualism, places more importance on social bonding, namely the depth of the relationship between the buyer and seller. On the other hand, structural bonding is more important in Canada, where society is more individualist, and where there is more emphasis on the process or task based elements of the relationship.

There is disagreement, however on the importance of cultural factors in building and maintaining relationships. Interestingly, Blankson et al. (2007) find a high degree of consistency in consumer bank selection across three different economies: an industrialized open market (USA), a newly industrialized open market (Taiwan), and a liberalized developing open market economy (Ghana). A study by Traylor et al. (2000) comparing Australian and US small business relationships finds significant differences in the way firms in the two countries approach the relationship. Personal relationships, location, and the product and service offerings are seen as the most important for US firms, whereas Australian firms consider prices, efficiency, and the willingness of the bank to provide a long-term relationship as the most important. The authors explain the differences as resulting from structural differences in the banking market in the two countries. The degree to which country, cultural, or institutional differences affect such choices is still to be determined and is an area that needs further research.

Trust in the business-to-business context

Theron and Terblanche (2010) find that trust, commitment, satisfaction, and communication are the most important dimensions of relationship marketing in B2B financial services, with competence, relationship benefits, bonding, customisation, attractiveness of alternatives, and shared values also significant. It is clear from most studies in this area that trust is a very important issue given the prevalence of asymmetric information and this has been the subject of considerable research in the provision of B2C services (as discussed in detail in Chapters 10 and 30). Theron and Terblanche's results emphasise the importance of the personal aspects of the relationship – empathy, politeness and similarity – compared to process aspects – customisation, competence and promptness (Coulter and Coulter 2002).

Gill et al. (2006) examined small business owners in the transportation industry and identified differences based on the length of their banking relationships. They found that the primary driver for trust is customization and, somewhat counter to expectations, found that newly established relationships are not more driven by personal characteristics. They conjectured that only after the basic survival needs of these small businesses are met do the person-related attributes begin to matter.

As Coelho and Henseler (2012) point out, service customization can create customer loyalty, in that it increases perceived service quality, customer satisfaction and trust. They find that customization has both direct and mediated effects on customer loyalty. Furthermore, there are also interaction effects between relationship quality, as modelled by customer satisfaction, and trust and customer loyalty. Guenzi and Georges (2010) find that a customer-orientated and expert salesperson increases the customer's trust in the salesperson; and unethical practice can do much to break trust down. These issues are explored further by Mulki in Chapter 34.

The above studies indicate that banking relationships are based on both affective and calculative commitment, but show a degree of variability due to different antecedents and dimensions that account for their complexity. Some of these complexities, such as the firm's life cycle, cultural differences, and the individual characteristics of both banks and firms, may account for the diverse results seen by researchers in this field. It remains to be seen whether future studies are able to establish a degree of consensus as to the relative strengths of the different elements of the relationship mix.

Investment management services

The bank-firm relationship can be seen as two-sided. There may be a number of actors involved on both sides, such as the relationship manager and service personnel on the bank side, and the treasurer and chief financial officer on the corporate side. However, the structure of pension fund investment management is more complex. Following Clark (2000), who examined the structure of the fund management industry, Figure 24.1 illustrates the number of parties involved and their different roles. It shows that plan sponsors will have multiple relationships with different service elements, such as the fund administrator, the internal and external investment managers, consultants, actuaries and so forth.

Nevertheless, given the importance of the services being offered, the principal relationship from a research perspective, and the one most subject to examination, is that between plan sponsors and the outside investment management firms hired to manage the pension plan's investments. Studies have focused on the antecedents of the hiring decision and the decision to terminate the appointment. A key issue that emerges in this literature is the credence aspect of the services on offer.

Strieter and Singh (2005) examine the factors that determine the choice of external investment management services. Using data from questionnaires, they apply an exploratory factor analysis approach to identify five latent characteristics that underlie the selection of investment managers in the equities, fixed income, real estate, and derivatives markets. These are listed in Table 24.1.

While it is clear that some determinants given in Table 24.1, such as past or portfolio performance, can be seen as objective, others, such as relationship characteristics, are far less easily determined as these include intangible elements such as direct communication, trust, and prior experience. Strieter and Singh point out that asset managers' promotional messages are

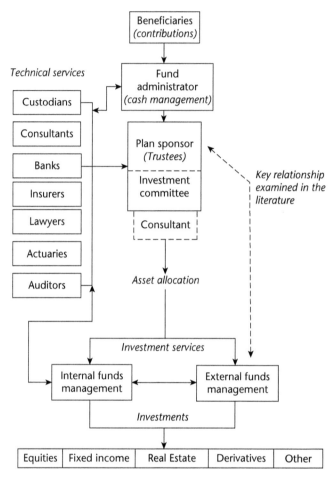

Figure 24.1 Pension fund investment management: institutions and services
Source: Based on Clark (2000).

dominated by past performance and supplementary support services (i.e. objective criteria), yet investment management is a service whose benefit and quality are largely uncertain (i.e. subjective). When viewed through the lens of the fiduciary relationship that exists between plan sponsors and outside investment managers, intangible characteristics become an important element of the business relationship. This is confirmed by the work of Parwada and Faff (2005) who, based on Australian data, find that prior performance, although important, is not the sole determinant. They cite the plan sponsor's conservatism and prudential concerns as selection factors.

Heisler et al. (2007), using a flow of funds approach, find a pattern of behaviour in plan sponsors that favours smaller products with longer track records and which exhibit a positive serial correlation of asset flows. They interpret this in the context of the appointment and termination of managers and asset allocation decisions as plan sponsors partly relying on qualitative factors such as subjective measures of manager skill, customer service and relationships with the manager.

In a quantitative study on the selection and termination of investment management firms, Goyal and Wahal (2008) find that investment managers are terminated for a number of reasons, not necessarily simply related to the underperformance of the funds under their

Table 24.1 Selection factors for equity, fixed income, real estate, and derivative portfolio investment management services

	Equities and fixed income[a]	Real estate[b]	Derivatives[b]
1	Past performance	Portfolio performance	Performance and personalisation
2	Professional standings	Performance reporting	Return and experience composite
3	Relationship characteristics		Relationship characteristics
4	Service quality		Service quality
5	Risk-adjusted return		

[a]Equities and fixed income are grouped together; risk-adjusted return was not a separate factor for fixed income.
[b]Real estate and derivatives had 2 and 4 factors, respectively. *Source* Derived from Strieter & Singh (2005).

management, and which in part appear to be related to the circumstances of plan sponsors. They argue that viewing the process as a whole, terminating investment managers may encourage competition and maintain discipline among existing management firms. Giller and Matear (2001) highlight the complex nature of inter-firm relationship termination and that, while there are common characteristics that govern terminations, they find that each is driven by a unique combination of the relationship factors involved. Interestingly, Goyal and Wahal find that for their sample the post-termination performance of managers is neutral or even positive compared to the benchmark.

As previously mentioned, plan sponsors largely rely on consultants to advise on the decision. Vaaland and Purchase (2005) examined a corporate (not financial services example) and found that the effect is to reduce the uncertainty in the decision process through the consultant providing additional information, although at the same time their presence adds to the uncertainty involved. They argue that the consultant's advice may increase uncertainty to a level that ultimately leads to termination. What is not evident is whether engaging consultants with their own agenda increases the likelihood of termination, in particular in the financial services sector. In this regard, Goyal and Wahal find no quantitative evidence that plan sponsors are more likely to hire and fire managers if they use the services of a consultant. Clearly this is an area that needs more research given the significant role played by consultants in the process.

In addition, what current studies in this area do not do is to look simultaneously at the termination and appointment decisions since hiring and firing investment managers mostly involves switching providers. This is a potential area for future research. Understanding the dynamics of this "switching" behaviour would provide insights into a key B2B financial marketing issue. Ellis (2006) points out that the literature in this area is largely exploratory and aims to identify individual incentives and deterrents to switching rather than providing an integrated explanation of the complexities of the underlying termination process.

A useful starting point might be the work of Yanamandram and White (2006) who identify a range of switching barriers in B2B services such as the availability of alternative providers, switching costs, inertia, relationship issues, service recovery, as well as other determinants that affect customer loyalty and hence the propensity to switch. In a follow-up paper that looks at dissatisfied customers, White and Yanamandram (2007) identify five deterrents that act to prevent switching to an alternative service provider: switching costs, interpersonal relationships, the attractiveness of alternatives, service recovery and inertia. In their model, these barriers are mediated by dependence and calculative commitment. In investment management, dependence is not likely to be very strong as the barriers to switching are likely to be quite low. On the other hand, calculative commitment is likely to be quite high.

The evidence on pension plan sponsor and investment management hiring and firing identifies both objective and subjective factors as important. The research tends to assume that plan sponsors are a homogenous group, although they will have different individual characteristics. This is clearly unrealistic and a richer portrayal of the behaviours of plan sponsors is called for. For instance, a possible line of research in this area is to expand on the insights made by Rowley (2005). She proposes that loyal customers can be categorised as either captive, convenience-seeker, contented or committed. It is clear that plan sponsors do not generally fall into the captive category since there are many potential investment managers and switching costs are relatively low. On the other hand, it is possible that they fall into the other three categories or new categorisations may be required to fully capture the differences involved.

Given the current state of knowledge, a lot more research is still needed to provide a good understanding of the dynamics of the hiring and firing process for investment management services. Research is also lacking on the way the marketing relationship works between plan sponsors, their advisors, and investment management firms. For instance, it would be useful to understand how asset managers are short-listed for the beauty contest. Clearly with a large number of potential candidates, how successful bidders are selected would provide insights into the antecedents involved. In particular, it would be interesting to see how they differ from those in other areas, such as banking relationships.

Insurance Services

The study of relationship marketing of insurance, a complex, high credence product whose benefits are hard to establish, seems greatly neglected and certainly is the poor relation of studies that look at bank marketing. A literature search revealed very little research that specifically looked at B2B marketing of insurance services, although there are a large number of studies that look at consumers' attitudes to insurance.

One paper that specifically looks at the institutional insurance service industry is Wong et al. (2008). They develop a vulnerability-commitment interactive relationship model that deals with the dynamic nature of insurance, the problems of its objective evaluation as a product, customization, and resource-dependence. In their model, successful relationships are built through client evaluation of the seller's capabilities, learning from the provider, cooperation, and involvement in customization. They find significant statistical support for their model from their data of institutional clients for commissioning general insurance in Hong Kong. They conclude that customization and trust increase vulnerability-commitment which, in turn, affects the client's loyalty to a particular provider.

Mäenpää and Voutilainen (2011) using a qualitative approach examine the cross-selling of bank and insurance products to SMEs. They find that the SMEs see banking and insurance as non-related products and they explain this in terms of the lack of loyalty programs in the B2B marketing context, as well as the unsuitability of hybrid banking-insurance products that are of questionable value to SMEs. They highlight two major issues with cross-selling, high switching costs and the reluctance of buyers to become dependent on a single provider. Their findings are generally in accord with the findings for cross-selling in the B2C context.

Conclusions

The challenge for B2B financial services marketing is to build long-term loyalty and ensure repeat business. A key problem for providers is that the buyer's evaluation of the offering goes beyond the technical attributes of the services and includes a wide range of dimensions, some of which are very subjective. A key challenge to any marketer is to manage the service relationships in such a way as to build and maintain client loyalty. The evidence in this chapter indicates that the ability to form and maintain such relationships varies across the types of financial services being offered. At one end, bank services can create strong, longer-lasting relationships, whereas asset management and insurance tend to create less loyal customers. Camarero (2007) argues that service quality and relationships are two aspects of a more fundamental attribute; namely, market orientation, the ability of the seller to capitalize on the current and future needs of customers. By building relationships, sellers can acquire the necessary intelligence on their clients and respond to their needs.

The research evidence presented in this chapter indicates the importance of building and maintaining strong customer relationships. However, strong relationships require an equally compelling service offering. Iyer and Bejou (2008) point out that providers have become increasingly conscious of the need to build these relationships and that the employer-customer relationship is just as important as the client's perception of the service offering. What the literature on this topic indicates is that, in order to build successful relationships in B2B marketing, financial service firms need to address both the objective and quantifiable elements of their offering as well as addressing subjective issues. Chief among the latter are trust, integrity, and commitment.

One conclusion that can be drawn from the research so far is that relationships matter in this area. A number of the studies reviewed here provide concrete evidence for the benefits of relationships, most of this evidence coming from the banking context. It would appear that providers are likely to emphasize the objective criteria of their offerings rather than subjective, relational ones. Perhaps the reason here is that it is hard to provide a compelling marketing narrative that captures the essence of these subjective criteria, in spite of their importance in building the attributes of a relationship. Consequently, it remains a real challenge for B2B financial marketers and their organizations to "get it right" given the complexities and dynamics involved.

Further research

If research in B2B marketing of financial services is to progress, it will have to overcome the issues identified in the introduction to this chapter. Clearly better access to data is required. The large data sets that are available about consumers are less available in relation to corporate customers. It is no accident that quite of bit of the literature relates to SMEs where banks relationships share some of the characteristics of retail customers. That researchers do not have access to similar data for large corporates is due to the way that financial service providers deal with these customers. There are sensitive commercial issues involved in disclosing information about significant customers. So until these can be resolved, progress in this area is likely to be patchy.

A further complicating factor is the customized and divergent nature of the product offering. Without adequately addressing this, researchers can never be confident that their results are not being driven by this rather than some other factor. Hence, ways to build this into their models need to be considered.

A further issue that this chapter highlights is that while the area of B2C marketing has been extensively examined and its determinants charted, by comparison B2B research remains relatively under-researched. Of particular note in this regard is the absence of papers that look at issues in the corporate insurance market, where very little empirical work and model building seems to have taken place. On the other hand, there is a growing literature on selling insurance to retail consumers. Given that insurance is a distinct financial product compared to banking and investment, this is all the more remarkable.

Other key areas of B2B financial services marketing still need clarification, in particular the role of antecedents and determinants, and our understanding of how factors such as customization, personalization, and personal relationships affect B2B financial services relationships. These are areas that have largely been examined in the context of retail consumers; adapting or developing testable models for the B2B market remains to be done. Given the significant changes that have taken place in financial services markets since the credit crunch some research, such as that by Rosenblatt et al. (1988) on bank selection criteria in the B2B context, could usefully be re-examined in the present context.

It would also be valuable to see studies that examine issues in different countries. This is a weakness in the current literature in that many studies are both very country specific and use relatively small samples. One has to reflect whether what applies in Australia, Finland, or Hong Kong can be assumed to apply elsewhere. It would be good to see other country-specific studies but also broader research that goes on to compare and contrast between countries. It is surely the case, as the extant literature seems to suggest that some of what we know is driven by country-specific factors and is not generalizable in another context.

Consequently, there exists a big future research agenda to examine the "how", "why" and "what" drivers of business-to-business purchase, retention, and termination decisions in financial services marketing.

References

Blankson, C. J., M-S. Cheng and N. Spears (2007), Determinants of banks selection in USA, Taiwan and Ghana, *International Journal of Bank Marketing*, 25(7): 469–89.

Brick, I.E. and D. Palia (2007), Evidence of jointness in terms of relationship lending, *Journal of Financial Intermediation*, 16: 452–76.

Camarero, C. (2007), Relationship orientation or service quality? What is the tiger of performance in financial and insurance services? *International Journal of Bank Marketing*, 25(6): 406–26.

Carey, M.M. Post and S.A. Sharpe (1998), Does corporate lending by banks and finance companies differ? Evidence on specialization in private debt contracting, *Journal of Finance*, 53(3): 845–78.

Clark, G. (2000), The functional and spatial structure of the investment management industry, *Geoforum*, 31: 71–86.

Cocco, J.F., F.J. Gomes and N.C. Martins (2009), Lending relationships in the interbank market, *Journal of Financial Intermediation*, 18(1): 24–48.

Coelho, Pedro S. and Jörg Henseler (2012), Creating customer loyalty through service customization, *European Journal of Marketing*, 46(3/4): 331–56.

Coulter, K.S. and R.A. Coulter (2002), Determinants of trust in a service provider: the moderating role of length of relationship, *Journal of Services Marketing*, 16(1): 35–50.

Dalziel, N., F. Harris and A. Laing (2011), A multidimensional typology of customer relationships: from faltering to affective, *International Journal of Bank Marketing*, 29(5): 398–432.

Dash, S., E. Brunning and K.K. Guin (2009), A cross-cultural comparison of individualism's moderating effect on bonding and commitment in banking relationships, *Marketing Intelligence and Planning*, 27(1): 146–69.

Ellis, Paul D. (2006), Factors affecting the termination propensity of inter-firm relationships, *European Journal of Marketing*, 40(11/12): 1169–77.

Elyasiani, E. and L.G. Goldberg (2004), Relationship lending: a survey of the literature, *Journal of Economics and Business*, 56: 315–30.

Engelberg, J.P. Gao and C.A. Parsons (2012), Friends with money, *Journal of Financial Economics*, 103: 169–88.

Farinha, L.A. and J.A. Santos (2002), Switching from single to multiple bank relationships: determinants and implications, *Journal of Financial Intermediation*, 11: 124–51.

Freixas, X and J.C. Rochet (1997) *Macroeconomics of Banking*, Cambridge, MA: Massachusetts Institute of Technology Press.

Gambini, A. and A. Zazzaro (2013), Long-lasting bank relationships and growth of firms, *Small Business Economics*, 40: 977–1007.

Gill, A.S., A. B. Flaschner and M. Shackar (2006), Factors that affect the trust of business clients in their banks, *International Journal of Bank Marketing*, 24(6): 384–405.

Giller, C. and S. Matear (2001), The termination of inter-firm relationships, *Journal of Business and Industrial Marketing*, 16(2): 94–112.

Goyal, A. and S. Wahal (2008), The selection and termination of investment management firms by plan sponsors, *Journal of Finance*, 63(4): 1805–47.

Guenzi, P. and L. Georges (2010), Interpersonal trust in commercial relationships: antecedents and consequences of customer trust in the salesperson, *European Journal of Marketing*, 44(1/2): 114–38.

Guo, X., A. Duff and M. Hair (2010), The antecedents and consequences of commitment in bank—corporate relationships: evidence from the Chinese banking market, *Asian Pacific Business Review*, 16(3): 395–416.

Guo, Y., J. Holland and N. Kraender (2013), Establishing bank-corporate relationships and building corporate advantages, *Journal of Financial Services Marketing*, 18(1): 27–39.

Heisler, J., C.R. Knittel, J. J. Newman and S.D. Stewart (2007), Why do institutional plan sponsors hire and fire their investment managers? *Journal of Business and Economic Studies*, 13(1): 88–115.

Iyer, G.R. and D. Bejou (2008), Managing service relationships: an overview, *Journal of Relationship Marketing*, 7(4): 323–25.

Korniotis, G.M. and A. Kumar (2010), Cognitive abilities and financial decisions, in *Behavioral Finance: Investors, Corporations, and Markets*, H.K. Baker and J.R. Nofsinger, ed, Holoben, N.J: John Wiley and Sons.

Mäenpää, I. and R. Voutilainen (2011), Value through combined offerings of bank and insurance, *International Journal of Bank Marketing*, 29(7): 535–54.

Nath, P. and A. Mukherjee (2012), Complementary effects of relational bonds in information asymmetry contexts, *Journal of Services Marketing*, 26(3): 168–80.

Ongena, S. and D.C. Smith (2001), The duration of bank relationships, *Journal of Financial Economics*, 61: 449–75.

Ongena, S., G. Tümer-Alkan and B. Vermeer (2011), Corporate choice of banks: decision factors, decision maker, and decision process_first evidence, *Journal of Corporate Finance*, 17(): 326–51.

Peltoniemi, P. (2007), The benefits of relationship banking: evidence from small business financing in Finland, *Journal of Financial Services Research*, 31: 153–71.

Rosenblatt, J., M. Laroche, A. Hochstein, R. McTavish and M. Sheahan (1988), Commercial banking in Canada: a study of the selection criteria and service expectations of treasury officers, *International Journal of Bank Marketing*, 6(4): 19–30.

Rowley, J. (2005), The four Cs of customer loyalty, *Marketing Intelligence and Planning*, 23(6): 574–81.

Strieter, J.C. and S. Singh (2005), The determinants of acquisition of outside investment management service providers in public and corporate pension plans and endowments, *International Journal of Bank Marketing*, 23(3): 218–36.

Theron, E. and N.S. Terblanche (2010), Dimensions of relationship marketing in business-to-business financial services, *International Journal of Market Research*, 52(3): 383–402.

Traylor, R., J. Nielson and R. Jones (2000), How small business firms select a bank: Comparisons between the United States and Australia, *Journal of Financial Services Marketing*, 5: 73–85.

Tyler, K. and E. Stanley (2001), Corporate banking: the strategic impact of boundary spanner effectiveness, *International Journal of Bank Marketing*, 19(6): 246–60.

Uchida, H., G.F. Udell and N. Yamori (2012), Loan officers and relationship lending to SMEs, *Journal of Financial Intermediation*, 211: 97–122.

Udell, G.F. (2008), What's in a relationship? The case of commercial lending, *Business Horizons*, 51: 93–103.

Wong, Y.H., R.Y.K. Chan, T.K.P. Leung and J.H. Pae (2008), Commitment and vulnerability in B2B relationship selling in the Hong Kong institutional insurance service industry, *Journal of Services Marketing*, 22(2): 136–48.

Yanamandram, V. and L. White (2006), Switching barriers in business-to-business services: a qualitative study, *International Journal of Service Industry Management*, 17(2): 158–92.

Yavas, U., E. Babakus and S. Eroglu (2004), Bank choice behaviour of small and medium-sized construction firms, *Journal of Business and Industrial Marketing*, 19(4): 258–66.

25

Competition and cooperation in partnership arrangements in financial services

Sandeep Singh and Joon Yong Seo

Introduction

The importance of collaborative relationships in the financial services industry is widely recognized. Environmental changes, such as globalization of the finance industry, increasing capital movements between countries, financial regulation, and technological advances in transaction processing (Lambkin and Muzellec 2008) have led to growing competition and difficulties in product differentiation. As a result, firms face increasing pressure to offer superior customer value. Value enabling activities can involve outright institutional purchase of a service or can be collaboration (partnership) with a third party that becomes an integrated component of an offering. Additionally, distribution channels have become a major strategic battle ground for financial institutions. This is probably because collaborative relationships with multiple financial intermediaries provide access to multiple segments. Serving new customers or providing existing customers with a wider range of financial products often requires new partnerships with new channels (Easingwood and Storey 1996).

Vitale et al. (2011) provide a framework for understanding institutional relationships with third parties that enable the organization to present an offering of superior value to customers. According to these authors, the combination of value enabling and value creating activities form the value chain that provides an offering perceived to be of value by the target market. In this chapter we examine the collaboration aspect of this part of the value chain as it pertains to the offering of financial services. Failing to build an effective channel partnership can lead to a firm's decline in the long term, and selecting the right partner can contribute to a financial firm's overall success (Howcroft 1992). This chapter complements Chapter 13 by Michel that focuses on customer value co-creation. Although partnerships with intermediaries and other firms are very common in financial services marketing, there is relatively little research on collaborations in this industry. Further, the extant literature fails to provide a framework that can be useful in understanding and guiding partnerships in this area. In this chapter we intend to remedy some of these deficiencies.

To provide a better understanding of issues pertaining to collaborations in financial services marketing, the following topics are addressed in this chapter. First, we provide a comprehensive review of the body of knowledge on the topic of partnership marketing as relevant to financial services. This is followed by a classification paradigm of the unique nature of these collaborative relationships in the institutional context. Then, we present a framework along with short guides that will assist practitioners in building successful collaborative relationships. Finally, we discuss the legal environment affecting the use of collaborative marketing arrangements.

Prior to the detailed discussion of the above topics, we begin with a description of what in our understanding constitutes partnership marketing in the financial services industry. We define partnership marketing in a broad sense. To us, a partnership marketing arrangement constitutes various types of collaboration between two or more firms to enhance the perceived benefit from the value chain by the customer. It might be a simple re-selling agreement where one partner acts as a distributor for the other for a fee. For example, securities brokers like E-Trade in the United States provide a selling platform to Blackrock, an investment management company, for their Exchange Traded Funds. Alternatively, the partnership can be complex where each partner has significant input in product development and marketing. For example, JP Morgan Chase in the United States teams up with Hyatt Hotels to offer an affinity credit card to Hyatt customers, the characteristics and marketing of which are jointly determined by both the companies.

Framework for marketing partnerships in financial services

Limited assistance is available to academics and practitioners in terms of a theoretical framework and empirical evidence to guide them in the design and use of collaborative relationships for enhancing value of a financial services offering. Nevertheless, the literature on the marketing of manufactured products does provide useful guidance on the nature of the relationship between partners in collaborative marketing arrangements. Partnership and collaborative marketing in the financial services arena share similarities with channel relationships in the manufacturing sector. The structure of institutional relationships in the manufacturing sector (for example, manufacturer-distributor relationships) can provide a basis for developing a framework for understanding institutional partnerships in the financial services sector.

Carlson et al. (2011) present a conceptual framework for the understanding of new physical product alliances. This framework is relevant to collaborative marketing in the financial services industry. We adapt and modify the framework to be applicable to collaborative marketing in the financial services industry. The adapted framework appears in Figure 25.1 and illustrates various internal and external factors that influence collaborative relationships in the financial services area.

According to this framework, the success of any partnership marketing arrangement in the financial services industry hinges upon five sets of factors: organizational, collaborative, relational, environmental and market orientation. Our discussion focuses on the first three factors as they are particularly pertinent to partnerships in the financial services area. The last two are indirectly addressed in Chapters 1 and 2 in this book.

Organizational factors

Financial services firms can depend on the prospective partner's reputation for an initial position in building a relationship. Research shows that a positive reputation can increase commitment and trust in partnerships (Ganeson 1994), which in turn results in enhanced cooperation between the partners.

Alliance orientation refers to a firm's capabilities to "scan its environment for partnering opportunities, coordinate its alliance strategies, and learn from its alliance experiences" (Kandemir et al. 2006: 325). While market orientation is concerned with a firm's focus on customers and creating superior customer value, alliance orientation is concerned with achieving

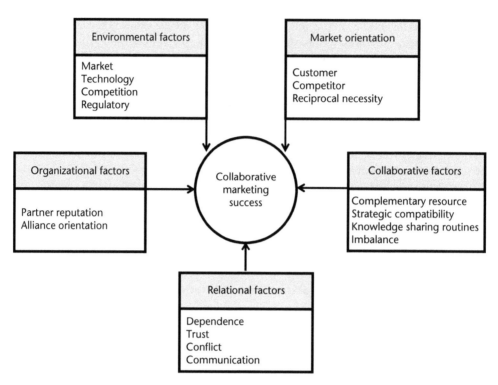

Figure 25.1 Conceptual framework for understanding financial services marketing collaboration
Source: Adapted from Carlson et al. (2011).

superior alliance management (Carlson et al. 2011). Alliance orientation has been shown to positively affect partnership performance and eventually overall market performance (Kandemir et al. 2006). Firms that adopt alliance orientation can be attractive partners since they are likely to provide the partner with evidence of resources that foster a committed and rewarding partnership.

Collaborative factors

Another motivation and success of partnership marketing may be derived from the resource-based view of organizations (Barney 1991). The dynamic capabilities construct (Teece et al. 1997) posits that thriving organizations anticipate changes in consumer needs and the marketplace and adjust the deployment of resources to retain the competitive advantage that challengers will find difficult to overcome. Researchers adopting the resource-based view propose that an alliance between partners with complementary abilities and orientations is more likely to be successful than a partnership between partners with unique and non-complementary abilities and orientations (Jap 1999). Similarly, in the financial services industry, collaborative marketing can be used to fill "resource gaps" for organizations. Advances and alliances in the payment processing industry provide excellent examples of such resource motivated partnerships. American Express, in order to retain its lead in use of technology, partnered with Twitter to allow card holders to charge for certain purchases using a specific "tweet". The partnership provides American Express extra revenue opportunities utilizing social media, while Twitter avails of the much needed monetization opportunity of its platform.

Dyer and Singh (1998: 665) define knowledge-sharing routine as a "regular pattern of inter-firm interaction that permits the transfer, recombination, or creation of specialized knowledge". They claim that knowledge-sharing routines between collaboration partners reduce uncertainty and increase trust and commitment, thereby facilitating collaboration.

In a study of 98 co-marketing alliances involving 70 firms in the technology industry, Bucklin and Sengupta (1993: 43) determine that "imbalances in power and in the managerial resources that each partner provides are significant drawbacks to alliance success". They suggest that a partnership of equals and high priority alliances is more likely to succeed. Other success factors include prior familiarity among partners and compatibility of culture, operations and goals. By contrast, high frequency of interaction and high transactions costs negatively impact success probability, and these negative influences can be mediated through the incorporation of elements of formality, exclusivity, exit barriers and incentives.

Relational factors

Relational factors are probably the most studied topics in collaboration marketing and are discussed in detail by Moles in Chapter 24. In this stream of research, dependence and trust seem to be the most significant contributor of a successful partnership. Utilizing a Social Exchange Theory (SET) framework to study manufacturer-distributor relationships, Anderson and Narus (1990: 42) observe "the success of each firm depends in part on the other firm, with each firm consequently taking actions so as to provide a coordinated effort focused on jointly satisfying the requirements of the customer marketplace". They analyze relational components as an influence upon and determinant of collaborative satisfaction. Lambe et al. (2001) list the following as the basic building blocks of SET: (1) interaction between partners results in economic or social outcomes, (2) dependence on the exchange relationship is a key variable determining behavior of the partners, (3) positive outcomes over time increase firms' trust of their partner(s) and their commitment to the relationship, (4) positive interactions over time produce norms and behaviors that guide the relationship.

Anderson and Narus (1990) find that relative dependence is a significant determinant of the extent to which a partner will influence, and be influenced by, the other partner(s). A firm with less dependence can enact independent influence strategies while dependent firms should seek to provide value to the exchange. Heide and John (1988) argue that the degree of dependence can be determined by four factors: magnitude, munificence, opportunity for other partners, and partner expertise. Magnitude is the volume of business provided by the partner. When a partner provides a significant portion of a firm's business, the firm is more dependent on the partner. Munificence is "the availability of critical resources" (Dowling et al. 1996). Dependence increases when there are fewer alternate sources for overcoming resource deficiency. Next, a firm is more dependent on its partner when there are fewer other potential partners. If a firm needs to operate in a partnership and there is only one potential partner, then the firm is significantly dependent on that partner. Finally, dependence increases because of partner expertise. When the partner provides the best alternative for job completion, or when it is the only firm that can accomplish a task, a firm is more dependent on that partner. Jarratt and Morrison (2003: 235) further the dependence framework and argue that "general measures of dependence, such as 'imbalance' mask the effect of dependence on relationship management practice in specific contexts". They investigate three factors affecting dependence in a partnership: need to access unique resources, relationship imbalance, and competitive vulnerability (i.e., replace ability). They find that a need to access unique resources enhances relationship quality, while an increase of imbalance in a business-to-business relationship neither increases relationship management nor decreases controlling behavior. They further determine that the absence of competitive vulnerability reduces the incentive on the dependent partner to resolve conflict expeditiously. Finally and quite interestingly, firms in dominant positions perceive to apply norms of fair behavior but do not feel the same about their partners when they themselves are in a dominated position.

The role of trust in collaboration has received significant attention from researchers. It has been shown as an important determinant for the purchase of financial services by individuals. Trust in a marketing partnership is best described as "the willingness of a party to accept perceived vulnerability to the actions of another party based on the expectation that the other has the ability, benevolence, and integrity to perform a particular action important to the trustor, irrespective of the ability to monitor or control that other party" (Clark et al. 2010: 218). As can be observed from the definition, parties contemplating entering into a partnership arrangement need to recognize that the degree of trust required for the relationship to be successful will be affected by the degree of dependence and how vulnerable one party is to the actions and competence of the other. One of the practical suggestions provided by the research is periodic review of the relationship with the intent of recalibrating expectations and outcomes in light of the changes in the relationship and competitive offerings.

In Chapter 24 of this book, Moles provides valuable insights into understanding business-to-business marketing relationships in financial services. One of the observations relevant to this chapter relates to trust building between partners as often the product being jointly offered is subject to evaluation on dimensions that may not arise from rational decision making. This fact becomes significant for partnerships offering services to individual customers where the resources to rationally evaluate the characteristics and benefits of the service may not be present. In such circumstances trust between partners becomes quite a significant variable.

Analytical framework for partnership marketing arrangements in financial services marketing

In marketing, classification and categorization enables a better understanding of the situation and enables the possibility of an increased efficiency in the deployment of resources. It may be beneficial to understand and categorize the nature of the partnerships and possibly offer some marketing advice for each category. To that end, we extend and modify Estelami's (2012) work on this subject.

The financial services market is initially analyzed on three dimensions. The first dimension builds on Estelami's proposed product classification metric. Using his classification as a basis, we provide a discussion on the broad categories of financial products. The second market dimension is a categorization based on the end consumer; whether it is an institution or an individual making the purchase decision. Finally, and perhaps most significantly, the market is classified based on the nature of the relationship.

Financial products can be broadly classified based on the industry in which they are sold. For analytical and simplicity purposes, we classify them into four areas; banking, insurance, asset management and back office services. Although this list is not comprehensive, our classification does cover the major segments of the financial services market, and to these we add the ever present category of other. A schematic framework for understanding the collaborative marketing space is provided in Figure 25.2.

The primary focus of the categorization is to develop an understanding of nature of the relationship, though we integrate end markets and product categories in the analysis. Deriving

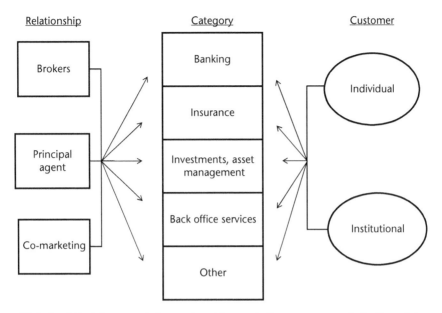

Figure 25.2 Analytical framework for partnership marketing arrangements in financial services marketing

from the understanding of exchange theory (Anderson and Narus 1990) where any relationship is predicated on the ultimate exchange of a good, service or an idea, we believe this to be the guiding principle behind partnership marketing arrangements. In financial services perhaps more than in other marketing situations, the channel relationship acquires a significant importance in the success of an organization and its offerings. The menu of mutual funds that are available to participants of a retirement plan (for example, a 401(K) in the US) is selected by the plan sponsor, not the eventual purchaser. Therefore, a mutual fund company should build a strong partnership with intermediaries with access to plan sponsors.

Classification of collaboration relationships

We classify institutional collaborative relationships based on their nature in three broad categories: Brokers, principal agent, co-marketing. We admit that the lines between these categories are blurry, yet, we expect the following discussion to highlight the subtle differences.

Brokers

The selling of a financial service involves the broker representing multiple vendors and often providing the buyer a menu that has offerings from multiple financial services firms. In such a selling arrangement, the broker may have a slightly superior position of power over the "manufacturer", as they determine the manner in which the product is presented to the final consumer. Most often, the broker needs to be compensated and essentially the manufacturer of the product to "sell" to two customers in the value chain; the broker and the ultimate consumer. Brokers are not an employee of the firm or an agent; they merely facilitate the transaction. An example can be cited from the placement of Exchange Traded Funds (ETF) by brokerage houses. The ultimate success in the placement of the ETF is dependent not only upon the choice by the customer but also the ease and magnitude of access to the broker's platform. Success of the ETF sponsor is affected not only by the choice of the consumer but also of the broker who provides the trading platform.

Principal agent

Financial services firms often use a network of agents to sell their products to customers. For instance, UBS, a Swiss bank, partners with Deutsche Bank to issue commercial mortgage bonds in the US in an effort to strengthen its fast-growing commercial-mortgage-backed-securities business. Although agents are not employees of the firm, they represent the firm and its products to customers. The agent who is required to represent only a single company's products is referred to as a captive agent, whereas one that represents multiple financial service firms is referred to as an independent agent. In either case, the principal is almost always responsible for the actions of the agent.

Agents are different from brokers in that brokers carry financial products from various (often competing) companies, whereas agents often have a responsibility to help their clients select the best product among the available choices. Since agents are not an employee of the company, they may have objectives and motivations that are different than the firms'. This conflict of interest poses several challenges, such as achieving coordination in marketing activities and maintaining consistent service quality. Moral hazard occurs when an agent places the firm at risk by violating the firm's policies. In order to make a sale, an agent may sell insurance policies to customers who are in high-risk categories. Moral hazard could be controlled through mechanisms such as explicit contracts between the firm and its agents or surveillance technologies that monitor the interaction between an agent and customers.

Co-marketing

The last type of collaboration is co-marketing. Co-marketing is a type of business alliance which can be referred to as a contractual relationship between two or more firms that pool their resources in an effort to achieve mutually compatible goals that they could not achieve easily alone (Hunt et al. 2002). Co-marketing alliances have become increasingly common in the financial services sector as more firms seek to develop partnership with other firms to achieve sustainable competitive advantage beyond their own boundaries. A financial services company can pursue partnership within and beyond the financial services industry. For instance, Royal Bank of Scotland teamed up with a UK retail giant Tesco to expand its market coverage. For Tesco, this was an opportunity to widen the range of its financial services. The firms estimate that the co-marketing alliance generated 400,000 extra customers (Feuchtwanger 1997). The alliance provided Royal Bank of Scotland with a very cost-effective channel. (Tesco Bank is now a subsidiary of Tesco as the firm later acquired the RBS shareholding. Chapter 2 provides further discussion).

American Express has broadened its bank relationships in the US through co-marketing, following a US court ruling that requires Visa and MasterCard to allow their member banks to issue competing cards. For instance, the firm has partnered with UBS and Juniper Bank (Wilmington, Delaware) to issue UBS-American Express-branded charge and credit cards. This program provides UBS clients with access to charge card, credit card, and automated-teller-machine services through their UBS management accounts. Through the partnership, UBS can provide its wealth management clients with a highly customized, distinctive reward program. What distinguishes co-marketing from brokers or principal agents is that both partners have significant input in the determination of product characteristics and the message.

Category of the financial services market

The category of the market being served affects the characteristics and capabilities of partner being sought. In the US, market restrictions on financial institutions were virtually removed in 1999 when President Clinton signed the Gramm-Leach-Bliley Act, also known as the Banking Modernization Bill. The wall between commercial and investment banking was removed. However, over the years it has become apparent that, with a few exceptions, developing competences in all categories of financial services remains challenging. The idea of a "one stop shop" of financial services has been proven difficult to achieve. Overcoming the competitive advantage of specialization in a category remains hard to overcome for firms serving other categories. This assertion can also be made with some confidence for non-US financial markets.

The financial services market has also become highly globalized. A cursory survey of top 20 commercial banks or top 20 investment banks in 2013 compared to those 15 years earlier provides preliminary evidence to this effect. While US banks still have a significant presence in the later list, their dominance is now shared by Chinese banks in the arena of commercial banking and by the Europeans in the area of investment banking. Moreover, partnership arrangements can provide a firm that has competence in one category, say commercial banking, access to the customers of a firm with competence in another category, for example, insurance.

As mentioned earlier, our categorization builds on Estelami's (2012) classification of financial services market. As many of these categories are discussed in detail in other chapters of this book, we provide a brief overview and focus on issues relevant to forming collaborative arrangements in each of these categories.

Banking

Banking is perhaps the largest category of the financial services market. It serves both institutional and individual consumers. Partnership marketing arrangements of firms with competence in this sector are primarily co-marketing arrangements with insurers and asset management services providers. A significant segment of bank lending is residential and commercial mortgages, where banks utilize what we have previously classified as brokers, and that classification of the relationship arrangement is significant for partnership marketing in this segment. Examples of co-marketing in the banking sector are primarily in marketing of insurance and asset management services, like mutual funds to retail customers.

Insurance

The insurance segment is primarily dominated by principal–agent relationships both in the service of individual and institutional customers. Lately, with the advent of Internet-based sales, many companies have dispensed with an agent-based marketing structure and are relying heavily on direct selling, especially for the individual consumer segment of the market. This phenomenon portends a trend away from partnerships or towards partners with web based capabilities.

Asset management

The asset management category of the financial services market perhaps provides the most instructive examples of, and lessons in, collaborative arrangements in financial services marketing. The broad category of asset management services encompasses a plethora of service providers. The spectrum ranges from traditional brokers to the modern day hedge funds and private equity firms, all vying for the individual or the institutional dollar. This category has a wide smattering of all three types of collaborative relationships involved in the delivery of financial services to the consumers.

Back office services

Back office services providers like transaction processors (Visa and MasterCard), payroll processors and securities transaction processors (black pools) require a high degree of technical competence and marketing is in a highly institutional framework. Collaborative arrangements in this sector might be a necessity as no one firm, with the exception of very large ones, can possess the technical competence to serve the needs of a wide array of customers and generate the economies of scale needed to survive in this market.

As might be evident, the above categories are not comprehensive and do not include all categories of financial services, for example tax advice. In Figure 25.2 we retain the "other" category for all services that do not neatly fit in any categories previously discussed.

The customer

Though intuitively simple, the nature of the ultimate consumer being served affects the choice of the partner. Financial services customers can be broadly classified in two categories: the individual consumer and the institutional buyer. To serve each, a separate kind of partner is needed. With a few exceptions, most financial services are complex products whose characteristics and value cannot be easily and directly assessed.

Devlin and McKechnie (2007) report that individual consumers of financial services often find financial products complex and intimidating. Additionally, the wide variety of choices and information often prove overwhelming. They cite earlier research indicating "that financial services markets can be characterized as having a high degree of opacity and complexity" (Devlin and McKechnie 2007: 31). On the other hand, institutional customers of financial products tend to be more sophisticated and have the resources to sift through and evaluate the products and information. In Chapter 3 of this book, Huhmann points to another possibility for improving an individual's ability to evaluate an experience product like financial services: improving financial literacy. He posits that financial literacy helps reduce the information asymmetry that exists between the provider of the service and the individual buyer. Essentially, the effort should be to provide tools to individual buyers that increase their parity to institutional buyers in product evaluation.

The choice of the partner is influenced by the type of ultimate consumers. Individual consumers often cannot "test drive" the product until after the purchase decision (McKechnie 1992). A firm contemplating offering financial services to individual consumers through a partnership arrangement will prefer a partner that has competence in trust building or fosters trust in the minds of individual consumers. If the firm itself has such capabilities, it would like to partner with a firm that will provide access to a volume of individual consumers that have the characteristics that the firm has capabilities to serve, for example, the mass affluent.

Institutional buyers, on the other hand, often are themselves agents of individual consumers (for example, a defined benefit pension plan) or seeking technical services (for example, back office processing capabilities). In most cases, these customers have the technical expertise and the resources to evaluate the financial product. In the case of a firm seeking to serve institutional clients, the technical competence of the partner should be one of the key characteristics sought. In marketing terminology, the firm seeks to overcome "competitive vulnerability" (Jarratt and

Morrison 2003) through the partnership. This vulnerability can be in the form of knowledge, technical competence or access to markets.

Some practical suggestions

As mentioned in the development of the theoretical framework, for any collaborative marketing effort in the financial services industry to succeed, each partner must understand the motivation and benefits for entering the collaborative marketing arrangement, the nature of the relationship and factors that are known to assist or hinder in the successful attainment of collaboration goals. In this section, the first topic of direct use to practitioners relates to advice on the partner selection process. Next we assimilate the theoretical knowledge of use to practitioners for understanding the collaborative relationship once it is established.

Collaboration partner selection process

Collaborative relationships have an enduring effect. The commitment involving collaboration arises from heavy investments of resources that are often required in building partnerships as well as the social and political character of collaboration (Coelho and Easingwood 2003). The enduring commitment often makes it difficult to change or terminate the partnership. Given the lasting impact of collaboration, it is critical to employ a systematic evaluation procedure in selecting partners. Drawing upon Holmberg and Cumming's (2009) research on building successful strategic alliances, in this part we aim to provide a practical partner selection process and guidelines, which will assist managers to assess new collaboration opportunities and identify most desirable partners.

The first step in the selection process is developing collaboration objectives and ensuring these objectives match overall corporate objectives. This calls for clarifying how a potential partnership will be aligned with a certain corporate goal. For instance, filling financial service gaps can be a collaboration objective that matches strengthening customer value proposition which can be a higher level corporate strategic objective. Common collaboration goals include, but are not limited to, attracting new customers, strengthening existing customer relationships, achieving economies of scale in operations, increasing website traffic, introducing new financial products and others. For instance, Bank of America built a partnership with the China Construction Bank (CCB) in order to achieve its objective to expand its global credit card business. Although it seems rather obvious that collaboration only makes sense if it leverages corporate objectives, this first and crucial step is often overlooked by managers in the process of forming partnerships (Sleuwaegen et al. 2003).

The second step is developing a set of critical success factors (CSFs) based on the firm's broader list of collaboration objectives. CSFs are the specific capabilities the firm should possess and serve as sources of competitive advantages over its competitors (Coelho and Easingwood 2003). CSFs are used in evaluating whether firms/individuals are worth considering as a potential partner by determining how well each of them fits with potential partners. For example, compared to foreign banks, Chinese banks have a significant advantage in their domestic market due to their strong corporate relationships as a majority of Chinese cardholders preferred to pay their credit card bills in cash at a local bank (Reuters 2007).

The third step is creating a potential partner map. This begins from identifying the most attractive industry groups, then the most promising segments within the industry groups, and finally the most attractive firms/individuals in the segments. Estimating how attractive a prospective partner should be based on the specific CSFs developed in the previous stage.

The mapping should relate back to collaboration objectives and the firm's overall goals identified in the first step. The China Construction Bank (CCB) is one of the largest commercial banks in China and is considered to have the capability to help Bank of America (BOA) to gain a strong base in China. Conversely, BOA possesses the expertise to enable CCB broaden its product offering to its customers.

The final step is systematically evaluating how well a prospective partner may help or hinder the firm's strategic objectives. Managers first assign relative importance weights to each CSF and then rate the extent to which each potential partner may help the firm achieve its CSFs. Coelho and Easingwood (2003) suggest that simply listing CSFs without weighting their relative importance can lead to erroneous conclusions about a collaboration opportunity. Thus, thorough consideration of relative importance of each CSF is important. For example, a manager may give more weight to attracting new online customers than to lowering market access costs. The tradeoff between the benefits and the costs of collaboration should be carefully considered. The benefits may include improved scale and operating efficiencies, while the costs may include inefficiencies resulting from sub-optimal operation. In the previous example, Bank of America acquired a nine percent stake in the CCB and agreed to provide the CCB with advice on developing credit cards, more customer-focused management, and improving its risk management.

In aggregate, utilizing this systematic approach to partner selection will help managers avoid paying only cursory attention to overall corporate objectives and other factors that may interfere with a successful partner selection process. Our advice is that the same degree of care should be exercised in the selection of a new partner as is in collaborative new product development or other types of strategic alliances. Previous interactions and vetting of multiple possible partners, if available, tend to increase the probability of success. A partnership of equals is more likely to succeed rather than a small partner seeking to leverage the capabilities of a large partner. Some imbalances can be removed through clearly laid out expectations and contractual arrangements (Bucklin and Sengupta 1993).

Managing collaborative relationships

A significant volume of theoretical research, though not directly focused on financial services, is available in this area and can be of help in the choice and design of a successful financial services partnership marketing program. The first variable shown to influence success and conflict in partnership marketing arrangements is referred to as dependence. There are multiple dimensions of dependence discussed in the marketing literature. We briefly discuss and explain a few prominent ones.

Relative dependence refers to the degree one partner is dependent on the other for their own success and for the success of the partnership arrangement. In other words, the success of the partnership may be more crucial to one of the partners. The more dependent partner should make an effort to follow least cost strategies to the success of the partnership. By contrast, the less dependent partner should try to follow exchange strategies like frequent interaction or request for information from the more dependent partner (Anderson and Narus 1990).

The strategic importance for each partner is the key dependence variable influencing partnership marketing arrangement success. Dependence arising from the need to access a partner's unique resources reduces controlling behavior by the partner and increases better relationship management thereby increasing relationship equity (Jarratt and Morrison 2003). It has been determined that the greater the disparity in mutual dependence, the lower the probability of success of the partnership marketing arrangement.

Trust has been mentioned prominently in academic literature as a factor affecting success of collaborative arrangements. In the context of this topic, trust refers to the ability, benevolence and the integrity of one partner to perform a task that is ultimately beneficial to the other partner without monitoring. As can be seen, trust is derived from the dependence of one partner on another for desired outcomes. It is important that interacting personnel (boundary spanners) in partnerships understand the three dimensions of trust to better build on their interactions with personnel on the other side. The depth of the partnership is directly correlated to the importance of benevolence and integrity aspects of the situation while shorter term relationships might require an ability focus (Clark et al. 2010).

Once established, the recommendation is of a periodic review of the partnership and additional alternatives available. This interaction clarifies continued expectations and often ensures mutual satisfaction (Anderson and Narus 1990). Even in the best run partnership arrangements disagreements and conflicts can sometimes arise. In this section we provide some useful guidance on actions partners can take to avoid disharmony and dysfunction.

Personnel interacting with the other party should be cognizant of trouble spots and be given authority to act quickly to resolve the situation. If the co-marketing effort involves multiple partners, then a council that represents the interests of all partners is useful. An independent ombudsman who has credibility with both parties is appointed at the initiation of the partnership, and can mediate conflicts before they become destructive to the achievement of the collaborative goal (Anderson and Narus 1990).

It is important to pay attention to the behavioral aspects of the partnership, not only the economic aspects. Depending on certain circumstances, it might be better to dissolve the partnership rather than spending effort and resources on salvaging it. Simply stated, it might not be a good idea to throw good money after bad (Purinton et al. 2007).

The legal environment of partnership marketing

In a broader context, the findings on co-marketing arrangements provide some useful lessons for managing the ethical and legal aspects of the partnerships. For example, one of the findings suggests that a partnership of equals is more likely to succeed than one of partners with disparate reputation and resources. Adhering to this suggestion might enable firms to reduce the possibility of being liable for the actions of the partner or risk compromising the ethical beliefs of the firm.

While increasing market share or revenues is often the motivation for partnerships, the regulatory environment often acts as a constraining variable for such goals. Partnerships that preclude competition, for example, a partner is given priority over others in access to markets, are likely to draw attention of regulators. In this regard, the suggestion from research studies on successful partnerships of periodic reviews and resets of expectations would include a review of legal, ethical and antitrust issues.

The regulatory landscape for financial services is significantly altered after the financial crisis on both sides of the Atlantic. In this section a brief overview of significant changes in the regulatory landscape affecting marketing partnerships on both sides of the Atlantic is provided. Given the breadth of the topic, it might not be possible to cover all the details. Hence, only a broad overview of salient changes and how they might affect partnership arrangements in financial services marketing is provided. The reader is also referred to two other chapters in this book. The first is on the topic of the role of regulation of competition in commercial and investment banking (Chapter 1 by Rai, Papaioannou and Cebenoyan) and the second is focused on the ethics of selling in financial services (Chapter 34 by Mulki).

In the US, calls to regulate marketing practices of financial services were being made well before the financial crisis of 2008. Demands to protect consumers from predatory marketing practices in the areas of credit card, personal loans and mortgage finance were gaining momentum. The first salvo in this area was fired by the signing of the Credit Card Accountability, Responsibility and Disclosure Act of 2009, popularly known as the Credit CARD Act to prevent abusive practices by credit card issuers. Of significance for partnership marketing efforts was Title III of the Act entitled "Protection of Young Consumers". In the US, credit cards are usually marketed to college students through "affinity" (co-marketing) arrangements or through "agents" whose primary purpose is to sign up new accounts for a fee. The new law prohibited the issuance of a card to anyone under 21 without a co-signor, who had to be above 21 years of age. Notable was the change in regulatory philosophy of providing the consumer with the information to make an educated choice to one of protecting the consumer from predatory practices.

In the US, the marketing landscape for financial services was forever altered by the establishment of the Bureau of Consumer Financial Protection (CFPB) as a part of the Dodd-Frank Wall Street Reform and Consumer Protection Act (Dodd-Frank) of 2010. The new law provided broad regulatory power to the Bureau so that it may "protect the American taxpayer by ending bailouts, [and] to protect consumers from abusive financial services practices" (Dodd-Frank Wall Street Reform and Consumer Protection Act 2010: 1). Notable and of interest to partnership marketing arrangements was the shift in legislative philosophy from one of rational economic choice to behavioural law and economics. According to Wright (2012: 2220–21):

> Behavioural law and economics is built upon the foundational assumption that consumers make predictable and systematically irrational decisions, and, indeed, that individual choice is not a reliable predictor of individual economic welfare; this observation in turn has inspired both commentators and legislatures to propose various restrictions on consumer choice. Behaviourists broadly contend that consumers systematically make choices that are both to their detriment and unrepresentative of their true preferences, and much of the behaviourist literature dedicates itself to establishing one or more of these biases in a specific context.

The broad implication of the shift in legislative philosophy for partnership marketing arrangements is the expectation of the enactment of more restrictions and disclosures going forward.

On a more practical level, according to Burr (2010), based on estimates by the law firm of Davis Polk, the Dodd-Frank Act will ultimately trigger 243 rule makings and 67 studies. As expected, a significant amount of legislative energy was devoted to the regulation of and attempting to eliminate abusive practices in the mortgage lending market. Residential and commercial mortgage lending is most often either directly originated by banks at their branches or through mortgage brokers. It is the use of these brokers that is most likely to be altered going forward, for two reasons. First, the new law requires that the mortgage originator retain at least five per cent of the mortgages that are securitized to create residential mortgage backed securities (RMBS). Second and more importantly in this regard, is the prohibition of directing incentives like the "yield spread premium". This is a marketing incentive offered by financial institutions to direct consumers to more lucrative products. Consequently, some of the money that lubricates these partnerships is being removed. Financial institutions will have to rely less on these partnerships for origination and incur higher costs for due diligence and credit appraisal going forward. Based on the knowledge provided by resource based explanations for marketing partnerships, there might be a shift from partnerships to developing capabilities internally by firms in this industry. It might also engender an era of consolidation in the industry where stronger players outright buy firms that previously were complementing partners.

In Europe it appears that the crisis was not sourced from abuses in the residential mortgage markets but from the precipitous decline in the value of securitized instruments held by European financial institutions. Later, governments of small and not so small European countries like Portugal, Italy, Ireland, Greece and Spain (PIIGS) saw a virtual shut out from access to capital markets. After much feet dragging and debate, in September 2010 the European Union decided to introduce a new, extensive regulatory regime for financial supervision. This is intended to address both micro- and macro-prudential supervisory aspects. At the core of this reform is the introduction of three new supervisory authorities: the European Banking Authority (EBA), the European Securities and Markets Authority (ESMA) and the European Insurance and Occupational Pensions Authority (EIOPA). Moreover, a European Systemic Risk Board (ESRB) has been created to foresee a role for the ECB (European Central Bank) (Amentbrink 2011). A comprehensive summary of regulation of the banking industry in the European Union can be found in Chapter 1 on regulation of competition in this book.

Broadly, this comprehensive set of legislative action was aimed to affect partnership marketing arrangements in four industries, namely banking, insurance, pension services and securities issuance and transactions. While the specific impact on each of the industries still remains to be determined, participants can be reasonably assured to expect a less hands off and self-regulating stance from rule making and regulating bodies.

In summary, over the foreseeable future, it might not be unrealistic for firms seeking partnership marketing arrangements to assume increased regulatory scrutiny and intervention, irrespective of geography.

Conclusion and suggestions for future research

Changes in the regulatory environment, globalization of the financial services industry and increasing complexity of financial products have created a need for firms to investigate and utilize collaborative arrangements. Delivering financial products/services of value increasingly requires supplementing the value chain with resources, knowledge of markets, or partners.

Limited guidance is available to marketers in the financial services industry when seeking or fostering marketing partnerships. We provide an adapted framework for understanding the theoretical constructs underpinning partnership relationships. We draw heavily from knowledge and empirical evidence from the marketing of manufactured products. Dependence and trust are found to be key constructs in the understanding of collaborative relationships. The literature also suggests that partnership of equals has the greatest possibility of success and partnership imbalances are best mitigated through clearly laid out contracts and constant and pre-emptive communication of differences, if any.

For a better understanding of the financial services marketing partnership a three-segment structural framework is provided. The partnership relationship is classified based on the nature of the relationship, category of the financial service and the status of the final customer of the financial product. Based on a survey of the literature and knowledge of the financial services industry, it is our opinion that it is the nature of the relationship that is perhaps the most significant determinant of partnership success.

Finally, we provide guidelines to practitioners on partner selection, characteristics of sustainable partnerships "dos and don'ts" when issues arise in a partnership. The key advice from the knowledge of manufactured products marketing on partner selection is "know thyself" prior to evaluating partners. Only then will a partnership map and desirable partner characteristics be helpful. A partner of equals is more likely to succeed than one with some kind of strategic imbalances. Imbalances become less significant if the partnership provides a needed resource to each other and many competitive alternatives are unavailable. Partnerships are sustained if there is constant communication between partners and clear expectations laid out in contractual documents. Partner differences are best addressed pre-emptively by boundary spanners who should be providing the resources to maintain a constant understanding of partner expectations and are given the authority to address problems pre-emptively.

The scope and depth of the research on partnership arrangement in financial services is very limited. In particular, a thorough literature review of the topic reveals the lack of a theoretical framework to guide partnership arrangements in the financial services industry. Our recommendation is for researchers to develop an initially agreed upon theoretical framework or competing frameworks for understanding partnership arrangements in the financial services industry. Subsequently, such models can be empirically tested as in the case of physical goods. In the financial services area, partnership arrangements take place between various types of financial organizations and nonfinancial organizations. Guidelines for partnership arrangements in one sector (for example, banking) may not be applicable to another area (for example, insurance). Therefore, in addition to a general theoretical framework, practical guidelines for various types of financial institutions will be useful. In our view, a wealth of questions remains to be answered.

We end the chapter on a cautionary note. We draw heavily from knowledge gained from partnerships in the marketing of manufactured goods. What might be good for the goose may not be good for the gander. The marketing and distribution of electronics components requires a slightly different partner and relationship than the placement of a hedge fund or a private equity position.

Acknowledgement

The authors would like to thank Mrs. Debbie Lester for her valuable assistance in the creation of Figures 25.1 and 25.2.

References

Anderson, J and Narus, J 1990, 'A model of distributor firm and manufacturer firm working partnerships', *Journal of Marketing*, 54, 1, pp. 42–58.

Barney, JB 1991, 'Firm resources and sustained competitive advantage', *Journal of Management*, 17, 1, pp. 99–120.

Bucklin, LP and Sengupta, S 1993, 'Organizing successful co-marketing alliances', *Journal of Marketing*, 57, 2, pp. 32–47.

Burr, SI 2010, 'Practitioner's Corner: The Dodd-Frank Act,' Real Estate Finance, 27, 3, pp. 10–13.

Carlson, B, Frankwick, G and Cumiskey, K 2011, 'A framework for understanding new product alliance success', *Journal of Marketing Theory and Practice*, 19, 1, pp. 7–26.

Clark, W, Ellen, SP and Boles, J 2010, 'An examination of trust dimensions across high and low dependence situations', Journal of Business-To-Business Marketing, 17, 3, pp. 215–48.

Coelho, F and Easingwood, C 2003, 'Multiple channel structure in financial services: A framework', *Journal of Financial Services Marketing*, 8, 1, pp. 22–34.

Devlin, JF and McKechnie, S 2007, 'Financial advice: What consumers need to know', *Consumer Policy Review*, 17, 1, pp. 31–35.

Dodd-Frank Wall Street Reform and Consumer Protection Act, 2010, *Dodd-Frank Wall Street Reform and Consumer Protection Act of 2010*, Pub. L. No. 3173–1.

Dowling, MJ, Roering, WD, Carlin, BA and Wisnieski, J 1996, 'Multifaceted relationships under competition', *Journal of Management Inquiry*, 5, 2, pp. 155–67.

Dyer, JH and Singh, H 1998, 'The relational view: Cooperative strategy and sources of interorganizational competitive advantage', *Academy of Management Review*, 23, 4, pp. 660–79.

Easingwood, C and Storey, C 1996, 'The value of multi-channel distribution systems in the financial services sector', *The Service Industries Journal*, 16, 2, pp. 223–41.

Estelami, H 2012, 'Marketing Financial Services', 2nd ed, Dog Ear Publishing, Indianapolis, IN.

Feuchtwanger, A 1997, 'Business day: Supermarkets are queuing up to be the superbanks', *Evening Standard*, 28, November.

Ganeson, S 1994, 'Determinant of long-term orientation in buyer-seller relationships', *Journal of Marketing*, 58, (April), pp. 1–19.

Heide, JB and John G 1988, 'The role of dependence balancing in safeguarding transaction-specific assets in conventional channels', *Journal of Marketing*, 52, 1, pp. 20–35.

Holmberg, SR and Cummings, JL 2009, 'Building successful strategic alliances: Strategic process and analytical tool for selecting partner industries and firms,' *Long Range Planning*, 42, 2/3, pp. 164–93.

Hunt, SD, Lambe, CJ and Wittman, CM 2002, 'A Theory and model of business alliance success', *Journal of Relationship Marketing*, 1, 1, pp. 17–35.

Jap, SD 1999, 'Pie-expansion efforts: collaboration processes in buyer-seller relationships', *Journal of Marketing Research*, 36, 6, pp. 461–75.

Jarratt, D and Morrison, M 2003, 'Dependence and the application of power and control in major business relationships: a study of manufacturing and service firms in the business-to-business sector', *Journal of Strategic Marketing*, 11, 4, pp. 235–53.

Kandemir, D, Yaprak, A and Cavusgil, ST 2006, 'Alliance orientation: Conceptualization, measurement, and impact on market performance', *Journal of the Academy of Marketing Science*, 34, 3, pp. 324–40.

Lambkin, M and Muzellec, L 2008, 'Rebranding in the banking industry following mergers and acquisitions', *International Journal of Bank Marketing*, 26, 5, pp. 328–52.

Lambe, CJ, CM Wittmann and RE Spekman (2001), 'Social Exchange Theory and Research on Business-to-Business Relational Exchange', *Journal of Business-to-Business Marketing*, 8, 3, pp. 1–36.

McKechnie, S 1992, 'Consumer buying behaviour in financial services: An overview', *International Journal of Bank Marketing*, 10, 5, pp. 5–39.

Purinton, EF, Rosen, DE Curran, JM 2007, 'Marketing relationship management: Antecedents to survival and dissolution', *Journal of Business-to-Business Marketing*, 14, 2, pp. 75–103.

Reuters (2007), No quick profit in China credit card market: survey, available at www.reuters.com/article/2007/06/26/us-china-creditcards-idUSSHA29521120070626

Sleuwaegen, L, Shep, K, den Hartog, G and Commandeur, H 2003, 'Value creation and the alliance experiences of Dutch companies,' *Long Range Planning*, 36, 6, pp. 533–42.

Teece, DJ, G Pisano and AA Shuen (1997). 'Dynamic capabilities and strategic management', *Strategic Management Journal*, 18, 7, pp. 509–33.

Vitale, R, Giglierano, J and Pfoertsch, W 2011, *Business to Business Marketing: Analysis and Practice*, Prentice Hall, Boston, MA.

Wright, Joshua D 2012, 'The Antitrust/Consumer protection paradox: Two policies at war with each other,' *Yale Law Journal*, 121, 8, pp. 2216–68.

Part IX
Alternative banking models

26

Islamic banking

Hussain Rammal

Introduction

The Islamic financial system is based on the teaching of the Qur'an, which prohibits the use of interest in economic activities (Saeed 1996). This prohibition meant that historically a section of the Muslim population stayed away from conventional money markets. The development of the Islamic banking and finance sector and the establishment of Islamic banks have provided an alternative for Muslims to have access to interest-free *halal* (permissible to consume) financing options (Siddiqui 1994).

Since the commercial introduction of the Islamic banking system in the 1970s, Islamic financing has received widespread acceptance in both the Muslim and non-Muslim worlds. The positive performance of the sector during the Global Financial Crisis, where the Islamic banks not only outperformed their conventional counterparts but also registered positive growth, has confirmed the sector's reputation as an ethical alternative to the conventional financing system (Chapra 2011). The Islamic financial system has grown at a rapid pace and the global assets of the sector are expected to reach the $4 trillion mark by 2020 (Karim 2012).

The Islamic financing system is regarded as the key to financial inclusion of Muslim communities around the world and is seen as the ethical alternative to conventional banking and investment systems. The purpose of Islamic financing is to help ensure equality in society and in the distribution of wealth. This chapter provides an overview of the Islamic financing system, its historical development and governance structure and a discussion on the various financial products offered by Islamic financial institutions.

The Islamic financing system

The Qur'an encourages trade and commercial activities but prohibits *riba*. There are two views of what *riba* means: one is that *riba* translates to all forms of interest, whereas the other is that *riba* refers to usury, which is defined as an exorbitant rate of return (Warde 2000) (see Table 26.1 for translation of Arabic terms used throughout the chapter). Muslim scholars have argued that a similar prohibition is found in Judaism and Christianity, and that there was no distinction between the use of the terms 'interest' and 'usury' until the Reformation in Europe

Table 26.1 Translation of some Arabic words used in the Islamic finance sector

Adl:	Refers to God's divine justice.
Fatwa:	Legal pronouncement in Islam, issued by a religious law specialist on a specific issue.
Fiqh:	Islamic jurisprudence that complements Islamic law with evolving rulings/ interpretations of Islamic jurists.
Gharar:	Uncertainty. Also refers to risky or hazardous sale, where details concerning the sale item are unknown or uncertain.
Hadith:	Oral traditions relating to the words and deeds of Prophet Muhammad.
Haj:	The pilgrimage to the Islamic holy city of Mecca undertaken by Muslims.
Hajis:	The pilgrims who undertake the pilgrimage to Mecca.
Halal:	Products or actions that are permitted under Islamic law.
Haram:	Products or actions that are prohibited under Islamic law.
Ijarah:	A lease based Islamic financing agreement.
Madhab:	Islamic schools of thought.
Mudaraba:	A profit-and-loss sharing Islamic financing agreement.
Mudarib:	The entrepreneur responsible for the management and execution of a project under the *mudaraba* contract.
Murabaha:	A mark-up based Islamic financing agreement.
Musharaka:	A profit-and-loss sharing partnership based Islamic financing agreement.
Qard hasan:	A loan which is given in the name of Allah. These loans are usually given to the poor and destitute.
Qist:	Refers to equity, fairness or balance.
Qur'an:	The holy book of followers of Islam.
Rabb-ul-mal:	The financier of the project under a *mudaraba* contract.
Riba:	Refers to interest charged on the lending and borrowing of money.
Shariah:	Islamic law based on the teachings of the *Qur'an.*
Sukuk:	Islamic investment certificates; sometimes also referred to as Islamic bonds.
Sunnah:	The traditions, practices and actions of Prophet Muhammad.
Takaful:	Referred to as Islamic insurance.
Ulema:	Muslim legal scholars who are known as arbiter of *Shariah* law.
Zakat:	The amount of money that every adult Muslim is obliged to pay to support specific categories of people.

(1500–1700 A.D.) (Saeed 1996). Hence, Muslims believe that any form of interest constitutes *riba* (Gafoor 1996).

Islam teaches Muslims to strive for equality in society and to pursue social justice. The Qur'an uses two words to describe this goal: *qist* and *adl*. These words express the ideals of equality in the world and in the relationship humans should have with each other (Kamla et al. 2006). To establish such a justice system, Islam has a number of rules that relate to the distribution of wealth in society. These include the payment of *zakat*, a 2.5 per cent tax on wealth paid to help the poor and needy in society, and *qard hasan* (gracious loan without interest). The prohibition on interest in financial transactions is related to the achievement of this social goal. The use of interest is seen to prohibit the distribution of wealth in society, where the rich would continue to hold the wealth and make a guaranteed return from lending money (Kamla 2007, Rammal 2006). The issue of socially responsible investment is discussed in detail in Chapter 33 by Nilsson, readers are encouraged to examine that chapter for modern perspectives on socially motivated investment practices.

In the Islamic economic system, money is treated as a means of exchange and does not hold any intrinsic value. Islamic financial institutions are therefore not permitted to make a return by lending money and are expected to share in the risks associated with a commercial venture by investing in physical assets (Usmani 1998). The Islamic financing system is therefore an asset-backed system. Any return made by a financial institution without taking risks is considered to be similar to interest, and is prohibited.

In addition to the prohibition of *riba*, financing agreements under the Islamic system are also required to avoid *gharar* or uncertainty. Under the conventional financing system the repayments on a loan may change over the life of the loan to reflect the change in interest rates. This creates uncertainty in relation to the amount of payment and leads to speculation over interest rate rises (Chapra 2007, Usmani 2002). Under the Islamic financing system all the details agreed upon remain the same for the life of the agreement. This means that the repayment of rent on the use of an asset remains the same, which helps the bank client know exactly what their obligations would be. The requirement also means that Islamic financial institutions are not permitted to finance high-risk activities that have an element of speculation. These are some of the reasons why the Islamic financing sector demonstrated positive performance results during the Global Financial Crisis. Further discussion on Islam's perspective on risk is provided in Chapter 27 by Wilson and Abdul Rahman.

Islamic financing is also sometimes categorised under ethical finance, as the sector is prohibited from dealing with certain industries. For example, Islamic financial institutions cannot finance activities that harm human life or are seen to promote immoral behavior. These include industries such as tobacco manufacturing, weapons and ammunition manufacturing, consumer products that include alcohol or pork, gambling centres such as casinos, interest-based financing, pornography, and some activities categorised under the entertainment sector (Rammal 2003). The products of Islamic financial institutions are available to people of all faiths and beliefs as long as the commercial activity being financed does not involve any of the industries mentioned earlier. In Malaysia, for example a large number of non-Muslim consumers use Islamic financial products (Abdullah et al. 2012, Rammal 2003).

Islamic financial products are offered globally through fully-fledged Islamic banks, stand-alone Islamic branches or 'Islamic windows' or Islamic cooperatives. Fully-fledged Islamic banks are banks that were established only to offer Islamic financial products and do not provide any conventional products. Their charter usually refers to the goals of social justice and equality in society. Stand-alone Islamic branches or 'Islamic windows' are operations of a conventional bank that offers Islamic products. This is usually achieved by either creating a stand-alone branch or by providing Islamic products from their existing branch facilities. In countries where the banking regulations do not facilitate the establishment of an Islamic bank, Islamic financial products are offered through Islamic cooperatives. In addition to fully-fledged Islamic banks, the market leaders in Islamic financing include conventional banking groups such as HSBC and Citicorp Banking Corporation.

Studies on Islamic bank marketing have found that the Muslim population in general has a positive view about the Islamic banking sector but remains unclear on the features of the system (Butt and Aftab 2013, Muhamad et al. 2012, Rammal and Zurbruegg 2007). The key institutions in the Islamic financial sector are seen to be weak at communicating and engaging with the community, which has led to questions being raised about the lack of transparency in the way Islamic financial institutions operate (Ghose 2013). In order to demonstrate their Islamic credentials to the sector, Islamic financial institutions are expected to adhere to Shariah governance principles (Haniffa and Hudaib 2007).

Shariah governance

One of the strengths of the Islamic financial system is the governance structure it follows. In addition to complying with international accountability requirements of having appropriate internal and external audits of the bank's records, Islamic financial institutions are also required to demonstrate appropriate governance measures to ensure compliance with Shariah. Islamic financial institutions achieve this by employing the services of a Shariah Supervisory Board (SSB). The SSB consists of a number of individuals with knowledge of and experience in Islamic jurisprudence (Khan 2007). The presence of an SSB in every Islamic financial institution is mandated by the central banks of most Muslim countries.

The SSBs have a number of responsibilities they fulfil. Although hired by the financial institution, the SSBs are expected to operate independently and to ensure the institution's compliance with Shariah. This is done by the SSB validating the transactions of the financial institution and providing a statement in the annual report that validates that the activities did not breach the regulations (Rammal 2006).

In case any breaches are identified, the SSB is required to inform the bank management and to ensure that any gains made from the breach are paid to a charity. If however, the SSB finds that the financial institution deliberately violated the rules of Shariah then the board is required to report the breach to the central bank of the country. Therefore, the SSB acts as a representative of the central bank but is remunerated by the Islamic financial institution. The SSB also ensures that the financial institution does not make a return from late fees or penalties imposed on clients. Under Islamic financing, the financial institution cannot count any late payment fees as income. While the financial institution can collect such fees, it is expected that the collected fees will be deposited to a charity that the institution selects.

The members of the SSB are also expected to answer queries about Islamic financing that the general public may have (Banaga et al. 1994). The websites of many Islamic financial institutions provide the biographies and contact information of the SSB members. For some Islamic financial institutions the reputation of the Shariah advisors is seen to help the brand of the bank and to differentiate them from their competitors. Therefore, large international banks tend to hire Shariah advisors who have a global reputation in Islamic jurisprudence and can be recognised by the members of the community (Haniffa and Hudaib 2007). In addition to the SSB, Islamic financial institutions may have an internal Shariah audit and review committee. The presence of these committees is mandated in some countries such as Malaysia (PricewaterhouseCoopers 2011).

Historical development of the Islamic financing system

The Qur'an was revealed in the seventh century, laying the foundations for the Islamic form of financing. However, the system's commercial implementation became a reality in the twentieth century (Lewis and Algaoud 2001). This was the period when many Muslim economies like those of Bahrain, Indonesia, Malaysia and Pakistan gained independence from colonial rule. During the 1950s and 1960s, some Muslim scholars and economists published studies arguing for Islamic countries to align their economic activities to the teachings of Islam and provided a roadmap for the introduction of Islamic finance (Rammal 2008, Warde 2000).

Some small-scale limited scope interest-free financing was attempted between the mid-1940s and 1960s, including one in Pakistan where rural landlords created an interest-free credit network (Gafoor 1996, Rammal and Parker 2013). According to Maali et al. (2006) the philosophy of these institutions was based on social initiatives to achieve social goals. Similar movements were initiated by many Indian subcontinent loan cooperatives that were influenced by European mutual loan experiments and religious ideals (Warde 2000). However, these experiments were short-lived as they did not receive any government support and there was limited guidance available of how Islamic financing should be implemented. In Malaysia, the Muslim Pilgrims Savings Corporation was set up in 1963 to help pilgrims save for the expenses associated with performing *haj* (religious pilgrimage to Mecca). The Muslim Pilgrims Savings Corporation has since evolved into Tabung Haji, an Islamic savings bank, which invests the savings of prospective *hajis* (pilgrims) in accordance with Islamic religious rulings (Wilson 1995).

The first commercial application of Islamic finance was undertaken in 1963 by Egypt's Mit Ghamr Savings Bank, which earned its income from engaging in trade and through profit-sharing investments (Lewis and Algaoud 2001, Warde 2000). The bank did not charge or pay interest but made no explicit reference to Islam or Shariah (Warde 2000). By the 1970s, the push for Islamic finance had gained momentum: in 1973 the conference of foreign ministers of Muslim countries decided to establish the Islamic Development Bank with the aim of fostering economic development and social progress of Muslim countries in accordance with the principles of Shariah (Rammal and Parker 2013). The second summit of the Organisation of the Islamic Conference was held in the Pakistani city of Lahore in February 1974. It was during this summit that the commercial introduction of Islamic finance was agreed upon and in 1975, the Dubai Islamic bank commenced operations as the world's first commercial fully-fledged Islamic bank (Dubai Islamic Bank 2012).

In 1979, the Government of Pakistan declared that it would Islamise its entire economy within a few years, making it the first country to attempt to have an interest-free Shariah compliant economy. However, Pakistan was unable to achieve this goal due to the lack of appropriate structure and external debts (Rammal and Parker 2013). Similarly, Iran attempted to Islamise its economy after the Islamic revolution of 1979. After nationalising the banking sector, Iran passed the Usury Free Banking Act in 1983, paving the way for Islamisation of the economy (Khan and Mirakhor 1990). Today Iran's banking sector only offers products that are considered to be Shariah compliant and no conventional financing products are permitted. Some of the largest Islamic banks in the world are based in Iran.

Similarly, countries such as Malaysia and Indonesia made changes to their Banking Act to facilitate the growth of the Islamic finance sector. However, these countries, and indeed most Muslim countries, operate a dual banking system, where both conventional and Islamic financial institutions operate in the economy. The growth of the Islamic financial system has not been limited to just Muslim majority countries. Islamic financial products are available in countries such as Australia, Thailand, Singapore, Hong Kong, the United States and across Europe. In Britain, the Islamic Bank of Britain was established in 2004 as the first fully-fledged Islamic bank in Western Europe (Islamic Bank of Britain 2013).

There are no regulatory bodies at the global level that control the activities of Islamic financial institutions. However, there are a number of organisations that have issued accounting, auditing and governance standards. Although the implementation of these standards is not compulsory, the central banks of Muslim countries are working with these institutions for the adoption of the standards. Two of these organisations are the Accounting and Auditing Organisation for Islamic Financial Institutions (AAOIFI) and the Islamic Financial Services Board (IFSB). The AAOIFI is located in Bahrain and was registered in 1991 as an autonomous body that prepares standards relating to accounting, auditing, governance, ethics and Shariah for Islamic financial institutions (AAOIFI 2012). In 2003, the IFSB commenced operations in Kuala Lumpur as a standard-setting body of regulatory and supervisory agencies. The IFSB promotes the development of the Islamic finance sector through the introduction of new standards that are consistent with Shariah requirements (IFSB 2013). The membership of both organisations include the central banks of many Muslim countries, whose participation is seen as important in achieving consistencies in application of the standards globally.

The Islamic finance sector is still in its infancy and despite the growth, the sector only constitutes a minor part of the banking and finance assets of the Muslim world. There is considerable opportunity to make further gains in existing markets and to explore the potential for the sector in new markets. At present, the key markets for the Islamic finance sector are Bahrain, which is considered the global hub for the sector, and Malaysia, which acts as a regional hub. The Gulf Cooperative Council region, Indonesia, Pakistan, Bangladesh, Turkey and India are seen as markets where future gains could be made.

Islamic financial products

Islamic financial institutions face the challenge of convincing consumers that their product offerings can match those of the conventional banks. While Islamic banks have succeeded in attracting those Muslims that had in the past refused to use interest-bearing bank products, this group only constitutes a small percentage of the total population. Islamic financial institutions have therefore had to be innovative in introducing products that are Shariah compliant but can also meet the needs of consumers. Some of the popular financing arrangements include the profit and loss sharing products known as *mudaraba* and *musharaka*, the lease based *ijarah* and the mark-up based *murabaha*.

In the profit and loss sharing based agreements, the parties share the profits of the venture at a pre-determined rate (Usmani 1998). Two commonly-used profit and loss sharing products are *mudaraba* and *musharaka*. *Mudaraba* is an agreement between parties, where one provides finance to another for utilisation in an agreed manner. The financier of the venture is known as the *rabb-ul-mal* and the entrepreneur responsible for the management and execution of the project is referred to as the *mudarib*. In keeping with the Islamic principles, the *rabb-ul-mal* cannot ask for a guaranteed return and the rate of return would depend on the profit the venture earns (Rammal 2003). The parties can only agree on the percentage that each party would receive from the profits. After the business is completed the financier receives the principal amount invested and the pre-agreed share of the profit. The remainder of the profit is the entrepreneur's compensation for their ideas and services (Gafoor 1996, 2001).

The *mudaraba* agreement is seen as risky from the financier's perspective. Whilst the agreement is seen to be profit and loss sharing, for the financier it is in fact profit sharing and loss bearing. As discussed previously the *rabb-ul-mal* and *mudarib* agree on the rate that they would use to distribute the profits but all the losses of the venture are borne by the *rabb-ul-mal*. As the *mudarib's* income is dependent on the venture making a profit, any losses in the venture would result in no income for the *mudarib*.

The other profit-and-loss sharing instrument is *musharaka*. The term literally means sharing and refers to a joint partnership where two or more persons combine either their capital or labour together to conduct business. Similar to *mudaraba*, the partners share the profit according to a pre-agreed ratio. However, unlike *mudaraba*, the losses in *musharaka* are shared by the parties according to the ratio of their respective contributions (Usmani 2002). In *musharaka*, all partners have a right to take part in the management of the business and to work for it (Gafoor 2001). The partners may agree upon a condition where the management is carried out by one of them. In such an instance, the other partner is only entitled to the profit to the extent of their investment, and the ratio of profit allocated to them should not exceed the ratio of his investment. All the partners are also treated as agents of the partnership and are permitted to make decisions on behalf of the partnership (Haron et al. 1994, Usmani 1998).

The profit and loss sharing agreements have their roots in the trade finance arrangements used by Arab traders predating the advent of Islam. Arab merchants financed the caravan trade by carrying goods on behalf of the producers from one city to another. They would share in the profits of a successful operation but could also lose all or part of their investment, if, for example, the merchandise was stolen, lost or sold for less than its cost (Gafoor 2001). The Prophet Muhammad was a trader himself and for these historical reasons the profit and loss sharing agreements are considered to be the most authentic form of Islamic financing products. However, the fact that under this agreement the financier could experience a loss makes it a less desirable product for many consumers with bank deposits and for financial institutions. The Islamic financial institutions offering these products tend to be conservative in the assessment of profitability of a venture to ensure that their depositors do not have to bear losses.

The *ijarah* agreement uses the leasing form of financing. Under *ijarah* the Islamic financial institution would buy an asset such as machinery or equipment on behalf of their client and then lease it out to them. The financial institutions therefore become the lessor and the client the lessee, who pays rent for the use of the asset. The amount of rent is agreed upon in advance. The financial institution thus transfers the right to the use of the property to the client, but keeps ownership. Theoretically, the maintenance of such an asset should remain with the owner of the asset. However, in practice as the client uses the asset exclusively, all repairs and maintenance costs associated with the assets are borne by the client. In instances where the clients would like to have the option to purchase the items at the end of the lease period, a lease-purchase form or *ijarah* agreement is required (Gafoor 1996). In such agreements the monthly payments consist of two components: rental for the use of the equipment; and instalments towards the purchase price.

Another popular form of financing is the mark-up based *murabaha*. In the *murabaha* agreement the financial institution purchases an asset on behalf of the customer and later sells it to the customer charging them the cost of the asset plus mark-up (Lewis 2001). This financial instrument was developed for use in foreign trade and working capital financing where the financial institution purchases raw materials and goods and sells them to a client at cost, plus a negotiated profit margin which would be paid normally within a fixed period of time or in instalments (Ahmed 1997). While murabaha remains one of the most popular Islamic financing instruments, it is also one of the most controversial. Some jurists claim that the mark-up amount in the agreement strongly resembles an interest amount charged by conventional banks. Instead of a percentage, the return is guaranteed in the form of a mark-up rate and this seems to be in contradiction of the Islamic principles. Financial institutions that provide this product argue that the return is justified as the banks do not lend the money but rather invest in the asset and also bear the risk that the client may refuse to take possession of the asset after it has been purchased.

Due to the criticism *murabaha* faces, some Islamic financial institutions have refused to offer this financing arrangement to clients. In 1991, the Federal Shariat Court of Pakistan (the country's highest religious court) ruled that financial products such as *murabaha* offered by the Islamic finance industry in Pakistan do not meet the Shariah requirements and are not acceptable (Federal Shariat Court 1991). However, this decision was later overturned on appeal and *murabaha* financing continues to be offered by many Islamic financial institutions worldwide.

Two other agreements used frequently in financing projects under the Islamic system are *takaful* and *sukuk*. Commercial insurance is seen to be incompatible with Islamic finance principles as it includes elements of uncertainty, interest and may be viewed as a way of gambling. All three of these components are strongly prohibited in Islam and cannot be used by practising Muslims. As an alternative, the Islamic finance industry has introduced an Islamic insurance concept called *takaful* (Ayub 2002; also discussed in detail in Chapter 27 by Wilson and Abdul Rahman). It is a form of mutual insurance that is based on mutual co-operation, responsibility, assurance, protection and assistance between groups of participants (Thomas 2005). Policyholders pay their subscription to help those within the group who need assistance. The resulting losses are divided and the liabilities are spread according to the community pooling

Table 26.2 Key features of select Islamic financial products

Product name	Financing arrangement	Key features
Mudaraba	Profit-and-loss agreement	• Form of venture capital. • Parties share profits according to a pre-determined rate. • All losses are borne by the financier.
Musharaka	Profit-and-loss agreement	• Form of partnership. • Parties share profits according to a pre-determined rate. • Losses are shared by parties according to the ratio of their investments.
Ijarah	Leasing	• The financier purchases the asset on behalf of the client, and then rents out the asset to the client in exchange for rental value. • Parties can enter into a hire-purchase agreement where the client can have the option of purchasing the asset at the end of the agreement.
Murabaha	Cost plus mark-up	• The financier purchases the asset on behalf of the client. • The client pays the financier the cost of the asset and an additional amount based on a pre-determined mark-up rate.
Takaful	Form of mutual insurance	• Pooling of funds via subscription fees by a group of people. • Policyholders who require assistance can access funds and the losses are shared amongst the group members.
Sukuk	Investment certificates or bonds	• Often used for capital projects. • Represents a collection of assets in the form of a bond that can be traded at the market price.

system. The system overcomes certain problems associated with traditional insurance by eliminating uncertainty and interest bearing payments (Thomas 2005).

Sukuk can be described as Islamic investment certificates and are sometimes also referred to as Islamic bonds. *Sukuk* are often used for capital projects and have been previously issued by both private firms and the governments of some Muslim countries. *Sukuk* is considered to be an authentic means of Islamic financing as it represents a collection of assets in the form of a bond. This bond can be sold at a market price provided that the majority of the rights in the bond relate to physical assets. Table 26.2 summarises the key features of some of the popular Islamic financial products.

Although the profit-and-loss sharing products are seen to be the most authentic form of Islamic financing, the most popular financing product is the mark-up based *murabaha*. It is estimated that about 80–90 per cent of financing agreements of some Islamic financial institutions are based on *murabaha* (Institute of Islamic Banking and Insurance 2013).

Introduction of products

The process of introducing and seeking approval for new Islamic financial products varies across countries. As highlighted earlier, the presence of a Shariah Supervisory Board (SSB) in the Islamic financial institutions is considered necessary and most countries tend to have this requirement. However, the scope of their responsibilities tends to vary from one jurisdiction to another. Historically Islamic financial institutions would introduce new financial products that had been approved by the bank's SSB. This led to disagreements between jurists as to which products were Shariah compliant (Kamla and Rammal 2013). The *murabaha* product is one such example where some Muslim jurists have claimed that the mark-up charged represents interest and not an earning for the financial institution. This was the basis of the case in Pakistan in 1991, where the banking system was declared to be non compliant with Shariah principles. These issues not only created confusion but also damaged the reputation of the sector.

To avoid a repetition of such incidents, the central banks of Muslim countries have constituted new committees and regulations to ensure consistency within their jurisdiction. The SSBs continue to work with the bank management in the development of new products but in many countries the final approval for introducing a new product to the market is held by a central Shariah board that exists within the central bank. For example, in Malaysia, Indonesia and more recently Pakistan, the central Shariah body of the country have issued fatwas (religious rulings) regarding the features of Islamic financial products (Bank Negara Malaysia 2011, State Bank of Pakistan 2010). The SSBs in financial institutions are required to follow these rulings when introducing new products. If the SSB feels that the features of the new product are not covered in the previous ruling, then they are required to seek approval from the central Shariah board. In other countries, such as Bahrain, the financial institutions are free to introduce new financial products. However, they are expected to comply with the regulations set by the Accounting and Auditing Organisation for Islamic Financial Institutions (AAOIFI) regarding accounting, auditing and governance principles. These developments indicate efforts to bring consistencies to Islamic banking at the global level. The central banks of Muslim countries have given indications that they will work with AAOIFI and the Islamic Financial Services Board (IFSB) to help future enforcement of their standards.

Challenges facing the Islamic finance sector

The Islamic finance sector continues to grow at a rapid pace. However, the system faces a number of challenges that may affect this growth. Some of these challenges include inconsistencies in the application of the system, the shortage of qualified Shariah scholars and the limited awareness about the system in the general population (Iqbal 2007, Rammal and Zurbruegg 2007). There are concerns about innovation and product development in Islamic financial institutions. As discussed earlier, the development of new products has been affected by the introduction of new regulations that give more control to the central banks. Despite these changes, Islamic financial institutions have continued to innovate and introduce new products. However, new financing products and instruments introduced in one country are not always accepted throughout the Muslim world. One such example is that of credit cards. In many parts of the Muslim world, Islamic financial institutions do not offer credit cards as it is seen as a form of lending and there is little control over the products and services that are purchased by the credit card holder. However, in Malaysia Islamic financial institutions have introduced credit cards as Islamic scholars in Malaysia recognise this as compatible with Shariah requirements.

These inconsistencies in the application of Shariah regulations can in part be explained by the variance in interpretation of Islamic teachings by different Islamic schools of thought (*madhab*). Scholars who are trained in Islamic jurisprudence under a specific school of thought are influenced in the way they interpret religious text and review the activities of the Islamic financial institutions. There are two main sects in Islam: Sunnis and Shias. The majority of the Muslim world falls in the Sunni category. Sunni Islam has four schools of law that are named after the scholars whose views on Islamic teachings are used to interpret Shariah: Hanafi (named after Imam Abu Hanifa), Hanbali (named after Imam Ahmad ibn Hanbal), Maliki (named after Imam Malik ibn Anas) and Shafi'i (named after Imam al-Shafi'i) (Usmani 1998; Warde 2000). The Shia sect tends to follow Ja'fari jurisprudence (named after Imam Ja'far ibn Muhammad al-Sadiq).

These differences are exacerbated due to the lack of an international central governing body. The standards issued by the AAOIFI and IFSB are aimed at introducing standard practices in the industry. However, these standards are not mandatory and financial institutions are required to follow the standards issued by their national central banks. While the central banks are attempting to incorporate some of the AAOIFI and IFSB standards in the regulations for Islamic banking, there is no timeframe for when this would be achieved.

Another issue facing the Islamic finance system is the lack of supporting infrastructure, in particular training institutions. The introduction of Islamic financing commenced without the appropriate educational infrastructure in the industry. This resulted in skills shortages, with the bank staff trained only in conventional banking practices and the Shariah jurists lacking knowledge about the banking and finance sector. The growth of the Islamic finance sector has increased the demand for more qualified and experienced Shariah scholars. With a limited pool to select these advisors from, Islamic financial institutions are forced to hire advisors who serve on multiple boards (El Baltaji and Anwar 2010). This has led to concerns about potential for conflicts of interest, where the advisors are working on boards for competitors. While the IFSB recommends that Shariah scholars hold a minimum of a bachelor degree in Islamic jurisprudence with strong Arabic and English language skills, only a few countries enforce this as a requirement. For example, Malaysia follows this requirement and has established the International Centre for Education in Islamic Finance (INCEIF), a university that specialises in Islamic finance. But in Pakistan, the requirement is for the Shariah advisor to have completed a basic Shariah jurisprudence course. A study on the number of Shariah scholars worldwide revealed that the current number of experienced and qualified Shariah scholars was not even sufficient to fulfil the demand in the Middle East (Abbas 2008).

The lack of knowledge about the sector remains a concern. Studies have shown that the majority of Muslims are open to the idea of using Islamic finance, but do not understand how the system operates (Rammal and Zurbruegg 2007). There are also concerns about whether current practices in the sector are truly Islamic in nature. These concerns highlight the inability of the banks to explain and promote their product offerings to the wider population. As the sector is relatively new, Islamic banks will have to develop ways of educating their potential consumers about the system and its features.

Future of the Islamic financing sector

The Islamic financing system is yet to become the dominant banking and finance system in the Muslim world, this presents opportunities for new entrants and existing Islamic financial institutions to gain and increase their market share. For example, the Islamic banking share of total banking assets in Malaysia and Pakistan is 19 per cent and 10 per cent, respectively. Both countries have set an ambitious target to double the share of Islamic banking assets to 40 and 20 per cent by the year 2020 (Anwar 2013, The Malaysian Insider 2013). The relatively untapped markets in Indonesia, India and Bangladesh are home to some of the largest Muslim populations in the world, and opportunities for further market penetration in Pakistan, the Gulf Cooperative Council (GCC) region and other parts of the Muslim world will help with the growth of the sector. However, the limitations the system is facing can slow this growth and can have a negative influence on the reputation of the sector. There are also concerns about inconsistencies in the application of rules and regulations and how this would influence innovation in the Islamic finance industry.

To address these concerns, there is a need for a global governing body, whose standards and regulations could be enforced in all national jurisdictions. The example of Malaysia shows that developing the infrastructure and supporting industries is critical for the continued growth of the sector. The establishment of training centres will help overcome the current shortage of qualified Shariah scholars, and would lead to the development of best practices in the sector.

Future research could look at the role central banks could play in initiating policies and procedures that would bring consistency in the operations of Islamic banks worldwide. Other studies could also examine how Islamic banks could communicate the key benefits and features of their products and services to potential clients to help increase their market share, and strengthen their ability to compete with conventional financing institutions.

References

AAOIFI. (2012). "Overview": Accounting and Auditing Organisation for Islamic Financial Institutions Homepage. Retrieved 8 April 2012 from www.aaoifi.com/aaoifi/TheOrganization/Overview/tabid/62/language/en-US/Default.aspx

Abbas, M. (2008). *Shortage Of Scholars Troubles Islamic Banks*. International Herald Tribune.

Abdullah, A. A., Sidek, R. and Adnan, A. A. (2012). Perception of Non-Muslim Customers towards Islamic Banks in Malaysia. *International Journal of Business and Social Science*, 3(11), 151–63.

Ahmed, M. (1997). The Political Economy of Loan Default – A Quest for a Socio Political Explanation. *Bank Parikrama*, 22(2), 10–45.

Anwar, Y. (2013). 'Developments of Islamic Banking in Pakistan'. Keynote address by Mr. Yaseen Anwar, Governor of the State Bank of Pakistan at the Islamic Finance News Pakistan Roadshow, Karachi, 27 August.

Ayub, M. N. (2002). *Islamic Banking and Finance: Theory and Practice*. Karachi: State Bank of Pakistan Press.

Banaga, A., Ray, G. H. and Tomkins, C. R. (1994). *External Audit and Corporate Governance in Islamic Banks*. Aldershot: Avebury.

Bank Negara Malaysia. (2011). *Shariah Advisory Council of the Bank*. Retrieved 22 December 2011 from www.bnm.gov.my

Butt, M. M. and Aftab, M. (2013). Incorporating attitude towards Halal banking in an integrated service quality, satisfaction, trust and loyalty model in online Islamic banking context. *International Journal of Bank Marketing*, 31(1), 6–23.

Chapra, M. U. (2007). The case against interest: Is it compelling? Thunderbird *International Business Review*, 49(2), 161–86.

—— (2011). The global financial crisis: Some suggestions for reform of the global financial architecture in the light of Islamic finance. *Thunderbird International Business Review*, 53(5), 565–79.

Dubai Islamic Bank. (2012). *About DIB. Retrieved 11 January 2012*, from www.alislami.ae/en/about_dib.htm

El Baltaji, D. and Anwar, H. (2010). *Shariah Scholar on more than 50 boards opposes limit plan: Islamic finance*. Bloomberg, 23 November.

Federal Shariat Court. (1991). Judgement on Riba (Interest). *Cabinet Report Document 1991*. Islamabad: Government of Pakistan.

Gafoor, A. L. M. (1996). *Interest-Free Commercial Banking*. Malaysia: A.S.Noordeen.

—— (2001). *Mudaraba-based investment and finance*.

Ghose, G. (2013). *Islamic banks need to reorient operations*. Gulf News, 26 November.

Haniffa, R. and Hudaib, M. (2007). Exploring the Ethical Identity of Islamic Banks via Communication in Annual Reports. *Journal of Business Ethics*, 76(1), 97–116.

Haron, S., Ahmad, N. and Planisek, S. L. (1994). Bank patronage factors of Muslim and non-Muslim customers. *International Journal of Bank Marketing*, 12, 32–40.

IFSB. (2013). *Background*. Retrieved 10 May 2013, from www.ifsb.org/background.php

Institute of Islamic Banking and Insurance. (2013). *Murabaha on Shari'ah ruling*. Retrieved 15 November 2013 from www.islamic-banking.com/murabaha_sruling.aspx

Iqbal, M. (2007). International Islamic Financial Institutions. In M. K. Hassan & M. K. Lewis (Eds.), *Handbook of Islamic Banking* (pp. 361–83). Cheltenham: Edward Elgar.

Islamic Bank of Britain. (2013). *Bank Website.* Retrieved 20 October 2009, from www.islamic-bank.com

Kamla, R. (2007). *Critically appreciating social accounting and reporting in the Arab Middle East: a postcolonial perspective.* Advances in International Accounting, 20, 105–77.

Kamla, R. and Rammal, H. G. (2013). Social Reporting by Islamic Banks: Does Social Justice Matter? *Accounting, Auditing and Accountability Journal,* 26(6), 911–45.

Kamla, R., Gallhofer, S. and Haslam, J. (2006). Islam, Nature and Accounting: Islamic Principles and the Notion of Accounting for the Environment. *Accounting Forum,* 30(3), 245–65.

Karim, D. R. A. (2012). Islamic Finance: An alternative funding source for the African Development Bank? *African Development Bank,* 3(3), 1–8.

Khan, M. F. (2007). Setting standards for Shariah application in the Islamic financial industry. *Thunderbird International Business Review,* 49(3), 285–307.

Khan, M. S. and Mirakhor, A. (1990). Islamic Banking: Experiences in the Islamic Republic of Iran and in Pakistan. *Economic Development and Cultural Change,* 38(2), 353–75.

Lewis, M. K. (2001). Islam and accounting. *Accounting Forum,* 25(2), 103–27.

Lewis, M. K. and Algaoud, L. M. (2001). *Islamic Banking.* Cheltenham, UK: Edward Elgar.

Maali, B., Casson, P. and Napier, C. (2006). *Social Reporting by Islamic Banks.* Abacus, 42(2), 266–89.

Muhamad, R., Melewar, T. C. and Alwi, S. F. S. (2012). Segmentation and brand positioning for Islamic financial services. *European Journal of Marketing,* 46(7/8), 900–21.

PricewaterhouseCoopers (2011). *Shariah Audit: Industry Insights.* Malaysia.

Rammal, H. G. (2003). Mudaraba in Islamic finance: Principles and application. *Business Journal For Entrepreneurs,* 4, 105–12.

—— (2006). The importance of Shari'ah supervision in Islamic financial institutions. *Corporate Ownership and Control,* 3(3), 204–8.

—— (2008). Political Motivations: The Nationalization of the Pakistani Banking Sector. *Corporate Ownership and Control Journal,* 6(2), 342–46.

Rammal, H. G. and Parker, L. D. (2013). Islamic banking in Pakistan: A history of emergent accountability and regulation. *Accounting History,* 18(1), 5–29.

Rammal, H. G. and Zurbruegg, R. (2007). Awareness of Islamic banking products among Muslims: The case of Australia. *Journal of Financial Services Marketing,* 12(1), 65–74.

Saeed, A. (1996). *Islamic Banking and Interest: A study of the prohibition of Riba and its contemporary interpretation.* Leiden, The Netherlands: E.J. Brill.

Siddiqui, M. N. (1994). *Issues In Islamic Banking:* Selected Papers.

State Bank of Pakistan. (2010). *Islamic Banking Department.* Retrieved 10 January 2010 from www.sbp.org.pk/ibd

The Malaysian Insider. (2013, 21 February). *Malaysia banks on reforms to spur Islamic finance growth.* 21 February.

Thomas, A. (2005). 'Understanding the Shari'a Process'. In A. Thomas, S. Cox & B. Kraty (Eds.), *Structuring Islamic Finance Transactions.* London: Euromoney Books. pp. 32–44.

Usmani, M. I. (2002). *Meezanbank's Guide To Islamic Banking.*

Usmani, M. T. (1998). *An Introduction To Islamic Finance.* Karachi: Idaratul Ma'arif.

Warde, I. (2000). *Islamic Finance in the Global Economy.* Edinburgh: Edinburgh University Press.

Wilson, R. (1995). 'Islamic Development Finance in Malaysia'; In S. Al-Harran (Ed.), *Leading Issues in Islamic Banking and Finance.* Malaysia: Pelanduk Publications. pp. 59–81.

27

Islamic perspectives on risk and insurance marketing

Jonathan A. J. Wilson and Zuriah Abdul Rahman

Introduction

This chapter sets out to achieve two key aims: to present the philosophical and critical perspectives underpinning the marketing of Islamic insurance products and services and to provide the foundation and basis for recommending appropriate stepwise marketing practices. A final point of reference is that it is assumed within this chapter that the insurance products in question have been created already and so discussions focus on branding, marketing communications, consumer behaviour and service delivery of these products. Product issues surrounding the design and Sharia' compliance (codes and laws derived from Islam) fall outside of the scope of this chapter, but are covered in Chapter 26.

The chapter thus bridges the gap between conventional marketing theory and practice that calls for specialized understanding, positioning and execution. Having stated this, it is also important to assert that in this chapter, marketing, Islam and Muslims are not viewed as monolithic entities or homogenous units, nor does the marketing of Islamic financial services necessarily signal a complete departure from conventional marketing concepts or simply a niche area. Rather, each are interconnected, culturally rooted and subject to environmental factors. The three key factors argued for are the call to evaluate Muslims' perspectives concerning risk, appraising the needs of a broad base of stakeholders and modes of communication subject to cultures and geographies.

The foundations of Islamic ontological arguments

Islam offers a code of conduct, way of life and an explanation of existence, as defined by God (*Allah* in Arabic). This is elucidated and preserved within the Qur'an (the words of Allah), and the documented sayings and practices of most notably the Prophet Muhammad and his close companions. As cited by Wilson and Liu (2011: 40):

> It is worth mentioning that of the 25 named prophets from Adam to Muhammad in Islam: Noah, Abraham, Moses, Jesus and Muhammad brought with them the Sharia'.

Expanding on this point within the same Islamic theological context, not all prophets (*nabi* in Arabic) are messengers, but all messengers (*rasul* in Arabic) are prophets. Messengers are defined as those individuals who are given a new *sharia'* through divine revelation, which abrogates previous laws. So, for example, in the case of Muhammad, believers in a monotheistic God, were commanded to pray five times a day and commanded to fast in the month of *Ramadan*.

For something to be *Islamic*, it must be attributable to that which is considered praiseworthy and pure. A Muslim is one who submits to the will of Allah in belief and actions. In Islam, Allah creates, controls and permits the creation of everything. However, evil would not be considered Islamic. Following this, a nuance pertaining to Islam, in comparison to Christianity, is that this position renders evil as an absolute construct. Islamic textual evidence supports this, citing Satan (*shaytan* in Arabic), a symbol of absolute evil, at times having offered valid Islamic guidance, albeit with the wrong intention. Furthermore, Satan and other lesser devils (*shayateen* in Arabic) are creations of God.

From this point it can be argued that, potentially, Muslims are open to considering perspectives from varied sources when filtered according to an Islamic paradigm. Abusulayman (1998) states that the oneness of Islam presents a vertical relationship between the creator (God) and humans that is manifest also in horizontal inter-human relations. As an extension of Abusulayman's (1998) observations, the argument is that Islam is a multi-dimensional and dynamic construct, which evolves and expands according to context, reality and human intentions from a grounded set of basic principles and articles of faith. Therefore, Islamic financial products and services cannot simply be created in isolation from their environment, or without an appraisal of the intentions of their producers and consumers.

Islam and Muslims articulate that they are not so much about being a religion by conventional interpretations; rather more accurately, a culture, a way of life and lifestyle choice as a holistic participatory experience, with Islam being intended to underpin and govern all decisions and judgements. The key Arabic term used by Muslims is *deen*, which goes beyond the restricted sense of religion. *Deen* has no direct translation but is used to describe faith, judgement, decision, allegiance, path, and way of life.

Wilson and Liu (2011) write that a significant amount of non-Muslim literature continues to overlook monotheistic theological differences. An example of this observation can be seen in the flawed assumption by Adair (2010) that Muslims and Christians use terms, such as prophet and messenger in the same way. For reasons like these Wilson and Liu (2011) argue that they can lead to erroneous interpretations. A further case in practice occurs when Adair (2010) derives what appears to be a rather Biblically based and Christian conclusion: "*If 'man is made in the likeness of God', then personal integrity reflects the oneness of God*" (Adair, 2010: 64).

In Islam, "man" is creation and bears little resemblance to that of Almighty God (Allah). Furthermore, Muslims are warned against attempts to make direct comparisons between them and Allah. Following this, the same belief applies to the Muslim view of Jesus Christ (*Isa* in Arabic), in that he is not the Son of God, nor is he God in human form. Rather, he is a prophet and messenger of God who one day will come back to earth, lead prayer in the same way that Muhammad has instructed previously, marry, have children and die a human death, as he is yet to die.

The reasons for highlighting these issues in detail are because multinational companies, producing Islamic financial services, face conceptual challenges in being able to preserve, communicate and deliver product and service offerings, which resonate with and reassure the faithful. At their inception, marketing activities have to demonstrate a clear link between submission to the will of Allah first and foremost, and a pull to draw human thoughts, feelings and actions towards God-consciousness and obedience through a Muslim lens.

The Islamic paradigm of acculturation

Dutton (2002) asserts that after the death of Muhammad, cultural practices became central in understanding how to derive, interpret and apply Islamic law. Ibn Khaldun (2005) and Dutton (2002) paint a picture of Muslim acculturation built around urban centres of knowledge, as opposed to the desert plains.

In 1377, the classical North African Islamic Scholar, Ibn Khaldun, wrote *The Muqaddimah* (translated as "Introduction to Universal History") (Ibn Khaldun 2005). He argues that people fall into two general categories: city dwellers, who enjoy an urban sedentary lifestyle, and those who live in harsh nomadic conditions. IbnKhaldun also groups Muslims into two broad camps which differentiates individuals according to linguistic and cultural Arabization.

With these in mind, Wilson (2012a) offers a new perspective on the driving factors behind Muslim existence, past and present. Wilson's model highlights the key factors in Islamic influence. It notes that Islamic acculturated experiences balance, and at times oscillate between orthodoxy and heterodoxy, that Muslims mediate between several cultures, driving homogenisation under an Islamic belief system, underpinned by Arab-esque artefacts and urbanites are the driving force behind the practice of Islam.

In Islam, whilst Bedouin nomadic culture plays a pivotal role in didactic stories, there has always been a movement towards economic development. Furthermore, key individuals from urban backgrounds, including the Prophet Muhammad, have been most influential in this process and have attempted to harmonise diverse cultures, especially through trade, commerce, education and hospitality. Clear differences in interpretation and cultural fusions can perhaps be most visibly seen today by the styles and ways in which Muslim females who choose to wear headscarves dress. More specifically within countries, there also appear to be both regional differences and individual fashionable expressions, which govern how headscarves are worn. For example, the distinct differences in Morocco, between the shorter and more colourful headscarf styles in cities, in comparison with longer black cloaks sported in villages close to the Sahara. These observations concur with the views expressed by Ibn Khaldun (2005), where urbanisation changes tastes and encourages fashionable cultural consumption.

Muslim consumption and behavioural patterns

Drawing on theories of consumer behaviour this section explores some of the key considerations in Muslim consumption, taking into account risk reduction-avoidance of doubt versus an article of faith, heuristics, dissonance reducing behaviour, high and low involvement, rationality versus emotion and religiosity.

Vaughn (1980) illustrates how in consumer behavioural psychology the FCB grid (reference to Foote, Cone and Belding) has four quadrants, ascribing the order through which consumers choose to think-feel-do (cognitive-affective-conative). These are subject to two variables: the level of involvement which the product necessitates and the messages appealing to and/or providing emotion or rationality.

An alternative interpretation could be presented for the second variable, in that consumers' predisposition towards emotion or rationality frames/reframes communication. Wilson and Liu (2010, 2011) argue that observant Muslim consumers seek high involvement in all products, due to their faith and a tendency toward risk aversion. Therefore, this removes the two quadrants, which commence with the conative, namely: Do-Think-Feel and Do-Feel-Think.

Instead, the variable that exists is the level of risk, rather than involvement. Here, once perceived risk has been reduced through cognitive and affective processes, a conative cue is created. When this has been achieved, then it is possible to facilitate compliant and conative consumption.

Muhamad and Mizerski (2010) understand religion to affect Muslim consumer behaviour according to religious affiliation, knowledge, orientation, and commitment. The consultancy firm Ogilvy Noor (2010, 2011) presents an alternative perspective, which suggests that traditionally Muslim consumers have been classified according to a scale of religious observance, however, it concludes that their findings point towards other factors being of more significance. In support of Ogilvy Noor's position Wilson and Liu (2011) suggest that culture remains the rate-determining step. Islam is a divine standard, which is interpreted by Muslims and therefore subject to the "fingerprints" of mortals, which imbibes it with culture. Herskovits (1948, 1955), is of the view that culture "is the man-made part of the environment" (Herskovits 1955: 305). Smith and Bond (1998) explain that this includes both material objects and social institutions and suggest that it does not help with deciding what conceptual units allow for cross-cultural comparisons.

From this, Wilson and Liu (2011) conclude that Muslim consumer behaviour is largely a cultural construct, which necessitates that marketers should understand Islam through the varied lenses of Muslim consumers. In doing so, it will inevitably point towards the grouping of Muslims into smaller homogenous segments. This also separates social sciences' marketing insights from Islamic scholastic Sharia'-based postulations. As an adjunct however it is suggested that the two positions need to work in tandem. In support, Arham (2010: 154), states that "the objectives of Islamic Marketing cannot be separated from the objectives of the Sharia'".

Agencies Ogilvy Noor (2010, 2011) and J. Walter Thompson (JWT) (2010) present their own criteria by which they have segmented the Muslim market. Notably, research from JWT (2010) points towards Saudi Arabian Muslim consumers expressing a preference for business role models above all others, and Iranian Muslims holding educators in prestige above Islamic scholars. This perhaps goes against generally held views of these two societies, in that their societies and citizens are seen to be highly religious in their beliefs and practices.

The Halal Paradigm: pre-consumption decision-making

Muslim consumer behaviour and corporate practices point towards perspectives that reframe the *halal* (permissible according to Islamic teachings). Wilson and Liu (2011) present "The Halal Paradigm" as demonstrating an area where cognitive, affective and conative decision-making patterns are affected by risk minimisation. These are related to the Muslim consumer cultural lens and Islam. The Halal Paradigm is a nub where the perceived importance of halal is brought into the Muslim consciousness. This is a dynamic and cyclical process, whose final verdict is finite and perishable due to hypersensitivity and environmental factors influencing Muslim perceptions of what is halal. Central to the model is the notion of At-Talaazum, a halal heuristic hybrid-deconstruction approach. *At-Talaazum* is Arabic for fusing and moulding and is used in an Islamic context to describe the correct approach for a Muslim to adopt. The model produces two outcomes, one rational and one emotional. Think-Feel-Do is a halal value-chain rational approach in which every stage and component is scrutinised rationally, according to their functional and materialistic elements. Feel-Think-Do is a halal cultural emotional approach. The resulting feelings, emotions and behavioural traits of collective consumerism ratify the validity of an approach.

The value chain approach represents the safest and most common brand position, appealing to rationality; however it restricts creative brand expression. Whilst more recent cultural artefact approaches to brand strategies, outlined by Holt (2004) and Holt and Cameron (2010), are able to offer greater opportunity for emotive brand strategies; both rational and emotional approaches still run the risk of opposition and scrutiny through offering an absolute position of purity. Wilson and Liu (2011) observe that halal ingredient branding and overtly branded Islamic financial services products still tend towards brand messaging which evokes Think-Feel-Do. Therefore it is suggested that there remains an alternative currently under-used approach, which requires further consideration as to how more overt emotional messages can be transmitted.

With the advent of a brand economy, where the differentiation of commodities is spearheaded by branding, Wilson and Grant (2013) examine the edifice of Brand Personality as one of the central tenets of current marketing practices. The idea being that people make decisions not on functional and financial criteria alone, but because of a felt "fit" between the brand personality and their own lifestyle, demographic and identity. From this, brands have become progressively viewed according to schools of thought, which judge them less on hard economics and more according to identities, personalities, relationships, communities and most recently cultures. Over time, this evolution has become enshrined as a universal theory of brands, with the messianic idea that brands (as modern deities) and their personalities are consumers' friends, say something about them and shape who they are.

In addition, Wilson et al. (2013) observe that it is often argued under the umbrella of postmodern social sciences, that the hallmarks of professionalism and rigor are grounded in hermeneutic principles of interpreting art and science from a position of relative dispassion. Traditionally, marketers are the messengers who convey messages, which shape perceptions of marketplace realities but this does not necessitate that they place themselves within these meanings, instead preferring to take a back seat, as architects and encoders.

However, with the increased efficacy and impact of phenomena such as user generated content, social media, expressions of marketplace tensions such as anti-branding movements and single issue politics, consumer-centric models of co-creation, celebrity endorsers and corporate and social responsibility, it is becoming increasingly difficult and even divisive for marketers to remain behind the scenes of the marketing theatre. For urban, savvy, engaged and information hungry sedentary tribes of consumers crave the knowledge that they are being served by marketers who share the same ideals and values. The inference is that *authenticity* is ratified by those who practice what they preach, and openly stand alongside their communications and offerings.

In support of these arguments, the phenomenon of products and services which profess to be *Islamic* exemplify such a movement. Bringing faith, the divine, and the sacred as well as the profane so forthrightly into the marketing mix attracts greater scrutiny from all stakeholders, regardless of faith. Furthermore, it is clear that rather than this phenomenon being a passing fad, it in fact appears to be a rapid heterodox evolutionary development in modern marketing.

Brand Islam and the halal

Alserhan (2010) states that "*Halal* is the norm and *Haram* is the exception" (p. 105). Whilst Wilson and Liu (2011) concur with this statement as a general principle, within the *halal* paradigm of consumption attached to consumerism, the argument they put forward is that this is increasingly being reversed due to a trait of risk aversion, which is attached to fear and suspicion (Wilson and Liu 2010).

This is especially interesting, as the phenomenon of branding products as halal is also being practiced in countries, such as Saudi Arabia, with almost exclusive Muslim majorities. Whilst some may see this as a positive movement encouraging Muslim commerce and consumption, underpinned by Islam, it is possible that a by-product may be the repositioning of halal labelling as an aesthetic factor, whose absence could encourage greater perceived consumer risk.

Wilson et al. (2013) also find that when identifying the emergent phenomenon of Islamic marketing it has been seen to provide a fertile ground for new concepts critical to generative theory building. They state that literature on Islamic marketing, arguing for its significance and relevance, can be grouped largely into three observations and by extension, three standpoints: (1) the economic argument, where data is presented and calculated to demonstrate the market potential through financial value and future sustainability through population figures, (2) the consumer-based perspective, which articulates that beyond the market value and size, there exists a consumer-based religious obligation to develop the sector and (3) the geopolitical imperative, where commerce linked with Islam is influenced by geopolitics, which reciprocally affects factors such as international relations, political stability and national brand equity.

Furthermore, these points can be summarised under one paradigm, which argues for Islamic marketing reaching out beyond one religion and beyond Muslims. To this end, Islamic marketing and its offerings are positioned as being similar to other previous movements and groups, which have gravitated towards the mainstream, such as with Chinese management as an analogy (Barney and Zhang 2009) and also Feminism, Fair Trade, Japanese culture and Total Quality Management and Black entertainment, amongst others.

As Islam is classified as a religion, such a positioning may be viewed by some as an inflammatory statement. However, the argument remains, as has been stated, that Islam and Muslims articulate that they are not so much about being a religion by conventional interpretations; rather more accurately, a way of life and lifestyle choice, as a holistic lived experience, with Islam being intended to govern all decisions and judgements.

Therefore, whilst awareness generated by branding commodities as "Islamic", or by using Islamic terms such as halal may have created great opportunities in Muslim markets, they also muddy the waters with regards to conventional marketing practices and their acceptance by Muslim consumers. Moreover, there is a risk that with such over religious signalling, potentially interested non-Muslim consumers may feel less of a connection.

Insuring the Muslim faithful

Having presented an overview of the underpinning of Islamic and Muslim thought, behavioural activities and consumption patterns, this section takes a critical and theoretical perspective, examining Islamic insurance (*takaful*) and what risk translated into insurance means conceptually and practically from a Muslim perspective.

Commoditization of Islamic Insurance: Takaful

The term insurance can have both a religious and a commercial interpretation. In terms of the former, insurance could signify faith, i.e. insurance against the negative values which are attributed to the faithless (Khorshid 2004). "It is enjoined upon Muslims to keep their promise in terms of the contract that they had entered into, and if they breached the terms, God would forfeit His protection (insurance) against fear, poverty, sadness and ill health" (Quran 24:55). A faithful Muslim will be protected from loss if he keeps his faith in God. To a Muslim, prayer is also a form of insurance, in which God will reward those who have turned to him in prayer and reward them with His protection.

Sherif and Shaairi (2013: 28) write that insurance, from conventional and Islamic perspectives *"is referred to as compensation or a promise of compensation for specific potential future losses in exchange for a periodic payment"*. *Takaful* is an Arabic word now used to refer to Islamic insurance. Literally, it means to guarantee each other through mutual co-operation and donation (Sherif and Shaairi

2013, Browne and Kim 1993, Li et al. 2007). *Takaful* as a financial product was first introduced in 1979 in Sudan. Whilst Malaysia ranks as the 20th largest Muslim population in terms of population figures, with approximately 17 million Muslims, it is reported to be the largest *takaful* market outside of the Arab region, accounting for $1.44 billion USD (Ernst & Young 2012). The world's Muslim population is expected to rise by about 35 percent in the next 20 years, from 1.6 billion to 2.2 billion (Pew Research Center, 2011). With these observations in mind, *takaful* and the Muslim population are both relatively young and present great market opportunities. Nevertheless there are a number of Muslim countries that, due to political, socio-cultural or economic instability and other issues, have not offered nor marketed *takaful* to their citizens. These include countries such as, Nigeria, Algeria, Morocco, Iraq, Afghanistan, Uzbekistan, Yemen and Syria (Abdul Rahman 2009).

Islamic perspectives concerning Risk or Rizq?

A key component in Islamic financial services is the concept of risk, which has its linguistic roots derived from the Arabic word *rizq* and the Classical Greek ριζα. *Rizq* is a wider and more inclusive term, which more correctly translated means "sustenance"; with sustenance ultimately being attributable to God. Its passage into English has restricted the term, largely to focusing on loss of current or future wealth. It is worth considering therefore that risk, as far as Muslim consumer behaviour is concerned, should be seen as being more inclusive and more closely aligned with the term *rizq*. *Takaful* is a bilateral contractual agreement, where there is a collective ownership of risk. Risk is inseparable from human life and Muslims as well as non-Muslims alike have to deal with it in the best way they can. Insurance was introduced as a financial instrument necessary to mitigate the presence of risks. *Takaful* was introduced to suit the requirements of Muslims in times of need due to the absence of Shariah compliance in conventional insurance products.

Wilson and Hollensen (2013) argue that Muslims believe in a life beyond current existence, the *afterlife*. The Muslim view on death is that it does not signal the termination of benefit seeking as there is value to be gained in the afterlife. When linked to Wilson and Liu's (2011) arguments of commercialisation and consumption, this would appear to signal a change in the way that Muslim consumers perceive risk and decide upon the purchase of insurance products. Such products have to fulfil the needs of the transient and the transcendent. Beyond legal requirements, in many ways, reliance on insurance is a tacit indicator that the individual is attempting to address both their transient physical existence and those of their associated and protected parties and the notion that, in their absence, safeguarding the wellbeing of others is an obligation and a form of charity, for which they will be rewarded now and in the hereafter, spiritually.

As to whether investment in a financial product can deliver greater levels of spiritual wellbeing than other activities, such as investment in commodities, or charitable donations, is an area of debate. Some Muslims would argue that the activities which insurance covers should instead be regarded as tests and products of fate and therefore accepted rather than shielding themselves from them. Over time, if nurtured, it is likely that wider adoption will lead to acceptance of insurance products in the same way as the Halal certification of food has become a necessary dissonance reducing strategy, signal of Muslim permissibility and a promotional tool.

According to Islam, risks are there to test and try humans, but individuals are not left unaided in facing risk. Islam has provided ways and means by which uncertainties can be lessened. First, it has provided rules of behaviour and a catalogue of decision-making tools and techniques and the associated payoffs in the Qur'an. However, Muslims are given the freedom to decide on whether to comply with these rules. Rules reduce the burden on human cognitive capacity, particularly in the process of making decisions under uncertainty. Second, Islam has always advocated economic activities, involving risk sharing among capable fellow human beings to enable them to mitigate uncertainty. Risk sharing would entail the risk to be spread and lowered for each participant. *Takaful* serves this purpose today, in a way not too dissimilar from ancient practice at the time of the Prophet Muhammad.

For example, merchants of Makkah, Saudi Arabia, conducting extensive trading with neighboring countries would band together to pool funds helping each other from various calamities, such as sand storms or caravans being attacked by bandits. Funds accumulated from the pool were used to help alleviate the financial burdens faced by individuals and their families. Compensation was calculated based on the price of the merchandise (for example, the value of camels and houses destroyed). Subsequently, Caliph, Umar Al-Khattab widened the practice through another scheme called the *Qasamah*, to pay compensation to the victims in the event of death where the killer could not be identified. Hence there appeared to be a form of life insurance that existed well before conventional forms came into practice (Abdul Rahman and Redzuan 2009).

How is *takaful* different from conventional insurance?

The distinction between Islamic and conventional insurance is the need for *Sharia'* compliance. Sherif and Shaairi (2013) identify the key distinguishing features as the condemnation of *riba* (usury), the elimination of *gharar* (uncertainty), the elimination of *maisir* (gambling) and the embedding of *tabarru'* (donation).

In order to establish a cooperative system (*ta'awun*) in any group which desires to help its members in the event of unforeseen calamity, a number of conditions must be met in regard to the funds collected. Every member who contributes his allotted share of the funds does so as a donation (*tabarru'*), in the spirit of brotherhood. From this pool of funds, help is given to those who are in need when certain unfortunate events occur. If any part of the collected funds is to be invested, it should be done in *halal* or permissible business that is free from usurious business activities. A member is not permitted to donate his share on the condition that he will receive a pre-determined amount in the event of an unforeseen calamity. Rather, he will be paid an amount which will compensate his loss or part of it, depending on the resources of the group, from the pooled monies. What has been donated (*tabarru'*) is a gift from the donor and taking it back is *haram* (not permissible).

Hence, a collective agreement among members of a pooled fund with the intention to compensate its members is allowable, as long as it conforms to Shariah. However, the collected funds must be kept in trust and a trustee or custodian of such funds has to be appointed to ensure that the collected funds are used for their intended purposes and also to ensure that the members' rights are protected. The trustee has to be appointed from a regulated financial institution which practices Islamic law in its commercial undertakings. For example, in Malaysia the Central Bank of Malaysia (the regulator of both conventional and Islamic financial institutions through the Shariah Advisory Council) approves several types of commercial *takaful* models to be practiced, suitable to the role and undertakings of the trustee. Since its inception, Malaysian *takaful* offerings have evolved from practicing a *Mudharabah* Model (profit sharing) to a *Wakalah* Model (agency or representative) or a hybrid of both of these models.

In conventional insurance, the risk or potential loss is assumed by the insurer as well as the insured. Participants in *takaful* schemes are not involved in fund management as well as the day-to-day operation of the business. A *takaful* operator is delegated to manage the fund commercially as a business venture for profit.

Basic *takaful* model

The setting up of a *takaful* entity requires the establishment of two separate funds: the *takaful* fund (or the participants'/policyholders' fund) and the operator's fund (or shareholders' fund). The contributions (premiums) made by the participants are accumulated in the *takaful* fund, a portion of which is relinquished as a donation (*tabarru'*) to pay claims or compensation to fellow participants who suffer from defined losses. The balance constitutes the participants' savings and investments. Initial start-up capital resides in the operator's fund. All management expenses and commissions or fees are charged to the fund.

Unlike conventional insurance, the participant is not entering into a bilateral contract. This eliminates the uncertainty as to the price of the premium and the subject of the insurance. The contract of *takaful* is unilateral because one party (participant) is donating ("*tabarru*") his share of the contributions to enable compensation to be paid to unfortunate members of the scheme, without asking for anything in return. This concept has to be understood by all in the mutual scheme that they are donating part of their contributions to alleviate the sufferings of their members. The other portion, which is not deemed to be a donation, is put into another fund which is then invested to gain profits and is shared by all parties. What a *takaful* scheme does is to create risk sharing amongst all the participants. The operators, however, do not share this risk, but merely manage the funds to ensure its economic viability and sustainability. All parties stand to gain from this commercial venture; the participants who will receive compensation if losses occur and the operator who receives profits from the invested portion of the fund. Investment returns on the capital will be added to the operator's fund while the returns earned on the contributions will be credited into the *takaful* fund. Depending on the operational model adopted, the operator may be able to share investment returns earned by the *takaful* fund. The profit sharing percentage is usually 30:70 (30 percent to the operator and 70 percent to the participants).

As the concept of profit sharing also involves loss sharing, all participants in the *takaful* fund will have to share in any losses equally. The sharing of profits or surplus is effected only after the obligation of assisting fellow participants has been fulfilled. If there is a loss (deficit) in the *takaful* fund, the operator is obligated to provide *Qard Hassan* (interest-free loans) from the shareholders' capital. This loan has to be repaid before any future surpluses are distributed. The possibility of this occurrence is very real; hence, it provides an incentive to *takaful* operators to be more prudent in managing the fund, paying out claims, and other related expenses, in order to ensure the adequacy of the fund.

Strategic marketing communications, branding and positioning

If Islamic marketing is to be taken as an equivalent term to Islamic Finance in the financial services sector, then there are currently comparable debates that question what *Islamic Marketing* actually means. For example, does it only consider how marketers should communicate with Muslims? Or whether being a Muslim is an essential element needed to execute Islamic marketing? A fundamental development is that now the field is more than simply marketing a religion, or marketing to the faithful. Furthermore, if Islamic marketing is posited as a subset of religion, it runs the risk of being a fad.

Wilson (2012b) presents a hierarchy of Islamic marketing approaches from Sharia' compliant to Sharia' sympathetic, to Muslim sympathetic, to Muslim targeted and finally ethnocentric marketing. The suggestion here is that the bedrock of marketing *takaful* products and services successfully should rely upon an approach that is predominantly ethnocentric. However, currently many *takaful* marketing promotional activities highlight Sharia' compliance and target predominantly those partners and consumers who seek compliance, rendering the product offering as niche and rational, which does not necessarily achieve full market penetration. Instead, the argument is that moving down the pyramid from Sharia' compliance to ethnocentric marketing could be a strategic corporate objective, but equally there is no reason why the same objectives could not be attempted in tandem, instead of in a sequential hierarchy.

Following the same train of thought, marketing communications should contain a depth of encoded messages that appeal to a selection of homogenous segments. Shared culture and ethnocentrism are held to be unifying factors that can mediate heterogeneity. Cases in practice outside the financial services industry can be seen with airline companies originating from the Muslim world, such as Emirates, Etihad, Garuda, Qatar and Malaysia. By framing Islam as a cultural experience rather that a religious edict, they have encouraged greater levels of inclusion, taking a bottom-up approach.

In support of marketing communications and promotional activities, strategic branding is another key factor. It is suggested that the following brand strategies and approaches should be considered, which take into account positioning, profiling, place and perception: whether to profile *takaful* products as being premium, match substitutes or incentivized value offerings, whether *takaful* is a generic, ingredient, or co-brand, whether *takaful* is exclusively, predominantly, or partially for Muslims, and whether *takaful* be standardized or adapted according to Muslim majority and minority markets and different geographies due to ethnocentric and cultural factors?

Human resources linked to the marketing imperative

Finally, as with any service industry, the delivery of service quality relies upon the calibre of employees and the management structure under which they operate. Relevant staff providing *takaful* products to customers need to have a good grounding and understanding of the particular nuances of Muslim consumer behaviour and their underpinning cultures. As an insurance organisation, they should understand the norms, values, rituals, modes of socialisation, greetings and language used by their audience, alongside technical Islamic terms. Beyond this, the ideal would be that employer and employee branding are central to all marketing and communications. The corporate brand and employees should make efforts to practice what they preach. This does not necessarily mean that staff in *takaful* operations have to be Muslims, but care should be taken to ensure that the needs of Muslim staff and customers are met and celebrated, such as providing prayer facilities and making efforts to demonstrate that relative to the locality they are employing a proportional number of Muslims. Without these elements, product and promotional efficacy will eventually be undermined.

Conclusions

The core argument presented in this chapter is that whilst *takaful* is a different insurance product, simply to treat it as a product that can be marketed using solely conventional marketing methods and practices has limitations. As *takaful* products have necessitated the synthesis of Islamic and conventional methods within an existing and well-established global industry, the associated branding and promotional activities require comparable treatment too. However, the call for bespoke methods and approaches to branding and promotions are especially crucial, due to the emotional or affective elements of consumer behaviour, which have a strong pull beyond purely rational and functional evaluations. In addition, as in conventional global marketing thought, attention should be given to the standardization and adaptation of messages and offerings according to regions and cultures.

Furthermore, across the board, there is evidence that Muslim consumer behaviour has inherent differences to other segments, which are being further complicated by the fact that there may be a drift between consumption patterns and traditionally held views of religious observance in response to globalization and commerce. Due to the strong effects of culture on Muslim consumers and its influence on the sacred, profane and mundane; the marketing of *takaful* products and services will resonate largely when they tend towards ethnocentrism, rather than pure Sharia' compliance. Therefore, there is a call for the use of images and messages in promotional materials, which mirror the feelings and aspirations of the audience and minimise cognitive dissonance. An example of this could be the use of models in advertisements who appear to be not as religiously observant; judged according to conventional perceptions of religious symbolism and piety evident in them having less facial hair for males and more relaxed interpretations of modest clothing for females. Here the argument is similar to that in conventional advertising, where consumers are exposed to a 'slice of life' with individuals and messages that they can relate to, rather that icons, exemplars and ideal images of religious piety.

References

Abdul Rahman, Z. (2009), *Wealth Management in Islam*, University Press (UPENA), Shah Alam, Selangor: Malaysia.

Abdul Rahman, Z. and Redzuan, H. (2009), *Takaful: The 21st Century Insurance Innovation*, McGraw-Hill, Kuala Lumpur: Malaysia.

Abusulayman, A.A. (1998), "The theory of the economics of Islam", *Journal of Islamic Economics*, Vol. 6 No. 1, pp. 79–122.

Adair, J. (2010), *The Leadership of Muhammad*, London: Kogan Page.

Alserhan, B.A. (2010), "On Islamic branding: brands as good deeds", *Journal of Islamic Marketing*, Vol. 1 No. 2, pp. 101–6.

Arham, M. (2010), "Islamic perspectives on marketing", *Journal of Islamic Marketing*, Vol. 1 No. 2, pp. 149–64.

Barney, J.B. and Zhang, S. (2009), "The Future of Chinese management research: A theory of Chinese Management versus a Chinese Theory of Management", *Management and Organization Review*, 5:1 pp. 15–28.

Browne, M. and Kim, K. (1993), "An international analysis of life insurance demand", *Journal of Risk and Insurance*, Vol. 60 No. 4, pp. 616–34.

Dutton, Y. (2002), *The Origins of Islamic Law: The Qur'an, the Muwatta and Madinan 'Amal*, London: Routledge Curzon.

Ernst & Young (2012), *The World Takaful Report 2012*, Dubai: Ernst & Young.

Herskovits, M.J. (1948), *Man and his Works: The Science of Cultural Anthropology*, New York: Knopf.

—— (1955), *Cultural Anthropology*, New York, NY: Knopf.

Holt, D.B. (2004), *How Brands Become Icons*, Boston, MA: Harvard Business School Press.

Holt, D.B. and Cameron, D. (2010), *Cultural Strategy: using innovative ideologies to build breakthrough brands*, New York: Oxford University Press, Inc.

Ibn Khaldun (2005), *The Muqaddimah – An introduction to History*, Translated by Franz Rosenthal, Princeton, New Jersey: Princeton University Press.

J. Walter Thompson (2010), "Reaching the Muslim market: opportunities and challenges", Keynote address by Roy Haddad, CEO, JWT MENA, *Oxford Global Islamic Branding and Marketing Forum*, 26–27 July, Saïd Business School, University of Oxford, Oxford.

Khorshid, A. (2004), *Islamic insurance: A modern approach to Islamic Banking*, Routledge Curzon. London: United Kingdom.

Li, D., Moshirian, F., Nguyen, P. and Wee, T. (2007), "The demand for life insurance in OECD countires", *Journal of Risk and Insurance*, Vol. 74 No. 3, pp. 637–52.

Muhamad, N. and Mizerski, D. (2010), "The constructs mediating religions' influence on buyers and consumers", *Journal of Islamic Marketing*, Vol. 1 No. 2, pp. 124–35.

Ogilvy Noor (2010), "Brands and Muslim consumers", Keynote transcript address by Miles Young, CEO, Ogilvy & Mather Worldwide, *Oxford Global Islamic Branding and Marketing Forum*, 26–27 July, Saïd Business School, University of Oxford, Oxford.

—— (2011), "Branding Halal – The Rise of the Young Muslim Consumer", Shelina Janmohamed and Nazia Du Bois, *Sparksheet*, (Online), 4th October, http://sparksheet.com/branding-halal-the-rise-of-the-young-muslim-consumer (accessed 9 November 2012).

Pew Research Center (2011), *The Future of the Global Muslim Population*, Pew Research Center's Forum on Religion & Public Life, January 2011, www.pewforum.org/Global-Muslim-Population.aspx (accessed 25 June 2013).

Sherif, M. and Shaairi, N.A. (2013), "Determinants of demand on family *Takaful* in Malaysia", *Journal of Islamic Accounting and Business Research*, Vol. 4 No. 1, pp. 26–50.

Smith, P.B. and Bond, M.H. (1998), *Social Psychology Across Cultures*, (2nd Ed.), Harlow, Essex: Prentice Hall Europe.

Vaughn, R. (1980), "How advertising works: a planning model", *Journal of Advertising Research*, Vol. 20 No. 5, pp. 27–33.

Wilson, J.A.J. (2012a), "Islamic Leadership: Bedouins in the Boardroom and profiting from Prophethood – Lessons from John Adair", *TMC Academic Journal*, Vol. 6 Iss. 2, pp. 48–62.

—— (2012b), "The new wave of transformational Islamic Marketing – reflections and definitions", *Journal of Islamic Marketing*, Vol. 3 Iss. 1., pp. 5–11.

Wilson, J.A.J., Belk, R.W., Bamossy, G.J., Sandikci, O., Kartajaya, H., Sobh, R., Liu, J. and Scott, L. (2013), "Crescent Marketing, Muslim Geographies and Brand Islam: Reflections from the JIMA Senior Advisory Board", *Journal of Islamic Marketing*, Vol. 4 Iss. 1, pp. 22–50.

Wilson, J.A.J. and Grant, J. (2013), "Islamic Marketing – a challenger to the classical marketing canon?", *Journal of Islamic Marketing*, Vol. 4 Iss. 1, pp. 7–21.

Wilson, J.A.J. and Hollensen, S. (2013), "Assessing the implications on performance when aligning Customer Lifetime Value Calculations with religious faith groups and *After* Lifetime Values – A Socratic elenchus approach", *International Journal of Business Performance Management*, Vol. 14, No. 1., pp. 67–94.

Wilson, J.A.J and Liu, J. (2010), "Shaping the Halal into a brand?", *Journal of Islamic Marketing*, Vol. 1 Iss. 2., pp. 107–23.

Wilson, J.A.J. and Liu, J. (2011), "The Challenges of Islamic Branding: navigating Emotions and Halal", *Journal of Islamic Marketing*, Vol. 2 Iss. 1, pp. 28–42.

28

Microfinance

Supporting micro and small enterprises

Atul Mishra, Paul Igwe, Jonathan Lean and Phil Megicks

Introduction

Financial services marketing in developing countries poses challenges that are very different from those in the developed world. In addition, the problems of financial services marketing in the corporate world are very different from those of marketing to micro and small enterprises; this is because the products and services which may be appropriate to the corporate world may not serve the best interests of micro and small enterprises. For similar reasons the solution to the problem of financial services marketing may require not only new product development but also greater market orientation. In the context of developing countries, microfinance has emerged as a unique institution to address the challenges of financing micro and small enterprises.

Microfinance refers to "the provision of a broad range of financial services such as deposits, loans, payment services, money transfers and insurance to poor and low-income households and their micro-enterprises" (African Development Bank 2000: 2). The micro and small enterprises (small-scale farmers, traders, agro-processing, transportation, manufacturing and mining, etc.) need access to financial services, including credit and savings products, through micro financing, as the formal sector financial services exclude them from their ambit as explained below. Microfinance as a panacea for the problems of rural credit markets to serve the micro and small enterprises has gone from celebration of success (Yunus 1998, Rutherford 2001) to doubt and self-doubt (Banerjee et al. 2010, Morduch 1999, Bateman and Chang 2012).

This chapter focuses on the contribution of microfinance towards supporting the development of micro and small enterprises in rural areas in developing countries. The main objective of this chapter is to provide the broad meaning and scope of the concept of microfinance. It reviews some of the relevant literature of existing published and grey empirical literature on the barriers that micro and small entrepreneurs encounter in their attempt to access credit facilities and financial services. It also discusses the reasons behind the failure of microfinance policy to support micro and small enterprises, especially in the rural areas in developing countries. The chapter complements Chapter 35 that focuses on understanding the poor and how best to market financial services to them.

History and growth of microfinance

The origin of microfinance stems from the popularity of microcredit which started in the late 1970s. Its main objective during the early stages was mainly to serve as a tool for poverty alleviation. Now its mechanism has been expanded to target poverty reduction for the poor, women's empowerment, economic growth and human development. As such, in the last thirty years, it has emerged from a grassroots movement to a global industry, with about 70 million clients in 40 countries (Harris 2005).

During the last few decades the microfinance sector has experienced substantial growth, but eventually this resulted in market saturation, a rise of non-performing loans and multiple lending across a few key markets, according to the Economic Intelligence Unit (2012). This situation has arisen because of the global financial crisis, which seems to have increased the focus on risk management, corporate governance and regulatory capacity in the financial sector.

In recent years, the growth of microfinance has been much slower than anticipated due primarily to the recent global financial crisis of 2008. According to Gonzalez (2010), the aggregate number of borrowers served by microfinance institutions (MFIs) grew 21 percent per year on average in the period 2003–8, while the loan portfolio grew 34 percent per year on average in the same period. For many microfinance practitioners and analysts, this level of growth is a reason for celebration, as it points towards microfinance's success in increasing access to financial services for poor and low-income households and businesses. However, according to the Microfinance Summit Campaign (Reed 2013), fewer of the world's poorest families received access to microcredit and other financial services in 2011 than in 2010, thus marking the first time that both the total number of clients and the number of poorest families reached by microcredit has declined from one year to the next since 1998.

The microfinance industry is highly concentrated (Reed 2013). Just twenty organizations serve over three-quarters – 95 million – of the world's poorest clients. The National Bank of Agriculture and Rural Development in India accounts for over 36 percent of the global total, followed by the Grameen Bank in Bangladesh that serves almost 7 percent of the global total. Nine of the top 20 institutions by volume of clients served are located in India and five are located in Bangladesh.

While India and Bangladesh lead in terms of volume of microfinance business globally, the "Microscope 2012" ranking (Economist Intelligence Unit 2013) reveals that in terms of the regulatory and operating conditions for microfinance it is the Latin American countries that are in the lead. The "Microscope 2012" ranking by country evaluates microfinance sectors in 55 countries globally according to two key dimensions: (1) national regulatory frameworks and practices and (2) supporting institutional frameworks. The result is an index that distinguishes between those countries that provide support for a greater availability of financing options for the poor from those countries where there is still work to be done. The analysis indicates that Peru holds the number one position in terms of performance, followed by Bolivia (second) and Pakistan (third). The Philippines, Kenya, El Salvador, Colombia, Uganda, Ghana and Brazil remained in the top 20 in 2012 with rankings of fourth, fifth, sixth, seventh, fourteenth, fifteenth and sixteenth places respectively. India ranked 22nd, followed by Nigeria (29th), China (36th), Argentina (47th), Egypt (50th) and Vietnam (55th) out of 55 countries.

In what follows, we first introduce microfinance in the context of rural credit markets. Next we provide a brief survey of microenterprise in the context of developing countries. We then bring the world of microfinance and micro enterprise together and finally confront the problems in microfinance with a new thrust towards market orientation. The chapter concludes with a new agenda for future research.

Rural credit markets

Of the 1.2 billion people living in extreme poverty in developing countries about 75 percent live in rural areas (Wermer 2010). However, the rural communities where the majority of the poor live in developing countries lack access to basic financial services, which are essential for people to manage their business, assets and livelihoods. Good management of assets and resources can be crucial to very poor people, who live in precarious conditions, threatened by lack of income, food and employment. In order to overcome poverty, households need to be able to borrow, save and invest, and to protect their investments against risk and uncertainties. But with little education, income and collateral assets, poor people are excluded from obtaining loans from banks and other formal financial institutions.

The informal market, comprising money lenders and thrift associations, receives wide patronage because of the accessibility and flexibility of services, but the loans are usually short term since the scale of operation of the average individual lender is small (Attah 2008). For example, of the over 140 million Nigerians (2006 Census), the formal financial system provides services to only about 35 percent of the economically active population; while the remaining 65 percent are excluded from financial services (Juma 2007: 31). Faced with the situation of discrimination against peasant farmers in terms of credit in most developing countries, credit guarantee schemes were implemented by governments in many developing countries throughout the twentieth century as a way of promoting private sector-led growth and development (Attah 2008: 24).

Financial exclusion refers to a situation where the poor and other disadvantaged groups are unable to access formal financial services owing to their perceived vulnerability (Juma 2007) (see Chapter 36 for a detailed discussion of financial exclusion). The rural reality is that few households and small firms can meet their need for credit and other financial services: in a survey of 6,000 households in two Indian states, results showed that 87 percent of the marginal farmers surveyed had no access to formal credit and 71 percent had no access to a savings account in a formal financial institution (World Bank 2008).

As a result, households have traditionally patronized informal credit lenders, some of whom charge higher interest rates and only issue short-term loans. The World Bank (2008) maintains that informal financial arrangements serve rural communities, but they tend to fragment along lines of household location, asset ownership, or membership in kin– or ethnic–based networks, all affecting the transaction costs of contracts, the size of the possible transactions and the rate of interest charged.

It has been suggested that financial services to low income entrepreneurs and producers may well be the single most effective means to tackle poverty and support microenterprise (Mishra 2002). In recognition of the importance of financial capital in promotion of growth and poverty reduction, many governments and development agencies have set up several programs for direct financial assistance. For example in Nigeria, the Central Bank of Nigeria has licensed about 850 microfinance banks but the majority of these banks operate in the urban centres. The World Bank (2008) notes that financial contracts in rural areas involve higher transaction costs and risks than those in urban settings because of the greater spatial dispersion of production, lower population densities, the generally lower quality of infrastructure, seasonality and often high covariance of rural production activities.

Characteristics of rural credit markets

Rural credit markets are characterized by high rates of interest and small volumes of credit availability. Mainstream economics explains the high rate of interest charged by the money lender either in terms of monopolistic behaviour or in terms of high default rates (Basu 2003). However, developments in the economics of imperfect information and the recognition of transaction costs has considerably altered our understanding of the problems in the rural credit markets as well as the policy solutions that emerge from them (Stiglitz 1993).

Problems of asymmetric information have resulted in credit being supplied at very high cost and in very small amounts in the rural sector. Problems with screening, incentives and enforcement are so pervasive that without addressing them, a large segment of the population gets left out of the market. For the non-collateralized poor the credit market may fail completely. One way in which the rural credit market seeks to overcome this problem is by interlinking the credit contract with contracts in other markets such as land, labor or commodity markets. "Interlinking describes the simultaneous fixing of transactions between two parties over several markets, with the terms of one transaction contingent on the terms of another" (Hoff et al. 1993: 6). One form of inter-linkage is between credit and marketing:

> A lender may require a prospective borrower to use the lender as his exclusive wholesaler for his output for several periods before a significant loan is made, as well as during the period of the loan itself. This improves the potential lender's ability to judge the farmer's capacity and willingness to pay (thus reducing adverse selection problems), and thereby may improve the farmer's opportunities to borrow(ibid).

Thus, while interlinked transaction serves the lender in making information available about the borrower, the same mechanism serves the borrower in making some loans available where none were available before.

Because the trader/moneylender generally has greater bargaining power than the borrower, there is scope for exploitation. Further, such transactions may continue to exist even after the formal sector steps in; indeed such transactions may thrive in the presence of the formal sector (Harriss-White and Janakrajan 1997). This is because, for several reasons, the loan from the formal sector is not a substitute for the loan from the trader/money lender.

First, the formal sector caters only to the collateralised borrower that, in the rural sector, rules out the landless and the marginal farmers; this is a case of lack of substitutability in terms of clients. Next, the formal sector caters to only a few well defined demands for loans; in particular, it fails to address the loan requirements of working capital in the informal sector (where book-keeping may be weak) and consumption loans (which smooths consumption and insures against wild fluctuations in net incomes). This is a case of lack of substitutability in product. This means that the state cannot step in and overcome the problems of market failure. "Rural credit markets behave the way they do because of the problems of screening, incentives and enforcement. Government credit institutions face these same problems relative to borrowers. They may be in a worse position in terms of informational asymmetry, monitoring and enforcement" (Hoff et al. 1993: 49).

An institutional innovation in the form of a self-help group and peer monitoring has shown promise in overcoming these problems. In such cases, Stiglitz (1993) notes that a small group is formed by individuals that become jointly liable for the debts of each group member. The group then takes on the responsibility for the selection, monitoring and enforcement that would otherwise be the responsibility of the lender. This type of practice can be inefficient, since a small group is less able to bear the risk compared with a lender with a larger and more diversified portfolio. Group borrowing may suffer from other problems too, one such problem is the problem of commons:

> While group borrowing provides many advantages, it can also cause severe inefficiencies and has many of the same problems that are associated with common ownership and team

production. Non-cooperative behaviour usually yields an inefficient outcome if joint output or liability is fully shared among the agents... Most of the successful cases have accounted for the incentive problems, while most of those that have failed have not.

(Braverman and Guasch 1993: 69)

Stiglitz (1993) recognizes the cost of peer monitoring-it transfers risk from the bank, which is in a better position to bear risk, to the co-signor. It can be shown that under certain circumstances, the benefits more than outweigh the costs. However there is an externality in the institutional innovation.

An individual who bears the initial cost of organizing such an institution is providing a form of social capital from which all members of the group will benefit. As is well known, when this type of externality arises, there will be an under supply of the socially beneficial service, and there is therefore a role for the government to help organize and act as a catalyst in the formation of such institutions. There are notable successes in the provision of rural credit when the governments have acted in this way.

(Hoff et al. 1993: 49)

There are other ways of reducing enforcement and information costs in the credit market by intervening in other markets. Greenwald and Stiglitz (1986) have shown that markets with imperfect information give rise to externality like effects and it is here that government intervention may be most successful. The authors state that in the context of credit markets, one externality that they have identified is the reduction of enforcement and information costs brought about by development in other markets.

It has been widely recognized that government investment in infrastructure that makes agriculture less risky will reduce the importance of informational asymmetries between borrower and lender and therefore lower the rate of interest. This prediction has indeed come true (World Development Report 1994). Using data for West Bengal in India, Ghatak (1983) showed that infrastructurally more developed districts had a lower rate of interest charged by the money lender than those which were less developed. Renkow et al. (2004) also establish that provision of rural infrastructure reduces transaction costs in other contexts as well.

To understand the role of microfinance in the area of micro and small enterprise (MSE), however, we need to understand the forces which impact the birth, death and expansion of MSEs, as the role of microfinance assumes a dynamic form changing with the needs of survival and expansion.

Microfinance uses

Microfinance institutions insist that their loans be used for economically productive purposes, mainly because they want to help creditors generate revenues and also because they want to ensure that beneficiaries of the loans will be able to repay them. Although lenders insist that loans be used for productive purposes (such as purchase of inputs, land, raw materials and equipment), there have been some reported cases where some people have used the loans to cater for personal or households needs. These needs include payment for children's school fees, home improvements, consumption expenditures and social spending.

Many people who wish to start businesses have unrealistic expectations when it comes to the funds needed to start a business. Often the poor lack the necessary start-up funds and cannot raise adequate financing. The poor have virtually no cash or liquid assets and expect either a bank or microcredit institutions to provide 100 percent financing. The fundamental principle in establishing microfinance therefore is primarily as a tool in the fight against poverty.

The rapid growth of the industry over the past fifteen years has reached approximately 130 million clients, according to recent estimates by the International Financial Corporation of the World Bank, yet microfinance still reaches less than 20 percent of its potential market among the world's three billion (IFC 2013). IFC maintains that financial services for poor people are a powerful instrument for reducing poverty, enabling them to build assets, increase incomes and reduce their vulnerability to economic stress. In its project, helping small business grow in Colombia, IFC finds that formal financial services such as savings, loans and money transfers enable poor families to invest in enterprises, better nutrition, improved living conditions and the health and education of their children. Microfinance has also been a powerful catalyst for empowering women.

There are several organizations whose primary function includes the provision of a broad range of financial services, such as deposits, loans, payment services, money transfers and insurance to people for either business investment or expansion. They include Microfinance Banks, Financial Intermediary NGOs, Savings and Credit Cooperatives, Small Farmers Cooperatives, International Development Partners, Commercial Banks, Development Banks, Government Agencies, Insurance Companies, NGOs, Universities and various local, national and international organizations. As previously indicated, the microfinance industry remained highly concentrated in 2012 with twenty institutions accounting for 76 percent or 95 million of all clients (Reed 2013).

The role of micro and small enterprises in the national economy

The World Bank (2013) estimates that in 2020 there will be a need for 600 million more jobs in the world compared to 2005 if the ratio of employment to working age population has to remain constant. In recent years, approximately 40 percent of the increase in the labor force in developing countries has found work in Micro and Small Enterprises (MSEs). This includes MSEs in both the urban informal sector and the rural sector. However, three quarters of these jobs have been in the rural sector (Liedholm and Mead 1999). "Most of these new employment openings (three quarters, taking good years and bad together) come into being through new businesses being established. The remaining quarter comes through the expansion of existing opportunities" (ibid: 67).

Liedholm and Mead (1999) carried out a large survey of micro and small enterprises (MSEs) in six countries of Africa. Supported by the United States Agency for International Development, a baseline questionnaire was administered to 28,000 respondents in six countries: Botswana, Kenya, Malawi, Swaziland, Zimbabwe and Dominican Republic. Most of the respondents in the study were from rural areas. Three categories of problems were predominant in these countries: access to capital, problems of markets and access to raw materials and intermediate inputs. The aim of the study was to understand the conditions of start-up, failure and survival of micro and small enterprises in these countries and isolate the significant development collaterals. The study provided some of the most important insights into new firm formation in rural sectors in developing countries.

It was found that the nature of new jobs created by new enterprises is fundamentally different from new jobs created from the expansion of existing enterprises. Liedholm and Mead (1999) maintain that new start up jobs are more likely to reflect people seeking a way of sustaining themselves (supply push), while expansion jobs are more likely to arise as entrepreneurs seek to respond to a growing demand for their products in expanding sectors (demand pull).

Unlike in developed countries, where new start-ups of micro and small enterprises vary directly with the aggregate level of economic activity, in developing countries new business birth rates vary inversely with the aggregate level of economic activity (ibid: 12). We have two kinds of job creation in the rural non-farm micro enterprises: first, by the coming into being of new units and second, by the expansion of existing units (Mishra 2005). The former types come into being mostly during economic recession and are more in the nature of distress activity, are low skilled, low value-adding and are more transient. Most of these jobs disappear either when farming conditions improve (when people revert to farming) or when businesses fail. The latter come into being during expansion of the level of aggregate economic activity, reflect more accurately genuine economic opportunity, create higher value-adding jobs and are more durable.

> A higher proportion of the new jobs arising from new start-ups reflect survival efforts by people with few options. A significant proportion of new enterprise starts are driven by the necessity of finding any source of income, even those providing only minimal returns, in situations where few alternatives are available. New MSE jobs arising from an expansion of existing enterprises are more likely to reflect a response to an identified business opportunity. Entrepreneurs take on additional workers primarily because they have tried a particular pattern of doing business, have found a market, and would like to expand their participation in that market.
>
> *(Liedholm and Mead 1999: 65)*

Start ups of new firms

A survey by the Global Entrepreneurship Monitor (2002) carried out across 37 countries showed that of about 472 million entrepreneurs worldwide attempting to start 305 million companies, approximately 100 million new businesses (or one third) will open each year around the world. The survey found that 12 percent of the workforce in these countries is engaged in starting or running a new business, implying a global figure of about 460 million. Reynolds (2002) noted that firm start up and failure rates are about equal: the ratio is almost one failure for each start-up. The GME survey also noted that the developing countries of Asia and Latin America are far ahead of Europe in starting new businesses.

Empirical relationships between new start rates of micro and small firms and other variables have not been systematically examined in any developing country. According to Liedholm and Mead (1999), one might expect new micro firm start rates to increase during a period of declining economic activity in developing countries, where the establishment of a new micro firm provides the only viable option of employment to individuals who would otherwise be unemployed. However, Mitra (2001) provides a different sort of evidence for India. Rural non-farm employment in India grew in the early 1980s at impressive rates, whereas when the rest of the economy grew at a higher rate in the 1990s after the 1991 liberalisation, rural non-farm employment failed to keep up its growth rate. According to Mitra (2001), the earlier growth was supported by a high level of deficit financing by the state, whereas post liberalisation, even though the economy grew at a higher rate, the level of deficit financing was severely curbed.

Most of the demand for rural non-farm activities in the 1980s was supported by artificially boosted demand led by deficit financing of the state. When this source of demand was curbed, growth in non-farm activity was severely reduced. However, from this study we do not know whether the initial increase in employment in the eighties and the later decline in employment in the nineties took place through jobs being created and subsequently lost in new firms or whether they were jobs created and lost by firm expansion and contraction. Fisher and Mahajan (1997) assert that most of the new jobs created in the rural non-farm sector in India during the nineties were by the coming into being of new units.

For Africa, there is a strong inverse relationship between new starts and enterprise size. The average annual new start rate for a one person firm is almost 30 percent, while the corresponding rate for ten person firms is typically less than 10 percent (Liedholm and Mead 1999: 29). It has long been recognised that what goes by the name of micro and small enterprises covers a wide array of activities in size, employment and productivity.

Daniels (1995) distinguishes between high and low profit activities. Looking at MSEs in Zimbabwe he finds the determinants of the two are different:

> For high return activities, the initial capital requirements, experience of the entrepreneur, and level of regulation are all inversely related to the new start rate. For low return activities, the rate of new start is related (inversely) only to the aggregate level of economic activity; for these firms, the lower the level of aggregate economic activity, the higher the rate of new starts, reflecting the importance of the push factors in firm creation.
>
> *(Daniels 1995, cited in Mishra 2005: 293)*

Firm closures

Somewhat more empirical evidence exists on the closure rates of small firms in developing countries. Firm mortality studies have been undertaken in Sierra Leone, Nigeria, Colombia, the Philippines and India. Liedholm and Parker (1989) reviewed the data generated from these studies and found that the closure rates of micro firms average between 9 and 10 percent per year. The empirical evidence on the relationship between location and closure rates has been meagre. Chuta and Liedholm (1985) found for Sierra Leone that the closure rates of small firms in rural villages (11.1 percent) were somewhat higher than those for firms located in the largest urban areas (9.5 percent).

Liedholm and Mead (1999) report the relationship found most consistently in empirical studies of firm dynamics between firm closures and the age of firm, in particular that there is a strong inverse relationship between the age of the firm and the failure rate and that most disappearances occur during the early years of a firm's existence. Nag (1980) found that almost two-thirds of all small firm closures in India took place during the firm's first four years. In an analysis of age specific closure rates in Sierra Leone, Liedholm (1990) generated estimates of a typical micro firm's "hazard rate", "which is the probability that the firm would fail during the following year, given that it has survived until the beginning of that year. At the beginning of the firm's fourth year, for example, the hazard rate was 22 percent, but in the fifth year it declined to 16 percent and in the sixth year it declined to 12 percent" (Liedholm and Mead 1999:14).

Many of these relationships have been studied for developed countries but not for developing countries. Liedholm and Mead (1999) suggest that firm closure rates might also be affected by the aggregate level of economic activity; but note that this relationship has not been examined in developing countries. This constitutes an important agenda for future research.

Poor business conditions have been found to be responsible for only half of business failures. Among these, Liedholm and Mead (1999) found that "lack of demand" and "shortage of working capital" accounted for the majority of business failures. Personal reasons, such as illness or retirement, accounted for about one quarter of MSE closures and around 10 percent of closures were due to the entrepreneur moving on to better opportunities. More than half of business failures have been found to occur in the firm's first three years, this is one of the most consistent relationships identified from studies. Firms that grow are more likely to survive the first three years than those that remain stagnant. However, firms that start small are more likely to survive than firms that start large, other factors being held constant. This finding indicates that smallness, by itself, is no impediment to survival.

The Global Entrepreneurship Monitor (2002) report finds that two-thirds of new employer firms survive at least two years and about half survive at least four. Owners of about one-third of firms that closed said their firm was successful at closure. Major factors determining whether a firm remains open include an ample supply of capital, whether the firm is large enough to have employees, the owner's education level and the owner's reason for starting the firm in the first place, such as freedom for family life or wanting to be one's own boss (Headd 2001).

In most cases people starting new businesses do not have enough cash to carry them beyond the first year of opening. In such cases, the prospect of survival or success is often slim. In this situation many of these aspire to borrow from micro-credit institutions to further their business aspirations. Borrowing in most parts of world though is not simple and straightforward and in most cases there are not the existing lending institutions to assist people in this situation.

Given this understanding of the dynamics of micro and small enterprises and with the context of rural credit markets in developing countries discussed above, we can now proceed to understand the role of microfinance in micro and small enterprises in developing countries.

The importance of microfinance to rural micro and small enterprises

In rural areas where there is less access to credit, the capacity to invest and manage economic activities is primarily based upon capital accumulation from personal savings. In communities where agriculture is the primary activity, financial capital often represents farm capital (savings), which are resources available to households for production and/or diversification, expansion or further investment. In rural areas, farm income is an important source for starting up non-farm businesses and also income from non-farm sources provides extra income for expansion of farm production. International Fund for Agricultural Development (IFAD 2009) states that raising capital to start farm or non-farm activities can be a daunting task in rural areas, where personal savings serve as the most important source of financing. However, less financial capital is needed to start up non-farm businesses, unlike farming, which requires more capital investment (for example, land, equipment and other inputs).

Igwe (2013) found that the four most important sources of start-up capital for farm businesses among rural households in Nigeria were income from parents or remittances from migrated family members and income or savings from non-farm work or business. Other common sources were sale of land and other family assets and income or savings from farm work. Loans/credit from formal money lenders was not a widely reported source of start-up funds for farm and non-farm businesses among rural households.

Several reasons were identified by Igwe (2013) as to why rural households were unable to access formal loans/credits. The reasons ranged from high interest rates, non-availability of financial institutions in local areas, lack of knowledge on how to apply and inability to meet collateral requirements. Access to loans/credit is a major obstacle that faces rural people in developing countries. For example, the Nigerian informal sector employs over 70 percent of the population and has 80 million micro entrepreneurs, who do not have access to financial services (Central Bank of Nigeria 2007).

Financial constraints are more pervasive in agriculture and related activities than in many other sectors, reflecting both the nature of agricultural activity and the average size of firms (World Bank 2008). Fabusoro et al. (2010) found that capital availability was a significant factor in the extent of diversification among rural people. They suggested that the significance of capital sources to livelihood diversification implies that availability of alternative sources of income will enhance an individual's capacity towards uptake of non-farm activities. In the absence of credit and microfinance, savings, to a large extent, determine the ability and capacity of people to invest or expand their income activities.

Financial capital is needed to create favourable economic conditions (for example, buy land, purchase inputs, equipment, hire labor, adopt new technology, increase or diversify production and embark on other day to day activities). Barrett et al. (2001) state that the fact that *ex ante* endowment of financial capital, skills, education or market access appear to increase the profitability of participation in higher-return non-farm activities, must not be misinterpreted as suggesting that all the wealthy move out of farming. They note that the key point is that the wealthy have greater freedom to choose among a wider range of options than the poor.

On the other hand, the poor have little choice but to diversify out of farming into non-farm employment due to lack of capital. Lack of micro-finance is one of the reasons why agricultural productivity has been on the decline, since it requires higher capital investment than non-agricultural activities. Lack of capital drives people to seek non-farm income in the form of trading, manufacturing, non-farm and agricultural paid employment. Rural non-farm activities are especially suitable for poor households because they require little capital and generate more employment per unit of capital than farm activities (IFAD 2009). This is one of the reasons why diversification has become a norm in rural communities of developing economies, especially in Africa.

The relative poverty situation of the rural population hampers savings and investment options and this has continued to perpetuate low income and output. Low level of income and lack of credit sources in the rural areas have considerable impact on a household's ability to secure a better livelihood, thereby affecting access to other livelihood opportunities. There is thus a tremendous need for financial innovations that can place smallholders on a ladder of ascending financial market access as well as for innovations that can complement financial services by managing the systemic risks that undercut their supply (World Bank 2008).

Many programs of direct assistance to rural non-farm enterprises have been cost effective. Credit projects, especially those supplying working capital, have enjoyed greater success. An evaluation of seven small enterprise credit projects found that all have benefit-cost ratios in excess of one (Kilby and D'Zmura 1985). Overall, as Kilby (1971) originally suggested and subsequent appraisals have confirmed, programs that aim to provide a complete package of financial, technical and management assistance – nursery industrial estates, for example – are generally less effective than programs that identify and provide a single missing ingredient necessary for enterprise success.

Bennett and Cuevas (1996) regard a sustainable financial services system for poor people relevant from three perspectives. First, it represents an important progress in reaching banking in a sustainable way to people who were earlier thought unreachable either because of high costs or high risk. Second, the availability of stable sources of funding and deposit services contributes to the start up and running of micro and small enterprises. Finally access to reliable, monetary savings facilities helps the poor smooth their consumption over periods of crisis, thus insuring them against risky outcomes of productive investments.

Our interest here is primarily in the second role mentioned above; for example the role of microfinance in helping the small and micro enterprise to start and survive, as well as potentially in the third. For some, the importance of financial services to small and micro entrepreneurs is firmly established and may be the single most effective means to tackle poverty (Women's World Banking 1995).

However, not everyone agrees on the primacy or even the relevance of credit constraint in the growth of rural non-farm enterprises. What has now come to be known as the Ohio School (Adams 1984, von Pischke 1991) doubt the hypothesis that it is the credit constraint that is binding in the growth of the rural non-farm sector. According to them, other factors such as infrastructure and rural incomes may be more relevant and credit will flow in the form of money lenders' and traders' advance once the need grows sufficiently. They regard the informal credit market as efficient and regard the high rate of interest as reflecting correctly the objective realities of lending in the rural sector. Finally, they do not think that access to credit can encourage economic activity; for them credit plays a passive not an active role in facilitating economic activity.

Remenyi (1991: 105–6) makes a number of observations on the economic and financial impact of Non-Governmental Organizations' (NGOs) credit based income generation projects (CIGP) on the poor. First, where there are project-level statistics on the impact of small loans on the income of borrowers they are overwhelmingly positive and appear to be very significant. Second, the few internal rate of return studies done and reported have indicated that CIGPs may be the most profitable way in which society can invest its scarce development funds. Diminishing returns have not yet arisen in this field of development assistance. Third, if on-time repayment rates are any sort of indicator of programme effectiveness, then this data also confirms that banking on and with the poor are very good things to do for development generally and the alleviation of poverty in particular. Fourth, the typical successful CIGP examined in this study required an investment well below $1,000 per sustained wage-paying position created (one-tenth of the ratio in the formal sector). Finally, the impact of CIGPs on the livelihood and prospects of the poor is dramatic rather than marginal due to the serious under-investment in micro enterprises of the poor in most developing countries, and the substantial impact a relatively small increase in earning capacity can have on the cash flow and the range of economic choices available for investment, saving and consumption.

However, with more than two decades of experience behind us it is now possible to look at the successes and failures of microfinance more objectively in its role of providing finance for micro and small enterprises.

Critique of microfinance for microenterprise

A number of criticisms can be levelled at microfinance for microenterprises. Bateman and Chang (2012) identify four key criticisms. First, microfinance ignores scale economies. The experience from Italy (Weiss 1988), South Korea and Taiwan (Wade 1990, Chang 1993) and China (Naughton 1995) shows that sustainable jobs can only be created by investing in microenterprises that can quickly achieve a minimum efficient scale of operations. However, MFIs promote a large number of microenterprises none of which have a high survival chance, creating a high turnover.

Second, microfinance ignores the fallacy of composition. Most new microenterprises merely redistribute the total volume of business instead of creating additions to the aggregate level of business.

Third, microfinance "crowds out" industrial microenterprises with prospects of technological upgrading, thus local savings are increasingly mobilised to invest in simple enterprises with short repayment schedules and which are unable to absorb new technologies, instead of industrial microenterprises with the potential of technological upgrading. Since the total volume of investible surplus is given at any point in time, this leaves fewer savings to be invested in microenterprises that can be scaled up and which can absorb new technology. This is also because the culture of microfinance does not encourage longer repayment periods which may be essential at the higher end of technology.

Finally, microfinance ignores the need to promote vertical and horizontal connectivity, whereas all successful industrial developments rely on clusters and subcontracting.

These are serious criticisms and, if microfinance is to have a successful role in microenterprise development, these criticisms must be addressed. One possible view to take is that microfinance caters precisely for the sector that is lacking in the above. The other is to hold that microfinance itself is evolving through continuous learning and sifting ways which work from those which do not, and this is the way forward.

Banerjee and Duflo (2013) conducted the first randomised evaluation of microfinance for micro enterprise and found that although households with access to microfinance were more likely to have a microcredit loan, they were no more likely to start a new enterprise than those who did not. However, their investment in capital goods increased. Other outcomes, such as health, education and women's empowerment remained unaffected.

Although microfinance institutions (MFIs) in India have had some success in overcoming many of the structural barriers that have militated against the provision of financial services to the poor, their role in supporting micro enterprises is yet to receive full recognition. The reason for such failure on the part of MFIs has been suggested to be a lack of market orientation within the supplying organisations (Woller 2002). In particular it has been argued that these MFIs are essentially product rather than customer-led in their approach to business. Their main focus is regarded as being on institutional rather than customer requirements, which is evidenced through offering standardized products to a market which is perceived as homogeneous, but which is in reality highly variable in its constituency.

Given that the market orientation of MFIs is seen to be a critical determinant of success in microfinance provision, Megicks et al. (2005) argue for a greater understanding of the implementation of the marketing concept in this context as a highly desirable research direction.

> Moreover, if a market-led approach to new financial service development and delivery is to be implemented within these MFIs, then the factors that influence the extent and nature of market orientation within MFIs require further investigation. The existing literature relating to market orientation and organisational performance is well defined and provides a strong theoretical platform from which to build an understanding of MFIs.
>
> *(Megicks et al. 2005:108)*

Evidence from a plethora of empirical studies across a large number of nations and contexts suggests that market orientation facilitates the attainment of organisational goals through acquiring a deeper understanding of customer requirements and competitive conditions, and the implementation of integrated marketing effort to deliver value-based propositions to the market.

As Attah (2008: 25) puts it:

> Finance is essential in the commodity-dominated rural world and determines people's ability to invest in farm or non-farm activities. There are two sides in the financing of the commodity: (I) the demand side, with strategies for processors, producers and traders; and (II) the supply side, with strategies for financial institutions. Closing the supply and demand gap is a daunting task, but not impossible. The two issues are crucial in combating poverty in a sustainable way: (I) on the demand side, a move is necessary from a sole emphasis on commodity production towards value creation through processing and marketing goods that respond to market pull; (II) on the supply side, there has to be a shift away from charity and interest rate subsidies towards dynamically growing and sustainable financial services at commercial terms

The provision of financial services has been a long-standing challenge in development, and access to insurance products is generally much weaker in developing countries, a fact reflected in the general lower penetration of financial services in the rural areas (World Bank 2010). A small farm size, lack of information on individuals' credit history, insufficient collateral, high levels of transaction and supervisory costs, uncertainties due to climate and low market prices for farmers' produce, among other factors, make lending and extending other financial services to rural communities risky and often unprofitable in poorer countries. On the demand side, the missing market for agricultural land, insufficient cash flow planning and lack of education are challenges facing micro-financing (World Bank 2005).

Conclusion

Nearly three billion people in developing countries have little or no access to formal financial services. Microfinance is one way of supporting micro and small enterprises, since it puts credit, savings, insurance and other basic financial services within the reach of poor local people. Through microfinance institutions poor people can access small loans, receive remittances from migrant relatives and expand or maintain their income activities and investments. Despite the success of microfinance in some areas, it has proven difficult to provide accessible microfinance services to remote rural areas in developing countries and the spread and scope of lending by micro-finance institutions in many countries remains very poor.

Research and financial policies need to focus more efforts on how to reach more people in remote places and provide types of products and services that will contribute to rural economic development. Most of the financial services in developing countries focus on the urban areas and cities and they are unable to reach rural households. This leads to the growth of informal lending services in rural areas providing credits and financial services. Microfinance has the capacity to fill this gap.

References

Adams, D.W. (1984) *Undermining Rural Development with Cheap Credit*, Boulder CO: Westview Press.

African Development Bank (2000) *Finance for the Poor: Micro-finance Development Strategy*, 2000, African Development Bank, p. 2.

Attah, J.A. (2008) *Micro-finance Banking needs for proper orientation: The Nigerian Micro-finance Newsletter* (7) January–June 2008.

Banerjee, A. et al. (2010) Microfinance miracle? *Evidence from a randomized trial* bread working paper No. 278 June, 2010.

—— (2013) *The miracle of microfinance? Evidence from a randomized evaluation* (Unpublished) Working paper series. Working paper 13–09.

Banjerjee, A. and Duflo, E. (2013) *Poor Economics: A Radical Rethinking of the Way to Fight Global Poverty.* Random House.

Barrett, C., Reardon, T. and Webb, P. (2001) Non-farm income diversification and household Livelihood strategies in rural Africa, Concept, dynamics and policy implications. *Food Policy* 26: 315–331.

Basu, K. (2003) *Analytical Development Economics* MIT Press.

Bateman, M. and Chang, H. (2012) Microfinance and the Illusion of Development: From Hubris to Nemesis in Thirty Years. *World Economic Review* Vol 1: 13–36, 2012.

Bennet and Cuevas (1996) "Sustainable Banking with the Poor", *Journal of International Development* vol. 8 (March–April).

Braverman and Guasch (1993) "Administrative Failures in Government Credit Programs" in Hoff, K. et al (ed.) (1993) *The Economics of Rural Organisation*, New York: Oxford University Press 1993.

Central Bank of Nigeria (2007) *CBN Annual Report and Statement of Account for the Year Ended 31st December,* 2007.

Chang, H-Joon (1993) The Political Economy of Industrial Policy in Korea, *Cambridge Journal of Economics* vol. 17 (2).

Chuta, E. and Liedholm, C. (1985) *Employment and Growth in Small-Scale Industry: Empirical Evidence and Policy Assessment from Sierra Leone*, London: St Martins Press.

Daniels, L. (1995) "Entry and Exit behavior and Growth Patterns among Small Scale Enterprises in Zimbabwe", PhD Dissertation, Michigan State University.

Economic Intelligence Unit 2012, Global microscope on the microfinance business environment, *The Economist*, London.

Economist Intelligence Unit (2013) *Global microscope on the microfinance business environment 2012.* The Economist. www.microfinancegateway.org/gm/document-1.9.59312/EIU_MICROFINANCE_2012_WEB.pdf

Fabusoro, E., Omotayo, A.M., Apantaku, S.O. and Okuneye, P.A. (2010) "Forms and Determinants of Rural Livelihoods Diversification in Ogun State, Nigeria", *Journal of Sustainable Agriculture*, 34:4, pp. 417–38.

Fisher, T. and Mahajan, V. (1997) *The forgotten sector: Non-farm employment in rural enterprises in rural India.* IT Publications London.

GEM (2002) *Global Entrepreneurship Monitor*, 2002 Executive Report, Babson College.

Ghatak, S. (1983) "On inter regional variation in rural interest rates" *Journal of Developing Areas* 18, pp. 21–34.

Greenwald and Stiglitz (1986) "Externalities in Economies with Imperfect Information and Incomplete Markets" *Quarterly Journal of Economics* vol. 101 issue 2, pp. 229–64.

Gonzalez, A. (2010) *Is Microfinance Growing Too Fast? Microfinance Information Exchange*, Mix Data Brief No. 5.

Harris, S.D. (2005) "The State of the Microcredit Summit Campaign Report 2005" Washington D.C. Microcredit Summit Campaign.

Harriss-White, B. and Janakrajan, S. (1997) From green revolution to rural industrial revolution in South India. *Economic and Political Weekly*, 32 (25), pp. 1469–77.

Headd, B. (2001) *Business Success: Factors Leading to Surviving and Closing Successfully*, Center for Economic Studies, U.S. Bureau of the Census, Working Paper CES-WP-01-01, January 2001; Advocacy-funded research by Richard J. Boden (Research Summary 204).

Hoff, K. and Stiglitz, J. (1993) "Imperfect information and Rural Credit Markets: Puzzles and Policy Perspectives" In Hoff, K., Braverman, A. and Stiglitz, J. (Eds.) (1993) *Economics of rural organization: theory, practice and policy.* New York: Oxford University Press.

IFAD (2009) Rural Enterprise and Poverty Reduction, Asia and the Pacific Division, *International Fund for Agricultural Development.*

IFC (2013) *International Finance Corporation Annual Report.*: World Bank Group.

Igwe, P.A. (2013) Rural Non-farm Livelihood Diversification and Poverty Reduction in Nigeria, University of Plymouth, *Rural Micro and Small Enterprises*, 2013 http://hdl.handle.net/10026.1/1561

Juma, L. (2007) "Solving Problems of Financial Exclusion of the Low-Income Rural and Urban Dwellers in Nigeria", The Nigerian Microfinance NEWSLETTER, *The Newsletter of the International letter of Microcredit 2007*, vol. 5, July–December 2007, pp. 24–32.

Kilby, P. (1971) *Entrepreneurship and Economic Development*, New York: The Free Press.

Kilby and D'Zmura (1985) *Searching for benefits United States Agency for International Development*: Washington DC.

Liedholm, C. 1990 "The dynamics of small scale industry in Africa and the role of policy" GEMINI Working Paper #2 Washington DC.

Liedholm, C. and Mead, D. (1999) *Small Enterprises and Economic Development: The Dynamics of Micro and Small Enterprises*, London and New York: Routledge.

Liedholm, C. and Parker, J. (1989) "Small Scale Manufacturing Growth in Africa: Initial Evidence" MSU International Development Working Paper No. 33, East Lansing MI: Department of Agricultural Economics, Michigan State University.

Megicks, P., Mishra, A. and Lean, J. (2005) "Enhancing microfinance outreach through market-oriented new service development in Indian regional rural banks" *International Journal of Bank Marketing* Vol. 23 issue 1 pp. 107–25.

Mishra, A. (2002) *Start-up and Survival of Rural Non-Farm Activities, PhD Thesis*, Department of Economics, University of Reading, Unpublished.

—— (2005) "Entrepreneurial motivations in Start-up and Survival of Micro- and Small Enterprises in the Rural Non-Farm Economy" *Journal of Small Business & Entrepreneurship.* Volume 18, Issue 3, 2005, pp. 289–326.

Mitra (2001) "Rural Non-farm Employment and Poverty" *Indian Journal of Labour Economics* vol. 41 no. 4.

Morduch, J. (1999) *The Microfinance promise Journal of Economic Literature* vol. 37 no. 4 Dec., pp. 1569–614.

Nag, A. (1980) "Small Industries: Aspects of their mortality", *The Economic Times*, October 6, Delhi, India.

Naughton, Barry (1995) *Growing out of the plan: Chinese Economic reform, 1978–1993*, Cambridge: Cambridge University Press.

Reed, L. R. (2013) *Vulnerability: the state of the microcredit summit campaign report, 2013. Microcredit Summit Campaign.* http://stateofthecampaign.org/multimedia/print-version

Remenyi, J. (1991) *Where Credit is Due: Income Generating Programmes for the Poor in Developing Countries*, London: Intermediate technology publications.

Renkow, M., Hallstrom, D.G. and Karanja, D.D. (2004) "Rural infrastructure, transactions costs and market participation in Kenya" *Journal of Development Economics*, Vol 74 issue 1, pp. 349–67.

Rutherford, S. (2001) *The Poor and Their Money* (Oxford India Paperbacks) 2001.

Reynolds, P.D. (2002) *Worldwide Business Start-Ups*, In Moya K. Mason: Email communication with Dr. Paul D. Reynolds, Director, Research Institute, Global Entrepreneurship Center.

Stiglitz, J.E. (1993) "Peer monitoring and Credit markets" In Hoff, K., Braverman, A. and Stiglitz, J. (Eds.) (1993) *Economics of rural organization: theory, practice and policy.* New York: Oxford University Press.

Von Pischke, J.D. (1991) *Finance at the frontier: Debt capacity and the role of credit in the private economy.* Washington DC Economic Development Institute of the World Bank.

Wade 1990, *Governing the market: Economic theory and the role of government in East Asian industrialization,* Princeton University Press, Princeton, New Jersey, USA.

Weiss, Linda (1988), *Creating Capitalism: The state and small business since 1945,* Oxford: Blackwell.

Wermer, N. (2010) Literature Review: Social Protection of the Rural Poor, in: *UNRISD Flagship Report: Combating Poverty and Inequality* (Geneva: United Nations Research Institute for Social Development).

Woller 2002, "The promise and peril of microfinance commercialization" *Small Enterprise Development* vol 13 no.4

Women's World Banking (1995) *Draft Policy* Paper World Bank Washington DC.

World Bank (2005) Rural Finance Innovations: Topics and Case Studies, the World Bank Agriculture and Rural Development Department, Report No. 32726 GLB in Igwe, P.A. (2013) *Rural Non-farm Livelihood Diversification and Poverty Reduction in Nigeria,* University of Plymouth, Rural Micro and Small Enterprises, 2013.

World Bank (2010) *World Development Report: Development and Climate Change.* Washington, DC: The World Bank.

World Development Report (1994) *World Development Report* World Bank: Oxford University Press 1994.

Yunus, M. (1998) *Banker to the poor Penguin* India Ltd, New Delhi.

Part X
Marketing malpractice and financial fiascos

29

The scale and scope of financial mis-selling

John K. Ashton

Introduction

As an introduction to this section considering financial services malpractice, this chapter assesses the scale, scope and characteristics of the phenomenon of mis-selling. Financial mis-selling is a widely used term attributed to many meanings including: aggressive, ignorant or incompetent sales tactics; a failure to appropriately advise customers; deliberate strategies to sell financial services that customers do not need; all circumstances where a customer is financially disadvantaged due to reasons they were neither aware of, nor desired (Black and Nobels 1998). This examination is undertaken through the content analysis of all the final notices issued and reported by the UK financial regulator (the Financial Services Authority, hereafter the FSA) to financial organizations for mis-selling over the ten-year period, 2002–11.

A range of findings are reported. The frequency of mis-selling cases and level of fines associated with financial mis-selling are increasing with time. The type of firm involved in financial mis-selling is diverse and includes large international banks and insurers and a number of smaller non-financial retailers, yet predominately smaller financial advisory firms. While a substantial proportion of recent research on financial mis-selling has emphasised single causes for this phenomenon such as commission based sales (Inderst and Ottaviani 2012a, 2012b, 2012c) or product or product line complexity (Carlin 2009, Carlin and Manso 2010, Kamenica 2008), we observe mis-selling to be a complex phenomenon with multiple causes. These causes include insufficient qualification of advisors, commission bias, failed management systems for collecting customer information and mis-leading advertising. A number of these factors are discussed in some detail in Chapter 34 in relation to the ethics of the selling process. Finally, the types of financial services mis-sold are assessed. We report many financial services have been mis-sold due to their high and often mis-understood risks and also their complexity; in many cases product features are not even fully comprehended by suppliers' advisors. Other mis-sold financial services have been poorly explained or sold as an add-on service appended to other financial services sought by the customer. The chapter concludes with discussion of recent UK regulatory developments to alleviate future financial mis-selling.

The significance of mis-selling

Assessment of financial mis-selling is important for many reasons, including its international scope, repeated occurrence, costs to firms and customers and on-going regulatory developments. Financial mis-selling is a persistent international phenomenon reported within the U.S., the European Union, India, Germany and the United Kingdom, amongst other nations. The scale of mis-selling in these nations is striking. Within India, Anagol et al. (2013) reported those selling life insurance overwhelmingly recommend unsuitable products which provide high commissions and provide correct advice in only 9 percent of cases. In Germany, Hacketal et al. (2012) report that both independent financial advisors and banks provide investment advice to customers which lowers investment returns, increases financial risks, enhances product turnover and encourages investment in products associated with high commission payments. Across the EU 27, Synovate (2011) reports the quality of retail investment advice is variable with many salespersons overlooking a customers' personal needs when advising and tending to be more interested in the ability rather than the need to invest. These mis-selling episodes have occurred repeatedly in many nations and have resulted in increasing corporate costs including fines, loss of reputation and in some cases customer redress. Customer redress paid to compensate customers for the costs incurred in an inappropriate sale are substantial. Within the UK, these have varied from over £10bn for pensions mis-selling in the 1990s, to £2.8bn for endowment mortgage mis-selling in the 1980s and 1990s (see Ferran 2012) to over £8bn paid to customers in redress for mis-sold payment protection insurance in the 2000s (Ashton and Hudson 2012).

In addition to corporate costs, customers are exposed to uncertainty and can incur financial costs due to financial mis-selling. While many purchase decisions have financial implications for a customer, the purchase of many financial services, such as mortgages, pensions, insurance or investments can have life changing implications. Obtaining an inappropriate mortgage contract could leave a household exposed to losing the family home, a poor pension decision might engender retirement on limited means and a poor investment decision can obliterate lifetime savings. These customer risks have also increased as individuals have had to take increasing responsibility and autonomy for their financial decisions (Benartzi 2001, Benartzi and Thaler 2002). Historically low levels of saving exist in many nations (Kirsanova and Sefton 2007) and a high proportion of households internationally already face financial fragility (Lusardi et al. 2011) and have little money to lose.

Responding to these concerns financial regulation to alleviate financial mis-selling has developed and expanded in many nations, particularly since the financial crisis of 2008. In the U.S. consumer financial services regulations have been substantially amended by the Dodd Frank Wall Street Reform and Consumer Protection Act (2010) which created the Consumer Financial Protection Bureau to write and enforce rules, conduct examinations and track customer complaints in financial services markets. In the UK, the financial regulator, the FSA, was split into two regulators for prudential and conduct of business regulation in financial markets respectively to address regulatory concerns more effectively, including mis-selling (FSA 2009). More widely the G20 Finance Ministers and Central Bank Governors have called for common principles for consumer protection to be developed in all financial services markets (Financial Stability Board 2011) reflecting the international scope of these concerns and the major risks to financial stability posed by financial services mis-selling.

Current literatures examining financial mis-selling

There is a varied multidisciplinary literature examining financial mis-selling, why customers' may make poor purchase decisions and buy inappropriate financial services. This literature spans a range of concerns from why some customers have decision making challenges, the role of commission in influencing advisors' recommendations, to the product design and complexity of financial services.

Central to most explanations of financial services mis-selling has been customers' limited comprehension of financial services. In order to make an appropriate financial service purchase decision an individual might be expected to have a clear understanding of the financial services' features and characteristics, how their own preferences relate to these characteristics and their future demands for this service. Despite these expectations a substantial proportion of consumers have a poor comprehension of financial services (Bucks and Pence 2008, FSA 2006a) particularly the young, old and less wealthy. These concerns are compounded as many individuals face challenges when comprehending money and monetary yields (for example, Shafir et al. 1997) and persons with distinct lifestyles, levels of education and politics have very different abilities to make decisions in personal financial services markets (Aldridge 1998, Peggs 2000). The challenges of financial literacy are discussed in detail in Chapter 3.

We can therefore characterise financial service purchase decisions as challenging for many customers. This results in a high proportion of financial sales undertaken with advice (Inderst and Ottaviani 2012b) where a successful and appropriate financial services sale is contingent upon the expert knowledge and competence of the supplier. This is a point of concern if financial decisions are presented to investors in a manner which does not assist optimal decision making (Hirshleifer 2001) or if firms adapt their behaviors to exploit observed decision making anomalies (Frey and Eichenberger 1994). These potential conflicts of interest between suppliers, advisors and consumers are well documented in retail financial services sales (Kane 1997) and emerge from the position of trust and commercial pressure faced by financial services suppliers. If we plausibly assume the financial supplier or advisor knows more about the financial services' characteristics than the consumer (Emons 2001) this enables a financial services advisor or salesperson to mislead customers and mis-sell financial services. While opponents to such views argue market discipline and reputational concerns motivate advisors to provide useful financial advice and customer education (Anagol et al. 2013), compounding this concern has been the widespread use of commission based sales in the financial services industry. Financial services are often sold using the advice of financial advisors and these persons are often remunerated on a commission basis. This creates incentives to inflate the perceived value of a financial service if it pays more commission (Inderst and Ottaviani 2009).

An associated and compounding factor is the design of financial services and how these services are presented within the product line. Perceptions of financial services complexity arise despite many retail financial services having similar functions, be this providing funds for house purchase, a return on investment or a degree of financial protection. One explanation to why complexity arises is the need for customers to perceive that a financial service offered by one provider differs and reflects a "better" or higher quality than products provided by other suppliers. This process involves firms developing products characterised by promotional features, where the provision of information and persuasion of the customers are closely linked (Aldridge 1998). This involves a host of marketing tools including providing additional features to differentiate financial services, presenting and applying pricing differently to distinct elements of the service and managing the product line of financial services.

One way in which such perceptual differences are established is within pricing. Parrish and Frank (2011) argue financial services pricing is representative of a "*peacock*" market, where price signals are designed to take maximum advantage of information shortages, limited attention and behavioral biases held by customers. Such pricing arises as financial services firms attempt to undercut competitors with lower prices on selective parts of the financial service, and through deceptive innovations, such as presenting prices differently from competitors. This competitive process is expected to produce a market where products are characterised by features of limited functional value yet significant perceived or symbolic value. These issues are discussed in detail in Chapter 16.

A further concern is that many financial services are marketed as a bundle of distinct financial services. Situations where multiple services are offered in combination has spawned a theoretical literature examining circumstances where customers make sub-optimal choices when jointly purchasing additional or add-on services (for example, DellaVigna and Malmendier 2004, Ellison 2005, Gabaix and Laibson 2006). This literature assumes the add-on good is offered at a relatively high price, allowing the base good, actually desired by the customer to be lowered by cross-subsidies flowing from the add-on good. These situations are amplified when, what is described as "naïve", "myopic" or "less sophisticated" customers with weaker decision making abilities populate markets, together with more "sophisticated" or "informed" customers with more refined decision making abilities. Given the existence of "naïve" customers, firms can use shrouding techniques, including small print and limited informative advertising, to conceal the true costs of add-on goods (Gabaix and Laibson 2006) encouraging their purchase. This feature, while applicable to many markets is observed repeatedly in financial services, for example in the sale of payment protection insurance offered as an additional service in credit transactions. Price bundling is discussed in more detail in Chapter 18.

Product line management, the degree of product churn or turnover and the overall scope of the product line have also raised concerns that firm actions can engender consumer confusion and poor purchase decisions in financial services markets. For example, Carlin and Manso (2010) report financial firms frequently change their product line to constrain customer comprehension through a marketing strategy of obfuscation. These authors theorise the issue of new financial services and phasing out of old financial services can reduce learning by customers, limiting and even reducing customer comprehension. Ultimately it is proposed that firms strive to populate markets with a greater proportion of poorly informed customers as selling to such customers is profitable for financial firms.

Customer regret can also influence decision making as customers desire to avoid poor or suboptimal decisions and regret such outcomes when these occur. This is a genuine concern as approximately 20 percent of simple choices might be mistakes (Fehr and Rangel 2011). When confronted by more complicated or unfamiliar decisions individuals often feel responsibility for making a correct or appropriate decision, increasing the fear of making poor decisions and influencing both what decisions are made and even if a decision is made at all (Iyengar and Lepper 2000). This concern is amplified when firms offer multiple similar services; a profitable strategy for firms (Kamenica 2008), long observed in financial services markets (Costanzo and Ashton 2006). For example, customer behavior within the US retirement savings market has repeatedly been associated with non-rational behaviors arising from such "excessive" choice. More choice of investment funds has been associated with lower participation rates (Choi et al. 2004) and has little influence over the funds chosen (Huberman and Jiang 2006).

From this brief review mapping the contours of a large and multidisciplinary literature, we can state the appropriate sale of financial services faces many challenges. Some customers have constrained decision making abilities, financial services can be complex and many academics have argued such complexity can be enhanced and used by firms for commercial benefit through the presentation of financial services both individually and in combination. Finally, how financial services are sold is believed to be influenced by conflicts of interest, asymmetric information and the use of commission based sales.

Methodology and data

In this section we outline the data employed, the content analysis methodology and the regulatory context of the data considered. To quantify the scale, scope and characteristics of financial services mis-selling we must first acknowledge mis-selling is a regulatory construct and the act of mis-selling exists only when it is judged to be outside what is legally appropriate at a point in time. Regulatory data, the final notices issued by the UK financial regulator, operating over the sample period (2002–11) are therefore assessed. These documents provide details of the offences or breach of regulations identified, including what punishments have been accorded. They vary in size from a couple of pages to over twenty pages and are publically available.

While this data has the benefit of allowing all the identified mis-selling cases in the UK to be considered, there are drawbacks; not least sampling difficulties which make inference challenging. The sample selection of mis-selling cases reflects the legal regime in which the cases were considered and selected by regulator to pursue. This sample is therefore influenced by the resources, politics and bureaucracy of the FSA; all factors varying over the sample period. Further and common to all crime statistics (see Simpson and Koper 1997) we only know what has been officially prohibited and investigated by the FSA; the mis-selling cases we examine are therefore a sample of all the financial mis-selling within the UK. The FSA also represents a certain type of financial regulator – a "super" financial regulator with a wide scope of regulatory concerns, including systematic, prudential and conduct of business regulation. However, competition concerns in some credit markets over the sample period were considered by a distinct competition regulator, the Office of Fair Trading.

This form of regulator, whist also seen in Germany, Japan, Sweden and the Netherlands, is not employed universally (see Masciandaro 2002). Finally, the approach to financial regulation seen in the UK over the sample period, while sharing commonalities with other nations, particularly in the EU, reflects the history and culture of UK financial regulation. In light of these concerns, it is important to consider the context of UK financial regulation of financial service marketing, a subject to which we now turn.

The UK regulatory context for financial services marketing

Throughout the sample period UK regulation has influenced the sales process of financial services. The standard economic justification for the regulation of financial markets during this period is associated with the correction of market failures to enable the efficient allocation and distribution of resources within a free market (see Llewellyn 1999). With respect to financial mis-selling such market failures could be understood as limited customer comprehension, product complexity and information asymmetry where regulation is used as a tool to reduce such inefficiencies and market imperfections.

While UK regulation of financial services marketing has evolved overtime from only addressing fraud concerns related to share pushing in the 1930s (Gower 1988) to specialist regulation of financial services conduct of business at the time of writing, the basis of the regulatory regime over the sample period is encapsulated within the Financial Services and Markets Act (2000). This legislation was introduced by the FSA (see Foot 2004) and has affected virtually all aspects of financial services operations, training and competence and consumer compensation over the sample period. Under this legal regime, regulation was enacted from a common set of rules and regulatory principles. Of pertinence for mis-selling, any person advising on or recommending a regulated financial service has to obtain sufficient information from the customer as to their financial circumstances as part of a "regulated sales" process (see FSA 2000). These prior to sale investigations would include subjective factors such as the investors' age and attitude to risk (Black and Nobels 1998) in addition to possible future circumstances. Once this 'fact find' has been undertaken and documented, a financial service should then be recommended which best serves the customers' circumstances; a decision which also requires justification and documentation. Following this sales process the advisor should then also disclose any interests and their status. Two key aspects of this regime include the "know your customer" requirements, that information on the customer characteristics is recorded and used to inform best advice using the "treating customers fairly" principle.

Methods

The form of content analysis employed is observational or manifest in form. This approach adopted within law (for example, Posner 1970), economics (for example, Davies et al. 1999), finance (for example, Wisniewski and Lambe 2013) as well as marketing (for example, Pass et al. 1994, Ashton and Pressey 2008, 2011) considers the frequency of values and common terms of pertinence to the research questions. While this content analysis method is common in many academic disciplines, it is distinct from that practiced in some academic fields, such as accounting, education or media studies (see Bos and Tarnai 1999).

The process of classifying cases was conducted both independently and with reference to the annual reports of the FSA, where many cases have been already reported in a coded form. During coding, data were captured from the reports considering salient characteristics of the mis-selling cases. The key characteristics of these cases reflects explanations of why mis-selling occurs, the features of these cases and the type of market (investments, pensions, insurance and mortgages) affected. Case features recorded include the duration of the mis-selling, the level of fine, the market and approximate number of customers affected by the mis-selling, remedial actions and the types of firms involved. Further qualitative information is recorded on the particular offence and the type of financial service mis-sold.

Dataset

The distribution of all final notices from which the mis-selling cases are selected is displayed in Table 29.1. The final notices have been issued by the FSA for a range of different activities grouped to represent different regulatory concerns. The largest group by frequency is reporting and compliance cases including circumstances where a firm or individual has failed to submit appropriate regulatory returns or has displayed failings with regards to the compliance with or reporting of business. Resource cases consider circumstances where a firm or an individual has insufficient resources to operate; be these financial or appropriate regulated human resources. Money laundering cases relate to breaches of money laundering rules to prevent proceeds of crime entering the monetary economy. Deception and theft include cases where a person or corporate entity has stolen or deceived clients or other interested parties. Complaint handling cases refers to concerns with how a firm has dealt with customers' complaints and rulings of the Financial Ombudsman Service. Market abuse cases involve insider dealing and other circumstances where the transparency and efficiency of financial markets has been compromised.

We can observe the number of mis-selling cases overall is a small proportion of all final notices issued by the FSA; an eighth of all cases and consisting of 164 cases overall. This sample also consists of both individual and corporate cases; reflecting the UK approach of also regulating individuals holding certain positions in financial firms. As this individual approach to financial regulation is distinct from that practised in many other nations, we only examine corporate

Table 29.1 Characteristics of final notices issued by the FSA (2002–11) and descriptive statistics

	All cases			Corporate cases		
	Freq.	*% of final notices*	*Average fine (357 cases)*	*Freq.*	*% of final notices*	*Average fine (203 cases)*
Money laundering	15	1%	£1,005,750	10	1%	£1,202,000
Reporting and compliance	455	34%	£893,999	272	41%	£1,145,635
Resources	339	25%	£25,800	188	28%	£31,500
Technical problems	5	0%	£1,308,000	5	1%	£1,308,000
Other	16	1%	£555,837	12	2%	£739,975
Mis-selling	163	12%	£1,441,061	107	16%	£2,919,377
Market abuse	96	7%	£833,628	30	4%	£3,031,663
Deception and theft	220	16%	£794,929	27	4%	£920,917
Complaint handling	34	3%	£880,379	17	3%	£1,302,854
Total	1342	100%*	£1,005,750	669	100%	£1,202,000

Descriptive Statistics

	Freq.	*Minimum*	*Maximum*	*Mean*
Fine level (£)	88	£7000	£10,500,000	£748,188
Duration (months)	104	2	120	28.11
Number of customers affected	72	6	1,300,000	18,943
Redress value	13	£1,000,000	£140,000,000	£24,507,000

*There is a 1% loss due to the rounding of percentages.

Source: Compiled from information contained in the Final Notices issued by FSA. The Final Notices may be accessed at www.fsa.gov.uk/library/communication/notices/final

cases of mis-selling to enhance the comparability of our results; these final notices are listed in Table 29.2. The corporate final notices account for over half of the mis-selling cases, with 107 cases over the sample period. In Table 29.1 we also include values of fines levied in all mis-selling cases and also just for mis-selling by firms. It can be seen that the level of fines is highest for mis-selling and when just corporate cases are considered mis-selling has the second highest level of fines. In all excepting five cases, mis-selling was undertaken by distinct firms. In the five cases, three cases related to different subsidiaries from the same firm at the same point in time and two cases consider the same firm at different points in time.

Table 29.1 also includes descriptive statistics for key variables collected. It is observed that there are some very large and small cases and a diversity of mis-selling cases which have occurred in the sample period. In many variables there are missing observations. This arises due to the data assessed and methodology adopted where some variables, such as customer redress are reported only in a limited number of cases reflecting the selective use and reporting of this remedy. Other variables such as duration are recorded for the majority of cases.

Results

Assessment of the scope, scale and characteristics of financial mis-selling is undertaken in three stages. First we report the frequency and scale of mis-selling cases over time in Table 29.3.

Table 29.2 Corporate financial mis-selling final notices issued by the FSA (2002–11)

Abbey Life Assurance Company Limited	G D Tancred Financial Services Ltd	Penn Financial Services Unlimited
Abbey Mortgages Ltd	GE Capital Bank Ltd	PB Roberts Ltd
Approved Financial Solutions Ltd	Gillen Farrelly Independent Mortgage Advisers	Perspective Financial Management Ltd
Alliance & Leicester plc	George White Motors Ltd	PMSG Insurance Services Ltd
AWD Chase de Vere Wealth Management Ltd	GK Group Ltd	Read Independent Financial Advisers Ltd
AXA Sun Life Plc	GMAC-RFC Ltd	Redcats Brands Ltd
Barclays Bank Plc	Hadenglen Home Finance plc	Regency Mortgage Corp. Ltd
Berkeley Jacobs Financial Services Ltd	Hargreaves Lansdown Asset Mngt. Ltd	Regency Investment Services Ltd
Best Advice Mortgage Network Ltd	Hemscott Investment Analysis Ltd	Ringways Garages (Leeds and Doncaster) Ltd
Bradford & Bingley plc	Henry Neil Ltd	Rockingham Independent Ltd
Braemar Financial Planning Ltd	HFC Bank Ltd	Royal & Sun Alliance Life and Pensions Ltd and Linked Insurances Ltd
Cantor Index Ltd	Highbury Financial Services Ltd	Royal Liver Assurance Ltd
Capita Trust Company Ltd	Home and County Mortgages Ltd	Scottish Amicable Life plc
Capital Mortgage Connections Ltd	HSBC Bank Plc	RSM Tenon Financial Services Ltd
Capital One Bank (Europe) Plc	Hythe Securities Ltd	Scotts Private Client Services Ltd
Cathedral Motor Company Ltd	Integrity Financial Solutions Ltd	Sesame Ltd
Chariot Mortgage Services Ltd	Kings	Sett Valley Insurance Services
Chase de Vere Financial Solutions plc	Knowlden Titlow Financial	Specialist Solutions plc
Cheshire Life & Pensions Cons.	Land of Leather Ltd	Square Mile Securities Ltd
City Gate Money Managers Ltd	Langtons (IFA) Ltd	St James's Place Int. plc
City Index Ltd	Leybridge Ltd	St James's Place UK plc
Combined Insurance Company of America	Lincoln Assurance Ltd	St James's Place Unit Trust Group Ltd
Courtover Investment Management Ltd	Liverpool Victoria Banking Services Ltd	Standard Life Assurance Ltd
Coutts & Company	Lloyds TSB Bank plc	TBO Investments Ltd
Cricket Hill Financial Planning Ltd	Loans.co.uk Ltd	The Ancient Order of Foresters Friendly Society Ltd
Credit Suisse (UK) Ltd	MLP Private Finance Plc	Garrison Finance Centre Ltd
DB UK Bank Ltd	Moneywise IFA Ltd	The Loan Company
DBS Financial Management plc	Mortgageland Ltd	The Matrix Model Group Ltd
Derrick Hales Financial Planning	Mortgages Remortgages Ltd	The Minel Group Ltd
Direct Sharedeal Ltd	Next Generation Mortgages Ltd	Thinc Group Ltd
Eastern Western Motor Grp Ltd	N-Hanced LLP	Thorntons Law LLP
Egg Banking plc	Norwich and Peterborough BS	Trigon Pensions Ltd
Exclusive Asset Management Ltd	Orchid Financial Ltd	Wheatcroft Fox & Company
Falcon Securities (UK) Ltd	Pacific Continental Securities (UK) Ltd	Wills & Co Stockbrokers Ltd (2007)
Fastmoney.co.uk	Park Row	Wills & Co Stockbrokers Ltd (2010)
Fox Hayes	Park's of Hamilton Ltd	

Table 29.3 The frequency of mis-selling over time

	Freq.	Average fine £	Average duration of mis-selling (months)	Average number of customers affected (73 cases)
2002	1	£1,000,000	60	52,000
2003	10	£520,000	19	113
2004	9	£273,333	37	275
2005	5	£40,000	13	901
2006	12	£170,800	21	287
2007	11	£105,450	18	145,365
2008	22	£633,233	29	438
2009	8	£718,375	36	47
2010	14	£463,510	31	440
2011	15	£2,943,481	35	414

Table 29.4 Characteristics and causes of mis-selling cases

Punishment	Freq.	%	Cause of Mis-sales	Freq.	%
Fine	89	83%	Misleading advertising	27	24.5
Public censure	15	14%	Failed information needs	72	65.5
Customer redress	24	22%	Unsuitable advice	75	68.2
Removal of regulatory permissions	3	3%	Monitoring staff	56	50.9

Institution type undertaking mis-selling	Freq.	%	Target market	Freq.	%
Bank/Building society/Friendly society/Credit issuing firm	17	16	All retail customers	83	75.5
Other retailers	9	8	Elderly or near retirement	7	6.4
Stockbroker/Investment/Financial advisor/Law or accounting firm	69	64	Less experienced investors	2	1.8
Insurer	12	11	High net worth	4	3.6
			Young singles	2	1.8
			Sub-prime market	7	6.4
			Other	2	1.9

In Table 29.4 we examine the characteristics of mis-selling and what types of firms have been involved. In Table 29.5 we examine what financial services appear to be mis-sold.

In Table 29.3, the frequency of mis-selling cases increases over time from 1 case in 2002 (Abbey Life Assurance Company Limited involving endowment mortgage mis-selling) to an average of 15 cases in 2011. The annual average number of mis-selling cases increases from 7.6 in the 2002–6 period to 14.4 cases in the 2007–11 period. The level of fines has also risen over time, from an average of £400,826 in the 2002–6 period to £972,810 in the 2007–11 period. Over time mis-selling cases investigated by the FSA have become more frequent and the level of corporate fines higher. The average duration of mis-selling is static at 30 months. The average number of customers affected by individual mis-selling cases varies over time and in some years is quite low reflecting the variation in the scale of mis-selling cases.

Table 29.5 Markets affected by mis-selling

		Freq.	Duration	Fine level	Average no. customers affected
Panel A	Insurance	22	20.59	£794,773	109013
	Investment	50	31.74	£1,013,984	417
	Mortgage	21	28.36	£483,235	3324
	Pensions	14	27.57	£86,500	399

		Percentage of cases with concern			
		Misleading advertising	Information needs	Unsuitable advice	Monitoring staff
Panel B	Insurance	5%	82%	77%	68%
	Investment	40%	60%	63%	50%
	Mortgage	13%	71%	75%	42%
	Pensions	29%	57%	71%	50%

In Table 29.4 characteristics of mis-selling cases are outlined including different remedial actions, types of firm mis-selling, identified causes of mis-selling and whether the mis-selling firm had a target market. When punishing firms, fines are used in the majority of cases and customer redress is reported in over a fifth of cases. Other punishments include public censure where the FSA publicises a mis-selling incident and in 3 percent of cases the regulatory permission for a financial firm to operate has been removed or amended.

The different types of firm involved in mis-selling cases varies substantially from very large banks and insurers, including HSBC, Credit Suisse and Standard Life, to relatively small advisory firms acting as intermediaries in this market. Most mis-selling cases are associated with firms undertaking this intermediary role, distributing rather than writing or funding financial services. Intermediaries mis-selling financial services include nationally important law and accounting firms and more frequently small, often one person, investment and financial advisory firms. The total number of mis-selling cases associated with banks and insurers is just over a quarter of all cases. Finally, fewer than 10 percent of cases of mis-selling emerged from non-financial firms, such as motor dealers and furniture retailers. These firms have gained regulatory permissions for the supply of credit and in most cases have mis-sold payment protection insurance with credit.

The causes of mis-selling are also outlined in Table 29.4. For brevity, these are classified into four main groups: mis-leading advertising; failed information needs; provision of unsuitable advice; and failures in monitoring staff. These classifications are not mutually exclusive and in most cases involve two or more causes.

"Mis-leading advertising" was observed in just under a quarter of these cases and involves presenting customers with an inaccurate perspective of the financial service. This outcome is linked with adverse customer outcomes and often the incomplete description of risks posed by a financial service. For example in the sale of precipice bonds, concerns were raised when "the description of the products as 'fantastic' and 'excellent' investments was not accompanied by any explicit mention of the risks involved on that page" (Chase de Vere Financial Solutions plc (FSA 2004a: 9).

"Failed information needs" considers circumstances where errors occurred in recording information, most commonly customer information, and the justification of why the sale was advised. This failure is observed in 65 percent of cases and is a particular concern for intermediary firms. "Unsuitable advice" considers circumstances where an advisor has mis-lead a customer or recommended an inappropriate financial service and is reported in 68 percent of cases.

"Monitoring staff" considers all cases where advisors have operated outside of or despite of management control and without regulatory compliance. Common in these cases has been an advisor not fulfilling information requirements when recommending financial services, having insufficient training and encouraging customers to obtain financial services associated with higher commission levels. For example in the MLP Private Finance PLC case (2003), unqualified new graduates with little or no previous financial services experience were recruited to act as advisers. These advisers were instructed to develop final year university graduates as potential clients; a business model of allowing inexperienced and unqualified advisers to provide investment advice to young and inexperienced clients. In other cases commission bias is significant. In the Park Row case (2010), despite strong and clear guidance from management that commission bias is unacceptable, and removing the option for advisors to suggest financial services with the highest commission rates, commission bias was still identified in 19 percent of all cases.

In Table 29.5, customer groups targeted in mis-selling cases are described. Overall in three quarters of cases there is not a specific target market. In the remaining cases, firms have targeted customer groups for both genuine commercial reasons such as providing specialised services to high net worth or recently retired individuals, and also for less justifiable reasons. Concerns arise when firms target vulnerable customers, particularly the elderly (6 percent of cases) or inexperienced (2 percent of cases). For example in the HSBC (2011) case elderly customers were advised to obtain long term asset-backed investment products in order to fund long-term care costs. This advice and sale was unsuitable as the customers' life expectancy was below the recommended five-year investment period requiring customers to make early withdrawals from these investments at a high personal cost.

In Table 29.5, we examine the different financial services mis-sold. Four groups of products (insurance, investments, mortgages and pensions) are assessed relative to other case characteristics and also the causes of mis-selling. These product groups are considered in turn.

While a range of different insurances have been mis-sold in the UK within the 2002–11 period, most cases (86 percent) involve payment protection insurance (hereafter PPI). Most of the concerns arising in the sale of insurance have been failed information needs, such as appropriately recording customer information, the provision of unsuitable advice and problems with monitoring staff.

Turning to PPI, this insurance provides varying combinations of accident, sickness and unemployment insurance and is used to protect the loan payments of policyholders in the event of them losing their income. This financial service is unusual in that it provides cover to both the borrower if they default on their debt after an unexpected event or circumstance and also to the lender which is assured the loan will be repaid; an outcome attractive to many lenders (see Ashton and Hudson 2012, Ferran 2012). Subsequently many firms have encouraged customers to purchase PPI with lending often by suggesting the purchase of PPI is an expected or "normal" action in lending transactions. For example in the Alliance and Leicester PLC (2008) case an "assumptive" approach to sales was adopted where advisers sought to find a reason to recommend and sell PPI whenever customers applied for a personal loan.

There is significant diversity in the type and forms of investment mis-selling with concerns raised as to how sales are undertaken and also the complexity or value of these investments. Investments have been sold by a variety of sources, from financial advisors, and investment advisors, law and accounting firms as well as banks and building societies. Investment sales are linked to many causes of mis-selling including misleading advertising, failed information needs, unsuitable advice and monitoring staff.

Complex products are also frequently observed in this market. For example Geared Traded Endowment Policies have been sold in 4 cases. This form of investment involves the purchase of traded with-profits endowment policies which were no longer required by their original holder and have been sold on the secondary market. The purchaser of such policies agrees to pay the remaining premiums on the policy and in return receives the value of the policy at maturity or when the original owner dies, depending on which occurs first. The gearing in these investments involves the use of loans to purchase these investments in the hope of obtaining the pay-out. Of course borrowing to invest for an uncertain return is a specialised and high risk form of investment particularly when customers were encouraged to re-mortgage their homes for this purpose (for example, Integrity Financial Solutions Limited, FSA 2010). Concerns also arose when advisors recommending these services did not fully comprehend the inherent risks of these investments (for example, Knowlden Titlow Financial, FSA 2008). Concerns also arise with how firms have promoted a complex and higher risk investment to investors seeking a lower risk service. In such circumstances firms are "tempted to 'gild the lily' to such an extent that they mislead consumers, either by presenting a seriously unbalanced impression of their own products, or by way of misleading comparisons with alternatives" (The Ancient Order of Foresters Friendly Society Limited, FSA 2006b: 6).

In total, 24 mortgage mis-selling cases are reported and are particularly associated with poor information management and the provision of poor advice (71 percent and 75 percent of cases respectively). In most cases mortgage mis-selling involved equity release or residential mortgages although a substantial minority of cases considered more specialised mortgage products such as life time mortgages, interest only mortgages, self-certification mortgages, and endowment mortgages. Major concerns exist with the provision of poor advice to customers, an outcome linked with poor collection of customers' information. For example in the DB UK Bank Ltd (2010) case, mortgage advisors did not check that customers were less than 60 years of age at the time of application, with the danger that the mortgage would need to be repaid during a period of retirement. A number of cases also consider aspects of staff training and commission bias. For example in the Fastmoney.co.uk (2011) case advisors gave personal recommendations to customers, did not ensure customers had read and understood the mortgage details and offered many customers one particular mortgage based on their own judgement rather than presenting all options to the customers.

In total, 14 cases of pensions mis-selling are identified. Many of these cases involved pensions switching where individuals give up their occupational pension rights in exchange for a personal pension scheme. This is a long term problem in UK financial services with over 2 million sales of personal pensions in the 1990s (Black and Nobels 1998). Other concerns exist with pensions unlocking, withdrawal and early vesting – a practice involving the removal of funds from a pension prior to retirement. While this practice is legal, this service is expensive for the customer. While the FSA advice is that pension unlocking is rarely in anyone's long term financial interests and should only be considered in exceptional circumstances some firms presented these services in a more positive light. For example Read Independent Financial Advisers Limited (FSA 2004b: 7) were fined £150,000 for placing an advertisement on nineteen occasions stating "So you can pay off debts, pay for home improvements, holidays or a new car – all without the costs of borrowing someone else's money", clearly not indicating the associated risks and costs.

Conclusion

This chapter has examined the scale, scope and characteristics of financial mis-selling by firms in the UK over a ten-year period. The occurrence of mis-selling in the UK has risen over the 2002–2011 period and the level of fines has grown. Mis-selling is undertaken by a diversity of firms including both large and small and financial and non-financial firms, yet particularly financial advisory firms. The number of customers affected by financial mis-selling varies substantially year to year as mis-selling cases have also varied in scale. In most instances no specific type of customer is targeted in financial mis-selling yet where this does occur serious harm to customers can occur. The types of financial services mis-sold are considered. Insurance mis-selling is dominated by the mis-sale of payment protection insurance, especially through assumptive sales approaches. For investments, product complexity, the mis-representation of risks and limited customer and advisors' comprehension are all common concerns. For mortgages, mis-selling is associated with commission bias, poor information collection and subsequently inadequate product recommendations. For pensions, mis-representation of the costs of pension switching and early vesting services is a major concern.

While financial services mis-selling can appear to be an intractable problem, there have been a range of regulatory solutions forwarded to combat these practices in the UK (see HM Treasury 2010). One area of development has been the prohibition of commission based sales for financial services in 2013. While this change may reduce financial advice offered to customers, this move will eliminate commission bias. Secondly, there has been a tentative start at standardising financial services (Sergeant 2012). While this process needs to progress beyond deposit savings and protection financial services currently considered in the UK, this process of standardisation can reduce financial services complexity. The new financial regulator considering financial services marketing in the UK, the Financial Conduct Authority, also has new powers to alleviate some of the worst excesses of mis-selling. The new power to ban the sale of certain financial services to the retail market (FSA 2011) is a welcome step to reduce cases where clearly inappropriate services have been sold to all customers. The developing regulated status of persons undertaking financial services marketing decisions is also a significant development. How financial services marketing is undertaken can have far reaching implications for both firms and customers, costing billions in customer redress, destroying corporate reputations and harming customers' lives. Regulating and holding financial services marketers legally responsible for their actions is a long needed requirement in the financial services industry. Assessing the success or otherwise of these regulatory initiatives is a research priority going forward.

References

All the cases considered including the enforcement cases cited are publically available at www.fsa.gov.uk/pages/library/communication/notices/final

Aldridge, A. 1998. Habitus and cultural capital in the field of personal finance. *The Sociological Review*, 46(1) pp. 1–23.

Anagol, S., Cole, S. and Sarkar, S. 2013. Understanding the advice of commissions-motivated agents: evidence from the Indian life insurance market. *Working Paper* 12–055, Harvard Business School.

Ashton, J. K. and Hudson, R. S. 2012. The Mis-selling of payments protection insurance in mortgage and unsecured lending markets. In Juan Fernández de Guevara Radoselovics and José Pastor Monsálvez (eds.) *Bank Behaviour in Modern Banking*, Basingstoke: Palgrave McMillan.

Ashton, J. K. and Pressey, A. D. 2008. Regulatory Perception of Marketing: Interpreting UK Competition Authority Investigations from 1950 to 2005. *Journal of Public Policy and Marketing*, 27(2) pp. 156–64.

—— 2011. The Regulatory Challenge to Branding: An Interpretation of UK Competition Authority Investigations 1950–2005. *Journal of Marketing Management*, 27(9–10) pp. 1027–58.

Benartzi, S. 2001. Excessive extrapolation and the allocation of 401(k) accounts to company stock, *Journal of Finance*, 61(6) pp. 1747–64.

Benartzi, S. and Thaler, R. H. 2002. How much is investor autonomy worth. *Journal of Finance*, 62(4) pp. 1593–1616.

Black J. and Nobels, R. 1998. Personal pension misselling: the causes and lessons of regulatory failure. *The Modern Law Review*, 61(6) pp. 789–820.

Bos, W. and Tarnai, C. 1999. Content analysis in empirical social research. *International Journal of Educational Research*, 31(8) pp. 659–71.

Bucks, B. and Pence, K. 2008. Do borrowers know their mortgage terms? *Journal of Urban Economics*, 64(2) pp. 218–33.

Carlin, B. I. 2009. Strategic price complexity in retail financial markets. *Journal of Financial Economics*, 91(3) pp. 278–87.

Carlin, B. I. and Manso, G. 2010. Obfuscation, learning and the evolution of investor sophistication. *Review of Financial Studies*, 24(3) pp. 754–85.

Choi, J. J., Laibson, D. and Madrian, B. C. 2004. Plan design and 401(k) savings outcomes. *National Tax Journal*, 62(2) pp. 275–98.

Costanzo, L. and Ashton, J. K. 2006. Product Innovation and Consumer Choice in the UK Financial Services Industry. *Journal of Financial Regulation and Compliance*, 14(3) pp. 285–303.

Davies, S. W, Driffield, N. L. and Clarke, R. 1999. Monopoly in the UK: what determines whether the MMC finds against the investigated firms? *The Journal of Industrial Economics*, 47(3) pp. 263–83.

DellaVigna, S. and Malmendier, U. 2004. Contract theory and self-control: theory and evidence. *The Quarterly Journal of Economics*, 119(2) pp. 353–402.

Ellison, G. 2005. A model of add on pricing. *Quarterly Journal of Economics*, 120(2), pp. 585–637.

Emons, W. 2001. Credence goods monopolists. *International Journal of Industrial Organization*, 19(3–4) pp. 375–89.

Fehr, E. and Rangel, A. 2011. Neuroeconomic foundations of economic choice – recent advances. *Journal of Economic Perspectives*, 25(4) pp. 3–30.

Ferran, E. 2012. Regulatory lessons from the payment protection insurance mis-selling scandal in the UK. *European Business Organization Law Review*, 13(2) pp. 247–70.

Financial Services Authority (FSA) 2000. Informing consumers: a review of product information at the point of sale DP4. *The Financial Services Authority Discussion Papers*, London: The Financial Services Authority.

—— (2004a). *Final Notice – Chase de Vere Financial Solutions plc*, London.

—— (2004b). *Final Notice – Read Independent Financial Advisers Limited*, London.

—— 2006a. *Financial Capability in the UK: Establishing a Baseline*. London: The Financial Services Authority.

—— (2006b). *Final Notice – The Ancient Order of Foresters Friendly Society Limited*, London.

—— (2008). *Final Notice – Knowlden Titlow Financial*, London.

—— 2009. *The Turner Review. A regulatory response to the global banking crisis*, London: The Financial Services Authority.

—— (2010). *Final Notice – Integrity Financial Solutions Limited*, London.

—— 2011. *Product Intervention*, DP 11/1, London: The Financial Services Authority.

Financial Stability Board 2011. *Consumer finance protection with particular focus on credit*, Bank of International Settlements, Basel: Financial Stability Board.

Foot, M. 2004. The FSA: The first 6 years. *Journal of Financial Regulation and Compliance*, 12(3) pp. 201–5.

Frey, B. S. and Eichenberger, R. 1994. Economic incentives transform psychological anomalies. *Journal of Economic Behaviour and Organization*, 23(2) pp. 215–34.

Gabaix, X. and Laibson, D. 2006. Shrouded attributes, consumer myopia, and information suppression in competitive markets. *The Quarterly Journal of Economics*, 121(2) pp. 505–40.

Gower, L. C. B. 1988. "BIG BANG" and City Regulation *The Modern Law Review*, 51(1), pp. 1–22.

Hackethal, A, Haliassos, M. and Jappelli, T. 2012. Financial advisors: A case of babysitters? *Journal of Banking and Finance*, 36(2) pp. 509–24.

Hirshleifer, D. 2001. Investor psychology and asset pricing. *Journal of Finance*, 56(4), pp. 1533–97.

HM Treasury 2010. *A new approach to financial regulation: judgement, focus and stability*, Cm 7874, London: HM Treasury.

Huberman, G. and Jiang, W. 2006. Offering versus choice in 401(k) plans: equity exposure and number of funds. *Journal of Finance*, 61(2), pp. 763–801.

Inderst, R. and Ottaviani, M. 2009. Misselling through agents. *American Economic Review*, 99(3), pp. 883–908.

—— 2012a. How (not) to pay for advice: A framework for consumer financial protection. *Journal of Financial Economics*, 103(2) pp. 393–411.

—— 2012b. Financial advice. *Journal of Economic Literature*, 502(2) pp. 494–512.

—— 2012c. Competition through commissions and kickbacks. *American Economic Review*, 102(2) pp. 780–809.

Iyengar, S. S. and Lepper, M. R. 2000. When choice is demotivating: can one desire too much of a good thing? *Journal of Personality and Social Psychology*, 79(6), pp. 995–1006.

Kamenica, E. 2008. Contextual inference in markets: on the informational content of product lines. *American Economic Review*, 98(5) pp. 2127–49.

Kane, E. J. 1997. Ethical foundations of financial regulation. *Journal of Financial Services Research*, 12(1) pp. 51–74.

Kirsanova, T. and Sefton, J. 2007. A comparison of national saving rates in the UK, US and Italy. *European Economic Review*, 51(8) pp. 1998–2028.

Llewellyn, D. T. 1999. The economic rationale of financial regulation. *Occasional Paper* No. 1, London: The Financial Services Authority.

Lusardi, A, Schiender, D. and Tufano, P. 2011. Financially fragile households: evidence and implications. *Brooking Papers on Economic Activity*, Spring pp. 83–150.

Masciandaro, D. 2002. E Pluribus Unum? Authorities' design in financial supervision: trends and determinants. *Open Economies Review*, 17(1) pp. 73–102.

Parrish, L and Frank, L. 2011. An analysis of bank overdraft fees: pricing, market structure and regulation. *Journal of Economic Issues*, 45(2) pp. 353–61.

Pass, C., Sturgess, B. and Wilson, N. 1994. Advertising, barriers to entry and competition policy. *Journal of Product and Brand Management*, 3(3), pp. 51–58.

Peggs, K. 2000. Which pension? Women, risk and pension choice. *The Sociological Review*, 48(3) pp. 319–64.

Posner, R. A. 1970. A statistical study of antitrust enforcement. *Journal of Law and Economics*, 13(2) pp. 365–419.

Sergeant, C. 2012. *Sergeant Review of Simple Financial Products: Interim Report*, London: HM Treasury.

Shafir, E., Diamond, P. and Tversky, A. 1997. Money illusion. *The Quarterly Journal of Economics*, 112(2) pp. 341–74.

Simpson, S. S. and Koper, C. S. 1997. The changing of the guard: top management characteristics, organizational strain and antitrust offending. *Journal of Quantitative Criminology*, 13(4) pp. 373–404.

Synovate 2011. *Consumer market study on advice within the area of retail investment services final report*, Brussels: European Commission.

Wisniewski, T. P. and Lambe, B. 2013. The role of the media in the credit crunch: The case of the banking sector. *Journal of Economic Behaviour and Organization*, 85(1) pp. 163–75.

30

A framework for understanding and restoring trust in universal banks

Robert F. Hurley, Xue Gong and Adeela Waqar

Introduction

Those of us living in market economies are well removed from the time of our ancestors when each household was its own self-contained economic unit taking on the simultaneous roles of producer and consumer. Today, in many parts of the world, specialization and markets for converting goods into currency are so developed that a 14-year-old can sell goods using eBay to people he has never met. But we forget that none of this economic progress would have been possible without the social, structural, institutional and cognitive preconditions that enable market exchange, namely trust. Without the willingness of parties to rely on one another to fulfill obligations, markets break down and exchange grinds to a halt (as we saw during the height of the global financial crisis in 2008 when money stopped moving among banks). Experts and industry leaders agree on the integral role of trust in market exchange. Lloyd Blankfein, CEO of Goldman Sachs, testifying on April 27, 2010 at the US Senate Permanent Subcommittee on Investigations, described the effect on exchange when trust is lost at the firm level: "If our clients believe that we don't deserve their trust, we cannot survive." (Harper 2010). Joseph Stiglitz, the Nobel Prize-winning economist, suggested that trust was not only needed at the firm level but also at the industry or system level when he wrote: "Financial markets hinge on trust, and that trust has eroded." (Stiglitz 2008)

For the purposes of this chapter we define trust as a judgment of confident reliance by a person (a trustor) on a person, group, organization or system (a trustee) where there is uncertainty and risk (Hurley 2006, 2012). This definition emphasizes agents, not objects, but it is consistent with other marketing definitions of trust: a confidence and a willingness to rely on an exchange partner (Moorman et al. 1992), the perception of confidence in a partner (Morgan and Hunt 1994), a belief that a partner is able to perform effectively (Doney and Cannon 1997) and a willingness to rely on the brand to perform (Chaudhuri and Holbrook 2001).

When customers make purchases they are willing to become vulnerable by exchanging their money. They have a degree of confidence that these goods or services will, at some future time, meet their needs and perform as advertised. This represents a complex combination of product, brand and firm-level trust. For high-involvement products and services (for example, a real estate agent) one's decision to trust may involve calculation. For low-involvement products (for example, a candy bar), it may be a more emotional and even unconscious process (Laurent and Kapferer 1985). In either case, once the decision to trust or not to trust is made, it fundamentally affects that customer's, or for that matter any stakeholder's (for example, employee, investor, regulator), relationship to the trustee. For example, if a real estate agent betrays a client's trust, they may end the relationship or stop relying on their assertions. When trust is offered and validated by experience, all parties in an exchange (for example, employees, customers, investors, suppliers) develop improved relationships (Dirks and Ferrin 2001). When trust is violated, relationships end or enter into a challenging process of trust repair, as with the financial system post 2008 (Gillespie and Hurley 2013).

There is a rich body of research concerning the virtues and benefits of trust. Trust facilitates business transactions (Williamson 1993, Noteboom 1996), increases customer satisfaction (Doney and Cannon 1997), enhances employee motivation (Brockner et al. 1997, Tyler 2000) and promotes cooperative behavior within organizations (Gulati and Westphal 1999, Dirks and Ferrin 2001) and between organizational stakeholder groups (Gulati 1995, Jensen 2003). Trust also fosters commitment (Ganesan 1994, Mayer and Gavin 2005), creativity, innovation, and knowledge transfer (Edmondson 1999). From a financial return perspective, there is research that supports the view that firms with higher levels of employee trust perform better than peers as measured by return on assets and market-to-book value ratios (Fulmer et al. 2003).

The state of trust in financial services and banks

Research on trust and financial services has explored a number of important topics. Researchers have examined the importance of trust in brand identity of financial services firms (Chaudhuri and Holbrook 2001), the extent to which trust facilitates initial purchase (Dwyer et al. 1987) and the effect of trust on repeat purchase and loyalty (Doney and Cannon 1997, Delgado-Ballester et al. 2003, Ennew et al. 2011). They have found that perceived competence is critical to consumer perceptions of trustworthiness and loyalty intentions. These perceptions are affected by two aspects of banks: front-line service employees, management policies and practices (Shainesh 2012). Trust also affects behavioral loyalty of retail bank consumers (El-Manstrly et al. 2011).

Research on trust in financial services has been conducted at the individual consumer level (Liang and Wang 2005), the organizational level (Johnson and Grayson 2005) and even the institutional level of the financial system as a whole (Gillespie and Hurley 2013). This chapter will focus on how research on individuals' decisions to trust can be applied at the macro level in financial institutions and the financial system as a whole. It provides a framework to restore trust in banks after the devastating effects of the global financial crisis.

Trust is especially challenging to foster in the financial services industry. Financial services are highly intangible and therefore can be harder to understand, often involve pronounced information asymmetries where there is a heavy reliance on credence, qualities and advice and involve particularly high perceived risk when dealing with buyers' livelihoods (Harrison 2003). Within financial services, there is compelling evidence that trust in banking is at an all-time low but most of the public's ire is directed at the large universal banks with trust scores for regional and community banks and credit unions showing higher levels (Hurley et al. 2014). Trust scores for community banks, regional banks and credit unions are substantially higher than large banks (Hurley et al. 2014). We will argue that these differences in trust ratings have a great deal to do with the differences in how universal and community banks operate.

As this chapter discusses later, universal banks are large organizations that deal in commercial and investment services. They take savings deposits and also engage in lending, investment banking, underwriting of securities, trading and market making. Notable examples of such universal banks include BNP Paribas and Société Générale of France, HSBC, Standard Chartered Bank and RBS of the United Kingdom, Deutsche Bank of Germany, ING Bank of the Netherlands, Bank of America, Citigroup, JP Morgan Chase and Wells Fargo of the United States and UBS and Credit Suisse of Switzerland. Investment banks were historically separated from commercial banks and focused on advisory for mergers and acquisitions, securities underwriting, asset management and trading. Examples of traditional investment banks would include Morgan Stanley and Goldman Sachs. In the United States, this separation of commercial and investment banking ended with the repeal of the Glass-Steagall Act in 1999. Citibank coined the term "financial supermarket" to describe the strategy of lobbying for repeal of the act to enable the combining of commercial and investment banking to enable one-stop shopping. Credit unions, regional and community banks are other forms of financial institutions that concentrate on taking deposits and lending money to a more narrowly targeted group of stakeholders.

Gallup polls in the late 1970s showed that 60 percent of North Americans trusted big banks "a great deal" or "quite a lot". But by 2012 that number was down to 21 percent (Jacobe 2012). The decline of trust among the general public after the financial crisis was a global phenomenon (Edelman 2013). At the level of the financial system as a whole, Luis Aguilar, a commissioner at the US Securities and Exchange Commission, cited data showing that "79 percent of investors have no trust in the financial system" (Partnoy and Eisinger 2013). Similar skepticism is found among institutional stakeholders. A survey by Barclays Capital found that more than half of institutional investors did not trust how banks measure the riskiness of their assets (Partnoy and Eisinger 2013). When hedge-fund managers were asked how trustworthy they found the numbers that banks use to calculate their required capital cushions, about 60 percent gave a 1 or 2 rating on a five-point scale, with 1 being "not trustworthy at all". None of the hedge-fund managers gave the banks the highest rating (Partnoy and Eisinger 2013).

Distrust of universal banks has even become embedded in the culture. For example, the July 2, 2012 cover of the Economist about the LIBOR scandal was titled "Banksters" (gangsters) and the image of villainous, greedy bankers has provided the subject of a number of popular movies (for example, *Inside Job, Freefall, Margin Call, Rogue Trader, Too Big To Fail, Wall Street, Money Never Sleeps*).

A marketing foundation for organization level trust

The Blankfein and Stiglitz quotes presented earlier highlight the multi-level dimensions in which trust operates in markets. For decades, marketing scholars have recognized the need to consider additional stakeholders beyond customers, in order to develop a robust view of how firms compete, develop legitimacy and navigate the larger societies in which they operate (Achrol 1997, Greenley and Foxall 1998, Gummesson 1994, Kimery and Rinehart 1998, Menon and Menon 1997, Polonsky 1996, Polonsky et al. 1999, Reidenbach and McClung 1999, Slater 1997). Unfortunately, this call has gone largely unheeded and marketing has provided little in the way of thought leadership on the legitimacy of broader stakeholders' demands for firms to be more sustainable and socially responsible to maintain their license to operate (Sheth et al. 2000).

Some scholars have called the lack of research on diverse stakeholders the "new marketing myopia" referencing Ted Levitt's seminal article (Levitt 1960) on defining markets based on underlying needs rather than wants (Smith et al. 2010). A special issue in 2010 of the Journal of Public Policy and Marketing partially fills the void in marketing's attention to social responsibility, but stakeholder trust was not a central focus or theme of that issue. It is clear that marketing is well behind the curve in addressing how firms can develop relations of trust among the wider stakeholder groups that affect companies today. The lack of thought leadership in marketing is particularly unfortunate in banking given the dire state of stakeholder trust in the universal banks.

The dearth of marketing research on stakeholder trust in financial services is underscored in a landmark paper by Grayson et al. (2008). They showed that trust must be considered from both a firm level (narrow scope trust) and the wider industry context in which exchanges occur (broad scope trust). They also established a critical theoretical foundation for marketing research on trust in financial services. Specifically they found that marketing has exclusively been focused on narrow scope trust (product, salesperson, firm level) and ignored broad scope trust (social and industry system context); broad scope trust in the financial system affects consumer behavior and is fully mediated by firm level, narrow scope trust. This means that the proper way to understand trust related customer behavior is to measure both context-related (industry) and firm level trust factors, and purchase behavior and customer satisfaction in financial services requires the establishment of a high level of broad scope trust (financial system) and narrow scope trust (firm-level). These three findings argue for a more macro-focus on trust in banks.

Research conducted by Gillespie and Hurley (2013) on the loss of trust during the global financial crisis support the Grayson et al. (2008) formulation. They found that stakeholder trust was undermined not only by violations at the company level (for example, Bear Stearns, Lehman Brothers, Countrywide Financial, UBS, RBS) but also due to a lack of trustworthiness at the system level (regulators, government, central banks, etc.). Hurley (2010) points to aggressive government promotion of homeownership, lack of regulation (mortgages, credit default swaps, ratings agencies) and allowing exceptions to bank leverage ratios as some of the more egregious failures of governance of the financial system. The implication is that the work of restoring trust must happen at both the individual organization level and within the broader financial system.

An integrated and robust theoretical framework to properly understand trust in banks must encompass a trust ecosystem. This ecosystem is the interdependent chain of relationships that extends from suppliers to groups within the organization and ultimately to external groups including customers, investors, communities and regulators. The theoretical underpinnings of such a framework encompass relationship marketing, market orientation and stakeholder theory.

Scholars in relationship marketing suggested early on that marketing should be focused on successful relationship exchanges and that trust was a central aspect to relationship commitment in all exchanges (Morgan and Hunt 1994). From a market orientation perspective, researchers have argued that marketers needed to provide "superior customer value while considering the interests of other stakeholders" (Slater 1997, Kohli and Jaworski 1990, Slater and Narver 1995). However, while recognizing the importance of other stakeholders, there has been little research in market orientation beyond customers (Ferrell et al. 2010).

Stakeholder theory concerns itself with the relationships between the firm and constituent groups (stakeholders) that affect and are affected by its decisions (Freeman 1984). Scholars typically examine firm relationships with stakeholders including customers, employees, investors, local and national communities and other interest groups (for example, environmental groups). A central tenet of stakeholder theory is that the interests of all legitimate stakeholders have value and it is critical that firm decisions consider all of these interests (Donaldson and Preston 1995). Instrumental stakeholder theorists argue that exchange with stakeholders, where there is mutual trust and cooperation, can lead to competitive advantage (Jones 1995). Interestingly, trust relations are at the core of relationship marketing, stakeholder theory, market orientation and resource-based theory of competitive advantage. These theoretical perspectives can be used to build a more comprehensive framework to understand trust in banks.

A framework for restoring trust in banks

Drawing on the theoretical foundations in marketing and management research, we offer a Stakeholder Trust Model of Organizations that provides a framework for understanding and managing trust. While the model can be applied to companies in any industry, this chapter will concentrate on its application to trust in banks, with a particular focus on universal banks. The model in Figure 30.1 describes this integrated framework. It considers the wider set of firm relations (stakeholder theory), locates the firm within the context of value creation and markets (market orientation) and articulates a chain of trust built both outside of and within the organization in order to sustain reputational advantage (relationship marketing). This model attempts to move marketing from a narrow focus on customers to encompass other stakeholders. It underscores the need for internal marketing throughout the value chain to develop high-quality relationships and competitive advantage.

In this model, firms are embedded within a context in which regulators create externalities that affect both stakeholders and companies directly. The desire, but often not the result, is that regulations will provide a common and understandable set of norms and practices that are trust enabling. Other stakeholders (investors, suppliers, potential customers, potential employees and communities) provide resources to, affect and are affected by the organization. These stakeholders may choose to initiate, end or maintain a relationship with the firm. If they choose to enter into a relationship with the firm, they may also choose a trust or distrust orientation to the relationship that affects their degree of cooperation with the firm. For example, the supplier that believes the firm will act opportunistically to take advantage of vulnerability (win/lose competitive orientation) may engage with the firm but will lack trust and take on a competitive orientation to maximize gains and minimize losses. Conversely, when a stakeholder decides that the firm is trustworthy (can be confidently relied upon) there will be more cooperation, collaboration and value creation (a win/win cooperative orientation). These dynamics of high and low trust and the effect on exchange relationships, are well documented in the literature on trust (Dirks and Ferrin 2001, McEvily and Zaheer 2006).

The stakeholder model of organization trust follows research on organization level trust and shows that most major trust violations have systemic root causes (Hurley et al. 2013). For example, both internal and external investigators of BP's 2010 Gulf of Mexico oil spill revealed that there were systemic operational flaws on the rigs and an operational culture emphasizing profit over safety. Toyota's reputational damage from unintended acceleration was due to a Tokyo-centric and overly centralized recall system. Barclays LIBOR and other trust violations were caused in part by weak HR and compliance functions and a company culture focused more on rapid growth than stakeholder trust (Salz 2013).

The research on systemic roots of trust and distrust shows that the firms able to successfully avoid trust violations do so because trustworthiness is deeply and pervasively embedded throughout the organization (Hurley et al. 2013, Gillespie and Hurley 2013). For example, Proctor and Gamble has strong core processes, along with effective executive development and succession routines, to ensure ethical and trustworthy leadership. Other firms that manifest the organizational systems that enable high trust are Ernst & Young, Microsoft, Quiktrip, Zappos and Starbucks, among others (Hurley 2012).

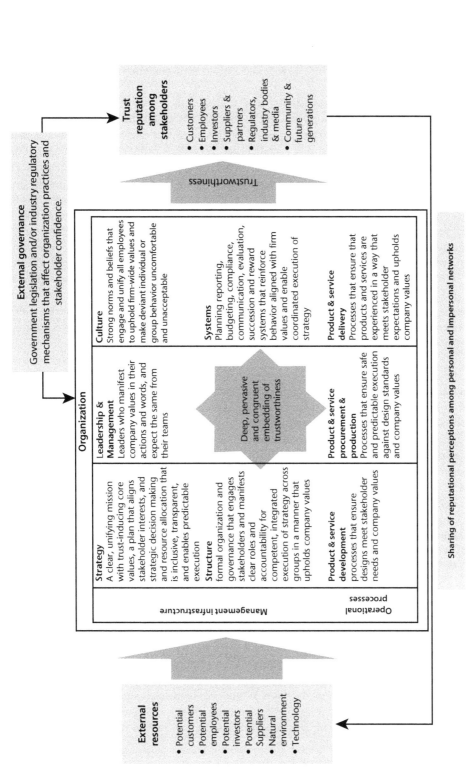

External governance
Government legislation and/or industry regulatory mechanisms that affect organization practices and stakeholder confidence.

Organization

Management infrastructure

Strategy
A clear, unifying mission with trust-inducing core values, a plan that aligns stakeholder interests, and strategic decision making and resource allocation that is inclusive, transparent, and enables predictable execution

Structure
formal organization and governance that engages stakeholders and manifests clear roles and accountability for competent, integrated execution of strategy across groups in a manner that upholds company values

Leadership & Management
Leaders who manifest company values in their actions and words, and expect the same from their teams

Culture
Strong norms and beliefs that engage and unify all employees to uphold firm-wide values and make deviant individual or group behavior uncomfortable and unacceptable

Systems
Planning reporting, budgeting, compliance, communication, evaluation, succession and reward systems that reinforce behavior aligned with firm values and enable coordinated execution of strategy

Deep, pervasive and congruent embedding of trustworthiness

Operational processes

Product & service development
processes that ensure designs meet stakeholder needs and company values

Product & service procurement & production
Processes that ensure safe and predictable execution against design standards and company values

Product & service delivery
Processes that ensure that products and services are experienced in a way that meets stakeholder expectations and upholds company values

Trust reputation among stakeholders
• Customers
• Employees
• Investors
• Suppliers & partners
• Regulators, industry bodies & media
• Community & future generations

Trustworthiness

External resources
• Potential customers
• Potential employees
• Potential investors
• Potential Suppliers
• Natural environment
• Technology

Sharing of reputational perceptions among personal and impersonal networks

Figure 30.1   Stakeholder trust model of organizations

While the stakeholder trust model of organizations provides a framework for understanding the process of how the various elements of organization and regulation can influence stakeholder trust, it does not answer the key content question: what attributes signal trustworthiness?

Russell Hardin, a preeminent scholar on trust, was one of the first to suggest that the crisis we are experiencing is not of trust but of trustworthiness (Hardin 2002). Hurley (2012) has outlined a conceptualization that supports this by suggesting that trust is something that trustors extend to a trustee when they consider that agent trustworthy. Trustworthiness has to do with the cues and signals which research shows are used to make the trust judgment. Ennew and Sekhon, in Chapter 10, provide a detailed discussion of trust and trustworthiness. In the trust literature, the elements comprising trustworthiness are often described as the antecedents to trust. In fact, an examination of how trust is measured shows that some scholars have used global measures of trust (degree of confidence, willingness to be vulnerable and degree of trust/distrust) and others have measured trust using perceptions concerning specific facets of trustworthiness (ability, benevolence, integrity) which aggregate into an overall measure of trust (Dietz and Den Hartog 2006, McEvily and Tortoriello 2011). Marketing researchers have explored this antecedents approach to trust, but as noted earlier, the emphasis has been more at a micro level (product, service or salesperson level) than macro level (organization or system level). For example, Johnson and Grayson (2005) noted five dimensions as the antecedents of trust in a financial services context (expertise, product performance, firm reputation, satisfaction with previous interactions and similarity).

One way to understand the erosion of trust in banks is to examine the original multi-level cues, which undermined perceptions of trustworthiness. This approach is also helpful in restoring trust because it helps to locate the elements of the socio-technical systems within and around the banks that caused signals of untrustworthy behavior to be emitted. To understand how to manage trust, Hurley (2006, 2012) developed a "decision to trust" model based on an exhaustive review of the literature on trust that identifies the fundamental cues that define and signal trustworthiness across a wide range of stakeholders and situations. Recognizing that there will be situational and stakeholder differences in the relative importance of elements of trustworthiness, no weighting scheme is advanced in the general "decision to trust" model. The full model has 4 variables that reflect trust or dispositional and situational risk factors and 6 broad relational dimensions of trustworthiness. For the purposes of this chapter, because dispositional and situational risk factors are difficult to change, we will concentrate on the six relational elements of the model that define how stakeholders make trust judgments:

- Similarities: does the trustee share the trustor's values, beliefs or identity?
- Aligned interests: do the trustee's interests coincide rather than conflict with those of the trustor?
- Benevolent intentions: does the trustee care about the trustor's welfare?
- Capability: is the trustee capable of delivering on commitments?
- Predictability and integrity: does the trustee abide by commonly accepted ethical standards (for example, honesty, fairness, and deeds match words) and is the trustee predictable?
- Open and transparent communication: does the trustee listen and engage in open and mutual dialogue?

The elements of trustworthiness and how they can manifest in the social and operating systems of a bank will be further illustrated in the next section.

Illustrating the trust framework in banking

The stakeholder trust model of organizations and the decision to trust model are helpful in diagnosing trust issues and conceptualizing interventions to restore trust. It is important to note at the outset that there are different types of banks with different business models, cultures and operating systems. Interestingly, some of these differences have been shown to relate directly to trust (Gangahar 2011). For example, when community banks focus on local development, they naturally develop similarity and identity bonds with savers and their communities.

Table 30.1 offers some data to compare universal banks and community banks. We will use this comparative analysis to illustrate the root causes of the erosion of trust among certain universal banks, many of which have been labeled "too-big-to-fail", and the growth of trust among some community banks. Given the very small sample on cases used here, this analysis should be considered an exploratory attempt to apply the model to understanding trust in banks. The data for Table 30.1 comes from the 2013 Salz Review on Barclays, newspaper accounts and two case studies on community banks (Arena 2011). Many, if not all, of the facts noted for Barclays are also true for Citibank, Bank of America, RBS, UBS and the other big banks. What makes Barclays unique is that they conducted a fully independent investigation of their practices and made the entire review public in early April of 2013. So as not to punish this trust-inducing act of transparency, we will refer to universal banks in the text and not single out Barclays, because there is ample evidence showing that these underlying issues are also factors at these other banks.

Similarities

Social identity theory confirms that when trustees are seen as different, strange, out of touch or otherwise dissimilar in identity and values, trust is inhibited. Table 30.1 points out some fundamental differences in how universal and community banks differ on value congruence and common identity bonds that enhance trust. As the stakeholder trust model of organization shows, creating value congruence among firm members and the external stakeholders they serve begins with mission, strategy and culture, which influences firm actions concerning external stakeholders. This process seemed to break down in Universal banks where there were different cultures in different parts of the banks and strong values concerning compensation and market returns. Various press reports and reviews (for example, Salz 2013) have suggested that the general public does not understand how investment banks contribute to the economy and why management compensation levels are so high. This feeds into a narrative that greedy, elite bankers are reaping oversized compensation at the expense of average citizens. At the community banks, employees and stakeholders were united by more common values and the media and reputational narrative were quite different.

Restoring the similarities aspect of trustworthiness to pre-violation levels is not simply a PR challenge for the Universal banks. These banks must embed more value congruence with legitimate publics in their mission and strategies. This will require them to revisit their purpose and reason for being in a very fundamental way. Once they have done this, the banks need to develop an education, engagement and public relations approach that communicates some value congruence, justifying the bank's business model and compensation schemes. As an example, Barclays has adopted the mission statement: "Helping people achieve their ambitions – the right way". To the degree that this notion is genuinely integrated into their strategy, culture and external communications it may, over time, help the public see the bank as making a contribution to society and therefore increase value congruence.

Table 30.1 Comparison between universal and community banks in terms of trustworthiness

Trustworthiness Factors	Universal banks	Community banks	
	Barclays	Wainwright	People's United
Similarities	• Lack of common culture. • Market risk-focused more than client-focused. • Compensation of elite seen as unfair.	• Empowerment of savers. • Social justice focus. • Community identity. • Common values embedded among employees.	• Strong common culture. • Community identity. • Quality of life.
Alignment of interests	• Incentives over emphasized financial returns for the bank. • Bank-client conflicts of interests that were not disclosed.	• Keeps an interest in community mortgages. • Strong multi-stakeholder focus not just shareholders. • Diverse board of directors. • Social benefit business model.	• Focused on the thrift and saver benefit.
Capability	• Good at fixing compliance issues but not addressing underlying causes. • Poor organizational learning from mistakes. • Rapid growth of investment banking and failure to grow organizational capabilities.	• Slow growth model and internal development of capability.	• Slow growth model and internal development of capability. • Prudent leverage. (Halted mortgage lending in 2006)
Benevolent intentions	• Numerous due care violations (LIBOR, Mortgages).	• Strong service and long term orientation to savers and community.	• Strong service and long term orientation to savers and community.
Predictability and integrity	• Under emphasis on compliance. • Challenged and tested regulatory boundaries. • Illegal credit card default charges. • High degree of customer complaints.	• Strong core processes centered around limited product and service offers. • Consistent ratings of service quality and customer satisfaction.	• Strong core processes centered around limited product and service offers. • Consistent ratings of service quality and customer satisfaction. • Clean balance sheet.
Communication	• Lack of candor. • Failure to engage and listen to external stakeholders. • Deception in disclosing mortgage insurance fees.	• Leadership promotes listening and responding.	• Intense community engagement.

Source: Salz Review of Barclays April 2013; Spitzeck, H., Pirson, M., and Dierksmeier, C., ed. 2011. *Banking with Integrity: The Winners of the Financial Crisis?.* London: Palgrave McMillan.

Alignment of interests

To the degree that interests of trustors and trustees are conflicting rather than aligned, distrust is often the prudent decision. Chapter 34 of this book, concerning ethics and selling, points out numerous instances where compensation schemes create conflicts of interest in financial services. As Table 30.1 points out, the strategy and business models of the community banks created strong alignment with trustors but weak alignment at the universal banks. The size and scope of the one-stop shopping banks makes conflicts of interests more likely. Consider for example the Merrill Lynch analyst who was under pressure to write reports about Enron that would help his company acquire Enron's equity underwriting business (Oppel 2002). Goldman Sachs was labeled as "unethical" in Senate hearings and fined 550 million dollars by the SEC for failing to disclose conflicts of interests in selling clients instruments that were described as "designed to fail". Barclays' advisory service was fined for steering its client, Del Monte, to structure a transaction in a way that may have hurt the client but helped Barclays win more business (Salz 2013). The Volcker Rule, which prohibits large banks from engaging in risky proprietary trading when it takes in government guaranteed deposits, is also an attempt to create more alignment with public interests.

Alignment of interests to enhance stakeholder trust requires an evaluation of the scope of the banks' products and services and elimination of conflicts that have the potential to create legal and reputational damage. Some banks, such as UBS and Morgan Stanley, have already begun shrinking or shedding businesses to narrow their focus to reduce conflicts, risks and complexity. This creates better alignment of interests with the remaining stakeholders and it should improve trust. It should also be noted that it is possible that in some ways reducing the scope of offered products and services could create competitive disadvantages. If this is the case banks must engage regulators to create a level playing field that extends industry-wide.

Capability

Distrust follows perceptions of incompetence. Table 30.1 points out systemic differences between universal and community banks concerning the scope of their products and services and their capabilities. Various agents sorting through the rubble of the global financial crisis have noted a number of trust violations that occurred because of basic competence issues (Salz 2013, McDonald and Robinson 2010). In fact, the apt title of the book about the failure of Lehman Brothers was "*A Colossal Failure of Common Sense*".

A number of highly prominent bankers (for example, Paul Volcker, Sallie Krawcheck, Robert Rubin, Sandy Weill) came out and suggested that the large banks had grown too large and too complex to be effectively managed (Volcker 2010, Toonkel and Grenon 2012, Belvedere 2013, Rattner 2012). The changes required in capability needed to improve trust include more effective risk management (Van Greuning and Bratanovic 2009), improved responsiveness to customer complaints (Salz 2013) and improved ability to evaluate new business in terms of potential reputation risk (Goldman Sachs Grp. 2011, Salz 2013). To the degree that universal banks develop the competencies needed to deliver on all stakeholder expectations, trust will be improved.

Benevolence

In making the trust-distrust decision, trustors' view of trustees' intentions and motivations has a powerful framing effect. We tend to trust those who we believe have an internal disposition to treat others as they would like to be treated and maintain positive relations (for example, with fairness, honesty, kindness). Table 30.1 points out some major differences among banks concerning benevolence. In newspaper reports and investigative hearings, large banks have been characterized as vampire squids, sharks and out for themselves at clients' expense (Taibbi 2010, Levin and Coburn 2010). Email exchanges between ratings agencies and investment bankers used the expression, IBGYBG which stands for "I'll be gone, you'll be gone" to suggest that the deal should just get done without concern for the negative effect on others (Levin and Coburn 2010).

Moving from low to high benevolence will require a fundamental culture change in these institutions. All of these reports and investigations point to a culture of doing deals, having a transactions focus and less emphasis on client service and long-term relationships. While the universal banks may never match the benevolence of many community banks where savers are their neighbors, to the degree that banking can facilitate economic progress and creation of jobs, an opportunity for expressing benevolence and altruism is real. Developing a culture of stewardship offers an opportunity to repair trust. Such a culture would be far from the annual bonus tournament where participants (individuals and firms) compare the size of their bonus trophies to see who is "best".

Predictability and integrity

Before we can trust a person or a firm we must be able to predict how they will behave at some time in the future. People and companies that are impulsive and erratic tend not to be trusted. Table 30.1 presents a sharp distinction between universal and community banks and the integrity of their practices versus their espoused values. As the stakeholder trust model shows, these integrity violations stem from a lack of congruence in the mission, values, leadership, culture and incentives at play within the universal banks.

Regulation and compliance will never create perceptions of trustworthiness unless the spirit of operating in an ethical and reliable manner is internalized in the culture of the firm. The Salz Review (2013) noted that Barclays had a very weak compliance function and their compensation schemes emphasized growth and profit, not operational excellence and compliance. Wal-Mart recently took the innovative step towards embedding compliance into its culture by linking executive compensation with compliance targets (Mont 2013). Banks could do the same and take the added step of assessing integrity and trustworthiness as part of 360-degree performance reviews and selection and promotion criteria for all managers.

Communication

Productive and trusting relationships, whether personal or corporate, require clear and open communication to avoid differences in expectations that are at the heart of most, perhaps all, trust violations. Poor communication, a lack of engagement and perhaps arrogance and deception on the part of banks has led to trust and reputation problems. It would be unfair and unreasonable to expect larger universal banks to match the level of community engagement noted in Table 30.1 for community banks. However, for the large universal banks a few areas warrant re-assessment. One area is improvement in product and service disclosures. For example, Goldman Sachs created an instrument (Abacus) which was designed-to-fail (default) with the help of one client (the Paulson project) and sold it to other Goldman clients to whom the Paulson project was not disclosed. Barclays was criticized for deceptive disclosures in selling mortgage insurance. Borrowers were left with no option for refund if the loan was paid off early, the impression that they would not get the loan if they did not take the insurance, and an overall confusion about the real cost of the insurance (Salz 2013). In general, banks need to re-examine how they communicate offers to clients. Information must be presented clearly and clients should be encouraged to take the time to read and understand disclosure statements prior to signing agreements. Behavioral science should be used to structure default options and client communications to protect customers' interests (Sunstein 2013).

Going forward, it seems clear that the communications function in banks should be given more power and influence. While some might argue that the C-Suite as a group must own trust, as a practical matter someone must drive the agenda and hold management accountable. The Chief Communications Officer (CCO) often has the wide strategic purview and the communication skills to perform this role well. Elevating the role of the CCO will also signal a cultural change that insularity and firm profits will no longer trump long-term stakeholder trust as a priority.

Conclusion

While this chapter has applied a broad, theory-based model in answering the question of why universal banks have struggled with trust, the framework certainly has applicability in other financial services contexts. For example, credit card companies, financial advisors and insurance companies all rely on trust for exchange and must therefore create organizations that can consistently demonstrate alignment of interests, benevolent concern, predictability and other signs of trustworthiness. To the degree that these and other markers of trustworthiness are embedded into the DNA of financial services companies, they will be more likely to create a chain of trust that sustains positive relations between the organization and its various stakeholders. More work is needed in order to connect the essential macro-organizational aspects of trustworthiness to loyalty and profitability of financial services firms.

Researchers in marketing should add more macro-level thinking and measures to understand banks. They have been too myopic and must broaden their focus to include all stakeholders' trust relationships. Developing more robust frameworks to think about building and repairing trust at multiple levels and within different constituencies requires new ways of thinking about marketing and how firms manage the internal-external value chain. As it relates to trust, we cannot understand the phenomenon accurately by only focusing at the transaction or product level. We must include the brand and firm level reputational factors as well as industry level perceptions. All of this requires a broader multi-level stakeholder perspective in our research.

As it relates to executives at universal banks, development is needed in a number of areas. Banks require more integrated, influential and powerful leaders in the areas of marketing, corporate social responsibility, sustainability, communication and compliance. These bank leaders and the C-Suite in general across industries, need a new strategic framework that goes beyond the new marketing myopia and silos of compliance towards building authentically trustworthy organizations. Barclays has made a very good start with its independent and highly transparent "warts and all" review. Hopefully others will follow Barclays' lead and begin a slow and steady journey towards building a foundation of trustworthiness that warrants renewed trust.

References

Achrol, R.S., 1997. Changes in the theory of inter-organizational relations in marketing: toward a network paradigm. *Journal of the Academy of Marketing Science*, 25(1), pp. 56–71.

Arena, C., 2010. Wainwright Bank and Trust Case Study-Humanistic Management in Practice. In: Spitzeck, H., Pirson, M. and Dierksmeier, C., eds. 2011. *Banking with Integrity: The Winners of the Financial Crisis?* London: Palgrave McMillan. Ch. 13.

Belvedere, M. J., 2013. Breaking up banks won't solve 'Too big to fail:' Rubin. *CNBC.com*, available at www.cnbc.com/id/100443238 (accessed on 7 February 2013).

Brockner, J., Siegel, P.A., Daly, J. P., Tyler, T. and Martin, C., 1997. When trust matters: The moderating effect of outcome favorability. *Administrative Science Quarterly*, 42, pp. 558–83.

Chaudhuri, A. and Holbrook, M.B., 2001. The chain of effects from brand trust and brand affect to brand performance: the role of brand loyalty. *The Journal of Marketing*, 65(2), pp. 81–93.

Delgado-Ballester, E., Munuera-Aleman, J.L. and Yague-Guillen, M.J., 2003. Development and validation of a brand trust scale. *International Journal of Market Research*, 45(1), pp. 35–54.

Dietz, G. and Den Hartog, D.N., 2006. Measuring trust inside organisations. *Personnel Review*, 35(5), pp. 557–88.

Dirks, K.T. and Ferrin, D. L., 2001. The role of trust in organizational settings. *Organization Science*, 12(4), pp. 450–67.

Donaldson, T. and Preston, L.E., 1995. The stakeholder theory of the corporation: Concepts, evidence, and implications. *Academy of Management Review*, 20(1), pp. 65–91.

Doney, P.M. and Cannon, J.P., 1997. An examination of the nature of trust in buyer-seller relationships. *Journal of Marketing*, 61, pp. 35–51.

Dwyer, F.R., Schurr, P.H. and Oh, S., 1987. Developing Buyer-Seller Relationships. *The Journal of Marketing*, 51(2), pp. 11–27.

Edmondson, A., 1999. Psychological safety and learning behavior in work teams. *Administrative Science Quarterly*, 44(2), pp. 350–83.

Edelman, R., 2013. *Edelman trust barometer 2013*.

El-Manstrly, D., Paton, R., Veloutsou, C. and Moutinho, L., 2011. An empirical investigation of the relative effect of trust and switching costs on service loyalty in the UK retail banking industry. *Journal of Financial Services Marketing*, 16(2), pp. 101–10.

Ennew, C., Kharouf, H. and Sekhon, H., 2011. Trust in UK financial services: A longitudinal analysis. *Journal of Financial Services Marketing*, 16(1), pp. 65–75.

Ferrell, O.C., Gonzalez-Padron, T.L., Hult, G.T.M. and Maignan, I., 2010. From market orientation to stakeholder orientation. *Journal of Public Policy & Marketing*, 29(1), pp. 93–96.

Freeman, R.E., 1984. *Strategic Management: A stakeholder approach*. Boston, MA: Pitman.

Fulmer, I. S., Gerhart, B. and Scott, K. S., 2003. Are the 100 best better? An empirical investigation of the relationship between being a "great place to work" and firm performance. *Personnel Psychology*, 56(4), pp. 965–93.

Ganesan, S., 1994. Determinants of long-term orientation in buyer-seller relationships. *Journal of Marketing*, 58(2), pp. 1–19.

Gangahar, A., 2011. People's United Bank-Humanistic Management in Practice. In Spitzeck, H., Pirson, M., and Dierksmeier, C., ed. 2011. *Banking with Integrity: The Winners of the Financial Crisis?* London: Palgrave McMillan. Ch. 10.

Gillespie, N. and Hurley, R.F., 2013. Trust and the global financial crisis. In Bachmann, R., and Zaheer, A., *Handbook of trust research*. Cheltenham: Edward Elgar.

Goldman Sachs Grp., Inc., *Goldman Sachs Announces Publication of Business Standards Committee Report*, 2011. available at www.goldmansachs.com/media-relations/press-releases/archived/2011/bsc-rep.html (accessed 11 January 2011).

Grayson, K., Johnson, D. and Chen, D.R., 2008. Is firm trust essential in a trusted environment? How trust in the business context influences customers. *Journal of Marketing Research*, 45(2), pp. 241–56.

Greenley, G.E. and Foxall, G.R., 1998. External moderation of associations among stakeholder orientations and company performance. *International Journal of Research in Marketing*, 15(1), pp. 51–70.

Gulati, R., 1995. Does familiarity breed trust? The implications of repeated ties for contractual choice in alliances. *Academy of Management Journal*, 38(1), pp. 85–112.

Gulati, R. and Westphal, J. D., 1999. Cooperative or controlling? The effects of CEO-board relations and the content of interlocks on the formation of joint ventures. *Administrative Science Quarterly*, 44(3), pp. 473–506.

Gummesson, E., 1994. Making relationship marketing operational. *International Journal of Service Industry Management*, 5(5), pp. 5–20.

Hardin, R., 2002. *Trust and Trustworthiness*. New York, NY: Russell Sage.

Harper, C., 2010. Goldman's Blankfein Says Firm Didn't Bet against Clients. *Bloomberg BusinessWeek.* April 26th.

Harrison, T., 2003. Why trust is important in customer relationships and how to achieve it. *Journal of Financial Services Marketing*, 7(3), pp. 206–9.

Hurley, R. F., 2006. The decision to trust. *Harvard Business Review*, 84(9), pp. 55–62.

——, 2010. A systems approach to restoring trust in the financial markets. In: EIASM (European Institute for Advanced Studies in Management), *5th Workshop on trust within and between organizations*. Madrid, Spain, 28–29 May, 2010.

——, 2012. *The decision to trust: how leaders create high trust organizations*. San Francisco, CA: Jossey-Bass.

——, 2012. The trustworthy leader: The first step toward creating high-trust organizations. *Leader to Leader*, 12 Sep. pp. 33–39.

Hurley, R.F., Gillespie, N. Ferrin, D.L. and Dietz, G., 2013. Designing trustworthy organizations. *MIT Sloan Management Review*, 54(4), pp. 75–82.

Hurley, R., Gong, X., and Waqar, A. 2014. Understanding the loss of trust in large banks. *International Journal of Bank Marketing*, 32(5), pp. 348–366.

Jacobe, D., 2012. *American's Confidence in Banks Falls to Record Low*. available at www.gallup.com/poll/ 155357/americans-confidence-banks-falls-record-low.aspx (accessed 27 June 2012).

Jensen, M.C., 2003. *A Theory of the firm: governance, residual claims, and organizational forms*. Cambridge, MA: Harvard University Press.

Johnson, D. and Grayson, K., 2005. Cognitive and affective trust in service relationships. *Journal of Business Research*, 58(4), pp. 500–507.

Jones, T.M., 1995. Instrumental stakeholder theory: a synthesis of ethics and economics. *Academy of Management Review*, 20(2), pp. 404–37.

Kimery, K.M. and Rinehart, S.M., 1998. Markets and constituencies: an alternative view of the marketing concept. *Journal of Business Research*, 43(3), pp. 117–24.

Kohli, A.K. and Jaworski, B.J., 1990. Market Orientation: the construct, research propositions, and managerial implications. *Journal of Marketing*, 54(2), pp. 1–18.

Laurent, G. and Kapferer, J.N., 1985. Measuring consumer involvement profiles. *Journal of Marketing Research*, 22(1), pp. 41–53.

Levin, C. and Coburn, T., (2010). Memorandum to the members of the Permanent Subcommittee on Investigations, 2010. *Wall Street and the financial crisis: the role of high risk loans*, Available at www.levin. senate.gov/newsroom/press/release/?id=adbfc45a-1147-4a3f-9547-9f3c9efa4848 (accessed 27 April 2010).

Levitt, T., 1960. Marketing myopia. *Harvard Business Review*, 38(4), pp. 24–47.

Liang, C.J. and Wang, W.H., 2005. Integrative research into the financial services industry in Taiwan: Relationship bonding tactics, relationship quality and behavioral loyalty. *Journal of Financial Services Marketing*, 10(1), pp. 65–83.

Mayer, R.C. and Gavin, M.B., 2005. Trust in management and performance: who minds the shop while the employees watch the boss? *Academy of Management Journal*, 48(5), pp. 874–88.

McDonald, L.G. and Robinson, P., 2010. *A colossal failure of common sense: The inside story of the collapse of Lehmann Brothers*. New York, NY: Crown Business.

McEvily, B. and Tortoriello, M., 2011. Measuring trust in organisational research: Review and recommendations. *Journal of Trust Research*, 1(1), p. 23–36.

McEvily, B. and Zaheer, A., 2006. Does trust still matter? Research on the role of trust in inter-organizational exchange. *Handbook of trust research*, pp. 280.

Menon, A, and Menon, A., 1997. Enviropreneurial marketing strategy: the emergence of corporate enviromentalism as marketing strategy. *Journal of Marketing*, 61(1), pp. 51–67.

Mont, J., 2013. Walmart links executive pay to success of compliance programs. *Compliance Week*, available at www.complianceweek.com/walmart-links-executive-pay-to-success-of-compliance-programs/ article/290190 (accessed on 23 April 2013).

Moorman, C., Zaltman, G. and Deshpandé, R., 1992. Relationship between providers and users of market research: the dynamic of trust within and between organizations. *Journal of Marketing Research*, 29(3), pp. 314–28.

Morgan, R.M. and Hunt S.D., 1994. The commitment-trust theory of relationship marketing. *Journal of Marketing*, 58(3), pp. 20–38.

Noteboom, B., 1996. Trust, opportunism and governance: A process and control model. *Organizational Studies*, 17(6), pp. 985–1010.

Oppel Jr, R.A., 2002. Merrill replaced research analyst who upset Enron. *New York Times*, 30 Jul. p. A1.

Partnoy, F. and Eisinger, J., 2013. What's Inside America's Banks? *Atlantic Monthly*, available at www.theatlantic.com/magazine/archive/2013/01/whats-inside-americas-banks/309196 (accessed 2 January 2013).

Polonsky, M.J., 1996. Stakeholder management and the stakeholder matrix: potential strategic marketing tools. *Journal of Marketing-Focused Management*, 1(3), pp. 209–29.

Polonsky, M.J., Suchard, H. T. and Scott, D. R., 1999. The incorporation of an interactive external environment: an extended model of marketing relationships. *Journal of Strategic Marketing*, 7(1), pp. 41–55.

Rattner, S., 2012. Regulate, don't split up, huge banks. *New York Times*, available at www.nytimes.com/2012/08/01/opinion/sanford-weills-glass-steagall-distraction.html?_r=0 (accessed on 31 July 2012).

Reidenbach, R.E. and McClung, G.W., 1999. Managing stakeholder loyalty. *Marketing Health Services*, 19(1), p. 20.

Salz, A., 2013. *The Salz Review*: An independent review of Barclays' Business Practices. Available at www.salzreview.co.uk/web/guest/home (accessed 3 April 2013).

Shainesh, G., 2012. Effects of trustworthiness and trust on loyalty intentions: validating a parsimonious model in banking. *International Journal of Bank Marketing*, 30(4), pp. 267–79.

Sheth, J.N., Sisodia, R.S., and Sharma, A., 2000. The antecedents and consequences of customer-centric marketing. *Journal of the Academy of Marketing Science*, 28(1), pp. 55–56.

Slater, S.F., 1997. Developing a customer value-based theory of the firm. *Journal of the Academy of Marketing Science*, 25(2), pp. 162–67.

Slater, S.F. and Narver, J.C., 1995. Market orientation and the learning organization. *Journal of Marketing*, 59(3), pp. 63–74.

Smith, N.C., Drumwright, M.E. and Gentile, M.C., 2010. The new marketing myopia. *Journal of Public Policy & Marketing*, 29(1), pp. 4–11.

Spitzeck, H., Pirson, M. and Dierksmeier, C. eds., 2011. *Banking with Integrity-The winners of the Financial Crisis?* London: Palgrave McMillan.

Stiglitz, J., 2008. The fruit of hypocrisy: dishonesty in the finance sector dragged us here, and Washington looks ill-equipped to guide us out. *The Guardian*, 15 Sep, p. 30.

Sunstein, C.R., 2013. *Simpler: the future of government*. New York, NY: Simon & Schuster.

Taibbi, M., 2010. The great American bubble machine. *The Rolling Stone Magazine*, available at www.rollingstone.com/politics/news/the-great-american-bubble-machine-20100405 (accessed 5 April 2010).

Toonkel, J. and Grenon, A., 2012. Sallie Krawcheck: JPMorgan Chase loss raises concern over too big and complex banks. *Huffpost Business*, available at www.huffingtonpost.com/2012/06/12/sallie-krawcheck-jpmorgan-chase-loss_n_1588989.html (accessed on 12 June 2012).

Tyler, T.R., 2000. Social justice: Outcome and procedure. *International Journal of Psychology*, 35(2), pp. 117–25.

Van Greuning, H. and Bratanovic, S.B., 2009. *Analyzing banking risk: a framework for assessing corporate governance and risk management*. Washington, DC: World Bank Publications.

Volcker, P., 2010. How to reform our financial system. *New York Times*, available at www.nytimes.com/2010/01/31/opinion/31volcker.html?pagewanted=all (accessed on 30 January 2010).

Williamson, O., 1993. Calculativeness, trust, and economic organization. *Journal of Law and Economics*, 36, pp. 453–86.

31

Nine 'tricks' in financial services marketing

Vesa Puttonen

Introduction

Financial fiascos have received considerable media attention in the last few decades. Reported high profile cases of fraud have shaken the confidence and the trust the average investor has in the financial system (Mesly 2012). Lack of trust is an inherent characteristic of many financial services transactions and a continuing challenge to the practice of marketing financial services. A survey by Oliver Wyman (2012) suggests that most consumers do not trust banks and insurers to manage their savings and in fact only trust themselves. This is particularly acute in developed nations where individuals have the most experience of the financial sector.

In the wake of the global financial crisis, one might assume that companies have become more aware that they are under strict public scrutiny and therefore must commit to ethical marketing practices under such circumstances. One might also assume that consumers have become more careful in choosing financial products. Evidence, however, suggests the opposite. Financial services marketers are facing customers who are neither financially literate nor very interested in financial services. The assumptions that consumers carry out the necessary amount of information search to identify their best options and that they are rational and unemotional in their decisions have consistently been disproved in empirical research.

Consumers tend to base their financial decisions on discriminatory prescreening, which refers to simplifying decision-making by narrowing down the choices and then eliminating choices that do not possess certain desired attributes (Estelami 2012). This is followed by compensatory decision-making, in which consumers evaluate the choices such that they compensate weak attributes with strengths in other attributes. In many cases, this may lead to discarding choices that would eventually perform better than the ones that were not excluded in the screening, resulting in not considering the best deals in the market. Research has found that there are certain mental shortcuts for problem solving (called heuristics) which consumers use in order to deal with complex decision-making in financial services (Estelami 2012, provides an extensive overview of research on these issues). They can be divided under three general categories: limitations in human cognitive capacity in conducting complex numeric computations that force consumers to simplify financial decision data, emotions that guide consumer decisions in a non-objective and irrational manner and insufficient consumer knowledge and motivation that translates into uninformed decisions.

What responsibilities, therefore, do consumers have in choosing the financial services they commit to? There seems to be very little research on the topic but it is evident that consumers are not necessarily to blame for buying products and services from financial companies that practice unethical marketing. Human cognitive circuitry does have some limitations and consumers do not have access to all the information available to companies selling financial services. However, it is legitimate to assume that consumers would use some common sense in their decisions. Some of the recent examples of marketing malpractice beg the question of whether consumers are unable to comprehend that the deals they are offered are simply too good to be true.

This chapter provides an analysis and categorisation of the variety of strategies and actions used by financial services firms to further their economic goals that have also disadvantaged or misled customers in some way. The analysis is based on eleven case examples to illustrate nine 'tricks' of financial services marketing malpractice. The tricks range from clear cases of fraudulent behaviour to lack of transparency in fees and the promise of unrealistic returns, all of which to some degree take advantage of the inherent weaknesses and limitations of investors. This chapter complements Chapter 29 on mis-selling and Chapter 34 on the ethics of the sales process.

Nine 'tricks' in marketing malpractice

Clear fraud

The most scandalous cases in financial services have been pure frauds. A case in point is Bernard L. Madoff Investment Securities LLC which operated as a securities broker-dealer. It provided executions for broker-dealers, banks, financial institutions and wealthy individuals. The returns were strikingly consistent, especially during market downturns. Often when asked about his ability to deliver such stable returns, Madoff would emphasize how his strategy's use of options and futures helped 'cushion' the returns against market volatility.

For decades, Madoff built a desired and trustworthy reputation for his funds. Only the few and most privileged investors were given the opportunity to invest in them. The impression of Madoff's magical skills was spread by word of mouth from one investor to another; for instance he typically refused to meet directly with clients, playing 'hard to get' and building a magical, myth-like aura around him. In addition, the fact that Madoff was a highly appreciated person in the financial world and the former non-executive chairman of NASDAQ, enhanced this image of which he took advantage. Madoff did not promise to deliver high returns but he delivered consistent returns. The consistency appealed to Madoff's client base.

The Madoff case turned out to be a classic example of a Ponzi scheme: where the returns for existing investors were paid with the money received from new investors (Ross 2009). According to Federal investigators, Madoff began his illegal activities in the 1970's. With hindsight, it can be said that several very clear warning signs of Madoff's scheme were totally ignored by both the financial regulators and Madoff's investors. Outside analysts raised concerns about Madoff's firm for years. The first one was Harry Markopolos in May 2000, a financial analyst who, when trying to simulate Madoff's returns, just could not reproduce the results; he even alerted the Securities and Exchange Commission (SEC) that the returns produced by Madoff were mathematically impossible. The SEC decided not to take any action.

It required a financial crisis of a once-in-a-generation amplitude to unravel Madoff's scheme. As general market downturn accelerated, investors desperately in need of capital started withdrawing funds. In December 2008, Madoff's clients tried to withdraw as much as $7 billion from their accounts. Following this mass withdrawal, he started desperately going through his unique contact network in search of emergency financing; he realized that the pyramid was close to collapsing. Madoff's sons reported him to the police and in March 2009 Madoff pled guilty to being the mastermind behind the largest ever Ponzi scheme (the prosecutors estimated the size of the fraud at $64.8 billion) and altogether to eleven federal crimes. He was sentenced to 150 years in prison with restitution of $17 billion. Thousands of wealthy clients, philanthropic organizations and middle-class individuals whose pension funds found their way into Madoff's investment fund lost their life savings (Collins 2013).

Misrepresenting risky products as safe

One example of misrepresenting risky products as safe can be seen in the issue of preferred shares by Spanish banks. When the real estate bubble burst, Spanish banks needed to raise money from their retail customers in order to finance the large deficits. The banks started to offer preferred shares to their retail customers to cover their substantial needs for additional capital. When promoting the preferred shares, the banks took advantage of the customers' lack of awareness of the risks involved with these financial instruments. The preferred shares were commonly marketed as riskless options for bank deposits. In some cases customers believed that they were making a deposit into the bank and were not in fact aware that they were investing in the bank's shares. However, preferred shareholders, unlike depositors, are not insured by the government against losses.

Between 1999 and 2004, some £18.3 billion worth of preferred shares were sold in Spain to around 50,000 individuals, mainly pensioners. In the period up to 2011, as the impact of the global financial crisis was biting harder and banks were desperate for cash, £31 billion worth of preferred shares were sold. Most of Spain's major banks and savings institutions were involved (El Pais 2012).

Another example of a 'safe' financial product was 'Minibonds'. The term was used to describe a series of financial notes issued under the control of Lehman Brothers both in Hong Kong and Singapore, since 2002. The Minibonds were promoted by Pacific International Finance Limited (PIF) which guaranteed investors that they would receive a fixed annual return of about 5 percent on their investments. The Minibonds were promoted to guarantee investors' interest payments at regular intervals, which made them appear as a bond. In reality, the Minibonds were three-layered high-risk credit-linked products with a Synthetic Collateralized Debt Obligation (CDO) hidden in their structure. After the bankruptcy of Lehman Brothers in 2008, more than 30,000 Hong Kong and Singapore based investors lost their money in Minibonds. In 2011 a settlement was announced providing most of the retail investors in these structured products with a 70–93 percent recovery rate on their initial investments (Economist 2011).

Excessive return expectations

In the U.S. throughout the 1980s and 1990s, investment clubs, previously known mainly in their local communities, started to become popular nationwide. During these years, investment clubs were at their peak: club membership numbers were high, various clubs received notable attention in the media and there seemed to be a generally positive public image of investment clubs as a viable means of investing. The significant financial media attention to a few particularly well performing investment clubs seemed to create a public consensus that investment clubs tended to outperform financial markets. Public opinion was reinforced by surveys conducted by the National Association of Investors Corporation (NAIC), also known as Betterinvesting, an umbrella organization of investment clubs, as noted by Barber and Odean (2000: 24) in their study on investment club performance:

The financial press makes frequent and bold claims regarding the performance of investment clubs. One oft quoted figure from a NAIC survey of clubs: 60 percent of investment clubs beat the market.

Yet, Barber and Odean (2000) challenge the view of investment clubs being "serious investment alternatives" on a more general level. Their findings denounced the widely suggested claims of general outperformance of the clubs relative to the market, finding in their study that 60 percent of their sample of 166 investment clubs actually underperformed the market during 1991–97.

What makes NAIC interesting from the perspective of financial services marketing is that while investment clubs are forbidden to directly promote their services, NAIC seemed to actively endorse investment clubs as a 'market-beating' investment alternative and generally built up a positive public perception of returns achieved by investment clubs, with sometimes questionable means.

Overcharging

The Kardashian credit card, also known as the 'Kard', was a pre-paid credit card launched in the U.S in 2010 by Dash Dolls, LLC, the Kardashian Corporation. The underlying idea was to use the image of Kim Kardashian and her luxurious lifestyle in the card's promotion in order to attract her fans. The main target groups were teenagers and young adults.

The cost of holding the card was $99.95, including a card purchase fee of $9.95 and a monthly fee of $7.95 per month. After the first year, consumers had to continue to pay the $7.95 monthly fee; a six-month option would cost $59.95. Moreover, ATM withdrawals cost $1.50 and customers were charged $1 to make a deposit. Automatic bill pay cost $2 per item. Closing the account cost $6.

Only one month after the card's initial launch it was withdrawn from the market. This was mostly due to the high criticism it received, primarily because of its exceptionally high fees. According to a statement by University National Bank, only 250 customers had purchased the card. The bank promised that customers who bought the Kard could continue using it for 30 days and thereafter they would receive refunds of any balances and any pre-paid fees (Ellis 2010).

It should be noted that the Kard's general concept was in no sense unique to the U.S. prepaid debit card market, as many other prepaid cards in the U.S. are characterized by various charges, including activation fees as high as $40, monthly fees that go up to $10 plus inactivity fees, balance inquiry fees and other fees. This practice of excessive charging has been viewed in different ways by the public; some criticize the credit card issuers for exploiting the financial illiteracy of individuals, which is highly prominent in their target markets, whilst others have viewed the seemingly high costs of such cards as a 'punishment' for the lack of credit history among many of the cards' customers and as compensation for the inconvenience this causes the issuers.

Another well-known example of overcharging are SPARQS (Stock Participation Accrediting Redemption Quarterly-pay Securities) issued in the U.S. by Morgan Stanley. SPARQS were introduced to the market for the first time in 2001 and were targeted specifically to retail investors. The product is a quarterly interest-paying, callable note which, upon maturity, is exchanged for shares of the underlying company. If called, holders are paid out all the future interest payments of the note, whilst waiving their rights to underlying equity at maturity. As with index-linked bonds, SPARQS are obligations of the issuer (in this case Morgan Stanley), not of the company whose shares act as the underlying equity of a specific SPARQS contract. During their short life-time, SPARQS evolved quickly into a billion dollar industry. Morgan Stanley issued only 69 different SPARQS from 2001 to 2005 with proceeds of approximately

$2.2 billion. Other major financial institutions also issued significant volumes of essentially identical products during the same period, for example YEELDS offered by Lehman Brothers and STRIDES offered by Merrill Lynch.

Referring to previous research on financial innovations, Henderson and Pearson (2011) note that much of the hype surrounding financial innovations in structured products similar to SPARQS has been that such products allow investors to achieve desired payoff patterns not commonly achievable via traditional financial instruments. This is valuable to individual investors as such products can help them to better structure their portfolios to provide desired payoffs at specific times or events, which is also valuable to the economy in general. However Henderson and Pearson (2011: 228) continue with a different tone:

> But there is a dark side to the ability to create instruments with tailored payoffs. If some investors misunderstand financial markets or suffer from cognitive biases that cause them to assign incorrect probability weights to events, financial institutions can exploit the investors' mistakes by creating financial instruments that pay off in the states that investors overweight and pay off less highly in the states that investors underweight, leading the investors to value the new instruments more highly than they would if they understood financial markets and correctly evaluated information about probabilities of future events.

Products such as SPARQS seem naturally predisposed towards potential agency problems or conflicts of interest between issuers and their clients and therefore there exists a strong need to critically examine pricing of such products.

Henderson and Pearson (2011) in fact studied the pricing of 69 issues of SPARQS, offered for sale between 2001 and 2005. Each of the issues was linked to a single, well-known, large-cap stock (for example, Oracle, Cisco Systems, Apple, Nokia and eBay) and with an average maturity of 14 months and was callable after 6 months. Henderson and Pearson (2011) estimated the fair values for each SPARQS issue as of the dates they were offered for sale. They found that the average offering price of a SPARQS issue on its offering date was 8.77 percent above the 'fair value' calculated by their model, which utilized the most up-to-date and appropriate asset pricing techniques.

Exaggerating historical returns

Mutual fund incubation is a strategy for initiating new funds, where several funds are first launched privately and then at the end of a specific evaluation period (incubation period) some of the funds are opened up to the investing public. Naturally, the funds that are marketed to the public and eventually grow into full-scale funds are those that have been beating the market during the incubation period; the funds that perform poorly are usually closed.

Such, 'lab-grown' funds have become increasingly popular in the mutual fund industry. According to Evans (2010), in his sample of newly created U.S. domestic equity funds offered between 1996 and 2005, approximately 23 percent of new funds were incubated. This practice has long been publicly advocated by the industry as a way of identifying the most effective investment strategies and promising fund managers for new mutual funds. The argument implies that this is a beneficial practice from the client's perspective as it allows the companies to offer clients funds with the best possible returns.

Critics of the incubation practice, however, have long argued that incubation period returns are produced under rather different conditions (i.e. significantly smaller fund sizes) compared with the conditions governing full-grown mutual fund returns, thus rendering the strategies not applicable and the produced returns not comparable to full-grown mutual funds.

In his study, Evans (2010) finds that funds in incubation outperform non-incubated funds by 3.5 percent risk-adjusted returns, more than double Sharpe ratios. When they are eventually opened to the public, they attract higher net dollar flows compared to non-incubated funds. This attraction of higher fund flows is explained by the fact that historical fund performance is known to be one of the most significant determinants in mutual fund choices by investors. However, post-incubation this outperformance seems to disappear, as there is no evidence for any statistically significant outperformance by incubated funds relative to non-incubated funds.

Even the U.S. Securities and Exchange Commission (SEC) has indicated its concern of incubator funds. SEC made an attempt to regulate incubation by forbidding the use of private funds (funds not registered with the SEC) for fund incubation. However, in practice, mutual fund companies work around the SEC regulation by making their funds public *de jure*, by registering them with the SEC, but keeping them *de facto* 'private' by not registering them with Morningstar and other data-reporting companies, and by gathering the needed fund capital mainly from the company's employees internally (Evans 2010).

To illustrate, Putnam Research Fund was set up in October 1995, with approximately $3 million in net assets. All of the starting capital was provided by Putnam Investments and inflow from outside investors was minimal, until July 1998 when Putnam finally began advertising the fund (Evans 2010). During the incubation period from October 1995 to July 1998, the fund's average annual return was 28 percent and it outperformed funds with similar investment objectives by an annual average of 5.3 percent.

Today the Putnam Research Fund has total assets of over $232 million. In its marketing material, Putnam shows the value development of $10,000 invested in the fund at inception to a current value of $34,979 (i.e. a total cumulative return of 249.8 percent) and states the annual average return rate of the fund as 7.4%; both of these calculations however involve the incubation period returns. When calculating these same figures for the period during which retail investors could actually invest in the fund (i.e. starting from July 1998, when Putnam began for the first time publicly advertising its fund) the fund shows a rather different performance. From July 1998 to March 2013, the fund produced a total cumulative return of 169.7 percent and an annual average return of 3.6 percent.

Complex products for untrained investors

Leveraged and inverse ETFs are a subcategory of exchange-traded funds (ETFs) that aim at either amplifying (leveraged ETFs) and/or inversing (inverse ETFs) the returns of the benchmark index they are designed to track. In contrast to ordinary ETFs, these are complex products that use both leverage and different financial derivatives to achieve desired payoff patterns; a fact that not all investors buying these products seem to realize. A typical leveraged ETF has a 2:1 or 3:1 leverage ratio, which it aims to maintain constant throughout the period of its activity. Leveraged ETFs are offered for most major international equity indices tracked by ordinary ETFs (for example, S&P 500, FTSE 100, Dow Jones Industrial Average).

These products were first introduced in 2006, but quickly grew in just a few years to encompass a notable volume of the ETF market. This rapid growth is not surprising. Mulvey et al. (2013) suggest that the global investment community viewed the products as a convenient alternative to the traditional approach for leveraging a portfolio, by taking out a margin loan from a brokerage and investing the proceeds in the desired securities (in this case the desired ETFs). According to Mulvey at al. (2013: 1), "introduction (of leveraged ETFs) was heralded as a convenient mechanism for investors to enhance performance over traditional borrowing and leverage strategies".

However, with the rapid growth in popularity of these instruments, finance academics and experts have expressed their concerns by pointing out that a large number of unsophisticated and naïve retail investors may fail to fully grasp the true nature of these complex products. The main issue of concern has been that, contrary to what the typical names of the products might suggest (such as "ABC's 3xS&P 500"), leveraged ETFs only aim to and are capable of accurately replicating, amplifying or inversing daily returns of the index they are tracking, *not* the long-term returns. In other words, a leveraged ETF promising to provide three times the returns of the Standard and Poor's 500 index, only aims to (and is designed to) deliver three times the daily return of S&P 500. However, over the long-run this successful daily mimicking does not add up to an exact amplification of the index's long-term returns by the fund's leverage ratio. Investors buying such ETFs and expecting them to amplify/inverse long-term returns of their underlying indices may be heavily disappointed by the resulting investment outcomes.

There exists a possibility that these novel products hold the potential for enormous tracking error, which, if not fully understood by investors, can lead to very large losses. This point has stirred the interest of financial regulators with regards to leveraged ETFs. For example, in 2009 the Financial Industry Regulatory Authority (FINRA) stated its concerns regarding the possibility of investors expecting long-term returns from these products that are consistent with the leverage ratios. Since the SEC also issued an alert regarding leveraged ETFs (Avellaneda and Zhang 2010), it is clear that the concern of potential mismatch between investor expectations and the reality of the product is highly relevant; several studies have found that investors hold leveraged ETFs on average for significantly longer periods than one day. Both the SEC and FINRA called for the ETF issuing companies to communicate more explicitly the funds' aim to mimic daily (rather than long-term) returns of the index it is tracking.

Abuse of cognitive biases

There exists a plethora of academic research in the field of behavioural finance, which is concerned with how different heuristics (mental shortcuts for problem solving) influence decision-making of investors. The impact of heuristics on financial decision-making is discussed in detail in Chapter 4. One of the most studied heuristics has been the so-called affect heuristic; it means that if peoples' evaluations/perceptions of an object are positive on one dimension, these tend to 'stick' to the evaluation of the same object on another dimension as well (for example, perceptions of a company's reputation as good often lead one to perceive the financial prospects of the company also as good). Decision-makers are known to fall for this decision-making fallacy when estimating risks and benefits of specific actions, such that if they have a positive disposition towards an action, they are more likely to judge the related risks as low and the benefits as high (Finucane et al. 2000).

Glamour stocks are well-known, widely held, popular among investors and belong to companies whose earnings are expected to grow at an above industry average rate. These stocks are often from so-called 'hot' companies, in the sense that their product offering or line of business is fashionable and timely, the company's reputation is at its peak and growth prospects are good.

Investors are likely to extend the generalization of good characteristics of a glamour company to their evaluations of the company as an investment; namely, investors would see such glamour stocks as a good investment and expect them to generate better returns than other stocks. This intuition has been supported empirically by Kaustia et al. (2009), who find that professional financial advisors fall for the affect heuristic. In their experimental study, financial advisors were shown to anticipate higher expected returns from 'good' companies (evaluated on general firm-level characteristics, such as low leverage, good management, good growth prospects) compared to 'not so good' companies. Unfortunately for the investors (as well as for financial advisors), this is the opposite of what finance theory would suggest. According to conventional asset pricing models, any good firm characteristic that is priced by the market is associated with lower, not higher, return expectations; a good evaluation on this characteristic causes a decrease in the required return, leading to a higher current price, and a lower future return on average.

Statman et al. (2008) compared how returns on companies' stocks differed in accordance to their ranking on Fortune magazine's annual list of "America's Most Admired Companies". They found that for the years 1982–2006, the mean annualized return of the "Spurned portfolio" was 19.7 percent higher than the mean annualized return of the "Admired portfolio" by 4.6 percentage points. The advantage of the "Spurned portfolios" over the "Admired portfolios" remained intact when assessed using the CAPM (Capital Asset Pricing Model).

Affect is the specific quality of "goodness" of a company. The immediate effect of an increase in affect is an increase in stock prices, but higher stock prices set the stage for lower future returns. One could assume that financial services providers operating in the best interests of their clients would highlight this in their marketing material and advisory services. However, some financial services providers offer products which could be perceived to be exploiting the misconception that good companies are also good investments and forget the pricing component.

Gambling dressed up as investing

The foreign exchange market (FX) is a global market for trading currencies. With an estimated daily volume of $5.3 trillion it is generally considered as the world's largest marketplace (Bank for International Settlements 2013). The main economic task of foreign exchange transactions is to assist international trade and investment by enabling currency conversions. However it is estimated that as much as 90 percent of this daily volume is generated by currency speculation, usefulness and benignity which has been widely debated among finance professionals for decades. Even though a significant majority of the speculation volume is generated by institutional investors, with the growing number of online FX trading platforms, more and more ordinary, home-based retail investors have joined the speculation game, amounting now to a notable proportion of the overall volume.

The interesting point about FX trading, in contrast to most of the 'investment alternatives' offered to retail investors, is that it is a zero-sum game. Numerous studies have shown (for example, Mitchell and Pearce 2007) that even the world's top economic experts and academics are not capable of predicting/modeling currency rates better than a naïve random walk model (i.e. better than chance alone). Mitchell and Pearce (2007) come to the conclusion that experts perform worse than a random walk model, implying that their estimates would be more successful if executed by the toss of a coin. Considering such a low prediction success rate for the world's top economic professionals, who have enormous resources supporting their forecasting efforts in comparison to the limited resources of retail investors, the possibility of outperforming the 'success rate' of these experts would seem quite unlikely for the average retail investor.

Making promises not supported by evidence

Socially responsible investing (SRI) is an investment approach that integrates social, environmental and ethical considerations as part of the investment process. The SRI approach has become an increasingly popular defining investment philosophy of asset management funds over the past decade (Renneboog et al. 2008). These funds are widely offered to both retail and institutional investors as mutual funds or other types of investment products. Nilsson, in Chapter 33, provides an overview of SRI.

According to Haigh and Hazelton (2004), there appears to be essentially two key selling arguments that SRI funds tend to emphasize in their promotions. The first one is the claim that by affecting corporations' access to capital, SRI funds can change prevailing corporate practices (i.e. investing in socially responsible companies will encourage other companies to adopt higher social and environmental standards in fear of becoming less competitive on the capital markets). Haigh and Hazelton (2004) refer to this category of promises as the 'corporate change' category. The second promotional claim used actively in marketing of SRI funds is that SRI funds can outperform conventional actively managed funds, as stable long term returns come from sustainable businesses that foresee the problems of the future. They classify such promises as the 'outperformance' category.

However ambitious the claims might be, academic findings do not seem to provide much support for them. For example, Statman et al. (1993) find that socially responsible mutual funds do not earn statistically significant excess returns and that the performance of such mutual funds is not statistically different from the performance of conventional mutual funds. Support for this view is also provided by Haigh and Hazelton (2004), who cite several studies that show that SRI funds are actually more correlated with general market indices rather than with socially responsible market indices and conclude that: "The distinction between SRI funds and conventional mutual funds, then, may largely be in name". Also Renneboog et al. (2008) conclude that given the existing and most up-to-date evidence on SRI performance, SRI funds outperforming conventional actively managed funds would seem highly unlikely.

Conclusion

Customers in financial markets represent varying levels of expertise, interest and financial literacy. This leads to opportunities for those with higher levels of financial capability to affect the decision-making of those less knowledgeable, or even to mislead them.

The overwhelming variety of financial services offerings and the complexity of many of them, has made it hard, even for finance professionals, to fully understand all features of modern financial products. The challenge is even more significant among customers with low levels of financial literacy. As the examples in this chapter show, there is indeed a wide array of 'tricks' that are used in financial services marketing. The tricks vary from extremely dramatic, completely illegal Ponzi schemes to minor offenses such as obscuring fees or implicitly promising excessive high returns. Most financial offerings are not limited to one trick only. For example, the Madoff case was a clear case of fraud but an elementary part of the story was the exaggeration of historical returns. Madoff also utilized his good reputation so that even professional investors, influenced by the affect heuristic, were not open to seeing the warning signs presented to the public. Table 31.1 summarizes the nine tricks in light of the eleven examples presented in this chapter.

The financial services industry could address the problem of potential marketing malpractice by generating internal regulations, codes of conduct and promoting good marketing practices. Decreasing the number and complexity of products and services would be a good start. Also, the industry needs to solve the problems of information flow and accuracy of information. In advertisements, emphasis should be on realistic expected risk-adjusted returns, and pricing should be transparent to customers.

Financial institutions have a central role in educating customers about the features associated with the financial products and services they offer. The financial services industry, its

Table 31.1 Nine tricks in financial services marketing

Examples	1 Clear fraud	2 Misrepresenting risky products as safe	3 Excessive return expectations	4 Overcharging	5 Exaggerating historical returns	6 Complex products for untrained investors	7 Abuse of cognitive biases	8 Gambling dressed up as investing	9 Making promises not supported by evidence
Madoff	*				*		*		
Kardashian Kard				*			*		
SR Investments			*				*		*
Spanish Preferred S.		*				*	*		*
Incubator funds			*		*		*		*
Good companies = good returns?			*						*
SPARQS			*	*		*	*		*
Investment clubs			*		*		*		*
Forex trading platform		*	*			*	*	*	
Leveraged ETF's			*			*			
Minibonds in Hong Kong		*				*			

management, salespeople and regulators have a responsibility in developing financial solutions that are both profitable for the producer and cost-effective to the customer.

Acknowledgement

The author would like to thank the research assistance of Ilja Tauber and the input of students in the *Marketing Financial Services* course at Aalto University School of Business in the Fall 2013 term. Comments provided at the Finnish Financial Supervisory Authority and Aalto Finance Brown Bag seminars are also warmly acknowledged.

References

Avellaneda, M. and Zhang, S. (2010). 'Path-dependence of leveraged ETF returns'. *Journal of Financial Mathematics*, 1(1), pp. 586–603.

Bank for International Settlements (2013). *Triennial Central Bank Survey: foreign exchange turnover in April 2013: preliminary global results*. Bank for International Settlements, September 2013. Online: www.bis.org/publ/rpfx13fx.pdf

Barber, M. B. and Odean, T. (2000). 'Too many cooks spoil the profits: Investment club performance'. *Financial Analysts Journal*, 56(1), pp. 17–25.

Collins, D. (2013). 'Bernie Madoff's Ponzi scheme: reliable returns from a trustworthy financial adviser', Case study. Edgewood College.

Economist (2011). 'The good inside the bad. A settlement in Hong Kong reveals substantial value inside dud securities'. March 31, 2011.

El Pais (2012). *The great preferential share swindle.* August 6, 2012.

Ellis, B. (2010). Kardashian Kard kanceled by "fun-loving" sisters. www.money.cnn.com, November 30, 2010.

Estelami, H. (2012). *Marketing Financial Services*. Indianapolis, IN: Dog Ear Publishing.

Evans, R. B. (2010). 'Mutual fund incubation'. *The Journal of Finance*, 65(4), pp. 1581–1611.

Finucane, L. M., Alkhami, A., Slovic, P. and Johnson, M. S. (2000). 'The affect heuristic in judgments of risks and benefits'. *Journal of Behavioral Decision Making*, 13(1), pp. 1–17.

Haigh, M. and Hazelton, J. (2004). 'Financial Markets: a tool for social responsibility?' *Journal of Business Ethics*, 52(1), pp. 59–71.

Henderson, B. J. and Pearson, D. N. (2011). 'The dark side of financial innovation: A case study of the pricing of a retail financial product'. *Journal of Financial Economics*, 100(2), pp. 227–47.

Kaustia, M., Laukkanen, H. and Puttonen, V. (2009). 'Should good stocks have high prices or high returns? *Financial Analysts Journal*, 65(3), pp. 55–62.

Mesly, O. (2012). 'The dark side of organizations – the story of financial predation and inadequate regulations'. *Journal of Finance & Accountancy*, 9, pp. 96–116.

Mitchell, K. and Pearce, K. D. (2007). 'Professional forecasts of interest rates and exchange rates: evidence from the Wall Street Journal's panel of economists'. *Journal of Macroeconomics*, 29(4), pp. 840–54.

Mulvey, J., Nadbielny, T. and Kim, W. C. (2013). 'Levered exchange-traded products: theory and practice'. *Journal of Financial Perspectives*, 1(2) pp. 105–18.

Oliver Wyman (2012). *The real financial crisis: Why financial intermediation is failing. The state of the financial services industry in 2012*. Marsch & McLennan Companies.

Renneboog L., Ter Horst J. and Zhang, C. (2008). 'Socially responsible investments: institutional aspects, performance, and investor behavior'. *Journal of Banking and Finance*, 32(9), pp. 1723–42.

Ross, B. (2009). *The Madoff Chronicles: Inside the Secret World of Bernie and Ruth*. New York: Hyperion Books.

Statman M., Fisher, K.L. and Anginer, D. (2008). 'Affect in a behavioral asset-pricing model'. *Financial Analysts Journal*, 64(2), pp. 20–29.

Statman, M., Jo, H. and Hamilton, S. (1993). 'Doing well while doing good? The investment performance of socially responsible mutual funds'. *Financial Analysts Journal*, 49(6), pp. 62–66.

Part XI

Moral and ethical issues in financial services marketing

32

Corporate Social Responsibility (CSR) in banking

What we know, what we don't know and what we should know

Lynette McDonald

Introduction

The international media is awash with tales of banking scandals, ranging from money laundering and rogue trading to interest rate fixing and potential criminal indictment (McDonald 2012). Coupled with the fallout from the recent international financial crisis, banks have experienced a loss of credibility (Bravo et al. 2012). In the wake of the crisis, the banking industry has been perceived as possessing serious moral flaws and as having engaged in wild speculation (Bennett and Kottasz 2012). In a recent 34-country survey, financial and banking institutions were ranked alongside the resources sector as industries least likely to behave in a responsible way towards society (European Commission 2013).

The intense media and public scrutiny focused on the banking industry means that banks are increasingly concentrating on protecting their reputational assets (Soana 2011) and image (Bravo et al. 2012). One of the main avenues for banks to improve their corporate image and re-engage with communities is via a corporate social responsibility (CSR) programme (Pomering and Dolnicar 2009). Banks use CSR as a form of impression management to shape public perceptions and to maintain or create organizational legitimacy (Pérez and del Bosque 2012). For the financial sector, where customer involvement with the service is high, CSR not only positively influences perceptions of the bank but also service evaluations (Matute-Vallejo et al. 2011). For banks, involvement in CSR creates a liking of the bank by customers, positively impacting its reputation for caring (Marin and Ruiz 2007). CSR also improves banks' financial performance and reduces potential risks (de la Cuesta-González et al. 2006).

The emphasis on CSR as part of a long-term strategy to regain lost reputation and reshape public perceptions accentuates the potential value that may accrue from a review of research findings on CSR practised by banks internationally. This is especially timely as Soana (2011) warns that research results for CSR activities cannot be generalized to all markets and sectors. Consequently, this chapter aims to conduct an integrative review of international empirical research on CSR in the banking industry. The primary goal of an integrative review is to summarize the accumulated state of knowledge concerning the topic of interest and to highlight important issues that research has left unresolved (Taveggia 1974).

The first step in such an investigation is to define the domain of the construct under examination (Albaum and Peterson 1984), in this case, corporate social responsibility (CSR). The second step in the integrative review is to delimit the area of investigation, which is conducted via an analysis of literature published in the research domain (Albaum and Peterson 1984). This research will investigate CSR in banking, conducted via a review of journal articles empirically investigating CSR in the bank marketing literature. Although CSR research is a relatively recent phenomenon, a twenty-year period was investigated to ensure that early empirical CSR research in banking was included.

The third step is to summarize the cumulative findings. In this regard, this review has several objectives: to identify the specific topics and areas that are being investigated, the populations being studied and the methodologies being employed, to identify the key findings of this research and the specific knowledge gaps that exist, indicating potential future research directions. After a discussion of the findings, the chapter also seeks to make evident what we should know and concludes with suggestions for future research directions.

What is CSR?

Researchers frequently conceptualize CSR as the requirement for corporations to make additional contributions to the well-being of society (Carroll and Shabana 2010 cited in Lin-Hi and Müller 2013). However, there is no general consensus on the precise meaning of CSR (Lin-Hi and Muller 2013). Indeed, Dahlsrud (2008) provided an analysis of 37 definitions of CSR. Two widely-cited CSR definitions provided by Carroll (1979) and the European Community (2011) are now discussed.

Carroll's (1979; 1991 cited in Mandhachitara and Poolthong 2011) CSR definition emphasizes four principle responsibilities and expectations that society has of organizations: economic, legal, ethical and philanthropic; the expectation that businesses accomplish these goals is driven by social norms.

The European Community's (2011) definition, while incorporating several areas congruent with Carroll's (1979; 1991) definition – economic, ethical and philanthropic concerns – also includes collaboration with stakeholders. Its definition states that, to fully meet their social responsibility, enterprises *"should have in place a process to integrate social, environmental, ethical human rights and consumer concerns into their business operations and core strategy in close collaboration with their stakeholders"* (European Community 2011).

The inclusion of stakeholder concerns in many CSR definitions is congruent with the increasing application of Freeman's (1984) stakeholder theory to CSR research. Stakeholder theory states that an organization has multiple stakeholders, each of whom has different expectations of organizations (Freeman 1984). Stakeholders refer to any group or individual who can affect, or is affected by, organizational activities and is vital to the successful operation of the organization. Primary stakeholder groups comprise customers, employees, local communities, suppliers and distributors and shareholders.

Dahlsrud (2008) found that stakeholders constituted one of the five dimensions consistently referred to in the 37 CSR definitions, along with economic, social, voluntariness and environmental dimensions. Because CSR is a socially constructed phenomenon, these five dimensions make the lack of one universally accepted definition less problematic (Dahlsrud 2008). As there are no universally-used indicators of CSR activities, these five dimensions, later discussed, are used in this research.

Method

This section discusses the data collection and analysis process. In doing so, this research aims to elucidate the existing knowledge about CSR in banking; that is, what we know and what we don't know.

Data collection

After completing the first step in an integrative review (construct definition), the second step is to delimit the subject matter of the investigation (Albaum and Peterson 1984): journal articles investigating CSR in banking institutions. In this investigation, CSR banking research is defined as any study which empirically examined CSR in banking-only settings or studied stakeholders of banks (including retail banks, co-operative banks, savings banks, social banks and universal banks), rather than within the broader financial industry sector. Empirical research refers to studies that propose research questions, and collect and analyse data (Yin 2003). Banks were selected because, in most nations, they are subject to more stringent government regulations than other financial institutions.

Journal articles for this review were retrieved following several procedures. First, a search was made for peer-reviewed articles drawn from two major business journal databases, ABI Inform Global and Business Source Premier, covering a twenty-year period from 1993 to 2013. This time period was selected to be sufficiently broad, yet current enough to provide a meaningful and balanced representation of empirical research in international banking. Second, the keywords search used "corporate social responsibility", "social responsibility", "CSR" and "bank" and "banking" in the abstract, title and keywords, and "marketing" in the text. This search yielded 57 and 55 articles respectively from each database.

Abstracts were reviewed to ensure each article's appropriateness for the current investigation. After deleting duplicates, foreign-language, non-empirical (for example, descriptive case studies) and non-banking articles, 41 articles remained. Two further reductions occurred. The first involved removing from the sample articles on non-banking financial institutions. The second reduction involved discarding studies that examined practices in multi-industry settings which confounded banking results with that of other institutions. Other suitable articles may have been overlooked in this process. The number of reviewed articles was 34 across 15 journals. Five additional 2013 articles were identified, resulting in 39 articles across 16 journals. Table 32.1 lists the journal sources and article numbers, with the *Journal of Business Ethics* providing the largest article source.

The third step in an integrative review is to summarize the cumulative findings to make evident, via an examination of multiple studies, any inconsistent or contradictory results as the findings of any single study may have occurred by chance (Taveggia 1974). This involved a thematic analysis of each journal article according to its content. Thematic analysis is a process for encoding qualitative information and as such requires use of an explicit "code" or list of themes (Boyatzis 1998). A theme is a pattern found in information that may be generated deductively from theory and prior research or inductively, developing new themes (Boyatzis 1998). With a small sample size, descriptive use of thematic coding is advisable (rather than content analysis) due to the lack of reliable statistical generalisation to the population sample (Marks and Yardley 2004). It is also appropriate when the study methodology requires enhancing the clarity of the findings (Boyatzis 1998). As no prior coding categories exist, Dahlsrud's (2008) earlier-listed CSR dimensions were used as coding categories: economic (referring to financial or socio-economic aspects, for example, a focus on business operations or profitability), social (referring

Table 32.1 Publications with empirical research on CSR in banking

Journal	Number of articles	Journal	Number of articles
Corporate Communications: An International Journal	2	Journal of Communication Management	1
Corporate Social Responsibility and Environmental Management	2	Journal of International Consumer Marketing	1
Critical Perspectives on Accounting	1	Journal of Services Marketing	1
International Journal of Bank Marketing	8	New Zealand Journal of Employment Relations	1
International Journal of Business and Social Science	1	Psychology and Marketing	1
Issues in Social and Environmental Accounting	1	Social Responsibility Journal	4
Journal of Banking and Finance	2	Supply Chain Management	1
Journal of Business Ethics	11	The TQM Magazine	1
Total 39			

to the relationship between business and society, for example, integrating social concerns into business operations or considering the scope of impact on communities), stakeholders (referring to interaction with, and treatment of, multiple stakeholders or stakeholder groups, for example, customers, employees, communities, suppliers), environment (referring to the natural environment, for example, considering environmental concerns in business operations) and voluntariness (actions not prescribed by law, for example, based on ethical values).

The next section first tabulates then expands on the findings from research undertaken on CSR in banking, reporting on topics according to their degree of coverage.

What we know: results

The search revealed that research on CSR in banking is a recent phenomenon. No empirical articles were identified prior to 2002. This investigation therefore spans only a twelve-year period. In regards to publishing trends, Table 32.2 shows an erratic, but overall upward tendency for an increase in the number of empirical publications on CSR in banking in bank marketing journals.

The results have highlighted the international nature of research on CSR in banking with single-country studies involving more than 20 countries across multiple regions and nine multinational studies investigating up to 22 countries and 162 banks. Studies in Spain (eight) and

Table 32.2 Year of publication

Year	Number of articles	Year	Number of articles
2002	1	2008	3
2003	0	2009	6
2004	2	2010	2
2005	1	2011	7
2006	3	2012	4
2007	3	2013	7

Australia (six) dominate, with possible reasons for this regional dominance addressed in the discussion section. Apart from the two countries mentioned, no other country or regional trends were identified.

Using Dahlsrud's (2008) five CSR dimensions as coding categories, the studies were sorted into four overarching themes: stakeholders (consumers, employees, community, supply chain), social, economic and voluntariness. No studies were identified which fitted the environment dimension. One further main theme was inductively identified, CSR communication, comprising studies on reporting of CSR activities and those investigating advertising themes. To clarify the findings of the review, results were categorized in Table 32.3 under these five themes, with themes ordered from the most to the least researched: CSR communication (reporting and advertising), CSR and stakeholders (consumers, employees, community, supply chain), social, economic and voluntariness.

Two articles (Pérez and del Bosque 2012, Pomering and Dolnicar 2009) each reported on the results of more than one study and these results were separately included in two content areas, while two disparate findings from Wu and Shen (2013) were included in two separate content areas. Results for the tabulated summary are now discussed according to each heading.

CSR communication: CSR reporting and advertising

The most researched area of banking CSR was communication, with articles totalling 13 of the 39 (33 percent) studies, 11 of these focusing on how banks reported their CSR practices and a further two addressing CSR advertising themes. Most studies investigating CSR reporting by banks used content analysis to investigate publicly available material (for example, website content, annual reports, annual CSR reports). Overall, the studies revealed the extent of CSR reporting by banks, that banks reported CSR activities according to categories (for example, environmental, consumers, community) and that various communication materials and methods were used to disseminate CSR information. Two discourse studies investigated how banks presented themselves in regards to their CSR activities.

Four of the 11 studies highlighted the low levels of CSR reporting by banks in Ireland (Douglas et al. 2004), Spain (de la Cuesta-González et al. 2006), Bangladesh (Khan et al. 2009) and the Middle East (Haniffa and Hudaib 2007, Zubairu et al. 2011). However, one study (Branco and Rodrigues 2006) indicated that the amount of reporting was dependent upon bank type, with listed banks reporting more CSR information than unlisted banks.

Eight of the nine studies which reported CSR categories used a stakeholder approach, organizing activities according to benefitted or targeted stakeholder groups, such as consumers, community, employees, or the environment (see Branco and Rodrigues 2006, Douglas et al. 2004, Hinson et al. 2010, Khan et al. 2009, Pérez and del Bosque 2012, Raubenheimer 2008, Reinig and Tilt 2009, Zubairu et al. 2011). However, different countries appeared to have a different stakeholder focus. The ninth study (Haniffa and Hudaib 2007) used different dimensions.

Banks used multiple communication materials to provide information on their CSR activities. Banks provided publicly-available CSR information via websites, CSR reports, annual reports, financial reports, media releases, HR documentation, and media stories (see Branco and Rodrigues 2006, Douglas et al. 2004, Haniffa and Hudaib 2007, Hinson et al. 2010, Khan et al. 2009, Pérez and del Bosque 2012, Raubenheimer 2008, Zubairu et al. 2011). CSR website reporting was common.

Two discourse analysis studies (Bartlett et al. 2007, Coupland 2006) on bank reporting on CSR activities highlighted that the banks' discourse focused on meeting stakeholder expectations or "doing good" via their CSR activities and business practices.

Table 32.3 Analysis of results

Authors	Research topic	Research design and analysis	Bank sample/setting	Results
CSR Communication: CSR reporting				
Bartlett et al. (2007)	Investigated Australian banks' internal and external reporting of CSR.	Discourse analysis of print media articles and company documents from 1999 to 2004. 5 in-depth interviews.	1257 media articles, 28 documents from 4 major Australian banks.	Over 6 years, banks shifted from 1-way communication focusing on bank profits to 2-way focusing on stakeholder engagement and meeting societal expectations.
Branco and Rodrigues (2006)	Portuguese banks' use of web sites and annual reports for CSR reporting.	Content analysis of web sites in 2004 and annual reports in 2003 in 4 categories (environmental, human resources, products and consumers, community involvement).	Web sites and annual reports of 15 Portuguese banks (7 listed on Euronext).	Listed banks disclosed more CSR information than unlisted banks. Banks with more local branches (higher consumer visibility) had higher CSR reporting. Annual reports focused on environment and human resources, web sites on community and consumer information.
Coupland (2006)	Investigated how UK banks portrayed their CSR activities on their web pages.	Discourse/textual analytic analysis of online CSR and financial reports.	Online CSR and financial reports from 5 UK banks.	Banks' reports of their CSR activities focus on doing good (community CSR), being good (environmental, internal CSR) and funding good (values-based CSR) with few reports on the latter.
Douglas et al. (2004)	Evaluation of six Irish banks' CSR reporting against four "best practice" international banks.	Content analysis of corporate annual reports and web sites from 1998 to 2001.	Annual reports and web sites of 6 Irish banks, 4 international banks (UK, Germany, Switzerland, Denmark).	Compared to "best practice" banks, Irish banks reported substantially less CSR in annual reports and web sites with minimal reporting on community involvement or environment. Websites more content-heavy than annual reports.
Haniffa and Hudaib (2007)	Extent of CSR reporting in Middle Eastern Islamic banks (IB) and conformance with Shari'ah ethical ideals.	Content analysis of annual reports from 2002–2004. CSR activities coded into 8 dimensions using an Ethical Identity Index (EII).	Annual reports from 7 Islamic banks in Abu Dhabi, Bahrain, Dubai, Kuwait.	Little CSR communication in IBs' annual reports. Only 1 IB had an overall EII mean above average. 6 IBs had disparities between their communicated and ideal ethical identities.

Author	Aim	Method	Sample	Findings
Hinson et al. (2010)	Extent of CSR reporting on bank websites in Ghana.	Content analysis of 16 bank websites for 4 CSR activity areas (environmental, HRM, community involvement, customer/product).	Websites of 16 out of 25 banks in Ghana.	One bank that had won the most CSR awards had the least CSR website communication. Non-award winning banks had better structured CSR website reporting.
Khan et al. (2009)	Investigated Bangladesh banks' CSR reporting and users' perceptions of this.	Content analysis of banks' annual reports (2004–2005). Survey of 50 annual report users (share-holders, analysts, suppliers, staff, customers).	Annual reports from 20 (18 private, 2 nationalized) of the largest listed banks in Bangladesh.	Banks had minimal CSR reporting, with most focus on reporting on human resource issues. Half reported community activities. Annual report users wanted more extensive CSR reporting.
Pérez and del Bosque (2012)	Analysed the perceived role of CSR reporting and CSR in identity in Spanish banks.	Content analysis of CSR reports, stock market indices, corporate communications, media publications.	CSR and other reports in two banks and 4 savings banks in Spain.	Banks take a stakeholder approach, reporting CSR activities according to the benefitted group. Multiple communication channels used, dependent on targeted stakeholder groups.
Raubenheimer (2008)	Investigated employee-related CSR reporting in banks in Australia/New Zealand and Europe.	Content analysis of CSR reports, annual reports, HR documentation, bank websites against 10 CSR criteria.	CSR and other reports in 4 Australian/New Zealand banks vs 3 English, 1 German, 1 Danish bank.	Environmental and community CSR dominate CSR reports. 4 Australian/New Zealand banks rated in the top three and last for employee CSR initiatives, with Deutsche Bank equal third best.
Reinig and Tilt (2009)	Investigated extent of CSR reporting via media releases targeting specific stakeholders in Australia.	Content analysis of 315 media releases from bank websites in 2006.	Media releases from 4 major banks in Australia.	More than 1/3 of media releases contain CSR content with 83% addressing customer concerns (e.g., security) and 73% discussing the banks' community involvement. Customers and community are targeted audiences.
Zubairu et al. (2011)	Extent of Islamic banks' CSR reporting.	Content analysis of annual reports.	Annual reports from 4 Islamic banks in Saudi Arabia.	Poor CSR reporting with least for environment and most for debtor commitment. Reporting practices congruent with conventional, not *Shari'ah*-based banks.

(Continued)

Table 32.3 Continued

Authors	Research topic	Research design and analysis	Bank sample/setting	Results
CSR communication: CSR advertising				
Peterson and Hermans (2004)	CSR themes in USA bank advertising over a decade.	Content analysis of 1879 (total) TV advertisements (3 major networks, 2 local, 6 cable stations). Bank numbers not provided.	In US, TV ads examined three times (1992, 1997, 2002).	CSR themes in advertising rose from 18.7% to 21.1% to 25.7% in 10-year period. CSR issues evolved over time. Most depict bank action on such areas as patriotism, consumerism, environment.
Scharf and Fernandes (2013)	Analysed CSR advertising by a retail bank in Brazil.	Critical discourse analysis of 5 double-page magazine ads.	Magazine ads from 1 retail bank in Brazil.	Bank was portrayed as socially-minded and environmentally concerned, tied into a discourse of rescuing the planet. Ads contrast with Brazilians' perception of banks' solely corporate interests.
CSR stakeholders: Consumers				
Chang et al. (2009)	Influence of social marketing (public-issue-promoted vs revenue-related) on customer-perceived value.	Survey of bank customers. Data analysed using structural equation modelling (SEM).	600 customers of 30 commercial banks in Taiwan.	Public-issue-promoted social marketing increases perceived service quality and decreases perceived risk. Revenue-related social marketing reduced risk perceptions.
Chomvilailuk and Butcher (2013)	Effect of community CSR initiative and CSR reputation beliefs and information on customers' liking of bank.	Survey bank customers in Australia and Thailand analysed with ANOVA and regression.	204 Australian customers and 219 Thai customers.	Both CSR reputation beliefs and new CSR initiative information positively impacted liking for the bank, with almost double effects for reputation in the Australian sample.
Mandhachitara and Poolthong (2011)	Examined the effect of CSR and service quality on attitudes and loyalty in Thailand.	Survey of banking customers. Data analysed using partial least squares (SEM path analysis variant).	275 customers in Thailand.	CSR strongly related to perceived service quality (PSQ) and attitudinal loyalty, but not to loyalty behaviour. PSQ mediated the relationship between CSR and behavioural loyalty.
Matute-Vallejo et al. (2011)	Does CSR and price fairness determine Spanish banking customer loyalty?	Survey of retail and savings bank customers. Data analysed using EFA and SEM.	300 customers in Spain.	CSR influenced customer perceptions of price fairness; both CSR and price fairness determined customer loyalty via a path through satisfaction and commitment.

Source	Research focus	Method	Sample	Findings
McDonald and Lai (2011)	Taiwanese retail banking customers' response to 3 CSR initiative sets (customers, community, environment).	Survey of banking customers. Data analysed using MANOVA and regression.	130 customers in Taiwan.	Customer-favouring initiatives produced more positive attitude and behaviour. Environmental initiatives produced less positive attitude and behaviour. Preferred CSR ranking: customer, community, environment.
Pérez and del Bosque (2013a)	Does customer support for CSR influence their perceptions of CSR practices in the banking industry in Spain.	Survey of banking customers. Cluster analysis used to identify customer groups. ANOVA, SEM.	1124 banking service customers in Spain.	Study 1 identified 4 customer clusters: high vs low CSR support; those seeking benefits to self; those seeking legal and ethical benefits. Different clusters differed in their CSR perceptions.
Pérez and del Bosque (2013b)	Do customer characteristics influence CSR perceptions in the banking industry in Spain.	Survey of banking customers. Confirmatory factor analysis (CFA), SEM.	1124 banking service customers in Spain.	Customer age, collectivism, customer novelty-seeking and customer support for CSR moderate CSR perceptions, but not gender or education.
Pomering and Dolnicar (2009)	Consumer awareness of CSR initiatives and perceptions of CSR communication channels in Australian banks.	Survey of representative sample of retail bank users. Data analysed using descriptive statistics, chi-square tests.	415 customers of 4 major Australian banks.	Low consumer awareness of CSR initiatives. Consumers have a high, but unsatisfied, interest in consumer-related CSR. Bank communication channels considered highly trustworthy for product-related information, but independent sources (e.g., media) are more trusted for CSR information.
Pomering et al. (2013)	Influence of key message variables in Australian bank customers' response to CSR advertising.	Online survey analysed using ANOVA.	176 retail banking customers in Australia.	CSR ads providing detailed information about the social topic are more helpful at contextualising the firm's CSR initiatives than those with less detail.
Poolthong and Mandhachitara (2009)	CSR effects on perceived service quality and brand for Thai retail bank customers.	Survey of retail bank customers. Data analysed using partial least squares (SEM path analysis variant).	275 customers in Thailand.	CSR determined perceived service quality, which influenced trust and affective attitude towards the bank. CSR is directly related to affective attitude.

(Continued)

Table 32.3 Continued

Authors	Research topic	Research design and analysis	Bank sample/setting	Results
CSR stakeholders: Employees				
de Gilder et al. (2005)	Effect of employee volunteering on attitude and behaviour towards the bank in the Netherlands.	Survey of employees in 3 groups: employer-sponsored volunteers (ESV), non-volunteers (NV), community volunteers (CV).	274 employees in 1 bank in the Netherlands.	ESV (vs NV and CV) had more positive work attitudes. These were highly correlated with organizational commitment and citizenship, and negatively correlated with leaving intentions. ESV were more highly educated, with 55% being first-time volunteers.
Ruiz-Palomino et al. (2012)	Does person-organization (P-O) fit mediate ethical culture (EC) and employee outcomes?	Survey of employees in commercial, savings, and credit union banks. Data analysed using partial least squares (SEM path analysis variant).	436 employees in multiple banks in 5 provinces in Spain.	EC was positively related to recommending the firm, affective commitment, job satisfaction, intent to stay. P-O fit partially mediated the EC-employee response relationship.
CSR stakeholder : Community				
Barroso et al. (2012)	Extent of Spanish savings banks' CSR contribution to developing nations' poverty alleviation.	Financial reports for 2009 were analysed for 45 savings banks using descriptive statistics (7 omitted due to no activity, 1 due to no data).	Financial reports of 37 savings banks in Spain.	Banks spent €31million on development programs in 15 countries (9 Latin American): 58.4% for development projects, 14.2% for humanitarian action, 11% for NGO collaboration.
Ragodoo (2009)	Extent of banks in Mauritius contribution to community poverty alleviation.	Semi-structured interviews with CSR-responsible managers in top 100 companies. Analysed using descriptive statistics for each industry.	Managers in 19 locally incorporated banks in Mauritius.	All banks had CSR, contributing an average 1.2% of before-tax profits; Top 3 initiatives: education and training, environmental, sports. Approx. 13% of CSR funds for poverty alleviation.

CSR stakeholder: Supply chain

Keating et al. (2008)	Best approach to develop a sustainable supply chain management (SSCM) system for an Australian bank.	Suppliers of 1 Australian bank.	Suppliers need time and support to recognize sustainable SSCM system benefits. Develop and implement 2 key governance tools: a sustainable supply chain policy; a supplier code of conduct.

Social: CSR practices in banks

Bravo et al. (2012)	Investigated Spanish banks' use of CSR practices to communicate corporate identity.	Online information from 42 banks and 40 savings banks in Spain.	CSR activities classified according to 5 main stakeholders. Most CSR activities targeted customers and the community, with fewer activities for the environment, then employees, then suppliers.
de la Cuesta-González et al. (2006)	Compared the ranking of Spanish banks' CSR practices against EIRIS ranking of international banks.	Public information on 4 banks in Spain vs data on 129 ethical international banking institutions.	Little publicly available CSR information. Two Spanish banks ranked lowest of all banks. Spanish banks just starting to address such issues as financial inclusion of low-income customers or investment selection using ethical and social criteria.
Moure (2011)	Investigated the relationship between organizational charts (OC) and CSR activities in EU banks.	CSR reports from 51 banks in 15 EU countries.	No clear conclusion about relationships between 10 types of OC adopted by banks and likelihood of reported CSR activities.
Narwal (2007)	Investigated (CSR) initiatives used in the Indian banking industry.	CSR personnel in 33 banks in northern Indian state of Haryana.	Banks are undertaking similar core CSR activities focusing on education, development programmes, health, environmental protection and value-added customer services.

(Continued)

Table 32.3 Continued

Authors	Research topic	Research design and analysis	Bank sample/setting	Results
Scholtens (2009)	Investigated CSR practices (social, environmental) in international banks with a €100 billion+ balance sheet in 2000 and 2005.	Using standardized scores, banks scored on 29 indicators in 4 CSR categories (ethics, environment, responsible products, social conduct) from publicly-available information (e.g., reporting, websites).	Public information on 32 banks in 15 countries in 3 regions (North America, Europe, Pacific).	Major improvement in banks' CSR scores between 2000 and 2005. No significant differences between banks in 3 regions. Highest CSR scores: banks from the Netherlands, Germany, France, UK. Lowest scores: 2 Scandinavian banks.
Economic effects				
Bouvain et al. (2013)	Investigated the relationship between 4 CSR dimensions (employees, community, environment, governance) and brand value in banks in three regions.	Tested scores from CSRHub data against brand value data from BrandFinance using ANOVA and multiple regressions.	Data on 84 major banks in China, Hong Kong, Japan, Taiwan, South Korea, USA.	Brand value is positively related to CSR. Brand value in East Asia (Japan and South Korea) is linked to employee management; in China, to community involvement; in the USA to environmental performance and governance.
Goss and Roberts (2011)	Examined the link between USA bank loan practices and CSR.	Companies receiving loans were ranked on 13 CSR concerns and strengths using KLD Research data. Data analysed using cluster, factor, and regression analyses.	3996 banking loans to US firms collected from Dealscan from 1991–2006.	Banks charge firms with CSR concerns 7 to 18 basis points more than more responsible firms. Low-quality borrowers that spend on CSR face higher loan spreads and shorter maturities, but banks are indifferent to CSR spending by high-quality borrowers.
Simpson and Kohers (2002)	Investigated the relationship between corporate social performance (CSP) and financial performance (FP) in USA banks.	CSP measured with the USA's CRA (government) rating. FP measured by return on assets and loan losses to total loans. Analysed using t-tests, regression, OLS regression.	Data on 385 US banks in 1993–1994: 284 high CSP, 101 low CSP.	A strong positive relationship found between CSP and FP. Return on assets for high CSP banks almost twice that of low CSP banks; Loan losses for high CSP banks almost half that of low CSP banks.

Study	Aim	Method	Data	Findings
Soana (2011)	Corporate social performance (CSP) effect on corporate financial performance (CFP) in multinational banks.	CSP evaluated (using 5 proxies) against CFP (measured by market and accounting ratios) using linear bivariate correlations.	Data on 13 Italian banks and 21 international banks.	No statistically significant link between CSP and CFP.
Wu and Shen (2013)	CSR's effect on financial performance (FP) in 162 banks.	Each bank's CSR index is compiled from the EIRIS database. Analysed using multinomial logit method with correlation coefficients, t-tests, regression, chi-square tests.	Banking data from 162 banks in 22 countries from 2003 to 2009.	CSR positively associated with FP for return on assets and equity, net interest income and non-interest income, yet it is negatively associated with non-performing loans.

Voluntariness

Study	Aim	Method	Data	Findings
Angus-Leppan et al. (2010)	Leadership styles influencing CSR practices in a major Australian bank.	Content analysis of 11 in-depth interviews with emergent CSR leaders within the bank using Leximancer software.	Managers in 1 Australian bank highly awarded for its CSR practice.	Two opposing CSR and leadership systems: Explicit CSR (voluntary, deliberate, strategic) linked to autocratic leadership style; Implicit CSR from embedded social norms aligned with emergent, authentic leadership styles.
Pérez and del Bosque (2012)	Analysed Spanish bank managers' CSR perceptions and attitudes.	Content analysis of in-depth interviews with 6 CSR bank managers.	Managers in Spain, 2 banks and 4 savings banks.	Compared to national banks, savings bank managers define CSR as an integral part of their mission.
Pomering and Dolnicar (2009)	Australian bank managers' perceptions of banks' responsibilities and CSR responsibilities.	Content analysis of in-depth interviews with 4 leading bank executives.	Managers in 4 major Australian banks.	Although the prime responsibility was shareholder profitability, executives viewed CSR initiatives as relationship-building, particularly with employees and consumers.
Wu and Shen (2013)	Motivation for CSR engagement: either altruistic, strategic or greenwashing in 162 banks.	Each bank's CSR index is compiled from the EIRIS database. Analysed using multinomial logit method with correlation coefficients, t-tests, regression, chi-square tests.	Banking data from 162 banks in 22 countries from 2003 to 2009.	Banks engage in CSR for strategic motivations.

In addition, two studies (Peterson and Hermans 2004, Scharf and Fernandes 2013) investigated CSR in US or Brazilian advertising. Both studies noted that banking CSR activities were portrayed according to "helping" themes, although the content of these themes differed between the countries.

CSR stakeholders

The stakeholder dimension suggested by Dahlsrud (2008) was used to identify banking CSR studies that focused on different stakeholder groups: consumers, employees, community and the supply chain. Consumers were the dominant stakeholder category, with 10 studies, then two studies on employees, two studies on community and one on the supply chain.

Consumers

Nine consumer studies in Spain, Taiwan, Thailand and Australia investigated banking consumers' response to CSR activities and one investigated consumer response to CSR advertising messages. All studies used surveys and statistical methods of analysis, including structural equation modelling (SEM) or path analysis, MANOVA, ANOVA, regression and partial least squares. All ten studies indicated that banks' CSR activities resulted in positive consumer outcomes.

Six studies identified that CSR positively impacted customer value and risk perceptions (Chang et al. 2009), was positively related to service quality perceptions (Mandhachitara and Poolthong 2011, Poolthong and Mandhachitara 2009), attitudinal loyalty (Mandhachitara and Poolthong 2011), affective attitude (Poolthong and Mandhachitara 2009) and influenced price fairness perceptions (Matute-Vallejo et al. 2011).

Two studies examined the effects of differing types of CSR activities on customer outcomes. CSR initiatives that assisted customers resulted in more positive company-directed attitudes and behavior than environmental initiatives (McDonald and Lai 2011). Ethical activities positively impacted trust, while philanthropic activities positively impacted identification with the bank, with both indirectly influencing loyalty (de los Salmones et al. 2009).

Two studies (Pérez and del Bosque 2013a, 2013b) highlighted that different psychological and demographic traits (gender, age, educational level, occupation, collectivism, novelty-seeking, CSR support) influenced how customers formed their perceptions of a bank's CSR activities.

In sum, banks' CSR activities positively influenced customer perceptions of value, price fairness, risk, and quality, as well as attitudes, loyalty, and trust, indicating the value of CSR in improving relationships with customers.

Employees

Two survey-based studies (de Gilder et al. 2005, Ruiz-Palomino et al. 2012) investigated the influence of CSR on employee-employer relationships within organizations. The first examined employee response to employer-sponsored volunteering, finding that, compared to either non-volunteers or employees who volunteered in their own time, employer-sponsored volunteers had more positive work attitudes, higher organizational commitment and citizenship and lower-leaving intentions (de Gilder et al. 2005). The second study examined the influence of ethical culture indicators (which included employee-favouring initiatives) on employees, finding that an ethical culture resulted in job satisfaction and employees recommending the company and was linked to affective commitment and the intent to stay (Ruiz-Palomino et al. 2012). In sum, CSR improved bank employees' relationships with their organization, although neither investigation examined any spill-over effect onto customer relationships.

Community

Two studies (Barroso et al. 2012, Ragodoo 2009) investigated bank spending on poverty alleviation within communities; one investigating total money spent, the other examining the percentage spent from pre-tax profits. Spanish savings banks contributed substantially to development programmes in less-developed Latin nations (Barroso et al. 2012), however, metrics, such as the percentage of profit allocated to CSR programmes, were not reported. In Mauritius, banks contributed an average of 1.2 percent of pre-tax profits to various CSR initiatives, but only 0.16 percent of these profits were aimed at measures to alleviate poverty; instead, the focus was on three other initiatives (Ragodoo 2009). Neither study provided comparative indicators regarding the amount of spending or percentage of profit expended by banks in other countries on poverty alleviation.

Social: CSR practices in banks

Dahlsrud's (2008) social dimension refers to the relationship between business and society and considers how companies integrate their social concerns into business operations, the scope of impact on communities and how companies contribute to a better society. Five studies were identified which investigated the nature of CSR practices in a total of 202 banks internationally. The studies garnered evidence from publicly available material (for example, CSR reports, website information) and in one case, via interviews with bank CSR personnel. As there are no universally-used indicators of CSR activities, all five studies used different CSR dimensions or indicators for their investigation. Methods of analysis included content and cluster analysis, use of EIRIS database ratings, and use of standardised scores.

Researchers either classified CSR activities according to stakeholders benefitted, such as the community and customers (Bravo et al. 2012, Moure 2011), core areas of CSR funding, such as health and education (Narwal 2007), a combination of both (de la Cuesta-González et al. 2006), or identified key areas indicating CSR practice: ethics, environment, responsible products and social conduct (Scholtens 2009).

Banks clustered activities according to stakeholder groups (consumers, community, employees), dimensions (social, environmental), or themes (health, education, community development). Due to this variance in reporting CSR activities (by CSR stakeholders, by activity areas, by a score), no conclusive picture has emerged about common CSR practices in banks.

Economic

In Dahlsrud's (2008) CSR dimensions, the economic dimension refers to financial or socio-economic aspects, such as a focus on business operations or profitability. Five empirical bank studies were located that investigated economic effects of CSR practices. Three studies (Simpson and Kohers 2002, Soana 2011, Wu and Shen 2013) focused on the effects of CSR or corporate social performance (CSP) on corporate financial performance (CFP). One study (Bouvain et al. 2013) investigated the effect of CSR data on brand value. The final study (Goss and Roberts 2011) examined the link between companies' CSR practices and bank-provided loans. All studies used statistical methods to investigate scores for CSP against CFP indicators.

Two studies (Simpson and Kohers 2002, Wu and Shen 2013) found a strong positive link between CSP and CFP, indicating that CSR practices resulted in a positive financial outcome for companies. Simpson and Kohers (2002) found that high CSP banks produced double the profitability and half the loan losses of low CSP banks. Wu and Shen (2013) found that CSR affects both cost and revenue functions: even though costs increase when a bank engages in

CSR, revenues increase even more. In contrast, Soana (2011) found no significant CSP-CFP link. Measuring such a complex theoretical construct as CSP is challenging, especially when using different CSP proxies such as the KLD index or the Domini 400 Social Index (Simpson and Kohers 2002). In this case, all three studies used CSR proxies, none identical for either CSP or CSP, which may have influenced results. The fourth study (Bouvain et al. 2013) also examined CSR's economic effects, establishing that CSR positively affected major banks' brand value, with between 18 and 66 percent of that variance being explained by CSR practices. The final study reported here examined CSR effects on banking loan policies. Goss and Roberts (2011) found that banks charge more responsible firms a lower loan rate than firms with CSR concerns. These studies indicate that CSR affects both business operations and profitability.

Voluntariness

According to Dahlsrud (2008), voluntariness refers to whether CSR is driven by legal reasons (for example, CSR in India is legally mandated), or by other motivations. Four bank studies investigated managerial values or motives for CSR activity: two in Australia, one in Spain and one multinational study. Three studies used content analysis of managerial interviews, the fourth took a statistical approach, analyzing each bank's CSR index against financial performance.

The study of 162 banks in 22 countries (Wu and Shen 2013) indicated that strategic motives are the main drivers of banks' CSR activities, rather than either altruistic or greenwashing reasons; greenwashing banks paid only "lip service" to CSR, unlike banks with altruistic motives, while strategic banks used CSR to increase profit. Congruent with this finding, bank executives viewed their main responsibility as being profit-oriented, but following a crisis of confidence in banks, recognized that CSR also helps to re-build relationships with both employees and customers (Pomering and Dolnicar 2009). Similarly, national bank managers had a more strategic perspective of CSR, although managers of the smaller savings banks viewed CSR as integral to their mission (Pérez and del Bosque 2012). Taking a different approach, Angus-Leppan et al. (2010) found that CSR motivation was linked to leadership style: strategic CSR was preferred by autocratic leaders, whereas implicit CSR was preferred by authentic leaders. These studies indicate that strategic motivations remain the main driver of banking CSR.

Discussion and managerial implications

This chapter conducted an integrative review of international empirical research on CSR in the banking industry in order to summarize the accumulated state of knowledge. The review has highlighted that research on CSR in the bank marketing literature is still emergent, with the earliest empirical research identified in 2002, but is gaining more research attention each year.

Banking CSR has been investigated in multiple countries and regions. Studies in two culturally divergent countries (Spain and Australia) dominate, perhaps prompted by two very different types of crises. Following the global financial crisis of 2008 (Bennett and Kottasz 2012), Spain experienced the restructuring of its banking system: 45 savings banks or "cajas" were either merged or dissolved to improve their financial prospects (Fund for Orderly Bank Restructuring 2013). The Australian banking sector, in contrast, experienced a crisis of consumer confidence (Pomering and Dolnicar 2009) with high levels of consumer dissatisfaction resulting from unpopular operational practices (Kohler 2003 in Pomering and Dolnicar 2009). These factors may have prompted CSR research in the two countries.

Four themes suggested by Dahlsrud (2008) were used in this integrative review: stakeholder, social, economic and voluntariness, plus one additional theme inductively derived; CSR communication. No literature was identified which fitted Dahlsrud's (2008) fifth dimension, environment. One potential reason for this gap is that, as banks are service organizations, they may be considered to have minimal environmental impact, attracting little research attention.

This analysis identified factors that may provide improved outcomes for companies and tangible benefits to business and are now discussed.

The dominant CSR theme in CSR banking research was CSR communication, more specifically, CSR reporting practices. Even though some banks had low levels of CSR reporting, most banks ensured that details of the CSR activities were communicated via publicly available documents. CSR was predominantly reported according to stakeholder activities. Banks mainly reported on community, customer, and environment initiatives, providing early indications that CSR communication favours these particular stakeholder segments, although this was not consistent between countries. Use of standardized guidelines for CSR reporting according to stakeholder segments would facilitate comparisons of the extent of CSR practice and stakeholder-favouring activities.

Some studies on CSR reporting (for example, Khan et al. 2009) highlighted stakeholder demand for more extensive CSR reporting. This is allied with a widespread low level of awareness of CSR initiatives, as stakeholders often do not actively seek CSR information. Yet CSR activity enables an organization to be differentiated from its competitors (Balmer et al. 2007 cited in Bravo et al. 2012), providing a competitive edge. Studies (Branco and Rodrigues 2006, Pérez and del Bosque 2012) suggest that CSR communication is most effective when messages are tailored to particular stakeholder groups, using as a carrier the medium best suited to each group. For example, targeted innovative social media strategies may be the most effective way to reach Generation Y, as they are heavy social media consumers.

As some banking institutions underestimate the strategic importance of CSR reporting, they face the risk of their CSR activities going unnoticed, thus wasting their investment (Pérez and del Bosque 2012). Further, they may underestimate the growing sophistication in stakeholder expectations about CSR communication. For example, a Cone Communication (2012) study indicated that 84 percent of surveyed US citizens wanted a company to not just communicate about its CSR activities, but to clearly demonstrate the programme outcomes. This carries significant implications for companies engaged in CSR to go beyond simply spending on initiatives, reported via publicly-accessible information, to report on the results-oriented effectiveness of their CSR spending via key performance indicators.

The use of CSR advertising is increasing in order to meet consumer demands for information on how firms manage social and environmental expectations (Dawkins 2004 in Pomering et al. 2013). Although the use of CSR themes in advertising is on the rise (Peterson and Hermans 2004), advertising through mass media may result in the disbelief of stated claims and a distrust of the firm's motives (Pomering and Johnson 2009b in Pérez and del Bosque 2012). For example, Pomering et al. (2013) found that providing detailed CSR commitment information in advertising did not mitigate consumer scepticism. Effective CSR communication has largely proved elusive (Dawkins 2004 in Pomering et al. 2013).

Investigation of stakeholder studies revealed a focus on consumers. It was consistently demonstrated that consumers respond positively to various CSR initiatives, with these responses including increased loyalty and trust. The influence of ethical behavior in driving banking customer loyalty is also discussed by El-Manstrly (Chapter 11). Further, as distrust of banks has been embedded into popular culture (see Hurley, Gong and Waqar Chapter 30), it is evident that an effective CSR strategy is a key tool for banks to mitigate negative perceptions and regain consumer trust. Studies on customer segmentation variables (Pérez and del Bosque 2013a; 2013b) highlighted the possibility that managers more effectively could target different CSR activities to different customer segments possessing different psychological and demographic traits, based on their support for CSR.

The stakeholder studies revealed that three stakeholder groups – employees, community and supply chains – were little studied in the bank marketing literature. While this reflects a similar research focus in the broader CSR literature, a lack of CSR reporting does not imply a lack of company initiatives. The two studies on employee CSR revealed that employees positively respond to CSR activities, in particular, to employee volunteering schemes, highlighting the need to integrate employee initiatives into CSR programming. The two studies on communities investigated spending on various community CSR initiatives, rather than community response to CSR initiatives, providing no guidelines for managing community initiatives. However, Mishra et al. (see Chapter 28) suggest that microfinance to low income entrepreneurs and producers may be the single most effective way to compact poverty. Further insight is also provided by Koku (see Chapter 35) on financial services for the socially disadvantaged. The supply chain study by Keating et al. (2008) highlighted that managers need to include supply chain initiatives to develop more fully-integrated stakeholder programmes. In investigating the best method to develop a sustainable supply chain, the authors suggested that banks could develop two tools: a supply chain policy and a supplier code of conduct.

From the analysis of the social dimension of CSR practices, it was clear that the banking industry lacks commonly-used indicators to identify CSR practice areas. More widespread use of identical indicators would progress understanding of trends in the banking industry's initiative development and implementation. Further, it would provide more clear-cut evidence of whether the banking industry favours particular practices or stakeholder segments. However, from the earlier review on CSR communication, it appears evident that CSR activities are increasingly being reported according to stakeholder groups. This may be due to the recent focus on taking a stakeholder approach to CSR practice.

Despite evidence that the banking industry is one of the main investors in CSR worldwide (Marín and Ruiz 2007 in Pérez and del Bosque 2012), only two studies were located investigating spending. Although the banking industry is considered to be a sustainability leader that often claims that it builds a better world in which to live (Scholtens 2008), evidence regarding banks' actual spend on CSR as a percentage of banking income or profits is little investigated.

Congruent with Dahlsrud's (2008) economic dimension, the review found that CSR had financial impacts on banking institutions. As well as stakeholder relationships, CSR affects an organization's management, its production and commercial activities (de la Cuesta-González et al. 2006). Three studies (Bouvain et al. 2012, Simpson and Kohers 2002, Wu and Shen 2013) identified a strong positive relationship between corporate social performance and financial performance indicators, such as profitability. Although Soana's (2011) own study determined no clear link between these indicators, the author identified 28 studies in other business domains that confirmed a positive relationship between corporate social performance and corporate financial performance. In terms of profit measures, banks conducting CSR activities outperform banks that do not engage in CSR.

The studies investigating CSR motivations indicated that banks CSR programmes remain driven by strategic or profit-driven motives, with only a sub-set of smaller banks having more altruistic motivations. However, the studies in this review indicate that banking leaders are developing the vision to see that CSR aligns with strategic goals, counters negative stakeholder perceptions and promulgates positive stakeholder responses.

What we should know: future research directions

The final objective of this review was to highlight important issues that research has left unresolved, suggesting potential research directions.

As stakeholders want more information about banks' CSR activities (Khan et al. 2009, Pomering and Dolnicar 2009), future studies might investigate preferred methods of CSR reporting and whether this differs between stakeholder groups.

Although consumers remain the dominant researched stakeholder group in non-banking CSR studies, little research exists on banking customer response to differing CSR initiatives. Customers may prefer customer-oriented CSR activities (McDonald and Lai 2011), which has implications not only for CSR reporting, but also for funds allocation.

Employee response to, and preference for, CSR initiatives is also neglected, both in banking research and in the broader research domain. As managers frequently take a "top-down" approach to establishing CSR programmes based on individual or corporate preferences (Carroll 1999 cited in Mandhachitara and Poolthong 2011), it is crucial to evaluate employee preferences to better inform CSR strategies.

Even though the banking industry heavily invests in CSR internationally (Marín and Ruiz 2007 in Pérez and del Bosque 2012), the banking industry would benefit from further evidence on CSR spending as a percentage of banking income or profits, in particular, to supply comparative spending guidelines.

Ragodoo (2009) noted that research on CSR in the developing world is scarce (also see Chapter 28 by Mishra et al. and Chapter 35 by Koku). Further, Lindgreen et al. (2009) question whether expectations of CSR in developing countries are the same as expectations found in well-developed economies. The answer to this question and to whether CSR is practised in the same way by banks in developed and developing nations has yet to be addressed.

The Islamic banking model (see Rammal, Chapter 26), which has CSR processes integrated, has received little investigation. However, as Islamic banks have social goals based on the Shari'ah which has society's betterment as its ultimate goal, banks may be expected to portray a high level of corporate social responsibility (Zubairu et al. 2011). Whether CSR reporting is viewed as unnecessary in Islamic society requires investigation.

Following scandals and the fallout from the global financial crisis, the international banking industry has accumulated negative stakeholder perceptions. Many consider bank CSR as a means of responding to criticism, rather than as part of a proactive stakeholder strategy (Reinig and Tilt 2009). Soana (2011) noted that CSR has a risk mitigation undertone, safeguarding reputation and profits in a crisis. When examining CSR initiatives' effect on consumers' response to a crisis, Assiouras et al. (2011) found that positively perceived CSR initiatives enhanced customers' sympathy and moderated anger. With Hurley, Gong and Waqar (Chapter 30) noting that movies portraying villainous, greedy bankers tap into the popular *zeitgeist*, generating audience's emotional involvement via anger, this suggests that there is scope for further investigation into the role of CSR and its effect on emotions.

References

Albaum, G. and Peterson, R.A., 1984. Empirical research in international marketing: 1976–82. *Journal of International Business Studies*, 15(1), pp. 161–73.

Angus-Leppan, T., Metcalf, L. and Benn, S., 2010. Leadership styles and CSR practice: An examination of sensemaking, institutional drivers and CSR leadership. *Journal of Business Ethics*, 93(2), pp. 189–213.

Assiouras, I., Ozgen, O. and Skourtis, G., 2011. The effect of corporate social responsibility on consumers' emotional reactions in a product-harm crisis. *American Marketing Association*, pp. 163–70. Available at *www.academia.edu/1140169/the_effect_of_corporate_social_responsibility_on_consumers_emotional_reactions_in_product-harm_crisis*

Barroso, M.J., Galera, C., Valero, V. and Galán, M.M., 2012. Corporate social responsibility: a study of savings banks. *International Journal of Bank Marketing*, 30(6), pp. 414–35.

Bartlett, J., Tywoniak, S. and Hatcher, C., 2007. Public relations professional practice and the institutionalisation of CSR. *Journal of Communication Management*, 11(4), pp. 281–99.

Bennett, R. and Kottasz, R., 2012. Public attitudes towards the UK banking industry following the global financial crisis. *International Journal of Bank Marketing*, 30(2), pp. 28–147.

Bouvain, P., Baumann, C. and Lundmark, E., 2013. Corporate social responsibility in financial services: A comparison of Chinese and East Asian banks vis-á-vis American banks. *International Journal of Bank Marketing*, 31(6), pp. 420–39.

Boyatzis, R.E., (1998). *Transforming qualitative information: Thematic analysis and code development*. Sage.

Branco, M.C. and Rodrigues, L.L., 2006. Communication of corporate social responsibility by Portuguese banks: A legitimacy theory perspective. *Corporate Communications: An International Journal*, 11(3), pp. 232–48.

Bravo, R., Matute, J. and Pina, J.M., 2012. Corporate social responsibility as a vehicle to reveal the corporate identity: A study focused on the websites of Spanish financial entities. *Journal of Business Ethics*, 107(2), pp. 129–46.

Carroll, A.B., 1979. A three-dimensional conceptual model of corporate social performance. *Academy of Management Review*, 4, pp. 497–505.

Carroll, A. B., 1991. The pyramid of corporate social responsibility: toward the moral management of organizational stakeholders. *Business Horizons*, 34(4), pp. 39–48.

Chang, H.-S., Chen, T.-Y. and Tseng, C.-M., 2009. How public-issue-promoted and revenue-related types of social marketing influence customer-perceived value in Taiwan's banking industry. *Journal of International Consumer Marketing*, 21(1), pp. 35–49.

Chomvilailuk, R. and Butcher, K., 2013. The effect of CSR knowledge on customer liking, across cultures. *International Journal of Bank Marketing*, 31(2), pp. 98–114.

Cone Communications, 2012. Cone Communications Corporate Social Return Trend Tracker. Available at *www.conecomm.com/2012corporatesocialreturntrendtracker*

Coupland, C., 2006. Corporate social and environmental responsibility in web-based reports: Currency in the banking sector? *Critical Perspectives on Accounting*, 17(7), pp. 865–81.

Dahlsrud, A., 2008. How corporate social responsibility is defined: An analysis of 37 definitions. *Corporate Social Responsibility and Environmental Management*, 15(1), pp. 1–13.

de Gilder, D., Schuyt, T.N.M. and Breedijk, M., 2005. Effects of an employee volunteering program on the work force: The ABN-AMRO case. *Journal of Business Ethics*, 61(2), pp. 143–52.

de la Cuesta-González, M., Muñoz-Torres, M.J. and Fernández-Izquierdo, M.A., 2006. Analysis of social performance in the Spanish financial industry through public data: A proposal. *Journal of Business Ethics*, 69(3), pp. 289–304.

de los Salmones, M.D.M.G., Perez, A. and del Bosque, I. R., 2009. The social role of financial companies as a determinant of consumer behaviour. *International Journal of Bank Marketing*, 27(6), pp. 467–85.

Douglas, A., Doris, J. and Johnson, B., 2004. Corporate social reporting in Irish financial institutions. *The TQM Magazine*, 16(6), pp. 387–95.

European Commission, 2013. How companies influence our society: Citizen's View. Flash Eurobarometer 363, available at *http://ec.europa.eu/public_opinion/archives/flash_arch_374_361_en.htm* (accessed 12 March 2013).

European Community, 2011. *Sustainable and responsible business Corporate Social Responsibility(CSR)*, available at *http://ec.europa.eu/enterprise/policies/sustainable-business/corporate-social-responsibility/index_en.htm* (accessed 12 March 2013).

Fund for Orderly Bank Restructuring, (FROB, 2013). *April 2013 Report*. 20130425_Presentacion_abril2013[1].pdf, retrieved 30.9.13 from *www.frob.es*

Freeman, R. E., 1984. *Strategic Management: A Stakeholder Perspective*. Englewood Cliffs, NJ: Prentice Hall.

Goss, A. and Roberts, G.S., 2011. The impact of corporate social responsibility on the cost of bank loans. *Journal of Banking & Finance*, 35(7), pp. 1794–1810.

Haniffa, R. and Hudaib, M., 2007. Exploring the ethical identity of Islamic banks via communication in annual reports. *Journal of Business Ethics*, 76(1), pp. 97–116.

Hinson, R., Boateng, R. and Madichie, N., 2010. What does my website say about my CSR activities? An investigation of banks' operating in Ghana. *International Journal of Bank Marketing*, 28(7), pp. 498–518.

Joffe, H. and Yardley, L. (2004). Content and thematic analysis. In Research Methods for Clinical and Health Psychology (Marks, D. F. and Yardley, L. eds) Sage, London, pp. 56–68.

Keating, B., Quazi, A., Kriz, A. and Coltman, T., 2008. In pursuit of a sustainable supply chain: insights from Westpac Banking Corporation. *Supply Chain Management*, 13(3), pp. 175–79.

Khan, M.H.U.Z., Halabi, A.K. and Samy, M., 2009. Corporate social responsibility (CSR) reporting: a study of selected banking companies in Bangladesh. *Social Responsibility Journal*, 5(3), pp. 344–57.

Lindgreen, A, Swaen, V. and Johnston W. J. 2009. Corporate Social Responsibility: An empirical investigation of U.S. organizations. *Journal of Business Ethics*, 85 (2), pp. 303–323.

Lin-Hi, N. and Müller, K., 2013 (in press). The CSR bottom line: Preventing corporate social irresponsibility. *Journal of Business Research http://dx.doi.org/10.1016/j.jbusres.2013.02.015*

Mandhachitara, R. and Poolthong, Y., 2011. A model of customer loyalty and corporate social responsibility. *Journal of Services Marketing*, 25(2), pp. 122–33.

Marin, L. and Ruiz, S., 2007. "I need you too!" Corporate identity attractiveness for consumers and the role of social responsibility." *Journal of Business Ethics*, 71(3), pp. 245–260.

Matute-Vallejo, J., Bravo, R. and Pina, J.M., 2011. The Influence of Corporate Social Responsibility and Price Fairness on Customer Behaviour: Evidence from the Financial Sector. *Corporate Social Responsibility and Environmental Management*, 18(6), pp. 317–31.

McDonald, C. (2012, September 1), 'Banks behaving badly', *CFO Magazine*, viewed 21 September 2012, *www.cfo.com/article.cfm/14658803*

McDonald, L.M. and Lai, C.H., 2011. Impact of corporate social responsibility initiatives on Taiwanese banking customers. *International Journal of Bank Marketing*, 29(1), pp. 50–63.

Moure, R.C., 2011. Is there any relationship between organizational charts and corporate social responsibility? The EU-15 banking case. *Social Responsibility Journal*, 7(3), pp. 421–37.

Narwal, M., 2007. CSR Initiatives of Indian Banking Industry. *Social Responsibility Journal*, 3(4), pp. 49–60.

Pérez, A. and del Bosque, I. R., 2012. The role of CSR in the corporate identity of banking service providers. *Journal of Business Ethics*, 108(2), pp. 145–66.

——, 2013a. How customer support for corporate social responsibility influences the image of companies: Evidence from the banking industry. *Corporate Social Responsibility and Environmental Management*, published online, wileyonlinelibrary.com DOI: 10.1002/csr.1331

——, 2013b. Customer personal features as determinants of the formation process of corporate social responsibility perceptions. *Psychology and Marketing*, 30(10), pp. 903–17.

Peterson, R.T. and Hermans, C.M., 2004. The communication of social responsibility by US banks. *The International Journal of Bank Marketing*, 22(3), pp. 199–211.

Pomering, A. and Dolnicar, S., 2009. Assessing the prerequisite of successful CSR implementation: are consumers aware of CSR initiatives? *Journal of Business Ethics*, 85(2), pp. 285–301.

Pomering, A., Johnson, L.W. and Noble, G., 2013. Advertising corporate social responsibility: Results from an experimental manipulation of key message variables. *Corporate Communications: An International Journal*, 18(2), pp. 249–63.

Poolthong, Y. and Mandhachitara, R., 2009. Customer expectations of CSR, perceived service quality and brand effect in Thai retail banking. *International Journal of Bank Marketing*, 27(6), pp. 408–27.

Ragodoo, N.J.F., 2009. CSR as a tool to fight against poverty: the case of Mauritius. *Social Responsibility Journal*, 5(1), pp. 19–33.

Raubenheimer, K., 2008. A Research Note: Employee-focused corporate social responsibility reporting in the banking industry. *New Zealand Journal of Employment Relations*, 33(3), pp. 91–104.

Reinig, C.J. and Tilt, C.A., 2009. Corporate social responsibility issues in media releases: A stakeholder analysis of Australian banks. *Issues in Social and Environmental Accounting*, 2(2), pp. 176–97.

Ruiz-Palomino, P., Martínez-Cañas, R. and Fontrodona, J., 2012. Ethical culture and employee outcomes: the mediating role of person-organization fit. *Journal of Business Ethics*, pp. 1–16.

Scharf, E. R. and Fernandes, J., (2013). The advertising of corporate social responsibility in a Brazilian bank. *International Journal of Bank Marketing*, 31(1), pp. 24–37.

Scholtens, B., 2009. Corporate Social Responsibility in the International Banking Industry. *Journal of Business Ethics*, 86(2), pp. 159–75.

Simpson, W. G. and Kohers, T., 2002. The link between corporate social and financial performance: Evidence from the banking industry. *Journal of Business Ethics*, 35(2), pp. 97–109.

Soana, M.-G., 2011. The relationship between corporate social performance and corporate financial performance in the banking sector. *Journal of Business Ethics*, 104(1), pp. 133–48.

Taveggia, T., 1974. Resolving research controversy through empirical cumulation. *Sociological Methods and Research*, 2(4), pp. 395–407.

Wu, M-W. and Shen, C-Hu., 2013. Corporate social responsibility in the banking industry: Motives and financial performance. *Journal of Banking & Finance*, 37, pp. 3529–47.

Yin, R.K., 2003. *Case Study Research Design and Methods*. Thousand Oaks, California: Sage Publications.

Zubairu, U.M., Sakariyau, O.B. and Dauda, C.K., 2011. Social reporting practices of Islamic banks in Saudi Arabia. *International Journal of Business and Social Science*, 2(2), pp. 193–205.

33

Marketing challenges and strategies for socially responsible investment initiatives

Jonas Nilsson

Introduction

The financial services industry, in general, is not an industry that is known among the public for its adherence to social responsibility and ethics. In many ways this is not surprising given the number of highly publicized scandals that have been associated with the finance industry, such as Enron, WorldCom, Nick Leeson and the Barings Bank, to name a few (Boatright 2008). However, while people have never rated the ethical standards of Wall Street highly, it seems that public opinion has hit new lows with the recent credit crunch and subprime crisis. For example, in a summary of attitudes towards the finance industry, Owens (2012) highlights that only 23 per cent of Americans agreed that bankers had a 'high' or 'very high' level of honesty and ethical standards in 2010. Moreover, 8 per cent of respondents said that they had 'only some' or 'hardly any' confidence in the people running Wall Street. These extremely negative perceptions are beginning to be recognized by the industry itself. For example, in a survey among financial services professionals, 96 per cent agreed that they have invited this negative attention through their own acts or omissions (Makovsky 2012).

Within the finance industry, however, there is a growing sector that challenges this perception of greed, scandals, and selfishness. Growing out of investment practices used by religious institutions for centuries, the Socially Responsible Investment (SRI) movement has grown during the last couple of decades (USSIF 2012, Eurosif 2010). Catering to socially concerned investors who want to invest their money in a socially responsible manner, SRI is an investment process which actively incorporates environmental, social, or governance (ESG) criteria (SIF 2007, Sparkes 2002). By incorporating various ESG criteria into mutual funds, the SRI industry gives socially concerned consumers the opportunity to invest their money in a manner that is in line with their social, environmental, or ethical concerns. Given the general trend of consumers increasingly demanding products and services positioned as socially responsible, fair trade, green, or eco, it is not surprising that many consumers have decided to take the opportunity to act in a socially responsible manner in their investment behavior as well.

In many ways, mutual funds profiled as SRI are becoming a recognized and important part of the modern financial services landscape. While this area could often have been overlooked a number of years ago, it has become increasingly important for financial services institutions to understand the nature and drivers of SRI. In order to meet this need, this chapter is intended to serve as a general starting point for an enquiry into the nature of SRI and how SRI practices impact financial services marketing. In order to accomplish this, the two purposes of this chapter are to introduce the background as well as the contemporary practices of SRI and to discuss the implications of SRI for financial services providers and financial services marketing.

The rest of this chapter is structured as follows: first, the focus will be on the historical roots and the development of SRI practices into the form we see today, then the financial characteristics of SRI will be discussed, finally, the chapter examines the implications and challenges of socially responsible investment to financial services providers today along with a look at current strategies that companies use when working in this area.

Historical development and contemporary practices

When tracing the history and development of the phenomenon of socially responsible investing, we clearly note that the roots of SRI are mainly of a religious nature (for example, Schwartz 2003, Bengtsson 2008). In many cases, these roots may arguably date back thousands of years. For example, Schwartz (2003) outlines aspects such as the Jewish doctrine, unchanged for over 3500 years, as well as the policies of the Catholic Church during the Middle Ages, as indications of the roots of responsible investment. With respect to a later period, Quakers are often considered to be pioneers of responsible investment as they refused to do business with firms involved with activities that were considered to go against their religious principles, such as the slave trade, tobacco and alcohol (Sparkes 2002, Schwartz 2003, Sparkes 2006).

While these examples extend far back into the past, it was not until about half a century ago that SRI started to take the mutual fund form and become available to the public. However, even here, the first mutual funds were closely connected to, and inspired by, religious organizations and principles. For example, it has been argued that the first ever publicly available mutual fund that used some sort of social screen was the AktieAnsvar Aktiefond, established in Sweden by the Temperance movement and the Baptist church as early as 1965 (Bengtsson 2008). In America, the first such fund open to the public was Pax World Fund, funded on Methodist principles (Pax 2013). In the United Kingdom, the Friends Provident Stewardship Fund, based on Quaker principles, became the first SRI fund available to the public in 1984 (Sparkes 2006).

In many ways, it was the needs and desires of religious organizations to invest their assets in accordance with their principles that triggered and guided the development of SRI in its early days. However, while this influence has historically been important, in more recent times, other issues and events, not necessarily connected to religious beliefs, have helped SRI-profiled mutual funds to develop into a mainstream financial product. While there are many factors that deserve mentioning here, Sparkes (2006) highlights four events or aspects that were particularly important in popularizing and mainstreaming SRI. These include public opinion against the Vietnam War, where some of the first ESG resolutions were filed and the boycott of South Africa during the apartheid era where several investment funds pressured companies to stop doing business in that country. Another important aspect for the development of SRI according to Sparkes (2006), was the environmental crises and public awareness of environmental issues in the 1980s, which made the environment an important issue for many people, as well as the legal developments that oblige private pension funds (in the UK context) to consider ESG issues. An important event that occurred later, and so was not included in the review by Sparkes (2006), is also the founding and growth of the UN-backed initiative Principles for Responsible Investment (UNPRI), which has helped to bring responsible investment to a wide range of mainstream asset owners and investment managers. To date, the initiative has around 1,200 signatories all over the world, and has acted as an important organization for enabling SRI initiatives, (Gond and Piani 2013) and contributing to the accessibility of SRI (for example, Sievänen et al. 2013).

Although it is beyond the scope of this chapter to go in depth into how each of these events have had an impact on the development of SRI, they have all, each in their own way, sparked interest for, popularized, or legitimized the integration of ESG factors into the financial investment process (for example, Schwartz 2003, Sparkes 2006, Domini 2001, Gond and Piani 2013, Sparkes 2002). Given that these events are diverse in both their nature and substantive area, it is not surprising that the current nature of SRI differs significantly from its previous form. Today, SRI has grown to encompass a multitude of ESG issues, methods and strategies. While some of these are based on 'original' religious roots (Sparkes 2006), others are much newer and based on modern ideas of Corporate Social Responsibility (see, for example, the review in Berry and Junkus 2013). This diverse nature of SRI is also reflected in the contemporary terminology that surrounds the area. While Socially Responsible Investing (or just Responsible Investing) in many ways is the dominant term to describe the process of incorporating ESG issues into the financial investment process, there are numerous other terms and concepts used such as 'impact', 'green', 'ethical', 'faith-based', 'social' or 'sustainable investing', to mention a few. In many ways, each of these terms indicates a different approach to integrating ESG issues into the investment process.

In essence, the wide variety of terms and concepts used to describe ESG integration indicates one important fact: SRI today is not a single uniform procedure or process (Sandberg et al. 2009). Instead, it has developed into a heterogeneous collection of strategies and issues, sometimes with little in common other than the fact that they all deal with the inclusion of some form of non-financial ESG concern in the financial investment process. This diverse nature of mutual funds that practice SRI can be better understood by examining the two major components where SRI practices today differ: the ESG issues that are involved and the methods or strategies through which these issues are incorporated into the investment process. This is explored in the following sections.

The ESG issues present in contemporary SRI funds

Current SRI practices incorporate a large number of ESG issues. This wide scope of SRI becomes clear when we consider the issues that are dealt with in contemporary SRI initiatives. In many ways, it could be said that although the ESG acronym provides the overarching framework, what actually is included in the environmental, social and governance categories differs considerably among various mutual funds.

At the heart of this diversity is the sheer number of possible ESG issues. For example, Socialfunds, a website specializing in providing consumers with information on SRI funds, categorizes SRI mutual funds according to ten different ESG issues (Socialfunds 2014). Here, a wide range of issues is addressed, such as environmental concerns, product safety and animal rights. However, while one may think that these ten issues provide quite a broad scope, they actually represent the tip of the iceberg that is visible to consumers. Considering that issues such as the environment, human rights and employment are broad, and actually contain many separate issues, it is hardly surprising that in actual ESG analysis many more indicators are used to evaluate the socially responsible nature of companies. For example, according to Louche and Lydenberg (2010), the SAM group (RobecoSAM, an asset management company focusing on sustainable investing) uses 130 indicators in its process while Asset 4 (an organization that provides investors with ESG information) uses as many as 250 performance indicators to evaluate the ESG nature of potential investment objects. While many of these are indicators or subcategories of the ten issues above, the fact that there are hundreds of relevant issues and factors nevertheless says quite a lot about the current nature of SRI. Thus, although the ESG acronym may initially seem fairly straightforward, it actually covers many different complex issues.

In all, it is safe to say that SRI encompasses a multitude of non-financial issues. This fact is also reflected in the market offerings related to SRI mutual funds. In this context, it is possible to practice SRI by only taking one ESG issue into account, or be much broader in focus and address a multitude of issues. This gives rise to mutual funds that focus on specific ESG categories or issues, such as faith-based investing or environmentally profiled mutual funds. However, there are also numerous funds that have a general orientation, targeting several ESG issues in different areas.

Nevertheless, while these differences create many different types of SRI-profiled mutual funds, this discussion on the ESG issues involved only tells part of the story of the diversity of current SRI practices. The other aspect important here relates to the methods or strategies used to actually incorporate the issues into the investment process. These are discussed in the next section.

The methods and strategies used in contemporary SRI funds

Much like the ESG issues used in current SRI practices, the methods and strategies used to incorporate these issues into the investment process are also broad in scope and diverse in nature. Here, the literature on SRI evidences the existence of many different strategies that all can be used to incorporate ESG issues into the investment process. While there is some disagreement among commentators as to the main strategies of SRI (for example, Sandberg et al. 2009, USSIF 2012, Sparkes 2002, Eurosif 2010), Louche and Lydenberg (2010) summarize four of the strategies that are considered central to the SRI movement. These include: avoidance, inclusion, relative selection and engagement.

Avoidance according to Louche and Lydenberg (2010), basically means seeking to avoid investing in companies engaged in activities perceived to be problematic from an ESG perspective, such as the production of goods or services that are harmful to individuals or society. Generally, subscribers to this strategy tend to use one or more of several exclusionary screening tools related to the investment object's products or activities. Examples here include production of alcohol, tobacco, weaponry, as well as companies in breach of certain international treaties.

Inclusion means seeking to invest in companies or industries that are considered to benefit society. This is essentially a positive version of the avoidance screening described above, actively including companies especially beneficial to society rather than focusing on excluding companies engaged in activities perceived to be problematic from an ESG perspective.

Relative selection means selecting companies who are leaders in their particular industry or sector. In contrast to many avoidance strategies, no general exclusions based on products or industry are made. Instead, the selection is made from the best companies in each industry or sector.

Engagement means establishing contact with a company and using influence as a shareholder to attempt to change conduct and practices regarding ESG issues. Examples here include proxy voting, filing of shareholder resolutions, and dialogue with management (Louche and Lydenberg 2010).

As is evident from the discussion above, these strategies differ in many ways. As a consequence of this, SRI-profiled mutual funds may take on completely differing forms not only depending on the issues that are addressed, but also on what strategy (or combination of strategies) is used. While a strict avoidance strategy, for example, would exclude entire industries from the mutual fund, a relative selection strategy would open the doors to include many companies in these industries. An engagement strategy, on the other hand, would not set inclusion limitations, thus enabling companies that are not traditionally associated with social responsibility to be included into the investment portfolio.

The impact of ESG factors on financial performance

One of the main questions focused on in research on SRI is how the integration of ESG issues into the investment process impacts a fund's financial metrics. This issue is important for both providers and consumers of SRI. Providers need to be able to accurately communicate financial prospects and create realistic expectations. Consumers, on the other hand, need to be informed about the financial opportunities when investing in SRI-profiled mutual funds. A selection of the research on actual (objective) financial performance as well as the perceived (subjective) financial performance of SRI is subsequently reviewed.

Objective financial performance of SRI

How then does the financial performance of SRI stack up compared to regular investments? Is it poor enough to discourage consumers from investing, or does SRI do so well that it could even serve as a potential point of attraction for investors? To date, a large amount of research has been performed on the topic (for example, Statman 2000, Derwall et al. 2005, Adler and Kritzman 2008, Humphrey and Lee 2011). However, while this question may seem straightforward in theory, in practice it is one that is surrounded by conflicting results (for example, Chegut et al. 2011, Climent and Soriano 2011). In the literature, this debate holds seemingly good arguments for both sides. On the one hand, the fact is that companies with a good CSR record often also are profitable, indicating potential for a good financial return in funds that invest in these companies. On the other hand, there are issues such as a limited diversification (due to screening away possible investment objects) and possibility of higher management fees (because managers have to perform extra work to identify companies with a good possibility for financial return and a good CSR record), that would suggest a lower return in SRI type mutual funds (for example, Kalev and Wallace 2012, Renneboog et al. 2008).

Against this somewhat diverse background, it is not surprising that there still seems to be room for some debate on the issue of financial performance of SRI. In an ambitious review of past research on the topic, Kalev and Wallace (2012: 65) sum up the current status of research: 'It may be argued that SRI funds underperform conventional funds, [...], however [...] although the SRI alpha (or average alpha) is less than the conventional fund alpha, few of the papers reviewed can show that there is a significant difference between the two'. In other words, the current state of research seems to indicate that while there are components of financial theory that largely imply that SRI should underperform and that some papers seem to indicate this, actual empirical research on the topic has failed to come up with a conclusive answer on the issue.

Perceived financial performance of SRI

While the objective financial performance is important, consumers of mutual funds are not likely to be completely familiar with, and knowledgeable of, the latest research in the area. Moreover, consumer perceptions are influenced by many things that are not necessarily that 'objective', such as advertising, financial advisers, interest groups, and family and friends. While they obviously are related, in the consumer domain, the perceived return of SRI among consumers is likely to differ from the actual objective financial metrics. As consumers make decisions on their personal knowledge and opinions, these perceptions are likely to be important determinants of the decision to invest in SRI.

What then, are consumers' perceptions of the financial performance of SRI? Given that this may be a relevant predictor of investing in SRI, it is quite surprising to see a lack of research on the topic. This is especially remarkable considering the abundance of research that attempts to address the objective financial performance of SRI. However, while it is difficult to generate any in-depth insight into consumer perceptions, the literature contains some indications of consumer perceptions on this topic. Table 33.1 is a summary of a selection of empirical data, gathered from studies in the UK, Sweden and Spain, on the topic.

Although the limited amount of data in Table 33.1 means that it should be viewed only as an indication of possible consumer perceptions, it nonetheless generates an interesting insight into consumers' perceptions of financial performance in SRI. In many ways, a similar pattern emerges in the three surveys. While some people think that investing in SRI may generate an above-average financial return, the majority of people do not hold these positive beliefs. Instead, most people seem to think that SRI mutual funds generate a similar or lower level of return than a conventional alternative: more than 80 per cent in each of the three surveys. Given that the surveys were performed in three different European countries, the fact that they show similar results is interesting as it indicates that these perceptions are not necessarily country-specific.

In general, these perceptions among consumers are important as previous research has shown that perceived financial performance actually impacts socially responsible investment behaviour. For example, Nilsson (2008) and Pérez-Gladish et al. (2012) both find a relationship between financial performance and investment in SRI. From this perspective, the fact that consumers often perceive that there is a financial penalty for investing in SRI, as displayed in Table 33.1, is clearly of concern to providers of SRI. However, looking to the broader literature, although a positive perceived financial return will impact behavior in a positive manner, financial return may be less important to SR-investors than it is for conventional investors. For example, looking at mutual fund flows, both Benson and Humphrey (2008) and Renneboog et al. (2011) find that past return is less important for SR-investors than for their conventional counterparts. Several studies, such as Lewis and Mackenzie (2000), Beal and Goyen (1998), as well as Berry and Yeung (2012) show that there is at least some willingness among SR-investors to not always attempt to maximize financial returns.

The nature of this willingness to trade-off some return is in many ways tied to the investors' own characteristics and preferences. For example, in Nilsson (2009) several groups of SR-investors were profiled. Here, the group that put the least emphasis on financial return in their investment decision-making also showed other characteristics that testify to their pro-social commitment. For example, this group was likely to donate significant amounts to charity and they also believed that SRI was a good way to address perceived social, environmental, and ethical problems.

Table 33.1 Perceptions of SRI performance among (potential) retail investors

Perceived return of SRI among (potential) retail investors

	Much lower	Slightly lower	Similar	Slightly higher	Much higher
Lewis and Mackenzie (2000)	1.7%	40.7%	40.8%	12.9%	0.8%
Nilsson (Unpublished)*	1.2%	36.5%	53.4%	7.4%	0.6%
Escrig-Olmedo et al (2013)**	5%	35%	50%	10%	0%

*Previously unpublished data from a survey to Swedish SR-investors in 2009,
**Of respondents characterized as "socially responsible consumers" (not investors), Slightly different scale used: Much lower, Lower, Similar, Better, Much better.

SRI-profiled mutual funds and financial services marketing

In general, the previous discussion of the strategies, issues, and financial characteristics paint a fairly diffuse picture of SRI today. There is a wide range of issues and methods that can be classified as components and characteristics of SRI, and financial return is likely to vary with the issues and methods used. In this sense, SRI is not one clearly defined process or goal like many other products and services that are positioned as socially responsible. Instead, it is up to the individual investor and the mutual fund provider to decide what ESG issues should be addressed and how these socially responsible characteristics should be brought into the investment process.

For marketers in financial services institutions, this active inclusion of social responsibility, as well as the ambiguity as to how this inclusion should be performed, has brought about a new set of challenges that they have to address. For example, dealing with customers who not only care about their financial bottom line, but also care about the ESG characteristics of their investments, will require different marketing tools and strategies than traditionally used. Moreover, introducing new 'socially responsible' services, attracting expertise and skill in new areas related to sustainability and ethics, and changing ideas on how to communicate and deliver results to consumers, could also represent significant challenges for marketers. In this section, some of the challenges associated with the integration of social responsibility into the investment context will be discussed. The end of the section will address four strategies on the role of SRI-profiled mutual funds in financial services providers' overall strategies.

Marketing SRI-profiled mutual funds

Perhaps the most obvious challenge that SRI has brought to financial services marketing is the need to start dealing with customers who are socially and environmentally concerned. Whereas other industries have a longer tradition of offering pro-social products and services, this phenomenon is fairly new to the financial services industry. Knowing socially concerned customers' desires and wants, how to communicate with them and how to design products that appeal to these customers, represent somewhat new tasks for many financial services institutions.

Knowing customer preferences

For companies that provide investment services, knowing the preferences of their clients, at least according to financial theory, has traditionally been a fairly easy task. While marketers, of course, would highlight the role of aspects such as service, convenience and personal relationships, investment services traditionally often focus on the fundamental financial characteristics, financial return and risk. Investing is often described as a process where these two components are the only ones that really matter to the investor (Statman 2005). Implicitly, it is assumed that investors will always prefer a high level of return to a lower one, and that 'rational' investors thus search for alternatives that will give them the highest possible returns at the lowest level of risk. Based on this view of investors, it is up to the mutual fund provider to try to meet these financial preferences, and to deliver as high financial return as possible.

Although there is obviously a case for companies to try to deliver as high returns as possible, what happens to financial services marketing and strategy when return and risk are not the only things that are desired by consumers? As reported previously, there is much research that shows that private (SR) investors do not always maximize profits (Berry and Yeung 2012, Nilsson 2009, Barreda-Tarrazona et al. 2011), and care about more than just the utilitarian financial characteristics of their investment (for example, Statman 2004, Statman 2011, Aspara and Tikkanen 2011).

At least in the case of SRI, there may be a case made for marketers of investment services to broaden the scope beyond the conventional risk and return variables, and try to understand and meet the non-financial desires of consumers.

While this notion of understanding non-financial needs and wants may be relevant in many different scenarios, when applied to the specific SRI context, it implies answering (at least) two separate issues. First, financial services providers need to understand how social responsibility can be understood as a desire or want from the consumer's point of view. That is, what issues do investors care about and how can these be included into the investment service to meet investor preferences? Second, financial services providers also need to understand how far customers are willing to go in their pursuit of social responsibility. While, as argued above, some investors may not always prefer as high financial return as possible, the question of how far this willingness goes, and what they want in terms of social impact for this trade-off, is something that remains unclear.

Like most tasks that marketers perform, neither of these questions have definite answers. Instead, like most marketing decisions, these are tasks that involve marketing research, targeting of relevant customer groups, as well as positioning towards these groups. Whereas some investor segments may prefer a thorough initiative focused primarily on making some sort of social or environmental impact, other segments may be much more focused on achieving a high level of financial return. Similarly, whilst some segments may prefer mutual funds focused on environmental issues, others may be more concerned about social or governance issues.

Addressing these questions is likely to be central to launching a successful SRI initiative. However, understanding the needs of the socially concerned investors is not always easy, especially when the familiar financial characteristics, metrics and fundamentals, have traditionally been such predominating factors in understanding the needs of investors.

Implementing a new socially responsible investment service

In addition to the challenges associated with understanding the consumer, another important challenge for financial services providers is to actually implement and set up a new type of investment service that, by integrating social responsibility with financial criteria, is fundamentally different from traditional investment products. Although the process of developing and introducing a new investment service obviously involves many different stages and aspects, two of the most important issues for marketers to address are how the SRI fund can be implemented in a genuine manner and how to communicate social, environmental, and ethical results.

The relevance of these issues is commonly addressed in marketing of green, pro-social, or fair trade products and services. This is largely due to the fact that any product or service that claims to be socially responsible and later, in one way or another, fails to live up to this claim, often suffers from it. This practice, where companies portray themselves as 'greener' or more socially responsible than they actually are is known as 'greenwashing', and is a popular topic among NGOs as well as in the media (for example, Delmas and Burbano 2011). For example, Greenpeace frequently provides the public with information on companies that portray themselves better than they actually are. Being accused of greenwashing is certainly not something that any company would want, as this could result in negative publicity and distrust among consumers. For companies that actively sell pro-social products or desires a pro-social positioning, being accused of greenwashing also risks hurting the company's fundamental credibility in the marketplace. Moreover, as many socially responsible initiatives are intangible, it may be difficult to restore any lost trust at a later stage.

For financial services providers, it is crucially important that their SRI funds are implemented in a way that is perceived as genuine and that marketers communicate results in a way that does not exaggerate the pro-social efforts made. This is especially relevant as the actions, practices and strategies used in SRI funds have been the target of much criticism in the media. For example, at the same time as the Swedish-Finnish telecom operator TeliaSonera was in the headlines for alleged bribery in Uzbekistan, many SRI funds kept or increased their ownership in the company (Hugo 2012). Similar criticism has been levelled against many SRI funds that invest in controversial sectors, such as big oil and energy companies. One should bear in mind, however, that some of the strategies, discussed earlier in this chapter, allow investments in industries and sectors that are perceived as socially irresponsible. Although this is often communicated clearly, SRI funds still find themselves in a position where they often have to endure, arguably unbalanced or unfair, criticism in the media.

As in the case of the two issues discussed previously, there is no simple answer as to how financial services providers can implement SRI-profiled mutual funds in a manner that is perceived as genuine, and thereby navigate past the pitfalls of greenwashing. Just based on the discussion above, there are a few principles that can help marketers. First, it is necessary that financial services providers view their SRI-profiled mutual funds as more than just a shiny surface that can complement other products in their offering. Any attempt to implement SRI should be genuine, and go beyond mere superficialities. Moreover, it is also important to clearly communicate the implications of certain strategies to avoid creating any false hopes or ideas of what SRI-profiled mutual funds do. Engagement and best-in-class strategies, for example, imply that the fund actually invests in companies that are perceived by many people (and members of the media) as irresponsible. If the nature of these strategies are not communicated clearly, this could invite criticism. Further, there is a need to recognize that many SRI strategies are fairly blunt and indirect tools with which to achieve social and environmental change. Making far-reaching claims of social change may be thus be risky. It may be better to be cautious when making promises of social and environmental change, at least in the short run.

The role of SRI: four corporate strategies

As previously discussed, financial services providers face many challenges in adapting to an environment where social responsibility plays an integral part. It is thus not surprising to see a multitude of different strategies surrounding SRI-profiled mutual funds in the marketplace. Whereas some providers have chosen to provide few or no SRI-profiled mutual funds to their customers, others have chosen to develop and introduce a wide range of different SRI funds. Moreover, while some view social responsibility as a niche, other providers use social responsibility as a way to position themselves in the marketplace.

Based on these two factors – the importance of social responsibility to the firms positioning and the number of SRI funds provided – it is possible to distinguish between four separate strategies dealing with social responsibility, in general, and SRI, in particular. These are displayed in Figure 33.1.

SRI defensive strategy

Although this discussion shows that social responsibility, in general, and SRI, in particular, has changed certain fundamental aspects of the investment industry, not all financial service providers have chosen to change their ways. Some mutual fund providers simply choose to ignore the SRI phenomenon, and keep focusing on providing investment products with no explicit socially responsible component. Even though some of these companies may offer their customers one or two SRI mutual funds, this is arguably not done proactively to develop SRI, as such, but more

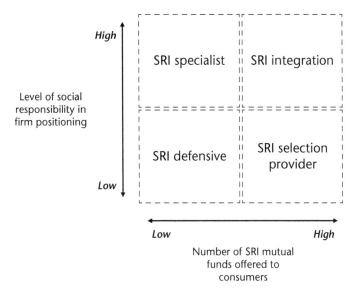

Figure 33.1 Four separate strategies for dealing with SRI profiled mutual funds

likely as a defensive measure to stop customers with a social conscience from going to other providers. Offering one or two SRI-profiled mutual funds may also be good if the media decides to do a story on SRI or social responsibility in the financial services industry.

This strategy seems to be popular with some of the larger conventional banks who may already have a strong brand based on their financial characteristics. Few of the providers using this strategy have their own ESG analysts, but rather pay external advisers to provide them with relevant data.

Selection provider strategy

Given that SRI has become a respectable niche in many countries, some providers may want to keep their normal positioning, yet provide their customers with a good selection of SRI funds. This strategy, of providing customers with a good selection of different mutual funds, is a viable alternative for larger providers who already have built a strong position in the marketplace, but still believe that there is potential in providing a large selection of SRI-profiled mutual funds. Many larger fund houses also have the financial capability to carry internal ESG analysts enabling them to develop high-quality products.

Following this strategy does not mean that anything necessarily is done to the older conventional funds. These types of funds can still constitute a key component of the providers' offering. In many ways, these are likely to represent the main component of the firms positioning efforts.

SRI specialist strategy

While the two strategies used above are common among older and larger providers, social responsibility can also be seen as an opportunity for smaller providers to establish a distinct positioning in the marketplace. Several smaller investment service providers have started to build their overall positioning on social responsibility. Here, SRI-profiled mutual funds are naturally a key component of the overall positioning strategy.

As these types of firms usually are fairly small, the actual number of SRI funds offered can be limited. However, as SRI-profiled mutual funds are largely the only type of funds they offer, following this strategy means that they still attract attention for being specialists in the area of responsible investment and social responsibility.

SRI integration strategy

The final strategy is to integrate social responsibility into most mutual funds as well as into any other type of financial services offered to consumers. Here, social responsibility becomes one of the key positioning attributes, likely to be backed up by strategies that emphasise social responsibility in all business operations visible to consumers. This strategy basically implies that the company only offers few (if any) conventional funds, and also incorporates social responsibility into any other products offered such as insurance, mortgages, and retirement savings plans. Social responsibility is also likely to be an important component of external communication efforts.

This strategy has the potential to be met with a good response among consumers. However, it is also vulnerable to accusations of greenwashing, indicating that it is important that this type of strategy be backed up by genuine products and services. Also, as there is a perception among many consumers that SRI products perform worse financially than conventional investments, this strategy may also risk alienating some consumers who care primarily about the financial aspects of their investments.

Conclusions and some words for the future

At the outset of this chapter, two separate purposes were outlined: to introduce the background as well as contemporary practices of SRI and to discuss the implications of SRI for financial services providers and financial services marketing, in general. In addressing these two issues, a few key conclusions, relevant to financial services marketing, have been reached. Perhaps the most important of these is that SRI is not one uniform financial service. Instead, there are a multitude of strategies and issues that could be characterized as SRI. As discussed in this chapter, this creates problems for consumers, who may have a difficult time making informed and educated choices. However, it also poses a challenge to financial services providers who have to develop and introduce a new type of service with few guidelines. In order to be successful in this task, it is important for providers to understand consumer preferences as well as to know how to develop and communicate products positioned as socially responsible. Going into this type of 'green marketing' is not an easy task. However, completely disregarding the area of SRI may risk losing customers who appear to have become more and more committed to social responsibility. It may thus be something that many providers, whether they like it or not, will become required to engage in to varying degrees.

As to the future, it is likely that we have only started to see the beginning of a trend in which social responsibility is integrated into the strategies of financial services providers. The UN-backed initiative, Principles for Responsible Investment was established in 2006 and has attracted many mainstream financial services providers, not otherwise known for social responsibility, as signatories. Moreover, sustainability is often described as a 'megatrend' and many actors in society will continue to demand certain levels of social responsibility from financial services providers. Just as an illustration, Chapter 32 in this book dedicated to CSR shows the relevance of sustainability and CSR for financial services providers. In many ways, it is likely that companies in the forefront of this trend will have an advantage over competitors. For example, it may be easier for these companies to adapt to new demands on social responsibility that will arise in the future. Moreover, actively working with social responsibility may also result in a favourable public perception. In this context, working with SRI-profiled mutual funds in a genuine manner may well help companies dealing with the demands of sustainability in the future.

Future research

This chapter has focused on the current nature and practices of socially responsible investment and has outlined several insights on the challenges and strategies that financial services providers encounter when dealing with this service. However, while these insights serve as a starting point for future enquiries into the area of SRI, given the fairly recent development of this area much research remains until a more complete understanding of the topic is reached.

Within the marketing discipline, there are at least two areas that need further attention from researchers. More insight is needed on the motivations and preferences of consumers who choose to invest in SRI profiled investment schemes. Sparkes (2002: 69) noted that there has been a 'general silence' on this topic. Whilst there has been an increase in research on the topic since Sparkes's observation in 2002 (for example, Berry and Yeung 2012, Barreda-Tarrazona et al. 2011, Nilsson 2008), it has only scratched the surface in understanding how the consumer values social responsibility in the financial services and investment context. While research has highlighted the concept of perceived value in the investment context in general (Puustinen et al. 2013), questions regarding the specifics of the intricate balance between financial and social, ethical, and environmental issues in the SRI context remain unexplored. For example, understanding how investors evaluate the value of the different types of (financial and socially responsible) characteristics of their mutual funds in both a pre-purchase and a post-purchase (on-going) setting would add considerable insight into the behavior of SR-investors. Also, while much research has been on a general level, future research could look at issue-specific aspects (such as specific events or social, environmental, and ethical categories) to understand how different types of ESG factors impact SR-investment behavior.

A second relevant research area within the marketing discipline could be to address how firms might use information about investors' SRI motivations and preferences to develop viable strategies. For example, four strategies on how companies deal with social responsibility and SRI are presented in this chapter. Future research could focus on evaluating these strategies in an in-depth manner, to reach insights on targeting and positioning strategies for SR-investments.

References

Adler, T. and Kritzman, M. 2008. The cost of socially responsible investing. *The Journal of Portfolio Management*, 35(1), pp. 52–56.

Aspara, J. and Tikkanen, H. 2011. Individuals' affect-based motivations to invest in stocks: beyond expected financial returns and risks. *Journal of Behavioral Finance*, 12(2), pp. 78–89.

Barreda-Tarrazona, I., Matallin-Sáez, J.C. and Balaguer-Franch, R. 2011. Measuring investors' socially responsible preferences in mutual funds. *Journal of Business Ethics*, 103(2), pp. 305–30.

Beal, D. and Goyen, M. 1998. "Putting your money where your mouth is" A profile of ethical investors. *Financial Services Review*, 7(2), pp. 129–43.

Bengtsson, E. 2008. A History of Scandinavian Socially Responsible Investing. *Journal of Business Ethics*, 82(4), pp. 969–83.

Benson, K. L. and Humphrey, J. E. 2008. Socially responsible investment funds: Investor reaction to current and past returns. *Journal of Banking and Finance*, 32(9), pp. 1850–59.

Berry, T. and Junkus, J. 2013. Socially responsible investing: an investor perspective. *Journal of Business Ethics*, 112(4), pp. 707–20.

Berry, R. H. and Yeung, F. 2012. Are investors willing to sacrifice cash for morality? *Journal of Business Ethics*, 117(3), pp. 477–92

Boatright, J. R. 2008. *Ethics in finance, foundations of business ethics*, 2nd edition, Malden, Mass: Blackwell Publishing.

Chegut, A., Schenk, H. and Scholtens, B. 2011. Assessing SRI fund performance research: best practices in empirical analysis. *Sustainable Development*, 19(2), pp. 77–94.

Climent, F. and Soriano, P. 2011. Green and Good? The Investment Performance of US Environmental Mutual Funds. *Journal of Business Ethics*, 103(2), pp. 275–87.

Delmas, M. A. and Burbano, V. C. 2011. The Drivers of Greenwashing. *California Management Review*, 54(1), pp. 64–87.

Derwall, J., Guenster, N., Bauer, R. and Koedijk, K. 2005. The eco-efficiency premium puzzle. *Financial Analysts Journal*, 61(2), pp. 51–63.

Domini, A. 2001. *Socially responsible investing: making a difference and making money*, Chicago, Ill: Dearborn.

Escrig-Olmedo, E., Muñoz-Torres, M. J. and Fernández-Izquierdo, M. Á. 2013. Sustainable development and the financial system: Society's perceptions about socially responsible investing. *Business Strategy and the Environment*, 22(6), pp. 410–28.

Eurosif 2010. *European SRI study 2010*. Available at www.eurosif.org, The European Sustainable Investment Forum.

Gond, J.-P. and Piani, V. 2013. Enabling institutional investors' collective action: the role of the principles for responsible investment initiative. *Business & Society*, 52(1), pp. 64–104.

Hugo, K. 2012. Trots skandal ökar etiska fonder i Telia. *Svenska Dagbladet*, Available at www.svd.se/naringsliv/branscher/teknik-och-telekom/etiska-fonder-okat-i-telia_7550960.svd (accessed: February 6, 2014).

Humphrey, J. and Lee, D. 2011. Australian Socially Responsible Funds: Performance, Risk and Screening Intensity. *Journal of Business Ethics*, 102(4), pp. 519–35.

Kalev, P. S. and Wallace, D. 2012. Performance of socially responsible investment funds. In Jones, S. and Ratnatunga, J., (eds.), *Contemporary Issues in Sustainability Accounting, Assurance and Reporting*, Bingley: Emerald, pp. 43–69.

Lewis, A. and Mackenzie, C. 2000. Morals, money, ethical investing and economic psychology. *Human Relations*, 53(2), pp. 179–91.

Louche, C. and Lydenberg, S. 2010. Responsible Investing. In Boatright, J. R., (ed.) *Finance Ethics: Critical issues in theory and practice*, Hoboken, New Jersey: John Wiley & Sons, pp. 393–418.

Makovsky 2012. *The 2012 Makovsky Wall Street reputation study: insight into reputational challenges faced by financial companies*. Available at www.makovsky.com

Nilsson, J. 2008. Investment with a conscience: Examining the impact of pro-social attitudes and perceived financial performance on socially responsible investment behavior. *Journal of Business Ethics*, 83(2), pp. 307–25.

—— 2009. Segmenting socially responsible mutual fund investors: The influence of financial return and social responsibility. *International Journal of Bank Marketing*, 27(1), pp. 5–31.

Owens, L. A. 2012. The Polls–Trends. *Public Opinion Quarterly*, 76(1), pp. 142–62.

Pax 2013. *Our History*. www.paxworld.com/about-pax-world/history. Pax World Investments.

Pérez-Gladish, B., Benson, K. and Faff, R. 2012. Profiling socially responsible investors: Australian evidence. *Australian Journal of Management*, 37(2), pp. 189–209.

Puustinen, P., Maas, P. and Karjaluoto, H. 2013. Development and validation of the Perceived Investment Value (PIV) scale. *Journal of Economic Psychology*, 36, pp. 41–54

Renneboog, L., Ter Horst, J. and Zhang, C. 2008. The price of ethics and stakeholder governance: The performance of socially responsible mutual funds. *Journal of Corporate Finance*, 14(3), pp. 302–22.

——. 2011. Is ethical money financially smart? Nonfinancial attributes and money flows of socially responsible investment funds. *Journal of Financial Intermediation*, 20(4), pp. 562–88.

Sandberg, J., Juavle, C., Hedesström, T. M. and Hamilton, I. 2009. The heterogeneity of socially responsible investment. *Journal of Business Ethics*, 87(4), pp. 519–33.

Schwartz, M. S. 2003. The "ethics" of ethical investing. *Journal of Business Ethics*, 43(3), pp. 195–213.

Sievänen, R., Sumelius, J., Islam, K. and Sell, M. 2013. From struggle in responsible investment to potential to improve global environmental governance through UN PRI. *International Environmental Agreements: Politics, Law & Economics*, 13(2), pp. 197–217.

SIF 2007. *Report on Socially Responsible Investing Trends in the United States, Executive summary*. Available at www.ussif.org

Socialfunds.com 2014. *Mutual funds center.* www.socialfunds.com/funds/chart.cgi?sfChartId=Social+Issues (accessed February 6, 2014).

Sparkes, R. 2002. *Socially responsible investment: a global revolution,* New York: J. Wiley.

—— 2006. A historical perspective on the growth of socially responsible investment. In Sullivan, R. and MacKenzie, C., (eds.), *Responsible Investment,* Sheffield: Greenleaf Publishing, pp. 39–54.

Statman, M. 2000. Socially responsible mutual funds. *Financial Analysts Journal,* 56(3), pp. 30–39.

—— 2004. What do investors want? *Journal of Portfoilio Management,* 30(5), pp. 153–61.

—— 2005. Normal investors, then and now. *Financial Analysts Journal,* 61(2), pp. 31–37.

—— 2011. *What Investors Really Want: Discover What Drives Investor Behavior and Make Smarter Financial Decisions,* New York: McGraw-Hill.

USSIF 2012. *Sustainable and responsible investing trends in the United States 2012,* Available at www.ussif.org: The Forum for Sustainable and Responsible Investment.

34

The ethics of the selling process in financial services

Jay Mulki

Introduction

On September 14, 2008 there were four major standalone investment banks and they were considered essential for the flow of capital to and investment in American business. Within a week, there were none.

> *Dick Fuld, testifying before the House of Representatives three weeks after the collapse of Lehman Brothers (Bloomberg BusinessWeek 2013: 8).*

A recent survey of trust in the professions found that businesses and bankers came last, along with politicians.

> *(Economist 2013: 66).*

A spate of corporate financial scandals during the first decade of the twenty-first century have rocked the industry and increased public scrutiny of companies in the US and worldwide. The 2008 financial crisis highlighted the importance of financial services to the world economy as well as the hidden issues of the industry. This chapter examines some of the underlying causes of ethical transgressions in the financial services industry. In addition, we provide some insights into the motivations behind the sales and service employees' propensity to pursue unethical behavior. Existing literature, research studies and trade publications were used to develop an understanding of the various forces contributing to unethical practices in the financial services industry. In addition, discussion with field salespeople provided unique insights into customer interactions.

Between 2000 and 2012, there were more than thirty scandals that were either initiated or supported by individuals associated with financial institutions (see Table 34.1). The year 2002 seems like a banner year for scandals, with more than twenty-five firms conducting unethical practices, many with tacit help from accounting firms to make these acts appear legal. While some of the scandals listed in Table 34.1 were Ponzi schemes by individuals, others were from financial service firms who sold securities of questionable value to unsuspecting consumers. Some of these firms also used accounting tricks ranging from inflating figures for sales, revenues

Table 34.1 Partial list of major financial scandals since 2000

No	Firm	Year	
1	Peregrine Financial Group Inc.	2012	CEO embezzled $200 million from customers for personal use.
2	MF Global Inc.	2011	Misappropriation of customer funds, declared bankruptcy.
3	Galleon Group	2009	Insider trading.
4	Bernard L. Madoff Investment Securities LLC	2008	Largest Ponzi scheme $65 billion.
5	Lehman Brothers Scandal	2008	Went bankrupt as they hid over $50 billion in loans disguised as sales.
6	AOL Time Warner	2003	Inflated sales volume.
7	IMClone Systems	2003	Insider trading.
8	HealthSouth	2003	Manipulation to inflate earning by $1.4 billion.
9	Tyco	2002	Improper use of company funds.
10	Global Crossing	2002	Inflate stock value.
11	Peregrine Systems, Inc.	2002	Inflated revenue through fake reselling trades.
12	Mirant	2002	Inflated various asset values and deflated costs.
13	Waste Management	2002	Manipulated books to meet earning targets.
14	Qwest Communications International	2002	Manipulation to inflate revenues.
15	AOL Time Warner	2002	Manipulation to inflate sales figures.
16	Global Crossing	2002	Manipulation to inflate sales figures.
17	Homestore.com	2002	Manipulation of barter transactions to inflate sales figures.
18	Bristol-Myers Squibb	2002	Manipulation of books, forced wholesalers to accept more inventory than they can sell.
19	WorldCom	2002	Manipulation of books to inflate cash flow.
20	Adelphia Communications	2002	Manipulation of books to overstate results.
21	CMS Energy	2002	Manipulation to boost energy trading volumes using "round-trip" trades.
22	Duke Energy	2002	Manipulation to boost energy trading volumes using "round-trip" trades.
23	Dynegy	2002	Manipulation to boost energy trading volumes using "round-trip" trades.
24	El Paso	2002	Manipulation to boost energy trading volumes using "round-trip" trades.
25	Halliburton	2002	Manipulation to boost energy trading volumes using "round-trip" trades.
26	Peregrine Systems	2002	Manipulation to boost energy trading volumes using "round-trip" trades.
27	Reliant Energy	2002	Manipulation to boost energy trading volumes using "round-trip" trades.
28	Nicor Energy	2002	Manipulation to boost revenues and underestimate expenses.
29	Merck	2002	Manipulation to income.
30	WorldCom	2002	Largest bankruptcy in US history, misuse of funds and manipulation of books.

(Continued)

Table 34.1 (Continued).

No	Firm	Year	
31	Kmart	2002	Declared bankruptcy, misleading share holders, company funds for personal use.
32	Arthur Andersen	2001	Hid important information from SEC about ENRON by shredding documents.
33	The Baptist Foundation of Arizona	2001	Unrecoverable loans and risky transaction using Church member deposits.
34	Enron	2001	Manipulation of results to boost profits.
35	Xerox	2000	Manipulation of financial results to inflate market value.

Source: Compiled from information contained in (1) Penelope Patsuris (26/8/2002), Forbes Corporate Scandal Sheet. www.forbes.com/2002/07/25/accountingtracker.html; (2) Michael G. Foster, The decade's worst financial scandals, School of Business, University of Washington www.foster.washington.edu/centers/facultyresearch/Pages/karpoff-scandals.aspxSource.

or profits, to boosting cash flow estimates, to hiding debt in order to attract investors. A detailed categorization and discussion of such "tricks" is provided in Chapter 31. As the global financial crisis unfolded, consumers became skeptical of the intentions of even the most reputable financial institutions. General opinion that banking and investment advisors are greedy and unethical only solidified. Financial advisors and salespeople were increasingly seen as unscrupulous individuals bent on pursuing profits without consideration of the damage to others. These sentiments have impacted salespeople in general and especially salespeople in financial institutions. The general public is convinced that the financial crisis resulted from the greed of financial salespeople at the expense of customers (Owens 2011).

In 2008, as the stock markets around the world began to implode, the global financial system teetered on the brink of collapse and the world economy was plunged into the Great Recession. The 2008 collapse of several major financial institutions, namely Lehman Brothers, Bear Stearns and U.S. Government-sponsored Fannie Mae and Freddie Mack, led to the worst financial crisis in 80 years (Economist 2013). The root causes of the crisis were attributed to indiscriminate and often unethical transactions involving complex securities.

Individual consumers, businesses and governments across the world depend on financial industry professionals for access to capital, along with avenues through which to invest, borrow and to assume transaction risk. Financial industry professionals include brokers and commercial bank CEOs, salespeople from investment banks and savings and loans institutions, insurance agents, financial planners, securities firms and hedge fund brokers. These individuals provide a vital service to the economy by developing and marketing products that fit the needs of individuals and institutions. Financial instruments can be equity-based or debt-based. Financial services are involved in the sale of cash instruments, such as securities, loans and deposits as well as derivatives that derive their value from their underlying assets. In addition, financial services provide investors with insurance as well as hedge funds to mitigate risks. Even in an electronic age, given the nature of their products, financial professionals rely on personal selling of financial instruments to the general public and to institutions. As a product, a financial instrument's perceived value is dependent upon the credibility of the firm as well as the credibility of the individuals representing that firm (Eisingerich and Bell 2006). A financial firm's reputation for ethical behavior reassures a sense of fairness and helps to gain the confidence of the buyer (investor).

Financial services and regulations

Asked why his bank kept making risky loans even as markets looked bubbly, Chuck Prince, then head of Citigroup, said that "as long as the music is playing, you have got to get up and dance.

(Economist 2013: 69)

Given its importance to the economy, legislators and lawmakers keep a close watch on the financial industry and its transactions, using regulations to prevent questionable practices. In 1933, after the failure of about 5,000 American banks during the Great Depression, the U.S. Congress passed the Glass-Steagall Act of 1933. This act drew a strict line between commercial and investment activities of a bank by prohibiting commercial banks from tendering investment business using customer deposits. In 1999, under pressure from the business lobby, legislators enacted the Financial Services Modernization Act of 1999, ostensibly to remove barriers that "prevented" modernization of the financial industry. This act by Congress repealed sections of the Glass Steagall Act of 1933 and allowed financial institutions to conduct all three functions, namely, commercial banking, investment management and insurance sale and underwriting (Gramm-Leach-Bliley Act 1999).

As a result of this act, the line of strict separation that existed between consumer banking and investment institutions prior to 1999 blurred. In addition, this act repealed the Glass–Steagall conflict of interest clause that prohibited "simultaneous service by any officer, director, or employee of a securities firm as an officer, director, or employee of any member bank". Freed from the regulatory shackles, financial services firms grew through mergers and acquisitions and became very creative in their offerings. Financial firms started developing increasingly complex financial instruments to differentiate themselves in a competitive marketplace and to find new avenues for growth. While the availability of countless investment options increased opportunities for average investors, the complexity of financial instruments increased customer dependency on financial advisors for investment decisions.

Financial services in general are complex and intangible, such that clients often do not have the technical knowledge or expertise to evaluate the financial advice they receive. As noted in Chapter 6, the pension purchase decision is typically a once-in-a-lifetime decision and provides limited opportunity of gaining knowledge through repeat purchases. For most people, the selection of a financial advisor is a careful deliberate process as their investment decisions can have an enormous impact on their life (Eisingerich and Bell 2006). Individual investors are acutely aware that a financial advisor's quality of recommendations can determine the investor's long-term financial security. As a service, financial advice is evaluated and chosen based on credence values resulting from past records and the reputation of the service provider (Zeithaml et al. 2006), thus, a firm's ethical reputation plays a major role in attracting business.

Jack Waymire (2013), a prominent advisor and founder of Investor Watchdog recommends that the selection of advisors should be objective and customers should assess an advisor's competence, ethical practices and past results before choosing them. However, the average customer often finds it difficult to assess the capabilities or the recommendations of a financial advisor (Eriksson discusses the general difficulties of assessing quality in Chapter 12). Hence, customers end up using the firm's reputation as a surrogate for quality of the investment advice. A customer's trust and repeat business is driven by perceptions of an advisor's integrity, along with the institution's ethical reputation and past performance (see Chapters 10 and 30). This reputation and integrity can suffer immensely when perceived to be engaging in unethical behavior, especially when that organization is censored or punished by regulators for unscrupulous practices.

Research shows that a firm's reputation for ethical behavior determines the investor's comfort level and influences the decision to trust a financial institution and its salespeople (Mulki and Jaramillo 2011).

Financial institutions and service professionals are sensitive to negative publicity and are aware of the impact of bad image on interpersonal trust developed with their investors. Lloyd Blankfein, of Goldman Sachs, is reported to have said to the U.S. Senate Committee investigating the financial meltdown, "If our clients believe that we don't deserve their trust, we cannot survive" (Harper 2010). By nature of the industry, professionals in financial services are involved in the transaction of massive monetary sums. As providers of financial services, they are operating in a competitive global market where salespeople are under enormous pressures to reach performance and profitability goals. Some of the major transactions create potential for big profits and also temptations for unethical behaviors.

As active sellers of securities and financial instruments, salespeople are aware of the consumer's inability to understand more complex transactions and position themselves as the knowledgeable advisor to investors. This information asymmetry allows for ambitious financial services providers to game the system with risky instruments or to indulge in questionable transactions in order to increase their own volume of business and profits at any cost. Martin et al. (2007) suggest that an individual's unchecked ambition or lack of success may lead to decay of normative structures and increase the temptation to pursue deviant behaviors.

Salespeople can become vulnerable to the lure of big money and often walk the fine line between ethical and unethical activity. Many cross this line in pursuit of profits relying on their customer's inability to catch fraud in time and the regulators' reliance on the industry's "self-regulation" norms. This can lead to unethical behaviors, unlawful transactions and ethical scandals. Table 34.1 provides a list of major financial scandals in the last ten years. While not all the scandals listed were caused by financial services salespeople, most of the transactions leading to the crisis in 2008 involved financial services salespeople who were aware of the potential negative impact of these transactions on the investing public (Zeidan 2013).

A rash of financial scandals coupled with huge compensation to people who created the financial crisis exacerbated public perception of a financial services industry that was manipulating the rules and could not be trusted (Sweene 2012). For example, in 2007, the CEO of Goldman Sachs was reported to have received a total compensation in excess of $70 million. This has not changed much since the 2008 crisis. Bloomberg BusinessWeek reports that employees in Goldman Sachs averaged a compensation of over half a million on an annualized basis for 2013 (Moore 2013). Kane (2002: 1920) posits that financial services employees' single-minded pursuit of profits led them to circumvent the regulatory protocols in the area of "disclosure, truth-telling, promise-making, promise-keeping, and conciliation" and proposed that financial regulators should be made responsible for implementing regulations in three major areas: to limit risk of fraud, discrimination and contract non-performance in financial transactions; to operate a safety net designed to virtually eliminate risk of fire-sale losses associated with financial-institution insolvencies and unjustified customer runs; and to operate the fraud controls and safety net honorably and at minimum opportunity cost to the taxpayer.

Ethics and financial services salespeople

Vulnerable elderly people were mis-sold unsuitable investment policies over five years by advisers working for the high street bank HSBC.

(The Independent, 2011: 1)

Financial transactions are based on trust and fairness. However, there is a general feeling that salesperson ethics is an oxymoron, resulting from the perception that all sales activities are "shady" and that salespeople will promise anything to get a sale. Trade sources indicate that salespeople misrepresent or lie on sales calls about 50 percent of the time (Strout 2002). About 33 percent of salespeople admitted making unrealistic promises to get the sale and 20 percent say that they managed to persuade customers to buy products that they do not need (Mulki et al. 2009). Given the importance of trust and potential for misuse of the trust, the financial industry is highly regulated and has to ensure compliance with the framework established by governments. In addition, the financial industry has set up self-regulating agencies to ensure fairness and transparency. Agencies such as the Financial Industry Regulatory Authority (FINRA) act as independent regulators to monitor securities firms with a view to maintaining fairness in the U.S. capital markets.

Unethical behavior in the financial industry, however, is rampant. Salespeople in the financial industry indulge in activities that comply with legal requirements but are often unethical in nature (Jin et al. 2013). This can range from making false promises, selling questionable investments, inflating claims of benefits, misleading by hiding disadvantages or highlighting advantages, manipulating results, padding expense accounts, conflicting interests, "churning" to increase commissions and "boiler room" operations to push stocks to unsophisticated consumers (Boatright 2000). As shown in Table 34.1, a firm's senior management becomes complicit by manipulating company balance sheets. In addition, there are Ponzi Schemes, the manipulation of numbers to inflate sales and the provision of soft loans for senior officers and the like. Most often many of these schemes are not only unethical but also illegal. Even otherwise honest salespeople are known to operate in an ethical grey area and resort to activities that include withholding of critical information, the use of fear tactics or aggressive sales pitches to intimidate the elderly or vulnerable into buying products they do not need and the extensive use of fine print to wiggle out of inflated promises (Hair et al. 2009, Sparks and Johlke 1996).

Who or what motivates unethical behavior?

A half-truth is a whole lie.

Yiddish Proverb

The most dangerous untruths are truths moderately distorted.

Georg Christoph Lichtenberg

Role of the organization and the supervisor

Organizations have an obligation to maximize shareholder value without violating trust and commitment to customers (Sternberg 2013). Firms achieve this by developing a long-term trusting relationship with customers who feel confident buying the firm's goods and services. Customers feel confident when they trust the firm; the trust that results from a proven track record of providing reliable, high-quality goods and services on a consistent basis. Sternberg (2013) believes that business should be conducted with "ordinary decency", which is represented collectively "by honesty and fairness, and without physical violence or coercion" (Sternberg 2013: 19).

An organization's ethical climate is one of the key factors that influence behavior of its salespeople. Studies show that when salespeople believe that the organization's practices are guided by strict adherence to ethical norms, they tend to be ethical in their transactions (Mulki et al. 2009, Valentine et al. 2011). Jaramillo et al. (2012) study of bank employees found that when firms follow ethical guidelines, employees respond better as this environment preserves their personal values and also makes the job both meaningful and worthwhile. In line with this, when salespeople encounter ethically questionable situations, their actions are likely to be guided by their perception of the manager's reaction. Litzky et al. (2006) study of employee deviant behaviors and unethical conduct indicated a strong influence of leadership style and organizational structure. Some of the organizational factors that encourage unethical behavior include the compensation/reward structure, role conflict and role ambiguity and organizational climate, role modeling and procedural justice.

Sales organization compensation structures range from 100 percent salary to 100 percent commission and also a combination of salary and commission. Manning et al. (2009) use industry survey information to indicate that about 20 percent of consumer companies used 100 percent salary, 15 percent used pure commission and 65 percent used a combination of salary and commission. For business-to-business product sales, a combination of salary and commission was used in about 75 percent of the firms. The financial institution that employs independent sales agents, brokers or insurance agents generally uses a compensation plan that relies heavily on commission to motivate higher performance. Research shows that compensation structures heavily based on commissions or bonuses push salespeople to aggressively pursue business, cut corners and encourages employee self-interest (Litzky et al. 2006). In addition to false promises and other unethical practices, insurance agents who work strictly on commission are known to lie about quotas, pad expense accounts, undercharge for services to make the sale and offer to pay the first premium to get the customer to buy a policy (Callahan 2004).

Salespeople must meet the needs of customers and the organization without jeopardizing the firm's interests. However, when the organization's (supervisor's) goals and customers' interests are in conflict, salespeople often have to compromise their ethical norms in order to satisfy either the organization or the customer (Eddleston et al. 2002). For example, if the firm directs a salesperson to sell a financial instrument that profits the firm but does not meet the customer's objectives, then the salesperson has to convince the customer to buy it, knowing that the product does not serve the customer's interest. Salespeople also encounter ambiguity of goals and lack of direction in their organization. When a manager asks the salesperson to get sales at any cost to meet quota, the salesperson perceives this instruction as a "tacit" approval for the use of unethical behavior to get the sale. Several studies have shown a strong relationship between role conflict, role ambiguity and unethical behavior (DeConinck 2010, Mulki et al. 2008).

There is an abundance of research that shows the right organizational climate and leadership practices influence a salesperson's ethical behavior (Ingram et al. 2007, Mulki et al. 2009). Prominent ethics researchers, Victor and Cullen (1988: 177) define the ethical climate of an organization as "a group of prescribed climates reflecting the organizational procedures, policies, and practices with moral consequences". Managers are the major conduit to organizational resources for salespeople and are seen as surrogates for the firm by their salespeople. They set the tone for the organizational ethical climate by setting clear guidelines for ethical behavior and by modeling their behavior. They also have to be fair in their dealings with the salespeople by supporting them with resources and treating all salespeople equally.

If salespeople develop the perception that a manager bends the rules for his convenience or as a favor to an employee, it signals that the rules can be bent and ethical transgressions are tolerated. Research also shows that when managers show favoritism in handing out praise and penalties, salespeople begin to distrust the supervisor and may resort to unethical behaviors (DeConinck 2011, Mulki et al. 2009). The scandals listed in Table 34.1 are examples of senior officers manipulating company rules and guidelines for short-term gain. It should be noted that many of the scandals in Table 34.1 did not originate from financial services salespeople.

However, financial salespeople in these organizations did not have any qualms about selling complex securities designed to profit the firm irrespective of market conditions. Often, salespeople did not fully understand the workings of these securities but were aware that they were not in the best interest of the customers. So long as these sales earned higher commissions moral standards and obligations were largely neglected.

Role of self-interest

Cullen et al. (2003) posit that employee ethical behaviors are driven by several factors including, egoism, benevolence and principles. Some individuals are driven by self-interest (egoism), while others are motivated by an inner need to be benevolent and their desire to do good to others. Many individuals are driven by the principle of doing the right thing irrespective of the outcome (Mulki et al. 2009). Forsyth (1990) posits that relativism and idealism, the two dimensions of personal moral philosophies, guide individual behavior. Idealists believe in avoiding harming others while non-idealists assume harm is necessary to produce good. Relativists do not accept any exceptions to moral principles while non-relativists see these principles as useful "guidelines". This would suggest that financial services employees' evaluations of unethical behavior may be guided by the acceptance of various moral dimensions.

In general, a firm's ethical climate has a very strong influence on its employees' ethical conduct, as they are motivated to align their behavior with the firm's ethical guidelines (DeConinck 2011, Valentine and Barnett 2007). However, when egoism and self-interest exert their influences, some employees may willfully resort to unethical behavior. Often these employees take a calculated risk when they perceive that the cost of violations and the probability of getting caught are far less compared to the potential benefits (Zeidan 2013).

As boundary-spanning employees, salespeople have to balance the demands of their customers, supervisors and organization; they often have to comply with group norms and behavioral expectations of coworkers. Their interactions expose them to numerous customer requests that pose ethical dilemmas. Financial service salespeople with the hope of making a quick sale may resort to behaviors that lead customers to develop unrealistic expectations. Most common in this category are money-doubling guarantees, promises of higher than market returns, downplaying of penalty clauses, waivers of (phantom) fees and the promise of ease of withdrawals. Salespeople couch these in "vague" statements and use small print to qualify these statements. While the "vague" language and "qualifiers" provide legal cover, salespeople are violating customer trust and behaving in an unethical manner by hoping for the most optimistic scenario.

Another type of unethical behavior includes the provision of special treatment for some customers at the expense of others. Large discounts or concessions may be exclusively provided to one customer in return for placing the order to meet a quota. Salespeople often perform favors for their customers that violate company norms. These may include "softening" loan qualification terms for one loan applicant but not for another, modifying offers based on race or ethnic background, giving a break on points, or knowingly making a loan even when the customer is neither credit worthy nor has the capacity to repay the loan. Other unethical practices include, misrepresenting cost and risk, predatory lending and pressurizing customers to take out a loan. In addition, gifts and promotional items are commonly used for getting business and to retain customers. While it is possible to accept these practices as a routine part of sales and relationship building, there is also concern about crossing ethical boundaries (Mulki et al. 2009). Some of the minor ethical transgressions, like padding expense accounts and using company resources for personal work, are prevalent in most organizations.

Since the deregulation of the industry by the Financial Services Modernization Act 1999, the marketing of financial services has become extremely competitive. Professional financial service providers are under tremendous pressure to generate revenue and profit (Jin et al. 2013). In addition, a very large portion (60–100 percent) of the financial services salespersons' compensation is based on commissions. This often puts the sales professional in a position to choose between a customer's best interests and earning a livelihood. The asymmetric nature of information held by financial service providers relative to that of their customers gives them an advantage to serve their self-interest (Falconer 2005, Harrison 2003). This, along with the lag between purchase and benefit realized from a purchase, affords the financial services salesperson opportunities to provide questionable investment advice.

Role of customers

Customer demands often steer salespeople to engage in unethical behaviors. When customers demand special favors in terms of discounts, preferential delivery terms, etc. at the expense of other customers, a salesperson may have to comply in order not to lose sales. Some customers ask for personal favors, indirectly but often directly (Federwisch 2006). There are plenty of anecdotal cases of customers demanding free samples, new year gifts, request for personal use of supplier's resources and even vacations at the supplier's expense. Some buyers are known to put pressure on salespeople to contribute to their fund raising events or their favorite charities. There have been instances where customers have offered to share competitor information (such as prices, delivery terms) with a supplier in return for gifts or unofficial payments.

Role of co-workers/peers

Bandura's (1976) social learning theory posits that employees look to peers when adopting workplace norms. This suggests that employee behavior results from a process of learning through observation of others' behaviors, using peers as role models and taking cues from them to develop behavioral norms (Bandura 1976, Deshpande et al. 2006). The theory of differential association indicates that salespeople are most likely to emulate the ethical behaviors of others at their workplace (Deshpande and Joseph 2009). The potential for adopting ethical or unethical behavior increases with frequency of interaction with peers (Hoffman et al. 1991). Furthermore, the practice of ethical behavior becomes real and norms are set based on how ethical standards are applied by an individual's coworkers.

In general, salespeople are very competitive by nature and are under pressure to meet quotas or to win bonuses (Steenburgh and Ahearne 2012). When their peers are seen as very successful in their sales, they may feel the need to win at any cost and may compromise their values in the process to do so. The need to secure business becomes intense in a competitive high-pressure environment as encountered in the financial industry (McLaughlin 2011). If sales people perceive that the success of their peers is due to "questionable" transactions, it provides the impetus to win by any means if the benefits of the sale exceed the perceived cost of ethical transgression. Greater regulation can discourage this by making the cost of ethical misconduct substantial and longer-lasting.

Research findings

Numerous studies have explored the relationship between an organization's ethical climate and outcomes for salespeople. McClaren's (2000, 2013) review of the literature provides a summary of findings. However, studies of financial services salespeople have been relatively scarce and

Table 34.2 Partial list of research of financial services salespeople and ethical behavior

Author	Sample	Independent	Dependent	Results
Jin et al. (2013)	466 financial services professionals	Organization type	Ethical behavior	Financial professionals working for organic (democratic) firms perceive higher financial performance compared to employees in mechanistic (authoritarian) firms.
Tseng and Su (2013)	227 Taiwanese life insurance salespeople	Fraud size and social consensus	Ethical behavior	Unethical decisions influenced by perceived fraud size and social consensus. Findings in turn showed that small fraud size may lead to the belief that peers would accept the salesperson misconduct.
Mulki and Jaramillo (2011)	299 customers of major financial institutions in Chile.	Ethics	Customer satisfaction and loyalty	Ethical reputation increases the perceptions of value received, increases customer loyalty.
Valenzuela et al. (2010)	299 customers of financial institutions in Chile.	Inducement, ethical reputation	Customer loyalty	Ethical reputation provides a positive perception of inducements.
Lu et al. (1999)	American and Taiwanese life insurance salespeople.	Cultural dimensions	Ethical decision-making	No difference between countries in industry-wide deontological norms. In ethical decision making Taiwanese agents placed greater value on the company and fellow employees compared to US
Schwepker and Good (1999)	Financial services salespeople in USA.	Annual quota	Ethical behavior	Concern over goal achievement may promote unethical behavior.
Bejou et al. (1998)	568 customers of financial services company in USA.	Ethics, trust	Customer satisfaction	Ethics, trust, customer orientation contribute to relationship quality with customers.

mostly have focused on bank employees and insurance salespeople. As shown in Table 34.2, research indicates that the annual quota or goals tempt financial services salespeople to resort to unethical behavior. Studies have also found that the ethical reputation of a firm develops positive feelings in customers and increases loyalty (Mulki and Jaramillo 2011, Pirsch et al. 2007). A comparative study of Taiwanese and US insurance agents to assess the impact of cultural values found no difference in employees' adherence to company ethical norms between the two groups. However, Taiwanese salespeople considered their company and peer reputation in making ethical decisions while personal reputation was a primary concern for US salespeople reflecting the individualistic cultural norms (Lu et al. 1999).

Millennials and ethical behavior

About four years after the onset of the financial crisis, spurred by industry-wide scandals in the financial services sector, the industry still continues to attract a large volume of fresh graduates due to the potential for substantial compensation. A 2012 report published in the New York Times states that the financial industry was the top employer for the students who graduated from elite schools in 2012 (Newland 2012). Millennials (those born between 1979 and 2002) make up 25 percent of today's workforce (Bureau of Labor Statistics 2012). As an internet savvy generation that is in constant communication with other millennials around the world, millennials' attitudes towards ethics has generated considerable research interest. However, research findings on millennials' attitudes towards ethics and ethical conduct show mixed results.

Some researchers consider millennials to be more ethical and socially conscious than the generations that preceded them, thus reducing the potential for ethical scandals (McGlone et al. 2011). There is a belief that millennials are noticeable by their receptiveness to ethical behavior norms and known for their social, cultural and environmental consciousness (Boyd 2010). There is an expectation that these values are likely to influence their product choices and preferences for employment (Boyd 2010). Researchers also point out that millennials consider themselves to be global citizens, concerned about equity, fairness and the exchange of information on issues that matter to them (Bucic et al. 2012). In a 2013 article, Forbes indicated that about 75 percent of millennials donated to charity and 63 percent served as volunteers, which reflects their strong social values (Goudreau 2013). Studies show that, as a better educated generation, millennials are more inclined to consider ethical reputation and ethical investments in their purchase decisions as well as in their choice of place to work (Hofmann et al. 2009). In addition, a study of millennials from Australia and Indonesia has shown that in purchasing decisions, they consider a firm's social agenda important alongside price and quality (Bucic et al. 2012).

Another group of researchers who have conducted extensive studies of millennials, state that this expectation of altruistic behavior from millennials is misplaced. They believe that millennials are known for putting their needs first and characterize them as a "me" generation focused on feeling good about themselves (Twenge et al. 2012). They suggest that millennials' volunteerism and charitable work is not based on altruism, but rather on a "perceived image" that buttresses their resume and boosts their career. Twenge et al. (2012) also state that, given millennials' self-focus they are likely to be involved with unethical behaviors if it helps to further their careers. Another study posits that millennials take a teleological perspective to justify their stand on certain issues, such as illegally downloading music from the Internet; believing that music piracy provides greater access to people and that it increases overall benefit to society (Freestone and Mitchell 2004). Twenge et al.'s (2012) study of millennials found that money, image and fame were more important to this generation compared to community values, interest in social problems or taking actions to help the environment.

Verschoor (2013) cites a June 2013 report by the Ethics Resource Center to show the differences in attitudes toward ethical issues among the four generational groups, namely, the Veterans, Baby Boomers, Generation X and Millennials. Verschoor (2013) indicates that a higher percentage of Millennials reported misconduct when they observed unethical behavior compared to other generations. However, Millennials, by a large percentage, did not consider behaviors such as working less in response to reduction in benefits, using the company credit card for personal business, or taking company software home for personal use to be unethical (Verschoor 2013). Since the development and implementation of strong ethical guidelines promotes ethical behavior (Mulki et al. 2009), leaders should promote vigorous ethical training programs. More research over the next few years may provide a better understanding of millennials' ethical norms, especially in financial contexts.

Challenges in the emerging financial markets

Capital market globalization took off in the 1990's, resulting in the widespread integration of financial markets. When outside investments were allowed to enter emerging economies such as Brazil, Russia, India and China, it opened up enormous opportunities for international financial institutions. However, these firms had to face major challenges of navigating the rules and coping with the regulations imposed by the countries they were entering. In the initial stages of entering new markets, intervention by the host government seeking to ensure compliance with local laws is a common occurrence. At the same time some of these market-distorting rules and regulations allow for profiteering by the local bureaucracy and their cronies. It is well known that bureaucrats in these governments use regulations to extract payment at every step of the process, from the approval of licenses, the provision of infrastructure and the opening of resources such as land and capital necessary to conduct business.

Research shows that corruption and unethical behaviors are higher in markets where competition is absent and activities are not transparent (Venard and Hanafi, 2008). In many cases, when foreign firms enter the market, domestic financial institutions that have been sheltered from competition feel threatened. This feeling of vulnerability is exacerbated when domestic firms have to jockey for position in the market and compete with international firms. Gaining competitive advantage becomes critical and increases the potential for unethical behavior. The absence of strong enforcement and weak legal systems make it difficult to punish unethical behavior by these firms, thus fostering an environment where corrupt practices provide a competitive edge. Venard and Hanafi (2008) surveyed chief executives, general managers and directors of financial institutions in eighteen countries to seek their opinion on issues related to business conduct. Their study found that when the institutional framework, in terms of enforcement of rules and regulations, is weak, bribes and special payments to secure competitive advantage increase significantly. This means multinational organizations that have a reputation for a clean operation at home may have to resort to bribery and unethical behaviors to be able to compete in these corrupt markets.

Conclusion

> The way to stop financial "joy riding" is to arrest the chauffeur, not the automobile.
>
> *Woodrow Wilson*

Owens (2011) states that "Animosity toward Wall Street is at its highest level in at least 40 years". There has been much discussion of the reasons that led to the 2008 financial meltdown. While some blamed the lack of strong regulation, others bemoaned the decline of corporate core values and social responsibility orientations (Jin et al. 2013). There was also universal condemnation of financial services salespeople who were thought to be pursuing profits at the expense of ordinary citizens. However, it is unfair to put all the blame on individuals in the financial services industry who are responding to the corporate "mantra" for success. In the current marketplace, salespeople are walking a tightrope to balance their need to meet quotas while also being ethical in their sales practices. The pressure to hit the quarterly numbers for the CEO often translates into a push for salespeople to get the sales at any cost. The dictum to maximize shareholder value could push the customer orientation behavior off center stage. This also leads to an increased likelihood of salespeople trying to balance on the thin line between ethical and unethical behavior, often forcing them into the grey area. This is particularly true when salespeople perceive a supervisor's tacit approval of ethically questionable behavior in order to secure a sale. A lasting change in attitudes and behaviors would require firms to implement a long term strategy that truly places primary emphasis on customer oriented behaviors that can create customer trust.

What does the future hold? Heineman (2013) opines in his blog that most scandals in the financial services industry resulted from institutional behaviors that were noticeably questionable or wrong. The government took action by imposing fines on some of the institutions after the scandals became known. On January 7, 2013 the major US banks reached an agreement with the federal government. They agreed to pay a total fine of $8.5 billion for their part in illegal and unethical practices in the processing of mortgages, as well as with their foreclosure processes.

Industry reports (Lynch 2012) state that within three years after the financial collapse, financial institutions that were penalized for their unethical and illegal acts have come back stronger than before. Lynch (2012) observes that the assets of the five largest banks as a percentage of US GDP increased from 43 percent in 2006 before the crisis to 56 percent in 2011 some years after the crisis. The banks have also strengthened their positions by adding equity and are now again looking for opportunities. Their relentless focus on cost reduction and profit growth has resulted in lowering customer service and increasing the inequality of banking services.

The Federal Deposit Insurance Corporation (FDIC) estimates that about 8 percent (17 million) of the households in the US are "unbanked" (they do not have a bank account) and about 20 percent of households are "under banked" (must rely on alternative financial service providers such as check cashing and money order use) (Economist 2012). On the financial services sales side, "boiler room" operations (i.e. the use of high-pressure sales tactics to sell stocks to randomly selected clients) are springing up to push stocks. Faux (2013) reports of an operation where employees were required to cold call for 14 hours per day. The employees, calling the uninformed public, were trained to use high-pressure tactics to push stocks and were told to avoid people "whose names sounded as if they were black, Latino or Muslim, because they were apt to be too poor to invest" (Faux 2013: 41).

On the brighter side, it should be noted that many firms have modified their compensation structure by linking consumer satisfaction to prevent unethical short-term gains. LearnVest, a financial services company pays "their advisers a flat salary, with bonuses tied to customer satisfaction" (Faux 2013: 47). This salary-only structure is intended to foster long-term interests of their customers and should encourage behavior that puts customer benefit at the forefront. Jenkins et al. (2012) report that there is a great push in Europe to limit the size of compensation and bonuses to bank executives

In September 2013, on the fifth anniversary of the Lehman Brothers bankruptcy filing that is largely considered to be the catalyst for the financial meltdown, Alan Blinder, Former vice chairman of the Federal Reserve commented that the Financial Services industry had already forgotten the crisis (Wall Street Journal, Blinder 2013). He further stated that the laws formulated to prevent the onset of another crisis have already been watered down due to resistance from the financial industry.

This leads us to question whether it is in the best interests of the financial firms to strictly adhere to ethical behavior. Does ethical behavior help improve financial performance? Unfortunately there is no empirical evidence to demonstrate that adherence to ethical guidelines helps improve financial performance. In addition, research indicates that the commission based compensation structure encourages risk taking and increased propensity to cut corners (Chen et al. 2006). Indeed, Honeycutt et al.'s (2001) study of salespeople showed that commission based compensation was one of the strong predictors of unethical behavior.

While a series of studies have extolled the virtues of ethical and socially responsible behavior, none of the extant studies have provided support for a strong correlation between ethical behavior and financial performance. While there has been considerable anecdotal information about the benefits of corporate social responsibility (CSR), of which ethical behavior is a part, McWilliams and Siegal's (2000) study found that CSR had a neutral impact on firm profitability. On the other hand, Carroll and Shabana's (2010) review found a positive relationship between CSR and corporate financial performance but they admitted that there are some inconsistencies. Karnani (2011) disagrees and suggests that this positive relationship is nothing but an illusion. As long as the employee's performance is linked to the firm's financial performance and compensation is based on meeting sales and profit quotas, the temptation to cross the ethical line will still remain.

References

Bandura, A. 1976. *Social Learning Theory*. Englewood Cliffs, NJ, Holt, Rinehart and Winston.

Bejou, D., Ennew, C.T., and Palmer, A. 1998. Trust, Ethics and relationship satisfaction. *International Journal of Bank Marketing 16*(4): 170–75.

Blinder, A. 2013. Five years later, financial lessons not learned. A good-though-weak law sinks under the weight of special-interest lobbies. *The Wall Street Journal*, September 13th 2013.

Boatright, J. 2000. Globalization and the ethics of business. *Business Ethics Quarterly, 10*(1): 1–6.

Boyd, D. 2010. Ethical determinants for generations X and Y. *Journal of Business and Ethics 93*(3): 465–69.

Bucic, T., Harris, J., and Arli, D. 2012. Ethical Consumers among the Millennials: A cross-national study. *Journal of Business Ethics, 110*(1): 113–31.

Callahan, D. 2004. *The cheating culture: why more Americans are doing wrong to get ahead*. New York, NY, A Harvest Book/Harcourt Inc.

Carroll, A. B., and Shabana, K. M. 2010. The Business Case for Corporate Social Responsibility: A Review of Concepts, Research and Practice. *International Journal of Management Reviews, 12*(1): 85–105.

Chen, C., Steiner, T., and Whyte, A. 2006. Does stock option-based executive compensation induce risk-taking? An analysis of the banking industry. *Journal of Banking and Finance*, 30(3): 915–45.

Cullen, J., Parboteeah, K., and Victor, B. 2003. The effects of ethical climates on organizational commitment: a two-study analysis. *Journal of Business Ethics, 46*(2): 127–41.

DeConinck, J. 2010. The influence of ethical climate on marketing employees' job attitudes and behaviors. *Journal of Business Research 63*(4): 384–91.

—— 2011. The effects of ethical climate on organizational identification, supervisory trust, and turnover among salespeople. *Journal of Business Research 64*(6): 617–24.

Deshpande, S., and Joseph, J. 2009. Impact of emotional intelligence, ethical climate, and behavior of peers on ethical behavior of nurses. *Journal of Business Ethics 85*(3): 403–10.

Deshpande, S., Joseph J., and Prasad, R. 2006. Factors impacting ethical behavior in hospitals. *Journal of Business Ethics 69*(2): 207–16.

Economist 2013. Where's the next Lehman? Five years after the maelstrom of September 2008, global finance is safer. But still not safe enough. *The Economist*. September 7th 2013.

—— 2012. The fed's new thresholds: The mandate is willing but the tools are weak. *Economist*. December 13th 2012.

Eddleston, K., Kidder, D., and Litzky, B. 2002. Who's the boss? contending with competing expectations from customers and management. *Academy of Management Executive 16*(4): 85–95.

Eisingerich, A., and Bell, S. 2006. Relationship marketing in the financial services industry: the importance of customer education, participation and problem management for customer loyalty. *Journal of Financial Services Marketing, 10*(4): 86–97.

Falconer, S. 2005. Ethical marketing in financial services: the continuing importance of fiduciary responsibility. *Journal of Financial Services Marketing 10*(2): 103–6.

Faux, Z. 2013. The Other Side of Wall Street. *Bloomberg BusinessWeek*. New York 40–42.

Federwisch, A. 2006. Ethical Issues in the financial services industry. In *Markkula Center for Applied Ethics*, edited by Markkula Center for Applied Ethics: Santa Clara University, 2006.

Forsyth, D. R. 1990. *Group dynamics* (3rd ed.). *Pacific Grove*, Calif: Brooks/Cole Publishing Co.

Freestone, O., and Mitchell, V, 2004. Generation Y attitudes towards e-ethics and internet-related misbe-haviours. *Journal of Business Ethics 54*(2): 121–28.

Goudreau, J. 2013. Are Millennials 'Deluded Narcissists'? *Forbes*, Forbes.com. Jan 15.

Gramm-Leach-Bliley Act (1999) U.S. Senate. 106th Congress, 1st Session. *Pub.L. 102–102, Gramm-Leach-Bliley Act*, Washington: Government Printing Office, 1999.

Hair, J. F., Anderson, R. E., Mehta, R., and Babin, B. J. 2009. *Sales management*. Boston: Houghton Mufflin Company.

Harper, C. 2010. Goldman's Blankfein Says Firm Didn't Bet against Clients. *Bloomberg BusinessWeek*. April 26th.

Harrison, T. 2003. Why trust is important in customer relationships and how to achieve it. *Journal of Financial Services Marketing* Vol. 7 (3): 206–10.

Heineman, B. W. 2013. *Why Are Some Sectors (Ahem, Finance) So Scandal-Plagued? January 10th.* http://blogs.hbr.org/2013/01/scandals-plague-sectors-not-ju (accessed 04/05/2014)

Hoffman, D., Howe, V., and Hardigree, D. 1991. Ethical dilemmas faced in the selling of complex services: significant others and competitive pressures. *Journal of Personal Selling & Sales Management 11*(4): 13–25.

Hofmann, E., Penz, E., and Kirchler, E. 2009. The 'Whys' and 'Hows' of ethical investment: understanding an early-stage market through an explorative approach. *Journal of Financial Services Marketing 14*(2): 107–17.

Honeycutt, E.D., Glassman, M, Zugelder, M.T., and Karande K 2001. Determinants of ethical behavior: a study of auto salespeople. *Journal of Business Ethics, 32*(1): 69–79.

Ingram, T., LaForge, R., and Schwepker, C. 2007. Salesperson ethical decision making: the impact of sales leadership and sales management control strategy. *Journal of Personal Selling & Sales Management 27*(4): 301–15.

Jaramillo, F., Mulki, J., and Boles, J. 2012. Bringing meaning to the sales job: the effect of ethical climate and customer demandingness. *Journal of Business Research.*

Jenkins, P., Masters, B., and Barker, A, 2012. Banks bow to EU over limit to bonuses, *The Financial Times, June 13th.*

Jin, K., Drozdenko, R., and DeLoughy, S. 2013. The role of corporate value clusters in ethics, social responsibility, and performance: a study of financial professionals and implications for the financial meltdown. *Journal of Business Ethics, 112*(1): 15–24.

Kane, E. 2002. Using deferred compensation to strengthen the ethics of financial regulation. *Journal of Banking & Finance, 26*(9): 1919–33.

Karnani, A. 2011. Doing well by doing good: The grand illusion. *California Management Review, 53*(2): 69–86.

Litzky, B., Eddleston, K., and Kidder, D. 2006. The good, the bad, and the misguided: how managers inadvertently encourage deviant behaviors. *Academy of Management Perspectives 20*(1): 91–103.

Long-Chuan, L., Rose, G., and Blodgett, J. 1999. The effects of cultural dimensions on ethical decision making in marketing: an exploratory study. *Journal of Business Ethics 18*(1): 91–105.

Lu, L.-C., Rose, G. M., and Blodgett, J. G. 1999. The effects of cultural dimensions on ethical decision making in marketing: An exploratory study. *Journal of Business Ethics, 18*(1): 91–105.

Lynch, D. 2012. Big banks: now even too bigger to fail. *Bloomberg BusinessWeek* (April 19).

Manning, G. L., Reece, B. L., and Ahearne, M. (2009). *Selling today*. Upper Saddle River, New Jersey, Pearson.

McClaren, N. 2000. Ethics in personal selling and sales management: A review of the literature focusing on empirical findings and conceptual foundations. *Journal of Business Ethics, 27*(3): 285–303.

—— 2013. The personal selling and sales management ethics research: Managerial implications and research directions from a comprehensive review of the empirical literature. *Journal of Business Ethics, 112*(1): 101–25.

McGlone, T., Spain, J., and McGlone, V. 2011. Corporate Social Responsibility and the Millennials. *Journal of Education for Business, 86: 195–200, 2011*, 195–200.

McWilliams, A., and Siegel, D. 2000, Corporate social responsibility and financial performance: correlation or misspecification? *Strategic Management Journal*, 21(5): 603–9.

Martin, K., Cullen, J., Johnson, J., and Parboteeah, K. 2007. Deciding to bribe: a cross-level analysis of firm and home country influences on bribery activity. *Academy of Management Journal*, 50(6): 1401–22.

McLaughlin, M. 2011. Can you cut it as a financial advisor? *Special to CNBC.com (August 15).*

Moore, M. J. 2013. Goldman's Pay Pool Shrinks 1% in First Quarter After Job Cuts. *Bloomberg BusinessWeek* (April 16, 2013).

Mulki, J., and Jaramillo, F. 2011, Ethical Reputation and Value Received: Customer Perceptions, *International Journal of Bank Marketing 29*(5): 358–72.

Mulki, J., Jaramillo, J., and Locander, W. 2008, Effect of ethical climate on turnover intention: linking attitudinal- and stress theory. *Journal of Business Ethics 78*(4): 559–74.

—— 2009. Critical Role of Leadership on Ethical Climate and Salesperson Behaviors, *Journal of Business Ethics 86*(2): 125–41.

Newland, L. 2012, How Elite Colleges Still Feed Wall St.'s Recruiting Machine. *The New York Times.*

Owens, L. A. 2011. 40-year low in America's view of Wall Street. *CNN news.* www.cnn.com/2011/10/07/opinion/owens-wall-street-disapproval/index.html

Pirsch, J., Gupta, S., and Grau, S. 2007. A framework for understanding corporate social responsibility programs as a continuum: an exploratory study. *Journal of Business Ethics, 70*(2): 125–40.

Read, S. 2011. HSBC Faces £40m Bill after Mis-Selling to pensioners. *The Independent* www.independent.co.uk/news/business/news (6 December 2011).

Sparks, J. R., and Johlke, M. 1996. Factors influencing student perceptions of unethical behavior by personal salespeople: An experimental investigation. *Journal of Business Ethics, 15*(8): 871–87.

Steenburgh, T., and Ahearne, M. 2012. Motivating salespeople: what really works. *Harvard Business Review, 90*(7/8), 70–75.

Sternberg, E. 2013. Ethical misconduct and the global financial crisis. *Economic Affairs 33*(1): 18–33.

Bureau of Labor Statistics. 2012. *Labor force projections to 2020.* Washington DC: Bureau of Labor Statistics.

Strout, E. 2002. To tell the truth: call it what you like: a fib, an untruth, a fabrication. *Sales & Marketing Management, 154.*7 (July), 40.

Sweene, P. 2012. Sarbanes-Oxley – a decade later. *Financial Executives International* (July/August).

Twenge, J., Campbell, K., and Freeman, E. 2012. Generational differences in young adults' life goals, concern for others, and civic orientation, 1966–2009. *Journal of Personality and Social Psychology 102*(5): 1045–62.

Valentine, S., and Barnett, T. 2007. Perceived organizational ethics and the ethical decisions of sales and marketing personnel. *Journal of Personal Selling & Sales Management 27*(4): 373–88.

Valentine, S., Godkin, L., Fleischman, G., and Kidwell, R. 2011. Corporate ethical values, group creativity, job satisfaction and turnover intention: the impact of work context on work response. *Journal of Business Ethics 98*(3): 353–72.

Venard, B., and Hanafi, M. 2008. Organizational isomorphism and corruption in financial institutions: empirical research in emerging countries. *Journal of Business Ethics 81*(2): 481–98.

Verschoor, C. 2013. Ethical behavior differs among generations. *Strategic Finance 95*(8): 11–14.

Victor, B., and Cullen, J. B. 1988. The organizational bases of ethical work climates. *Administrative Science Quarterly, 33*(1): 101–25.

Waymire, J. 2013. How to choose a financial advisor. *Forbes.com.*

Zeidan, M. 2013. Effects of illegal behavior on the financial performance of us banking institutions. *Journal of Business Ethics, 112*(2): 313–24.

Zeithaml, V., Bitner, M. J., and Gremler, D. 2006. *Services Marketing: Integrating Customer Focus across the Firm.* New York, McGraw-Hill Irwin.

35

Reaching out to socially disadvantaged groups

Financial services and the poor

Paul Sergius Koku

Introduction

The exclusion of the poor from financial services is a topic discussed both in the academic arena (Koku 2009, Koku and Acquaye 2011, Beck and Demirguc-Kent 2008; Beck et al. 2007, Koveos and Randhawa 2004) and in international political fora (IMF 2010, United Nations Development Program 2002). Nevertheless, the plight of the poor in respect of access to financial services can still benefit from further debates and discussions. Why is that the case? This chapter not only tries to answer this question, but it also examines the evolving meaning of financial services and what they offer, particularly to the socially disadvantaged. Furthermore, it examines the composition of the consumer segment universally referred to as "the poor" (Daley-Harris 2007, Stiglitz 1990), and their need for financial services. Using the bottom of the pyramid theory (Prahalad and Hammond 2002, Prahalad 2005), this chapter not only makes an argument that it makes sense to devise financial services that meet the needs of the poor, but it also goes further to map out the kinds of financial services (such as revolving micro-credits, micro-loans, loaning livestock) that could be offered to meet the needs of the poor.

The rest of the chapter is organized as follows. The first section discusses the "poor" around the world and their predicament. Next is a review of the relevant literature on financial services for the poor. This is followed by a discussion of the bottom of the pyramid theory and how the financial services industry could benefit by designing services for the poor. Following this is a discussion on a range of financial services and how they could be of assistance to the poor. This section is broken into subsections on formal education, technical and vocational education, financial literacy programs, shelter, healthcare and insurance. Next is a discussion on public and private partnership (PPP). In addition to the traditional micro-lending provided by for-profit institutions such as banks and not-for-profit institutions such as NGOs, this chapter argues that poverty is a social ill that must be forcefully confronted by governments and social entrepreneurs around the world. The chapter concludes with the argument that by serving the poor, for-profit organizations will be more profitable and not-for-profit organizations and governments will realize a good social return on their investments in the form of less social unrest. Furthermore, as evidenced in the recent economic growth rates in Bangladesh, a reasonable increment in the gross domestic product (GDP) is realized when poverty is reduced (Muhammad 2009).

Not only do governments do better by reducing poverty but the world becomes a safer and better place when poverty is reduced or eliminated.

Who are the poor?

Understanding the poor is one of the major challenges in the path to developing an effective strategy to combat poverty, some scholars of the field (Koku and Acquaye 2011, Morduch 2000, Gulli 1998) have argued. Hence the first question that needs to be answered is, who are the poor? To compound the issue of solving problems associated with poverty is our inability to give a simple answer to even the simplest question that goes to the heart of who the poor are. Because different agencies that are involved in solving problems of the poor define the "poor" differently, there are several definitions of the poor. Microcredit Summit, for example, defines the "poor" or the "very poor" as people living on less than US$1 per day at international prices; the World Bank defines "extreme poverty" as living on less than US$1.25 per day and "moderate poverty" as living on less than US$2.00 per day (Daley-Harris 2007, Koku and Acquaye 2011).

So complex are the problems of the poor such that it is not unusual to have one agency or an entity with more than one definition for the poor. Take the case of the United States Government who uses two different definitions of poor, as an example. The Department of Health and Human Services (HHS) in its Federal Poverty Guidelines, for aid purposes, defines the poor as a household of four with an annual income of $23,550 or less or a single person household with an annual income of $11,490 or less (U.S. Department of Health and Human Services 2013).

On the other hand, the United States' Census Bureau uses a more complicated definition that takes into account such factors as whether the head of the household is older or younger than 65 years old and the number of adults versus children. The details of the Census Bureau's definition of the poor is a family of four (two adults, two children) with an income equal to or less than $23,283 or a single person under the age of 65 with an income of $11,945 or $11,011 if aged 65 or older (U.S. Census Bureau 2013).

Despite attempts to provide a comprehensive definition of poverty, it is clear that there are still some shortcomings as the definitions encountered in the literature do not take into consideration the fact that the cost of living can vary even within the same country. This problem is magnified by between country differences as the cost of living can change dramatically.

Some scholars and observers of poverty and social unrest in places such as some of the boroughs of London (Lewis 2011, Batmanghelidjh 2011), the poor suburbs of Paris (Silverman 1992, Peters 2005) or in developing countries such as Mali and the Central African Republic (Guterres 2012, Ngoupana 2013) have argued that poverty and political instability are somewhat intertwined even though poverty might not be the only causal factor of instability. The argument is therefore made that it is fruitless to expend efforts to try to establish peace without developing programs to eradicate poverty (Kai 2010). These arguments must have held sway given the current concerted global efforts towards poverty eradication. For example, the International Monetary Fund in 1996 established the Highly Indebted Poor Countries Initiative (HIPCI) which granted debt relief and provided low interest loans to cancel or reduce external debt repayments of a group of 39 poor countries (IMF 2013).

While many non-governmental organizations (NGOs) and civil societies, who maintained presence in these highly indebted countries and have in cases lobbied for the debt reduction, have praised the IMF's HIPC initiative, there are also many critics. For example, Easterly (1999) on the basis of empirical analysis suggested that debt relief is not helpful to highly indebted poor countries that do not change their long-run savings preferences because they would only end up running up new debts and running down assets.

In a later study, Asiedu (2003) analysed the economic performance of the 39 countries that have benefited from HIPC initiatives. The author found a relationship between the quality of governmental institutions in these countries and the achievement of the benefits of debt relief. The twelve institutional quality measures that the author used showed that HIPCs have much weaker institutions when compared to other developing countries. The study concludes that to attain the benefits for which debt relief was granted, highly indebted poor countries must attain a certain threshold of quality institutions. While taking care of economic reforms, the study suggests that to succeed in their efforts in reducing poverty, the highly indebted countries must also implement institutional reforms which must be an integral part of the economic reforms.

Literature review

Long before the recent "microfinance explosion", rural credit market programs have been in existence and attracted the attention of academics and the international financial communities. According to Hoff and Stiglitz (1990), in the effort to combat poverty and to provide alternatives to rural moneylenders who lent money at exorbitant rates, many governments with aid from multilateral and bilateral agencies had devoted considerable resources into channelling cheap credit to farmers. Sadly, however, many of those intervention programs ended in failure because of poor understanding of the workings of rural credit markets. To develop some real understanding of the problems, symposia were organized at which theoretical and empirical papers which examined the problem of "imperfect information" on rural credit markets were presented.

Commenting on the studies which were published in a special issue of *The World Bank Economic Review*, Hoff and Stiglitz (1990) suggested that it was clear that neither the traditional monopoly power nor the perfect market view could adequately explain the inability of institutional alternatives to drive moneylenders out of the credit market for rural farmers. Furthermore, empirical evidence suggests that the rates that moneylenders charge continue to increase in spite of the existence of the alternative government programs that provide low rates. In view of these observations, Hoff and Stiglitz (1990) called for further studies that investigate the sources and nature of imperfections of government intervention programs. These studies, according to Hoff and Stiglitz, should develop a generalized framework of alternative models that are effective.

Moneylenders and microfinancing

Even though moneylenders in economic terms render useful economic services, their unsavoury reputation as leeches, or opportunists abounds not only in Biblical and Shakespearian stories, but in the pages of contemporary publications. It is not uncommon for many, including governments, to regard the rates charged by rural moneylenders as usurious. However, a critical question that most people have overlooked is how much of this negative reputation is grounded in economic facts? Aleem (1990) sought to answer this question with data from Pakistan in the face of the failure of the establishment of government alternatives to drive moneylenders (who cater to individuals seeking small capital to start business) out of the market.

With a careful analysis of the data, Aleem (1990) finds that the estimates for resource costs such as screening, pursuing delinquent loans, overhead and cost of capital suggest that moneylenders' charges are equal to their average cost of lending, but exceed their marginal costs. He suggests that his findings are consistent "with the view that the informal credit market is characterized by excess capacity and monopolistic competition in the presence of imperfect information" (Aleem 1990: 329).

Following the much trumpeted high repayment rate of borrowers from banks that operate on a format such as the Grameen Bank in Bangladesh, Besley and Coate (1995) investigate the "impact on repayment rates of lending to groups which are made jointly liable for repayment" (Besley and Coate 1995: 1). The results of the study are mixed; they indicate that successful group members may have to repay the loans of group members who could not make payments because their projects may have performed poorly. On the other hand entire groups occasionally default even if some members could make the payment. Overall, the social collateral that group lending "harnesses" mitigates the negative effects of group lending. These findings are consistent with Koku (2009) who argued that commercial banks that were willing to serve the poor could creatively leverage cultural values such as "family ties" as collateral for lending in lieu of physical property.

The informal financial markets

Levenson and Besley (1996) reiterated the general feelings that not much is known about the nature of informal financial markets in developing countries. The authors therefore set on a journey to contribute to our understanding by analysing Rotating Savings and Credit Associations (ROSCAs) in Taiwan. The results of the study are rather interesting. Contrary to the belief that the poor rely on revolving credits and savings to raise small capital, the study finds that participation in ROSCAs in Taiwan is highest among high-income households and that ROSCAs may be an "alternative savings device to the formal financial sector" (Levenson and Besley 1996: 45). Furthermore, the researchers could not rule out the "possibility of tax evasion and rosca participation are intimately linked" (Levenson and Besley 1996: 60), given the high participation rate of high income households.

While Levenson and Besley's (1996) research was on Taiwan, the authors citing other studies such as Ardener (1964), Kurtz (1978), Adams and Canavesi (1992) and Mansell-Carstens (1995) observed that ROSCAs "play a role in many developing countries in Americas including Bolivia, the Dominican Republic, Jamaica and Mexico" (Levenson and Besley 1996: 47). Anecdotal stories in other countries in the Caribbean and Africa suggest that the informal financial sector and in particular ROSCAs are prevalent in several other countries in the Caribbean besides Jamaica and in other countries in Africa, Ghana, Nigeria, Kenya and South Africa to name only a few and have been used by the middle class to gain access to cash to buy targeted durable goods.

Mosley and Hulme (1998) examine the impact of thirteen microfinance institutions on poverty and other target-variables in seven developing countries. Realizing that microfinance institutions are not necessarily designed in the same manner, the study also examined the relationship between the design features of the institutions and their impact on poverty reduction. The results of the study suggest that the beneficiary's "household income tended to increase, at a decreasing rate as the recipient's income and asset position improved" (Mosley and Hulme 1998: 783). The authors explained these findings by suggesting that the poor become more vulnerable to asset sales as they show greater preference for consumption loans because of their "limited range of investment opportunities" (Mosley and Hulme 1998: 783). Furthermore, the results suggest that lenders were faced with a trade-off between lending to the poorest and settling for a relatively low total impact on household income, or lending to the not-so-poor to obtain a higher impact. The authors conclude that innovations that address savings and loan collections, features of the institutions, as well as incentives for borrowers and staff could significantly change the impact of the institution.

The absence of a consensus on why people are poor and disagreement on the role of governments in reducing poverty create another major stumbling block in developing a real understanding of the poor and developing an effective tool to fight poverty. Most free marketers argue that governments should play no role in reducing poverty because governments' efforts only lead to bureaucracy and wastage (Osei 2002). Another school of thought, however, espouses the view that the poor fail to better their condition because they are "wasteful, immoral and irrational" (Bouman 1990: 154, cited in Martin et al. 2002).

Progress and popularity of microfinance institutions

Martin et al. (2002) in an interesting and encyclopaedic review of the achievements of microfinance institutions around the globe observed that even though noticeable progress has been made, there is still room to innovate and improve. The authors argue that to truly offer financial services to the poor, particularly the "poorest", means that this sector must be provided with programs that allow it to turn "savings into sums large enough to satisfy a wide range of business, consumption, personal, social and asset-building needs" (Martin et al. 2002: 273). Implicit in this suggestion are the following: (1) The poor are not homogeneous, hence their problems cannot be solved through a one-size-fits-all type of policy; (2) Helping the poor with financial services is effective in reducing poverty; (3) Helping the poor helps society in general. Martin et al (2002) conclude their study by observing that whereas microfinance is not a magical solution to ending poverty, it can however be positioned in such a way that the poor can use it to escape the clutches of poverty.

The popularity of microfinance institutions (MFIs) as a "tool" for fighting poverty has also attracted research attention some of which focused on assessing their effectiveness. How effective are MFIs in meeting their objectives became an important question. Koveos and Randhawa (2004) tried to answer this question by analyzing the means by which MFIs perform their services. The authors first acknowledged that the roles played by MFIs are unique; i.e., they serve as a financial institution and as an instrument for development. Because of this dual role, the traditional measures that are used to assess financial intermediaries would be inappropriate when applied to MFIs; therefore the authors suggested the use of the balanced scorecard approach. In applying this approach, the authors found that the credit portfolios of MFIs outperformed the best managed portfolios at large multinational banks. This stellar performance was attributed to the fact that MFIs are extremely innovative and flexible in their approach. Their group surveillance and incentive-compatibility between lenders and borrowers offer lessons that the traditional financial institutions may learn from.

Koku (2009) observed that "poverty knows no boundaries", hence problems of the poor, particularly access to small capital and financial institutions is not a matter that is limited to developing countries alone. Researchers and organizations such the World Bank (WB) that studied conditions of the poor are in agreement that problems of the poor are world-wide; even advanced countries have not been spared. For example, in the United States 46 million people reportedly live below the poverty line, according to the United States' Census Bureau (2013). Similar dismal pictures are available in other statistics. For example, the 2012 "Innocenti Report Card" produced by the United Nations Children's Fund (UNICEF) lists Romania as the country with the highest percentage of children living in households that have the equivalent income of lower than 50% the national median (that is equivalent to living in poverty). The United

States is the second, followed by Latvia, Bulgaria, Spain, Greece and Italy. These statistics should move people with a conscience to action to redouble the fight against poverty.

The Grameen Bank and other approaches

The success stories of the Grameen Bank did not only spawn research/articles on microfinance (MFIs) but it also unleashed a slew of books on the subject. Johnson and Rogaly (1997) translated their collective experience with Oxfam and ACTIONAID into a book titled *Microfinance and Poverty Reduction*. The authors discussed a wide range of informal services that poor people use and explained several features of micro-financing. For example, on the issues of MFIs focusing on lending to women and the elimination of physical collateral, Johnson and Rogaly observed that even though some commentators have indicated that focusing on lending to women is a practical consideration about efficiency of operations, caution should be exercised because evidence has shown that loans given to women are not necessarily empowering by themselves. Such loans should be backed with other mechanisms if gender empowerment is their objective. Regarding the peer-group lending or the use of locally based loan-officers providing character references for individuals instead of reliance on physical collateral, Johnson and Rogaly explained that these substitutes are better "screeners" of borrowers since they have "inside" information that a distant banker might not have.

On the issue of small sizes of loans, the authors explained that such features are necessary to discourage well-off individuals from seeking them or crowding out the poor. Even though the loans are small and therefore unattractive to the well-off, they are significant and attractive to the poor. The authors observed further that the "compulsory savings" requirement of some microloans are necessary to inculcate the habit of saving on a regular basis from regular income, however, they also acknowledged that that aspect of microlending might not be applicable or necessary in every situation. In conclusion Johnson and Rogaly emphasized the need for flexibility in microlending since situations differ from person to person and from one region to the next.

A collection of articles reflecting the tripartite approaches to the problems faced in developing microfinance programs for the poor was compiled into an edited book by Zeller and Meyer (2002). The three common problems identified were: (1) reaching the poor in substantial numbers, (2) enabling them to move out of poverty and (3) creating financial institutions that are sustainable (Zeller and Meyer 2002). An interesting aspect of these studies is the fact that they were conducted in different countries around the world and therefore represent a multi-country cross-sectional view of the problems that are faced by the poor. The articles also reflect the thinking of the policy makers that design policies to fight poverty. Furthermore, they show the trade-offs that the policy makers have to grapple with as they balance within the delicate triangle of the three demands: outreach, sustainability and impact.

Vento (2006) observed that many microfinance institutions are more than a provider of financial services; they have a social service component to them. In fact, most of them offer financial services to those who are deemed "high risk" by the standards of conventional financial institutions and as such have been excluded from participating in mainstream financial services. For this reason, assessing the performance of microfinance institutions by the traditional risk-management benchmarks used in banking might detract from attaining their social objectives.

Islam (2007), in his book *Microcredit and Poverty Alleviation* critically examined the microfinance model of development in general and the "credit-alone" policy operations of the Grameen Bank in particular. On the basis of his analyses, the author concluded that "the rhetoric of promising poverty alleviation has moved far ahead of the evidence and that even most fundamental claims of success remain largely unsubstantiated" (Islam 2007: 5). In his critique, the author expressed doubts regarding the effectiveness of credit-alone policy that does nothing regarding training or skill-enhancement of the poor. In the end, in suggesting policy alternatives, the author advanced the proposition that instead of a credit-centred approach, microfinance organizations should adopt a client-led, flexible approach of financial services.

While Islam makes valid points, we are mindful of the fact that his study focused on Bangladesh and the Grameen bank, and the microfinance problems are far larger than these two alone.

At the bottom of the pyramid

People are often blinded to the realities that surround them until someone makes an insightful observation regarding them. Such was the case with the bottom of the pyramid theory (Prahalad 2005). Clearly, there are fewer millionaires in every country around the world than there are the poor. Or, put differently, a disproportionately larger percentage of the world is poor rather than rich. Four billion people around the world, according to Prahalad and Hammond (2002), earn per capita income below US$1,500 per year and are considered to be the underserved who are at the so-called bottom of the pyramid. However, when things are properly put in context, the rest of the world would realize that the poor have the same desires and aspirations as the rich. The poor desire to be healthy, safe and free from pain just as the rich do. This observation is not only philosophical but it should also be an eye-opener to an entrepreneur with conscience.

The bottom of the pyramid theory (Prahalad 2005) as originally postulated, recognized the fact that a poor person in India, Peru or the United States who has a headache may wish they had a headache medicine, be it "Aspirin" or "Panadol", just as the rich person in Bombay, Lima or the United States. In both cases the sick want to get well. Hence, one can conclude that the basic desires of both the rich and the poor are universal regardless of where they might be. The difference between the two comes from the fact that because of their financial conditions, one of these individuals can afford a bottle of the headache tablets whereas the other cannot afford to buy a whole bottle but may be able to afford only a few pills. In this example, by making the headache medicine such that it could be sold as individual pills as well as in bottles, the manufacturer could satisfy the needs of both the rich and the poor.

Recognizing this difference, Prahalad (2005) suggested that global firms might do much better by studying how the needs of the poor could be met, instead of overlooking them or trying to use the "one-size-fits-all" approach in which the same format is used to reach both the rich and poor. The theory offers three main lessons. First, global firms must have detailed knowledge of people at the "bottom of the pyramid", both as consumers and producers. Global firms must understand the needs, perceptions, means and behaviors of those at the bottom of the pyramid. Second, global firms must realize the folly in relying on a "one-size-fits-all" policy; not only will that be inefficient, it is also completely ineffective in reaching people at the bottom of the pyramid since their means are limited and therefore their purchasing patterns and habits are also different. Global firms need to develop different or separate business models for people in different segments or at different levels of the pyramid. Third, and perhaps the self-serving lesson, is that by serving the poor, not only will businesses be able to make more money, but they are also securing world peace.

Prahalad (2005) cited a series of success stories around the world where companies have been profitable serving the poor to buttress his points. In India, Prahalad cited the case of Hindustan Unilever which enjoyed tremendous success in marketing specially packaged shampoo targeted to low-income consumers in India as evidence that the theory works. In Nicaragua, Prahalad cited Tecnosol's successful efforts to provide access to energy to the bottom of the pyramid from renewable sources: solar and wind power. In addition to the aforementioned success stories, the case of Casas Bahia, a retailer in Brazil that not only sells homes to people at the bottom of the pyramid but also sells furniture and appliances, clearly illustrates Prahalad's point that there is money to be made by for-profit organizations even in serving the poor: the bottom of the pyramid. The task at hand for financial services that truly intend to reach and serve the poor is to make the "bottom of the pyramid" theory of retailing work for financial inclusion of the poor as well.

Even though the "bottom of the pyramid" theory appears logical, it is not without its critics. For example, Simanis (2012) observed that apart from the success of Unilever, several other companies such as Procter & Gamble and Du Pont failed in their attempts to make products that cater specifically to "the poor". Simanis blamed the failure of Procter & Gamble, Du Pont and many other companies like them on the extremely high penetration rate, the high margins, and the low prices that are required to make the theory sustainable. Others such as Crabtree (2007) criticized Prahalad's theory as having been based on a flawed methodology of case studies. However, Bellamkonda (2012) believes the theory is sustainable if only organizations will take their time to study their target markets carefully.

Financial services for the poor

As evidenced in the above discussions, the bottom of the pyramid theory deals primarily with selling to the poor, nevertheless lessons could be learned from the theory in designing financial services for the poor. First, the theory warns against a "one-size-fits all" approach which is in accord with the points made by Johnson and Rogaly (1997). Second, the theory recommends intimate knowledge of the consumers' needs, perceptions and behaviors for whatever the organization intends to sell. This point is also consistent with the points made by Hoff and Stiglitz (1990). Perhaps, this point is the overarching lesson for providing financial services to the poor: have an intimate knowledge of your customers' needs.

While the goal of financial services to the poor has never been unclear, what should be included in financial services to the poor, on the other hand, has never been clear. This is partly because the problems of the poor are complex and not homogeneous. Should financial services to the poor include such other services as formal education, skill/technical training, vocational education, financial literacy, shelter, healthcare or insurance? Or should it simply focus on providing credit to the poor? While we cannot provide a simple answer to these questions, we can provide a summary of lessons learned from several previous studies that have approached the above questions from varying perspectives. Such lessons, we hope, can inform the construction of a solution.

First, it is clear that reaching out to the financially disadvantaged or solving the problem of the "unbanked" might include all the above services, but in a different order; however, we do not intend to suggest by any means that the list of possible services is limited to only those discussed here. The list can indeed be endless, but the key should be flexibility and creativity and above all client-centered services that are coupled with the desire to make a difference.

Formal education

How does formal education solve the problems involved in providing financial services to the poor? The answer to this question lies in the fact the poor like any other segment of society also have children. Education does not only solve the problem of ignorance but also has the power to fuel the imagination. The children of the poor in most instances are caught-up in the cycle of poverty through the unfortunate incidence of being born poor. They grow up to replace their parents in the vicious web of poverty. However, with the opportunity and access to formal education, some of the children of the poor could emerge from poverty. They could also have the chance to be lawyers, engineers, doctors, etc. This fact is ironically not lost on the poor; that is why not too long ago, the completion of formal education by a "child" of a village in some African countries such as Ghana, Nigeria, etc. became a reason for celebration. Even though not many of them could afford to have their children formally educated, they understand the possibility it offers.

It is evident therefore that access and opportunity to formal education for the children of the poor could be a ticket out of poverty to a family, the question, however, is how or what is the best means to provide this education. Because the poor in many developing countries eke out a living sometimes as subsistence farmers or raise a few animals, they often live in isolated villages that are difficult to reach and are under harsh conditions. The decision to provide a formal education to their children will therefore revolve around the solutions of whether basic schools should be set up in those isolated villages, or whether the children should be sponsored and sent away to other cities and towns where there are established schools? These are not simple decisions but in the fashion of a client-centered approach, the correct decision will depend on the specific circumstances. Will a school in a remote village attract good teachers who can truly prepare the children in very deprived environments to be competitive in national exams? Are the parents willing to send their children away? These are only a few of the relevant questions.

It must also be realized that the decision to provide formal education to the children of the poor in a developing country entails more than setting up a school or hiring a teacher. Because of the financial circumstances of their parents, in most cases the children must be provided with books as well as clothes to wear to school.

The scenario of educating children of the poor presented above focuses mainly on developing countries, however, the argument that giving a good education to the children of the poor is a good way to break the cycle of poverty and to improve social mobility is true for advanced countries as well. In that respect, the decision by well-respected universities such as Harvard, Yale, The University of Michigan, Princeton, Virginia, Stanford, etc. (Brandon 2006), to give free tuition to academically able students from low-income households who gain admission to the institution is not only laudable and noteworthy but also consistent with the kind of forward-looking policies that good education can accomplish in alleviating poverty.

Skills/technical training and vocational education

Vocational/technical education that is geared at equipping individuals with skills that can make them either employable or self-employed has been shown to be another effective tool in fighting poverty (Koku and Acquaye 2011). The reasoning here is that when individuals are able to make money, they will be able to save and therefore can ultimately gain access to mainstream financial institutions. However, often individuals who have completed skills/vocational training remain unemployed and still in poverty because they lack the minimal capital needed to start their own enterprises. It is therefore not enough to pursue one particular course of action in combatting poverty at the exclusion of all others. For example, it would be more effective to couple skills/vocational training with a small loan program that would allow individuals who have demonstrated competency during the vocational training program to gain access to small loans to start their own small business if needed. The skills programs advocated here could be such that they could cater to both parents and children if necessary.

Financial literacy

In Chapter 3, Huhmann discusses the need, relevance and importance of financial literacy to consumers' savings and purchase decision-making. The need and importance of financial literacy is even greater for the poor. In fact, several studies (Jacob et al. 2000, Ginovsky 2003) have attributed some of the problems of the poor to financial illiteracy; this is particularly true in advanced countries such as the United States where it is not uncommon for large proportions of the working poor to be perpetually indebted to credit card and payday loan companies. In this context, one of the tools in tackling poverty is to make the poor financially literate. Teaching the poor financial literacy must be done so that the poor would either learn to properly manage the small amount of money that comes to them, for example, welfare checks from the government, or monies that they may earn from working in one form or the other.

Providing financial literacy to the poor as a way to reduce poverty is also championed by the school of thought that holds the view that a significant number of individuals have become poor simply because they do not know how to make logical financial decisions. These individuals will most likely become poor again, even if they were to "come in to money" unless they know how to make sound financial decisions. The preceding line of reasoning applies to the poor regardless of whether they live in the United States or elsewhere. Because judicious financial decision-making is necessary for not falling into poverty, it is equally necessary for breaking out of poverty. Earlier chapters in this book on financial literacy have made this point clear.

Shelter

How does shelter relate to poverty or financial inclusion of the poor? Most people think about money alone in terms of demarcating between the poor and the well-off. This reaction is probably correct given the fact that every definition of the poor is made on the basis of money. Nonetheless, providing shelter to the poor could be important and indeed related to thinking about financial inclusion of the poor, particularly in developed countries. Why is that? One of the basic pieces of information required in applying for a job in many developed countries is an address. However, which address does a homeless person provide? We often do not think of the homeless when we talk about the poor but they are a key sub-segment of the poor. Poverty may very well be the reason that some people are homeless in the first place. Hence, the fight against poverty will not be complete without mounting an assault on homelessness as well.

What is the best approach to tackling homelessness? Governments in many advanced countries seem to be the only entity fighting poverty along this front. However, not-for-profit organizations such as Habitat for Humanity (which operates in the U.S., South America and Africa) assist individuals from low income groups to own their own homes. The International Red Cross is active in providing shelter to the homeless, but there is room for many more organizations. While having an address may not be critical in getting a job in developing countries, the issue of providing shelter to the poor is no less critical. Perhaps, it is high time the governments of developing countries also started fighting poverty by providing shelter especially to the masses of homeless children that are found in the cities. These children need shelter and education and there is very little doubt that without such assistance, they would most likely not escape the clutches of poverty.

Healthcare

Even though we cannot say that providing affordable healthcare or free healthcare for the poor is a universal right, because of the high healthcare costs in a country such as the United States, many people are only a major illness away from bankruptcy. Those who do not have medical coverage provided through their employer or do not have a job at all often cope for longer than necessary with an illness that could be cured cost-effectively. However, because they have neglected the illness for a long period, it often turns into something more serious. For the poor, it needlessly means a death sentence or having to live in pain with a debilitating illness. It can also mean the loss of income or productive capacity/opportunity which could be the beginnings of a slippery descent into poverty for those who are on the margins but do have some form of employment.

A similar argument could be made for the provision of affordable healthcare in developing countries. The issue in most developing countries is not necessarily having to file for bankruptcy because of high healthcare costs (they probably do not even have that option); however, it is true that high healthcare costs in many developing countries (that is, if the sick have to use the services of a hospital or a physician) means living without healthcare as it is unaffordable. How will people get to feed their families for the rest of the year if they have to spend the equivalent of four to six months' salary on a single visit to a doctor?

Insurance

Insurance in its various forms is needed by the poor in developing countries just as much as it is needed in developed countries; however, the needs are not necessarily of the same form. While the working poor in advanced countries need health insurance, the poor in developing countries need more than health insurance. Because many of the poor in developing countries engage in subsistence farming or herding, drought or floods could cost a whole year's proceeds. Thus, some form of insurance that immunizes these farmers and herders against quirks of nature or natural disasters are sorely needed. Furthermore, insurance is needed that bridges the gap when income from farming, gardens and herding is absent because of illness or any other reasons for inability to generate income. For example, there is no insurance for loss of income for farmers in Ghana, Nigeria and many other countries in Africa and therefore, farming families are doomed to starve if they are unable to attend to their gardens or herd of animals because of a protracted illness. They would suffer the same fate if their farms were destroyed by accidental bush fire, drought or floods (Tsikirayi et al. 2013).

Public-private partnership

The discussion up to this point has provided financial, moral and ethical bases for the financial inclusion of the poor. However, the two more vexing questions concerning programs aimed at providing financial services for the poor are: Who is better positioned to provide such services? and What form should the service take?

With four decades of history of failure of several well-intentioned microfinance projects, it is important that the providers of future platforms that are intended to help the poor escape the clutches of poverty be better positioned to attain a reasonable success rate. Some of those who study government programs intended to help the poor in both advanced and developing countries argue that governments are ineffective in performing these services successfully (Hughes 1998). Similarly, those who study the performance of microfinance argue that governments of various developing countries are poorly equipped to deliver such programs effectively.

Government services invariably create bureaucracies that are inflexible and bloated (Minogue 1998). These criticisms do have merit; however, others also argue that funds from many non-government organizations (NGOs) that are active in the microfinance field in developing countries are spent on expensive four-wheel drive vehicles, laptop computers, staff, etc. that do nothing for the poor that they are supposed to help.

Given these criticisms, and the fact that it is not only crucial, but also in the interest of governments, to actively work to reduce poverty, we suggest a partnership between the various governments, private organizations, and individuals (social entrepreneurs) who are interested in working towards the financial inclusion of the poor. While these entities can work independently in certain regions, they could pool resources together and work on a larger scale. A partnership between all the entities could provide the necessary checks and balances that may be needed to avoid wastage and enhance output. Governments, particularly of developing countries, have to be interested in reducing poverty because the Bottom of the Pyramid theory suggests that a major impact on their economies could be achieved by doing just that. In fact, Yunus Mohammed, the 2006 Nobel Peace laureate remarked that the phenomenal growth in the Gross Domestic Product (GDP) of Bangladesh, for example, is attributed largely to the significant effects of microfinancing efforts in getting women to be microentrepreneurs (Nobel Peace Prize 2006).

Public-private partnerships have existed for decades in both advanced and developing countries. These partnerships have been forged as a more efficient means to develop one form of public good or the other. For example, in developing water management systems in China (Lee 2010), fighting corruption and financial crimes (Hardouin 2009), developing schools (Callet 2010), or developing a new and essential drug and biotechnology (Ko 1992). Despite the fact that the model seems to work well in many instances, except for a few scattered publications (for example, VanSandt and Sud 2012) there is virtually no one advocating such an approach in tackling poverty and creating a system for the financial inclusion of the poor. Such a model can offer the much-needed checks and balances so that one single entity does not get bogged down in quagmire. This may be actively pursued with three key modifications.

First, the system must have flexibility built in. Without flexibility, whatever approach is adapted becomes no more than a one-size-fits-all approach. As a segment, the poor are not necessarily homogenous, an approach that works very well in one place might not necessarily work everywhere, thus a standardized cookie-cutter approach is doomed to fail. Second, because possession of local information, particularly on borrowers, is key to the success of microlending, it is imperative that "locals" are employed as field officers. They will know the individual borrowers personally, and can work with them to achieve success. Third, because financial inclusion of the poor is the ultimate goal and therefore the benchmark for success, the field officers of the organizations that are committed to serving the poor must be carefully selected and trained. They must be encouraged to buy into the goals of the institution that has employed them and not see themselves as just working for a pay check, but rather on a mission to serve the poor. They must not cast value judgments about the poor, but rather be sensitive to the needs of the poor. Finally, they must also see themselves as advocates for the poor and want to see them succeed.

Conclusion

Even though this chapter has focused on strategies towards financial inclusion of the poor, our discussions have not by any means exhausted the possibilities and the opportunities that are available to reach out to those who have been so long excluded from mainstream financial networks. No single chapter or book can claim to have achieved such an objective. Several other areas, such as the giving of assets, such as livestock and land, to the poor to jump-start their journey out of poverty remain largely unexplored. Such strategies, admittedly, cannot work for the urban poor who have limited space. However, the effectiveness of such alternative methods must also be evaluated. If such strategies are found to be effective, then and only then must they be adopted on a larger scale as a tool to fight poverty and pave the way towards financial inclusion of the poor.

It is evident now that there is no single panacea for the world's most dangerous illness – poverty – and the journey toward ending its ravages will not be completed tomorrow. However, every step forward is most likely a step that will not be repeated again, hence the need to examine different strategies that have been tried for insights and lessons learned, and more importantly to avoid repeating the same mistakes in future.

References

Adams, D. W., and Canavesi, M. L., 1992. Rotating savings and credit associations in Bolivia, in Adams, D. W. and Fitchett, D. A. eds. *Informal Finance in Low-Income Countries*. Boulder: Westview Press.

Ardener, S., 1964. The comparative study of rotating credit associations. *Journal of the Royal Anthropological Society of Great Britain and Ireland*, pp. 201–29.

Aleem, I., 1990. Imperfect Information, Screen, and the Costs of Informal Lending: A Study of a Rural Credit Market in Pakistan. *The World Bank Economic Review*, ¾, pp. 329–49.

Asiedu, E., (2003), Debt Relief and Institutional Reform: A focus on heavily Indebted Poor Countries. *Quarterly Review of Economic Finance*, 43, (Fall 2003), pp. 614–26.

Batmanghelidjh, C., 2011. Caring costs – but so do riots – Commentators, Opinion. *The Independent* (UK). 9 August 2011. Retrieved 11 March 2013.

Beck, T., and Demirguc-Kent, A. 2008. Access to finance: An unfinished agenda. *The World Bank Economic Review*, 22 (3), pp. 383–96.

Beck T., Demirguc-Kent, A., and Levine, R., 2007. Finance, inequality and the poor: Cross-country evidence. *Journal of Economic Growth*, 12(1) pp. 27–49.

Bellamkonda, S., 2012. *Selling to the Bottom of the Pyramid, Small Business Trends* online, http://smallbiz-trends.com/2012/07/bottom-of-the-pyramid-concept.html, July 6 (accessed April 2, 2013).

Besley, T., and Coate, S., (1995), Group lending, repayment incentives and social collateral. *Journal of Development Economics*, 46, pp. 1–18.

Bouman, F. J. A., 1990. Informal Rural Finance: An Alladin's Lamp of Information. *Sociologia Ruralis*. 30(2), pp. 155–73.

Brandon, E., 2006. *Better Yet, No Tuition; More programs offer students free schooling.* U.S. News & World Report, 141.10 (Sep. 18), pp. 74–75.

Callet, V., 2010. *Problems Solved, Problems Created: A Critical Case Analysis of a Public-Private Partnership in Alternative Education for At-Risk Students*, A doctoral dissertation, Faculty of the USC Rossier School of Education, The University of Southern California, LA.

Crabtree, A., 2007. Evaluating the "bottom of the pyramid" from a fundamental capabilities perspective. (accessed April 2, 2007), http://openarchive.cbs.dk/handle/10398/6755

Daley-Harris, S., 2007. *Report of Microcredit Summit campaign*, Washington, D.C. Microcredit Summit.

Easterly, W., 1999. How Did Highly Indebted Poor Countries Become Highly Indebted? Reviewing Two Decades of Debt Relief, *International Monetary Fund*.

Ginovsky, J., 2003. Financial literacy. *ABA Bankers News* 11.14 (July 8): pp. 1–2.

Gulli, H., 1998. Microfinance and Poverty. *Inter-American Development Bank*. Washington, D.C.

Guterres, A., 2012. *Why Mali Matters, The New York Times*, September 4, *www.nytimes.com/2012/09/05/ opinion/why-mali-matters.html?_r=0.* (accessed on March 4, 2013).

Hardouin, P., 2009. Banks governance and public-private partnership in preventing and confronting organized crime, corruption and terrorism financing. *Journal of Financial Crime*, 16, pp. 199–209.

Hoff and Stiglitz, J. E., 1990. Introduction: Imperfect Information and Rural Credit Markets – Puzzles and Policy Perspectives. *The World Bank Economic Review*, ¾, pp. 235–50.

Hughes, O. E., 1998. *Public management and administration*, 2nd edn. London: Macmillan.

International Monetary Fund (IMF), 2010. Facsheet: Debt Relief under the Highly Indebted Poor Countries (HIPC) Initiative, *www.imf.org/external/np/exr/facts/hipc.html* (accessed on March 4, 2013).

—— 2013. *Debt Relief Under the Heavily Indebted Poor Countries (HIPC) Initiative*, Factsheet, April 2, Retrieved on April 3, 2013.

Islam, T., 2007. *Microcredit and Poverty Alleviation*, Ashgate Publishing Company, Burlington.

Jacob, K, Hudson, S., and Bush, M., 2000. *Tools for survival: An Analysis of Financial Literacy Programs for Lower-Income Families*. Chicago, Woodstock Institute.

Johnson, S., and Rogaly, B., 1997. *Microfinance and Poverty Reduction*, Oxfam, London, U.K.

Kai, Z., 2010. *Foreign Direct Investment Liberalization and the Political Economy of authoritarianism*, Doctoral Dissertation, Northwestern University, Evanston.

Ko, Y., 1992. An Economic Analysis of Biotechnology Patent Protection. *Yale Law Journal*, 102 (3), pp. 777–804.

Koku, P. S., 2009. Doing well by doing good-marketing strategy to help the poor: The case of commercial banks in Ghana. *Journal of Financial Services Marketing*,14(2), pp. 135–51.

Koku, P. S., and Acquaye, H. E., 2011. Who is responsible for rehabilitating the poor? The case for church-based financial services for the poor. *Journal of Financial Services Marketing*, 5(4), pp. 346–56.

Koveos, P., and Randhawa, D., 2004. Financial Services for the poor: Assessing microfinance institutions. *Managerial Economics*, 30(9), pp. 70–95.

Kurtz, D. F., 1978. The Tanda: A rotating savings and credit association in Mexico, *Ethnology* 17, pp. 65–71.

Lee, S., 2010. Development of Public Private Partnership (PPP) Projects in the Chinese Water Sector. *Water Resource Management*, 24, pp. 1925–45.

Levenson, A.R., and Besley, T., 1996. The anatomy of an informal financial market: Rosca participation in Taiwan. *Journal of Development Economics*, 51, pp. 45–68.

Lewis, P., 2011. "Tottenham riots: a peaceful protest, then suddenly all hell broke loose". *The Guardian* (London). Retrieved 7 April 1, 2013.

Mansell-Carstens, C., 1995. *Popular Finance in Mexico* (Centro de Estudios Monetarios Latino Americanos, Mexico, City).

Martin, I., Hulme, D., Rutherford, S., (2002), Finance For the Poor: From Microcredit to Microfinancial Services. *Journal of International Development*, 14, pp. 273–94.

Minogue, M., 1998. "Changing the state: Concepts and practice in the reform of the public sector". In Minogue, M., Polidano, C., and Hulme, D. (Eds.), *Beyond the new public management*. Cheltenham: Edward Elgar, pp. 17–37.

Morduch, J., 2000. The Microfinance Schism. *World Development*, 28(4), pp. 617–29.

Mosley, P., and Hulme, D., (1998). Microenterprise Finance: Is There a Conflict Between Growth and Poverty Alleviation? *World Development*, 26(5), pp. 783–90.

Muhammad, M., 2009. The Role of Small Enterprises in the Manufacturing Sector in Bangladesh, *International Council for Small Business (ICSB)*, Proceedings. pp. 1–15.

Ngoupana,P-M.,2013. *www.reuters.com/article/2013/03/24/us-centralafrica-rebels-idUSBRE92M0AU20130324* (accessed on April 10, 2013).

Nobel Peace Prize. 2006. *http://nobelprize.org/nobel_prizes/peace/lauraeates/2006/yunus-lecture-en.html* (accessed 24 April 2013).

Osei, P. D., 2002. A critical Assessment of Jamaica's National Poverty Eradication Programme, *Journal of International Development*, 14, pp. 773–88.

Peters, R., 2005. France's *Intifada, New York Post*, November 8, 2005.

Prahalad, C. K., 2005. *The fortune at the bottom of the pyramid*, Wharton School Publishing, Upper Saddle River.

Prahalad, C. K., and Hammond, A., 2002. Serving the world's poor profitably, *Harvard Business Review*, 9, pp. 48–57.

Silverman, M., 1992. *Deconstructing the Nation: Immigration, Racism, and Citizenship in Modern France*, London: Routledge

Simanis, E., 2012. *Reality Check at the Bottom of the Pyramid*, Harvard Business Review online. http://hbr.org/2012/06/reality-check-at-the-bottom-of-the-pyramid/ar/1 (accessed on April 3, 2013).

Stiglitz, J. E., 1990. Peer Monitoring and Credits Markets. *The World Bank Economic Review*, 4(3), pp. 351–66.

Tsikirayi, C. M. R., Makoni, E., and Matiza, J., 2013. Analysis of the uptake of agricultural insurance services by the agricultural sector in Zimbabwe, *Journal of International Business and Cultural Studies*, 7, 1–14.

U.S. Census Bureau, 2013. *Highlights; Poverty Thresholds.*

U.S. Department of Health and Human Services, 2013. *Federal Poverty Guidelines.*

United Nations Children's Funds, 2012. *Inocentia Report Card.* UNICEF Research Center, (May 2012) Italy: Florence.

United Nations Development Program, 2002. *Human Development Report*, 27 November.

VanSandt, C., and Sud, M., 2012. Poverty Alleviation through Partnerships: A Road Less Travelled for Business, Governments, and Entrepreneurs. *Journal of Business Ethics*, 110, pp. 321–32.

Vento, G., 2006. "The Main Features of Microcredit" in Microfinance, Eds. La Torre, M., and Vento, G. Palgrave Macmillan, New York, New York, pp. 38–53.

Zeller, M., and Meyer, R. L., 2002. *The Triangle of Microfinance: Financial Sustainability, Outreach, and Impact.* The Johns Hopkins University Press: Baltimore.

36

Financial exclusion

James Devlin

Introduction

Financial exclusion is a situation where individuals and households lack access to mainstream financial services. Financial exclusion is generally considered problematic as it is seen as fuelling wider social and economic exclusion. In addition, poor people without a bank account often find themselves paying more for basic services, such as utilities, as they cannot use beneficial payment mechanisms, such as automated monthly payments from bank accounts. For such reasons, it is generally considered undesirable for any significant proportion of the population to be suffering financial exclusion, either temporarily or on an ongoing basis.

Although precise estimates of the proportion of a population suffering exclusion are difficult, in the developed world, rates of well over 5 percent are commonly observed. Estimates for EU countries put the figure at 6 percent for the UK, 8 percent for Spain and well over 10 percent for Italy and Ireland. In contrast, the rate for Germany estimated at just 3 percent, with 2 percent for France and 1 percent for Denmark and the Netherlands (European Commission 2008). In the US, the number of those termed "unbanked" has been estimated at just over 8 percent (FDIC 2012a). Overall, commentary and government initiatives indicate that the issue has been considered as significant in many countries. That said, more recently the financial crisis and subsequent fallout have meant that the previous focus on exclusion issues has dissipated, as concerns over systemic risks and institutional solvency prevail.

Notwithstanding these more recent anxieties, financial exclusion remains very much a live issue and one which, arguably, will be exacerbated as financially-stretched banks seek to preserve their balance sheets and profitability. In such circumstances, if left to their own devices, as commercial entities, banks are likely to focus more on potentially profitable and "safe" customers and seek to avoid serving more marginal segments. Thus, financial exclusion is likely to be a significant issue for the foreseeable future in developed and developing economies. Therefore, this chapter provides a detailed overview of the topic, considering first questions of definition and scope, before discussing the impact and importance of financial exclusion. The various types of exclusion and antecedent causes are then considered in detail, after which potential policy interventions are discussed.

Definition and scope

In simple terms, financial exclusion is characterised as a lack of access to mainstream financial services on the part of some consumers. For instance, Panigyrakis et al. (2002: 55) defined financial exclusion as the "inability of some financial services segments to access financial services in an appropriate form". Alternatively, McKillop and Wilson (2007: 9) refer to the "inability, difficulty or reluctance" of some segments to access "mainstream financial services". Mitton (2008: 1) suggested that accessing inappropriate financial services could be characterised as exclusion from better choices and that exclusion could be contrasted with proper inclusion where consumers engage in "good financial decision-making" on the basis of adequate financial capability.

Such definitions are relatively broad-based, mentioning financial services in general, rather than just focusing on the ability to open a transaction backing account. These definitions also hint at a myriad of related causes, a topic analysed in detail below. Other commentators have distinguished between, *total* financial exclusion, where individuals use no mainstream financial services products at all and those *"on the margins"* of exclusion, with only a basic account that is rarely used (Collard et al. 2001). The UK government, through the auspices of Her Majesty's Treasury, clearly views financial exclusion primarily through the lens of access to banking services (HM Treasury 2013). The Treasury argues that it is the responsibility of banks to serve the economy and to provide transparent and accessible banking products and that tackling exclusion means ensuring that low-income consumers can use mainstream banking services. In the US, the issue is also largely seen in terms of access to banking services, with the term "unbanked" often used to characterise those suffering financial exclusion (see for instance Rhine and Greene 2013).

Clearly, there are differing views as to how broadly the concept of financial exclusion should be viewed, with the majority of sources referring to access to appropriate financial services and some focussing more specifically on banking services. As the UK House of Commons Treasury Select Committee (2006) points out, referring to access to appropriate mainstream financial services raises as many if not more questions than it answers, not least, how is "appropriate" defined and which financial services should and should not be included? To deal with this issue, the Centre for Social Inclusion at the National Australia Bank (Connolly, et al. 2011) focuses on three "essential" financial services and related needs: transaction banking, access to mainstream credit and access to general protection insurance, particularly home and (greater than mandatory) car insurance. The World Bank (2008) also recognises the issue and suggests that four financial services should be viewed as essential and, as a consequence, exclusion from such services should be considered a particular problem. These are transaction banking, savings or deposit accounts, credit and general insurance. While the World Bank's product grouping is an excellent starting point, it is suggested that a broader category of savings and long term investment products should be incorporated into discussions of financial exclusion. Although not suitable for everyone, long-term pensions saving (and related advice) is arguably essential for large swathes of the population in economies where the state has withdrawn from social provision and has placed the onus on individuals to provide for themselves in later life.

Importance and impact

Arguably, in the recent past, the perceived importance of financial exclusion relative to other areas of the personal finance domain has receded, as governments and their agents have focussed on financial stability and fiscal prudence in an extremely challenging general environment. For instance, in the UK, the Financial Inclusion Taskforce has been disbanded and the issue of exclusion has been described as "out of fashion" (Rahman 2011). This is understandable in a time of extreme crisis where systemic stability and the maintenance of institutional confidence are a priority and scarce resources of government time and priority are allocated accordingly. There may also be political factors at play, where governments of a more progressive nature are inclined to focus on the issue of financial exclusion to a greater degree.

Despite the lack of attention on financial exclusion presently, few would argue that serious individual and societal consequences result from being excluded from essential financial products. Bryson and Buttle (2005) argue that the debate surrounding financial exclusion must be viewed in the context of the discussion of social exclusion more generally and the Financial Services Authority (FSA 2000) argues that financial exclusion re-enforces social exclusion more generally, particularly exclusion from the "gateway" service of a bank account. Social exclusion is a term that is much used in European policy debates and it has clear links with commentary about poverty, disadvantage and deprivation. However, social exclusion is a much broader concept which is a shorthand term for what can happen when people or areas suffer from a combination of linked problems such as unemployment, poor skills, low incomes, poor housing, high crime rates, bad health care, poverty and family breakdowns. The impact of social exclusion is on both individuals and social cohesion as a whole.

Discussions linking financial exclusion to social exclusion have, in the past, mainly been framed with reference to access to mainstream transaction banking services. However, it is apparent that exclusion from the other types of essential financial services outlined above may also reinforce social exclusion. For instance, the fact that mandatory car insurance may be prohibitively expensive for certain segments of the population may hinder mobility in the workplace, thus prolonging unemployment. More recently, the societal impact of the fact that many people are, one way or another, excluded from making adequate provision for retirement has also been noted (Altman 2010). Overall, it is apparent that financial exclusion is likely to have a deeper more profound impact than merely being unable to access certain financial services, *per se*.

Financial exclusion: types and antecedent causes

Initially, discussions concerning financial exclusion were focussed very much on the lack of access from which certain individuals suffered due to the tendency of mainstream financial services providers to avoid areas of social deprivation. Many living in such areas will not have access to a car and will therefore be forced to rely on public transport to access financial services physically. They are also less likely to own/have access to the technology required to interact with such services remotely. Such a focus on physical and geographical factors (see Leyshon and Thrift 1993) could be characterised as location-based exclusion. Whilst location-based exclusion formed the initial focus of financial exclusion concerns, subsequent research and commentary has identified a range of further types of exclusion.

Kempson and Whyley (1999a, 1999b) argued that there are a number of facets to financial exclusion including: access exclusion, product condition exclusion, price exclusion, marketing exclusion and self-exclusion. Access exclusion is distinct from location-based exclusion as it is not concerned with a lack of access due to geographical factors, but that some may be excluded from accessing financial services on the basis of unfavourable risk assessments by organisations. Product condition exclusion is where individuals are excluded from financial services due to conditions attached to the product offering, or where such conditions render services inappropriate for certain people. For some, this may be viewed as closely related to access exclusion.

Price exclusion is where certain individuals cannot afford financial offerings at the current price and are therefore "priced out" of the market. A related concept is resource exclusion, which Devlin (2005) described as a lack of discretionary income from which to meet payments. Marketing exclusion refers to the overlooking of certain groups by the marketing activities of financial services firms as the marketers seek to only target the most profitable customers.

Finally, it should be remembered that certain individuals may choose to self-exclude (self-exclusion), perhaps due to past refusal/negative experience or due to encountering negative word-of-mouth from acquaintances. Equally, they may choose to self-exclude from a fully informed viewpoint, merely concluding that they do not need a particular financial service. Low levels of financial capability or confidence may also lead to self-exclusion as people choose not to engage rather than make an uninformed choice. This aspect of self-exclusion has been referred to as capability exclusion. Certain individuals may also choose to self-exclude due to the fact that they cannot find a mainstream product that matches or is suitable for their values, a situation known as values exclusion.

As there are a number of dimensions of financial exclusion, it is perhaps no surprise that a number of potential antecedents, or causes, have also been identified in previous research. The specifics of precisely who is likely to be excluded are returned to below. However, in general terms, the FSA (2000) noted some economic, sociocultural and demographic trends which have contributed towards financial exclusion. These include the group of individuals left behind on the margins of society, even in periods of strong growth before the recent financial crisis, increasingly referred to as "the underclass". Uneven income growth and low income mobility amongst the lowest income groups have also fed exclusion. There have also been significant demographic changes including more lone parents and older people living alone, as well as a rise in homelessness, all of which may have fuelled financial exclusion further. Devlin and Gregor (2008) also noted that social and income inequality are the main antecedent drivers of financial exclusion. The Resolution Foundation (2007) notes that financial exclusion is best predicted by poverty and low income across Europe. Other general demand-side explanatory factors include a low level of financial capability and financial confidence.

According to HM Treasury (2004) mutually reinforcing barriers operate from both the demand and supply side. The former concerns consumers and their actions in the marketplace, whilst the latter concerns the actions of firms. The European Commission (2008) also add societal factors to the list of drivers of exclusion. They studied exclusion in fourteen separate European countries and the resultant list of potential antecedent factors is shown in Table 36.1.

As can be seen from Table 36.1, the Commission distinguishes between access and use, but if either is prevented then the net result is the same, i.e. exclusion from the service in question. The Commission also highlights which particular types of financial service are affected by the factor in question and also in how many countries the factor has an impact on levels of exclusion.

In terms of societal, the Commission highlights demographic changes and the attendant technology gap as the most important drivers, noting that older people generally are more vulnerable to fall prey to the technological divide which drives exclusion and that younger people are more likely to become over-indebted and suffer exclusion as a result. These factors drive exclusion from banking and credit in particular. Other, less important demographic factors that may lead to exclusion include the fact that more young people are living at home longer and may find it less useful to open a bank account and also increased migration that may lead to cultural and language barriers when attempting to open and operate an account. Labour market changes have also driven exclusion from banking and credit in the majority of counties studied, as more flexible labour markets lead to less stable and predictable incomes, lower creditworthiness and

Table 36.1 Drivers of financial exclusion

Type of factors	Access or use	Type of service affected	Number of countries where this cause of financial exclusion has been identified*
Social factors			
Demographic changes technological gap	Access; use	Banking; credit	10/14
Labour market changes	Access	Banking; credit	8/14
Income inequalities	Access	Banking; credit	8/14
Liberalisation of markets less attention to marginal market segments	Access	Banking	6/14
Liberalisation of markets disappearance institutions targeted to low income	Access	Banking	5/14
Social assistance	Access; use	Banking	5/14
Demographic changes overindebted	Access; use	Banking; credit	4/14
Money laundering rules/ identity checks	Access; use	Banking	3/14
Fiscal policy	Access; use	Banking	3/14
Demographic changes young (1)	Access; use	Banking; credit	2/14
Demographic changes migrants/minorities (2)	Access; use	Banking; credit	2/14
Cash is common (3)	Access	Banking	1/14
Supply factors			
Risk assessment	Access	Banking; credit	8/14
Marketing	Access	Banking; credit; savings	8/14
Geographical access	Access	Banking; savings	7/14
Product design (terms and conditions)	Access; use	Banking; credit	7/14
Service delivery (eg internet)	Access; use	Banking; credit; savings	7/14
Complexity of choice	Access	Savings	7/14
Price	Access; use	Banking; credit	4/14
Type of product (4)	Access; use	Banking; credit; savings	1/14
Demand factors			
Concern about costs	Access; use	Banking; credit	8/14
Belief that not for poor / low self esteem	Access	Banking; credit; savings	8/14
Fear of loss of financial control	Access	Banking; credit	7/14
Mistrust of providers	Access	Banking; credit; savings	7/14
Preference for alternative providers and cultural factors	Access	Banking; credit; savings	4/14
Religion	Access	Banking; credit; savings	4/14
Opposition to use	Access	Credit	4/14
Bad past experience (5)	Access; use	Banking; credit	1/14
Fear of seizures (6)	Access; use	Banking; savings	1/14

*Fourteen countries have been studied: Austria, Belgium, Bulgaria, France, Germany, Ireland, Italy, Lithuania, Norway, Poland, Slovakia, Spain, the Netherlands and the United Kingdom
Source: European Commission (2008) "financial services provision and prevention of financial exclusion", European Commission, Directorate-General for Employment, Social Affairs and Equal Opportunities; reproduced with permission.

resultant exclusion from banking and credit services. Related income inequalities have also fuelled exclusion in the majority of countries surveyed, as there is a clear link between exclusion and levels of income inequality (Kempson 2006).

A general liberalisation of markets has also occurred in a number of countries, which has led to increased competition and complexity. This is classified as a societal factor by the European Commission, but it is actually a supply side factor. In any event, such developments have increased competition and have led firms to focus more ruthlessly on profitability, meaning that some more marginal segments are intentionally neglected. This has exacerbated exclusion from banking in particular. The British Bankers Association (2000) acknowledges that the structure of the personal banking market in the UK can exacerbate exclusion, particularly due to the increased competition faced by banks. Banking per se is not a particularly profitable operation, especially when serving segments of relatively modest means. In the UK, it has been estimated that current accounts do not make a profit unless the average annual balance is at least £1,175 (Cruickshank 2000). Other analysis has shown that just to break even an account would require an average daily balance of almost £1,300 (British Bankers' Association 2000). It is little wonder that, without the prospect of cross-selling or other avenues of profitability, banks are reluctant to serve poor customers. Bank profits derive ultimately from the "time value of money" (British Bankers' Association 2000), while the main short-term opportunities for profit are cross-selling and penalty charges. If viewed in the short-term, low income customers are not perceived as attractive profit opportunities for banks (Kempson and Whyley 1999a, 1999b, HM Treasury 2004), with their low average balances and little demand for other products. It should be noted, however, that commenting upon the role of financial services organisations in increasing the chances of exclusion for some customers does not necessarily imply that organisations are to blame for financial exclusion. Firms' activities can have undesirable social consequences, while still being commercially legitimate (Devlin 2009). In summary a basic lack of the potential for profitable engagement is a key driver of exclusion, particularly from banking services.

Changes in social assistance regimes can also fuel exclusion from banking, as rules may deter people from saving for fear of losing benefits. A more positive effect may result from the increased use of electronic payments and the related need to have some form of bank account. Money laundering rules have also been cited as a cause of financial exclusion from banking according to the European Commission report. Concerns over money laundering lead institutions to demand more stringent documentary evidence before allowing an account to be opened. However, in some instances, there is at least the suspicion that firms are using the excuse of money laundering regulations to avoid opening accounts for those they see as problematic or unprofitable (Devlin and Gregor 2008). The *fiscal policy* of some countries has also been identified as a contributory factor, as taxes and duties on banks are passed onto customers, meaning that it is harder for poorer segments to afford banking services. Finally, in terms of *societal factors*, in some less developed economies there may still be a strong preference for cash, particularly among the less sophisticated population segments.

For supply-side factors, the Commission cites the most important factor as risk assessment practices, which lead to exclusion from banking and credit. As these become more sophisticated and also more routinized with the use of computer models and information technology, they have a tendency to increase exclusion amongst poorer, more risky segments. Such developments are obviously linked to the increased liberalisation and competition mentioned above. Marketing practices are also an important supply-side factor, leading to increased exclusion from financial services generally. Firms, quite understandably, are likely to focus their marketing efforts on more wealthy, potentially profitable segments. Also connected to marketing, exaggerated claims and general marketing hype may engender mistrust and deter consumers from accessing services. Geographic factors have also been identified as key drivers of exclusion from banking and saving. Indeed, initial debates surrounding exclusion (see Leyshon and Thrift 1993) concentrated largely on geographical factors and in particular the tendency of banks to close branches in poorer, less profitable areas. The net result could be financial desertification, as some areas are completely abandoned by mainstream providers.

Product design, terms and conditions can also lead to exclusion, particularly as they have a tendency to be less than clear and straightforward and may put a number of potential customers off. In extreme cases, the type of product required may simply not exist in the marketplace, due to the fact that it is not profitable for firms to offer such a product. An increased tendency to deliver services through contemporary media such as the internet is also likely to lead to increased exclusion. Some services may well be "internet specials" and therefore not available through other channels and increasingly consumers will be charged more to access services through alternative channels, which may well price some people out of the market. Whilst differential pricing practices merely reflect the relative cost of channel maintenance on the part of firms, they remain controversial and lead to an accusation that the poor pay more. Indeed, pricing has also been noted by the Commission as a driver of exclusion, as the poor are less likely to be able to afford some financial services and are excluded as a result. The opacity of financial services markets and the complexity of choice have been cited as important contributory factors to the well documented problems that consumers have in terms of choosing appropriately in financial services (HM Treasury 2002) and in the extreme this may lead potential customers to give up altogether and suffer a lack of access as a result. Issues concerned with pricing and price perceptions are discussed in detail in Chapters 15, 16 and 17 of this book.

Many of the demand-side drivers of exclusion identified are closely linked to the societal and supply-side factors listed. For instance concern about costs on the part of users may well be linked to opaque terms and conditions that make prices unclear, or a general feeling of confusion on the part of consumers given the complexity of choice that they face. According to the European Commission, research in a number of countries has shown that there is a tendency for poor people to assume that banks will not be interested in serving them and that they would not be welcomed by financial institutions. This could be due to low self-esteem, confidence issues or a bad past experience, another factor noted as a driver of exclusion. The issues associated with reaching out to the socially disadvantaged are discussed in detail in the previous chapter. A fear of a loss of financial control is also a factor that contributes to exclusion from banking as some may find it easier to budget with cash and may consider their money to be less safe in a bank than in their possession. Such concerns have gained greater validity since the advent of "bail-ins" as a response to banks' difficulties in the light of the financial crisis. Closely allied to the loss of financial control is mistrust of providers and fear of seizures as some consumers may fear that potential financial impropriety on the part of providers could cost them dearly. Previous bad experiences, negative publicity and a climate of general hostility towards the financial services sector may exacerbate problems of mistrust and, hence, levels of exclusion. These issues are explored further in Chapter 30.

Some consumers may have a preference for alternative providers and could be considered to be excluded from mainstream services. At the extreme, this could mean going to a "loan-shark" rather than a bank, or, more positively, engaging in peer-to-peer saving/lending rather than using a mainstream financial institution as an intermediary. In some cases, religion may drive exclusion, particularly if the types of products required to satisfy religious beliefs/doctrine are not available in the marketplace (Chapters 26 and 27 discuss religion in the context of Islamic banking and insurance respectively). People may also oppose the use of certain types of financial service (for instance credit) for reasons other than religion and therefore may choose to self-exclude.

The aforementioned list of societal, supply-side and demand side causes of financial exclusion were generated by a large number of academic experts throughout Europe. However, the causes listed and explained undoubtedly apply more generally, although the balance of importance of the various factors will vary from country to country. In the US, Hogarth and O'Donnell (1997) noted that those on low income and those who are unemployed are more likely to be excluded and that there are notable regional variations in exclusion levels. They also showed that race and ethnicity are linked to financial exclusion, with those from ethnic minorities more likely to be excluded than white Americans. Those who are married are also less likely to be excluded than single person households. In the US, a gender influence on exclusion has been noted, with females more likely to be excluded. However, in some other countries, such as the UK, evidence on this point is more mixed (FSA 2000). In Australia, Connolly et al. (2012), found that young people aged 18–24 are far more prone to exclusion, as are students not in employment. Also, those who were not born in an English speaking country suffer greater levels of exclusion, as do the working poor. In Canada, Buckland and Dong (2008) find similar drivers to other developed countries and in particular low income and assets and being a single parent family. Overall, it is clear that the key drivers of exclusion such as poverty and ethnicity are instrumental in explaining exclusion in a number of countries.

Financial exclusion and policy interventions

As financial exclusion is widely considered a key driver of social and economic exclusion, especially lack of access to a transaction banking account which is seen as a gateway to genuine citizenship and societal participation, it is not surprising that governments have engaged in policy initiatives aimed at reducing levels of exclusion. Often, this has been done with the voluntary participation of the banking sector, rather than by imposition of mandatory changes of practice or statutory intervention. This has led to the questioning of governments' genuine desire to tackle such problems and to truly rein in the commercial instincts of banks and other financial institutions. However, others have countered that the banks are commercial organisations that should, in the main, be given the freedom to formulate commercial strategies in a competitive market situation.

In the UK, the government has tended to take a broadly voluntary, rather than mandatory approach, with the main actors being government, the industry and third sector organisations. The argument that interest and policy intervention in the area has passed the "high-water mark" is a strong one. The Financial Inclusion Task Force "completed its work" in early 2011 according to HM Treasury (2013) having issued its final report in 2010. The 2013 Parliamentary Commission on Banking Standards did little more than pay lip service to the issue. It incorporated a Joint Select Committee on Financial Exclusion and Basic Bank Accounts, however the committee has only two standing members and no committee business is currently scheduled (UK Parliament 2013) and the term financial exclusion did not appear in Volume I of the final report of the Commission (House of Commons/House of Lords 2013) detailing the main conclusions and recommendations from the Committee's extensive investigation into banking practices.

Prior to this, arguably the main policy initiative in the area was the introduction of "Basic Bank Accounts (BBA)" (Devlin and Gregor 2008). The BBA was developed and launched by the banks and the government in 2003. It is designed to be simple to open and run for customers who cannot access a current account or do not want access to credit, and to keep banks' running costs low. Although from the banks' perspective the BBA was a voluntary initiative, the main high street banks and a number of other providers offer such accounts, meaning that the degree of access and choice for customers is reasonable. Although the precise features and benefits vary from provider to provider, all accounts offer basic transaction banking services. Crucially, the procedures and documentation required to open such accounts are less onerous than for traditional current accounts, meaning that those from more impoverished and marginal backgrounds should be able to access such services in a more straightforward manner.

In the US, the main approaches to tackling the "unbanked" and "underbanked" could also be characterised as broadly of a partnership nature (FDIC 2012a), with many initiatives operating mainly at the state level. The unbanked are noted to rely to a greater degree on "alternative financial providers". Some of these, such as credit unions and micro-finance institutions are seen as part of the solution; however, others such as pay-day lenders are generally judged to exacerbate the problems. The Federal Deposit Insurance Corporation has responsibility for ensuring that all citizens have access to safe and secure banking services that they can afford. One notable initiative is the FDIC Model Safe Accounts Pilot (FDIC 2012b), similar to the UK's approach of BBAs. Although the pilot has now ended, the nine banks that took part reported relatively few problems in serving previously unbanked customers and the approach may well provide a template for future initiatives should the political will exist.

The EU also distinguishes between two distinct types of alternative providers in the financial sector (European Commission 2008), those that are non-stigmatising, such as credit unions and those that do stigmatise, such as pawn-brokers and payday lenders. Both are seen as variants of what the EU terms "market policy" approaches to tackling exclusion, which may be for profit or social in nature. For instance, the EU noted that commercial, for-profit banks have developed simple, low cost banking products to serve previously excluded sectors in Belgium, Germany, Italy and the Netherlands as well as the UK as mentioned earlier.

The EU also notes the importance of voluntary charters or codes of practice in ensuring that those at risk of exclusion receive fair treatment from banking organisations and indicates that such an approach is an integral part of the policy landscape in various forms in a number of European countries. National governments also have a crucial role to play, most often in the form of a high level facilitator, providing an understanding of the problem, ensuring that powerful agents consider how best to provide solutions and encouraging market based approaches. Finally, and arguably more reluctantly, governments can intervene directly to enshrine the right to a bank account in law. This would be politically and culturally unacceptable in more liberal, free-market minded countries such as the UK, but has been considered an appropriate policy intervention in countries such as France and Norway.

Overall, it is clear that a number of policy levers are available to governments and in essence these range from a cajoling approach incorporating voluntary agreements/codes of practice to statutory intervention guaranteeing in law the right to a bank account. Whilst the statutory approach is likely to prove most effective, in many countries, placing such statutory burdens on private-sector, profit-seeking organisations would not be considered appropriate. Therefore, arguably the dominant approach is one that sees the relevant government acting as facilitator and strongly encouraging voluntary agreements/codes of practice.

Conclusions

Financial exclusion can lead to wider social and economic exclusion and many individuals in developed and developing countries continue to suffer negative consequences as a result. Perhaps paradoxically, the problem tends to be treated as more serious in developed countries where the vast majority of the population are participating fully in the mainstream financial sector. In such circumstances, those without access to such services are more unusual and very much at the margins of societal and economic activity.

The drivers of financial exclusion have been shown to be complex and interlinked, meaning that precise cause and effects are difficult to establish. Factors from both the demand and supply side act in isolation and interact to drive exclusion from mainstream financial services. Financial exclusion can be a more or less permanent state for some, but for others it is a transitory state of affairs, with the former generally the cause of greater concern.

As the causes of financial exclusion are complex, then simplistic policy interventions are not a realistic option. This is especially the case as, in the main, government and policymakers have preferred to adopt a voluntary, partnership based approach rather than legislate to force institutions to serve marginal segments. Such an approach is no doubt viewed as politically more acceptable and more appropriate when dealing with profit-seeking private sector organisations. However, given the requirement to generate profits and reward shareholders, voluntary, code of conduct based approaches will always be limited in what they can achieve. Added to that, post the financial crisis the focus has been very much on strengthening balance sheets and ensuring systemic stability and robustness in the face of an extremely hostile economic and financial climate. In such circumstances, it is inevitable that concerns over matters such as financial exclusion decrease and the focus of government is diverted to other matters. Therefore, the issue is likely to remain a live one for some time.

References

Altman, R. 2010. *Response to Consultations on State Pensions Age Increase*. Dr Ros Altman, Director-General Saga Group. *www.rosaltmann.com/pr_spa_response_4aug10.htm* (accessed 15/06/2011).

British Bankers' Association 2000. *Promoting Financial Inclusion – The Work of the Banking Industry*. London: British Bankers' Association.

Bryson, J. R. and Buttle, M. 2005. Enabling inclusion through alternative discursive formations: the regional development of community development loan funds in the United Kingdom. *Service Industries Journal*, 25(2), pp. 273–88.

Buckland, J. and Dong, X-Y. 2008. Banking on the Margin in Canada. *Economic Development Quarterly*, 22, pp. 252–63.

Collard, S., Kempson, E. and Whyley, C. 2001. *Tackling financial exclusion: an area based approach*. Bristol and York, UK: The Policy Press and the Joseph Rowntree Foundation.

Connolly, C., Georgouras, M. and Hems, L. 2012. *Measuring Financial Exclusion in Australia*, Centre for Social Impact (CSI) – University of New South Wales, 2012, for National Australia Bank.

Connolly, C., Georgouras, M., Hems, L. and Wolfson, L. 2011. *Measuring financial exclusion in Australia*. Centre for Social Impact (CSI) – University of New South Wales, 2011, for National Australia Bank.

Cruickshank, D. 2000. *Competition in UK banking. A report to the Chancellor of the Exchequer*. March. London: The Stationery Office.

Devlin, J. F. 2005. A detailed study of financial exclusion in the UK. *Journal of Consumer Policy*, 28, pp. 75–108.

—— 2009. An analysis of influences on total financial exclusion. *Service Industries Journal*, 29(8), pp. 1021–36.

Devlin, J. F. and Gregor, M. 2008. *From access to inclusion: an evaluation of the role of basic bank accounts in promoting financial inclusion*. London: Toynbee Hall.

European Commission 2008. *Financial services provision and prevention of financial exclusion*. European Commission Directorate-General for Employment, Social Affairs and Equal Opportunities Inclusion, Social Policy Aspects of Migration, Streamlining of Social Policies, European Union, Brussels.

Federal Deposit Insurance Corporation (FDIC) 2012a. *2011 FDIC national survey of unbanked and under-banked households*. Federal Deposit Insurance Corporation, USA.

—— 2012b. *FDIC model safe accounts pilot: final report*. Federal Deposit Insurance Corporation, USA.

Financial Services Authority (FSA) 2000. *In or out? Financial exclusion: a literature and research review*. Financial Services Authority Consumer Research Paper 3, London.

H M Treasury 2002. *Medium and long term retail savings in the UK: A review.* (The Sandler Report), H M Treasury, London

—— 2004. *Promoting financial inclusion.* HM Treasury, London.

—— 2013. *Making it Easier for People to Access and Use Financial Services. www.gov.uk/government/policies/making-it-easier-for-people-to-access-and-use-financial-services* (accessed 04/11/2013).

Hogarth, J. M. and O'Donnell, K. H. 1997. *Being accountable: a descriptive study of unbanked households in the US.* Proceedings of the Association for Financial Counseling and Planning Education, pp. 58–67.

House of Commons/House of Lords 2013. *Changing banking for good: report of the parliamentary commission on banking standards: Volume One.* London: The Stationary Office.

House of Commons Treasury Select Committee 2006. *Financial inclusion: credit, savings, advice and insurance, twelfth report, Session 2005–06.* HC 848. London: The Stationery Office.

Kempson, E. 2006. *Policy level response to financial exclusion in developed economies: lessons for developing countries.* Personal Finance Research Centre, University of Bristol. Paper for the World Bank.

Kempson, E. and Whyley, C. 1999a. *Kept in or opted out? Understanding and combating financial exclusion.* Bristol: Policy Press.

—— 1999b. Understanding and combating financial exclusion, *Insurance Trends*, 21, pp. 18–22.

Leyshon, A. and Thrift, N. 1993. The restructuring of the UK financial services in the 1990s. *Journal of Rural Studies*, 9, pp. 223–41.

McKillop, D. and Wilson, J. 2007. Financial exclusion. *Public Money and Management*, 27 (1), pp. 9–12.

Mitton, L. 2008. *Financial Inclusion in the UK: Review of policy and practice.* Joseph Rowntree Foundation, York, UK.

National Australia Bank 2011. *Measuring Financial Exclusion in Australia.* The Centre for Social Impact for the National Australia Bank.

Panigyrakis, G. G., Theodoridis, P. K. and Veloutsou, C. A. 2002. All customers are not treated equally: financial exclusion in isolated Greek islands. *Journal of Financial Services Marketing*, 7(1), pp. 54–66.

Rahman, F. 2011. *Why ATM charges prove that financial inclusion is out of fashion.* The Guardian newspaper, 20th September 2011.

Resolution Foundation 2007. *In brief: financial inclusion.* London: Resolution Foundation.

Rhine, S. L. W. and Greene, W. H. 2013. Factors that contribute to being unbanked. *Journal of Consumer Affairs*, 47(1), pp. 27–45.

UK Parliament 2013. *Joint Select Committee Panel on Financial Exclusion and Basic Bank Accounts. www.parliament.uk/business/committees/committees-a-z/joint-select/professional-standards-in-the-banking-industry/panels/parliament-2010/panel-on-financial-exclusion-and-basic-bank-accounts* (accessed on 04/11/2013).

World Bank. 2008. *Finance for all? Policies and pitfalls in expanding access.* Washington, DC: World Bank.

Index

When the text is within a table, the number span is in *italic*. When the text is within a figure, the number span is in **bold**.

THE ROUTLEDGE COMPANION TO INNOVATION MANAGEMENT

Innovation contributes to corporate competitiveness, economic performance and environmental sustainability. In the Internet era, innovation intelligence is transferred across borders and languages at an unprecedented rate, yet the ability to benefit from it seems to become more divergent among different corporations and countries. How much an organization can benefit from innovation largely depends on how well innovation is managed in it. Thus, there is a discernible increase in interest in the study of innovation management. This handbook provides a comprehensive guide to this subject.

The handbook introduces the basic framework of innovation and innovation management. It also presents innovation management from the perspectives of strategy, organization and resource, as well as institution and culture. The book's comprehensive coverage on all areas of innovation management makes this a very useful reference for anyone interested in the subject.

Jin Chen is Professor at Tsinghua University, Beijing, China.

Alexander Brem is Professor at Friedrich-Alexander-Universität Erlangen-Nürnberg and University of Southern Denmark.

Eric Viardot is Director of the Global Innovation Management Centre and Permanent Professor of Strategy and Marketing at EADA Business School in Barcelona, Spain.

Poh Kam Wong is Professor in Entrepreneurship and Innovation strategy at the NUS Business School, National University of Singapore.

ROUTLEDGE COMPANIONS IN BUSINESS, MANAGEMENT AND ACCOUNTING

Routledge Companions in Business, Management and Accounting are prestige reference works providing an overview of a whole subject area or sub-discipline. These books survey the state of the discipline, including emerging and cutting-edge areas. Providing a comprehensive, up-to-date, definitive work of reference, Routledge Companions can be cited as an authoritative source on the subject.

A key aspect of these Routledge Companions is their international scope and relevance. Edited by an array of highly regarded scholars, these volumes also benefit from teams of contributors which reflect an international range of perspectives.

Individually, Routledge Companions in Business, Management and Accounting provide an impactful one-stop-shop resource for each theme covered. Collectively, they represent a comprehensive learning and research resource for researchers, postgraduate students and practitioners.

Published titles in this series include:

THE ROUTLEDGE COMPANION TO MANAGEMENT BUYOUTS
Edited by Mike Wright, Kevin Amess, Nick Bacon and Donald Siegel

THE ROUTLEDGE COMPANION TO CO-OPETITION STRATEGIES
Edited by Anne-Sophie Fernandez, Paul Chiambaretto. Frédéric Le Roy and Wojciech Czakon

THE ROUTLEDGE COMPANION TO REWARD MANAGEMENT
Edited by Stephen J. Perkins

THE ROUTLEDGE COMPANION TO ACCOUNTING IN CHINA
Edited by Haiyan Zhou

THE ROUTLEDGE COMPANION TO CRITICAL MARKETING
Edited by Mark Tadajewski, Matthew Higgins, Janice Denegri Knott and Rohit Varman

THE ROUTLEDGE COMPANION TO THE HISTORY OF RETAILING
Edited by Jon Stobart and Vicki Howard

THE ROUTLEDGE COMPANION TO INNOVATION MANAGEMENT
Edited by Jin Chen, Alexander Brem, Eric Viardot and Poh Kam Wong

For more information about this series, please visit: www.routledge.com/Routledge-Companions-in-Business-Management-and-Accounting/book-series/RCBMA

THE ROUTLEDGE COMPANION TO INNOVATION MANAGEMENT

Edited by *Jin Chen, Alexander Brem, Eric Viardot and Poh Kam Wong*

LONDON AND NEW YORK

First published 2019
by Routledge
2 Park Square, Milton Park, Abingdon, Oxon OX14 4RN

and by Routledge
52 Vanderbilt Avenue, New York, NY 10017

First issued in paperback 2020

Routledge is an imprint of the Taylor & Francis Group, an informa business

British Library Cataloguing-in-Publication Data
A catalogue record for this book is available from the British Library

Library of Congress Cataloging-in-Publication Data
Names: Chen, Jin, editor. | Brem, Alexander, editor. | Viardot, Eric, editor.
Title: The Routledge companion to innovation management / edited by Jin Chen, Alexander Brem, Eric Viardot and Poh Kam Wong.
Description: New York : Routledge, 2019. | Series: Routledge companions in business, management and accounting | Includes bibliographical references and index.
Identifiers: LCCN 2018046350| ISBN 9781138244719 (hardback) | ISBN 9781315276670 (ebook)
Subjects: LCSH: Technological innovations—Management. | Organizational change.
Classification: LCC HD45 .R756 2019 | DDC 658.4/063—dc23
LC record available at https://lccn.loc.gov/2018046350

ISBN 13: 978–0–367–65606–5 (pbk)
ISBN 13: 978–1–138–24471–9 (hbk)

Typeset in Bembo
by Apex CoVantage, LLC